Police Misconduct

The Legal Action Group is a national, independent charity which campaigns for equal access to justice for all members of society. Legal Action Group:

- provides support to the practice of lawyers and advisers
- inspires developments in that practice
- campaigns for improvements in the law and the administration of justice
- stimulates debate on how services should be delivered.

Police Misconduct

Legal remedies

FIFTH EDITION

Stephen Cragg QC and Sam Jacobs

LAG the access to justice charity | 50 YEARS 1972–2022

This edition published in Great Britain 2022
by LAG Education and Service Trust Limited
Gatehouse Chambers, 1 Lady Hale Gate, London WC1X 8BS
www.lag.org.uk

British Library Cataloguing in Publication Data

a CIP catalogue record for this book is available from the British Library.

print ISBN 978 1 913648 24 4
eBook ISBN 978 1 913648 25 1
bundle (print and eBook) ISBN 978 1 913648 26 8

Typeset by Refinecatch Ltd, Bungay, Suffolk
Printed in Great Britain by Hobbs the Printers, Totton, Hampshire

Preface

The book is edited by Stephen Cragg QC, who also co-edited the second edition in 1991, the third edition in 1995, and the fourth edition in 2005. For this, fifth edition, he is joined as co-editor by Sam Jacobs. We were supported by a formidable team of committed and talented colleagues at Doughty Street Chambers. The authors of each chapter are identified in the contents page to the book. We were also assisted by Tony Murphy and Carolynn Gallwey of Bhatt Murphy Solicitors who brought their considerable expertise as solicitors in police claims to author chapter 14 on the pre-issue considerations in bringing a claim against the police.

We remember John Harrison who wrote the first edition of this book in 1987 while working at Paddington Law Centre, with a £26,000 grant from the Greater London Council (GLC) and co-authored all subsequent editions. John was a trailblazer who saw that areas of law which were relevant to police conduct, such as the torts of false imprisonment, malicious prosecution and misfeasance had largely fallen into disuse over the years (more than half of the case references in the first edition's section on false imprisonment were from the nineteenth century). The first edition provided a straightforward guide which helped establish actions involving the police as a mainstream area of legal practice and provided the first proper guide to the police complaints system. Sadly, John died, much too young, in 2009, not long after he co-authored the fourth edition having, by that time, moved on to a successful career as a planning lawyer.

We express our gratitude to LAG, and acknowledge the contribution of LAG to this book, and to its published collection of books, which serves such an important role in promoting understanding and knowledge of the law and, ultimately, access to justice. Particular thanks go to our stellar editor, Esther Pilger, who has urged us on mightily when the going got tough, and has extended all known limits of patience as the book has ebbed and flowed over the last two years. We are told that cakes are also owed to the typesetters.

Particular thanks for the help in contributing to the text and ensuring the book got finished, in addition to the listed authors, is owed to Donnchadh Greene who wrote a first draft of the section on facial recognition technology for chapter 11, and Mel Warner, redoubtable practice manager at Doughty Street, who encouraged our wonderful team of contributors when deadlines loomed. Many thanks also to our senior practice manager, Sian Wilkins, and our practice assistants, Grace Walton and Ben Davis.

We are, of course, also indebted to the patience and support of our families: Steve (Debbie, Rosa and Cydney) and Sam (Claire, Reuben and Esme).

The law is up to date to 30 June 2022.

Stephen Cragg QC
Sam Jacobs
Doughty Street Chambers
July 2022

Contents

Table of cases

Case	Paragraph
Stewart v Commissioner of Police of the Metropolis [2017] EWHC 921 (QB), [2017] 4 WLUK 515	17.24, 17.71
Sutcliffe v Chief Constable of West Yorkshire [1995] 5 WLUK 293, (1995) 159 JP 770, [1996] RTR 86, (1995) *Times*, June 5, CA	9.77
Sutton v Commissioner of Police of the Metropolis [1998] 7 WLUK 864, CA	16.75
Swain v Hillman [2001] 1 All ER 91, [1999] 10 WLUK 703, [2001] CP Rep 16, [1999] CPLR 779, [2000] PIQR P51, (1999) *Times*, November 4, (1999) Independent, November 10, CA	15.56
Swales v Cox [1981] QB 849, [1981] 2 WLR 814, [1981] 1 All ER 1115, [1980] 11 WLUK 136, (1981) 72 Cr App R 171, [1981] Crim LR 235, (1981) 125 SJ 133, QBD	7.26
Swinney v Chief Constable of Northumbria [1997] QB 464, [1996] 3 WLR 968, [1996] 3 All ER 449, [1996] 3 WLUK 344, [1996] PNLR 473, (1996) 146 NLJ 878, (1996) *Times*, March 28, CA	11.171
Swinney v Chief Constable of Northumbria (No 2) [1999] 4 WLUK 160, (1999) 11 Admin LR 811, (1999) *Times*, May 25, QBD	11.171
Syed v DPP [2010] EWHC 81 (Admin), [2010] 1 WLUK 120, [2010] 1 Cr App R 34, (2010) 174 JP 97, (2010) 107(4) LSG 14, (2010) *Times*, January 26	9.34
TBS v Commissioner of Police of the Metropolis [2017] EWHC 3094 (QB), [2017] 12 WLUK 44	7.59
TLT v Secretary of State for the Home Department [2016] EWHC 2217 (QB), [2016] 6 WLUK 618, [2016] Info TLR 373	11.208, 11.209
TVZ v Manchester City Football Club Ltd [2022] EWHC 7 (QB), [2022] 1 WLUK 11	14.125
Tabernacle v Secretary of State for Defence [2009] EWCA Civ 23, [2009] 2 WLUK 103, (2009) 106(7) LSG 18, (2009) *Times*, February 25	10.20, 10.21, 10.52
Taylor v Anderton [1995] 1 WLR 447, [1995] 2 All ER 420, [1995] 1 WLUK 335, (1995) 92(11) LSG 37, (1995) 139 SJLB 66, (1995) *Times*, January 19, (1995) Independent, February 28, CA	15.85, 15.86
Taylor v Chief Constable of Thames Valley [2004] EWCA Civ 858, [2004] 1 WLR 3155, [2004] 3 All ER 503, [2004] 7 WLUK 116, (2004) 101(32) LSG 36, (2004) 148 SJLB 877, (2004) *Times*, July 13	6.144, 6.146, 6.155
Taylor v Director of the Serious Fraud Office [1999] 2 AC 177, [1998] 3 WLR 1040, [1998] 4 All ER 801, [1998] 10 WLUK 535, [1999] EMLR 1, (1998) *Times*, November 4, (1998) Independent, November 3, HL	8.154
Taylor v Jaguar Land Rover Ltd [2020] 9 WLUK 200, [2020] ET/1304471/2018, 14 September	12.49
Taylor Wimpey UK Ltd v Harron Homes Ltd [2020] EWHC 1190 (TCC), [2020] 5 WLUK 168, [2020] BLR 514, 191 Con LR 60	14.99
Tchenguiz and Rawlinson and Hunter Trustees SA v Director of the Serious Fraud Office [2014] EWCA Civ 472, [2014] 4 WLUK 541, [2014] CP Rep 35, [2014] Lloyd's Rep FC 519; *Affirming* [2013] EWHC 1578 (QB), [2013] 6 WLUK 355, [2013] Lloyd's Rep FC 535	9.27, 9.30
Tempest v Snowden [1952] 1 KB 130, [1952] 1 All ER 1, [1951] 2 TLR 1201, [1951] 11 WLUK 73, (1952) 116 JP 28, (1951) 95 SJ 817, CA	8.69
Thacker v Crown Prosecution Service 16 December 1997, unreported, CA	8.72
Thackeray v Information Commissioner [2012] UKFTT EA/2011/0082 (GRC)	11.117

Table of statutes

Table of statutory instruments

Table of EU and international legislation

Abbreviations

A1P1	Article 1 of the First Protocol to the European Convention on Human Rights
AAIB	Air Accident Investigation Branch
AAP	actions against the police
ACPO	Association of Chief Police Officers
ACRO	Criminal Records Office
ADR	alternative dispute resolution
AFR	automated facial recognition
APCC	Association of Police and Crime Commissioners
ASBCPA 2014	Anti-social Behaviour, Crime and Policing Act 2014
ASBI	anti-social behaviour injunction
ATE	after-the-event (insurance)
BCRP	business crime reduction partnership
BSL	British Sign Language
BTE	before-the-event (insurance)
BTP	British Transport Police
BTPA	British Transport Police Authority
BWV	body worn video
CAD	computer-aided despatch
CAPA	claims against public authorities
CCA 1984	County Courts Act 1984
CCA 2013	Crime and Courts Act 2013
CCC	criminal conviction certificate
CCG	clinical commissioning group
CCMC	costs and case management conference
CCMS	Client and Cost Management System
CEA 1995	Civil Evidence Act 1995
CED	conducted energy device (taser)
CEOP Command	Child Exploitation and Online Protection Command
CFA	conditional fee agreement
ChA 2004	Children Act 2004
CICA	Criminal Injuries Compensation Authority
CJA 2003	Criminal Justice Act 2003
CJPA 2001	Criminal Justice and Police Act 2001
CJPOA 1994	Criminal Justice and Public Order Act 1994
CLA 1967	Criminal Law Act 1967
CNC	Civil Nuclear Constabulary
Complaints and Misconduct Regs 2020	Police (Complaints and Misconduct) Regulations 2020 SI No 2
Conduct Regs 2020	Police (Conduct) Regulations 2020 SI No 4
COP	College of Policing

CPOSA	Chief Police Officers Staff Association
CPS	Crown Prosecution Service
CRC	criminal record certificate
DBA	damages-based agreement
DBS	Disclosure and Barring Service
DPA 1998	Data Protection Act 1998
DPA 2008	Data Protection Act 2008
DSI	death or serious injury
ECHR	European Convention on Human Rights
ECRC	enhanced criminal record certificate
ECtHR	European Court of Human Rights
EHRC	Equality and Human Rights Commission
FAA 1976	Fatal Accidents Act 1976
FOIA 2000	Freedom of Information Act 2000
FSP	forensic service provider
GDPR	General Data Protection Regulation
GLAA	Gangmasters and Labour Abuse Authority
HMCPSI	Her Majesty's Crown Prosecution Service Inspectorate
HMICFRS	Her Majesty's Inspectorate of Constabulary and Fire and Rescue Services
HMRC	Her Majesty's Revenue and Customs
HRA 1998	Human Rights Act 1998
ICO	Information Commissioner's Office
IMS	information management strategy
IOPC	Independent Office for Police Conduct
IPCC	Independent Police Complaints Commission (now the Independent Office for Police Conduct)
LA 1980	Limitation Act 1980
LAA	Legal Aid Agency
LASPO	Legal Aid, Sentencing and Punishment of Offenders Act 2012
LED	Law Enforcement Directive
LPP	legal professional privilege
LRMPA 1934	Law Reform (Miscellaneous Provisions) Act 1934
MAPPA	multi-agency public protection arrangements
MDA 1971	Misuse of Drugs Act 1971
MDP	Ministry of Defence Police
Merits Regs 2013	Civil Legal Aid (Merits Criteria) Regulations 2013 SI No 104
MHA 1983	Mental Health Act 1983
MOD	Ministry of Defence
MOPAC	Mayor's Office for Policing and Crime
MOPI	Management of Police Information 2005 Code of Practice
NAFIS	National Fingerprint Database and National Automated Fingerprint Identification System (IDENT1)
NCA	National Crime Agency
NCCU	National Cyber Crime Unit
NCRS	National Crime Recording Standard
Netpol	Network for Police Monitoring
NFA	no further action
NPCC	National Police Chiefs' Council
NPIA	National Policing Improvement Agency (now the National Crime Agency)
NRAC	National Retention Assessment Criteria
NRM	National Referral Mechanism

PA 1997	Police Act 1997
PACE	Police and Criminal Evidence Act 1984
PAT	police appeals tribunal
PCA	Police Complaints Authority (now the Independent Office for Police Conduct)
PCA 2017	Policing and Crime Act 2017
PCC	Police and Crime Commissioner
PCP	provision, criterion or practice
PD on Protocols	Practice Direction on Pre-Action Conduct and Protocol
PHA 1997	Protection from Harassment Act 1997
PI	personal injury
PII	public interest immunity
PNC	Police National Computer
PND	Police National Database
POA 1985	Prosecution of Offences Act 1985
POA 1986	Public Order Act 1986
PRA 2002	Police Reform Act 2002
PRSRA 2011	Police Reform and Social Responsibility Act 2011
PSD	professional standards department
PSED	public sector equality duty
PTSD	post-traumatic stress disorder
QOCS	qualified one-way costs shifting
Remuneration Regs 2013	Civil Legal Aid (Remuneration) Regulations 2013 SI No 422
ROA 1974	Rehabilitation of Offenders Act 1974
RPRP	reflective practice review process
RRA 1976	Race Relations Act 1976
RRAA 2000	Race Relations (Amendment) Act 2000
RTA 1988	Road Traffic Act 1988
RTSA 2003	Railways and Transport Safety Act 2003
SAR	subject access request
SCA 1981	Senior Courts Act 1981
SCCP	Surveillance Camera Commissioner's Code of Practice
SOCA	Serious Organised Crime Agency (now the National Crime Agency)
SOCPA 2005	Serious and Organised Crime and Police Act 2005
SSHD	Secretary of State for the Home Department
Super-complaints Regs 2018	Police Super-complaints (Designation and Procedure) Regulations 2018 SI No 748
TA 2000	Terrorism Act 2000
UPP	unsatisfactory performance procedures
VRR	Victim's Right to Review

CHAPTER 1

Introduction

1.1 This book aims to guide lawyers and advisers through the law, practice and procedure of the remedies available where there are allegations of misconduct by the police or the wrongful use of police powers. The kinds of situations covered by the book can range from incivility by police officers, right through to cases of deliberate abuse of powers, and can include cases which engage the Human Rights Act (HRA) 1998, the Equality Act 2010 or the Data Protection Act 2018.

1.2 In particular, the book addresses the police complaints and disciplinary process and the available civil remedies for torts such as assault and battery, false imprisonment and malicious prosecution, but other remedies and causes of actions are also covered in some detail.

Policing, controversy and the role of the law

1.3 As explained in chapter 2, the first formal police force in the UK was established under the Metropolitan Police Act 1829. Instructions issued by the then Home Secretary, Robert Peel, set out nine principles of policing (known as the 'Peelian principles' (see para 2.8)). In large part the principles encapsulate the notion of policing by consent. The police were instructed always to recognise that 'the power of the police to fulfil their functions and duties is dependent on public approval of their existence, actions and behaviour, and on their ability to secure and maintain public respect'.

1.4 A tension in policing, or at least a challenge of it, is that the police are equipped with significant coercive powers, but must deploy those powers in a manner that maintains the confidence and approval of the public on whom those coercive powers are visited.

1.5 History shows that the tension often resolves in to controversy. That has certainly been the pattern of recent decades. The 1970s and 1980s saw frequent and at times brutal clashes between the police and both political protestors, aggrieved groups in the community, and on trades' unionists such as the miners. There were the deaths of Kevin Gately in Red Lion Square in 1974, and Blair Peach in Southall in 1979, and the 'Battle of Orgreave' in 1984 which saw violent clashes between pickets and South Yorkshire Police. In 1989 there was the Hillsborough football stadium disaster resulting in 97 deaths. That was followed by a police cover-up of its own failures and a lengthy campaign by the bereaved family members, which ultimately resulted in the conclusion of the Hillsborough Inquests in 2016 that the supporters were unlawfully killed by the gross negligence of the senior officer in charge. The years 1989 and 1990 also saw the quashing of the convictions of the 'Guildford four' and 'Maguire seven' who had been convicted in respect of the Guildford pub bombings, only for it to transpire, almost two decades later, that there had been patently unlawful coercion and doctoring of evidence by the investigating police officers. In 1993 there was the racially motivated murder of Stephen Lawrence, and in 1999 Sir William Macpherson concluded that the investigation into the murder had been 'marred by a combination of professional incompetence, institutional racism and a failure of leadership'.[1]

1.6 The context for this fifth edition of this book is one in which the relationship between the police and the public appears to be as strained as ever. The Undercover Policing Inquiry was set up in 2015 amidst revelations that the Metropolitan Police had, over a period of decades, deployed undercover officers amongst protest groups and some of those officers engaged in romantic relationships with protestors on whom they provided intelligence. In September 2021 the Investigatory Powers Tribunal made findings as to violations of the rights of one victim and expressed that this was 'not just a case about a renegade police officer' and his 'sexual proclivities', but also the authorisations given by senior officers that revealed 'lamentable failings at the most fundamental levels'.[2] At the time of writing, the public inquiry is ongoing.

1.7 The May 2020 murder of George Floyd by police officers in Minneapolis in the US sparked global outrage and debate as to racism in society, including in the UK. It renewed focus on issues of policing and race. In recent years there has been a number of controversial deaths of black men following police contact (such as Sean Rigg, Leon Briggs, Azelle Rodney, Mark Duggan and Jermaine Baker). In July 2020 a black athlete, Bianca Williams, was stopped by police while driving and a video of the incident drew criticism, with Ms Williams complaining they had been targeted because they are black and drive a Mercedes.

1.8 On 3 March 2021, 33-year-old Sarah Everard was kidnapped, raped and murdered – and the horror was magnified by the perpetrator transpiring to be Wayne Couzens, a serving Metropolitan Police officer. The murder sparked broader debate as to the safety of women, and as to the culture within the police with regards to attitudes towards women. In December 2021 two Metropolitan Police officers were sentenced to terms of imprisonment for taking and sharing photographs of the bodies of two sisters who had been murdered. In February 2022, the Independent Office for Police Conduct (IOPC) published a report into nine linked inquiries, named Operation Hotton, which described a pattern of bullying, discrimination, and 'toxic masculinity, misogyny and sexual harassment' at Charing Cross police station.[3] The IOPC described an underlying culture which allowed such behaviour to permeate and go unchallenged.

1.9 In June 2021 a report was published into the police investigations into the death of Daniel Morgan in 1987 and concerns as to police corruption.[4] The authors criticised the Metropolitan Police for placing the reputation of the organisation above the need for accountability and transparency.

1.10 In February 2022, in the wake of the series of controversies, the then Commissioner of Police of the Metropolis, Cressida Dick, resigned.

1 Sir William MacPherson, 'The Stephen Lawrence Inquiry', February 1999, para 46.1, https://assets.publishing.service.gov.uk/government/uploads/system/uploads/attachment_data/file/277111/4262.pdf

2 *Wilson v Commissioner of Police of the Metropolis* [2021] UKIPTrib IPT_11_167_H at [344].

3 https://www.policeconduct.gov.uk/recommendations/thematic-learning-issued-addresscultural-concerns-nine-linked-investigations%E2%80%93/.

4 https://www.danielmorganpanel.independent.gov.uk/the-report/, 15 June 2021.

1.11 Even in the context of a history of controversy, public trust and confidence in the police is at a low ebb.[5]

1.12 Beyond conscious or malevolent wrongdoing, policing has always been challenged by developments in society, and continues to be. The COVID-19 pandemic brought unprecedented curtailments on individual freedoms with national 'lockdowns' which the police were required to enforce. Additionally, freedom of speech and freedom from hate continues to be a challenge, and one particularly important and delicate area is in relation to transgender rights.[6] Developments in technology, such as automatic facial recognition, provides new opportunities in policing, but also, potentially, new invasions of privacy.[7]

1.13 Centrally, the complaints and civil claims for damages with which this book is primarily concerned are about obtaining accountability and a remedy in individual cases. However, the tenacity often required of those who complain about police abuses of power, and the skill and knowledge required of those who represent them, also plays a broader role in ensuring accountability in respect of the use of police powers. That is, in ensuring that the often delicate and fraught but always fundamentally important balance between police powers and public freedoms is forever tested and preserved, and that transgressions are brought to light.

Legal and procedural developments since the last edition

1.14 The last edition of this book was published some 17 years ago in 2005. The HRA 1998 had been in force for almost five years and was becoming embedded in the law. The preface in 2005 described that the Act was 'capable of reaching into almost every aspect of the law and practice of police misconduct and it's effect is still only beginning to be felt'. That observation proved to be correct, and the impact of the Act can be seen in a number of the chapters in this edition. Some areas of the law have seen significant developments, such as in negligence and the decision of the Supreme Court in *Robinson v Chief Constable of West Yorkshire*.[8] In other areas, such as in relation to false imprisonment, the essential framework remains the same, but 17 years of cases and nuance nevertheless result in significant change. The police complaints system has gone through a major overhaul with the Independent Police Complaints Commission being replaced by the Independent Office for Police Conduct and a heavily amended complaints process introduced in February 2020. The fifth edition has therefore been a re-write rather than updating of the last edition.

5 See, further the data from the Crime Survey for England and Wales described at para 2.13.

6 See, for example, the decision of the Court of Appeal in *R (Miller) v The College of Policing* [2021] EWCA Civ 1926.

7 See, for example, the decision of the Court of Appeal in *R (Bridges) v Chief Constable of South Wales* [2020] EWCA Civ 1058, [2020] 1 WLR 5037.

8 [2018] UKSC 4, [2018] AC 736.

1.15 There have also been significant procedural developments. In particular, the review by Sir Rupert Jackson into civil costs resulted in reforms in 2013 including the abolishment of success fees, the non-recoverability of after-the-event (ATE) insurance premiums, and the introduction of qualified one-way costs shifting (QOCS) in personal injury claims. Those reforms, irrespective of their merit generally, have posed an access to justice problem in police misconduct claims. Many police claims, such as false imprisonment claims, raise issues of importance but do not fall within the QOCS provisions and do not attract sufficiently large awards of damages to cover significant ATE premiums. In such cases, the only costs protection available for claimants is that offered by the legal aid scheme, but that can only be accessed by those on very low incomes. Many potential claimants are financially ineligible for legal aid but have nothing like the necessary financial resources to face the risk of adverse costs if a claim is unsuccessful. For such potential claimants, pursing a claim is all but impossible.

1.16 A practical development since the last edition is that increasing numbers of cases are settled before trial, as is consistent with the drive in modern litigation to resolve cases at an early stage and amicably between the parties. The effect of provisions such as Civil Procedure Rules (CPR) Part 36 is such that it can be virtually impossible not to accept any reasonable offer of settlement. For many, that results in a more timely and welcome access to a remedy, although some claimants in police claims may have preferred the opportunity of a vindication of their rights in a public hearing and judgment. That opportunity is now generally illusive, in anything but the most difficult of claims which defendant police forces wish to resist to trial.

Structure of the fifth edition

1.17 Due to the extensive developments since the last edition, the structure of this edition has been amended as follows.

1.18 Chapter 2 addresses the constitution and organisation of the police, and chapters 3–5 address the police complaints and disciplinary processes as in force from 2020.

1.19 Chapters 6–12 address the substantive areas of law that give rise to civil claims for damages. Rather than structure the chapters with reference to causes of action, the chapters have been organised around the type of damage with which the claim is concerned. For example, chapter 6 on false imprisonment and liberty includes those causes of action that may be relevant to a claim in respect of a loss of liberty. Similarly, chapter 7 on personal injury considers the causes of action which may be of relevant to such a claim, being assault and battery, negligence, intentionally causing psychiatric injury, harassment and the relevant provisions of the HRA 1998. The intention is that practitioners will be directed to the causes of action relevant to a particular claim in a single chapter, rather than having to peruse a number of different chapters to identify and consider which causes of action may be relevant. Of course, given the number of overlapping areas, it is impossible to achieve that perfectly and we have endeavoured to provide effective cross-referencing where we can. Chapter 12 on discrimination claims concerning equality and discrimination can, for example, cut across a number of different areas.

1.20 Chapter 13 addresses prosecutions of and by the police, including the Victim's Right to Review (VRR) and judicial review of prosecutorial decisions.

1.21 Chapters 14–16 address the procedural aspects of bringing a claim, from initial instructions through to trial and appeal.

1.22 The principles relating to damages apply across a number of different causes of action and, accordingly, are addressed separately in chapter 17.

CHAPTER 2

The constitution and organisation of the police

Introduction

2.1 The accountability of the police to the citizens they serve is complicated and frequently incoherent. This is in part a result of the growth of the modern police from its origins as numerous local, voluntary enterprises without ties to central government. The current organisational framework of the police in England and Wales is not straightforward, and control over the police is exercised by a variety of different bodies with a patchwork of roles and responsibilities.

2.2 This is not helped by frequent tinkering with that framework by successive governments. The introduction of elected police and crime commissioners (PCCs), under the Police Reform and Social Responsibility Act (PRSRA) 2011, represented a more fundamental change to the accountability structure of the police, and introduced another level of complexity. Since then, the Policing and Crime Act (PCA) 2017 has made additional changes, in particular in relation to collaboration between police and other emergency services, and further developments have been introduced by the Police, Crime, Sentencing and Courts Act (PCSCA) 2022.

2.3 To effectively hold the police to account for unlawful behaviour or misconduct, it is important to understand the constitutional position of the police, and the principles underpinning that position, as well as the structure of police forces and the bodies that oversee them.

2.4 This chapter will consider these matters under the following headings:

- principles underpinning policing;
- the office of constable;
- civilian employees;
- police forces in England and Wales;
- organisation of the police in England and Wales:
  - PCCs;
  - chief officers of police;
  - role of the Secretary of State for the Home Department;
  - oversight and professional bodies.

Principles underpinning policing

2.5 There are two fundamental principles underpinning policing in England and Wales:

- policing by consent; and
- constitutional independence.

Policing by consent

2.6 A well-known, if somewhat elusive, concept said to underpin the role of the police in England and Wales is that of 'policing by consent'. This concept is said to distinguish the role and responsibilities of British police from many other police forces across the world, whose accountability is directly to the government from whom their authority stems.

2.7 'Policing by consent' has its origins in the way in which police and policing first emerged in England and Wales. No formal police force was established under statute until relatively late in Britain's history. This was a result, at least in part, of scepticism towards an organised force tasked with keeping law and order, and fear of what such a powerful force could do under malign influence. Such views were prevalent not only in the public mind, but also among its elected representatives. As a Parliamentary Select Committee put it in 1822 (with an emphasis on individual liberty rarely heard in the 21st century):

> . . . it is difficult to reconcile an effective system of police, with that perfect freedom of action and exemption from interference, which are the great privileges and blessings of society in this country . . .[1]

2.8 In the absence of organised police forces, the peace was kept by members of the public entrusted by their peers and neighbours to take on the role (see the discussion of the office of constable below). Thus emerged the concept of 'policing by consent', most clearly expressed in the 'Peelian Principles'. These principles are named for Sir Robert Peel, the Home Secretary 1828–1830, and were set out in the general instructions issued to every police officer in the first formal police force to be established in Britain, under the Metropolitan Police Act 1829.

The Peelian Principles of Policing

1) To prevent crime and disorder, as an alternative to their repression by military force and severity of legal punishment.
2) To recognise always that the power of the police to fulfil their functions and duties is dependent on public approval of their existence, actions and behaviour, and on their ability to secure and maintain public respect.
3) To recognise always that to secure and maintain the respect and approval of the public means also the securing of the willing co-operation of the public in the task of securing observance of laws.
4) To recognise always that the extent to which the co-operation of the public can be secured diminishes proportionately the necessity of the use of physical force and compulsion for achieving police objectives.
5) To seek and preserve public favour, not by pandering to public opinion, but by constantly demonstrating absolutely impartial service to law, in complete independence of policy, and without regard to the justice or injustice of the substance of individual laws, by ready offering of individual service and friendship to all members of the public without regard to their wealth or social standing, by ready exercise of courtesy and friendly good humour, and by ready offering of individual sacrifice in protecting and preserving life.
6) To use physical force only when the exercise of persuasion, advice and warning is found to be insufficient to obtain public co-operation to an extent necessary to secure observance of law or to restore order, and to use only the minimum degree of physical force which is necessary on any particular occasion for achieving a police objective.

1 *Report of the Select Committee on the Police of the Metropolis*, 17/6/1822.

7) To maintain at all times a relationship with the public that gives reality to the historic tradition that the police are the public and that the public are the police, the police being only members of the public who are paid to give full-time attention to duties which are incumbent on every citizen in the interests of community welfare and existence.
8) To recognise always the need for strict adherence to police-executive functions, and to refrain from even seeming to usurp the powers of the judiciary of avenging individuals or the State, and of authoritatively judging guilt and punishing the guilty.
9) To recognise always that the test of police efficiency is the absence of crime and disorder, and not the visible evidence of police action in dealing with them.

2.9 Policing by consent continued to be expressed as a core principle of British policing into the 20th century. It was explained in the 1929 Report of the Royal Commission on Police Powers and Procedure[2] as stemming from the public's:

> . . . instinctive feeling that, as a matter of principle, [the police] should have as few powers as possible which are not possessed by the ordinary citizen, and that their authority should rest on the broad basis of the consent and active co-operation of all law-abiding people . . . It follows that the police, in exercising their functions, are, to a peculiar degree, dependent upon the goodwill of the general public and that the utmost discretion must be exercised by them to avoid over-stepping the limited powers which they possess . . .

2.10 This view was endorsed by the Royal Commission on the Police in 1962. The 1962 Commission was established due to concerns at the time that 'that the police were not subject to adequate accountability; that their constitutional position in the state was ill-defined; and that the method of dealing with complaints against them was ineffective and not always fair to the complainant'.[3]

2.11 In the 21st century, the Peelian Principles have continued to be referred as the 'heart and soul' of British policing.[4] The 'Policing Vision 2025' adopted by the Association of Police and Crime Commissioners (APCC) and the National Police Chiefs' Council (NPCC) declares that the 'link between communities and the police will continue to form the bedrock of British policing'.[5]

2.12 Thus policing by consent suggests co-operation on the part of the public, but also concomitant restraint and respect on the part of the police. Without such restraint and respect, the foundations upon which the powers of the police are established are threatened.

2.13 The reality of this relationship can be more strained than the Peelian ideal. According to the *Crime Survey for England and Wales*, confidence in

2 *Report of the Royal Commission on Police Powers and Procedure*, Command Paper No 3297, 16 March 1929.

3 *Report of the Royal Commission on the Police*, Command Paper No 1728.

4 *Policing in the UK: a brief guide*, Association of Chief Police Officers (ACPO), 2012, p2.

5 *Policing vision 2025*, APCC and NPCC, 2016, p3.

the police was at about 62 per cent in 2017/18 and had fallen to 55 per cent in 2019/20. That level of confidence varies across forces and across demographics. While 53 per cent of Black people said the police were doing a good or excellent job, only 39 per cent of those from a Caribbean background were of that view.[6] Trust among women, in particular, has decreased in the aftermath of the 2021 murder of Sarah Everard by a serving police officer.[7]

Constitutional independence

2.14 Closely connected with the concept of policing by consent, and the historical concern over the potential for tyranny posed by an established police force, is the long-standing emphasis on the constitutional independence of the police. To the traditional separation of the power of the state between the legislature, executive and judiciary can be added the distinct power of law enforcement invested in the police. Thus the British police are not servants of the government, but rather of the rule of law.

2.15 This independence was famously expressed by Lord Denning in *R v Commissioner of the Police of the Metropolis ex p Blackburn (No 1)*:[8]

> I have no hesitation in holding that, like every constable in the land, [the Commissioner of Police of the Metropolis] should be, and is, independent of the executive . . . I hold it to be the duty of the Commissioner of Police of the Metropolis, as it is of every chief constable, to enforce the law of the land. He must take steps so to post his men that crimes may be detected; and that honest citizens may go about their affairs in peace. He must decide whether or no [sic] suspected persons are to be prosecuted; and, if need be, bring the prosecution or see that it is brought. But in all these things he is not the servant of anyone, save of the law itself. No Minister of the Crown can tell him that he must, or must not, keep observation on this place or that; or that he must, or must not, prosecute this man or that one. Nor can any police authority tell him so. The responsibility for law enforcement lies on him. He is answerable to the law and to the law alone.

2.16 Nevertheless, the independence of the police is not absolute. Clearly someone must be able to hold constables, and particularly chief constables, to account and thus wield power over them. This system of accountability is considered further below. However, in matters of *operational* policing, the independence of the police remains a key aspect of their constitutional role. This aspect is, however, not defined and the Home Office's Policing Protocol Order 2011 describes it as 'fluid and context-driven'.[9] Sir Chris Patten, in his landmark review of policing in Northern Ireland, preferred the term 'operational responsibility' to 'operational independence' because the former made clearer the police's freedom to exercise their responsibilities but also accountability for the exercise of those responsibilities.

6 See *Crime in England and Wales: annual supplementary tables*, Office of National Statistics (ONS), available at: www.ons.gov.uk.

7 YouGov/EVAW Survey, 27–28 October 2021, available at: www.endviolenceagainstwomen.org.uk.

8 *R v Commissioner of the Police of the Metropolis ex p Blackburn (No 1)* [1968] 2 QB 118, CA.

9 Policing Protocol Order 2011 SI No 2744 Sch para 35.

2.17 As policing has moved from a local to a national concern, central government has become more involved in setting strategic priorities for the police. For example, since 2012 the Secretary of State for the Home Department from time to time issues a document entitled the *Strategic policing requirement* to which all chief officers of police must have regard when exercising their functions.[10] This document sets out what the secretary of state considers to be national threats and the appropriate national policing capabilities to counter those national threats.[11] The role of the secretary of state, including more direct intervention in policing, is discussed further below.

The office of constable

Overview

2.18 A key element of police independence, which remains a cornerstone of the modern police force, is the office of constable. All members of a police force irrespective of their rank hold the office of constable.

2.19 The office of constable is an ancient one, deriving from the common law. Centuries ago, each parish was required to elect a parish constable. The constable acted as executive agent and representative of the village and had duties including keeping the peace (under supervision of justices of the peace). However, the office was unpopular and many parishes failed to make appointments. From the middle of the 17th century, the local justices of the peace had power to appoint a constable if elections were not held, but even then practice varied around the country and many areas effectively had no constable at all. Where constables did exist it was customary for them to be sworn into office by justices of the peace (as they continue to be). By reason of this oath, and because of the relationship with the local justices, constables were recognised as officers of the Crown.[12]

2.20 The lack of consistent and effective peacekeeping bodies across the country led inexorably to the establishment of modern police forces, within which constables retained their common law powers and their independent status. Modern police constables remain officers of the Crown and not employees of their police force.

2.21 The powers of a constable acting as a police officer, whether conferred by common law or now by statute, are exercised by virtue of the office of constable and cannot be exercised on the responsibility of any other person. A police officer is an officer whose 'authority is original, not delegated, and exercised at his own discretion by virtue of his office'.[13] A constable only exercises a delegated authority when acting in execution of a lawfully issued warrant.

10 The March 2015 version is available at: www.gov.uk/government/publications/strategic-policing-requirement. Plans for a *Strategic policing requirement* review, to coincide with elections of PCCs, did not result in any further version being published by the end of that year.

11 Police Act 1996 s37A (as amended by PRSRA 2011 s77).

12 *Mackalley's Case* (1611) 9 Co Rep 65b at 68b.

13 Viscount Simmonds in *Attorney-General for New South Wales v Perpetual Trustee Co Ltd* [1955] AC 457, PC (Australia).

2.22 A constable cannot therefore be ordered to exercise their powers in a particular manner by the Home Office, by any other emanation of the Crown or by a PCC. Nor can a constable rely upon a claim that they were simply obeying the orders of a superior officer as a defence to a civil, disciplinary or criminal charge of wrongdoing. Neither a superior officer, nor even the courts, can order a constable to exercise a power which can only be lawfully exercised if the constable forms a suspicion or belief on reasonable grounds.[14]

2.23 It remains somewhat difficult to square a constable's status as independent 'officer of the peace', exercising original powers at their own discretion, with their position as a member of a disciplined body subject to the lawful orders of superior officers. The police *Standards of professional behaviour*[15] state that:

> Police officers only give and carry out lawful orders and instructions.
> Police officers abide by police regulations, force policies and lawful orders.

2.24 In an earlier version, the statutory guidance that accompanied the above standards provided the following important qualification:

> 1.40 The police service is a disciplined body and therefore any decision not to follow an order or instruction will need to be fully justified.
>
> 1.41 There may however be instances when failure to follow an order or instruction does not amount to misconduct. This may be for example where the police officer reasonably believed that a lawful order was in fact unlawful or where a police officer had good and sufficient reason not to comply having regard to all the circumstances and possible consequences.[16]

2.25 These passages were removed in 'version 4' of the guidance.[17] They do not appear in the current guidance, which was recast in 2020, either.[18]

Attestation of constables

2.26 Every member of a police force maintained for a police area and every special constable appointed for a police area must on appointment be attested before a justice of the peace as a constable by making a declaration in the prescribed form.[19] It is the act of attestation that confers the status of constable.[20]

2.27 The modern form of attestation is:

> I do solemnly and sincerely declare and affirm that I will well and truly serve the Queen in the office of constable, with fairness, integrity, diligence

14 *R v Chief Constable of Devon and Cornwall ex p Central Electricity Generating Board* [1982] QB 458, CA.

15 Police (Conduct) Regulations 2020 SI No 4 Sch 2.

16 *Home Office guidance: police officer misconduct, unsatisfactory performance and attendance management procedures*, issued under Police Act 1996 s87(1), v2, November 2012.

17 Home Office, v4, May 2015.

18 *Home Office guidance: conduct, efficiency, and effectiveness: statutory guidance on professional standards, performance and integrity in policing*, v1.0, 5 February 2020, available at: www.gov.uk/government/publications/policing-professional-standards-performance-and-integrity.

19 Police Act 1996 s29.

20 *Sheikh v Chief Constable of Greater Manchester Police* [1990] 1 QB 637 CA.

> and impartiality, upholding fundamental human rights and according equal respect to all people; and that I will, to the best of my power, cause the peace to be kept and preserved and prevent all offences against people and property; and that while I continue to hold the said office I will, to the best of my skill and knowledge, discharge all the duties thereof faithfully according to the law.[21]

Vicarious liability

2.28 A consequence of police officers holding the office of constable rather than being employees is that there is no employer to bear vicarious liability at common law for their wrongful acts.[22]

2.29 As it was plainly undesirable, both for the police and for potential claimants, that there should be no form of vicarious liability for police wrongdoing, parliament has provided that the chief officer of any force shall be liable in respect of any unlawful conduct of constables under their direction and control in the performance or purported performance of their functions, in the like manner as an employer is liable in respect of any unlawful conduct of their employees in the course of their employment.[23]

2.30 Given that constables exercise their powers on their own authority and do not require authorisation from their superior officers, it follows that a chief officer can be vicariously liable for the actions of an off-duty officer, but only where there was a close connection between the officer's tortious actions and their position as a police officer.[24] See further para 14.120 below.

Duties of constables

2.31 There is no single and comprehensive statement of all the duties of constables. The duties derive from common law, and have been formulated in a number of ways in various leading cases. For example, in *Glasbrook Bros Ltd v Glamorgan* in 1925, Viscount Finlay stated that: 'There is no doubt that it is the duty of the police to give adequate protection to all persons and to their property.'[25] Forty years later, in *Rice v Connelly* it was said that:[26]

> . . . it is part of the obligations and duties of a police constable to take all steps which appear to him necessary for keeping the peace, for preventing crime or for protecting property from criminal injury. There is no exhaustive definition of the powers and obligations of the police, but they are at

21 Police Act 1996 Sch 4.

22 This is perhaps less of an issue in light of the development of vicarious liability beyond the confines of the traditional employer/employee relationship (eg *Various Claimants v Catholic Child Welfare Society* [2012] UKSC 56, [2013] 2 AC 1).

23 Police Act 1996 s88(1).

24 *Allen v Chief Constable of Hampshire Constabulary* [2013] EWCA Civ 967. In *N v Chief Constable of Merseyside* [2006] EWHC 3041 (QB) a claim of vicarious liability was rejected when an off-duty constable in uniform used his position as a police officer to take an insensible woman into his custody and then sexually abused her.

25 *Glasbrook Bros Ltd v Glamorgan CC* [1925] AC 270, HL.

26 *Rice v Connelly* [1966] 2 QB 414 at P419, DC.

least those, and they would further include the duty to detect crime and to bring an offender to justice.

2.32 The common law duty on the police to investigate effectively has been described as 'a bare minimum safeguard in any civilised State'.[27] These broad principles are echoed in the attestation made by each and every constable (see above). However, the common law does not go as far as the European Convention on Human Rights (ECHR) in this respect, which imposes a positive obligation to investigate potential violations of the right to life (Article 2), the prohibition on torture or inhuman or degrading treatment (Article 3) and the prohibition on slavery and forced labour (Article 4).[28]

2.33 There are limits to the broadly stated common law duties. Chief officers have 'the widest possible discretion' in their choice of the methods by which they discharge their duties to keep the peace and enforce the law.[29] The courts have taken the view that it is for the chief officer and individual members of a police force to weigh up the competing demands upon their limited resources in deciding how and when to exercise their duties. Provided they act in an even-handed way and not in a discriminatory manner, the courts will be reluctant to second-guess their judgments.

Jurisdiction of constables

2.34 A member of a police force has all the powers and privileges of a constable throughout England and Wales and the adjacent UK waters.[30]

2.35 Police powers across borders within the UK are dealt with in Criminal Justice and Public Order Act (CJPOA) 1994 Part X. Police officers from England and Wales may execute in Scotland or Northern Ireland an arrest warrant issued in England and Wales;[31] and where a crime is committed in England and Wales, they may pursue a suspect into Scotland or Northern Ireland and arrest them there (if it would have been lawful to have done so in their own jurisdiction).[32] Furthermore, a constable of a police force in England and Wales has the same powers to arrest a person in Scotland or Northern Ireland as would have a police officer from those jurisdictions (ie under local law) – and Scottish or Northern Irish police officers have the same powers of arrest in England and Wales as a constable of England and Wales.[33]

27 *DSD v Commissioner of Police of the Metropolis* [2014] EWHC 436 (QB) at para 230.

28 See the discussion in *DSD* on appeal to the Supreme Court: [2018] UKSC 11, [2019] AC 196.

29 *R v Commissioner of Police of the Metropolis ex p Blackburn (No 1)* [1968] 2 QB 118, CA; and, regarding Article 4, *OOO v Commissioner of Police of the Metropolis* [2011] EWHC 1246 (QB).

30 Police Act 1996 s30(1).

31 CJPOA 1994 s136. Scottish and Northern Irish police officers may equally enforce arrest warrants issued within their jurisdictions in England and Wales.

32 CJPOA 1994 s137. Again, Scottish and Northern Irish police officers have the same powers to arrest persons within England and Wales.

33 CJPOA 1994 s140. The person arrested will have the same rights as they would if arrested by an officer of the country's own police.

Special constables

2.36 Special constables are unpaid volunteers, serving as a part-time reserve for regular police forces. Each of the 43 territorial police forces in England and Wales, as well as the Scottish police forces and the British Transport Police (BTP), has its own special constabulary. They will often be called upon to assist in the policing of large public events and demonstrations or to help in major investigations. A special constable wears the same uniform and has all the same powers and privileges as a constable throughout England and Wales and the adjacent UK waters.[34]

2.37 Special constables are appointed by the chief officer for their area and are under the direction and control of, and subject to dismissal by, the chief officer.[35] Every special constable appointed for a police area must on appointment be attested as a constable by making a declaration before a justice of the peace in the prescribed form.[36] As with the regular members of a police force, it is the act of attestation that confers the status of constable.

2.38 Special constables are personally liable for their unlawful conduct in the civil courts in the same way as regular members of a police force. Equally, as special constables hold the office of constable, a chief officer will be statutorily vicariously liable for their unlawful conduct.[37]

Civilian employees

Overview

2.39 The police employ numerous staff to carry out administrative duties and other functions not directly associated with the detection and prevention of crime (eg clerical work, human resources, public relations, legal etc). Over the past few decades, there has also been a substantial increase in the recruitment of civilian staff to carry out functions formerly carried out by police officers. In 2010 the Police Federation recorded that the ratio of police officers to civilian staff across England and Wales had dropped from 2.3:1 in 2000 to 1.4:1 in 2009, although government figures indicate that by 2021 this had increased slighty to 1:6:1.[38]

2.40 In 2021 there were over 85,000 civilian staff carrying out a wide range of duties, including police community support officers (PCSOs; also known as community support officers (CSOs)), control room staff, front-desk staff, detention and escort officers, scene-of-crime officers, civilian investigating officers, computer forensic investigators, crime analysts and prosecution file preparation officers.[39]

34 Police Act 1996 s30(2).

35 Police Act 1996 s27.

36 Police Act 1996 s29.

37 Police Act 1996 s88(1).

38 See: https://www.gov.uk/government/statistics/police-workforce-england-and-wales-31-march-2021/police-workforce-england-and-wales-31-march-2021#headline-workforcefigures/.

39 *Police workforce tables*, Home Office, 31 March 2021, published 28 July 2021.

2.41 Civilian staff by definition do not hold the office of constable. They are, however, like constables, under the direction and control of the chief officer of police.[40]

2.42 Of the many different civilian roles, four are granted some of the powers of a constable. A person can only occupy one of these roles if so designated by the chief officer, and the chief officer is only permitted to so designate if satisfied that the person is suitable, capable and properly trained. The four roles are:

1) PCSO/CSO;
2) investigating officer;
3) detention officer; and
4) escort officer.[41]

2.43 The powers of each category of civilian officer are specific to that category and none has all the powers of a constable. Nevertheless the powers are extensive.[42] A person may be designated to more than one category.

Police community support officers

2.44 The most frequently encountered category of civilian staff in a traditional policing role is the PCSO (or alternatively CSO). These are uniformed civilian officers, primarily used to support the delivery of 'neighbourhood policing' and to deal with low-level anti-social behaviour and disorder.

2.45 Until 2017, all PCSOs had certain standard powers derived from statute with other powers that could be granted by the relevant chief constable. The PCA 2017 abolished the list of standard powers and provided that PCSOs shall only have those powers which the relevant chief constable considers necessary in their area.[43] The legislation reserved certain powers – such as arrest – to constables only.[44]

2.46 Complaints against civilian employees, as persons under the direction and control of the chief officer, come within the police complaints system. See further chapters 3 and 4 on police complaints and their resolution.

2.47 For the purpose of determining liability for unlawful conduct of a civilian police employee, conduct in reliance or purported reliance on a designation is taken to be conduct in the course of the person's employment. In the case of a tort the employer, be it the chief officer of police or the local policing body, is treated as a joint tortfeasor (see further 'Vicarious liability' above at para 2.28).[45]

Contracted-out staff

2.48 The contracting-out of police functions is an increasing reality of policing in England and Wales. The majority of contracting-out relates to support

40 PRSRA 2011 ss2(3) and 4(3).
41 Police Reform Act (PRA) 2002 s38.
42 PRA 2002 Sch 4.
43 PCA 2017 s38.
44 PRA 2002 Sch 3B, as inserted by PCA 2017 Sch 10.
45 PRA 2002 s42(7).

functions, but the private sector is extending into more core police functions, such as the management and operation of custody suites.

2.49 Where a private sector contractor provide services relating to the detention or escort of persons in custody, a chief officer can designate a civilian employee of that contractor as either a detention officer or escort officer.[46] Such a person will have the powers and duties conferred or imposed by the designation[47] and if those powers, if exercised by a constable, would carry with them a power to use reasonable force, the contracted out staff shall also have the same entitlement to use reasonable force.[48] Complaints against contracted-out detention or escort officers fall within the responsibility of the Independent Office for Police Conduct (IOPC), but under a distinct system.[49]

2.50 For the purpose of determining liability for unlawful conduct of an employee of a contractor, conduct in reliance or purported reliance on a designation is taken to be conduct in the course of the person's employment. In the case of a tort, the contractor is treated a joint tortfeasor.[50]

Police forces in England and Wales

Geographic forces

2.51 Policing in England and Wales is primarily organised on a geographical basis – in part as a consequence of the origins of the constable as a locally arranged function. There are 39 statutorily defined police areas in England (including the Metropolitan Police (in Greater London) and City of London Police areas) and a further four in Wales, for a total of 43.[51]

2.52 This arrangement has been described in 2020 as 'no longer fit for purpose' by Her Majesty's Inspectorate of Constabulary and Fire and Rescue Services (HMICFRS).[52] It is said to present problems 'for many aspects of policing, including in the flow of information and intelligence between forces, and the establishment and efficient operation of national ICT systems'.[53] Any significant reform would require primary legislation.

46 PRA 2002 s39.

47 PRA 2002 s39(6).

48 PRA 2002 s39(8).

49 Independent Police Complaints Commission (Complaints and Misconduct) (Contractors) Regulations 2015 SI No 431, as amended by the Independent Office for Police Conduct (Transitional and Consequential) Regulations 2017 SI No 1250.

50 PRA 2002 s42(9).

51 Police Act 1996 Sch 1.

52 *State of policing: the annual assessment of policing in England and Wales 2019*, HMICFRS, 2020, p35.

53 *State of policing: the annual assessment of policing in England and Wales 2020*, HMICFRS, 2021, p42. The 2018 report had elaborated: '... in too many respects, the lines on the map that delineate force boundaries act as barriers to the exchange of intelligence, to co-operation, and to true effectiveness and efficiency'. *State of Policing: the annual assessment of policing in England and Wales 2018*, HMICRFS, 2019, p13.

Non-geographic forces

2.53 There are also a number of forces not tied to a particular location. The most prominent of these are the BTP, the Ministry of Defence Police (MDP) and the National Crime Agency (NCA).

British Transport Police

2.54 Since 1 July 2004 the BTP has been maintained by the British Transport Police Authority (BTPA).[54] Its function is to police the railways, specifically the railways of England and Wales, Scotland, the London Underground system, the Docklands Light Railway, the Midland Metro Tram System, parts of the Tyne and Wear Metro and the Glasgow Subway, as well as the Croydon Tramlink and the Thames cable car. These functions are carried out under police services agreements with the private companies running the railways.[55]

2.55 The BTP has its own chief constable, deputy chief constable and assistant chief constable.[56] In contrast to the status of constables in the geographic forces, the BTPA appoints and *employs* constables of the force.[57] The authority may therefore be sued in vicarious liability for the wrongful acts of its constable/employees. The chief constable can appoint special constables and cadets.[58] As special constables are not employees of the BTPA, and the Authority therefore cannot be vicariously liable, the chief constable is made vicariously liable for their wrongful acts by statute.[59]

2.56 A constable of the BTP has all the powers and privileges of a constable on track; network; in a station; in a light maintenance depot; on other land used for purposes of or in relation to a railway; on other land in which a person who provides railway services has a freehold or leasehold interest; and throughout Great Britain for a purpose connected to a railway or to anything occurring on or in relation to a railway.[60]

Ministry of Defence Police

2.57 The MDP (separate and distinct from the military police, who are not covered in this chapter) has a wide variety of responsibilities covering UK military, naval and air force installations, dockyards and ordnance companies. The force was put on a statutory basis in 1987.[61] It consists of officers nominated by the Secretary of State for Defence and attested as constables before a justice of the peace.[62] MDP constables have the full powers and privileges of any other constable, and operate under the direction and

54 Railways and Transport Safety Act (RTSA) 2003 s20.
55 RTSA 2003 ss33–34.
56 RTSA 2003 ss21, 22 and 23.
57 RTSA 2003 s24.
58 RTSA 2003 ss25 and 26.
59 RTSA 2003 s25(5).
60 RTSA 2003 s31. Policing of the Channel Tunnel system is the responsibility of the Kent Constabulary: Channel Tunnel Act 1987 s14.
61 Ministry of Defence Police Act 1987.
62 Ministry of Defence Police Act 1987 s1.

control of the MDP chief constable.[63] Members of the MDP are both constables and civil servants in the employment of the Crown; any civil proceedings may be brought against the individual officer or the Ministry of Defence (MOD).[64]

2.58 In the aftermath of the strategic defence and security review in 2010,[65] and the context of government 'austerity', there has been a shift in the MDP responsibilities, and reduction in its personnel. The MDP's *Corporate plan 2020–2025* describes its purpose as 'to deliver unique specialist policing, to protect the nation's defences and national infrastructure'.[66] It is tasked by the MOD to enable the delivery of certain 'defence tasks' through provision of policing and protective security services:

- defence, security and resilience of the UK and its overseas territories;
- nuclear deterrence and the defence nuclear enterprise;
- strategic intelligence and the global defence network;
- overseas defence activity;
- promoting UK prosperity and civil society.[67]

2.59 The MDP's primary policing outputs are nuclear policing; territorial policing (specialist services in relation to defence and critical national infrastructure); national counter-terrorist response (in particular armed response to major incidents); and crime and intelligence (in particular in relation to defence equipment and assets).[68]

National Crime Agency

2.60 The NCA was established in 2013. It replaced the Serious Organised Crime Agency (SOCA) and part of the National Policing Improvement Agency (NPIA).[69]

2.61 The NCA is a non-ministerial government department with core functions of 'crime-reduction' and 'criminal intelligence' gathering.[70] In contrast to the largely local set-up of police forces in England and Wales, the NCA operates as a national law enforcement agency. It is made up of separate commands, including Border Policing; Economic Crime; Organised Crime; Intelligence; and Operations. It also houses the Child Exploitation and Online Protection (CEOP) Command and the National Cyber Crime Unit (NCCU).

2.62 The NCA is headed by a Director General, who has independent operational direction and control over the NCA's activities. The NCA takes up a position at the top of the police hierarchy, with the role of setting the

63 Ministry of Defence Police Act 1987 s1(3).

64 Crown Proceedings Act 1947 s2(1).

65 *Securing Britain in an age of uncertainty: the strategic defence and security review*, 2010, Command Paper No 7948.

66 *Ministry of Defence Police: Corporate plan 2020–2025*, 2020, p6.

67 *Ministry of Defence Police: Corporate plan 2020–2025*, 2020, p6.

68 *Ministry of Defence Police: Corporate plan 2020–2025*, 2020, p8.

69 The NCA was established by Crime and Courts Act (CCA) 2013 s1; SOCA and the NPIA were abolished under s15.

70 CCA 2013 s1.

overall operational agenda for tackling serious and organised criminality.[71] While the Director General can *request* that chief officers of the geographic police forces perform functions to assist the NCA, they also have the power to *direct* them to do so.[72] They are, however, accountable to the Home Secretary and, through the Home Secretary, to parliament.

2.63 The Director General may designate NCA officers as having the powers and privileges of a constable, an officer of Revenue and Customs or an immigration officer.[73] NCA functions are exercised on behalf of the Crown[74] and the NCA will be vicariously liable for the unlawful actions of its officers.

Rank structure

2.64 The geographic police forces are organised under a common rank structure:

- constable;
- sergeant;
- inspector;
- chief inspector;
- superintendent;
- chief superintendent;
- assistant chief constable;
- chief constable.

2.65 In the Metropolitan Police, the ranks above chief superintendent vary:[75]

- commander;
- deputy assistant commissioner;
- assistant commissioner;
- deputy commissioner;
- commissioner.

2.66 'Senior officers' are defined as those officers holding a rank above chief superintendent.[76]

Organisation of the police in England and Wales

Police and crime commissioners

Overview

2.67 The task of securing the maintenance of an efficient and effective police force within a police area used to fall to police authorities. However, under

71 *The National Crime Agency: A plan for the creation of a national crime-fighting capability*, Cm 8097, Home Office, June 2011.

72 CCA 2013 s5.

73 CCA 2013 s10.

74 CCA 2013 Sch 1 para 1.

75 In the City of London Police, the ranks above chief superintendent are commander, deputy commissioner and commissioner.

76 See, for example, Police Act 1996 s50(6B).

the PRSRA 2011, police authorities were abolished[77] and replaced with a PCC, or in certain places, the relevant mayoralty. In certain areas, the PCC also has responsibility for fire and rescue services.[78]

2.68 The aim of the reform was 'increasing local accountability and giving the public a direct say on how their streets are policed' and 'ensuring the police respond to local priorities and are directly accountable to the public for delivering safer communities and cutting crime and [anti-social behaviour]'.[79]

2.69 PCCs are directly elected and serve a four-year term. Elections were held in 2012, 2016 and 2021. The 2021 elections fell between two stages of a government review of the operation of PCCs. In March 2021 the Home Secretary informed parliament of the outcome of the first stage of the review, and the government's intention to strengthen accountability of PCCs and improve transparency. The government also committed to provide a 'brighter-line' on the boundaries of operational independence.[80] In March 2022 the second stage outcomes included focusses on offender management, partnerships with other agencies, improving public confidence in policing, and greater access to criminal justice data.[81]

2.70 The essential role of a PCC for a police area is to 'secure the maintenance of the police force for that area'; to 'secure that the police force is efficient and effective'; and to 'hold the relevant chief constable to account for the exercise of (a) the functions of the chief constable, and (b) the functions of persons under the direction and control of the chief constable'.[82]

2.71 PCCs are responsible for financing the police, receiving the police grant from central government, and other financial grants, that previously were provided to police authorities.[83]

2.72 The Metropolitan Police Service does not have a PCC, but falls under the supervision of the Mayor's Office for Policing and Crime which serves the same role,[84] and has essentially the same obligations.[85] Thus the elected Mayor of London effectively operates as the PCC for the Metropolitan Police Service. Similarly, in Greater Manchester, and in West Yorkshire, the role of the PCC is undertaken by the respective mayoralty for the area.

77 PRSRA 2011 s1(9).

78 PCA 2017 Sch 1 Pt 2 para 87(2)–(3).

79 The government's July 2010 white paper *Policing in the 21st Century: Reconnecting police and the people* (Cm 7925), paras 2.1 and 2.2.

80 Priti Patel MP, *Police and Crime Commissioner Review: concluding part one*, Statement of 16 March 2021.

81 Priti Patel MP, Update on Part Two of the Police and Crime Commissioner Review, Statement of 7 March 2022.

82 PRSRA 2011 s1(6)–(7).

83 Police Act 1996 ss46–48 and 92–94.

84 PRSRA 2011 s3.

85 The PRSRA 2011 refers to the PCC and Mayor's Office collectively as 'elected local policing bodies'.

Police and crime plans and other tasks

2.73 PCCs must issue a 'police and crime plan' (with regard to the views of the police and crime panel (see below) and in consultation with the chief constable),[86] which is a plan setting out matters such as police and crime objectives (essentially the objectives for policing and crime reduction in the area), what policing the chief constable is to provide and the financial and other resources to be provided to the chief constable.[87] The Home Secretary has the power to provide guidance on the matters to be dealt with in police and crime plans, to which a PCC must have regard.[88]

2.74 Both the PCC and the chief constable have a duty to have regard to the police and crime plan when exercising their functions.[89] The Home Secretary can issue guidance on how that duty is to be complied with, to which the body concerned must have regard.[90]

2.75 PCCs must also:

- co-operate with 'responsible authorities';[91]
- make arrangements with 'criminal justice bodies' (such as the Crown Prosecution Service (CPS) and youth offending teams);[92]
- provide the public with information to allow them to assess the performance of the PCC and chief constable;[93]
- publish annual reports;[94]
- provide relevant information to the police and crime panel (see below).[95]

2.76 PCCs must arrange to obtain the view of the community on policing (including views on the police and crime plan before it is published).[96] When carrying out its functions, the PCC must have regard to the views of people in the area about policing.[97] The statutory framework does not set out a process by which this is to be done. The College of Policing (COP) Authorised Professional Practice (APP) on 'Engagement' refers to this duty. It goes on to note that 'Community engagement needs to be effectively implemented to ensure community participation occurs at all levels of policing'.[98] A PCC that fails to discharge its duty to have regard to such views could be held to account by a judicial review claim.

86 PRSRA 2011 s5.
87 PRSRA 2011 s7(1)–(3).
88 PRSRA 2011 s7(4)–(5).
89 PRSRA 2011 s8.
90 PRSRA 2011 s8(5)–(7).
91 As defined in Crime and Disorder Act 1998 s5: PRSRA 2011 s10(2).
92 PRSRA 2011 s10(3) and (5).
93 PRSRA 2011 s11.
94 PRSRA 2011 s12.
95 PRSRA 2011 s13.
96 PRSRA 2011 s14.
97 PRSRA 2011 s17.
98 Available at: www.app.college.police.uk/app-content/engagement-and-communication/engaging-with-communities/.

Powers to appoint and remove chief officers

2.77 Significantly, the PCC for a police area is responsible for appointing the chief constable. The PCC also has the power to suspend chief constables and to require them to resign or retire.[99] The power to require resignation or retirement may only be exercised following a scrutiny process and an opportunity for the chief constable to make representations, and following review by the police and crime panel.

2.78 PCCs must also be consulted by the chief constable before any deputy or assistant chief constable is appointed.[100]

2.79 The Metropolitan Police Commissioner, and Deputy Commissioner, continues to be appointed by the Queen, following recommendation by the Home Secretary.[101] The Mayor's Office for Policing and Crime must be consulted before assistant commissioners, deputy assistant commissioners and commanders are appointed.[102]

2.80 The Mayor's Office for Policing and Crime, with the approval of the Home Secretary, may suspend the commissioner or the deputy commissioner or require them to retire or resign.[103]

Accountability of elected local policing bodies

2.81 While the PCCs hold chief constables to account, they themselves are held to account by 'police and crime panels'.[104] The appointment, structure and procedures of police and crime panels is dealt with in PRSRA 2011 Sch 6. Police and crime panels can either be established by local authorities or centrally by the secretary of state.[105]

2.82 If established by a local authority, a police and crime panel is a committee of the relevant local authority (if it is the panel for a single-authority police area), or joint committee of the relevant local authorities (if it is the panel for a multi-authority police area).[106] If established by the secretary of state, the panel is not a local authority committee.[107]

2.83 The responsibilities of these bodies include reviewing and scrutinising the actions of the PCC in the discharge of their functions and making reports or recommendations to the PCC in respect of the discharge of those functions.[108]

2.84 The police and crime panel reviews the draft crime and police plan and can provide reports or make recommendations on it. After the publication of the PCC's annual report it must hold a public meeting at which the PCC will answer questions on it, and then review the annual report. The panel also

99 PRSRA 2011 s38 and Sch 8, see further chapters 3 and 4 on police complaints.
100 PRSRA 2011 ss39–40 and Sch 8.
101 PRSRA 2011 s42–43.
102 PRSRA 2011 s45–47.
103 PRSRA 2011 s48.
104 If a PCC also has responsibility for fire and rescue services, then the relevant panel will be Police, Fire and Crime Panel: PRSRA 2011 s28, as amended by PCA 2017 Sch 1 Pt 2 para 89.
105 PRSRA 2011 Sch 6 Part 1.
106 PRSRA 2011 Sch 6 Part 2.
107 PRSRA 2011 Sch 6 Part 3.
108 PRSRA 2011 s28.

scrutinises, and makes recommendations in respect of, the appointment of chief and senior officers and senior appointments to the PCC's staff.[109]

2.85 The police and crime panel is not limited to making recommendations. It has the power of veto over an appointment as chief constable.[110] It also has the power to require the PCC or their staff to attend before it and ask questions at any time,[111] and the power to suspend the PCC, but only if charged with an offence punishable with more than two years' imprisonment.[112]

2.86 In respect of the Metropolitan Police Service, the same role is played by the London Assembly police and crime panel.[113]

Chief officers of police

2.87 The Commissioners of the Metropolitan Police and the City of London Police and the chief constables of the other 41 police forces in England and Wales[114] are collectively called 'chief officers' or 'chief officers of police'.[115] The direction and control of their respective forces is vested by statute in the Commissioner of the Metropolitan Police (a corporation sole) and the 41 chief constables.[116]

2.88 The Commissioners of the Metropolitan Police and the City of London Police have certain functions in addition to those of chief constables, eg concerning the routes to be followed by public processions.[117]

2.89 The PRSRA 2011 places obligations on chief officers of police with the aim of increasing the accountability of the police to the public. They must make arrangements for obtaining the views of persons within 'neighbourhoods'[118] about crime and disorder, and for providing them with information about policing (including through holding neighbourhood beat meetings).[119] The COP APP on 'Engagement' is relevant, again, here.[120] A failure to discharge the statutory duty could be subject to judicial review. Reflecting the focus on austerity at the time the PRSRA 2011 was passed, in exercising their functions chief officers are under a specific obligation to secure that 'good value for money is obtained'.[121]

2.90 By section 8 of the PCSCA 2022, chief officers of police are required to collaborate with the relevant authorities in each area to prevent and reduce serious violence, including by jointly preparing and implementing a

109 PRSRA 2011 Sch 1 paras 9–12 and Sch 8.
110 PRSRA 2011 Sch 8 para 5.
111 PRSRA 2011 s29 (reasonable notice must be given).
112 PRSRA 2011 s30.
113 PRSRA 2011 ss32–33.
114 Ie those listed in Police Act 1996 Sch 1.
115 Police Act 1996 s101(1).
116 PRSRA 2011 ss2 and 4. The Commissioner of the City of London Police is still governed by the City of London Police Act 1839. However, Police Act 1996 s88(1) applies to all chief officers including the Commissioner of the City of London Police and constables under their direction and control.
117 Metropolitan Police Act 1839 s52, as amended; City of London Police Act 1839 s22, as amended.
118 A unit that it is up to the chief officer of police to determine.
119 PRSRA 2011, s34.
120 COP, APP on Engagement.
121 PRSRA 2011 s35.

strategy which is required to be published. By section 14 of the Act, PCCs are empowered to assist.

Role of the Secretary of State for the Home Department[122]

2.91 The limits of the traditional independence of the police from government are reached in the Secretary of State for the Home Department's powers set out in the Police Act 1996.

2.92 Perhaps most stark is the secretary of state's power to direct local policing bodies to take specified measures if they are satisfied that the whole or any part of a police force, or the local policing body itself, is failing (or will fail) to discharge any of its functions in an effective manner. These powers can only be exercised once the local policing body, and HMICFRS,[123] have been given an opportunity to respond to the secretary of state's concerns.[124] If the secretary of state makes any such direction, they must lay it (and a report on it) before parliament.[125]

2.93 The secretary of state also retains a power to require the Mayor's Office for Policing and Crime to call upon the commissioner or deputy commissioner to retire or resign, but only following an inquiry.[126]

2.94 The secretary of state has further powers to:

- set minimum budgets for local policing bodies;
- require chief officers to report on the work of their forces;
- make regulations covering: the government, administration and conditions of service of police forces, special constables and cadets;[127] the standard and provision of equipment;[128] police procedures and practices.[129]

2.95 The secretary of state also influences policing by issuing a 'policing protocol' to which chief officers, local elected policing bodies and police and crime panels must have regard.[130] The Policing Protocol Order was made in 2011[131] and has been amended several times since – most recently by the Police (Complaints and Misconduct) Regulations 2020.[132] This protocol sets out ways in which these bodies should exercise, or limit, their functions in the interests of positive working relationships, and avoiding overlap or conflict, between them. The current protocol is subject to review as part of the government's consideration of the role and functions of PCCs. The secretary of state is also responsible for issuing

122 In relation to the geographical police forces, the relevant secretary of state is the Home Secretary.
123 The former Her Majesty's Inspectorate of Constabulary took on additional responsibility for fire and rescue services in 2017.
124 Police Act 1996 ss40–40A.
125 Police Act 1996 s40B(6).
126 Police Act 1996 s42.
127 Police Act 1996 ss50–52.
128 Police Act 1996 s53.
129 Police Act 1996 s53A.
130 PRSRA 2011 s79.
131 Policing Protocol Order 2011 SI No 2744.
132 SI No 2.

the Police and Criminal Evidence Act 1984 (PACE) Codes of Practice pursuant to section 66 of the Act.

2.96 Finally, the secretary of state has a 'general duty' to exercise the powers conferred by the Police Act 1996 and PRSRA 2011 in such manner and to such extent as appears best calculated to promote the efficiency and effectiveness of police.[133]

2.97 PCSCA 2022 s1 requires the secretary of state to make an annual 'police covenant report' to parliament. The report is required to address the health and wellbeing of members and former members of the police force, their physical protection, and any other matter the secretary of state considers relevant. The secretary of state is obliged to have regard to certain matters, including 'the obligations of and sacrifices made by members of the police workforce'.

Oversight and professional bodies

Her Majesty's Inspectorate of Constabulary and Fire and Rescue Services

2.98 Established in 1856, and expanded in 2017 to include fire and rescue services, HMICFRS inspect and report publicly on the efficiency and effectiveness of the police forces in England and Wales.[134] As independent holders of public office under the Crown, appointed under Royal Warrant, the four inspectors and the chief inspector are neither civil servants nor police officers. Acting under the direction of the secretary of state, their ultimate responsibility is to parliament – to whom the chief inspector must provide an annual report providing their assessment of the efficiency and effectiveness of policing in England and Wales.[135]

2.99 Local policing bodies may request HMICFRS to inspect the force in their police area.[136] They, along with the chief of police, may also publish comments on any report on the police in their area.[137]

Independent Office for Police Conduct

2.100 The IOPC was established under the PCA 2017, and is responsible for oversight of the police complaints system and related matters. It is responsible for maintaining suitable arrangements for the handling of complaints and for recording disciplinary matters and criminal offences committed by police officer. It replaced the Independent Police Complaints Commission (IPCC) which had undertaken that function since 2002. The IOPC has additional powers that the IPCC did not, including a power to initiate its own investigations without relying on referrals from police

133 Police Act 1996 s36; and PRSRA 2011 s78.

134 Police Act 1996 s54(2). HMICFRS's statement of purpose reads: 'Promoting improvements in policing and fire & rescue services to make everyone safer.'

135 Police Act 1996 s54(4)-(4A). Detail on the powers and responsibilities of HMICFRS is set out in Police Act 1996 Sch 4A.

136 Police Act 1996 s54(2BA).

137 Police Act 1996 s55.

forces.[138] The IOPC has responsibilities for the 43 geographic police forces and also for the NCA and independent police forces (discussed above).[139] Its functions are described in further detail in chapter 3.

College of Policing

2.101 Established in 2012 and beginning operation in 2013, the COP is the professional body for all those who work in policing in England and Wales. It is a limited company wholly owned by the Home Secretary and an arm's-length body of the Home Office. The COP has taken on functions previously carried out by the NPIA and the Association of Chief Police Officers (ACPO) (see below). It describes its functions as threefold:

- sharing knowledge and good practice within the policing community;
- setting service standards for policing;
- supporting the professional development of police personnel.

2.102 To this end, the COP has statutory powers to submit to the Home Secretary for approval draft regulations on the government, administration and conditions of service of police forces; to issue codes of practice to chief officers of police relating to the discharge of their functions; and to issue guidance on the appropriate qualifications, experience and training of civilian staff.[140]

2.103 The COP is responsible for delivery of the Policing Education Qualification Framework which, pursuant to the APCC's *Policing Vision 2025*, will standardise entry requirements and learning provision for new police officers.

2.104 The COP's 'Authorised Professional Practice' (APP) is a key form of non-statutory guidance for police officers. In *Catt*, both the Supreme Court and the European Court of Human Rights considered such guidance to be part of the framework relied upon for the purpose of an assessment of whether or not an interference with rights had a legal basis.[141] Key guidance relates to the use of force, the use of firearms, and discrimination.[142] APPs may be relied upon as setting standards of conduct in civil actions against the police,[143] in complaints and IOPC investigations,[144] and in judicial review challenges.[145]

2.105 In addition, the COP's guidance can itself be subject to judicial review, as in *Miller*, in which the Court of Appeal held that guidance on police

138 PCA 2017 s17.

139 The IOPC is also is also responsible for dealing with serious complaints and conduct matters relating to staff at Her Majesty's Revenue and Customs (HMRC) and Home Office immigration and enforcement staff.

140 Introduced into the Police Act 1996 by Anti-social Behaviour, Crime and Policing Act 2014 ss123–125.

141 *R (Catt) v Commissioner of Police of the Metropolis* [2015] UKSC 9, [2015] AC 1065; *Catt v UK* (2019) 69 EHRR 7.

142 All guidance is available online at: www.app.college.police.uk.

143 Eg *Watling v Chief Constable of Suffolk* [2019] EWHC 2342 (QB); *Gilchrist v Chief Constable of Greater Manchester* [2019] EWHC 1233 (QB).

144 Eg *R (W80) v Director General of the IOPC* [2020] EWCA Civ 1301, [2021] 1 WLR 418; *R (Ladkin) v IOPC* [2021] EWHC 122 (Admin).

145 Eg *R (Catt) v Commissioner of Police of the Metropolis* [2015] UKSC 9, [2015] AC 1065.

recording of 'non-crime hate incidents' was an unlawful infringement on the ECHR Article 10 right to freedom of expression.[146] Dame Victoria Sharp, giving the judgment of the court, made clear the importance of clarity in the guidance: 'The Guidance should truly reflect what the police are expected to do and should not mislead by omission either the police who have to use it or the public.'[147]

2.106 The secretary of state may direct the COP to exercise any of its functions or carry out other duties for the purpose of furthering the efficiency, effectiveness or integrity of the police.[148]

National Police Chiefs' Council

2.107 The NPCC was formed on 1 April 2015, a simplified body occupying the space left by the previous professional body, ACPO. ACPO was dissolved on 31 March 2015 following the recommendations of a review commissioned by PCCs.[149] ACPO's responsibility for setting standards, policy and guidance has been shifted to the COP. The NPCC has taken over ACPO's role as a forum for the senior leadership of the police service, and as a co-ordinating body for national operational responses.

2.108 The NPCC lists its key functions as:

- The co-ordination of national operations including defining, monitoring and testing force contributions to the Strategic Policing Requirement, and working with the National Crime Agency where appropriate;
- The command of counter terrorism operations and delivery of counter terrorist policing through the national network as set out in the Counter Terrorism Collaboration Agreement;
- The co-ordination of the national police response to national emergencies and the co-ordination of the mobilisation of resources across force borders and internationally;
- The national operational implementation of standards and policy as set by the College of Policing and Government;
- To work with the College of Policing, to develop joint national approaches on criminal justice, value for money, service transformation, information management, performance management and technology;
- Where appropriate, to work with the College of Policing in order to develop joint national approaches to staff and human resource issues, including misconduct and discipline, in line with the Chief Officers' responsibilities as employers.[150]

2.109 In legal terms, the NPCC is underpinned by an agreement under Police Act 1996 s22A, a statutory provision which provides for collaborations between chief officers and policing bodies, where it is in the interests of efficiency and effectiveness. The NPCC is a national unit hosted by the

146 *R (Miller) v College of Policing* [2021] EWCA Civ 1926 at para 123. For an unsuccessful challenge to an APP see *R (Delezuch) v Chief Constable of Leicestershire* [2014] EWCA Civ 1635.

147 *R (Miller) v College of Policing* [2021] EWCA Civ 1926 at para 123.

148 Police Act 1996 s40C.

149 General Sir Nick Parker, *Independent review of ACPO*, 14 November 2013 (known as the 'Parker Review').

150 See 'About' on the NPCC website: www.npcc.police.uk.

Metropolitan Police Service but formally independent of it.[151] It has a full-time chair,[152] supported by vice chairs who are acting chief officers of regional police forces. The NPCC is answerable to an Audit and Assurance Board made up of a non-executive chair, PCCs, non-executive members and a representative from the Chief Police Officers Staff Association (CPOSA).[153] The NPCC is subject to the Freedom of Information Act 2000 and the Data Protection Act 2018.

151 See 'Structure and membership' on the NPCC website: www.npcc.police.uk. Unlike ACPO, the NPCC is not a private company limited by guarantee.

152 At the time of writing, the Chair is Martin Hewitt QPM, former assistant commissioner of the Metropolitan Police Service.

153 See 'Governance and accountability' on the NPCC website: www.npcc.police.uk.

CHAPTER 3

Police complaints – overview, structure and initial stages

continued

Introduction

3.1 This chapter and the next provide a guide to the police complaints system as it has operated since 1 February 2020. They provide a detailed description of the working of the current system, making reference to the Acts, regulations, case law and statutory (and other) guidance issued by the Independent Office for Police Conduct (IOPC) and the Home Office. This chapter describes:

- legal and policy sources for the complaints process;
- the structure and functions of the IOPC;
- how and where to make a complaint;
- what and who can be complained about;
- the logging and recording of complaints;
- the decisions which are made about how a complaint will be handled;
- complaints that do not need to be dealt with.

The next chapter will deal more fully with the investigation of complaints; investigation reports and outcomes; and the system of reviews which follow. Complaints involving senior officers and officers who have left the force will be discussed, as will the new system of so-called super-complaints.

3.2 The situation where complaints are upheld and disciplinary proceedings and other subsequent procedures invoked is described in chapter 4.

3.3 There have been a number of iterations of the complaints system since the Police Reform Act (PRA) 2002 became law on 1 April 2004. The first version introduced the Independent Police Complaints Commission (IPCC), which superseded the Police Complaints Authority (PCA). The PRA 2002 has been much amended over last two decades, but is still the governing statute for the current version of the complaints system which is now overseen by the IOPC. The new name recognises the role of the IOPC in overseeing all aspects of police *conduct*, and not just issues which arise from complaints.

Sources

3.4 The statutory, regulatory and policy framework for the police complaints system and the linked system for disciplinary procedures is to be found in a number of different places. The following provides a brief overview:

- PRA 2002 Part 2 provides the basic structure for the IOPC and the complaints system.
- PRA 2002 Sch 3 provides the detail as to how the complaints procedure operates.
- Further detail for the complaints process is contained in the Police (Complaints and Misconduct) Regulations ('Complaints and Misconduct Regs') 2020.[1]

1 SI No 2.

- The Police (Conduct) Regulations ('Conduct Regs') 2020[2] are also relevant and contain the Standards of Professional Behaviour for the Police in Schedule 2.
- The IOPC has published detailed *Statutory guidance on the police complaints system*[3] using its powers under PRA 2002 s22. The guidance should be read in conjunction with:
  - *Guidelines for handling allegations of discrimination*;[4]
  - the IOPC's *Guidance on capturing data about police complaints*;[5]
  - the IOPC's *Statutory guidance to the police force on achieving best evidence in death and serious injury matters.*[6]
- The IOPC also publishes *Focus*[7] designed to give police force professional standards departments (PSDs) practical guidance on dealing with complaints, conduct matters and death or serious injury (DSI) cases. It supports police complaint handling and improves standards, and is also useful for police complaints advisers.

3.5 Of greater relevance to the performance and disciplinary aspects of the system, but also relevant for the police complaints practitioner, is the *Home Office guidance – Conduct, efficiency and effectiveness: statutory guidance on professional standards, performance and integrity in policing.*[8]

3.6 As well as the legislation and guidance governing the police complaints and disciplinary systems, the police and associated bodies must also consider and comply with legislation such as the Human Rights Act 1998, the Equality Act 2010 (including the 'public sector equality duty' (PSED) in section 149 of that Act) and the provisions of the Data Protection Act 2018.

3.7 For complaints that were made before 1 February 2020, the best place to glean information as to how the system works is the previous version of the *Statutory guidance* from 2015, available on the IOPC website.[9]

Background

3.8 The recent history of the police complaints system can be summarised as follows.

2 SI No 4.

3 February 2020, available at: www.policeconduct.gov.uk/sites/default/files/Documents/statutoryguidance/2020_statutory_guidance_english.pdf.

4 IPCC, September 2015, available at: www.policeconduct.gov.uk/sites/default/files/Documents/research-learning/guidelines_for_handling_allegations_of_discrimination.pdf.

5 Published February 2020, updated January 2021, available at: www.policeconduct.gov.uk/sites/default/files/Documents/statutoryguidance/Guidance_on_capturing_data_about_police_complaints_Jan2021.pdf.

6 January 2019, available at: www.policeconduct.gov.uk/sites/default/files/Documents/statutoryguidance/statutory-guidance-section-22-guidance.pdf.

7 See: www.policeconduct.gov.uk/research-and-learning/learning-and-recommendations/focus.

8 5 February 2020, available at: https://assets.publishing.service.gov.uk/government/uploads/system/uploads/attachment_data/file/863820/Home_Office_Statutory_Guidance_0502.pdf.

9 2015 guidance available at: www.policeconduct.gov.uk/complaints-reviews-and-appeals/statutory-guidance.

3.9 As mentioned above, the IPCC took over as the body dealing with complaints against the police from the PCA in 2004, having been created by the PRA 2002.

3.10 The IPCC regime was introduced after a lengthy period considering possible reforms. The two main criticisms of the PCA had been: a) that all police complaints had to be investigated by police officers as there was no provision for independent investigation; and b) that the system provided for very limited disclosure to complainants and others of information gleaned as a result of the complaints investigation (this especially referred to the routine non-disclosure of the investigating officer's report which was said to be covered by 'class' public interest immunity[10]). Both these criticisms were raised in the Home Affairs Committee report into police complaints and discipline in 1997[11] and the Stephen Lawrence Inquiry report in 1999.[12]

3.11 Following consultation, the government issued, in December 2000, a framework document entitled *Complaints against the police: framework for a new system*, which set out the emerging framework for the new complaints procedures, explained how this framework was developed, and eventually led to the statutory provisions in the original version of the PRA 2002 allowing for some independent investigation of police complaints and oversight by the IPCC.

3.12 Concerns remained about the independence of the IPCC, as the vast majority of complaints were still investigated by the police themselves. The number of independent investigations increased six-fold after 2013.

3.13 In 2017, the IPCC became the IOPC as a result of further amendments to the PRA 2002 introduced by the Policing and Crime Act 2017 as the IPCC had doubled in size and needed structural changes. As the IOPC says:

> We now have a single line of accountability running up to our Director General . . . He is ultimately responsible for the work of the organisation and its decisions – which are delegated to the various teams that make up the IOPC.
>
> Our investigations are delegated via the Deputy Director General, Operations to a network of five Regional Directors and a Director for Wales, who manage local operational teams. We no longer have Commissioners, which is why we are no longer called a 'Commission'.[13]

3.14 The IOPC commenced 687 new independent investigations in 2018/19 (out of 4,097 cases referred to it). This number dropped to 508 in 2019/20 (out of 4,379 referrals). It was said that this was an anticipated drop, as the system moved away from 'a target driven investigation start rate to a

10 *R v Chief Constable of the West Midlands ex p Wiley* [1995] 1 AC 274, HL.

11 See: https://publications.parliament.uk/pa/cm199798/cmselect/cmhaff/258-i/ha0102.htm.

12 By Sir William MacPherson, Cm 4262-I, available at: www.gov.uk/government/publications/the-stephen-lawrence-inquiry.

13 See: https://policeconduct.gov.uk/becoming-iopc.

phased implementation of thematic case selection'.[14] For 2020/21, the IOPC's *Impact report* states that from 4,674 referrals it 'began 465 independent investigations and completed 460. The number of investigations we are taking on has reduced as we take on increasingly more complex cases which take more resources'.[15]

3.15 Describing the most recent changes, the IOPC says that the legislative reforms include:

- reasonable and proportionate handling of complaints with greater flexibility in the way they are dealt with, and a stronger focus on service to complainants. Complaint handlers have more options open to them to resolve a complaint and must consider what is reasonable and proportionate in each individual case
- new powers for the IOPC to investigate without referral, all misconduct allegations against chief officers, and to present our own cases at police misconduct hearings
- focusing the formal discipline system on breaches of professional standards that would result in formal disciplinary action, enabling police line managers to concentrate on improving individual learning and behaviours in response to lower-level conduct matters – based on a new reflective practice review process.[16]

Structure and functions of the IOPC

Structure

3.16 The IOPC is a body set up by PRA 2002 Part 2. It consists of a director general, formally appointed by the Queen (and who is, therefore, not an appointee of the Home Secretary) and 'at least' six other members who can either be non-executive members or employee members (a majority must be non-executive members). At the time of writing, there are currently six non-executive members.[17] The director general must be independent of the police.[18]

3.17 The director general can be appointed for up to five years, and such period can be renewed.[19] The other non-executive members can be appointed for a renewable period of three years.[20] There are very limited provisions for removing the director-general or the non-executive members of the IOPC from office.[21] The non-executive members can terminate the

14 *Annual report and statement of accounts 2019/20*, IOPC, HC 511, p15, available at: https://policeconduct.gov.uk/sites/default/files/Documents/Who-we-are/accountability-performance/IOPC_annual_report_and_accounts_2019-20_web_accessible_version.pdf.

15 *Making a difference: IOPC impact report 2020/21*, p10, available at: https://policeconduct.gov.uk/sites/default/files/Documents/Who-we-are/accountability-performance/IOPC_Impact_Report_202021.pdf.

16 *Annual report and statement of accounts 2019/20*, IOPC, p21.

17 See: www.policeconduct.gov.uk/who-we-are/our-people.

18 PRA 2002 s9.

19 PRA 2002 Sch 2 para 1(3).

20 PRA 2002 Sch 2 para 2.

21 PRA 2002 Sch 2 paras 1(5) and 2(6).

appointment of an employee member with written notice.[22] The IOPC's powers to appoint staff include staff on secondment from the police.[23]

3.18 The IOPC has the power to set up regional offices, and has offices in the North West, the North East, the Midlands, the South East, London and Wales.[24]

Functions

3.19 The IOPC's functions are exercised in relation to three matters:

a) the handling of police complaints;
b) recording other matters where there may have been misconduct justifying criminal or disciplinary proceedings (known as 'conduct matters');
c) the manner in which complaints or conduct matters are dealt with by the police and police authorities.[25]

3.20 The arrangements must be kept under review, be efficient and effective, 'manifest an appropriate degree of independence' and ensure that public confidence is established and maintained in the arrangements.[26]

3.21 The IOPC has a proactive role in recommending changes to the arrangements, and also advising on 'police practice in relation to other matters' arising from its work as it feels necessary or desirable.[27] The IOPC has a number of formal reporting functions. In addition to the requirement to produce annual reports, the IOPC must also report to the Home Secretary, when requested, on the exercise of its general functions,[28] and there is a power to report to the Home Secretary on other issues as appropriate.[29] The IOPC can also submit other reports on exceptional or grave matters which the director general feels should be drawn to the Home Secretary's attention, and can produce reports containing advice and recommendations in relation to police practice.[30] The director general must set out a strategy for the performance of the IOPC's functions.[31]

3.22 The IOPC has the power to require that information from police forces is provided for the purposes of fulfilling its functions[32] and to impose time limits within which the information must be provided. The IOPC can also require a police force to allow them access to premises and to documents and other things on the premises to examine the efficiency and effectiveness

22 PRA 2002 Sch 2 para 2A.
23 PRA 2002 Sch 2 para 6.
24 See: www.policeconduct.gov.uk/who-we-are/our-people.
25 PRA 2002 s10(2).
26 PRA 2002 s10(1)(c), (d).
27 PRA 2002 s10(1)(e).
28 PRA 2002 s11(2).
29 PRA 2002 s11(2A).
30 PRA 2002 s11(3) and (4).
31 PRA 2002 s10C. See *Strategic plan 2018–22*, IOPC, November 2018, available at: www.policeconduct.gov.uk/sites/default/files/Documents/Who-we-are/accountability-performance/IOPC_Strategic_plan_2018.pdf.
32 PRA 2002 s17.

of the police force's arrangements for handling complaints,[33] and for the purposes of any investigation the IOPC is directing or carrying out itself.

3.23 The IPCC must keep a register of all the information provided to it by the police in relation to the complaints procedure and can publish or disclose all of this information for the purposes of learning lessons, raising public awareness and improving the system, so long as the rules restricting certain types of disclosure (see below at paras 4.56–4.75) are complied with.[34]

3.24 The Home Secretary has issued orders allowing the IOPC to engage in 'directed and intrusive surveillance' and the use of informers for the purposes of carrying out its functions.[35] The powers are similar to those enjoyed by the police themselves.[36]

3.25 The IOPC also has a role in issuing guidance to local policing bodies, chief officers and other officers about the complaints system, how it should be run, and the detection and deterrence of misconduct.[37] Some of this guidance is listed above (see para 3.4). Every person to whom the guidance relates must 'have regard' to it in carrying out their functions. The IOPC must consult with a number of policing bodies, and others as it is seen fit on any proposed guidance and the guidance must be approved by the Home Secretary.[38] The Home Secretary also retains the power to make regulations on a wide range of police complaints matters.[39]

3.26 Clearly, complainants and their advisers can have a role in drawing matters to the IOPC's attention and urging the organisation to concentrate on specific failings of the system which have been identified either locally or nationally; for example, the way lawful police policies and practices are deployed, stop and search, use of firearms, police pursuits, community policing, etc. The IOPC would be in a strong position to make credible contributions to these areas and to encourage improvements where possible to discourage misconduct and complaints arising from these areas of policing.

3.27 The Policing and Crime Act 2017 increased the role of local policing bodies which, for most areas, means the police and crime commissioner (PCC).[40] They have a statutory responsibility to hold their chief officer to account for the performance of the complaints system locally and for ensuring there are appropriate processes in place for dealing with conduct and DSI matters.[41]

3.28 The local policing body has an overarching duty to scrutinise, support and challenge the overall performance of forces, monitor complaints and

33 PRA 2002 s18.
34 Complaints and Misconduct Regs 2020 reg 45.
35 PRA 2002 s19.
36 Independent Police Complaints Commission (Investigatory Powers) Order 2004 SI No 815.
37 PRA 2002 s22.
38 PRA 2002 s22.
39 PRA 2002 s23.
40 Police Act 1996 s101.
41 *Statutory guidance on the police complaints system*, IOPC, 2020, para 1.10.

hold chief officers to account for the performance of officers and staff.[42] They are also able, where they consider that aspects of PRA 2002 Part 2 (which describes the police complaints system) are not being complied with, to direct chief officers to take steps to remedy this.[43]

3.29 Local police bodies can also choose to take on responsibility for certain additional police complaints functions that would otherwise be the responsibility of the chief officer of a police force. The local police body can adopt one of three models, described by the IOPC as follows:

- *Model 1 (mandatory):* all local policing bodies have responsibility for carrying out reviews where they are the relevant review body.
- *Model 2 (optional):* in addition to the responsibilities under model 1, a local policing body can choose to assume responsibility for making initial contact with complainants, handling complaints outside of PRA 2002 Sch 3, and recording complaints.
- *Model 3 (optional):* a local policing body that has adopted model 2 can additionally choose to assume responsibility for keeping complainants and interested persons properly informed of the progress of the handling and outcome of their complaint.[44]

3.30 At the time of writing, most local policing bodies are limiting their involvement to model 1. In addition where appeals were previously handled by either the chief officer or the IOPC, the new right to apply for a review is to either the local policing body or the IOPC.

3.31 In the text that follows, it is assumed that model 1 has been adopted. The statutory regime refers to the 'appropriate authority' when describing the functions that need to be performed. Depending on the context, that can mean the chief officer of the police force, the director-general of the IOPC or the local policing body. In the description of the system, the shorthand of 'the police' will be used to describe the powers of the chief officer, and 'IOPC' will be used instead of referring additionally to the director general.

Making a complaint

What is a complaint?

3.32 The IOPC explains that under the 2020 complaints system:

> 1.5 The complaints system was expanded to cover a broader range of matters. Formerly, the way that the term 'complaint' was defined meant that it needed to relate to the conduct of an individual officer. Now a complaint can be made about a much wider range of issues including the service provided by the police as an organisation. This was designed to increase access to the police complaints system.[45]

3.33 The statutory definition of a 'complaint' is that it is 'any expression of dissatisfaction with a police force which is expressed (whether in writing

42 Policing Protocol Order 2011 SI No 2744 Sch para 17.

43 PRA 2002 s15(2), (2A), (2B).

44 *Statutory guidance on the police complaints system*, IOPC, para 1.27.

45 *Statutory guidance on the police complaints system*, IOPC, para 1.5.

or otherwise) by or on behalf of a member of the public', so long as the other rules as to who is permitted to make a complaint (see below) are met.[46] Thus the word 'complaint' does not have to be used in the communication with the police. The complaint does not necessarily have to be about the individual conduct of an officer (although it usually will be). The IOPC says that it can, for example, 'be about force-wide crime initiatives, the organisation of policing resources and general policing standards'.[47]

Who can make a complaint?

3.34 There are detailed rules as to who can make a complaint. The rules are different depending on whether the complaint is about a person serving with the police, or a matter which does not concern the conduct of an individual. There are different rules if a police officer wishes to complain.

General complaints

3.35 If the matter complained about does not concern the conduct of an individual, then a complainant must either be adversely affected by the matter complained about, or acting on behalf of a person adversely affected.[48] Thus it is not possible to make a complaint if it is, for example, a general comment on the policy of a police force unless an adverse effect has been caused on the complainant. 'Adversely affected' is discussed further below (para 3.42).

Complaints about individuals

3.36 The three groups who can complain about the conduct of a person serving with the police are members of the public[49] who claim to be:

a) persons who claim that the conduct of a police officer took place in relation to them; or
b) witnesses (persons who claim to have witnessed the conduct); or
c) persons adversely affected by the conduct (although the conduct did not happen to them).[50]

3.37 In all these categories, someone can act on behalf of the complainant if they have been given the written authority to act.[51] The IOPC's statutory guidance states that although the written authority must be 'clear and unambiguous', it need not be in English.[52]

3.38 In addition, the IOPC can designate other organisations through which complaints can be made. These organisations can pass on complaints to

46 PRA 2002 s12(1).
47 *Statutory guidance on the police complaints system*, IOPC, para 5.3.
48 PRA 2002 s12(1A)(b).
49 PRA 2002 s29(4).
50 PRA 2002 s12(1B).
51 PRA 2002 s12(1), (6)(b).
52 *Statutory guidance on the police complaints system*, IOPC, para 5.11.

the police without the written consent of the complainant.[53] At the time of writing, no organisations have been designated.

3.39 The statutory law is silent as to how complaints from those under 18 should be dealt with. The IOPC recommends that usually a complaint from a parent, guardian or other appropriate adult should be accepted without the need for a written consent from a child under 16. If it becomes clear that there is a conflict between the views and wishes of a child and their parent or guardian, then the child's views should be taken into account. If a young person under 18 makes a complaint themselves that should be accepted by the police, who should ask whether a parent or guardian should be informed (and comply with the response), and consider offering support at the start when the complaint is made and throughout the process, for example, by providing the child with an advocate.[54]

Those in relation to whom conduct of a police officer took place

3.40 The statutory provisions and the IOPC statutory guidance do not define this group of complainants further than to say that their complaint must be that the conduct complained about happened to them. This will include the vast majority of complaints from people who have been on the receiving end of police misconduct. There is no suggestion that the complainant needs to have suffered any loss or harm to make a complaint in these circumstances.

Witnesses

3.41 To make a complaint as a witness a person must have acquired knowledge of the conduct in a manner which would enable them to be a witness in criminal proceedings and give admissible evidence of the conduct. Alternatively, the person must have in their possession anything which would constitute admissible evidence of the conduct.[55] Thus, eye witnesses are, of course, included but are not the only witnesses who can make a complaint. Someone who has evidence such as videotape would also be able to make a complaint.

Those adversely affected

3.42 A person is adversely affected by conduct if the person:

- suffers any form of loss or damage, distress or inconvenience; or
- is put in danger; or
- is otherwise put at risk of being adversely affected.[56]

3.43 Further, a person can only claim to have been adversely affected for the purposes of a claim against an individual, if they were physically present or

53 PRA 2002 s12(6).
54 *Statutory guidance on the police complaints system*, IOPC, paras 2.21–2.24, 5.11.
55 PRA 2002 s12(5).
56 PRA 2002 s29(5).

sufficiently nearby so as to be able to see the conduct complained about or its effects.[57] The exception to this is if the would-be complainant already knew the person to whom the conduct occurred, and this fact aggravated or caused the adverse effect said to be suffered.[58] Thus anyone who simply saw the conduct on television or social media would not be able to make a complaint about police misconduct unless they knew the victim already.

3.44 In general, police officers (or others serving with the police) cannot make complaints under this statutory mechanism[59] about their own force, or against officers they are on duty with when the alleged conduct occurs. Some uncertainty might arise if the partner of a person serving with the police makes a complaint about misconduct that has happened to such a person, but there might well be circumstances where a relative or partner has witnessed the misconduct or been adversely affected by it. One example might be where a person is distressed or inconvenienced by any trauma suffered by their partner who is a police officer (as a result of misconduct be another police officer) – it is hard to see how such a person would not come within the definition of being 'adversely affected'.

3.45 The IOPC points out that the exclusionary rule does not mean that a person serving with the police cannot raise concerns about people serving in their own force, but there should be alternative and confidential systems for ensuring that this can happen.[60]

Who can be complained about?

3.46 Under the complaints system, as mentioned above, a complaint can be made against 'a person serving with the police'. This is further defined to include:[61]

- a member of a police force;
- a civilian employee of a police force;
- a special constable who is under the direction and control of a chief officer;
- a person designated as a community support volunteer or a policing support volunteer;
- a special constable under the control of the chief officer.

Civilian employees

3.47 The role of civilian employees interfacing with the public includes police community support officers, designated escort and detention officers (both employed by the police authority and in some cases employed by a private contract provider), designated investigators, and staff dealing with telephone queries and front-desk duties.

57 PRA 2002 s12(3).

58 PRA 2002 s12(4).

59 PRA 2002 s29(4) and (4B) provides details, and see *Statutory guidance on the police complaints system*, IOPC, para 5.6.

60 *Statutory guidance on the police complaints system*, IOPC, paras 5.7–5.10.

61 See PRA 2002 s12(7) for the full list.

3.48 There is power for regulations to be made to bring contractors with the police within the police complaints system but, at the time of writing, none of have been made.[62]

3.49 There is nothing to prevent a complaint being made against a person who no longer serves with the police, so long as the conduct complained about occurred while they were still serving. There is also nothing to prevent a complaint being made about the conduct of a person serving with the police who was off duty at the time, although the IOPC advises that it may not be proportionate to take further action if the complaint is not relevant to the person's professional role.[63]

Other police forces

3.50 The provisions of the complaints regime apply primarily to the police forces in England and Wales. However, the police complaints system can also be used to complain about a range of other bodies who 'maintain a body of constables'.[64] At the time of writing, there are arrangements that cover the following:[65]

- the National Crime Agency (NCA);
- Her Majesty's Revenue and Customs (HMRC);
- staff who carry out certain border and immigration functions who now work within the UK Border Force and the Home Office;
- PCCs and their deputies;
- the Mayor's Office for Policing and Crime;
- officers carrying out certain functions of the Gangmasters and Labour Abuse Authority (GLAA);
- British Transport Police (BTP);
- Ministry of Defence Police (MDP);
- Civil Nuclear Constabulary (CNC);
- College of Policing (COP).[66]

3.51 Where there is no agreement in place between a given force and the IOPC, the Home Secretary can direct that an agreement be reached.[67]

IOPC staff and directors

3.52 It is not unusual for complainants to be dissatisfied with the actions of an investigating officer or other members of the IOPC staff. In these circumstances, it is possible to make a complaint about the staff member. Thus, a complaints system has been introduced which covers IOPC staff members.[68] In effect, these provisions require that serious complaints (as defined by the IOPC) are investigated by the IOPC and the complainant

62 PRA 2002 s12(8).
63 *Statutory guidance on the police complaints system*, IOPC, paras 5.5, 12.10.
64 PRA 2002 s26(1).
65 See: www.policeconduct.gov.uk/investigations/what-we-investigate-and-next-steps.
66 PRA 2002 s26BA.
67 PRA 2002 s26(2).
68 PRA 2002 s27; and Independent Police Complaints Commission (Staff Conduct) Regulations 2004 SI No 660.

is kept informed of the progress and outcome of the report. Less serious complaints are dealt with internally. There is also an internal procedure which deals with complaints about the director general, senior independent directors and non-executive directors.[69]

Where and how to make a complaint

3.53 People can only complain if they know how to do this and are not discouraged from doing so. The IOPC makes it clear that police forces should promote the complaints system and make information about the complaints system available online, at police stations (including in custody areas), and through Citizens Advice Bureaux, libraries and schools. It should be possible to make complaints in writing, online, through social media, in person and by telephone. Police force websites should contain clear, accurate and up-to-date information about complaints procedures.[70]

3.54 The legislation itself envisages complaints being made to three different places: the IOPC, a local policing body or the chief officer.[71] Although the IOPC urges complaints to be made to local police forces, the system also provides for complainants to complain directly to the IOPC (who will then forward the complaint to the police force unless there are exceptional reasons not to do this).[72]

3.55 The IOPC website has links to the complaints departments of all police forces, with a form to complain, and also has a link to the IOPC's own complaint form.[73]

3.56 Even with access to online complaint forms, the likelihood is that many people will make complaints orally to their local police station. If an oral complaint is made, the brief details at least should be recorded. Even with the best will in the world, this is likely to be less satisfactory than a statement made in the complainant's own words or with the help of a sympathetic adviser. In addition, if a complainant then decides to bring a civil action against the police (see chapter 14) in terms which differ from the record of an oral complaint, the police may well argue that the initial record is the best indicator as to the relevant facts.

3.57 In practice, complaints should be made as soon as possible after the event while recollections are still fresh in the mind. Furthermore, the police have the power to apply to dispense with any investigation if it is not possible to carry out a proper investigation because of the passage of time (see below, para 3.134).

3.58 Police forces should take steps to ensure that the complaints system is accessible to those who need additional assistance, and duties under the

69 *Making complaints about the IOPC director general, senior independent director and non-executive directors*, IOPC, November 2018, available at: www.policeconduct.gov.uk/sites/default/files/Documents/Complaint_forms/Director-General-and-non-exec-directors-complaint-policy.pdf.

70 *Statutory guidance on the police complaints system*, IOPC, paras 2.4–2.9.

71 PRA 2002 Sch 3 para 2.

72 PRA 2002 Sch 3 para 2(1) and (1A).

73 See: www.policeconduct.gov.uk/complaints-and-appeals/make-complaint.

Equality Act 2010 are highlighted by the IOPC, including the duty to make reasonable adjustments for disabled people to access the system.[74]

3.59 When a complaint is made to the chief officer (in practice often through a more junior officer acting on their behalf), the chief officer has to decide whether they are the chief officer of the officer or force complained about. If not, then the complaint must be referred to the correct chief officer, and the complainant informed that that has happened.[75] Complaints against the chief officer should be sent or referred to the chief officer's local policing body. In the paragraphs that follow, reference is made to the chief officer of a force (or 'the police').

3.60 When a complaint is made, the police are under a duty to take any steps that are appropriate for the purposes of the complaints system to obtain or preserve evidence relating to the conduct forming the subject of the complaint as soon as practicable. The duty is ongoing throughout the investigation.[76]

3.61 There is also a duty to comply with any directions given by the IOPC in relation to the obtaining and preserving of information.[77] This might involve such things as preserving documentary records, conducting searches, taking photographs and seeking medical examinations of the parties to an assault, both the complainant and the police officer(s). Medical examinations can be carried out only by consent. If an examination by a police doctor is carried out, the complainant should be warned not to discuss the circumstances of the injury with the doctor. Complainants should also arrange for an examination by an independent doctor as soon as possible. This is often achieved by a visit to a GP or to the local casualty department.

3.62 If the complainant is aware of any evidence that ought to be obtained or preserved, this should be specified in the letter of complaint, even if it has been mentioned orally. Failure by the police to obtain or preserve evidence may itself justify a further complaint.

Recording complaints

Overview

3.63 All complaints must be *logged* by the police, but not all complaints will be formally *recorded*. In overview, only complaints about one or more of a defined list of serious matters must be recorded under the legislation. The IOPC advises that complaints about certain other matters or of a certain amount of complexity should be recorded, and the complainant has the right to insist that a complaint is recorded.[78] However, neither the legislation nor the IOPC's guidance appear to require the complainant to be informed that they can insist on a complaint being recorded, and neither does the complainant advice page on the IOPC website.[79]

74 *Statutory guidance on the police complaints system*, IOPC, paras 2.13–2.20.

75 PRA 2002 Sch 3 para 2(3).

76 PRA 2002 Sch 3 para 1(1)–(3).

77 PRA 2002 Sch 3 para 1(5)–(6).

78 PRA 2002 Sch 3 para 2(6A).

79 See: https://policeconduct.gov.uk/complaints-reviews-and-appeals/make-complaint.

3.64 If a complaint is not recorded, then it will be dealt with outside the statutory complaints system (although the IOPC advises that if resolution is not achieved, recording the complaint can be considered again).

3.65 Thus, once a complaint has been received, the complainant must be contacted to establish how they wish the complaint to be handled.[80] Before that contact is made, the IOPC advises that the police can consider whether the complaint is about a matter that requires mandatory recording, and if it is then the complaint will be recorded in any event.

3.66 A complaint must be recorded[81] if it is an allegation that:

- the conduct complained about resulted in death or serious injury;
- if proved, might constitute a criminal offence or justify the bringing of disciplinary proceedings;
- if proved, might have involved the infringement of a person's rights under European Convention on Human Rights (ECHR) Articles2 (right to life) or Article 3 (prohibition of torture and inhuman or degrading treatment or punishment);
- meets any of the criteria for mandatory referral of the complaint to the IOPC.

3.67 It will be immediately clear that all these categories need further explanation. All these terms are discussed more fully in other parts of this chapter. What comes under the definition of 'death or serious injury' (often referred to as DSI) is discussed at paras 3.93–3.95. The kinds of matters which would justify the bringing of disciplinary proceedings is discussed at para 4.15. ECHR Articles 2 and 3 are discussed at various points in the book, and the IOPC has provided a glossary of explanation in the statutory guidance. The complaints which require mandatory referral to the IOPC are discussed at paras 3.92–3.110.

3.68 There is also a discretion for the police to record the complaint in any event (that is, even if the complainant does not want the complaint recorded and where the complaint does not come within the mandatory list set out above).[82] The IOPC provides some advice as when this discretion should be exercised. This includes the 'extent and nature of the enquiries' required to address the complaint, and so a complicated matter should be considered for recording. Complaints alleging potential breaches of other Articles of the ECHR should be considered (see elsewhere in the book for discussion of Articles 5, 8, 10, 11 and 14, for example). The police should also consider whether other similar complaints have been recorded (for example, about the same issue or the same officer).[83] The IOPC also comments that where the allegations, if proven, are likely to lead to a finding that there is 'practice requiring improvement' by an officer then a complaint should be recorded. This is a reference to a statutory process known as the 'reflective practice review process' (RPRP), whereby

80 PRA 2002 Sch 3 para 2(6).
81 PRA 2002 Sch 3 para 2(6B).
82 PRA 2002 Sch 3 para 2(6A).
83 *Statutory guidance on the police complaints system*, IOPC, para 6.30.

conduct which requires action short of disciplinary action is dealt with by the police.[84]

3.69 The IOPC also advises that a complaint would need to recorded where 'accounts need to be taken from officers' or other investigative measures will be necessary.[85]

3.70 Under previous iterations of the complaints system, a complainant had a right to appeal a failure or refusal to record a complaint. The IOPC received 1,305 non-recording appeals in 2019/20, and upheld 40 per cent of the appeals.[86] As there is now a general right for a complainant to insist on recording of a complaint, that route of appeal no longer exists. Any refusal, nevertheless, to record a complaint could be a matter for judicial review (see chapter 14 for further information).

Records

3.71 Chief officers and local policing bodies must keep records of all complaints and purported complaints made to them, every conduct matter (see below, para 4.44) recorded, every DSI matter and every exercise of a power or duty made during the complaints process.[87] The IOPC has issued guidance on capturing data about police complaints which deals with this issue in more detail. Appendix A of the guidance sets out a system for categorising complaints, and advisers may wish to satisfy themselves that the complaint has been properly categorised (for example, category F covers discriminatory behaviour, whereas category H covers matters like impolite language or tone).[88]

Copies of complaints

3.72 The police are under a duty to supply a copy of the record made of a recorded complaint to the complainant and to the officer complained about.[89] This could include the letter in which the complaint was made, or the record made of an oral complaint.

3.73 It is worth bearing in mind that the police have the power to anonymise the record disclosed to the officer complained about, and this should be pointed out in the initial complaint if it will be relevant.[90] The police also have the power not to provide a copy of the complaint at all if it may prejudice criminal investigations or proceedings or if it is otherwise in the

84 See *Home Office guidance – Conduct, efficiency and effectiveness: statutory guidance on professional standards, performance and integrity in policing*, 5 February 2020, section 4; and Conduct Regs 2020 Part 6.

85 *Statutory guidance on the police complaints system*, IOPC, para 6.23.

86 *Police complaints: statistics for England and Wales 2019/20*, IOPC, p17, available at: www.policeconduct.gov.uk/sites/default/files/Documents/statistics/complaints_statistics_2019_20.pdf.

87 Complaints and Misconduct Regs 2020 reg 44.

88 *Guidance on capturing data about police complaints*, published February 2020, updated January 2021, available at: https://www.policeconduct.gov.uk/sites/default/files/Documents/statutoryguidance/Guidance_on_capturing_data_about_police_complaints_Jan2021.pdf.

89 Complaints and Misconduct Regs 2020 reg 3.

90 Complaints and Misconduct Regs 2020 reg 3(2).

public interest not to do so.[91] It would be rare that this will be appropriate in relation to the complainant, as the complainant will know the content of their complaint in any event.

How will complaints be dealt with?

Overview

3.74 Once a complaint has been received and it has been decided whether or not to record the complaint, the police need to decide how it will be handled. This will depend on whether the complaint has been recorded, and how serious are the matters raised. The range of acceptable responses goes from a short telephone call, to an independent investigation carried out by the IOPC. This section explains the processes by which it is decided how to handle a complaint.

Reasonable and proportionate handling

3.75 An important feature of the police complaints system is the concept of 'reasonable and proportionate' handling of complaints. Although the complaints system is still very complicated, reasonable and proportionate handling is designed to be a touchstone for the process, and has enabled some of the more complex procedures to be simplified. However, inevitably the result of this is that a lot of leeway is handed to the police to decide just how they will deal with complaints, especially those that are deemed to be less important.

3.76 The IOPC provides guidance on what is meant by 'reasonable and proportionate' handling, and the police need to take this into account when dealing with complaints.

3.77 The IOPC states that reasonable and proportionate handling of complaints is necessary 'to ensure both public confidence in the complaints system, and the system's efficient and effective operation'.[92] Roughly speaking, this translates to mean that complainants need to feel that their complaints are being dealt with fairly, but regard must also be had to the time and resources to be devoted to complaint resolution. The principles of reasonable and proportionate handling apply to decisions about how a complaint should be handled, what steps are required to resolve it, and providing a reasonable and proportionate outcome.[93]

3.78 An important aspect of reasonable and proportionate handling is said to be delivering what the IOPC calls 'good customer service'.[94] Essentially this involves a complaint handler listening to the complainant, understanding the complaint, what they wish to achieve from the complaint, and explaining how the system works.[95] However, a complainant's expect-

91 Complaints and Misconduct Regs 2020 reg 3(3).

92 *Statutory guidance on the police complaints system*, IOPC, para 3.2.

93 *Statutory guidance on the police complaints system*, IOPC, para 3.4.

94 *Statutory guidance on the police complaints system*, IOPC, paras 3.5–3.6.

95 *Statutory guidance on the police complaints system*, IOPC, para 3.6.

ations should also be 'managed'.[96] There should be good and timely communication with a complainant and a defensive approach should not be taken.[97]

3.79 Key to the approach advocated by the IOPC is that reasonableness and proportionality should be assessed on a case-by-case basis:[98]

> All complaints should be handled in a way that takes account of the seriousness of the allegation, any actual or potential impact or harm caused, and the potential for learning and improvement. The more serious a complaint, the greater the need for accountability and scrutiny. For more serious complaints, this may mean that more wide-ranging enquiries need to be carried out, or that efforts need to be made to corroborate information, where it otherwise may not be considered to be reasonable or proportionate in the circumstances.

3.80 The IOPC advises that in some cases it might be helpful for the complaint to be dealt with by a specific person because of the subject-matter or circumstances of the complaint, or their expertise; and that where the subject-matter of the complaint is particularly serious or sensitive, the complaint handler should also consider having regard to the entitlements set out in the Ministry of Justice's statutory guidance, *Code of practice for victims of crime in England and Wales (Victim's Code)*.[99] An example is given of offering the opportunity to have a person of the same sex handle certain types of complaint.[100]

3.81 Complaint handlers 'should be alert to opportunities to identify learning and improve service delivery'[101] and this might particularly be the case where the complaint is about new police powers or techniques, or areas that are known to be controversial.[102] Advisers will be keen to ensure that police complaints decisions are properly made and explained. On this issue the IOPC says:[103]

> Complaint handlers should consider the fairness of their actions on all those involved in a complaint. They should ensure that the decisions they make:
>
> - are impartial, free from bias (or the appearance of bias) or discrimination, having considered the perspectives provided by all parties
> - are logical and justifiable with reference to the relevant available evidence
> - do not place undue weight on any given consideration
> - are accompanied by a clear, evidence-based rationale

96 *Statutory guidance on the police complaints system*, IOPC, para 3.7.

97 *Statutory guidance on the police complaints system*, IOPC, para 3.10.

98 *Statutory guidance on the police complaints system*, IOPC, para 3.12.

99 Published 1 October 2005, last updated 21 April 2021, available at: www.gov.uk/government/publications/the-code-of-practice-for-victims-of-crime.

100 *Statutory guidance on the police complaints system*, IOPC, para 3.13.

101 *Statutory guidance on the police complaints system*, IOPC, para 3.14.

102 Statutory guidance on the police complaints system, IOPC, para 3.16.

103 *Statutory guidance on the police complaints system*, IOPC, para 3.18

Handling complaints that have not been recorded

3.82 The intention is almost always that less serious complaints should be dealt with quickly and simply and not involve disproportionately expensive investigations. This clearly can have advantages for complainants and the police. However, there is a perceived danger that the police may attempt to record fewer complaints than they should, and thus deal with more complaints outside the formal investigation process. Prior to 2020, this was done through a local resolution procedure, and in 2019/20, 48 per cent of all allegations were dealt with by local resolution. It was striking, though, that the use of local resolution differed from force to force: for example, the Metropolitan Police used local resolution for only 21 per cent of allegations, whereas Thames Valley used it for 76 per cent of allegations.[104]

3.83 Complaints that are not recorded should be those that are less serious, and where a minimal element of investigation is necessary with an attempt at conciliation. Although not recorded, there is a statutory duty to handle the complaint in an appropriate manner 'with a view to resolving the complaint to the complainant's satisfaction'.[105] This allows the complainant to see whether the complaint can be resolved to their satisfaction without a formal investigation. The IOPC cite the example of a complainant who wants an explanation for what has happened or for concerns to be passed on.[106] As well as satisfying the complainant, any learning points can be identified by the police at the same time.

3.84 There is no set procedure to follow when handling a complaint which has not been recorded. The IOPC states that appropriate and effective actions could include:[107]

- providing information and an explanation – either by telephone or in writing
- providing an update on the complainant's outstanding matters
- answering questions the complainant has
- organising the return of property
- offering an apology for poor service
- confirming that steps have been taken to prevent an error occurring again
- signposting the complainant to appropriate processes – for example, the Information Commissioner's Office complaints process or Victim's Right to Review
- logging the complainant's concerns for consideration when a policy or procedure is next due for a review

3.85 The IOPC has published an edition of *Focus* which gives more practical detail as to how these complaints should be dealt with.[108] It provides a number of case studies and practical advice as to how to deal with things like old complaints, vague complaints, repeat complaints, and complaints

104 *Police complaints: Statistics for England and Wales 2019/20*, p10.

105 PRA 2002 Sch 3 para 2(9).

106 *Statutory guidance on the police complaints system*, IOPC, para 6.20.

107 *Statutory guidance on the police complaints system*, IOPC, para 6.21.

108 *Focus*, Issue No 14, February 2020, updated January 2022, https://policeconduct.gov.uk/sites/default/files/Documents/Focus/Focus_14_February2020.pdf.

about off- duty officers, as well as the kind of actions which might be taken to resolve a complaint. A complainant should be kept informed of the progress of the handling of the complaint. The IOPC advises that further steps can be taken if initial attempts to resolve the complaint are unsuccessful, but that once a point has been reached where resolution is not possible without delay or substantial additional steps, then it is likely that a complaint should then be recorded.[109]

3.86 The outcome of the complaint should be communicated to the complainant within five working days of the determination. This should be in writing unless the initial complaint was not in writing.[110] If the complainant is dissatisfied with the outcome, then there is no right to an appeal or review. However, the IOPC tells complaint handlers that a complainant should be reminded at this stage that they have the right for their complaint to be recorded, and if it is, then there will be the right to have the outcome of the recorded complaint reviewed (see below). A complainant should not be dissuaded from insisting that the complaint is recorded at that point.[111]

How to handle recorded complaints

3.87 Once a complaint has been recorded, the police need to decide how it will be dealt with. First, it needs to be decided whether a complaint must or should be referred to the IOPC to take a decision as to how the complaint should be handled. This applies to serious and high-profile complaints and there are detailed provisions as to when referral should happen and how the IOPC should then respond in deciding whether any investigation should take place and if so, what kind of investigation.

3.88 Second, if the complaint is not to be referred to the IOPC, the police must, themselves, decide how to deal with the complaint reasonably and proportionately. There are some cases where investigation will be compulsory and other cases where there the police have some discretion whether to investigate the complaint.

3.89 Third, if it is decided not to investigate, then in some circumstances the police can decide not to take any action, and in other cases will be able to take steps short of investigation in order to try to resolve the complaint.

3.90 In all this, the system provides little opportunity for the complainant to influence how the complaint is dealt with (unlike the statutory right to insist that a complaint is recorded). However, there is nothing to prevent a complaint seeking to persuade the police or the IOPC to deal with a complaint in a particular way (for instance by arguing that a complaint should be referred to the IOPC, or formally investigated) and, ultimately, decisions made in relation to statutory functions would be susceptible to judicial review.

109 *Statutory guidance on the police complaints system*, IOPC, para 6.22.
110 Complaints and Misconduct Regs 2020 reg 34(2) and (3).
111 *Statutory guidance on the police complaints system*, IOPC, para 6.25.

When a case will be referred to the IOPC

3.91 There are two categories of complaints which will be referred to the IOPC, for the IOPC to decide on the kind of investigation which is appropriate. The first relates to complaints that have to be referred to the IOPC ('mandatory referrals'). The second is where the police exercise their discretion to refer a case ('discretionary referrals').

Mandatory referrals

3.92 The police must refer a complaint to the IOPC:[112]

a) where the complaint alleges conduct which has led to death or serious injury (known as DSI matters);
b) where the conduct comes within a description set out in regulations;
c) where the IOPC decides to call in the complaint.

Death or serious injury matters

3.93 DSI matters are defined in legislation. They cover any circumstances in which, or in consequence of which, a person has died or has sustained serious injury, and where other conditions are met.[113] Thus, the person must be under arrest or otherwise detained by the police;[114] or there must have been contact (direct or indirect) at or before the time of the death or serious injury with a person serving with the police acting in the execution of their duty, and an indication that the contact may have caused or contributed to the death or serious injury.[115] The most recent figures for deaths following contact with the police for 2020/21 from the IOPC say that there were:[116]

- 25 road traffic fatalities;
- one fatal police shooting;
- 19 deaths in or following police custody;
- 54 apparent suicides following police custody;
- 92 other deaths following police contact that were independently investigated by the IOPC.

3.94 In effect, all deaths or serious injuries which occur when a person is in custody must be referred to the IOPC, whatever the circumstances, and whether the person is at a police station or not. In cases where there has been 'contact', the test to be met for referral is a low one as there only needs to be an 'indication' that the contact 'may' have 'caused or contributed to' the death or serious injury. The IOPC has indicated that the

112 PRA 2002 Sch 3 para 4(1)(a)–(c).
113 PRA 2002 s12(2A).
114 PRA 2002 s12(2B).
115 PRA 2002 s12(2C).
116 *Deaths during or following police contact: Statistics for England and Wales 2020/21*, IOPC, p3, available at: https://policeconduct.gov.uk/sites/default/files/Documents/statistics/deaths_during_following_police_contact_202021.pdf.

contact can involve both action and inaction.[117] All DSI matters which come to the attention of the police must be recorded.[118]

3.95 'Serious injury' for the purposes of a DSI matter is defined as 'a fracture, a deep cut, a deep laceration or an injury causing damage to an internal organ or the impairment of any bodily function'.[119] Clearly there is some room for interpretation here as to what is a 'deep' cut or laceration and what amounts to 'damage' or 'impairment'. There is no reason why a mental impairment cannot be included in this definition. If the police appear to be adopting a restrictive interpretation, it may well be worthwhile requesting the IOPC to call in the case in an event (see below, para 3.108).

Other mandatory referrals

3.96 The list of conduct falling within the current regulations,[120] complaints about which must be referred to the IOPC (in addition to DSI matters), includes the following:[121]

- a serious assault, as defined in guidance issued by the IOPC;
- a serious sexual offence, as defined in guidance issued by the IOPC;
- serious corruption, including abuse of position for sexual purposes or the purpose of pursuing an improper emotional relationship as defined in guidance issued by the IOPC;
- a criminal offence or behaviour which is liable to lead to disciplinary proceedings[122] and which in either case is aggravated by discriminatory behaviour on the grounds of a person's race, sex, religion or other status identified in guidance by the IOPC;
- an offence for which the sentence is fixed by law, or an offence where an adult may be sentenced to seven years imprisonment (known as a relevant offence).

3.97 In addition, any complaint that arises from the same incident as a DSI matter must be referred,[123] as must certain complaints against chief officers.[124] Thus, if the complaints are that an officer swore at a person and then broke their leg, then both complaints must be referred to the IOPC.

3.98 The relevant definitions by the IOPC are found in the *Statutory guidance on the police complaints system* at paras 9.7–9.30. Additional guidance by the IPCC from 2017 is still available on the IOPC website.[125]

117 *Statutory guidance on the police complaints system*, IOPC, para 7.3.
118 PRA 2002 Sch 3 para 14A.
119 PRA 2002 s29(1).
120 Complaints and Misconduct Regs 2020.
121 Complaints and Misconduct Regs 2020 reg 4(1).
122 Police (Complaints and Misconduct) Regulations ('Complaints and Misconduct Regs') 2012 SI No 1204 reg 1 for definition.
123 Complaints and Misconduct Regs 2020 reg 4(1)(b).
124 Complaints and Misconduct Regs 2020 reg 4(1)(c).
125 *Operational advice note (Mandatory referral criteria update, April 2017)*, IPCC, available at: www.policeconduct.gov.uk/sites/default/files/Documents/statutoryguidance/Operationa_%20advice_note_mandatory_referral_criteria_April_2017.pdf.

Serious assault

3.99 'Serious assault' is conduct that results in injury that amounts to actual bodily harm or a more serious injury. The offence is committed when a person intentionally or recklessly assaults another, thereby causing actual bodily harm. Psychological harm that involves more than mere emotions such as fear, distress or panic can amount to actual bodily harm. The IOPC states that the Crown Prosecution Service (CPS) legal guidance should be applied in deciding the seriousness of the injury (this can be found on the CPS website).[126]

Serious sexual offences

3.100 'Serious sexual offences' are defined as any sexual offence under the Sexual Offences Acts 1956 to 2003, other than 'summary-only' offences committed while off-duty by police officers. Allegations which amount to attempts, incitement or conspiracy to commit the offence, for example, must also be referred.

Serious corruption

3.101 'Serious corruption' is defined at length by the IOPC.[127] It includes:

- attempts to pervert the course of justice;
- offences of receiving benefits, payments and favours likely to be tried in the Crown Court;
- abuse of authority;
- corrupt controller, handler or informer relationships;
- providing confidential information for payment, benefits or favours in certain circumstances;
- extraction and supply of seized controlled drugs, firearms or other material.

Attempts or conspiracies to commit these offences are included.

3.102 Allegations should be referred even if there is insufficient information to arrest, and even where covert operations are, or are about to be put, in place.

3.103 The IOPC's predecessor, the IPCC, made it clear that cases where officers have deliberately lied in a statement about the actions of the complainant, leading to the perversion of the course of justice, should also be referred.[128]

3.104 Serious corruption also includes abuse of position for a sexual purpose or the purpose of pursuing an improper emotional relationship. The IOPC states that this should be interpreted widely, and should include any cases where an officer has sought to abuse their position for these purposes.[129]

126 See: www.cps.gov.uk/legal-guidance/offences-against-person-incorporating-charging-standard.

127 *Statutory guidance on the police complaints system*, IOPC, paras 9.15–9.23.

128 *Focus*, Issue Nine, p7.

129 *Statutory guidance on the police complaints system*, IOPC, para 9.20.

Criminal offences and behaviour (liable to lead to disciplinary proceedings) aggravated by discrimination

3.105 For criminal offences and behaviour (liable to lead to disciplinary proceedings) aggravated by discrimination, in addition to the definitions provided in the regulations (race, sex, religion), discrimination on the basis of the following statuses is included by the IOPC: age, sexual orientation, disability, gender reassignment, marriage and civil partnership, and pregnancy and maternity. The IOPC further explains:[130]

> The form of the alleged discrimination may be direct through language or behaviour, for example, the use of offensive and discriminatory words or use of stereotypes to describe individuals. The complainant or interested person may allege that the conduct was motivated by discrimination. They may allege treatment which amounts to discrimination when compared with the treatment given to others . . . The person dealing with the matter should encourage the complainant or interested person to provide as much information as possible about why they consider they were discriminated against. It is also possible that the complainant or interested person does not allege discrimination, but that the person dealing with the matter believes discrimination is a factor.

3.106 However, the IOPC also notes that when assessing the gravity of a discrimination complaint and whether it should be referred, the police have to assess both whether the alleged behaviour would, if proved, lead to criminal or disciplinary proceedings, and then whether discrimination is an aggravating factor.[131] Both elements must be met for a mandatory referral, but the police may consider a voluntary referral in a case of serious discrimination where the first element (criminal/misconduct proceedings) is not met.[132]

Appropriate referral to the IOPC

3.107 Making sure that cases are appropriately referred to the IOPC is important to ensure that the right cases are being considered by the IOPC. In a report published in 2015,[133] the IPCC researched 400 cases that it thought were likely to come within the referral criteria, but which had not been referred. It found that:[134]

> . . . 76 (18%) of these cases should have been mandatorily referred to us, including six deaths and twelve serious injuries, and that a further 17 (4%) were suitable for voluntary referral. The six deaths all followed some form of contact with the police, and in five of them there were issues about the management of known risks to the individual.
>
> . . . We also found that the majority of cases that should have been referred originated as complaints from the general public, particularly allegations of excessive force or discrimination.

130 *Statutory guidance on the police complaints system*, IOPC, para 9.27. See also the IOPC's *Guidelines for handling allegations of discrimination*, 2015.

131 *Statutory guidance on the police complaints system*, IOPC, para 9.27.

132 *Focus*, Issue Nine, p9.

133 *Referring complaints, conduct matters and death or serious injury matters to the IPCC – a review of current police force practice*, IPCC,2015, available at: www.policeconduct.gov.uk/sites/default/files/Documents/research-learning/IPCC_referrals_review.pdf.

134 At p1.

3.108 The IOPC has not set out the kinds of cases where it will exercise the power to call in complaints which do not fall within the above categories. However, the power can be used where, for example, the IOPC has a concern about a particular complaint. The IOPC can also decide that all complaints of a certain type should be referred to it. For example, in April 2022, the IOPC announced that it was considering whether to require referral of all cases involving use of tasers on those under 18.[135] It will be open to a complainant to make a case to the IOPC that they should require a particular complaint to be referred.

3.109 A case can be called in by the IOPC even where it has previously considered the complaint and even if it is already being investigated by the police.[136] The purpose of this is to allow a late referral where concerns arise after an investigation has started.

3.110 The IOPC also has an additional power to treat any complaint as having been referred, even if it has not been recorded. This allows the IOPC to consider whether an investigation is necessary (and what kind of investigation), without having to rely on the referral of a case.[137]

Discretionary referrals

3.111 Notwithstanding the above description of mandatory referrals and the IOPC powers to call in complaints, the police can refer a complaint to the IOPC because of a) the gravity of the subject-matter of the complaint; or b) any exceptional circumstances.[138]

3.112 The IOPC says that it encourages such referrals, for example, because the complaint could have a significant impact on public confidence, or it is felt that there is a need for independent involvement in the investigation.[139] Thus, complaints about the local exercise of stop and search powers against particular groups in the community might come within these examples.

3.113 Even where the police do not exercise these powers to refer, a local policing body can, for the same reasons, refer the case to the IOPC.[140]

3.114 The discretion to refer a case to the IOPC can be exercised even after an investigation has begun.[141]

Time limits for referral

3.115 A complaint about one of the matters for which referral is mandatory must be referred to the IOPC by the end of the day following the day when it became clear that the complaint should be referred.[142] If the IOPC calls

135 See: https://www.policeconduct.gov.uk/news/iopc-calls-forces-refer-taser-discharges-children-afterreview/.
136 PRA 2002 Sch 3 para 4(5).
137 PRA 2002 Sch 3 para 4A.
138 PRA 2002 Sch 3 para 4(2).
139 *Statutory guidance on the police complaints system*, IOPC, para 9.31.
140 PRA 2002 Sch 3 para 4(3).
141 PRA 2002 Sch 3 para 4(5).
142 Complaints and Misconduct Regs 2020 reg 4(2).

in a complaint, then it must be referred by the end of the day following the day the IOPC gave the police notice.[143]

3.116 Voluntary referrals should be made as soon as possible.

3.117 The IOPC emphasises the importance of referring cases as soon as possible where there is potential engagement of ECHR Articles 2 or 3,[144] including by out-of-hours telephone call (where necessary) for a list of very serious incidents.[145]

3.118 The IPCC can determine how it wants to be notified of a referral.[146] The statutory guidance note also contains a list of the information the IPCC would like to be provided with when cases are referred.[147] The complainant must be told that a referral has been made.[148]

The IOPC's decision on referred complaints

3.119 When a complaint is referred[149] to the IOPC or is called in, the IOPC must decide first whether it is necessary to investigate the complaint;[150] and if so, what form of investigation should take place.[151] If the IOPC decides that a complaint does not need to be investigated, then the case is referred back to the police. If the complaint was being investigated before the referral (that is, the case was referred to the IOPC while the police investigation was ongoing), then that investigation must be completed. Otherwise it is up to the police to decide to deal with the complaint in whatever manner it determines is reasonable and proportionate. This could include deciding to undertake a local investigation.

3.120 In deciding the form of the investigation the IPCC must take into account the seriousness of the case and the public interest.[152] There are three possible forms of investigation for the IOPC to consider:[153]

1) investigation by the police themselves (a local investigation);
2) investigation by the police under the direction of the IOPC (a directed investigation);
3) investigation by the IOPC itself.

3.121 If the IOPC decide, having regard to the seriousness of the case and the public interest, that a local investigation is appropriate, then that must be the determination made.[154] If a local investigation is not appropriate, then the IOPC must investigate the complaint, unless it is decided that an investigation by the police under the direction of the IOPC is

143 Complaints and Misconduct Regs 2020 reg 4(3).
144 *Statutory guidance on the police complaints system*, IOPC, para 9.42.
145 *Statutory guidance on the police complaints system*, IOPC, para 9.43.
146 Complaints and Misconduct Regs 2020 reg 4(2) and (3).
147 *Statutory guidance on the police complaints system, IOPC*, para 9.46.
148 PRA 2002 Sch 3 para 4(6).
149 In 2020/21, 4,674 cases were referred: *IOPC annual report 2020/21*, p28.
150 PRA 2002 Sch 3 para 15(1).
151 PRA 2002 Sch 3 para 15(2).
152 PRA 2002 Sch 3 para 15(2).
153 PRA 2002 Sch 3 para 15(4).
154 PRA 2002 Sch 3 para 15(4A).

appropriate.[155] At present, there is very little guidance as to how the IOPC will make these decisions, but they must be kept under review.[156]

3.122 It will be open to a complainant to make representations to the IOPC as to which method of investigation is appropriate. The IOPC is empowered to change its mind as to the method of investigation if it thinks another method has become more appropriate[157] for instance if there is a change of circumstances or further information comes to light. If the IOPC decides that a complaint investigation decision should be changed, then it must normally inform the complainant, the police and the complained about officer and provide reasons for its decision.[158] Both the police and the IOPC can decide to split or combine investigations if this would be more efficient, effective, or in the public interest.[159]

Cases that remain with the police

Overview

3.123 If a complaint is not one which must be or has been referred to the IOPC but has been recorded (see above), then the complaint stays with the police. There will be no input by the IOPC in the process. In reality, the vast majority of complaints are dealt with in this way.

3.124 The overriding duty of the police in such circumstances is to handle the complaint in a reasonable and proportionate manner.[160] This can include investigating the complaint, or telling the complainant that no further action will be taken.[161] The IOPC advises that between these two, the police can otherwise respond to concerns raised and seek to resolve them.[162]

3.125 There are some cases which must be investigated and these are discussed below. However, gauging what is 'reasonable and proportionate' for the police to do is a difficult matter to pin down, and does not allow for a precise definition. This is deliberate, and it is intended that the police should have a high degree of discretion as to how to deal with complaints. This means that there may be a wide divergence of approaches between different police forces as well. The IOPC sets out a list of matters which should be taken into account without providing much advice as to what should be consequences from doing so. These include:

- the seriousness of the matter, including:
  - what is alleged and the impact and/or harm that has, or could have been, caused
  - the public interest
  - whether any Articles of the ECHR are engaged

155 PRA 2002 Sch 3 para 15(4B), (4C).
156 PRA 2002 Sch 3 para 15(5).
157 PRA 2002 Sch 3 para 15(5).
158 PRA 2002 Sch 3 para 15(9).
159 Complaints and Misconduct Regs 2020 reg 14.
160 PRA 2002 Sch 3 para 6(2A).
161 PRA 2002 Sch 3 para 6(2B).
162 *Statutory guidance on the police complaints system*, IOPC, para 10.2.

   - the wider context and whether the matter gives rise to concerns additional to those alleged by the complainant
   - whether a number of previous similar complaints have been recorded or logged (either about the same issue, or, where appropriate, about the same officer or department)
   - the potential for learning for individuals, or local or national policing
   - whether there appears to be an indication that whilst the matter may not be misconduct or gross misconduct, it appears to be 'gross incompetence'
- what facts need to be established and whether they are in dispute
- how long ago any incident took place and whether evidence is still likely to be available
- what might be done to remedy any issues
- what outcome the complainant may have indicated that they are seeking.[163]

3.126 The IOPC advises further that when dealing with any matter in which discrimination is or may be a factor, the IOPC's *Guidelines on handling allegations of discrimination* should be followed.[164]

Complaints that will be investigated

3.127 There are some recorded complaints that must be investigated. Clearly, if the police have decided that it is reasonable and proportionate to investigate a complaint (taking into account the factors set out above), then it should be investigated. However, the complaint must also be investigated where there is an indication that an officer may have committed a criminal offence or behaved in a manner that would justify the bringing of disciplinary proceedings, or there may have been the infringement of a person's rights under ECHR Article 2 or 3.[165]

3.128 In addition, there must be an investigation where that has been decided by the IOPC in relation to any complaint referred to it or 'called in' (see below), or where an investigation is required as a result of a review.

3.129 The IOPC comments on the use of the word 'indication' in the test for a mandatory investigation as follows:[166]

> In making the decision about whether there is 'an indication', the appropriate authority should consider whether the circumstances, and the evidence readily available, show or reasonably imply that a person serving with the police may have committed a criminal offence or behaved in a manner that would justify the bringing of disciplinary proceedings, or that there may have been the infringement of a person's rights under Articles 2 or 3.

3.130 What is clear is that the test to be met is a low one. The IOPC advise the police to look at the facts set out in the complaint, and any readily available evidence, and seek further information and clarification from the

163 *Statutory guidance on the police complaints system*, IOPC, para 10.12.

164 *Statutory guidance on the police complaints system*, IOPC, para 10.14; and see paras 4.36–4.42.

165 PRA 2002 Sch 3 para 6(2C).

166 *Statutory guidance on the police complaints system*, IOPC, para 10.7.

complainant where necessary. However, the police should not take preliminary investigative steps in order to make the decision, such as obtaining accounts from officers and/or witnesses. Having said this, the IOPC goes on to advise that if a complaint is undermined by available 'contemporaneous real objective evidence' such as CCTV or body-worn video then there is unlikely to be an indication. If there is doubt whether the test is met, then it may be reasonable and proportionate to investigate. Any decision that there is no 'indication' can be reviewed later if it seems that the test may, in fact, be met, and the complaint then investigated.[167]

3.131 Regulations exclude from the duty to investigate a complaint in circumstances where substantially the same complaint has already been made and dealt with by the complaints system, and where there is no fresh evidence or indication which would justify an investigation.[168]

Complaints which cannot or need not be investigated

3.132 The previous iteration of the police complaints system had complicated procedures for deciding that police complaints did not need to be investigated. These included excluding complaints because they were filed outside a usual one year time limit, a process of 'disapplication' for repetitious or vexatious complaints, and where a complainant failed to co-operate with an investigation. There were also rules which governed how a complaint could be withdrawn by a complainant.

3.133 The rules for withdrawal largely remain and are discussed below. However, in other situations the police are required to take a 'reasonable and proportionate' response to a complaint, and told that in certain circumstances that can include not investigating or taking any steps in relation to a complaint. Despite the change in approach, the same concerns remain that the police will sometimes be too keen to find a way not to deal with a complaint if that is possible, while claiming that they have been acting reasonably and proportionately.

3.134 It has been explained above (paras 3.63–3.70) that many complaints do not need to be recorded by the police, unless the complainant requests it, and the police will have a wide discretion how to deal with such complaints.[169] This wide discretion can be used to explain to a complainant, on the telephone (or in writing if the complaint is in writing), the reason why the police have decided to take minimal or no action towards investigating the complaint. It might be explained that the complaint was about matters which occurred too long ago to enable proper enquiries to be made, or that the complaint simply repeats matters already dealt with. As has been explained though, there are some complaints which must be recorded in any event and, importantly, the complainant has the right to insist that a complaint is recorded if this is what they want at any stage of the process.

3.135 If a complaint has been recorded the police still have a discretion in many cases how to deal with the complaint (see paras 3.75–3.81). There

167 *Statutory guidance on the police complaints system*, IOPC, paras 10.8–10.9.

168 Complaints and Misconduct Regs 2020 reg 6.

169 *Statutory guidance on the police complaints system*, IOPC, paras 6.21–6.22.

has to be an investigation in some cases, but otherwise the rule is, again, that the police must take a reasonable and proportionate approach.[170]

3.136 There is also a specific provision which allows the police to dispense with investigation where the complaint concerns conduct already complained about, where there is no 'fresh substantive evidence' and the previous complaint has been dealt with, or his being dealt with (by investigation or otherwise), or the complaint has been withdrawn.[171] As the IOPC point out, such a complaint should still be dealt with reasonably and proportionately under PRA 2002 Sch 3,[172] and this would include providing the complainant with a full explanation as to why the complaint was not being investigated.

3.137 Otherwise, the IOPC gives general guidance as to when it will be reasonable and proportionate not to take any action on a complaint which has been recorded. It says that circumstances where it may not be reasonable to take any action in relation to a complaint include (but are not limited to):[173]

- complaints about the off-duty behaviour of an officer, which has no relevance to their police role and, even if proved, would not discredit the police service or undermine public confidence in it;
- 'fanciful' complaints which are patently of a nature that no reasonable person could lend any credence to it;
- complaints which would be better handled by another process, for example, a complaint to the Information Commissioner's Office;
- complaints where too little information has been provided to enable an enquiry to progress.

3.138 Not all cases are clear-cut and the IOPC recognises that 'there may be circumstances where some enquiries are needed before it can be established that it is reasonable and proportionate' to take no further action to handle the complaint after recording it.[174] Thus, there may be circumstances where it is worthwhile considering again complaints that have already been addressed to see if 'more can be done to handle the matter and respond to the complainant's dissatisfaction'.[175] Recognising the temptation not to take action in relation to complaints that are perceived as 'difficult' to deal with, the IOPC states that a positive resolution of a complaint should be sought whenever possible.[176] Where it is decided that no further action can be taken as part of the reasonable and proportionate handling of a complaint, a detailed rationale for this should be provided to the complainant along the lines of the communication duties for complaints.[177]

170 See *Statutory guidance on the police complaints system*, IOPC, Chapter 10.
171 Complaints and Misconduct Regs 2020 reg 6.
172 *Statutory guidance on the police complaints system*, IOPC, para 10.11.
173 *Statutory guidance on the police complaints system*, IOPC, para 12.10.
174 *Statutory guidance on the police complaints system*, IOPC, para 12.11.
175 *Statutory guidance on the police complaints system*, IOPC, para 12.11.
176 *Statutory guidance on the police complaints system*, IOPC, para 12.12.
177 *Statutory guidance on the police complaints system*, IOPC, para 12.13.

Withdrawn complaints

3.139 The provisions about withdrawal of complaints contain a number of safeguards against abuse by the police, and offer the possibility that the complaint will continue to be investigated in any event and against the complainant's wishes.

3.140 A number of things happen when the complainant or their representative notify the police or the IOPC (depending on the type of investigation) in writing that the complainant wishes to withdraw the complaint:

1) First, the police or the IOPC must record the withdrawal, and if the withdrawal is sent to the IOPC then it must be copied to the police.[178]
2) Second, if the police receive a withdrawal of a complaint which was referred to the IOPC (and was not referred back) (see above, para 3.119) then the police must inform the IOPC that it has recorded the withdrawal.[179] If there is an outstanding review then the review body must be informed of the withdrawal.
3) Third, in cases which have been formally referred to the IOPC (and not referred back) the IOPC must decide whether it is in the public interest to treat the complaint as a 'recordable conduct matter', and if so inform the police force of this,[180] and effectively, the investigation will continue).[181]
4) Fourth, in cases where withdrawal has been notified and there is an outstanding review being considered by the local policing body or the IOPC, the police must also make a decision whether to continue the investigation as a recordable conduct matter in the 'public interest'.[182] If the case is under review to the IOPC, then the police force must inform the IOPC whether it is treating a withdrawn complaint as a recordable conduct matter, and if it is not, the IOPCC can reverse that decision.[183]

3.141 There are sometimes difficulties if the complainant indicates orally to the police force or the IOPC that they do not wish to continue with a complaint. In these circumstances, the police must write to the complainant to ascertain their views. A 'nil response' after 28 days will be treated as a formal written withdrawal.[184] As this puts the onus on the complainant, advisers should be vigilant in ensuring that casual or ambiguous oral remarks are not misinterpreted by the police in such a way as to lead to attempts to treat a complaint as withdrawn, if that is not the complainant's real intention.

3.142 The complained about officer must be kept informed of all the decisions taken as part of this process, unless criminal or disciplinary proceedings would be prejudiced or unless it would be contrary to be the public interest to do so.[185]

178 Complaints and Misconduct Regs 2020 reg 38(2).
179 Complaints and Misconduct Regs 2020 reg 38(3).
180 Complaints and Misconduct Regs 2020 reg 38(5).
181 Complaints and Misconduct Regs 2020 reg 38(8).
182 Complaints and Misconduct Regs 2020 reg 38(6).
183 Complaints and Misconduct Regs 2020 reg 38(9).
184 Complaints and Misconduct Regs 2020 reg 39.
185 Complaints and Misconduct Regs 2020 reg 38(10).

Resumption of investigation after criminal proceedings and other situations where handling of complaint has been suspended

3.143 There are provisions for suspending the handling of complaints where to continue would prejudice any criminal investigation or proceedings.[186] Thus, a complaint investigation is often initially suspended if there are linked criminal proceedings against a complainant, and, for example, a complainant would have to provide the police with a statement setting out their version of events if a complaints investigation continued. In such circumstances, the complainant might argue that this would make the criminal trial unfair. A police force might also prefer to suspend investigation in the hope that the complainant (if they have been charged) is convicted. As a check on this, the IOPC has the power to overrule any decision by the police to suspend the handling of a complaint if it is in the public interest (although it must consult with the police before making such a direction).[187] Thus, it may be that there is little dispute as to the facts and the complainant is happy to give a statement, and the public interest in having complaints speedily resolved might outweigh any potential prejudice to the criminal trial.

3.144 The IOPC has issued guidance which indicates that the IOPC is keen for a complaint to continue wherever possible and the power to suspend should be exercised sparingly. The guidance says that there should be specific, identified prejudice, and that prejudice should be significant, and that it is necessary to consider the extent to which the complaint raises issues which are the same or closely connected to issues which arise in the criminal matter; and what particular prejudice would be caused if the complaint process was to continue.[188] The police should also consider any measures that could be put in place to reduce the prejudice, and also whether the public interest in a prompt consideration of the complaint would outweigh any prejudice caused to the continuation of the criminal matter.[189] Such measures might include carrying out a single interview with witnesses to cover the complaint and criminal proceedings, or 'interviewing witnesses to the matter in the presence of the solicitor for the defendant to the criminal proceedings'.[190]

3.145 Thus when deciding whether to exercise the power to suspend, a balancing exercise should be carried out which looks at matters such as the severity of the complaint allegation and the criminal matter, the strength of the evidence in either case, and the potential effect of delay. The police should look at whether suspending the complaint would risk the expiration of the six-month time limit for the bringing of summary-only charges against the complained about officer.[191] The IOPC advises that before the power to suspend is exercised, the views of the CPS and the police legal

186 Complaints and Misconduct Regs 2020 reg 40.

187 Complaints and Misconduct Regs 2020 reg 40(2).

188 *Statutory guidance on the police complaints system*, IOPC, para 15.2.

189 *Statutory guidance on the police complaints system*, IOPC, para15.3.

190 *Statutory guidance on the police complaints system*, IOPC, para 15.5.

191 *Statutory guidance on the police complaints system*, IOPC, para 15.4.

department should be sought on the issue. This might also help to identify steps that can be taken even if the power to suspend is activated, such as securing CCTV evidence or witness statements from those not involved in the criminal proceedings.[192]

3.146 Those advising the complainant might also want to consider whether it is possible for the complainant to make a statement for the purposes of the complaint in any event, rather than waiting for the outcome of the criminal case. The IOPC states that if this is done then the officer can be served with the notice of investigation.[193]

3.147 The complainant should be notified in writing about a decision to suspend, and provided with a rationale for the decision. The IOPC says that where a complainant objects to the suspension, they should also be informed that they may ask the IOPC to consider whether to direct that the investigation or other handling continue (see above).[194] Judicial review of the decision of the police and/or the IOPC may be possible if the complainant remains dissatisfied with the outcome.

3.148 In cases where a complaint investigation is suspended and, after the resolution of criminal proceedings, the complainant has not indicated that they want it to be restarted, certain steps must be taken by the police or the IOPC.[195] Essentially, all reasonable steps must be taken to obtain the views of the complainant. The investigation must be started or resumed if the complainant indicates that they want this. If the views of the complainant cannot be ascertained and they do not respond within 28 days to a letter, or if the complainant does not want to continue with the complaint, then the IOPC or the police (whichever has been investigating/directing the complaint) must decide whether it is in the public interest to treat the complaint as a 'recordable conduct matter' (see paras 4.43–4.52).[196]

3.149 The IOPC does advise that the police should take all reasonable steps to contact the complainant and to check that they have the right contact details. This might be especially important if the complainant is in prison as a result of the criminal proceedings.[197]

3.150 In cases which were being handled other than by way of investigation (see above, paras 3.87–3.90), the IOPC advises that the police should contact the complainant and resume the handling of the complaint.[198] The outcome of the criminal proceedings might mean that the case should be reconsidered as to whether investigation has become appropriate.

192 *Statutory guidance on the police complaints system*, IOPC, para 15.8.
193 *Statutory guidance on the police complaints system*, IOPC, para 15.8.
194 *Statutory guidance on the police complaints system*, IOPC, para 15.9.
195 Complaints and Misconduct Regs 2020 reg 41.
196 Complaints and Misconduct Regs 2020 reg 41(4).
197 *Statutory guidance on the police complaints system*, IOPC, para 15.12.
198 *Statutory guidance on the police complaints system*, IOPC, para 15.10.

CHAPTER 4

Police complaints – investigations and outcomes

continued

Introduction

4.1 The previous chapter described the relevant issues at the initial stages of making a complaint against the police. This chapter will deal more fully with the investigation of complaints, investigation reports and outcomes and the system of reviews which follow. Complaints involving senior officers and officers who have left the force will be discussed, as will the new system of so-called 'super-complaints'. This chapter will cover:

- the various methods of dealing with a complaint, including formal investigations;
- the nature of investigations, including special requirements and severity assessments;
- specific guidance relating to death or serious injury (DSI) complaints;
- specific guidance relating to complaints involving allegations of discrimination;
- investigation of 'conduct matters' where there is no complaint;
- unidentified officers and officers who have left the force;
- disclosure of information to the complainant and others;
- what happens after the investigation;
- applying for a review of a decision;
- the system of super-complaints.

Complaint investigations

4.2 The decision-making process by which it is decided whether a police complaint will be investigated and whether this will be by the police (in a local or directed investigation) or the Independent Office for Police Conduct (IOPC), was set out in the previous chapter.

4.3 Where it has been decided that there will be an investigation, the primary requirement for an investigation is that it must be 'reasonable and proportionate . . ., conducted promptly and allow effective participation from complainants or interested persons'.[1] The IOPC states that investigations 'will vary greatly in their scope, purpose and complexity depending on the nature of the complaint or matter under investigation'.[2]

4.4 In a local investigation or an investigation directed by the IOPC a police officer must be appointed as an investigator by the police force.[3] This can be an officer from another force and the complainant would be able to make representations about this if this is what would be preferred.

4.5 In a directed investigation, the IOPC has powers to confirm or veto the appointment, and to require a replacement investigator if not satisfied with the person investigating.[4]

1 *Statutory guidance on the police complaints system*, IOPC, February 2020, para 13.2; available at: www.policeconduct.gov.uk/sites/default/files/Documents/statutoryguidance/2020_statutory_guidance_english.pdf.

2 *Statutory guidance on the police complaints system*, IOPC, para 13.60.

3 Police Reform Act (PRA) 2002 Sch 3 para 16(3).

4 PRA 2002 Sch 3 para 18.

4.6 Practitioners may want to consider for themselves whether the investigator appointed is appropriate, and there are a number of statutory requirements which must be satisfied. Essentially, the investigator should have sufficient skill and experience to plan and carry out the investigation; must not work under the management of the person being investigated; and there must be no concerns about a possible lack of impartiality. If the investigation concerns a senior officer, then the investigator must be from a different force.[5]

4.7 There should be a written record of the appointment and a note of any concerns about impartiality, and what decisions have been taken if there are concerns. There is no reason why the complainant should not ask to see these records.[6]

4.8 If it has been decided that the IOPC will carry out the investigation, then the IOPC will appoint the investigator and the necessary staff to assist the investigation.[7] The IOPC investigator will have all the powers of a constable for the purposes of carrying out the investigation.[8]

The nature of investigations, including special requirements and severity assessments

Terms of reference

4.9 The IOPC expects all investigations to have terms of reference, even though these are only required, by law, in cases involving special procedures.[9] The terms will vary with the complexity of the investigation and can be very simple in straightforward complaints, but it is worthwhile here to set out the IOPC guidance advice in relation to the contents of terms of reference:[10]

> Terms of reference should:
> - provide focus and direction for the investigation
> - be clear, unambiguous and tightly drawn
> - describe the scope of the investigation that will be undertaken, including the time period and/or what will not be investigated, if appropriate
> - include a summary of any concerns, complaints or allegations
> - not be a list of all actions to be undertaken
> - include the identification of learning – both for individuals or organisations
> - spell out, where there is a parallel investigation, the relationship between the two investigations.

4.10 The terms of reference should be shared with the complainant (subject to the harm test (see below in the section on disclosure)) and the investigator

5 Police (Complaints and Misconduct) Regulations ('Complaints and Misconduct Regs') 2020 SI No 2 reg 12.
6 *Statutory guidance on the police complaints system*, IOPC, paras 13.5–13.8.
7 PRA 2002 Sch 3 para 19(2).
8 PRA 2002 Sch 3 para 19(4).
9 Complaints and Misconduct Regs 2020 reg 17(2); and *Statutory guidance on the police complaints system*, IOPC, para 13.9.
10 *Statutory guidance on the police complaints system*, IOPC, para 13.10.

should consider a meeting with the complainant to discuss the terms of reference.[11]

Special procedures

4.11 An important assessment to be made early in the investigation of a complaint (and then kept under review throughout) is whether the allegations made should be made subject to 'special procedures'. This is an assessment which is made at the start of a complaints investigation (although it can be revisited later, and can be raised in an appeal)[12] and which will determine some issues of procedure, possible outcomes and the review route.

4.12 Advisers need to be aware as to when the assessment is being made in order to make representations where appropriate. For example, it is only in a case where a decision has been made that special procedures apply, that the final outcome of the complaint investigation can be couched in the language as to whether the officer has a case to answer in respect of 'misconduct or gross misconduct'. Although the special procedures are primarily to provide safeguards for the complained about officer,[13] determinations are effectively being made at this early stage about the level of potential misconduct that is being investigated, and the potential sanctions that can be imposed.

4.13 Special procedures must be followed in a complaints investigation where it appears to an investigator that there is an indication that the police officer may have committed a criminal offence, or may have behaved in a manner which would justify the bringing of misconduct proceedings.[14] There is, therefore, a low threshold to meet, as there only needs to be an 'indication' that one or both of these matters 'may' have happened (although the IOPC advises that something more than a bare assertion by a complainant might be necessary).[15] The investigator is entitled to consider the circumstances and evidence available at the time, and whether or not a bare assertion (if that is what the complaint amounts to) is undermined by other material or is inherently unlikely.[16] Reasons must be provided for the special requirements decision.[17]

4.14 There is no immediate avenue of appeal or review for a complainant in relation to the 'special procedures' decision (although a judicial review of the decision may be possible). However, there may be circumstances in which it may be appropriate to consider on review (at the end of the

11 *Statutory guidance on the police complaints system*, IOPC, para 13.11.

12 *R (Yavuz) v Chief Constable of West Yorkshire* [2016] EWHC 2054 (Admin).

13 *Statutory guidance on the police complaints system*, IOPC, para 13.20.

14 PRA 2002 Sch 2 para 19A. 'Disciplinary proceedings' (misconduct proceedings) are defined in the Police (Conduct) Regulations ('Conduct Regs') 2020 SI No 4 reg 2 and relate to breaches of the Standards of Professional Behaviour, set out in Schedule 2 to the Conduct Regs 2020 – see para 5.8 below.

15 *Statutory guidance on the police complaints system*, IOPC, para 10.7.

16 *Statutory guidance on the police complaints system*, IOPC, para 10.8; and see *R (Yavuz) v Chief Constable of West Yorkshire* [2016] EWHC 2054 (Admin) at para 142.

17 *Statutory guidance on the police complaints system*, IOPC, para 13.23.

complaints process) the propriety of a decision not to certify a case as being subject to special procedures.[18]

4.15 If it is decided that special procedures apply, then the investigator must carry out a 'severity assessment'.[19] This is an assessment as to whether the misconduct, if proved, would amount to either misconduct so serious as to justify disciplinary action, or gross misconduct, and what form any disciplinary proceedings would take in relation to the conduct.[20] There are two terms which need definition in this formulation. Thus:

- 'Misconduct so serious as to justify disciplinary action' is any conduct which, if proved, would amount to a breach of the Standards of Professional Behaviour[21] so serious as to justify a written warning (including a final written warning), reduction in rank, or dismissal without notice.[22]
- 'Gross misconduct' is a breach of the Standards of Professional Behaviour so serious that dismissal would be justified.[23]

4.16 The severity assessment decision must be fully reasoned and documented.[24] The officer's disciplinary record should be consulted before a decision is made, as this may influence the decision if there have been previous disciplinary outcomes.[25] In relation to the type of disciplinary proceedings which would apply, the IOPC advise, subject to an officer's disciplinary record that:[26]

> Ordinarily, an assessment that the conduct amounts to misconduct that is so serious as to justify disciplinary action would result in a misconduct meeting and an assessment that the conduct amounts to gross misconduct would result in a misconduct hearing.

4.17 In a local investigation, the investigator makes both the special procedures decision and the severity assessment. In a directed investigation, the IOPC makes the special procedures decision and, after considering the opinion of the investigator, carries out the severity assessment. Where the IOPC is investigating the complaint, it will carry out both functions.[27] The severity assessment can be revised once it is made, and so if the complainant disagrees with the assessment, representations can be made to the investigator, the force or the IOPC.[28]

4.18 That the special procedures decision and the severity assessment are important decisions can be seen from the next step in the investigation, as ordinarily the complained about officer will be served with a notice (known

18 *R (Yavuz) v Chief Constable of West Yorkshire* [2016] EWHC 2054 (Admin) at para 160.

19 Complaints and Misconduct Regs 2020 reg 16(3).

20 Complaints and Misconduct Regs 2020 reg 1(2).

21 Contained in Conduct Regs 2020 Sch 2.

22 Conduct Regs 2020 reg 2. The IOPC advises (*Statutory guidance on the police complaints system*, para 13.27) consulting the College of Policing (COP) *Guidance on outcomes in police misconduct proceedings*, 2017, available at: www.app.college.police.uk/wp-content/uploads/2017/10/MIsconduct-C621I0617_Guidance-on-outcomes-in-police-misconduct-proceedings_12.10.17.pdf.

23 PRA 2002 Sch 3 para 29.

24 *Statutory guidance on the police complaints system*, IOPC, para 13.37.

25 *Statutory guidance on the police complaints system*, IOPC, paras 13.34–13.35.

26 *Statutory guidance on the police complaints system*, IOPC, para 13.34.

27 Complaints and Misconduct Regs 2020 reg 16.

28 Complaints and Misconduct Regs 2020 reg 19.

as a 'regulation 17 notice') which provides the officer with information about the allegations, the severity assessment conclusions, and contains the right to seek advice and make representations, and the right not to say anything, among other matters.[29] If the severity assessment is revised during the investigation then usually the complained about officer will be give written notice of this.[30] Representations from the complained about officer in response need to be considered and, if made orally, recorded.[31]

Accelerated procedures, suspension and early contact with the Crown Prosecution Service

4.19 Complaints investigations can often be lengthy and drawn out. The statutory framework contains provision for 'accelerated procedures'. Where the investigator or the IOPC believe that that there is sufficient evidence to establish on the balance of probabilities that there has been gross misconduct, and it is in the public interest for an officer to be dismissed without delay, then a statement supporting this and a report of the investigation to date will be made. If the police force or the IOPC (depending how the complaint is being investigated) agree, then the case is certified as meeting the special conditions for accelerated procedures.[32] Once again, the complainant can make representations to the police, the investigator or the IOPC if it is thought that the conditions for accelerated procedures are met.

4.20 There are also provisions for the force or the IOPC to suspend an officer who is subject of investigation (if temporary redeployment to alternative duties or an alternative location is not appropriate), where it appears that either the effective investigation of the case may be prejudiced unless the officer concerned is suspended, or having regard to the nature of the allegation and any other relevant considerations, the public interest requires that the officer should be suspended.[33]

4.21 The IOPC also encourages that there should be contact with the Crown Prosecution Service (CPS) where there is an 'early indication' that the complained about officer has committed a criminal offence, although it is only where the case has been certified as subject to accelerated procedures and the CPS are of the view that there are exceptional reasons not to delay criminal proceedings, that such proceedings can be brought before an investigation report is completed.[34] Otherwise the referral of the case to

29 Complaints and Misconduct Regs 2020 reg 17.

30 *Statutory guidance on the police complaints system*, IOPC, para 13.42.

31 Complaints and Misconduct Regs 2020 reg 20.

32 See Complaints and Misconduct Regs 2020 reg 25; *Statutory guidance on the police complaints system*, IOPC, paras 13.46–13.57; and *Home Office guidance: Conduct, efficiency and effectiveness: Statutory guidance on professional standards, performance and integrity in policing*, v1, 5 February 2020, chapter 12, available at: https://assets.publishing.service.gov.uk/government/uploads/system/uploads/attachment_data/file/863820/Home_Office_Statutory_Guidance_0502.pdf.

33 Complaints and Misconduct Regs 2020 reg 22; *Statutory guidance on the police complaints system*, IOPC, paras 13.58–13.59; *Statutory guidance on professional standards, performance and integrity in policing*, Home Office, chapter 5.

34 PRA 2002 Sch 3 para 20; and *Statutory guidance on the police complaints system*, IOPC, paras 13.74–13.79.

the CPS is only considered once the investigation report has been completed (see below, para 4.105). The IOPC advises that simply because there may be statutory time-limits to bring prosecutions for summary-only offences is unlikely to provide exceptional reasons (although it may be something to consider in relation to the timing of an investigation).[35]

The content of an investigation

4.22 In relation to the conduct of the investigation, the statutory guidance available is fairly vague as to what constitutes a reasonable and proportionate investigation. In general terms:[36]

> The investigator should take the reasonable steps available to them to secure the evidence concerning the incident, including witness statements and forensic evidence. Investigations may require only limited enquiries or more substantial activity to gather and analyse a wide range of evidence.

4.23 The investigator is told that they should try to obtain an account from the complainant.[37] Some complainants are happy to be interviewed by the investigator and for a statement to be produced for them to sign. In other cases, complainants prefer to provide their own statement which they have written themselves or which a solicitor has assisted with, and this is submitted to the investigator. As the investigator may well have very specific issues they need to address in a report, it is not uncommon for an investigator to have further questions for a complainant even if a statement is provided, and a decision will need to be taken whether more can be said. Often further clarification can be in writing. Thus in many cases, a complainant will decline to meet with the investigator and will provide a written statement and follow up answers only.

4.24 Even if a complainant decides to meet with the investigator, it will almost always be sensible to have provided a written statement from the complainant in advance of the meeting. If there is any possibility of a civil action being brought, an interview should take place, if at all, only with a solicitor present (see further on the relationship between a complaint and civil action at paras 14.101–14.110). In this event, such a statement should only be drafted by the solicitor acting in the civil action. Even if there will be no civil action, it is sensible for a friend or adviser to be present at any face-to-face interview. Many complainants feel uncomfortable if the interview is held at a police station, and may also be reluctant to allow the police into their home. Interviews can therefore be arranged to be held on neutral territory, such as an adviser's office or a solicitor's office where the complainant will feel confident and relaxed.

4.25 The IOPC also says that it will usually be reasonable and proportionate to obtain an account from the officer complained about, but also says it will not always be reasonable and proportionate to do this by way of an interview, and a written statement may suffice.[38] However, the difficulty with this approach is that the officer's account will not be challenged in the

35 *Statutory guidance on the police complaints system*, IOPC, para 13.76.
36 *Statutory guidance on the police complaints system*, IOPC, para 13.60.
37 *Statutory guidance on the police complaints system*, IOPC, para 13.60.
38 *Statutory guidance on the police complaints system*, IOPC, para 13.63.

way it can be in an interview, and it is open to the complainant to make representations to the investigator that an interview is necessary if the investigation is, in fact, to be reasonable and proportionate.

4.26 There are statutory procedures which must be followed by the investigator where it is decided to interview an officer in a case where special procedures apply.[39] These dictate the arrangements for the interview, the notice that must be given and the information which should be provided to the officer to prepare for the interview. Once the interview is arranged, the officer must attend and non-attendance may be a breach of the Standards of Professional Behaviour. An officer attending an interview does not have to answer questions (although they will have been warned that this may harm their case in any disciplinary proceedings if something not said is later relied upon). It is not uncommon for officers to provide a written statement at the start of the interview and then not to answer questions thereafter.

4.27 The IOPC emphasises the need for complaints to be investigated in a timely manner to secure confidence in the system and a fair result. Information has to be provided therefore if a complaint investigation has not been completed within 12 months which sets out the timetable of the complaint, the progress that has been made, why the investigation is taking so long, and the planned steps to bring it to a conclusion. This process has to be repeated every six months until the investigation is completed.[40]

Investigation of death or serious injury complaints

4.28 There is special statutory guidance issued by the IOPC to the police on achieving best evidence in DSI matters.[41] See above at paras 3.93–3.105 for what this covers. As the IOPC says: 'It is essential that the facts surrounding such incidents are fully and independently investigated in order to preserve and even enhance public confidence.'[42] The IOPC says that its fundamental approach is that police officers and staff involved in such incidents 'will continue to be treated as witnesses, unless and until the available evidence requires otherwise'.[43]

4.29 The guidance deals with the critical period immediately following a death or serious injury. As it is statutory guidance issued under PRA 2002 s22, the police need to have a sound rationale before departing from it, and that rationale needs to be recorded as soon as practicable. The IOPC notes

39 Complaints and Misconduct Regs 2020 reg 21; and see *Statutory guidance on the police complaints system*, IOPC, paras 13.64–13.73.

40 Complaints and Misconduct Regs 2020 reg 21; and see *Statutory guidance on the police complaints system*, IOPC, paras 13.80–13.86.

41 *Statutory guidance to the police force on achieving best evidence in death and serious injury matters* IOPC, January 2019, available at: www.policeconduct.gov.uk/sites/default/files/Documents/statutoryguidance/statutory-guidance-section-22-guidance.pdf.

42 *Statutory guidance to the police force on achieving best evidence in death and serious injury matters* IOPC, p1.

43 *Statutory guidance to the police force on achieving best evidence in death and serious injury matters* IOPC, p1.

that failures to follow the guidance may come under scrutiny in inquests or disciplinary proceedings, and of course in civil proceedings. As we have seen above, all DSI matters also must be referred to the IOPC as soon as possible, but the guidance applies 'from the moment a DSI matter comes to the attention of the police'.[44] There is a specific statutory duty to obtain and preserve evidence as soon as the police become aware of a DSI matter,[45] and systems should be in place to ensure that happens.

4.30 The IOPC lists some of the steps that can be taken to ensure that evidence in relation to a DSI is not lost or compromised. It can include 'establishing a perimeter to control and protect any scene and maintaining an accurate scene log recording details of everyone who enters and leaves, protecting samples of forensic evidence from damage or contamination and preventing the overwriting of visual or audio footage'.[46] It is important that the police do not take steps beyond obtaining and preserving evidence, pending directions from the IOPC, except where there are risks that the evidence could be destroyed or to protect the public from harm.[47]

4.31 The IOPC advises that, pending involvement from the IOPC, the police should obtain details and a brief description of their evidence from non-police witnesses to the DSI incident, and advise the witnesses not to discuss the incident with others.[48]

4.32 An important part of the guidance deals with the way key police witnesses are dealt with after a DSI incident. The guidance was issued following an unsuccessful judicial review[49] of guidance issued by the COP in relation to post-deployment issues in armed policing incidents,[50] which is still in force, covering some of the same issues. The concerns raised were that failure to separate police witnesses to a DSI could lead to collusion or contamination of evidence in a way that would breach the investigative duties in European Convention on Human Rights (ECHR) Articles 2 and 3 (see further in chapter 7).

4.33 Once key police witnesses have been identified, they will be dealt with as a witness unless 'there is any indication that a key policing witness may have committed a criminal offence or behaved in a manner which would justify the bringing of disciplinary proceedings'.[51] Clearly this test may apply in cases where a person has died or been seriously injured following a use of force by the police. In relation to witnesses conferring, the IOPC

44 *Statutory guidance to the police force on achieving best evidence in death and serious injury matters* IOPC, para 3.

45 PRA 2002 Sch 3 para 14B.

46 *Statutory guidance to the police force on achieving best evidence in death and serious injury matters* IOPC, para 8.

47 *Statutory guidance to the police force on achieving best evidence in death and serious injury matters* IOPC, pp4–5.

48 *Statutory guidance to the police force on achieving best evidence in death and serious injury matters* IOPC, pp5–6.

49 *R (Delezuch) v Chief Constable of Leicestershire* [2014] EWCA Civ 1635.

50 COP Authorised Professional Practice (APP) on Armed policing, Post-deployment, available at: www.app.college.police.uk/app-content/armed-policing/post-deployment/.

51 *Statutory guidance to the police force on achieving best evidence in death and serious injury matters* IOPC, para 18.

says that police witnesses should be routinely warned not to discuss the incident in question whether before or after giving their account because:[52]

> Any conferring between witnesses has the potential to undermine the integrity of their evidence, and to damage public confidence in the investigation. There is a risk that if officers discuss an incident their evidence could be contaminated, whether consciously or unconsciously. A truthful account may be doubted by a jury at a criminal trial or inquest where there has been extensive conferring.

4.34 The rule not to confer can be relaxed, says the IOPC, where it is necessary for the safety of the public or police officers, and where this happens it should be recorded. The IOPC says that to avoid contamination of police evidence its preference 'is to keep key policing witnesses separate from the moment it is operationally safe to do so, until after they have provided their personal initial account'.[53] In circumstances where key police witnesses are not separated then the IOPC advises other methods to ensure integrity of their evidence such as allowing an IOPC investigator to witness interactions and bodyworn camera evidence where for example officers have to travel together in a van after an incident. The rationale for any methods used should be recorded.

4.35 Key police witnesses are expected to record a 'personal initial account' of a DSI matter at the earliest opportunity, and before they go off duty, and the IOPC says that failure to do so 'damages not only the effectiveness of the investigation but also the public's confidence in the police service'.[54] Although this advice seems unremarkable, the IOPC accepts that no-one can be compelled to give an account, and that an officer may not be required to do so if they have been certified as medically unfit. Officers should not view any CCTV or bodyworn camera footage before providing their initial account. The aim is to obtain the officer's account unaffected by any extraneous factors, although it may be provided to provide them with incontrovertible facts such as times and dates. The IOPC provides guidance as to what should be expected in the personal initial account as follows:[55]

> It should be headed with the appropriate statutory declaration (in accordance with section 9 of the Criminal Justice Act 1967, and Part 16 of the Criminal Procedure Rules 2015) and should include the following as a minimum:
>
> - the witness' full personal details;
> - the officer's understanding of the nature of the incident, including any information they received before and/or during it;
> - the role they played in relation to the death or serious injury, and/or related incident(s);

52 *Statutory guidance to the police force on achieving best evidence in death and serious injury matters* IOPC, para 19.

53 *Statutory guidance to the police force on achieving best evidence in death and serious injury matters* IOPC, para 23.

54 *Statutory guidance to the police force on achieving best evidence in death and serious injury matters* IOPC, para 26.

55 *Statutory guidance to the police force on achieving best evidence in death and serious injury matters* IOPC, para 30.

- their decision making in respect of the incident or related incident(s), particularly when they have used force and/or have exercised any other police powers;
- their recollection of the incident and/or related incident(s) (it should be their honestly held belief of the facts, and their reasons for holding such a belief, including what they did and what they observed others doing).

Investigation of discrimination complaints

4.36 There is also special guidance which deals with complaints that allege discriminatory behaviour.[56] It was issued, initially, by the Independent Police Complaints Commission (IPCC – the predecessor of the IOPC) under its powers in PRA 2002 s22, and has been updated by the IOPC for complaints received after 1 February 2020.[57] Whether the investigation has followed this guidance in such cases will be something that advisers will want to consider carefully when deciding whether to ask for a review of a complaints outcome (see para 4.115).

4.37 The guidance flags up the relevant standard in the Standards of Professional Behaviour entitled 'Equality and Diversity', which states that 'Police officers act with fairness and impartiality. They do not discriminate unlawfully or unfairly',[58] as well as the corresponding advice in the COP Code of Ethics.[59]

4.38 The guidance outlines aspects of the Equality Act 2010, describing the difference between direct and indirect discrimination harassment and victimisation; and sets out the 'protected characteristics' of age; disability; gender reassignment; marriage and civil partnership; pregnancy and maternity; race; religion and belief; sex; and sexual orientation.[60] The requirement to make reasonable adjustments for disabled people is also explained.[61] It is emphasised that a complainant alleging discrimination will already have a low level of trust in the police and so empathetic engagement is especially important. When assessing the gravity of the complaint (see para 3.111), the impact on the complainant should be considered along with the intent of the officer concerned and any records of repeat behaviour. Investigating officers should have a good understanding of diversity and equality issues, and the terms of reference for the investigation should clearly refer to and address any discrimination allegations

56 *IPCC guidelines for handling allegations of discrimination*, IPCC, 2015, available at: https://policeconduct.gov.uk/sites/default/files/Documents/research-learning/guidelines_for_handling_allegations_of_discrimination.pdf.

57 *Applying the IPCC guidance on dealing with allegations of discrimination to cases after 1 February 2020*, IOPC, March 2020, available at: https://policeconduct.gov.uk/sites/default/files/Documents/research-learning/IOPC_discrimination_guidelines_updated_March_2020.pdf

58 Conduct Regs 2020 Sch 2.

59 COP Code of Ethics, 2014, p7; available at: www.college.police.uk/What-we-do/Ethics/Ethics-home/Documents/Code_of_Ethics.pdf.

60 *IPCC guidelines for handling allegations of discrimination*, pV.

61 *IPCC guidelines for handling allegations of discrimination*, pV.

raised.[62] It would not be good enough, for example, to refer to alleged racist comments as 'rudeness' or 'incivility'.

4.39 The discrimination guidance contains detailed examples of all kinds of discrimination based on the protected characteristics to assist investigators understand the complaint. When investigating the complaint, it is recognised that there is often little or no direct evidence to support the allegation. In deciding whether there is a case to answer in such cases, other factors should be considered. These might include the officer's complaint history and other 'patterns of behaviour evidence' such as 'trends in stop and search' where relevant, along with 'comparator evidence' as to how a person without the protected characteristic would have been treated, and an assessment of the language used in records relating to the incident which led to the complaint. A failure to follow these lines of enquiry could lead to a successful request for a review of the complaint outcome. The officer complained about should be asked about the way they acted, what assumptions they made and to reflect upon why the complainant may have felt discriminated against.[63]

4.40 In relation to findings in discrimination complaints the guidance describes what a complainant should see in the findings of the complaint investigation:[64]

> In many cases the investigating officer will need to assess the cumulative picture of circumstantial evidence which could include patterns of behaviour, comparator evidence, any language of concern or evidence that the officer/staff member acted in a way that fits with discriminatory stereotyping.

4.41 The guidance goes on to say that the assessment of the complaint should include a consideration of the cumulative weight of all the evidence and of credibility, whether reasons given by the officer for the behaviour are plausible, and whether the complainant would have been dealt with differently if they did not have the relevant protected characteristic (or race, age, gender reassignment etc).[65]

4.42 The section of the guidance dealing with outcomes and resolution emphasises the need for clear and empathetic responses to discrimination complaints, and for reflections on best practice and organisational learning. If the case goes to a disciplinary hearing then panels are expected to 'have regard for this guidance when considering allegations of discriminatory behaviour'.[66]

Investigation where there is no complaint

4.43 There are cases where there has been misconduct by police officers, but there has been no complaint about it. Sometimes this is because the victim or witness has decided not to the engage with the complaints system.

62 *IPCC guidelines for handling allegations of discrimination*, pVII.

63 *IPCC guidelines for handling allegations of discrimination*, pXIII.

64 *IPCC guidelines for handling allegations of discrimination*, pIX.

65 *IPCC guidelines for handling allegations of discrimination*, pIX.

66 *IPCC guidelines for handling allegations of discrimination*, pX.

Nonetheless, these cases have to be considered, and in certain cases these cases will have to be investigated. The IOPC says this is important to ensure individual accountability and to support learning and improvement for the officer and the force.[67]

4.44 Thus, a 'conduct matter' is defined in the PRA 2002 as being a matter which has not been subject of a complaint but where there is an indication that a 'person serving with the police' may have committed a criminal offence or behaved in a way which would justify the bringing of disciplinary proceedings.[68] This is a terminology which will be recognised from other parts of the complaints system (see para 4.15) and refers to the most serious kinds of complaints against police officers.

4.45 In addition, the regime ensures that civil claims against the police are examined for possible conduct matters.[69] This should happen when the police become aware that civil proceedings are likely to be brought. The police should consider whether a complaint has been brought about the same conduct, but if it has not, an initial assessment as whether conduct matters arise should be made and then kept under continual review.[70] In effect, all conduct matters which arise in this matter are treated as 'recordable' (see below) although the statutory regime does not describe them as such.

4.46 Where a conduct matter does come to the attention of the police, and it has not arisen from civil proceedings, then a decision has to be made as to whether it is 'recordable', and this will depend on whether the conduct falls within specific conduct.[71] This covers first, situations where it appears that the conduct has led to death or serious injury[72] of a person, or that a member of the public has been adversely affected by the conduct. It also covers situations as follows where there has been a serious assault, a serious sexual offence, or serious corruption (including certain sexual abuse scenarios). Conduct will also be recordable where it involves allegations that a criminal offence or behaviour which is liable to lead to disciplinary proceedings has taken place, and which in either case was aggravated by discriminatory behaviour, or certain serious offences in any event. Conduct can also be recordable if it is grave or exceptional conduct which makes it appropriate to record the matter, and will be recordable if it is conduct of a chief officer or the deputy commissioner of the Metropolitan Police.[73]

4.47 Once conduct has been identified as recordable, it will normally need to be referred to the IOPC,[74] for the IOPC to decide how it should be investigated. The IOPC has the power to treat a conduct matter that comes to its attention other than through referral from the police as having been referred.[75] This is an important power if a police force has, for whatever reason, decided not to refer a conduct matter to the IOPC.

67 *Statutory guidance on the police complaints system*, IOPC, para 8.4.
68 PRA 2002 s12(2).
69 PRA 2002 Sch 3 para 10.
70 *Statutory guidance on the police complaints system*, IOPC, para 8.9.
71 PRA 2002 Sch 3 para 11; and Complaints and Misconduct Regs 2020 reg 7.
72 'Serious injury' is defined in PRA 2002 s29 and has been explored above at para 4.28.
73 See *Statutory guidance on the police complaints system*, IOPC, paras 8,15–8.16,
74 PRA 2002 Sch 3 para 13; and Complaints and Misconduct Regs 2020 reg 7(3).
75 PRA 2002 Sch 3 para 13A.

4.48 Once a recordable conduct matter has been referred to the IOPC, then the IOPC must decide whether the matter needs to be investigated. If it decides not to do so then the case is sent back to the police.[76]

4.49 Given the strict time limits for referral of recordable conduct matters,[77] in practice a lot of serious cases involving the IOPC including those involving deaths and serious injuries will start as a result of the referral of recordable conduct matters rather than as complaints. This is because in these cases referrals will be made within hours of the incident by the police to the IOPC, sometimes before interested persons have even been told about it.

4.50 Once a case has been referred, there may be little incentive for a potential complainant to make a complaint. However, it should be considered that rights of review of the outcome of the investigation (where investigated by the police) will only arise where a complaint has been made, and so in most cases of this type, therefore, the potential complainant should be advised to make a complaint to enable them to have review rights at the end of the process.

4.51 There is probably no right or wrong answer as to whether the claimant in a civil action should co-operate with an investigation triggered through the 'recordable conduct matter' mechanism. In some cases, a finding of misconduct will lead to a rapid settlement of the civil action. In others, it may be thought so unlikely that the investigation of the matter will lead to disciplinary action (for whatever reason) that the claimant decides not to co-operate with the investigation and to concentrate on the civil action.

4.52 If the police are not under a duty to refer a recordable conduct matter to the IOPC, or decide not to exercise their discretion to refer, or the IOPC has sent a matter back to the police on the basis that it does not need to be investigated, then there is a power for the police to deal with the matter in any way they may determine[78] In many cases, of course this will mean that nothing further is done, but if the police decide to take further management action or to otherwise review the action of officers, then this will be open to them.

Unidentified officers and officers who have left the force

4.53 Two issues have, in the past, been a source of embarrassment for the effectiveness of the police complaints system:

- The first is when it is not possible to identify the officer whose misconduct has been complained about. This is especially frustrating when it is known that one of a group of officers is the alleged culprit, but none of the officers will provide information to identify that officer.
- The second is officers who are allowed to retire while a complaint is ongoing, thus making it impossible to proceed with disciplinary action against the officer.

76 PRA 2002 Sch 3 para 14.

77 Complaints and Misconduct Regs 2020 reg 7(4).

78 PRA 2002 Sch 3 paras 11(3E) and 14(2).

4.54 In the case of the unidentified officer, the complaint must still be investigated, but provisions which relate to notifying the complained about person are not applied and the decisions do not need to be made about criminal or disciplinary proceedings. If the officer is identified during the investigation, then the full requirements of the complaints process can be applied.[79] If it is known that the complaint is about a member of a group of officers (and the other members must know who is the culprit), then there should be nothing to stop the investigation of complaints against all members of the group for neglect of duty for failing to identify the guilty officer.

4.55 In relation to an officer 'who ceases to be a person serving with the police since the time of the conduct' (and after 15 December 2017) the complaint is investigated as normal, with consideration of criminal proceedings, and with modifications whose purpose is to allow a disciplinary process to take place where a police officer has ceased serving with the police, but has a case to answer for gross misconduct (as opposed to simple misconduct).[80] The IOPC has issued guidance which emphasises that throughout the complaints process this modification need to be borne in mind, explaining that:[81]

> As disciplinary proceedings can be brought only where the matter may amount to gross misconduct, the only disciplinary proceeding that can be brought for a former officer is a misconduct hearing. When considering whether there is an indication of behaviour 'justifying disciplinary proceedings' for a former officer, it is therefore necessary to consider whether the behaviour, if proven, is serious enough to have justified dismissal (had the person not ceased to be a member of a police force or special constable). This affects some of the handling decisions to be made under Schedule 3 to the Police Reform Act 2002. There are also some changes to the procedure for an investigation concerning a former officer, and changes to the opinions that should be given in the final report.

Disclosure

Overview

4.56 Disclosure is the information provided by the investigation to the complainant at various stages of the process. It includes information disclosed during the investigation and information disclosed at the end of the investigation.

4.57 Historically, the police complaints process was dogged with concerns about lack of disclosure of information to a complainant. Indeed, for years there was a statutory presumption against disclosure.[82] However, under the present system that presumption is now reversed in favour of disclosure to the complainant.

79 Complaints and Misconduct Regs 2020 reg 42.

80 Complaints and Misconduct Regs 2020 reg 41.

81 *Statutory guidance on the police complaints system*, IOPC, Appendix B, para B.5.

82 Police Act 1996 s80.

4.58 The requirements of the Human Rights Act (HRA) 1998 add further weight to the need for openness in the process (especially where complaints involve arguable breaches of ECHR Articles 2 and 3), and there is a duty to conduct an effective official investigation which includes the involvement of the complainant as one of its requisite factors.[83]

4.59 The general duty under the present regime is that the police (or the IOPC if it is investigating the complaint) is to provide the complainant with all such information as will keep the complainant properly informed, while the complaint is being handled and subsequently of a range of matters. This applies whether the complaint is being formally investigated or not.[84] The matters listed are:

a) the progress of the handling of the complaint;
b) the outcome of the handling of the complaint;
c) any right to apply for a review conferred on the complainant.[85]

4.60 The complainant must also be told the correct body to which the review request should be directed, the time limit for a review, and also should be told if there is no right to a review.

4.61 Additionally, the complaint must be kept informed of the progress of any criminal proceedings, disciplinary proceedings, performance proceedings, or reflective practice review process (RPRP – see below) which has been brought in relation to, or arising from the complaint. This includes the outcome of any such proceedings and, if there is an appeal, the fact and outcome of the appeal.[86] This ensures that the complainant remains informed about the consequences of the complaint if further action is taken.

4.62 The first notification of progress made must be within four weeks of the start of the investigation, and then at four weekly intervals.[87] This also applies to the other procedures and processes listed above. The outcomes of the complaint, appeals and other procedures should be communicated to the complainant within five working days.[88] Communication should be in writing unless the complaint was not in writing and has not been recorded (see above, paras 3.63–3.70).[89]

4.63 In practical terms the IOPC gives further guidance:[90]

> Forces and local policing bodies should ensure that communication is tailored to meet the needs of the individual, as far as possible. They should ask the complainant and/ or interested person how they wish to be kept informed of the progress, and take all reasonable steps to achieve this. They must also make any reasonable adjustments required under the Equality Act 2010.

83 See *R (Amin) v Secretary of State for the Home Department* [2003] UKHL 51, [2003] 3 WLR 1169 and *R (Green) v Police Complaints Authority* [2004] 1 WLR 725. See also the discussion around the Article 2 investigative duty in chapter 7.

84 PRA 2002 s20(3).

85 PRA 2002 s20(4).

86 Complaints and Misconduct Regs 2020 reg 33.

87 Complaints and Misconduct Regs 2020 reg 34(2).

88 Complaints and Misconduct Regs 2020 reg 34(2).

89 Complaints and Misconduct Regs 2020 reg 34(3).

90 *Statutory guidance on the police complaints system*, IOPC, para 11.8.

4.64 The IOPC states that 'failure to give regular, timely, updates, or providing poor updates, is highly likely to damage the complainant's and/or interested person's trust in the process'.[91]

4.65 As to the content of updates, the IOPC advises:[92]

> Updates on the progress of handling [the complaint] should include, for example, information about the stage reached, what has been done, what remains to be done and, where applicable, a summary of any significant evidence obtained. Updates should also include the likely timescale for completing the investigation or other handling and any revisions to this. If there are any revisions to timescales, the reason for this should be given.

4.66 A complainant should be updated even if there has been little progress, and any delays explained. As part of the duty to keep a complainant informed it might be appropriate to arrange a meeting with the complainant, and to provide a written record of the meeting.[93]

4.67 However, there may be circumstances in which the investigators are reluctant to disclose substantive documents, such as witness statements and CCTV footage if it is felt that this might contaminate future proceedings. Thus, in *R (Green) v Police Complaints Authority*[94] the House of Lords found, among other things, that the risk of contamination of evidence in criminal and disciplinary proceedings (for example, the complainant tailoring their evidence after having access to other witness' statements) would usually be too great to allow such disclosure. Such concerns might not apply to CCTV evidence where witnesses have already given a statement prior to seeing the CCTV evidence. In *R v Roberts*,[95] the Court of Appeal indicated that disclosing video evidence after a witness had made an initial statement was a desirable practice, and complainants should expect to have such evidence disclosed during the investigation after an initial statement has been taken from them.

4.68 The information that must be provided to the complainant at the end of the investigation is dealt with below (see para 4.110).

The restrictions

4.69 The Home Secretary has made regulations for exceptions to the various duties to disclose information during the complaints process using powers in the PRA 2002.[96] Thus, if the IOPC or the police are of the opinion that non-disclosure is necessary for one or more of a limited number of purposes then the duty to keep the complainant informed does not apply. The purposes are as follows:[97]

(a) preventing the premature or inappropriate disclosure of information that is relevant to, or may be used in, any actual or prospective criminal proceedings;

91 *Statutory guidance on the police complaints system*, IOPC, para 11.9.
92 *Statutory guidance on the police complaints system*, IOPC, para 11.10.
93 *Statutory guidance on the police complaints system*, IOPC, paras 11.11– 11.13.
94 [2004] UKHL 6, [2004] 1 WLR 725.
95 [1998] Crim LR 682, CA.
96 PRA 2002 s20(6).
97 Complaints and Misconduct Regs 2020 reg 35(3).

(b) preventing the disclosure of information in any circumstances in which its non-disclosure–
   (i) is in the interests of national security;
   (ii) is for the purposes of the prevention or detection of crime, or the apprehension or prosecution of offenders;
   (iii) is required on proportionality grounds; or
   (iv) is otherwise necessary in the public interest.

4.70 'Proportionality grounds' essentially refers to an adverse effect which would be disproportionate to the benefits arising from disclosure.[98] This appears to be a catch-all category to deal with unforeseen circumstances, but then its use should be properly explained to the complainant.

4.71 There are circumstances in which the police or the IOPC have a duty to consider whether non-disclosure is necessary under the above grounds (although it appears it is generally empowered to consider non-disclosure in other circumstances). These circumstances are where:[99]

- that information is relevant to, or may be used in, any actual or prospective disciplinary proceedings (or appeal against the outcome of such proceedings);
- the disclosure of that information may lead to the contamination of the evidence of witnesses during such proceedings (or appeal);
- the disclosure of that information may prejudice the welfare or safety of any third party; and/or
- that information constitutes criminal intelligence.

4.72 However, in all circumstances the IOPC and the police cannot conclude that a restriction on disclosure is 'necessary' unless there is a real risk that disclosure of the information will cause a significant adverse effect.[100] The IOPC advises that whether provision of information will cause a significant adverse effect may not be explicit on the face of one document, but may be implicit when a number of documents are considered together (for example, where the identity of an informer can be gleaned from the content and context of a number of documents).[101] The IOPC also advises that potential harm can sometimes be avoided by redacting material from a document, rather than refusing to disclose the document completely.[102]

4.73 There is some information that cannot be disclosed at all without the consent of the authority from which it comes. This includes intelligence service information, information about certain warrants issued under the Investigatory Powers Act 2016, and other very sensitive information from government departments.[103]

Disclosure to other parties

4.74 Certain interested parties have the right to be kept informed in the same way as complainants (so long as they consent to be so informed) about the

98 PRA 2002 s20(7).
99 Complaints and Misconduct Regs 2020 reg 35(5).
100 Complaints and Misconduct Regs 2020 reg 35(4).
101 *Statutory guidance on the police complaints system*, IOPC, para 11.18.
102 *Statutory guidance on the police complaints system*, IOPC, para 11.19.
103 PRA 2002 s21A.

progress or the outcome of a complaint or conduct matter investigation.[104] The individuals concerned are:[105]

- a relative (spouse, partner, parent or adult child[106]) of a person who it is alleged has died from misconduct;
- a relative of a person who it is alleged has suffered serious injury as a result of misconduct and who is incapable of making a complaint;
- someone who themselves was seriously injured as a result of the misconduct;
- anyone else who the IOPC or the police decide has a sufficient interest to be kept informed.

4.75 Thus, the police and the IOPC have wide powers to ensure that relatives, victims and others (who may include friends, community organisations, MPs etc) are kept fully informed about an investigation. The same considerations about openness and limited restrictions on disclosure as discussed above apply in relation to interested persons also. In all cases the person to whom it is proposed to disclose information must consent. Interested persons do not have the rights of appeal granted to complainants.

After the investigation

The investigator's report

4.76 An investigation report must be completed by the investigator at the end of the investigation.[107] This section deals with the procedures for what happens when it is completed.

4.77 Once the report has been completed, if the complaint has been investigated by the police with no formal involvement from the IOPC then a copy of the report must be sent to the chief officer.[108] If the investigation has been directed by the IOPC, then the IOPC should be consulted about the report's content before it is finalised,[109] and a copy of the report must then be sent to the IOPC and the police.[110] If the IOPC is investigating the complaint then its investigator will submit the report to the IOPC[111] and the IOPC must also ensure a copy of the report has been sent to the police.[112] The report in a DSI investigation, where there has been no related recordable conduct matter, must be submitted to the IOPC and a copy sent to the appropriate authority.[113]

4.78 As the IOPC states, the police will rely on the report 'to guide them through the evidence, as may others including the IOPC, the relevant

104 PRA 2002 s21.
105 PRA 2002 s21(3).
106 Complaints and Misconduct Regs 2020 reg 36.
107 PRA 2002 Sch 3 para 22.
108 PRA 2002 Sch 3 para 22(2).
109 *Statutory guidance on the police complaints system*, IOPC, para 14.6.
110 PRA 2002 Sch 3 para 22(3).
111 PRA 2002 Sch 3 para 22(5).
112 PRA 2002 Sch 3 para 23(2).
113 PRA 2002 Sch 3 para 24A.

review body, the CPS, a coroner, a court and/or those conducting disciplinary proceedings'.[114]

4.79 A complainant must be informed of the outcome of the handling of the complaint and the details of and time limits for any right to apply for a review[115] conferred on the complainant.[116] The IOPC explains that:[117]

> The complainant and/or interested person(s) must be provided with sufficient information to ensure that they are properly informed. This should include a written explanation of how the matter has been handled, the actions taken or to be taken, the findings and the outcome. Where appropriate, it should include the reasons for not taking certain actions where this was in line with reasonable or proportionate handling.

4.80 There is a further duty imposed on the IOPC or the police to disclose to the complainant the 'findings' of the investigation report.[118] The police or the IOPC are empowered to discharge this last duty by disclosing a copy of the investigation report itself.[119] The IOPC underlines the approach that the complainant should normally be provided with a copy of the investigation report, unless there is a reason under the disclosure provisions not to (see above).[120] This is the most transparent way of communicating the findings of the investigation. In practice the investigation report is now routinely shared at the end of an investigation. The IOPC advises that additional information may also need to be provided to explain the outcomes and any next steps.[121]

4.81 A complainant might also request further disclosure, such as statements gathered during the investigation, to understand better the decision and it would appear to be within the spirit of the law and guidance (at least) to provide these. The courts may be slow to review a decision of the appropriate authority (IOPC or police) not to disclose material, at least for national security reasons, although of course it must be shown that the correct test has been applied: see for example *R (Miah) v Independent Police Complaints Commission*.[122]

4.82 However the outcome is communicated, the IOPC provides detailed guidance to the effect that the information provided to the complainant is clear and accessible, providing reasons and detail for decisions[123] taken and actions taken, and shows a willingness to demonstrate organisational accountability and any learning opportunities identified. Reports and communications which use jargon or which do not have an evidence-based rationale are discouraged,[124] and may provide grounds to request a review of the findings of the complaint investigation.

114 *Statutory guidance on the police complaints system*, IOPC, para 14.4.
115 *Statutory guidance on the police complaints system*, IOPC, para 17.73.
116 PRA 2002 s20(4).
117 *Statutory guidance on the police complaints system*, IOPC, para 17.68.
118 PRA 2002 Sch 3 paras 23(10) and 24(8).
119 PRA 2002 Sch 3 para 23(5) or para 24(10).
120 *Statutory guidance on the police complaints system*, IOPC, para 17.71.
121 *Statutory guidance on the police complaints system*, IOPC, para 17.71.
122 [2017] EWCA Civ 2108, [2018] 1 WLR 3817.
123 See *R (Watson) v Independent Office for Police Conduct* [2020] EWHC 2859 (Admin) for more on the content of reasons.
124 *Statutory guidance on the police complaints system*, IOPC, para 17.72.

4.83 The contents of an investigation report depend on what kind of investigation has been carried out.

Special procedures not applied

4.84 If the investigation has not been made subject to special procedures (see above, para 4.11), the IOPC recommends that the reason for this is set out in the report. As explained above, if special procedures have not been applied, then a decision has already been taken that there was no indication of a criminal offence or behaviour that would justify disciplinary proceedings, and this will limit the findings that can be reached in the investigation report. (This may be an issue which can be raised in a review if the complainant is of the view that criminal or disciplinary proceedings should have been considered.)[125] Thus, the IOPC advises that 'the investigator should not express an opinion in the report on whether or not there is a case to answer for misconduct or gross misconduct'.[126] Instead the report in such cases should include an opinion, with a clear rationale, from the investigator as to whether:[127]

- the service provided by the police was acceptable;
- the service provided by the police was not acceptable; or
- we have looked into the complaint, but have not been able to determine if the service provided was acceptable.

4.85 The investigator should also identify areas of learning that have been identified and also draw attention to matters that would help the police, or the IOPC in a directed investigation, to decide whether there may have been unsatisfactory performance, practice requiring improvement or learning.[128] In a DSI case where special procedures have not been applied, the IOPC says that the report should:[129]

> . . . include an analysis of the evidence as to how, and to what extent, if any, the person who died or was seriously injured had contact with the police, and the degree to which this may have caused or contributed to the death or injury. It should seek to include questions or concerns raised by interested persons, such as the injured person or next of kin, or otherwise identified by the investigator. It should also highlight any areas of learning identified.

Special procedures applied

4.86 Additional information is required in a report where special procedures have been applied. In a local investigation carried out by the police the report must also include the investigator's opinion as to:[130]

- whether any person to whose conduct the investigation has related has a case to answer in respect of misconduct, gross misconduct or has no

125 See *R (Yavuz) v Chief Constable of West Yorkshire* [2016] EWHC 2054 (Admin).
126 *Statutory guidance on the police complaints system*, IOPC, para 14.9.
127 *Statutory guidance on the police complaints system*, IOPC, para 17.4.
128 *Statutory guidance on the police complaints system*, IOPC, para 14.10.
129 *Statutory guidance on the police complaints system*, IOPC, para 14.12.
130 Complaints and Misconduct Regs 2020 reg 27(1).

case to answer, and whether disciplinary proceedings should be brought (taking into account, in particular, the seriousness of any breach of the Standards of Professional Behaviour);

- whether or not any such person's performance was unsatisfactory and whether or not performance proceedings should be brought;
- whether or not any matter which was the subject of the investigation should be referred, to be dealt with under the reflective practice review process (see below).

4.87 In a directed investigation, it is for the IOPC, on receipt of the investigator's report, to give its opinion on these matters.[131]

4.88 There is some judicial guidance as to what constitutes misconduct. Thus in *R (Chief Constable of Northumbria) v Independent Office for Police Conduct*[132] the High Court explained that:

> . . . for behaviour to amount to misconduct it must fall below a recognised standard of probity or competence relating to the task in respect of which the misconduct is said to arise. If it does not, it cannot be characterised as particularly grave. For an error of judgment to amount to misconduct it must be the result of actions which fall below those standards.

4.89 The question as to whether there is a case to answer is one that has been the subject of case law and subsequent guidance. The IOPC defers[133] to the guidance issued by the Home Office on the test. The Home Office guidance points out that, in the police disciplinary context, the standard of proof is 'the balance of probabilities', and therefore the evidential threshold for deciding whether there is a 'case to answer' will be a low one.[134] The investigator is offering an opinion as to whether a disciplinary panel 'could' make a finding 'on the balance of probabilities' against an officer. Case-law makes it clear that the decision-maker on a 'case to answer' issue does not step into the shoes of the disciplinary body which will hear the case.[135] As the Home Office guidance says:[136]

> The person making the decision as to whether there is a case to answer should not make their own finding of misconduct or gross misconduct nor are they making an assessment as to whether there is a 'reasonable prospect' of the meeting or panel making such a finding (as for example, a decision-maker would under the Crown Prosecutors' Code). Instead, the person deciding whether or not there is a case to answer must evaluate and consider whether the evidence – both in its nature and quality – is sufficient to allow for a reasonable panel at hearing or meeting to properly reach such a finding. If they conclude that it is, then, they must make a finding of case to answer.

131 Complaints and Misconduct Regs 2020 reg 27(2).

132 [2019] EWHC 3169 (Admin) at para 55.

133 *Statutory guidance on the police complaints system*, IOPC, para 14.13.

134 *Statutory guidance on professional standards, performance and integrity in policing*, Home Office, para 8.62.

135 *R (Chief Executive of the Independent Police Complaints Commission) v Independent Police Complaints Commission* [2016] EWHC 2993 (Admin).

136 *Statutory guidance on professional standards, performance and integrity in policing*, Home Office, para 8.65.

4.90 The Home Office guidance addresses cases where there are conflicting witness accounts which are 'on an analysis of the evidence equally plausible'. In such cases, the Home Office says:[137]

> ... the case to answer decision-maker should not attempt to resolve that conflict between accounts or form a view on the reliability of witness evidence based on that witness evidence alone. In these circumstances, it will usually be correct to decide that there is a case to answer. It is ultimately the role of a misconduct meeting or hearing to take into account witnesses' evidence both in chief and under cross-examination along with the witnesses' demeanour in order to make a decision about which account to accept.

4.91 This is an important point to note when considering an investigation report which deals with the situation where the complainant's account does not accord with that of the complained about officer, and whether to apply for a review of the decision. The IOPC also notes that investigators 'should take particular care not to reach findings of fact that may be determinative of whether or not there has been misconduct' as this will also usurp the role of the disciplinary proceedings.[138]

Considering the report

4.92 As has been seen, the investigator offers an opinion in the investigation report of the matters required, depending on what kind of investigation that has been carried out. However, the investigator is not the ultimate decision maker of the outcome of the complaint, and that role reverts to the police in a local investigation, and to the IOPC in directed and independent investigations. Clearly, what will usually happen is that the police or the IOPC will agree with the investigator's opinion, but that is not required by the statutory framework.

Outcomes where special procedures do not apply

4.93 The police will need to make the final decision on whether the service provided by the police was acceptable, taking into account the view of the investigator (see above).[139] The approach to be taken is that:[140]

> It should be determined that the service provided by the police was not acceptable where handling has shown that the service provided (whether due to the actions of an individual, or organisational failings) did not reach the standard a reasonable person could expect.

4.94 If it is so determined, the police should consider what remedies will be appropriate for remedying dissatisfaction, including making a timely apology where appropriate.[141] The IOPC provides a possible list of other remedies for the police to consider. As well as obvious options such as

137 *Statutory guidance on professional standards, performance and integrity in policing*, Home Office, para 8.70.

138 *Statutory guidance on the police complaints system*, IOPC, para 14.16.

139 *Statutory guidance on the police complaints system*, IOPC, para 17.6.

140 *Statutory guidance on the police complaints system*, IOPC, para 17.6.

141 *Statutory guidance on the police complaints system*, IOPC, para 17.12.

explanations, mediation meetings, sharing evidence of learning and committing to reviewing policy, the following, more concrete, options are included:[142]

- Returning seized property, where it is appropriate, necessary and lawful to do so.
- Reviewing information on police records or databases. This may be appropriate where there is evidence that a complainant's details may have been kept on police records or other databases inaccurately or inappropriately.
- Removing police cautions. This may be appropriate where evidence indicates that a caution may have been issued outside of any guidelines.

4.95 There is also a procedure for the IOPC or the local policing body to make recommendations to the police with a view to remedying the dissatisfaction of a complainant where a review is upheld or at the end of an investigation.[143] This can include reference to the reflective practice review process (see below) or anything else that is appropriate, although not compensation.[144] However, the IOPC advises that the person making the recommendation should be 'mindful of whether there are, or are likely to be, any ongoing proceedings that may make a recommendation inappropriate.'[145] Clearly 'ongoing proceedings' could include a civil action, and inquest or a judicial review claim, as well as criminal or disciplinary proceedings. Additionally, if the police disagree with the recommendation then they can explain the reason for the disagreement to the IOPC or local policing body and do not have to abide by it.[146]

4.96 As mentioned above (para 3.21), the IOPC has other powers for making recommendations for organisational learning which it could chose to exercise at the end of an investigation, and the IOPC provides further detail as to when these powers might be used.[147]

Reflective practice review process

4.97 Reflective practice review process (RPRP) is a new procedure introduced in 2020. It is described in full in the Home Office guidance, and will be discussed further in the next chapter on police disciplinary procedures (paras 5.84–5.93). The IOPC explains that:[148]

> The Reflective Practice Review Process is not a disciplinary process or a disciplinary outcome. It is intended to provide an open environment to encourage all those involved in the process to reflect, learn and, where necessary, put things right and prevent any issues identified from reoccurring. It is important that this, and the steps involved in the process, are explained to complainants and any interested persons . . .

4.98 There are various routes under the PRA 2002 by which a complaint can result in a reference to the RPRP. These are as follows:

142 *Statutory guidance on the police complaints system*, IOPC, para 17.14.
143 PRA 2002 Sch 3 para 28ZA.
144 Complaints and Misconduct Regs 2020 reg 30.
145 *Statutory guidance on the police complaints system*, IOPC, para 17.17.
146 Complaints and Misconduct Regs 2020 reg 30.
147 PRA 2002 s10 and Sch 3 para 28A. See *Statutory guidance on the police complaints system*, IOPC, paras 17.30–17.37.
148 *Statutory guidance on the police complaints system*, IOPC, para 17.24.

- as the outcome to a complaint handled otherwise than by investigation;
- as the outcome of an investigation into a complaint or recordable conduct matter where a matter is assessed as amounting to practice requiring improvement;
- as a result of a recommendation under PRA 2002 Sch 3 para 28ZA (see above, para 4.95).

4.99 However the case has been 'handled' under the complaints process (by investigation or otherwise) will form part of the fact-finding stage for the subsequent RPRP.[149]

Unsatisfactory performance procedures

4.100 The purpose of unsatisfactory performance procedures (UPP) is to improve the performance of the officer and the overall performance of the force.[150]

4.101 There are various routes under the PRA 2002 by which a complaint can result in a reference to the UPP. These are as follows:

- as the outcome following an investigation into a DSI, complaint or recordable conduct matter where the performance of an officer has been a assessed as unsatisfactory;
- as directed by the IOPC following a directed or independent investigation into a complaint or recordable conduct matter;
- as recommended or directed by the IOPC following the consideration of the report of an investigation into a DSI;
- as recommended or directed as a result of a review of the outcome of a compliant handled by way of a local investigation.

4.102 The UPP procedures are explained more fully in the next chapter. The IOPC explains that unsatisfactory performance is different from misconduct and gross misconduct, as the latter will always involve a breach of the Standards of Professional Behaviour, whereas unsatisfactory performance or attendance concerns the inability or failure of an officer to perform their role to a satisfactory level *but* not enough to breach the Standards of Professional Behaviour.[151]

4.103 The IOPC accepts that it can sometimes be difficult to distinguish precisely between unsatisfactory performance and misconduct, but advises that the following principles, which suggest a degree of purposeful action or inaction for misconduct, should be taken into account:[152]

- a deliberate failure to perform the duties of a police officer or special constable satisfactorily would not normally be unsatisfactory performance;
- a failure to perform the role satisfactorily through lack of competence or capability on the officer or special constable's part should generally be dealt with as unsatisfactory performance;

149 *Statutory guidance on the police complaints system*, IOPC, para 17.23.
150 Police (Performance) Regulations 2020 SI No 3.
151 *Statutory guidance on the police complaints system*, IOPC, para 17.27.
152 *Statutory guidance on the police complaints system*, IOPC, para 17.29.

- unsatisfactory performance may be more readily identified by a pattern of behaviour, rather than a single incident (although a single incident may suffice).

4.104 The IOPC deals with complaints about lawfulness in its guidance. These kinds of cases are important where the allegation made is that the police have exceed their powers to arrest, detain or search a person for example. The IOPC says as follows:[153]

> . . . No determination should be reached, either during the handling of the complaint or in the outcome, as to whether there has been criminal behaviour or civil unlawfulness. Reaching determinations on these issues is for the criminal and civil courts and/or those conducting disciplinary proceedings.
>
> If there is a critical need to offer a view in order to address a complaint which has been made, it must be couched in the language of an indication of opinion on the matter. For example: 'Having considered the evidence and the relevant law, it is my opinion that a disciplinary tribunal could find that there was no lawful reason for the arrest and that it was an abuse of the officer's authority'.

Action on receipt of an investigation report of a complaint or recordable conduct matter – local investigations

4.105 When a police force receives a report of a local investigation of a complaint or recordable conduct matter, it must determine first of all, whether the report indicates that a criminal offence may have been committed by the complained about officer; and then whether the circumstances are such that it is appropriate for the CPS to consider it.[154] If these conditions are met, then the report must be sent to the CPS. The first part of the test for referral to the CPS is there only needs to be an indication that an offence may have been committed. However, the second part of the test suggests that there is a wide discretion to take factors into account when deciding whether to refer. The police force is required to inform the complainant about a decision made on this matter.[155]

4.106 When the CPS has considered its decision on a case referred to it, it must inform the police whether not it intends to take action.[156]

4.107 The IOPC provides guidance to the police in relation to the referral decision. A decision not to refer a case must be properly documented. Care should be taken to ensure that time limits for summary only offences (usually six months) are not missed.[157] There is no right of review of the police decisions on this issue, although an action for judicial review might be possible if there is a refusal to refer the case to the CPS. Chapter 13 describes remedies which might be available in relation to decisions of the CPS.

153 *Statutory guidance on the police complaints system*, IOPC, paras 17.38–17.39.

154 PRA 2002 Sch 3 para 24(1)–(2B).

155 PRA 2002 Sch 3 para 24(5).

156 PRA 2002 Sch 3 para 24(3).

157 *Statutory guidance on the police complaints system*, IOPC, paras 17.47–17.51.

4.108 Once criminal proceedings have been completed or (more commonly) where the CPS decides not to prosecute an officer, or the police force decides not to refer the case to the CPS in the first place, then the police force has to decide what further action to take in relation to the report. Decisions must be made:

a) whether or not the officer has a case to answer in respect of misconduct, gross misconduct or has no case to answer;
b) whether or not the officer's performance is unsatisfactory; and/or
c) what action, if any, police must or will take in respect of the matters dealt with in the report.[158]

The IOPC states that in making the decisions about misconduct, the Home Office guidance should be referred to (see para 4.19), and that this guidance 'must be read in conjunction with any College of Policing guidance on outcomes'.[159]

4.109 A notification sent to the complainant must include the findings of the report, what action the police are proposing to take and, importantly, the complainant's right to review (and to whom the request for review should be made).[160] The police force is specifically empowered to disclose the investigating officer's report as a means of informing the complainant of the findings of the report.[161] The process of disclosure is governed by the rules set out above at paras 4.56–4.75. The communication of the outcome should take place within five days of its determination.[162]

4.110 The IOPC provides guidance as to how the outcome should be communicated to a complainant:[163]

> 17.68 The complainant and/or interested person(s) must be provided with sufficient information to ensure that they are properly informed. This should include a written explanation of how the matter has been handled, the actions taken or to be taken, the findings and the outcome. Where appropriate, it should include the reasons for not taking certain actions where this was in line with reasonable or proportionate handling.
>
> 17.69 Where it was considered that it was reasonable or proportionate to take no further action in relation to a matter, the reasons for this should be explained clearly.

4.111 As well as the investigation report, the IOPC states that it may be helpful to provide supplementary explanation of the outcomes and any next steps. There is a long list of requirements for the communication which is worthwhile setting out in full:[164]

> Whether the outcome is communicated by way of an investigation report or otherwise, it should be communicated in a clear and accessible way. It should:

158 PRA 2002 Sch 3 para 24(6).
159 *Statutory guidance on the police complaints system*, IOPC, para 17.52.
160 PRA 2002 Sch 3 para 24(7).
161 PRA 2002 Sch 3 para 24(10).
162 Complaints and Misconduct Regs 2020 reg 34.
163 *Statutory guidance on the police complaints system*, IOPC, paras 17.68–17.69.
164 *Statutory guidance on the police complaints system*, IOPC, para 17.72.

- provide the recipient with sufficient information to properly understand and examine the handling of the matter, the decisions taken and the conclusions reached
- directly address the matters raised
- show that the objectives set – for example, in the terms of reference or during discussions with a complainant or interested person – have been met
- be written in plain language, free of technical jargon wherever possible
- be impartial and supported by evidence-based rationale
- provide a clear account of the information/evidence gathered and how it has been evaluated
- where appropriate, explain why information or action/lines of enquiry were not pursued
- not be defensive in tone
- acknowledge any concerns and harm caused, and the impact of this
- willingly demonstrate organisational accountability, where appropriate
- set out any learning opportunities for an individual or organisation, and how these will be acted on

IOPC outcome decisions

4.112 On receipt of an investigation report of a DSI matter, the IOPC must determine whether the report indicates that a person serving with the police may have committed a criminal offence or behaved in a manner that would justify the bringing of disciplinary proceedings, make a determination on any other matter dealt with in the report, in a process similar to that undertaken by the police in local investigations.[165] Where the IOPC determines that the report does not indicate that the officer may have committed a criminal offence or behaved in a manner that would justify the bringing of disciplinary proceedings, it may notify the police force that it must now determine whether any person's performance is unsatisfactory and, if so, what action (if any) it will take.[166] There is then a process for the police force to inform the IOPC what action it will take and for the IOPC to make directions as to unsatisfactory performance if it does not agree with the police force proposals.

4.113 In relation to directed investigations, it is the IOPC which decides whether to refer the case to the CPS where there is an indication that a criminal offence has been committed, but the IOPC seeks the views of the police force on other outcome matters.[167] Where the directed investigation is subject to special procedures (see above, para 4.11), the IOPC must inform the police of its views on the following matters:[168]

- any person to whose conduct the investigation has related has a case to answer in respect of misconduct or gross misconduct or has no case to answer;

165 Set out in PRA 2002 Sch 3 para 24A; and see *R (Ladkin) v Independent Office for Police Conduct* [2021] EWHC 122 (Admin) for an example of a challenge to this decision making process, as there is no statutory review of IOPC decisions.

166 PRA 2002 Sch 3 para 24C.

167 PRA 2002 Sch 3 para 23; and see *Statutory guidance on the police complaints system*, IOPC, paras 17.62–17.66.

168 Complaints and Misconduct Regs 2020 reg 27; *Statutory guidance on the police complaints system*, IOPC, para 17.63.

- whether or not any such person's performance was unsatisfactory;
- whether or not disciplinary proceedings should be brought, and, if so, what form those proceedings should take (taking into account, in particular, the seriousness of any breach of the Standards of Professional Behaviour);
- whether or not performance proceedings should be brought;
- whether or not any matter that was the subject of the investigation should be referred to be dealt with under the RPRP (see paras 4.97 and 5.84–5.93).

4.114 There are provisions for the exchange of views before the IOPC reaches conclusions on these matters. The IOPC can make a determination as to any matter dealt with in the report, and this may include a determination that a matter amounts to practice requiring improvement.

Reviews

Overview

4.115 There are now no appeals from police complaints decisions, for complaints made after 1 February 2020, either to the IOPC or to the police force that investigated the complaint. However, there is a general right of review of the outcome of any complaint which has been recorded under PRA 2002 Sch 3 (see above paras 3.63–3.73 as to when complaints are recorded whether the complaint has been subject to investigation or not.[169] As noted above, a complainant always has the right to insist that a complaint is recorded, and the subsequent right to seek a review is another reason for insisting on the complaint being recorded (see para 3.63 above). Where a complaint has not been recorded and the complainant is dissatisfied with the outcome to the complaint, the IOPC advises that a complainant can ask for the complaint to be recorded at that point, and that will then trigger the right to ask for a review.[170]

4.116 However, the right to review does not apply where there has been directed or independent investigation (see above). In these cases, the only way to challenge will be by way of judicial review.

4.117 A review is upheld when it is decided that the outcome of the complaint is not reasonable and proportionate.

4.118 In most cases the body that will review the complaint will be the local policing body. The local policing body can delegate complaints reviews.[171] Thus in London, for example, the Mayor's Office for Policing and Crime (MOPAC), which is the local policing body, has recruited complaints review staff to carry out the functions for which it is responsible.

4.119 However, there are a number of cases where the review body is the IOPC.[172] These include situations where the local policing body (rather than the police force) has taken responsibility for the complaint. The IOPC will

169 PRA 2002 Sch 3 paras 6A and 25.
170 *Statutory guidance on the police complaints system*, IOPC, para 6.25.
171 Complaints and Misconduct Regs 2020 reg 50.
172 PRA 2002 Sch 3 para 30; and Complaints and Misconduct Regs 2020 reg 30.

also be the review body in the more serious cases where, from the complaint alone, the police did not rule out that the conduct (if proved) would justify criminal or disciplinary proceedings or a breach of ECHR Article 2 or 3.

4.120 The IOPC is also the reviewing body where a complaint was referred to it, or it treated a complaint as having been referred using its so-called 'power of initiative'.[173] The IOPC is also the reviewing body where a complaint involves a senior officer over the rank of chief superintendent.

4.121 The request for a review should be received within 28 days, although there is provision for this to be extended taking into account a range of factors such as the importance of the issues, the reasons for delay and the length of the delay.[174] There are provisions which an application for a review should meet. The application should contain details of the complaint and the date it was made, the name of the relevant police force, and the date the complainant was told about the right of review.[175] These requirements can be met by making enquiries of a complainant, before deciding if the request is invalid.[176] A decision that an application for review is invalid would only be challengeable by way of judicial review.

4.122 Once the request has been received by the correct reviewing body, the complainant should be informed of this, and also informed about the process and timescale for the review. The officer complained about will usually be informed about the review request. The reviewing body must request any information from any person which it considers necessary to deal with the review.[177] In practice this will often mean requesting the investigation report and supporting documents from the police. The police will have a duty to provide these.[178]

4.123 The IOPC provides further guidance as to how a review should be conducted. Importantly, the IOPC confirms that:[179]

> An application for a review offers the opportunity to consider whether the complaint outcome is reasonable and proportionate and, if not, to put things right. Conducting a review should not be merely a quality check of what has happened before. The reviewer should come to their own conclusions about whether the outcome is reasonable and proportionate.
>
> When deciding whether the outcome is reasonable and proportionate, the focus should be on whether it is appropriate to the circumstances of the individual complaint, rather than the process followed to reach that outcome. However, where the handling of a complaint is found to be legally flawed in a manner that could have affected the outcome, the review should be upheld unless the reviewer finds that the same outcome would inevitably have been reached even without those flaws.

4.124 The IOPC also offers guidance as to how applications for reviews of different kinds of issues should be dealt with by a reviewer:

- A review of a **decision to take no further action** on a complaint (see above, para 3.75) should consider, for example, whether reasonable

173 *Statutory guidance on the police complaints system*, IOPC, para 19.36.
174 Complaints and Misconduct Regs 2020 reg 29.
175 Complaints and Misconduct Regs 2020 reg 29.
176 *Statutory guidance on the police complaints system*, IOPC, para 8.20.
177 Complaints and Misconduct Regs 2020 reg 29.
178 PRA 2002 Sch 3 para 25.
179 *Statutory guidance on the police complaints system*, IOPC, paras 18.29 and 18.33.

and proportionate steps were taken to obtain necessary further information from a complainant.[180] There may of course be a wide range of reasons why it was not appropriate for the police not to deal with a complaint which could form the basis for a successful review.

- The review should consider whether the complainant has been given **sufficient information to explain any findings**. The IOPC advises that a review should only be upheld where it is not possible for the outcome to be understood. Where that is because of missing information which the reviewer can provide from the evidence before them, although the review would be upheld, the reviewer would be able to provide the missing information without requiring any further action from the police.[181]
- In reviews of the **findings and determinations** of complaints, the IOPC provides a checklists for reviewers which provides examples of things to consider as follows:[182]
  - Was the complaint fully understood and were all allegations or concerns addressed?
  - Were reasonable lines of enquiries undertaken to be able to provide a reasonable and proportionate outcome?
  - Was due regard given to relevant guidance? (for example, operational guidance, the IOPC's Guidelines on handling allegations of discrimination, IOPC statutory guidance, Home Office guidance, College of Policing guidance)
  - If any aspects of the complaint were not addressed, or any lines of enquiry were not pursued, were there sound reasons for this?
  - Was information or evidence weighed appropriately and fairly?
  - Do the findings or determinations reached, logically follow from the information or evidence obtained?

4.125 However, as the review is to whether the complaint has been dealt with reasonably and proportionately, any point can be raised which throws this fundamental issue into question. Thus for example, the failure of the police to apply special procedures to the complaint (see para 4.11 above) might be an issue to raise on review if this omission casts doubt on reasonableness and proportionality.[183]

4.126 The reviewer can also review the actions proposed as a result of the complaint. The IOPC states that the reviewer should consider:[184]

- Whether due regard was given to the relevant legal tests and guidance (for example, Home Office and College of Policing guidance).
- Whether the complaint handler attempted to understand the outcome the complainant was seeking and gave that due consideration.
- Whether the proposed actions have sought to remedy the issues raised by the complainant, so far as is reasonably possible.
- Whether the proposed actions are reasonable and proportionate, considering all the circumstances.
- Whether actions have been proposed or taken in respect of any learning or other issues identified through the handling of the complaint.

180 *Statutory guidance on the police complaints system*, IOPC, para 18.35.
181 *Statutory guidance on the police complaints system*, IOPC, para 18.37.
182 *Statutory guidance on the police complaints system*, IOPC, para 18.38.
183 *R (Yavuz) v Chief Comstable of West Yorkshire* [2016] EWHC 2054 (Admin).
184 *Statutory guidance on the police complaints system*, IOPC, para 18.39.

4.127 These will all be factors that advisers will want to consider upon receipt of a review decision. The decision is not expected to be as 'tightly argued' as a judicial decision, but the conclusion should be clear and the reasons readily understood.[185]

Outcome of the review

4.128 The actions that a reviewing body can take where it decides that the outcome of the complaint is not reasonable or proportionate are set out in statutory provisions and depend on how the complaint was handled and who is the appropriate review body.

Cases dealt with other than by investigation

4.129 The first category of case is where the complaint was dealt with other than by investigation. Normally the local policing body will be the review body in such cases and it is able to do the following things when a review is upheld.[186]

4.130 First, it can recommend that the police refer the complaint to the IOPC, if the complaint has not been previously referred. This would be appropriate where the complaint appears to deal with matters that are more serious than the initial handling by the police appears to acknowledge. The IOPC would need to consider whether the complaint should be investigated and what kind of investigation is appropriate. Second, it can be recommended that the police investigate the complaint. Third, the reviewing body can make a recommendation with a view to remedying the dissatisfaction of a complainant pursuant to PRA 2002 Sch 3 para 28ZA (see above, para 4.95).

4.131 If the IOPC was the reviewing body, it can also make a recommendation under PRA 2002 Sch 3 para 28ZA, otherwise it has the power to determine that it is necessary for the complaint to be investigated.[187]

Cases which have been investigated by the police

4.132 If the complaint has been investigated by the police already, then the local policing body, where it is the reviewing body, has the power to do a number of things if the review is upheld.

4.133 First, the police can be recommended to re-investigate the complaint or recommend that the complaint is referred to the IOPC if that has not been done already. Second, the review body can make recommendations in relation to the police officer complained about. These include whether or not the officer has a case to answer for misconduct or gross misconduct, or whether or not the officer's performance was satisfactory, and recommend what kind of disciplinary proceedings should be brought. Third, the reviewing body can recommend that the police provide the CPS with a copy of the report and notify them that the local policing body considers

185 *R (Dennis) Independent Police Complaint Commission* [2008] EWHC 1158 (Admin); *R (Watson) v Independent Office for Police Conduct* [2020] EWHC 2859 (Admin).

186 PRA 2002 Sch 3 para 6A.

187 PRA 2002 Sch 3 para 6A.

that the report indicates that a criminal offence may have been committed by the investigated officer, and the reviewing body consider it is appropriate for the matters to be considered by the CPS. Fourth, the reviewing body can also make a recommendation under PRA 2002 Sch 3 para 28ZA as explained above at paras 4.130 and 4.95.[188]

4.134 In situations where the IOPC is the reviewing body, it has similar powers to make recommendations in respect to the officer complained about. However, it also has the power to make directions where necessary as to what should happen, and can also make its own findings in place of or additionally to the findings of the investigation, or direct that the complaint is re-investigated and the mode of such investigation. It can also refer the report to the CPS if it considers that the report indicates there has been a criminal offence, and it can make a recommendation under PRA 2002 Sch 3 para 28ZA as explained above at paras 4.130 and 4.95.[189]

Communicating with the complainant

4.135 The outcome of the review must be communicated to the complainant, any interested parties, the police and usually the complained-about officer.[190] The IOPC advises that where re-investigation has been recommended or directed, then it would be good practice to outline what issues should be addressed.[191] The remedy for a complainant at this stage will be a judicial review of the outcome of the review if it is felt that the reviewing body has reached an unlawful decision.

The police force response

4.136 The police must comply with any directions from the IOPC. In practice, the force can make representations to the IOPC who are entitled to change their minds about the directions.[192] If the IOPC maintains the directions, then judicial review can be an option for the police.

4.137 In relation to recommendations from the review process to the police, the police have 28 days to indicate whether a recommendation is accepted and what steps will be taken, or to explain why a recommendation is not accepted.[193] The IOPC says that it is acceptable for the police to discuss the recommendation with the reviewer and even suggest alternatives, but that normally it is expected that recommendations will be complied with.[194] The complainant should be provided with both the recommendation and the response.

4.138 If the police decline to follow a recommendation, then the IOPC has the power to direct that the recommendation is complied with.[195]

188 PRA 2002 Sch 3 para 25.
189 PRA 2002 Sch 3 paras 25 and 26.
190 PRA 2002 Sch 3 paras 6A and 25.
191 *Statutory guidance on the police complaints system*, IOPC, para 18.47.
192 See *R (Chief Executive of the Independent Police Complaints Commission) v Independent Police Complaints Commission* [2016] EWHC 2993 (Admin).
193 Complaints and Misconduct Regs 2020 reg 30.
194 *Statutory guidance on the police complaints system*, IOPC, para 18.50.
195 PRA 2002 Sch 3 para 27.

Super-complaints

4.139 The super-complaints system was launched in November 2018 and is administered by Her Majesty's Inspectorate of Constabulary and Fire and Rescue Services (HMICFRS), the IOPC and the COP, who are known as the 'decision-making authorities'. The system allows 'designated bodies' (such as charities and pressure groups) to raise broad or systemic issues that could affect public confidence in policing.

4.140 It is important to note that super-complaints are not an alternative way to raise an individual conduct matter.

4.141 The structure of legislation and guidance for super-complaints starts with PRA 2002 s29A,[196] which allows a designated body to make a complaint to the HMIC that 'a feature, or combination of features, of policing in England and Wales by one or more than one police force is, or appears to be, significantly harming the interests of the public'.

4.142 The designation of bodies which are able to make super-complaints is made by the Home Secretary.[197] Regulations set out how this is to be done,[198] and include a list of the current designated bodies:[199]

- Action on Elder Abuse;
- Advocacy After Fatal Domestic Abuse;
- Centre for Women's Justice;
- Children's Commissioner for England;
- Criminal Justice Alliance;
- Faith Matters;
- Galop;
- Hestia;
- Liberty;
- Missing People;
- Pathway Project;
- Southall Black Sisters;
- Suzy Lamplugh Trust;
- Tees Valley Inclusion Project;
- Welsh Women's Aid;
- Women's Aid Federation of England.

4.143 There are criteria for deciding which bodies should be designated.[200] Thus:

1) A designated body needs to have competence in and experience of representing the public.
2) It would represent the interests of the public effectively with the aim of improving policing.
3) The composition and governance of the body must be such that it can act independently and with integrity.

196 PRA 2002 s29A was added by Policing and Crime Act 2017 s25.

197 PRA 2002 s29B.

198 Police Super-complaints (Designation and Procedure) Regulations ('Super-complaints Regs') 2018 SI No 748.

199 Super-complaints Regs 2018 reg 3; and see www.gov.uk/government/publications/police-super-complaints-designated-bodies/designated-bodies.

200 Police Super-complaints (Criteria for the Making and Revocation of Designations) Regulations 2018 SI No 412 reg 3.

4) It has the capability necessary to carry out its role as a designated body effectively.
5) A body must have made arrangements for appropriately storing and handling data.
6) It can be relied upon to follow guidance about the making of complaints.
7) It must have activities in more than one police area.
8) It cannot be a trade union or a body representing the interests of police officers.
9) It would:
   a) collaborate effectively with bodies which are not designated bodies but which are, or may be, aware of matters which could form the basis of a complaint; and
   b) where appropriate, make a complaint on the basis of matters raised with it by such bodies.

Designation can be revoked if a body is no longer able to meet any of these criteria.

4.144 When making a complaint, a designated body must set out 'the feature, or combination of features, of policing to which it relates'.[201] It must be explained why the body is of the view 'that the feature, or combination of features, is or appears to be significantly harming the interests of the public' and this must be supported by evidence.[202]

4.145 So long as these requirements are met, and the complaint does not simply repeat a previous complaint that is being or has been investigated, the complaint will be eligible to be investigated as a super-complaint.[203] Progress reports of the investigation must be provided, along with a report of the investigation when it is completed.[204] If the decision-making authorities cannot decide on the contents of the investigation report, then each of the authorities must include its own opinion in the report.[205]

4.146 Statutory guidance has been issued about the making of super-complaints.[206] The guidance amplifies the statutory provisions for designated bodies, with an emphasis on discussing the subject-matter of the complaint before the complaint is made and during the investigation.

4.147 There is a list of the kind of evidence which could be provided with a super-complaint, which includes statistics; publicly available reports; academic research; research carried out by the body; and relevant correspondence.

4.148 A list is set out of the kind of results which come from a super-complaint as follows:

201 Super-complaints Regs 2018 reg 4(2)(a).
202 Super-complaints Regs 2018 reg 4(2)(b).
203 Super-complaints Regs 2018 reg 6.
204 Super-complaints Regs 2018 regs 7 and 8.
205 Super-complaints Regs 2018 reg 9.
206 Super-complaints Regs 2018 reg 5; *Police super-complaints: Guidance on submitting a super-complaint about policing*, IOPC, COP and HMICFRS, published 23 October 2018, last updated 18 April 2019, available at: www.gov.uk/guidance/police-super-complaints.

- an investigation by IOPC;
- changes to existing policing standards or support materials from the COP;
- a recommendation that another public body is better placed to deal with the issue;
- a recommendation to one or more police forces to change practices or local policies;
- a recommendation to another public body or government department to consider taking action to respond to the super-complaint or a related matter;
- finding the super-complaint needs no action;
- finding the super-complaint is unfounded.

4.149 The following indicates the subject-matter of some of the super-complaints that have been made to date:[207]

- police response to police-perpetrated domestic abuse;
- police response to BAME (black, Asian and minority ethnic)[208] victims of sexual abuse;
- police use of stop-and-search powers;
- police data sharing for immigration purposes;
- police use of protective measures in cases of violence against women and girls.

207 See 'Related content' at: www.gov.uk/guidance/police-super-complaints.

208 Updated 30 June 2022: https://www.gov.uk/government/publications/police-super-complaints-forceresponse-to-police-perpetrated-domestic-abuse/police-perpetrated-domesticabuse-report-on-the-centre-for-womens-justice-super-complaint/.

CHAPTER 5

Police disciplinary procedures

Introduction

5.1 Disciplinary or criminal proceedings can arise whether or not a complaint is made by a member of the public. However, if a complaint is upheld, the police may take disciplinary proceedings against the officer or, if a criminal offence has been committed, the Director of Public Prosecutions (DPP) may decide that a prosecution should be brought. In either case, the complainant may have a limited role to play and there are concerns that members of the public are not provided with sufficient information about how the case is progressing.

5.2 As was seen in the last chapter, a complaints investigation (or an investigation in a conduct matter) ends with decisions being made about an officer's conduct. Depending on the kind of investigation which has been carried out, decisions have to be made about whether criminal proceedings or disciplinary proceedings should be brought against an officer. Alternatively, decisions might have been made that an officer's performance was unsatisfactory and that unsatisfactory performance proceedings should be brought, or the case may have been referred to be dealt with under the reflective practice review process (RPRP).

5.3 The circumstances in which all of these decisions might be made has been discussed in the previous chapter. The process of considering criminal charges against officers is considered in chapter 13.

5.4 The purpose of this chapter is to, first, explain the sources of law and guidance, as well the terminology involved; and then to provide an overview for complainants and their advisers as to what happens during disciplinary and performance procedures and appeals. The procedures for misconduct meetings and misconduct hearings will be set out, and the differences between them, with special reference to the parts of the process where a complainant can be involved and/or be informed about what will happen or the outcomes of procedures. Next unsatisfactory performance procedures (UPP) (para 5.73) will be explained; following that, an overview of the RPRP (para 5.84) will be given. Finally the chapter will discuss appeals processes (para 5.94).

Sources of law and guidance

5.5 These following statutory provisions contain the legal framework for police discipline procedures:

- The Police (Conduct) Regulations ('Conduct Regs') 2020[1] deal with internal conduct matters brought to the attention of the police otherwise than under Police Reform Act (PRA) 2002 Sch 3 and operate alongside the Police (Complaints and Misconduct) Regulations ('Complaints and Misconduct Regs') 2020,[2] which deal with public complaints and discipline-related matters arising under PRA 2002 Sch 3. The Conduct Regs 2020 also deal with the procedures involved for misconduct hearings and meetings, which are discussed in detail below.

1 SI No 4.
2 SI No 2.

- The Police (Performance) Regulations ('Performance Regs') 2020[3] make provisions for cases which are not subject to misconduct hearings or meetings, and are also discussed in summary in this chapter.
- The Police Appeals Tribunals Rules ('PAT Rules') 2020[4] set out the circumstances in which a member of a police force may appeal to the PAT and the procedures governing such an appeal.

5.6 There is also guidance on police discipline procedures:

- Home Office Guidance (HOG) has been published entitled *Conduct, efficiency and effectiveness: statutory guidance on professional standards, performance and integrity in policing.*[5] It is the guidance which provides the details for all those involved in the disciplinary process. Thus, those responsible for discipline procedures must take its provisions into account when discharging their functions. The HOG says that its provisions 'must only be departed from when there is good reason to do so which can be clearly justified'.[6] This is an important document for complainants and advisers involved in disciplinary procedures which have arisen as a result of a police complaint that has been upheld and further action taken against an officer.
- The College of Policing has produced statutory guidance entitled *Guidance on outcomes in police misconduct proceedings*[7] which should be taken into account by those conducting misconduct proceedings. For those advising complainants, it is a useful resource as it underlines the seriousness with which misconduct proceedings should treat transgressions by police officers, especially where the allegations concern dishonesty, lack of integrity and discrimination. Thus, it should be consulted if a complainant is considering a challenge to the outcome of misconduct proceedings if it is thought that the sanction imposed has not been appropriately severe. The guidance contains reference to the main case-law at the time of its publication (2017) which has been referred to in many of the subsequent cases cited in this chapter.[8]
- The College of Policing has also produced a *Code of ethics: a code of practice for the principles and standards of professional behaviour for the policing profession of England and Wales*[9] which is 'a supportive, positive, everyday decision-making framework and is a constant reinforcement of the values and standards that policing is proud of' and is often referred to in misconduct proceedings as a tool for assessing the level and appropriateness of police officer behaviour.

3 SI No 3.

4 SI No 1.

5 V1, February 2020, issued pursuant to Police Act 1996 ss87 and 87A, available at: www.gov.uk/government/publications/policing-professional-standards-performance-and-integrity.

6 HOG para 1.25.

7 2017, available at:www.app.college.police.uk/wp-content/uploads/2017/10/Misconduct-C621I0617_Guidance-on-outcomes-in-police-misconduct-proceedings_12.10.17.pdf.

8 See especially *Salter v Chief Constable of Dorset* [2012] EWCA Civ 1047.

9 July 2014, available at: https://assets.college.police.uk/s3fs-public/2021-02/code_of_ethics.pdf.

- The Independent Office for Police Conduct (IOPC) has also published *Statutory guidance on the police complaints system.*[10]

Misconduct and gross misconduct

5.7 As has been seen, whether there is a case to answer for an officer in relation to either misconduct or gross misconduct is an important issue in the complaints process, and the level and type of misconduct necessary has already been discussed (para 4.15).

5.8 For there to be 'misconduct' at all, there must be a failure to meet the standard set out in the 'Standards of professional behaviour'. The current Standards are set out in the Conduct Regs 2020 Sch 2 and consist of the following:

> **Honesty and Integrity**
>
> Police officers are honest, act with integrity and do not compromise or abuse their position.
>
> **Authority, Respect and Courtesy**
>
> Police officers act with self-control and tolerance, treating members of the public and colleagues with respect and courtesy.
> Police officers do not abuse their powers or authority and respect the rights of all individuals.
>
> **Equality and Diversity**
>
> Police officers act with fairness and impartiality. They do not discriminate unlawfully or unfairly.
>
> **Use of Force**
>
> Police officers only use force to the extent that it is necessary, proportionate and reasonable in all the circumstances.
>
> **Orders and Instructions**
>
> Police officers only give and carry out lawful orders and instructions.
> Police officers abide by police regulations, force policies and lawful orders.
>
> **Duties and Responsibilities**
>
> Police officers are diligent in the exercise of their duties and responsibilities.
> Police officers have a responsibility to give appropriate cooperation during investigations, inquiries and formal proceedings, participating openly and professionally in line with the expectations of a police officer when identified as a witness.
>
> **Confidentiality**
>
> Police officers treat information with respect and access or disclose it only in the proper course of police duties.
>
> **Fitness for Duty**
>
> Police officers when on duty or presenting themselves for duty are fit to carry out their responsibilities.

10 February 2020, available at: www.policeconduct.gov.uk/complaints-reviews-and-appeals/statutory-guidance.

Discreditable Conduct

Police officers behave in a manner which does not discredit the police service or undermine public confidence in it, whether on or off duty. Police officers report any action taken against them for a criminal offence, any conditions imposed on them by a court or the receipt of any penalty notice.

Challenging and Reporting Improper Conduct

Police officers report, challenge or take action against the conduct of colleagues which has fallen below the Standards of Professional Behaviour.

5.9 'Gross misconduct' means a breach of the Standards that is so serious as to justify dismissal. Misconduct means a breach of the Standards that is so serious as to justify disciplinary action. 'Disciplinary action' means a sanction which is at least a written warning or higher.[11]

5.10 There is some judicial guidance as to what constitutes misconduct. Thus in *R (Chief Constable of Northumbria) v Independent Office for Police Conduct*[12] the High Court explained that:

> 55 . . . for behaviour to amount to misconduct it must fall below a recognised standard of probity or competence relating to the task in respect of which the misconduct is said to arise. If it does not, it cannot be characterised as particularly grave. For an error of judgment to amount to misconduct it must be the result of actions which fall below those standards.

Misconduct hearings

Standard procedures

Overview

5.11 A misconduct hearing takes place for cases where it has been decided that there is a case to answer in respect of gross misconduct or where the police officer has a live final written warning or has been reduced in rank less than two years previously and there is a case to answer in respect of a further act of misconduct. The maximum outcome at a misconduct hearing is dismissal from the police service without notice.

5.12 The presumption is that misconduct hearings must be held in public.[13] The HOG says that this is 'in keeping with a general principle that discipline proceedings should be as open, transparent and fair as possible for both the public and parties to the procedures. Restrictions on attendance should be the exception'.[14]

Independent Office for Police Conduct

5.13 The IOPC also has the potential to be significantly involved in misconduct hearings. There is a discretion for the IOPC to present the case if it is

11 Conduct Regs 2020 reg 2.

12 [2019] EWHC 3169 (Admin).

13 Conduct Regs 2020 reg 39. For discussion of the applicability of open justice and use of documents in misconduct proceedings, see *R (Newsquest Media Group Ltd) v Legally Qualified Chair of the Police Misconduct Tribunal* [2022] EWHC 299 (Admin).

14 HOG para 11.7.

brought after an investigation carried out by the IOPC itself or following a directed investigation (see chapter 4), and the police force disagreed that there was a case to answer.[15]

5.14 The IOPC can also decide to present the case if the IOPC had to direct that a misconduct hearing took place following a local investigation (see chapter 4) where the police force disagreed that there was a case to answer.[16] In other cases, the police force and the IOPC can agree that the IOPC will present the case. The IOPC also has a power to present a case where there is a compelling public interest for this to happen.

5.15 The complainant has no formal role in any of these considerations, but there is no reason why the complainant should not make representations to the IOPC if it is felt that the IOPC should present the case at a misconduct hearing, and a refusal to do so could be susceptible to an application for judicial review. If the IOPC does decide to exercise the discretion to present, then reasons for this should be put in writing.[17] Even if the IOPC decides to present the case, the police force retains control of the administration of the hearing, although the IOPC will set out the details of allegations to be served on the officer.[18]

Chair

5.16 The hearing will be chaired by a legal qualified person appointed from a pool held by the local policing body.[19] The chair hears the case with a layperson and an officer of superintendent or above (providing that the officer is at least one rank above the person subject to the misconduct hearing). If the subject of the hearing is above the rank of chief superintendent, then an inspector of constabulary will sit instead.[20]

5.17 The chair is responsible for the management of the hearing along with the police force and decides case management issues, points of law and issues about witnesses and evidence.[21]

5.18 The chair is also responsible for ensuring that the misconduct hearing begins within 100 days of notification being served on the officer concerned, although this time limit can be extended in the interests of justice,[22] although it is emphasised that 'it is in the interests of all parties to the hearing that the procedures are expedited as soon as practically possible'.[23]

Regulation 30 notice

5.19 The officer concerned will be served with a notice under Conduct Regs 2020 reg 30 and accompanying information, to which a reply is usually expected within 15 working days, setting out whether or not it is accepted that the alleged conduct amounts to misconduct or gross misconduct,

15 PRA 2002 Sch 3 para 23(5A); and Conduct Regs 2020 reg 24.
16 PRA 2002 Sch 3 para 27(4)(b).
17 HOG para 11.19.
18 See in detail for the arrangements, at HOG paras 11.29–11.34.
19 For details, see HOG para 11.35–11.39.
20 Conduct Regs 2020 reg 28; HOG para 11.40.
21 Conduct Regs 2020 regs 25, 29, 32 and 33.
22 HOG para 11.44.
23 HOG para 11.45.

together with the officer's account, legal submissions (for example, about inadmissible material) or mitigation, as appropriate, and any documents to be relied upon.[24] As the HOG notes:

> 11.50 The officer concerned's response to the Regulation 30 notice is critical to gathering the evidence needed for presentation at the hearing and understanding the officer's position. It is an important opportunity for the officer to put across their side of the case before the hearing and officers will be encouraged and supported by their police friend to give a full response.

Bundle and witnesses

5.20 Once the response has been received, a bundle of documents should be sent to the chair within 10 days,[25] and it is for the chair to resolve any disputes about the content of the bundle. There is provision for the police force and the officer to provide lists of proposed witnesses.[26] A witness will only be required to attend a misconduct meeting if the chair or person conducting the meeting reasonably believes their attendance is necessary, in the interests of justice, to resolve disputed issues in that case.

5.21 Of course, a complainant may be a witness in the hearing, and will sometimes be the main witness called in the case against the officer. It is important to note that the HOG says as follows:

> 11.60 It is important that the welfare of the witness should be considered by the appropriate authority, or the Director General [of the IOPC] as the case may be: they will be responsible for arranging their attendance and they should meet the reasonable expenses of any witnesses. In general terms, the hearing must recognise the individual needs and concerns of witnesses and treat them with dignity and respect. This may include completing a risk assessment on the impact of appearing at a misconduct hearing for a witness, given the responsibility which the appropriate authority, or Director General, has to the witness.
>
> 11.61 Particular care should be taken where cases involve individuals who are vulnerable or where the case is one of a sensitive nature which is likely to cause anxiety and stress for the individual involved. In these circumstances, every effort should be taken to provide the necessary support and adjustments to the individual to support their attending and participation in the misconduct proceedings.
>
> 11.62 The appropriate authority, or the Director General should make the chair aware of any needs of the witness and whether to allow for measures for certain groups of witnesses who may be vulnerable or feel intimidated. This could include giving evidence behind a screen or by video link.

Pre-hearing meeting

5.22 Whether a witness should be called will usually be discussed at a pre-hearing meeting after which the chair will make a determination. Provision is made for a pre-hearing meeting to take place in private.[27] It should be noted that the chair has the power to seek a summons from the High

24 Conduct Regs 2020 reg 31.
25 Conduct Regs 2020 reg 32(6).
26 Conduct Regs 2020 reg 31(4).
27 Conduct Regs 2020 regs 33 and 39.

Court to require a witness to attend, and this can apply to complainants and witnesses who support them.

5.23 Given the requirement to deal with vulnerable witnesses sensitively, if a summons is issued or threatened, then the complainant should write to the chair if there are particular reasons why the complainant does not want to attend as a witness, or requires special measures to be put in place if they do.

5.24 Other matters that can be discussed at the pre-hearing meeting are consideration of documents, preliminary legal submissions, and discussions on whether the hearing should be held, wholly or in part, in private.

5.25 The complainant will be one of the parties from whom the chair can take written representations at the pre-hearing meeting about any reporting restrictions or exclusions from the hearing, along with the main parties to the hearing, interested persons, witnesses and the media.[28] Following representations, the chair must make a determination on these issues. The HOG states that:

> 11.83 ... This decision should be based on the principle that misconduct hearings should be in public. 'In public' means that the public is able to attend and the media report on the proceedings. This is in keeping with long standing traditions in courts and tribunals and any restrictions should be on the basis of strict criteria.

5.26 There are a range of issues set out in the HOG which the chair may consider when making a decision as to whether any person should be excluded from a hearing or any part of a hearing.[29] The list includes issues such as the need for transparency, national security issues, and the need to avoid disclosure of sensitive police matters. It may also be the case, in hearings where the credibility of witnesses is at issue, that witnesses are excluded from the hearing until such time as they give their evidence.

5.27 The vulnerability, physical and mental health of witnesses, the complainant and the officer involved are also listed. Emphasising again the need for transparency, the HOG states that:

> 11.87 ... A hearing should not be held privately or notice withheld for administrative reasons or because of concerns to the reputation of the force or police arising from the hearing being public.

5.28 Complainants and interested persons are entitled to attend the misconduct hearing and must be informed of the date, time and place of the hearing.[30] The HOG makes it clear that if 'an individual has additional needs or special requirements, they also have the right to be accompanied at the hearing by someone who is helping them with that need and for reasonable adjustments to be made to facilitate their attendance'.[31] The chair of the misconduct panel has a discretionary power to require public

28 Conduct Regs 2020 regs 36 and 39.

29 HOG para 11.84. For discussion of the applicability of open justice and use of documents in misconduct proceedings, see *R (Newsquest Media Group Ltd) v Legally Qualified Chair of the Police Misconduct Tribunal* [2022] EWHC 299 (Admin).

30 Conduct Regs 2020 reg 40.

31 HOG para 11.88; and see Conduct Regs 2020 reg 40(4).

notification of a misconduct hearing to be given by way of publishing various details on the police force's website.[32]

5.29 As the hearing is usually in public, reasonable efforts must be made for people to attend in the room where the hearing takes place, but live-streaming of the hearing can also be facilitated.[33] Although not included in the regulations, the HOG suggests that the chair can impose conditions on those attending including the need to register or produce identification, although the HOG also states:

> 11.95 The rationale for the imposition of any condition(s) on attendance should be explained in the notice given to the public or, where a decision is made at the hearing itself, orally by the chair. Where information is required from members of the public as a condition of attendance the notice should explain how this data will be used and processed i.e. in accordance with the Data Protection Act and General Data Protection Regulation.

5.30 Once the hearing has started, the chair reaches a decision to exclude anyone from the hearing or any part of the hearing, the decision should be announced openly at the hearing with reasons, unless it is considered by the chair that it would be inappropriate to do so.[34]

5.31 If the chair decides that the public should be excluded from any part of the hearing, separate consideration should be given as to whether it would be appropriate in the circumstances to nonetheless allow any complainant and/or any interested person (and person accompanying such a person) to attend or remain in attendance.[35]

5.32 The complainant will have no right of appeal or review if any of the decisions made by the chair is not thought to be correct. It would always be open to make further representations in writing to the chair, and decisions may also be susceptible to an application for judicial review. If the decision impugned is made before the hearing of the case, it may be possible to make an application for judicial review which can be considered before the misconduct hearing – but if it is a decision made at the misconduct hearing itself, it will usually be necessary to make the application for judicial review once the hearing is completed.

5.33 The police officer against whom misconduct is alleged must attend the hearing[36] but, if they do not, the hearing may be may be conducted and concluded in the absence of the officer, whether or not they are represented.[37]

The misconduct hearing

5.34 The misconduct hearing itself will usually take the form of an adversarial hearing where a case is put against the officer, who will have the opportunity to defend the allegations. The chair of the hearing will determine the course of the hearing in accordance with the principles of natural justice and fairness. The hearing will be recorded.

32 Conduct Regs 2020 reg 36.
33 HOG para 11.92.
34 HOG para 11.97.
35 HOG para 11.100.
36 Conduct Regs 2020 reg 37.
37 HOG para 11.106.

5.35 Thus the case will be presented by the police force or the IOPC as appropriate (see above) who will usually appoint a lawyer to do this. The officer will also have the right to be represented by a lawyer. Witnesses who are called can be cross-examined. If a complainant gives evidence, then they can expect to be cross-examined by the officer's lawyer. This has the potential to be an unpleasant experience for the complainant, as it is likely that the officer is disputing their version of events, in circumstances where the officer's continued employment as a police officer is on the line. The most important thing for the complainant is to have read carefully any statement they have given to the police, as this will form the subject-matter of cross-examination as well as evidence in chief.

5.36 When considering the evidence of the officer, the hearing is entitled to draw inferences from any matter which is raised in the officer's defence, which could have been (but was not) raised by the officer when a statement was made upon being served with the regulation notice or in response to questioning from the investigating officer.[38]

5.37 When the evidence has been heard, final speeches can be made on behalf of the officer and the force.

5.38 The panel will have read the investigator's report together with any account given by the officer concerned during the investigation or when submitting their response. The panel will also have had the opportunity to read the relevant documents provided to the officer under regulation 30 (see para 5.19 above). When evidence is given, the chair can determine whether any question should be put to a witness.[39] The complainant does not have the right to put questions directly to the police officer. However, proposed questions for the officer can be sent in writing to the chair, who then has the discretion whether they are asked in the hearing.[40]

Findings

5.39 Following the end of the hearing, the panel needs to decide whether the case against the officer, on the balance of probabilities, amounts to misconduct or gross misconduct or neither. If the panel decides that the conduct amounts to neither, the panel may direct the matter to be referred under the RPRP or determine that no further action is taken.[41]

5.40 If the finding is one of misconduct (rather than gross misconduct), then there are a range of possible outcomes ranging from a written warning through to, reduction in rank to dismissal without notice.[42] In the case of misconduct, dismissal can only be imposed as a sanction where the officer concerned had a final written warning at the time of the risk assessment or where the officer's conduct arose from more than one incident and those incidents are not closely factually connected.[43] Where more than one allegation of misconduct against the officer concerned has been

38 Conduct Regs 2020 reg 41(12) and (14).
39 Conduct Regs 2020 reg 41(10).
40 Conduct Regs 2020 reg 40.
41 Conduct Regs 2020 reg 42(1)(b).
42 Conduct Regs 2020 reg 42(3); HOG para 11.122.
43 Conduct Regs 2020 reg 42(3)(a)(iv), (5) and (6); HOG para 11.145.

found proven, it is for the panel to decide whether, taken together, the misconduct may amount to gross misconduct.

5.41 If the finding is of gross misconduct, then the possible outcomes start with a final written warning, and then a reduction in rank or dismissal without notice.[44]

5.42 Written and final written warnings will be put on an officer's file, along with a copy of the written notification of the outcome and a summary of the matter, and will remain live for the period stipulated by the panel from the date the warning is given.[45] The HOG states that this 'means that in the case of a written warning any misconduct in that period is likely to lead to (at least) a final written warning'.[46]

5.43 The HOG has detailed advice about the use of reduction in rank as an outcome, noting of course that a constable cannot be reduced in rank, and that it is possible for reduction in rank to be by one or more ranks. Where reduction in rank is appropriate as an outcome, it will be because the misconduct justifies a reduction from the higher level in which the poor example of leadership was exercised, not that the person is unfit to lead at any level.[47]

5.44 Where dismissal is the outcome of the misconduct hearing, this is without notice and the police force must notify the College of Policing that the officer must be placed on the police barred list,[48] preventing the officer from taking up a role in a different police force.[49]

5.45 The officer is permitted to provide evidence of mitigating factors, including the record of police service,[50] to the misconduct hearing, and the earlier it is presented the more weight it may be given.[51] The panel must take care not to place too much weight on mitigation factors, especially in a gross misconduct case. Thus, in *R (Williams) v Police Appeals Tribunal*,[52] the court found that the tribunal had put too much weight on personal mitigating circumstances in a gross misconduct case involving dishonesty and a lack of integrity.

5.46 If the mitigation concerns sensitive matters of a private and personal nature or where medical matters involving the officer concerned are to be disclosed, it may be that the officer requests that persons are excluded from the hearing. This will be a matter for the chair to decide. The HOG states that:

> 11.99 . . . If any person has been excluded whilst mitigation is given, the chair must, subject to the need to keep them excluded for any other reason, invite them back into the hearing for the communication of the finding and the outcome of the proceedings.

44 Conduct Regs 2020 reg 42(3).

45 Conduct Regs 2020 reg 42(9) and (10).

46 HOG para 11.128.

47 HOG paras 11.133–11.143.

48 See the Police Barred List and Police Advisory List Regulations 2017 SI No 1135; and HOG chapter 21.

49 Conduct Regs 2020 reg 42(16); HOG para 11.144.

50 Conduct Regs 2020 reg 42(14).

51 Conduct Regs 2020 reg 42(14); HOG paras 11.146–11.152.

52 [2016] EWHC 2708 (Admin); and see *R (Chief Constable of Sussex) v Police Appeals Tribunal* [2017] EWHC 2333 (Admin); and *R (Chief Constable of Dorset) v Police Appeals Tribunal* [2011] EWHC 3366 (Admin).

Report

5.47 The chair of the misconduct hearing is responsible for compiling a report of the hearing within five working days and must submit it to the police force. The report should contain:[53]

- the findings of the misconduct hearing;
- the reasons for those findings;
- any disciplinary action imposed;
- any direction that the matter be dealt with under the RPRP.

5.48 The report needs to be sent to the main parties involved in the misconduct hearing and also to the complainant.[54] Unless the chair determines that the harm test set out in the regulations is met, or in line with any restrictions imposed on the disclosure of information during the course of proceedings, the police force must publish the full determination of the misconduct hearing as soon as practicable following the officer being informed of the outcome.[55] The report must remain on their website for at least 28 days.[56]

Right to appeal

5.49 As set out, below, a police officer has the right to appeal against the finding or outcome of a misconduct hearing to a PAT, and the officer must be informed of their right to appeal when notified of the outcome of the misconduct hearing.[57]

5.50 However, neither the complainant nor the chief constable of the police have a right of appeal and the only remedy at this stage will be an application for judicial review. In *Chief Constable of Thames Valley v Police Misconduct Panel*,[58] a chief constable brought a challenge to a finding by a misconduct panel (with an independent chair) against a finding that an officer was only guilty of misconduct (rather than gross misconduct). The challenge was unsuccessful, but the complainant would have similar standing to bring a challenge to the finding of a misconduct hearing or meeting. Thus in *R (Miller) v Chief Constable of Merseyside*,[59] a complainant successfully challenged as irrational decisions in favour of an officer at misconduct meeting, and the complainant's removal from the proceedings in breach of regulations was described as a breach of natural justice.

5.51 In *R (Chief Constable of the West Midlands) v Panel Chair (Police Misconduct Panel)*,[60] the High Court emphasised the seriousness of racist

53 Conduct Regs 2020 reg 43(1).

54 Conduct Regs 2020 reg 43(5).

55 Conduct Regs 2020 reg 49(3).

56 Conduct Regs 2020 reg 43(6) and (8). For an example of published reasons under the 2020 regime, see the report *In the matter of misconduct proceedings under the Police Act 1996 and the Police (Conduct) Regulations 2020 in the matter of Police Constable 41079 Cooling*, 27 July 2021, available at: www.surrey.police.uk/SysSiteAssets/media/images/surrey/misconduct/full-adjudication-of-misconduct-proceedings-pc-cooling.pdf.

57 Conduct Regs 2020 reg 43(2).

58 [2017] EWHC 923 (Admin).

59 [2014] EWHC 400 (Admin).

60 [2020] EWHC 1400 (Admin).

conduct by a police officer and quashed the decision to give the officer a final warning instead of a more serious sanction, finding that it was irrational. The panel had failed to take into account the need to maintain high standards and public confidence in the police force.

5.52 A similar approach was taken by the court in *R (Chief Constable of Dyfed Powys) v Police Misconduct Tribunal*[61] where the allegation was of a number of incidents where an officer had made unwanted comments to or physical contact with female colleagues, but the misconduct proceedings did not result in dismissal. The conclusion that the officer's behaviour was simply crass or inappropriate was found to irrational. Both cases demonstrate that the courts will look extremely carefully to ensure that guidance has been followed, that conclusions are supported by the evidence, that the importance of maintaining public confidence in the police is properly taken into account, and that discriminatory behaviour is not explained away by police misconduct panels.

Accelerated procedures

5.53 In the previous chapter it was described that, when a complaint is made, where the IOPC or police force form the view that there is sufficient evidence to establish on the balance of probabilities that there has been gross misconduct, and it is in the public interest for an officer to be dismissed without delay, then a statement supporting this and a report of the investigation to date will be made. If the police force or the IOPC (depending how the complaint is being investigated) agree, then the case is certified as meeting the special conditions for accelerated procedures.[62]

5.54 The procedures are set out in HOG chapter 12, and the Conduct Regs 2020. To a large extent, as might be expected, accelerated procedures are a faster version of the misconduct hearing procedures. The HOG explains:

> 12.5 These procedures are therefore designed to deal with cases where the evidence is incontrovertible in the form of statements, documents or other material (e.g. CCTV) and is therefore sufficient without further evidence to prove gross misconduct and it is in the public interest, if the case is found or admitted, for the officer to cease to be a member of the police service straightaway.

5.55 A complainant is entitled to be kept informed about an accelerated hearing and its outcome in much the same way as in a misconduct hearing.[63] However, other than the officer concerned, no other witness may be questioned.[64] As this is the case, there is a process for referring the case back to the standard procedures if a particular witness whose

61 [2020] EWHC 2032 (Admin).

62 See Complaints and Misconduct Regs 2020 reg 25, Conduct Regs 2020 reg 49, IOPC Guidance at paras 13.46–13.57; and HOG chapter 12.

63 Conduct Regs 2020 reg 59; HOG paras 12.12–12.13.

64 Conduct Regs 2020 reg 61; HOG para 12.28.

evidence is crucial to the case and is disputed must be called to give oral testimony.[65]

Officers who retire or resign

5.56 As described in chapter 4, procedures have now been changed to allow misconduct proceedings to be pursued against officers who resign after being served with misconduct proceedings, or in fact resigned before proceedings have commenced. The procedures provide for three categories of officer:[66]

1) Officers who resign after an allegation first comes to the attention of the police force under the Conduct Regs 2020. Where it is assessed that the allegation amounts to one of gross misconduct, the investigation may begin and lead to a hearing where there is a case to answer for gross misconduct.
2) Officers who have resigned or retired within 12 months of the allegation of gross misconduct being made. The investigation may begin and lead to a hearing where there is a case to answer for gross misconduct.
3) Officers who have resigned or retired more than 12 months before an allegation of gross misconduct being made, but only in the most serious and exceptional cases of gross misconduct likely to do damage to public confidence in policing.

5.57 In such circumstances, the Conduct Regs 2020 and Complaints and Misconduct Regs 2020 apply with important modifications set out in schedules to those Regulations. As the HOG explains:

> 20.13 . . . Those Regulations, as modified, should be read as if the former officer subject to the allegations were still serving and serving in the position in which they last served. The procedures for investigation and hearing will therefore be the same as those set out for serving officers in the Conduct Regulations and Complaints Regulations and this statutory guidance should be followed with some important differences . . .

5.58 In essence, and practically, the investigation and misconduct hearing process can only reach a conclusion as to whether there has been gross misconduct and whether an officer would have been dismissed if still in post. Full details of the procedures are set out in HOG chapter 20.

Misconduct meetings

Overview

5.59 Where a decision has been taken that there is a case to answer for misconduct, but not for gross misconduct, then a misconduct meeting (as opposed to a hearing, see para 5.11 above) will take place – unless the

65 Conduct Regs 2020 reg 50; HOG para 12.33; and see *R (Evans) v Chief Constable of Sussex* [2011] EWHC 2329 (Admin) for a case where use of fast-track procedures were found to be a breach of natural justice.

66 Conduct Regs 2020 reg 4.

officer concerned is already subject to a final written warning, or has been reduced in rank in the last two years, in which case a misconduct hearing will take place (see para 5.11 above).[67]

Procedure

5.60 Some of the procedure which applies to misconduct hearings also applies to misconduct meetings, and where that is the case, reference will be made to the previous section.

Regulation 30 notice

5.61 The officer concerned will be served with a notice under Conduct Regs 2020 reg 30 and accompanying information, to which a reply is usually expected within 15 working days, setting out whether or not it is accepted that the alleged conduct amounts to misconduct, together with the officer's account, legal submissions or mitigation, as appropriate, and any documents to be relied upon.[68]

5.62 It is usually expected that the meeting will take place at most 20 working days after the officer has replied to the regulation notice (or the end of the 15-day period for a response, but this can be extended, in the interests of justice.[69]

Who will conduct the meeting

5.63 For non-senior officers (up to the rank of chief-superintendent), the regulations provide for a more senior officer to conduct the misconduct meeting.[70] An appropriate manager (whether a police officer or police staff manager) may also be appointed as an adviser to the person appointed to hold the meeting.[71] The officer who is subject of the proceedings has a limited power to object, for compelling reason, to those appointed to conduct the misconduct meeting or to advise.[72] A misconduct meeting for a senior officer requires a legally qualified chair, and other senior members.[73]

Witnesses

5.64 There is provision for the police force and the officer to provide lists of proposed witnesses.[74] A witness will only be required to attend a misconduct meeting if the person conducting the meeting reasonably believes their attendance is necessary, in the interests of justice, to resolve disputed issues in that case. The HOG states that:

> 10.20 . . . Where there is a witness whose evidence is in dispute and who is material to the allegation then such witnesses should be made available to

67 Conduct Regs 2020 reg 23(10)((b) and (c).
68 Conduct Regs 2020 reg 31.
69 See HOG paras 10.15–10.17.
70 Conduct Regs 2020 reg 28.
71 Conduct Regs 2020 reg 8(6).
72 Conduct Regs 2020 regs 30 and 35.
73 See HOG para 10.14.
74 Conduct Regs 2020 reg 31(4).

attend. The appropriate authority should meet the reasonable expenses of any witnesses.

5.65 If the required witness is a police officer, then the person conducting the meeting can require them to attend, and other witnesses can be given notice to attend.[75]

No pre-hearing meeting

5.66 Unlike for misconduct hearings, the regulations do not provide for a pre-hearing meeting to discuss this and other matters for the meeting.

The misconduct meeting

5.67 Misconduct meetings, unlike misconduct hearings, are held in private.[76] However, where the investigation was carried out as a complaint investigation, the complainant and interested person can, subject to certain exceptions, attend the meeting as an observer and the police force must notify them of the date, time and place of the meeting.[77] A complainant or interested person may be accompanied at a misconduct meeting by one other person.[78] If a person has additional needs or special requirements, they also have the right to be accompanied at the meeting by someone who is helping them with that need and for reasonable adjustments to be made to facilitate their attendance. As at a misconduct hearing, the complainant or interested person will not be permitted to ask questions of the officer but the person chairing the meeting put any questions to the officer concerned that the complainant or interested person may request be put to the officer.[79] In practice it will often be sensible to put these questions in writing and send them to the chair in advance of the meeting, rather than doing this at the meeting itself.

5.68 The documents available to the misconduct meeting and the procedure adopted is likely to be similar to that adopted at misconduct hearings (see above) but ultimately it is for the persons conducting the meeting to ensure that whatever procedure is followed is fair and complies with natural justice.

Findings

5.69 After the meeting, the panel conducting the meeting must decide on the balance of probabilities whether the officer's conduct amounted to misconduct or not. If misconduct is not found, then the panel must decide whether to refer the matter to be dealt with under the RPRP, or that no further action be taken.[80] There are similar procedures for the panel to decide what the outcome should be if misconduct is established as for misconduct hearings, and for taking into account any mitigation on behalf of an officer.[81]

75 Conduct Regs 2020 reg 32(5).
76 Conduct Regs 2020 reg 39(2).
77 Conduct Regs 2020 reg 40(2).
78 Conduct Regs 2020 reg 40(4).
79 Conduct Regs 2020 reg 40(5).
80 Conduct Regs 2020 reg 42.
81 HOG paras 10.41–10.49.

5.70 Before informing the officer of the outcome of the misconduct meeting, the person conducting the meeting will summarise the case and set out the reasons for the outcome they are about to make. Where misconduct is established and it is decided that disciplinary action is appropriate, then either a written warning or a final written warning will be imposed,[82] and the details as to how these are to be applied are set out in the HOG and the regulations.[83]

5.71 The provisions for informing the officer of the outcome are the same as in a misconduct hearing (see above). A complainant and interested persons must be told of the outcome by the police force.

Right to appeal

5.72 Unless the officer is a senior officer (in which case there will be an appeal to the PAT (see below), an officer will have a right of appeal to an appeal meeting.[84]

Unsatisfactory performance procedures

Overview

5.73 As seen in chapter 4, a complaints investigation can result in a decision whether or not a police officer's performance was unsatisfactory and whether or not performance proceedings should be brought (as opposed to misconduct proceedings). The purpose of these procedures in to improve the performance of the officer and the overall performance of the force.[85]

5.74 The IOPC explains that unsatisfactory performance is different from misconduct and gross misconduct, as these latter will always involve a breach of the Standards of Professional Behaviour, whereas unsatisfactory performance or attendance concerns the inability or failure of an officer to perform their role to a satisfactory level but not enough to breach the Standards of Professional Behaviour.[86] The IOPC accepts that it can sometimes be hard to distinguish precisely between unsatisfactory performance and misconduct, and the factors to be taken into account were set out in the previous chapter at para 4.103.[87]

Procedure

Overview

5.75 A detailed description of the unsatisfactory performance procedures (UPP) is set out in the HOG chapter 14, and in the Performance Regs

82 Conduct Regs 2020 reg 42(2).

83 Conduct Regs 2020 reg 42(9)–(11); HOG paras 10.51–10.55.

84 Conduct Regs 2020 regs 45 and 46.

85 Performance Regs 2020.

86 IOPC Guidance para 17.27.

87 IOPC Guidance para 17.29.

2020, to which practitioners are referred. The procedures are more akin to employment guidance than disciplinary proceedings.

5.76 There are three potential stages to the UPP. The first stage is informal, with escalation if performance is still assessed to be unsatisfactory. Referral to a second stage meeting can also take place following a complaints or other investigation where there are reasonable grounds, based on evidence from an investigation to conclude that the officer concerned has demonstrated a serious inability or serious failure to perform the duties of their rank or role to a satisfactory standard or level, such that a referral to a second stage meeting is appropriate.[88] An officer can also be referred directly to a third stage meeting where there is an assessment of unsatisfactory performance amounting to gross incompetence.[89]

5.77 'Gross incompetence' means a serious inability or serious failure of a police officer to perform the duties of the officer's rank or the role the officer is currently undertaking to a satisfactory standard or level, without taking into account the officer's attendance, to the extent that dismissal would be justified.[90]

First and second stages

5.78 At the first and second stages, where it is found that the officer's performance or attendance is unsatisfactory, an improvement notice will be issued. Improvement notices require an officer to improve on their performance or attendance and must state:

a) in what respect the officer's performance or attendance is considered unsatisfactory;
b) the improvement in performance or attendance required to bring the officer to an acceptable standard;
c) a 'specified period' within which improvement is expected to be made; and
d) the 'validity period' of the written improvement notice (the period of 12 months beginning with the date of the notice within which the performance or attendance must be maintained).[91]

5.79 A complainant has no specific role if a case is considered at the first or second stage. However, if a case is referred to the third stage following a complaint, then the complainant (and any interested persons) will be permitted to attend and remain in the meeting until the conclusion of the proceedings, after having given evidence (if appropriate).[92] The complainant or interested person may be accompanied by one other person, and if the complainant or interested person has a special need, by one further person to accommodate that need. There are provisions for ensuring that a complainant is informed about a third stage meeting. An officer can apply for a complainant to be excluded from the meeting while mitigation is being considered, and this needs to be considered by the chair of the

88 Performance Regs 2020 reg 24; HOG para 14.20.
89 Performance Regs 2020 reg 32.
90 Performance Regs 2020 reg 4.
91 Performance Regs 2020 regs 18 and 26; HOG paras 14.27–14.33.
92 Performance Regs 2020 reg 41; HOG paras 14.40–14.45.

meeting. The regulations and the HOG also set out the circumstances in which a police force can be directed to take action (or where action can be recommended), following an investigation under PRA 2002 Sch 3 (see in more detail in chapters 3 and 4).[93]

Third stage

5.80 The procedure for third stage meetings is set out in detail in the HOG and in the regulations.[94] It is not dissimilar to the procedure for misconduct meetings (see para 5.59 above) and involves the service of a notice on the officer,[95] the appointment of a chair (a senior police officer or senior HR professional) and a panel to conduct the meeting, the service of documentation, and the calling of witnesses to give evidence where the panel chair reasonably believes that it is necessary in the interests of fairness for the witness to do so.

5.81 Where a witness attends to give evidence, any questions to that witness should be made through the panel chair. This does not prevent the panel chair allowing questions to be asked directly if they feel it appropriate. The panel chair can also put questions to a witness suggested by the complainant or interested person,[96] and it is therefore best to submit these questions before the meeting takes place, rather than to wait to do it at the meeting.

Findings

5.82 Having considered any representations, the panel will come to a finding as to whether or not the performance of the officer has been unsatisfactory or whether or not their behaviour constitutes gross incompetence, as the case may be. Where the panel make a finding of unsatisfactory performance or gross incompetence, before deciding on the appropriate outcome, the panel must have regard to the personal record of the officer and any mitigation or references put forward on behalf of the officer. The panel must prepare their decision in writing, and state reasons, why, if that is the case, the panel has found that the officer's performance has been unsatisfactory or that they have been grossly incompetent, and also state any outcome. The complainant should be told about the outcome of the meeting, whether they attend or not.

5.83 The sanctions available following a third stage meeting are dismissal with notice, dismissal with immediate effect, reduction in rank, extension of a period of final written improvement notice, the issue of a final written, and redeployment to other alternative duties.

Reflective practice review process

5.84 RPRP is a new process introduced in 2020. The detailed procedure is set out in HOG chapter 13, and the relevant statutory framework is contained

93 Performance Regs 2020 reg 12; HOG para 14.47.
94 Performance Regs 2020 regs 44-46; HOG chapter 17.
95 Performance Regs 2020 reg 33.
96 Performance Regs 2020 reg 41(7).

in Conduct Regs 2020 Part 6. The description in this section will focus on the role of the complainant in the process, while setting out the outline of the procedures.

5.85 There are various routes under the PRA 2002 by which a complaint can result in a reference to the RPRP. These are as follows:

- as the outcome to a complaint handled otherwise than by investigation;
- as the outcome of an investigation into a complaint or recordable conduct matter where a matter is assessed as amounting to practice requiring improvement;
- as a result of a recommendation under PRA 2002 Sch 3 para 28ZA (see above paras 4.130 and 4.95).

5.86 However the case has been 'handled' under the complaints process (by investigation or otherwise) will form part of the fact-finding stage for the subsequent RPRP.[97]

5.87 Following the conclusion of misconduct proceedings, the chair is also able to direct that a matter is referred to be dealt with under the RPRP.[98]

5.88 The IOPC Guidance explains that:

> 17.24 The Reflective Practice Review Process is not a disciplinary process or a disciplinary outcome. It is intended to provide an open environment to encourage all those involved in the process to reflect, learn and, where necessary, put things right and prevent any issues identified from reoccurring. It is important that this, and the steps involved in the process, are explained to complainants and any interested persons . . .

5.89 The Home Office explains that:

> 13.3 . . . Where a matter, whether raised/identified internally or via complaint, meets the definition of Practice Requiring Improvement and does not reach the threshold for disciplinary action, it should be handled locally by line managers and supervisors with a clear focus on reflection, learning from mistakes and focusing on actions / development to improve and, where necessary, put the issue right and prevent it from happening again.
>
> . . .
>
> 13.8 Many parts of the formal police disciplinary system can at times feel like an adversarial and combative process and often involve significant stress for all parties because of the nature of proceedings. The Reflective Practice Review Process for dealing with Practice Requiring Improvement is intentionally designed as a non-adversarial environment . . .

5.90 Where it has been decided that the RPRP is the correct way to deal with an issue then essentially the process consists of a discussion between a reviewer and the officer concerned to discuss the identified Practice Requiring Improvement and related circumstances, to identify lessons learned and set out actions to be taken in order to respond to, and prevent a reoccurrence of, the identified Practice Requiring Improvement. This leads to a Reflective Review Development Report setting out a summary of the matter, a summary of the discussion, the actions/next steps to be taken

97 HOG para 17.23.

98 Conduct Regs 2020 reg 42.

by the individual officer, the reviewer and the police force, lessons learned and a specified period for reviewing matters.[99]

5.91 Where a referral of practice requiring improvement has occurred as a result of a complaint, the complainant should be given the opportunity to be engaged in the reflective process. The Home Office says:

> 13.79 . . . It will be important for their views to be taken into account during the Reflective Practice Review Process, so what they have complained about is effectively considered and, where possible, resolved. This is in addition to any steps being taken with the member of the public to resolve issues they have complained about that fall outside the Reflective Practice Review Process.
>
> 13.80 As well as communicating to the complainant that the outcome of the handling of their complaint is via the Reflective Practice Review Process, the progress and outcome of the Reflective Practice Review Process should also be communicated, in accordance with Regulation 33 of the Complaints Regulations. This should explain what has happened as well as what action has been taken as part of the Reflective Review Development Report and information about any learning identified as a result of the complaint.
>
> 13.81 This would not necessarily involve the report being shared with the member of the public in full, unless it is felt that doing so would support resolving the issue to the satisfaction of the complainant and there are no significant issues raised by the parties involved that suggest it should not be disclosed.
>
> 13.82 In terms of the action taken, this could include, for example, a meeting with the complainant, an explanation or potentially an apology from the participating officer where it is appropriate.

5.92 It should also be noted that a complainant will have a right of review (see chapter 4) of the outcome of the handling of a complaint. The HOG says:

> 13.84 . . . Whether a matter has been referred to be dealt with under the Reflective Practice Review Process, following either a formal investigation under Schedule 3 (where it has been determined that there is no case to answer) or without a formal investigation (in circumstances where it is determined that there is no indication that disciplinary proceedings would be justified), the right to review will occur after the decision to refer the matter into the Reflective Practice Review Process . . .
>
> 13.85 In the vast majority of cases, it is expected that any right to review will not delay the Reflective Practice Review Process from taking place . . .

5.93 The HOG states that a complainant should continue to be updated every four weeks until the conclusion of the process, and that this 'would ordinarily be once the Reflective Review Development Report has been created as opposed to all of the actions completed'.[100]

Appeals

Police appeals tribunals

5.94 The procedures are set out in the PAT Rules 2020 and HOG chapter 26.

99 Conduct Regs 2020 regs 66–70; HOG paras 13.40–13.73.
100 HOG para 13.86.

5.95 All officers have a right of appeal to a PAT against any disciplinary finding and/or disciplinary outcome imposed at a misconduct hearing or a finding of gross misconduct and/or any disciplinary outcome imposed at an accelerated misconduct hearing held under the Conduct Regs 2020.[101]

5.96 Senior officers, in addition, have the right to appeal to a PAT against any disciplinary finding and/or outcome imposed at a misconduct meeting in addition to the right of appeal following a misconduct hearing.

5.97 All officers have a right of appeal to a PAT against a finding of unsatisfactory performance or attendance following a third stage meeting, held under Performance Regs 2020 reg 30. They may appeal against the following outcomes:

a) dismissal with notice;
b) reduction in rank;
c) redeployment to alternative duties.[102]

5.98 Where there has been a finding of gross incompetence or unsatisfactory performance following third stage meeting under Performance Regs 2020 reg 32, the officer may appeal against the following outcomes:

a) dismissal without notice;
b) reduction in rank;
c) redeployment to alternative duties;
d) the issue of a final written improvement notice;
e) the issue of a written improvement notice.[103]

5.99 The PAT is set up by statute. There are three members of the PAT. There must be a legally qualified chair from a list maintained by the Home Office, a senior serving police officer and a lay member who has no links to the police.[104] The HOG sets out good practice in appointing the legally qualified chair and lay member.[105]

5.100 For senior officers, the serving officer and lay members are replaced by an Inspector of Constabulary and a Home Office Director.[106]

5.101 An appeal hearing is not a re-hearing of the original matter. The grounds of appeal for matters dealt with under the Conduct Regs 2020 relate to whether the finding or disciplinary action was unreasonable,[107] whether there is new relevant evidence, or a breach in the conduct or complaints procedures, or other unfairness.[108]

5.102 If the appeal arises from proceedings under the Performance Regs 2020, then, in addition to grounds of unreasonableness, new evidence and unfairness, there is a ground of appeal that an officer should not have been required to attend a third stage meeting.[109]

101 PAT Rules 2020 r4.
102 PAT Rules 2020 r5.
103 PAT Rules 2020 r5.
104 Police Act 1996 Sch 6.
105 HOG paras 26.15–26.20.
106 Police Act 1996 Sch 6.
107 See *R (Wilby-Newton) v Police Appeals Tribunal* [2021] EWHC 550 (Admin), on the test to be applied.
108 PAT Rules 2020 r4(4); HOG para 26.21; and see *R (Ali) v Police Appeals Tribunal* [2022] EWHC 646 (Admin) for a discussion on issues which go to fairness.
109 PAT Rules 2020 r5(6); and see HOG para 26.22.

5.103 Where the officer concerned admitted the finding at the original proceedings brought in accordance with the Conduct or Performance Regs 2020, the appeal may only be brought in respect of the outcome or disciplinary action imposed, and may not appeal the finding.[110]

5.104 There are procedural rules which set out time limits for the various stages before a hearing. These provide for exchange of documents and grounds between the appellant officer and the respondent force.[111]

5.105 The role of a complainant at a PAT hearing is set out in the PAT Rules 2020 and in the HOG.[112] Where the substance of the appeal is related directly to a complaint made against the appellant or is a conduct matter involving an interested person, the chair of the PAT must give written notice of the time, date and place of the hearing to the complainant or interested person at the same time as this notice is given to the appellant and respondent. There is power for the chair to dismiss the appeal on the papers if the appeal has no real prospect of success.[113]

5.106 The PAT Rules 2020 make provision for publication of notice of the hearing including the name of the appellant, and the time, date of the hearing.[114] The complainant is specifically permitted to make representations as to whether the notice should be published and what should be contained in it.[115]

5.107 The complainant or interested person may attend the PAT as an observer. The complainant or interested person may be accompanied by one other person and, if the complainant or interested person has a special need, by a further person in order to accommodate that need. Where the complainant or interested person or any person accompanying them is to give evidence at the hearing, this individual may not attend the hearing before that evidence is given. The complainant is not entitled to be represented at the appeal or ask questions, but chair may put any questions to the officer that the complainant or interested person request be put.[116] A record of the hearing must be kept.

5.108 The PAT must determine if the grounds of appeal are made out, and prepare a written statement of the PAT's determination and its reasons for it. A PAT may make any decision that the original panel or person could have imposed at the original meeting or hearing, including increasing or reducing the original outcome. If there is procedural unfairness, the case can be remitted to be considered afresh. There are provisions for notification of the decision of the PAT, which include informing the complainant,[117] and the PAT can require publication of the decision and can consider representations from the complainant on this issue.[118]

5.109 There have been a number of judicial review cases against the PAT, often brought by chief constables aggrieved that the tribunal has found in

110 PAT Rules 2020 rr4(3) and 5(3).
111 PAT Rules 2020 rr9–134.
112 PAT Rules 2020 rr22–24; HOG paras 26.93–26.95.
113 PAT Rules 2020 r15.
114 PAT Rules 2020 r18.
115 PAT Rules 2020 r18(7) and (8).
116 PAT Rules 2020 r23.
117 PAT Rules 2020 r26(9).
118 PAT Rules 2020 r26(11), (13) and (16).

favour of an officer who had been disciplined by the force. In *R (Chief Constable of Thames Valley) v Police Appeals Tribunal*,[119] the Court of Appeal criticised the PAT for going behind a finding of the disciplinary process without an evidential basis for doing so. *In R (Commissioner of Police of the Metropolis) v Police Appeals Tribunal*,[120] the Commissioner unsuccessfully challenged a lenient approach taken by the PAT in relation to an inspector who acted without integrity. However, emphasising that racism should not be tolerated, the High Court quashed a decision of the PAT not to uphold the dismissal of an officer who made racist comments in public, in *R (Chief Constable of Northumbria) v Police Appeals Tribunal*.[121]

5.110 A PAT decision was quashed in *R (Chief Constable of Nottinghamshire) v Police Appeals Tribunal*[122] where the tribunal had not followed the three-stage test applied in the College of Policing's *Guidance on outcomes* (see para 5.6 above), namely to:

a) assess the seriousness of the misconduct;
b) keep in mind the purpose of imposing sanctions; and
c) choose the sanction which most appropriately fulfilled that purpose for the seriousness of the conduct in question.[123]

Appeals from misconduct meetings

5.111 There is a similar procedure of appeal available from decisions of misconduct meetings, set out in the Conduct Regs 2020[124] and in HOG chapter 25, but for which there are no appeal rules as there are for appeals to PATs (see para 5.95 above). The appeal is considered by a more senior police officer than the officer who chaired the misconduct meeting.[125] The complainant must be given notice of the appeal meeting and can attend the meeting as an observer.[126] However, the person determining the appeal may impose conditions regarding the attendance of a complainant or interested person in order to facilitate the proper conduct of the appeal meeting. This can include requiring the complainant or interested person to withdraw whilst a submission in mitigation is made on the officer's behalf.[127] The police force must provide the officer concerned with written notice of the determination and a summary of the reasons for the finding of the appeal.[128] There appears to be no provision for the complainant to be informed of the outcome of the appeal, but the IOPC must be informed in certain cases, and there would appear to be no reason why a complainant should not also be informed.

119 [2016] EWCA Civ 1315.
120 [2013] EWHC 1684 (Admin).
121 [2019] EWHC 3352 (Admin).
122 [2021] EWHC 1248 (Admin).
123 College of Policing, *Guidance on outcomes* (2017), para 4.4; and see *Fuglers LLP v Solicitors Regulation Authority* [2014] EWHC 179 (Admin).
124 Conduct Regs 2020 regs 45–47.
125 Conduct Regs 2020 reg 45(4).
126 Conduct Regs 2020 reg 46(7).
127 HOG para 25.15.
128 Conduct Regs 2020 reg 47.

CHAPTER 6

False imprisonment and deprivation of liberty

continued

Introduction

6.1 The right to liberty and the freedom to move about without fear of arbitrary arrest or detention is a fundamental civil liberty, and it is a human right. It is a civil right that is protected at common law by the ability to sue in tort for false imprisonment. It is also a human right protected by the right to liberty contained in European Convention on Human Rights (ECHR) Article 5, a right which is enforceable domestically under the Human Rights Act (HRA) 1998 by bringing a claim under HRA 1998 s7 for any breach.

6.2 The right to liberty and tort of false imprisonment most commonly arise in the context of police law when the police make an arrest, but it can also apply in situations short of arrest such as a stop and search or where police are seeking to contain people during a demonstration (often referred to as 'kettling'). In most cases, however, the right to sue for false imprisonment, or breach of Article 5, arises as a result of an unlawful arrest, and this may explain why people often refer to suing for 'wrongful arrest'. There is, however, no such tort in English law; rather, the act of an unlawful arrest usually occurs at the start of a period of false imprisonment.

6.3 Following an arrest there is very often a further period of detention, most usually in a police station. This again can lead to claims for false imprisonment or for breaches of Article 5. Police and Criminal Evidence Act 1984 (PACE) Part IV sets out detailed rules limiting the period of time a person can be detained in police custody, and also imposes the conditions in which a person is to be detained, and includes the need for regular reviews. Breach of these rules may also lead to claims in false imprisonment and or breach of Article 5.

6.4 This chapter is structured as follows:

- It first provides overviews of the tort of false imprisonment and the protection provided by Article 5, covering matters such as what is meant by 'loss of liberty' and 'false imprisonment', in addition to the procedural protections provided. There is some discussion around the similarities and differences between a claim in tort and a claim brought under the HRA 1998, and how to decide on the type of claim to pursue.
- There then follows a more detailed consideration first of the powers of arrest, and thereafter stop and search and the other police powers that restrict the right to liberty. The section on arrest considers the issues of 'reasonable grounds to suspect' and 'necessity' of arrest, which are topics that have led to extensive case-law and that form the basis for most claims for false imprisonment and or breach of Article 5.
- There are then sections dealing with issues around police detention and conditions of detention.
- Consideration is then given to the circumstances in which imprisonment might give rise to a claim in negligence.
- Finally, there is a brief consideration of potential legal remedies available apart from a civil claim for damages: escapes and habeas corpus and judicial review. This chapter does not deal with damages available and quantum – these are dealt with in chapter 17.

Basis for claims for false imprisonment and deprivation of liberty

The tort of false imprisonment: an overview

6.5 The tort of false imprisonment concerns the complete restraint of the liberty of the person for any time, however short, without lawful excuse. There are two elements which together constitute a false imprisonment: 1) a detention[1] and 2) a lack of a lawful authority for the detention.

6.6 The onus, or burden of proof, is on the claimant to prove that detention, in the sense required, has occurred. Having done so, the burden shifts to the police to prove that they had a lawful excuse, power, or authority for the detention. If the police fail to discharge that burden, then the claimant will succeed in proving the tort of false imprisonment. The police must prove that the detention was lawful minute-by-minute and hour-by-hour.[2] If the police cannot show that the detention was lawful, then the tort of false imprisonment is established.

6.7 False imprisonment is a tort of strict liability and is actionable without proof of special damage. The focus is on the claimant's right rather than the culpability of the defendant's conduct. It does not matter in terms of establishing that the tort has been committed whether the detaining power could have been used lawfully; so even if the claimant would in any event have been detained had the power been lawfully exercised the claimant will still be able to prove the tort. Causation is not in this way relevant to liability. In *R (Lumba) v Secretary of State for the Home Department*,[3] Lord Dyson JSC commented on the inappropriateness of applying a causation test when establishing liability in false imprisonment, saying:

> 66. The causation test shifts the focus of the tort on to the question of how the defendant would have acted on the hypothesis of a lawful self-direction, rather than on the claimant's right not in fact to be unlawfully detained. There is no warrant for this . . .
>
> 71. . . . Where the power has not been lawfully exercised, it is nothing to the point that it could have been lawfully exercised. If the power could and would have been lawfully exercised, that is a powerful reason for concluding that the detainee has suffered no loss and is entitled to no more than nominal damages. But that is not a reason for holding that the tort has not been committed.

6.8 In terms of remedy and damages, once the claimant has established the tort has been committed, they are entitled to a remedy and the usual remedy will be an award of damages. In *Lumba*, the Supreme Court re-affirmed that where the claimant had suffered no harm as a result of the false imprisonment then only nominal damages would be awarded, exemplary damages apart.[4] The circumstances in the context of police

1 Any restraint within confined bounds is an imprisonment: See *Collins v Wilcock* [1984] 1 WLR 1172 at pp1180F–1180H, DC; *Bird v Jones* (1845) 7 QB 742; and *Walker v Commissioner of Police of the Metropolis* [2014] EWCA Civ 897, [2015] 1 WLR 312.

2 *Mercer v Chief Constable of Lancashire* [1991] 1 WLR 367 at p373, CA per Lord Donaldson MR.

3 [2011] UKSC 12, [2012] 1 AC 245.

4 See paras 99–100.

arrest and detention that will give rise to nominal damages only are considered at paras 17.83–17.89 below. On damages generally, including 'vindicatory damages', see chapter 17.

6.9 If a person has been detained, the most common defences open to the police are that they were a) carrying out a lawful arrest or stop and search; or b) detaining a person at a police station in accordance with PACE; or c) lawfully acting on a warrant issued by a court.

What amounts to 'detention'?

Overview

6.10 Detention of a person by the police may occur in many common situations: in the course of a stop and search in the street; during questioning, whether at the police station or anywhere else; or on arrest.

6.11 The place of detention is irrelevant, but the restraint on freedom of liberty must be total, in that a person is prevented from leaving a defined area whether by means of physical barriers or by person(s) (whether by use of threats or use of legal process).[5] A person may, for example, be held in prison,[6] in a car,[7] in their own home,[8] or in the street.[9] Provided that the person is restrained within an area set by the police, all of these amount to detention. A person can also be imprisoned even if they are moved from one place to another, for instance to a police station from the place of arrest.

6.12 The means used for detention need not be physical – a threat of force can be used, and an assertion of authority by a police officer, such as saying, 'You're under arrest', is enough. There is no need to show that the person was touched by the officer,[10] nor is there any need to resist arrest. In *Alderson v Booth*,[11] Lord Parker CJ said:

> There are a number of cases, both ancient and modern, as to what constitutes an arrest, and whereas there was a time when it was held that there could be no lawful arrest unless there was an actual seizing or touching, it is quite clear that that is no longer the law. There may be an arrest by mere words, by saying 'I arrest you' without any touching, provided, of course, that the defendant submits and goes with the police officer. Equally it is clear, as it seems to me, that an arrest is constituted when any form of words is used which in the circumstances of the case were calculated to bring to the defendant's notice, and did bring to the defendant's notice, that he was under compulsion and thereafter he submitted to that compulsion.

6.13 Whether there has been an imprisonment is a matter of fact not law, and so will be for a jury to decide[12] (if there is a jury).

5 See *R (Jalloh) v Secretary of State for the Home Department* [2020] UKSC 4.

6 *Cobbett v Grey* (1850) 4 Exch 729.

7 *Burton v Davies* [1953] St R QD 26 (Queensland).

8 *Warner v Riddiford* (1858) 4 CB(NS) 180.

9 *Termes de la Ley* c1520; see *Meering v Grahame-White Aviation Co* (1920) 122 LT 44.

10 *Warner v Riddiford* (1858) 4 CB (NS) 180; *Chinn v Morris* (1826) 2 C&P 361; *Grainger v Hill* (1838) 4 Bing NC 212; *Wood v Lane and Cleaton* (1834) 6 C&P 774.

11 [1969] 2 QB 216 at 220H–221A, CA.

12 *R v Inwood* [1973] 1 WLR 647 at pp652–653, CA.

The duration of the detention

6.14 In terms of proving the fact of detention and establishing liability, there is no minimum period of confinement before a claim for false imprisonment can succeed.[13] In *Thomas James Parry v James Sharples (sued as the Chief Constable of Merseyside)* a person held at gun-point for two minutes was held to have been detained in the manner required to prove false imprisonment,[14] and in *Walker v Commissioner of Police of the Metropolis*[15] the police officer was found to have unlawfully detained Mr Walker in his doorway. At the time, the officer was not exercising his power of arrest, and although the detention was only brief, a few seconds, it still amounted to false imprisonment.[16]

6.15 The length of detention is however important with regards to the level of damages. A long period of unlawful detention will usually justify a larger sum of damages. However, being conned for even a short period can be serious. For example, a person wrongly arrested in a public place in circumstances that attracted a lot of attention, even if released after a few minutes, might suffer more embarrassment, distress and damage to their reputation than if they were arrested at home but kept for several hours.

Knowledge of detention

6.16 An action can be brought for false imprisonment even if the claimant did not know they were being detained unlawfully, or they were not harmed by the detention.[17] However, in cases where there is no knowledge and no harm caused a person 'can normally expect to recover no more than nominal damages'.[18] However, a person who is aware of their detention, but not that it is unlawful will be entitled to more than nominal damages.[19]

6.17 As noted above, once the fact of detention has been proved by the claimant, it falls to the defendant to establish that the detention was lawful, that is, that there was a lawful use of a power or authority in effecting and continuing the detention. Some of the relevant powers are dealt with below, from para 6.38 onwards.

Article 5, the right to liberty: an overview

What does Article 5 protect?

6.18 ECHR Article 5 sets out the right to liberty and the security of the person and lists the limited (and exhaustive) situations in which this right can be compromised. Any limitation on the right to liberty must not be arbitrary and must be prescribed by law. In addition to setting out the right to liberty

13 *Walker v Commissioner of Police of the Metropolis* [2014] EWCA Civ 897, [2015] 1 WLR 312 and see *Clerk and Lindsell on Torts*, 23rd edn, para 14-23.

14 [1991] 7 WLUK 235, CA.

15 [2014] EWCA Civ 897, [2015] 1 WLR 312.

16 Para 30.

17 *Murray v Ministry of Defence* [1988] 2 All ER 521, HL; and *P v Cheshire West and Chester Council* [2014] UKSC 19, [2014] AC 896 at para 35.

18 *Murray v Ministry of Defence* at p529 per Lord Griffiths.

19 *Roberts v Chief Constable of Cheshire* [1999] 2 All ER 326, CA; *R v Governor of HMP Brockhill ex p Evans (No 1)* [1997] 2 WLR 236, DC.

and the permitted limitations, Article 5 also provides for the procedural safeguards that must accompany any restriction on the right to liberty. Article 5(1) sets out the substantive right and the circumstances in which a person may be deprived of their liberty:

> **Article 5 – Right to liberty and security**
> 1. Everyone has the right to liberty and security of person. No one shall be deprived of his liberty save in the following cases and in accordance with a procedure prescribed by law:
>
> (a) the lawful detention of a person after conviction by a competent court;
> (b) the lawful arrest or detention of a person for non-compliance with the lawful order of a court or in order to secure the fulfilment of any obligation prescribed by law;
> (c) the lawful arrest or detention of a person effected for the purpose of bringing him before the competent legal authority on reasonable suspicion of having committed an offence or when it is reasonably considered necessary to prevent his committing an offence or fleeing after having done so;
> (d) the detention of a minor by lawful order for the purpose of educational supervision or his lawful detention for the purpose of bringing him before the competent legal authority;
> (e) the lawful detention of persons for the prevention of the spreading of infectious diseases, of persons of unsound mind, alcoholics or drug addicts or vagrants;
> (f) the lawful arrest or detention of a person to prevent his effecting an unauthorised entry into the country or of a person against whom action is being taken with a view to deportation or extradition.

Procedural protections

6.19 The procedural safeguards relevant to arrest are set out in Article 5(2) and (3), which read:

> 2. Everyone who is arrested shall be informed promptly, in a language which he understands, of the reasons for his arrest and of any charge against him.
> 3. Everyone arrested or detained in accordance with the provisions of paragraph 1(c) of this article shall be brought promptly before a judge or other officer authorised by law to exercise judicial power and shall be entitled to trial within a reasonable time or to release pending trial. Release may be conditioned by guarantees to appear for trial.

6.20 Many of the safeguards afforded by Article 5 are provided for within domestic law. For example, with regards to Article 5(2), PACE s28 requires a person who has been arrested to be informed they have been arrested and informed of the ground for the arrest at the time of, or as soon as is practicable after, the arrest. If this is not done the arrest will not be lawful (see further below at para 6.143).

6.21 Article 5(3) ensures that a detained person is brought promptly before a judicial authority with the power to assess the lawfulness of the arrest, to review the merits of the detention, and to order release if continued detention would be unlawful.[20] In domestic law, the provisions in PACE Part IV which provide detailed rules and impose strict time limits on

20 *Brogan v UK* (1991) 13 EHRR 439, ECtHR.

police detention provide the necessary safeguards in respect of Article 5(3).

6.22 A claim under Article 5(3) can arise in the police context where a person's detention is prolonged unjustifiably due to police action or inaction. An example is the case of *Zenati v Commissioner of Police of the Metropolis*,[21] where the police delayed informing the Crown Prosecution Service (CPS) for some 20 days that a passport thought to be counterfeit was in fact genuine. As a consequence, the claimant spent additional time remanded in custody unjustifiably, and in violation of Article 5. If it comes to the knowledge of the police that the person is innocent of the offence for which they are being prosecuted and remanded into custody, but the police fail to convey that knowledge to the CPS, then there will likely be a violation of Article 5 on the basis that the detention of the person no longer falls within Article 5(1)(c). A delay in bringing the matter to the attention of the CPS will also fall foul of the requirement of reasonable promptness in Article 5(3). Other investigative errors in circumstances that there remain reasonable grounds to suspect the accused will *not* give rise to a violation of Article 5. Thus, in *AAA v Chief Constable of Kent*, Spencer J referred to the need for 'some "game-changing" information or factor which was not before the court, but which should have been, and which would have made all the difference to the court's decision and approach'.[22]

6.23 Article 5 concludes by providing rights for a person to have the lawfulness of their detention speedily determined by a court, as set out in Article 5(4). The criminal justice system of England and Wales, together with the availability of judicial review and habeas corpus applications generally ensures compliance with the Article 5(4) procedural safeguards. In *X v UK*[23] the ECtHR found that the writ of habeas corpus satisfied the requirements of Article 5(4).

6.24 There is also contained in Article 5 an enforceable right to compensation where there has been a breach of Article 5.[24] The strict liability tort of false imprisonment will ensure that this right to compensation is for the most part provided for within domestic tort law. Alternatively, of course, there may be a claim under the HRA 1998.

What amounts to a deprivation of liberty?

6.25 For the purposes of Article 5(1), a distinction is drawn between a 'deprivation' of liberty and a 'restriction' of liberty – whether there has been a deprivation of liberty as opposed to a restriction of liberty is to be decided according to the individual and concrete circumstances of each case. Where there has only been a restriction on liberty, there will be no

21 [2015] EWCA Civ 80, [2015] QB 758.
22 [2017] EWHC 3600 (QB) at para 41.
23 (1982) 4 EHRR 188, ECtHR.
24 Article 5(5).

breach of Article 5. The degree or intensity of the restriction must be examined.[25] Examples of the relevant factors are:[26]

- the extent of the denial or loss of liberty;
- its duration;
- the degree of compulsion behind the restriction in the sense of the immediacy of any use of force, and/or the existence of penal sanctions;
- its characterisation in municipal law;
- its manner of implementation.

6.26 There are several examples of findings of 'deprivation of liberty' despite there being a degree of freedom of movement left to the citizen which possibly may not have had a similar outcome in a domestic court deciding whether a person had been detained at common law. In *Guzzardi v Italy*,[27] a suspected mafioso was required to reside within 2.5 sq kilometre of a Mediterranean island. His confinement, in all the circumstances, engaged Article 5(1). Similarly, in *Amuur v France*[28] there was a breach of Article 5(1) where a person was restricted to the international transit area of an airport, and an attached hotel.

6.27 The meaning of 'detention' in the context of the tort of false imprisonment and Article 5 was considered by the Supreme Court in *R (Jalloh) v Secretary of State for the Home Department*.[29] The case concerned the detention of the claimant under immigration powers when facing deportation. He had been released on curfew, so had to be at home between the hours of 11 pm and 7 am. The curfew was monitored by means of an electric tag and lasted 891 days. Breach of the curfew could lead to a fine or imprisonment. It was held that this amounted to an imprisonment at common law, notwithstanding that it did not amount to a deprivation of liberty for the purposes of Article 5. For the purposes of Article 5, the curfew was a restriction rather than deprivation of liberty. Lady Hale, giving the judgment of the court, said that the essence of 'imprisonment' was being made to stay in a particular place by another person. How this was achieved could be by various means – it could be physical, using bars or guards, or it could be by the use of the threat of a legal process: the 'point is that the person is obliged to stay where he is ordered to stay whether he wants to do so or not'.[30] The Supreme Court declined the invitation to align 'imprisonment' with a 'deprivation of liberty' within the mearing of Article 5, finding that doing so would be 'a retrograde step' that would restrict the meaning of what amounted to imprisonment at common law, and there was no need to align the two concepts.[31] Accordingly, there can be a false imprisonment at common law that does not also amount to a deprivation of liberty under Article 5. The Supreme

25 See *Guzzardi v Italy* (1981) 3 EHRR 333 at paras 92–93, ECtHR.

26 See eg *De Tommaso v Italy* (2017) 65 EHRR 19 at para 80, ECtHR; *Medvedyev and others v France* (2010) 51 EHRR 39 at para 73; and *Creanga v Romania* (2013) 56 EHRR 11 at para 91, ECtHR.

27 (1981) 3 EHRR 333 at paras 91–95, ECtHR.

28 (1996) 22 EHRR 533 at paras 42–49, ECtHR.

29 [2020] UKSC 4, [2021] AC 262.

30 Para 24.

31 Para 33.

Court left open the question of whether the reverse could also be true, although see *Zenati v Commissioner of the Police of the Metropolis* referred to a paras 6.22 and 6.29.[32]

Claim in tort or under the Human Rights Act 1998?

Overview

6.28 As can be seen from the brief overviews above, there are many similarities between the protection of the right to liberty under Article 5 and the tort of false imprisonment at common law, but there are also differences. A question that often arises is whether to issue a claim in tort, under the HRA 1998 – or, indeed, both.

6.29 Whether to bring a claim in the tort of false imprisonment or under the HRA 1998, or both, will depend on several factors. For example, there may be a difference in terms of damages as between the two causes of action. For a breach of the HRA 1998 the court will decide on what remedy will afford 'just satisfaction', and while it will invariably be the case that a breach of Article 5 will require the award of damages (see Article 5(5)),[33] the level of damages will be determined taking into account the ECHR jurisprudence (see HRA 1998 s8). Exemplary damages are not available for a breach of Article 5 (for a more detailed discussion on damages, see chapter 17). Where the lawfulness of an imprisonment is to be determined with reference to the relevant statutory provisions – such as those relating to arrest in PACE s24 – an Article 5 claim will ordinarily be superfluous as a breach of the statutory provision has the inevitable consequence of establishing a false imprisonment at common law. There may, however, be circumstances in which a detention is lawful at common law, but is unlawful pursuant to Article 5. An example is *Zenati v Commissioner of the Police of the Metropolis*[34] (considered above at para 6.22) in which the imprisonment was pursuant to a court order and was lawful at common law, but was considered arbitrary and contrary to Article 5.

6.30 There is also a difference in terms of time limits – the time limit for bringing a claim under the HRA 1998 is one year, or such other time as the court considers equitable in all the circumstances (see s7(5)); as opposed to a claim in tort where the time limit is three years, if the claim includes a claim for personal injury, or six years if not.[35]

6.31 In most cases, it will make little difference as to whether the claim is brought in the tort of false imprisonment, or under the HRA 1998, and where there is no obvious advantage to bringing a claim under the HRA 1998 it is likely that a claim should only be brought in the tort of false imprisonment, given the more generous time limits and the greater availability of damages.

32 Para 34.

33 See above at para 6.24; and also *Clerk and Lindsell*, 23rd edn, para 13-127.

34 [2015] EWCA Civ 80, [2015] QB 758.

35 See Limitation Act 1980 ss2 and 11, and chapter 14.

Human Rights Act 1998 or tort when challenging lawfulness of arrest

6.32 So far as any question as to the lawfulness of any arrest is concerned, the justification for detention on grounds of reasonable suspicion in Article 5(1) is very similar to the domestic test in PACE s24:[36]

> . . . having a 'reasonable suspicion' presupposes the existence of facts or information which would satisfy an objective observer that the person concerned may have committed the offence in question.[37]

6.33 In *O'Hara v UK*[38] the ECtHR emphasised that the 'reasonableness' of the suspicion on which an arrest must be based forms an essential part of the safeguard against arbitrary arrest and detention laid down in Article 5(1)(c). The court also commented that the standard imposed by Article 5(1)(c) does not presuppose that the police have sufficient evidence to bring charges at the time of arrest.

6.34 The object of questioning during detention under Article 5(1)(c) is to further the criminal investigation by way of confirming or dispelling the concrete suspicion grounding the arrest. Thus, facts which raise a suspicion need not be of the same level as those necessary to justify a conviction, or even the bringing of a charge which comes at the next stage of the process of criminal investigation.[39]

6.35 In relation to 'terrorist crime' and proving reasonable suspicion where information may be particularly sensitive the ECtHR in *O'Hara* said:[40]

> . . . the police may be called upon, in the interests of public safety, to arrest a suspected terrorist on the basis of information which is reliable but which cannot be disclosed to the suspect or produced in court, without jeopardising the informant. However, though Contracting States cannot be required to establish the reasonableness of the suspicion grounding the arrest of a suspected terrorist by disclosing confidential sources of information, the Court has held that the exigencies of dealing with terrorist crime cannot justify stretching the notion of 'reasonableness' to the point where the safeguard secured by Article 5(1)(c) is impaired. Even in those circumstances, the respondent Government has to furnish at least some facts or information capable of satisfying the Court that the arrested person was reasonably suspected of having committed the alleged offence.

6.36 The approach of the Strasbourg court to the lawfulness of arrests has, then, been very similar to the approach taken by domestic courts in the tort of false imprisonment and the test under PACE s24. It seems unlikely that there would be any advantage to bringing a claim under the HRA 1998 rather than in tort where the claim is based on a lack of reasonable suspicion.

6.37 There may arise, exceptionally, circumstances in which the officer making the arrest has acted lawfully in accordance with PACE s24, but there has nonetheless been a violation of Article 5. Whereas pursuant to section 24 the lawfulness of an arrest turns upon the mind of and what was known to the arresting officer, under Article 5 it is the knowledge of

36 See further below at para 6.38.

37 *Fox, Hartley and Campbell v UK* (1991) 13 EHRR 157 at para 32, ECtHR.

38 (2002) 34 EHRR 32, ECtHR.

39 *O'Hara v UK* (2002) 34 EHRR 32 at para 36, ECtHR.

40 *O'Hara v UK* at para 35.

the public authority[41] that is relevant (ie of the police force rather than the individual officer). Accordingly, where exculpatory information is known to the police force, but not to the arresting officer, it is possible that the arresting officer has acted lawfully at common law, but the detention is nonetheless contrary to Article 5. Similarly, where an arrest is effected pursuant to a warrant, the warrant may provide a defence at common law, but the detention may still be arbitrary and contrary to Article 5.[42]

Police powers to arrest and detain

Arrest without a warrant

6.38 The vast majority of arrests will be made by police officers using their powers under PACE s24 to arrest without having first obtained a warrant. This section will consider the structure of section 24, and the associated Code of Practice. It will consider in detail the central tests of 'reasonable grounds to suspect' and 'reasonable belief in the necessity' of arrest that must be satisfied for an arrest to be lawful. If an arrest is not lawful the subsequent detention will constitute a false imprisonment and/or a breach of Article 5.

Powers under PACE s24 and related Codes of Practice

Overview

6.39 PACE s24 firsts set out when the power of arrest arises (subsections (1), (2) and (3)) and then provides that the power is only exercisable where there exists a reasonable belief that arrest is necessary for one of the specified purposes (subsections (4) and (5)).

6.40 Broadly, PACE s24(1) empowers a constable to arrest anyone who is in the act of committing an offence, or is about to do so. Subsections (2) and (3) empower a constable to arrest anyone whom the constable reasonably suspects of having committed an offence.

6.41 Thus, while the circumstances as set out in PACE s24(1)–(3) give rise to a power of arrest, the arrest will only be lawful if the arresting constable also has 'reasonable grounds for believing' that the arrest is necessary for one of the purposes (or 'reasons') specified in PACE s24(5). These reasons are set out in s24(5)(a)–(f) as follows:

(a) to enable the name of the person in question to be ascertained (in the case where the constable does not know, and cannot readily ascertain, the person's name, or has reasonable grounds for doubting whether a name given by the person as his name is his real name);
(b) correspondingly as regards the person's address;
(c) to prevent the person in question–
   (i) causing physical injury to himself or any other person;
   (ii) suffering physical injury;
   (iii) causing loss of or damage to property;

41 HRA 1998 s6(1).

42 See *Zenati v Commissioner of Police of the Metropolis* [2015] EWCA Civ 80, [2015] QB 758, and the discussion above at para 6.22.

(iv) committing an offence against public decency . . .;[43] or
(v) causing an unlawful obstruction of the highway;

(d) to protect a child or other vulnerable person from the person in question;
(e) to allow the prompt and effective investigation of the offence or of the conduct of the person in question;
(f) to prevent any prosecution for the offence from being hindered by the disappearance of the person in question.

6.42 Both limbs of reasonable grounds to suspect and reasonable grounds to believe in the necessity for arrest include a subjective and objective requirement. The arresting officer must hold an actual (ie genuine) suspicion that the person has committed a criminal offence, and there must be objectively reasonable grounds for that suspicion.[44] Similarly, in respect of necessity, the arresting officer must actually believe that the arrest is necessary for one of the specified purposes, and there must be objectively reasonable grounds for that belief.[45]

6.43 The requirement for objectively reasonable grounds is based solely on what information is known to the arresting officer, at the time of arrest. It relates to what is in the mind of the arresting officer when the power is exercised.[46] For example, if there are no objectively reasonable grounds to suspect the person of having committed an offence at the time the arrest takes place, it does not matter that evidence subsequently comes to light corroborating the officer's suspicion.[47]

6.44 There may be circumstances in which the arresting officer has acted lawfully based on what is known to the officer at the time, but the arrest has, in effect, been procured by a briefing officer who has withheld or given incorrect information. While the arresting officer has acted lawfully, the briefing officer may be liable in false imprisonment, and that is considered further below (at paras 6.71–6.75).

6.45 The subjective questions are issues of fact to be determined by the jury (if there is one).[48] The objective questions are questions of law to be determined by the judge.

6.46 A further requirement of a lawful arrest, as provided by PACE s28, is that the person is informed that they are under arrest and of the ground for the arrest (see para 6.142).

6.47 That combination of requirements results in seven questions to be answered in determining the lawfulness of the arrest, as summarised in *Parker v Chief Constable of Essex* in the first instance decision of Stuart-Smith J:[49]

43 Subject to PACE s24(6).

44 See, for example, *Castorina v Chief Constable of Surrey* [1988] 6 WLUK 85, (1988) 138 NLJ Rep 180, CA.

45 *Hayes v Chief Constable of Merseyside* [2011] EWCA Civ 911, [2012] 1 WLR 517 at paras 40 and 42.

46 *O'Hara v Chief Constable of the Royal Ulster Constabulary* [1997] AC 286, HL (Northern Ireland) per Lord Hope (considering the similarly worded Prevention of Terrorism (Temporary Provisions) Act 1984 s12(1)).

47 See, for example, *Fittschen v Chief Constable of Dorset* [2022] EWHC 399 (QB).

48 The circumstances in which this factual question can properly be left to the jury are considered at paras 16.62–16.66 below.

49 [2017] EWHC 2140 (QB) at para 14. The judgment was overturned on appeal ([2018] EWCA Civ 2788 (QB)), but on the separate question of whether the claimant was entitled to more than nominal damages.

[1] Did the arresting officer suspect that an offence had been committed? The answer to this question depends entirely on the findings of fact as to the officer's state of mind.
[2] Assuming the officer had the necessary suspicion, did the arresting officer have reasonable grounds for that suspicion? This is a purely objective requirement to be determined by the Court.
[3] Did the arresting officer suspect that the person who was arrested was guilty of the offence? The answer to this question depends entirely on the findings of fact as to the officer's state of mind.
[4] Assuming the officer had the necessary suspicion, did the arresting officer have reasonable grounds for that suspicion? This is a purely objective requirement to be determined by the judge if necessary on facts found by a jury.
[5] Did the arresting officer believe that for any of the reasons mentioned in subsection (5) it was necessary to arrest the person in question? The answer to this question depends entirely on the findings of fact as to the officer's state of mind.
[6] Assuming the officer had the necessary belief, were there reasonable grounds for that belief? This is a purely objective requirement to be determined by the judge, if necessary on facts found by a jury.
[7] If the answer to the previous questions is in the affirmative, then the officer has a discretion which entitles him to make an arrest and in relation to that discretion the question arises as to whether the discretion has been exercised in accordance with the principles laid down by Lord Greene MR in *Associated Provincial Picture Houses Ltd v Wednesbury Corpn* [1948] 1 KB 223.

6.48 In *Magee v Chief Constable of Derbyshire* Saini J referred to these as the '*Parker* questions'.[50]

PACE Codes of Practice: Code G

6.49 PACE has associated Codes of Practice.[51] The Codes of Practice are issued by the secretary of state pursuant to PACE ss66 and 67. A failure to follow or have regard to a Code of Practice does not in and of itself give rise to liability in a civil claim,[52] but a court will take any such failure into account when deciding on a claim. The Court of Appeal in *Hayes v Chief Constable of Merseyside*[53] said of the Codes and their relevance in legal proceedings that:

> . . . in any court proceedings, criminal or civil, the code is admissible in evidence, and if its provisions appear to be relevant to any question arising, it is to be taken into account in determining that question.

6.50 The relevant related Code of Practice in respect of the power to arrest is Code G: Code of practice for the statutory power of arrest by police officers, which states that:[54]

50 [2020] EWHC 3569 (QB) at paras 44–47.
51 Available at: www.gov.uk/guidance/police-and-criminal-evidence-act-1984-pace-codes-of-practice.
52 PACE s67(10).
53 [2011] EWCA Civ 911 at para 38.
54 PACE Code G para 1.3.

> The use of the power [of arrest] must be fully justified and officers exercising the power should consider if the necessary objectives can be met by other, less intrusive means.

Reasonable grounds to suspect

6.51 A brief summary of the case-law surrounding 'reasonable grounds to suspect' was set out by Sir Brian Leveson in *Parker v Chief Constable of Essex*:[55]

> The bar for reasonable cause to suspect set out in s24(2) of the 1984 Act is a low one. It is lower than a prima facie case and far less than the evidence required to convict: *Dumbell v Roberts* [1944] 1 All ER 326, 329A and *Hussien v Chong Fook Kam* [1970] AC 942, 948–9; see also *Castorina* [(1996) 160 LG Rev 241] (at 21D) and *O'Hara* [[1997] AC 286] (at 293). Further, prima facie proof consists of admissible evidence, while suspicion may take account of matters that could not be put in evidence (*Hussien* at 949, and *O'Hara* at 293). Suspicion may be based on assertions that turn out to be wrong (*O'Hara* at 298D–E). The factors in the mind of the arresting officer fall to be considered cumulatively (*Armstrong* [[2008] EWCA Civ 1582] at [19], and *Buckley* [[2009] EWCA Civ 356] at [6]).

6.52 In the often-cited case of *Hussien v Chong Fook Kam*[56] Lord Devlin said:

> Suspicion in its ordinary meaning is a state of conjecture or surmise where proof is lacking: 'I suspect but I cannot prove'. Suspicion arises at or near the starting point of an investigation of which the obtaining of prima facie proof is the end.

6.53 Although the threshold is low, there may still be a need for something more than a 'speculative hunch'.[57]

6.54 Where the police have ostensibly reliable information concerning a crime from a third party that will generally constitute reasonable grounds to suspect a person of a crime.[58]

6.55 An arresting officer may, depending on the circumstances, need to either make further enquires to substantiate or verify the information provided on which the arrest is to be based, or check the accuracy of information held. In *Armstrong*[59] the court accepted, however, that there will be circumstances when due to the urgency of the situation further enquiries and checks cannot be made. Hallett LJ stated that 'there may be circumstances, provided there is no urgency, which makes it incumbent upon an officer to make further enquiries before "suspicion could properly crystallise" '.[60] Hallet LJ went on to say:[61]

> However, it is important to remember, in my view, that an arrest may be effected very early on in an investigation, and it is nonetheless lawful for that. It will not always be possible or indeed desirable to carry out further enquiries before making an arrest.

55 [2018] EWCA Civ 2788 at para 115.

56 [1970] AC 942 at p948, PC (Malaysia).

57 *Fittschen v Chief Constable of Dorset* [2022] EWHC 399 (QB) at para 62.

58 *Jones v Chief Constable of Bedfordshire* [1987] 2 WLUK 101, DC.

59 *Armstrong v Chief Constable of West Yorkshire* [2008] EWCA Civ 1582 at para 14.

60 Para 14. See also the judgment of the then Simon Brown LJ in *Hough v Chief Constable of Staffordshire* [2001] EWCA Civ 39 at para 17.

61 Para 14.

6.56 If the suspect provides an explanation when challenged, that should be taken into account by the officer in deciding whether their initial suspicion can be maintained or remains based on reasonable grounds.[62]

6.57 If suspicion falls on more than one person in circumstances where only one person could have committed that crime (for example, where the police suspect that one member of a group is responsible but cannot identify which) then it may be appropriate to arrest all the suspects until evidence is available to establish whether the suspicion is well-founded by interview.[63] However, the police should clearly take whatever steps they can to exclude any members of the group if possible.

Necessary to arrest

Overview

6.58 It is an essential prerequisite to a lawful arrest that the arresting officer has reasonable grounds for believing that it is 'necessary' to make the arrest for one of the reasons specified in PACE s24(5) (set out above at para 6.41).[64]

6.59 The statutory requirement of necessity was added by the amendments made to PACE by the Serious Organised Crime and Police Act (SOCPA) 2005.[65] Prior to 2005 a police officer's power of arrest depended upon either the offence being an 'arrestable offence' (within PACE s24) or, for other non-arrestable offences, the general arrest conditions provided by PACE s25 (now repealed) had to apply. As the law then stood, for an arrestable offence, the only formal condition for arrest without a warrant was that the officer had reasonable grounds for suspecting that an offence had been committed and that the suspect had committed it. There was no statutory requirement for a belief in the necessity of arrest. It was, however, recognised that the officer still had a discretion which they had to exercise. If the power to arrest was exercised in a manner which was *Wednesbury* unreasonable, the arrest would be unlawful.[66] For other (lesser) offences, the officer would have to seek a court summons authorising arrest, unless it was impracticable to do so or one or more of the 'general arrest conditions' in PACE s25 applied. The 'general arrest conditions' were similar to the necessity requirements which now exist in PACE s24(5).

6.60 SOCPA 2005 amended PACE by substituting a new section 24 and repealing section 25. The broad effect was to create a single code of arrest powers applicable to all offences and providing a statutory requirement, in

62 *Banjo v Chief Constable of Greater Manchester* [1997] 6 WLUK 618, CA; *Mabey v Chief Constable of Hampshire* (unreported 29 June 1995, CA).

63 *Clarke v Chief Constable of North Wales* [2000] 4 WLUK 102, CA; *Cumming v Chief Constable of Northumbria* [2003] EWCA Civ 1844, (2004) Times, January 2.

64 *Parker* at para 10. The judgment was overturned on appeal ([2018] EWCA Civ 2788), but on on the separate question of whether the claimant was entitled to more than nominal damages.

65 The effect of the changes brought about by SOCPA 2005 were clearly summarised in *Hayes v Chief Constable of Merseyside* [2011] EWCA Civ 911 at paras 12–15.

66 *Mohammed-Holgate v Duke* [1984] AC 437 at pp445E–446D, HL per Lord Diplock; *Castorina v Chief Constable of Surrey* (1996) 160 LGR 241, CA; *and Cumming and others v Chief Constable of Northumbria* [2003] EWCA Civ 1844 at paras 16, 26 and 42 per Latham LJ, all referred to in *Parker* at para 9.

respect of all arrests, for an officer to honestly and reasonably believe that the arrest is necessary.[67]

6.61 In *Hayes v Chief Constable of Merseyside* it was said that the 'effect of this is, in one sense, to tighten up the accountability of police officers, at least in the case of arrest for serious offences, because those arrests now become subject to the criterion of necessity, whereas previously only non-arrestable offences were'.[68] In *Shields v Chief Constable of Merseyside*,[69] Toulson LJ said of the new regime that it creates a single code for all offences, ensures conformity with ECHR Article 5 and incorporates the *Wednesbury* principle of review. It was said in the subsequent case of *B and others (former soldiers) v Chief Constable of Northern Ireland*[70] that there is no separate and overarching *Wednesbury* review to be' applied to the decision to arrest. The requirement for objectively reasonable grounds incorporated the *Wednesbury* principle of review.[71]

6.62 One of the significant consequences of the introduction of the requirement of necessity has been an increasing number of investigations proceeding without an arrest. The number of arrests overall has decreased significantly. When the new single code for arrests was introduced in 2006, there were over 1.424 million arrests (year ending March 2007). In the years thereafter, there has been a significant and consistent decline in the number of arrests such that in 2020/21 there were 631,217 arrests.[72]

The meaning of necessity

6.63 Necessity does not mean, as may be understood in ordinary usage, that arrest is the only, indispensable option. Rather, for the purposes of PACE s24, necessity has been said to mean 'the practical and sensible option', as was the language used in *Re Alexander's Application for Judicial Review*.[73] PACE Code G describes that the constable is 'not required to be satisfied that there is no viable alternative to arrest. However, it does mean that in all cases the officer should consider that arrest is the practical, sensible and proportionate option'.[74]

6.64 In *Richardson v Chief Constable of the West Midlands* it was said, slightly differently, that 'necessity ... is an ordinary English word which can be applied without paraphrase'.[75] In *R (TL) v Chief Constable of Surrey*, Jay J described that the concept of necessity 'cannot be envisaged as a synonym

67 For a useful summary and analysis of the introduction of the test of necessity into PACE see *Parker* at paras 8–10. Caution is needed when relying on pre-2006 case-law.

68 [2011] EWCA Civ 911 at para 15.

69 [2010] EWCA Civ 1281.

70 [2015] EWHC 3691 (Admin). While this case concerned the equivalent provisions in the PACE (Northern Ireland) Order SI No 1341 (NI 12), the court made clear that article 26 in the Northern Ireland legislation was equivalent to PACE s24 in England and Wales, so the court's analysis applies to arrests in England and Wales.

71 See para 23.

72 See: https://assets.publishing.service.gov.uk/government/uploads/system/uploads/attachment_data/file/1072832/arrest-police-powers-procedures-mar21-tables-2e.ods.

73 [2009] NIQB 20 at para 18. See, also, *Reay v Chief Constable of Northumbria* [2020] EWHC 3246 (Admin).

74 Note 2C.

75 [2011] EWHC 773 (QB) at para 62.

for "desirable" or "convenient" '.[76] It has been described as setting 'a high bar'.[77]

6.65 In *Rashid v Chief Constable of West Yorkshire* it was observed that, whereas the requirement in PACE subsections 24(2) and (3) is for reasonable grounds for *suspecting* a person to be guilty of a crime, the requirement in subsections 24(4) and (5) for reasonable grounds for *believing* that an arrest is necessary imposes 'a comparatively high hurdle'.[78]

6.66 The courts will generally be sensitive to the operational judgment of police officers. However, the lawfulness of arrest and the liberty of the subject is at stake, and so 'careful scrutiny' is required by the court.[79]

The reasons of the arresting officer

6.67 In *Hayes v Chief Constable of Merseyside*[80] the Court of Appeal rejected the proposition that it was necessary for the officer to have given active consideration to every possible alternative to arrest. The arresting officer need not give themself a self-direction on all material matters and all possible alternatives. It is not a 'full-blown public law reasons challenge'. Whereas in a public law reasons challenge a failure to take into account a material consideration may render the decision unlawful, that may not be so in respect of an officer conducting an arrest.

6.68 However, 'the officer who has given no thought to alternatives to arrest is exposed to the plain risk of being found by a court to have had, objectively, no reasonable grounds for his belief that arrest was necessary'.[81] Similarly, in *Re Alexander's Application for Judicial Review* it was expressed that the decision as to whether an arrest was necessary involves 'at least some thought about the different options'.[82] Were it otherwise, the necessity requirement would be 'watered down so as to provide an inadequate safeguard'.[83] PACE Code G emphasises that the use of the power of arrest 'must be fully justified and officers exercising the power should consider if the necessary objectives can be met by other, less intrusive means'.[84]

6.69 It is also important to note that what must be objectively reasonable is the actual reason (or reasons) of the arresting officer, at the time of the arrest. As expressed in *R (TL) v Chief Constable of Surrey*, the 'court does not ask itself whether any police officer could rationally have made the decision under challenge; it directs itself to the particular decision maker and his grounds'.[85] Similarly, in *Lord Hanningfield of Chelmsford v Chief*

76 [2017] EWHC 129 (Admin), [2017] 1 WLR 2047 at para 40.

77 *Commissioner of Police of the Metropolis v MR* [2019] EWHC 888 (QB) at para 47.

78 [2020] EWHC 2522 (QB) at para 25. See, similarly, *Fittschen v Chief Constable of Dorset* [2022] EWHC 399 (QB) at para 11.

79 *B and others (former soldiers) v Chief Constable of Northern Ireland* [2015] EWHC 3691 (Admin) at para 18 per Lord Thomas LCJ.

80 [2011] EWCA Civ 911, [2012] 1 WLR 517.

81 *Hayes v Chief Constable of Merseyside* [2011] EWCA Civ 911, [2012] 1 WLR 517 at para 34.

82 [2009] NIQB 20 at para 19.

83 *ST v Chief Constable of Nottinghamshire* [2022] EWHC 1280 (QB) at para 93.

84 Para 1.3.

85 [2017] EWHC 129 (Admin), [2017] 1 WLR 2047 at para 39.

Constable of Essex Eady J described that an objective assessment is made 'albeit having regard to the factors which actually informed any decision made at the relevant time'.[86] 'After the event' rationalisation by the officer (or the Chief Constable) should be rejected. Neither is it for the court to determine for itself as a primary question of fact whether the arrest was necessary, as opposed to the narrower question of whether the officer's actual reasons were objectively reasonable.[87]

6.70 The focus, however, will be on whether, in substance, the officer's reasons disclose an objectively reasonable belief in the necessity of the arrest, and not on whether the officer's wording precisely mirrors that of the statute: there is no need for a 'statutory mantra' to be recited in the officer's evidence.[88]

Reliance on information provided by others

6.71 It is often the case that an arrest is effected not by an investigating officer, but further to a briefing provided by an investigating officer, or, even, further to a request made to arrest on the Police National Computer (PNC). In *O'Hara v Chief Constable of the Royal Ulster Constabulary*,[89] the House of Lords considered the situation where an officer arrests a person on the basis of information they obtain at a police briefing. It was held that an officer could not simply be instructed to carry out an arrest as a result of such a briefing, but as long as the officer has information from the briefing which gives them suspicion of guilt which is reasonably held, then an arrest will be lawful.

6.72 The House of Lords in *O'Hara* was careful to ensure that arresting officers had an independent responsibility and accountability when exercising powers of arrest. Lord Steyn (at p291) quoted Lord Diplock in *Mohammed-Holgate v Duke*[90] in stating that:[91]

> . . . the arrest can only be justified if the constable arresting the alleged suspect has reasonable grounds to suspect him to be guilty of an arrestable offence. The arresting officer is held accountable. That is the compromise between individual liberty and public order.

6.73 The ECtHR approved the approach in *O'Hara* and found that it complied with the requirements of ECHR Article 5(1).[92]

6.74 It is not sufficient for an arresting officer to merely infer that their superiors must have had reasonable grounds to suspect prior to issuing an instruction to arrest. In *Raissi*[93] the court rejected such a proposition as

86 [2013] EWHC 243 (QB) at para 29.

87 *R (TL) v Chief Constable of Surrey* [2017] EWHC 129 (Admin), [2017] 1 WLR 2047 at para 38.

88 *Magee v Chief Constable of Derbyshire* [2020] EWHC 3569 (QB) at para 82.

89 [1997] AC 286, HL (Northern Ireland).

90 [1984] AC 437, HL.

91 [1997] AC 286, HL (Northern Ireland).

92 O'Hara v UK (2002) 34 EHRR 32, ECtHR.

93 *Raissi v Commissioner of Police of the Metropolis* [2008] EWCA Civ 1237, [2009] QB 564.

being inconsistent with *O'Hara*.[94] Similarly, in *ST v Chief Constable of Nottinghamshire* it was considered that:[95]

> The failure of others to provide adequate, basic information to an officer who is asked to arrest someone for a simple and straightforward matter cannot provide a justification for that arrest. If it were otherwise 'arrestograms' with limited information would provide an obvious route to circumvent the requirement to properly consider the necessity of arrest. If in doubt, as [the arresting officer] clearly was, an officer cannot 'play safe' and arrest someone because given all the circumstances as known to others it may be necessary.

6.75 If the briefing officer has told the arresting officer that there is reliable information when there is not, the chief constable may become vicariously liable for false imprisonment on the basis that the briefing officer has wrongly procured the arrest. That is considered below at paras 6.97–6.103.

Voluntary interview as an alternative to arrest

6.76 One of the issues that commonly arises is whether arrest was necessary for the purposes of a prompt and effective[96] investigation so as to fall within PACE s24(5)(e) or whether, alternatively, the investigation could proceed by way of voluntary interview as an alternative to arrest. The legal framework around a voluntary interview is considered further below at paras 6.104–6.106.

6.77 Arrest may be necessary in order to interview where, for example, there is some reason to believe that the person may not co-operate with a voluntary interview, or there is concern that the invitation for a voluntary interview will give the suspect opportunity to collude with others[97] or otherwise interfere with potential evidence prior to interview.

6.78 The arresting officer need not interrogate the person as to whether they will attend a police station voluntarily, but the officer must at least consider whether having a suspect attend in this way is a 'practical alternative'.[98]

6.79 In *Lord Hanningfield of Chelmsford v Chief Constable of Essex*,[99] Lord Hanningfield had been arrested for offences of fraud at home in the early hours of the morning and his home was searched. He claimed damages including for false imprisonment based on the lack of necessity of arrest. His arrest occurred just days after he had been convicted of false accounting relating to his expenses as a member of the House of Lords. The court dismissed arguments by the Chief Constable that the arrest was necessary in order to 'allow the prompt and effective investigation of the offence or

94 [1997] AC 286, HL (Northern Ireland).

95 [2022] EWHC 1280 (QB) at para 110.

96 In *B and others (former soldiers) v Chief Constable of Northern Ireland* [2015] EWHC 3691 (Admin) it was said that 'prompt and effective' had to be read conjunctively (paras 26–28).

97 As in *R (Norman) v Chief Constable of Essex and others* [2020] EWHC 3456 (Admin).

98 *Re Alexander's Application for Judicial Review* [2009] NIQB 20 at para 19.

99 [2013] EWHC 243 (QB).

of the conduct of the person in question' (PACE s24(5)(e))[100] and that Lord Hanningfield could not be trusted to attend an interview voluntarily. The court found that there were no grounds to believe that Lord Hanningfield would destroy or hide evidence and noted that Lord Hanningfield had previously voluntarily attended for police interviews. The arrest could not therefore be said to be necessary on the grounds asserted, namely PACE s24(5)(e). The court stated that the consideration of alternatives to arrest was 'not a matter of box-ticking'.[101] In the course of the judgment, the High Court referred to Code G, Note 2F, which states:

> An officer who believes that it is necessary to interview the person suspected of committing the offence must then consider whether their arrest is necessary in order to carry out the interview. The officer is not required to interrogate the suspect to determine whether they will attend a police station voluntarily to be interviewed but they must consider whether the suspect's voluntary attendance is a practicable alternative for carrying out the interview. If it is, then arrest would not be necessary. Conversely, an officer who considers this option but is not satisfied that it is a practicable alternative, may have reasonable grounds for deciding that the arrest is necessary at the outset 'on the street'. Without such considerations, the officer would not be able to establish that arrest was necessary in order to interview.

6.80 In *Commissioner of Police of the Metropolis v MR*[102] Thornton J said:[103]

> Whether a person attending at a police station voluntarily for the purpose of assisting with an investigation needs to be arrested is fact specific. The officer who has given no thought to alternatives to arrest is exposed to the risk of being found by a Court to have had objectively no reasonable grounds for his belief that arrest was necessary . . . The obvious alternative to arrest was to interview MR, establish his identity and require that he hand over his phone. Any difficulties in this regard could have necessitated his arrest at that juncture, but not before.

6.81 In *Hayes v Chief Constable of Merseyside* the Court of Appeal described that proceeding by way of a voluntary interview only for it to be disrupted 'the moment it reached a topic [the suspect] found difficult' may not be an effective way of proceeding and, on the facts of that case concerning a suspected drug dealer manipulating his customer.[104] On the facts in *Hayes,* the Court of Appeal considered that as a suspected drug dealer believed to be manipulating his customer, there was some basis to consider that a voluntary interview may be disrupted. In *Mouncher v Chief Constable of South Wales*[105] it was similarly contended that an arrest was necessary because the suspect could have left a voluntary interview at any time 'thereby frustrating the inquiry'.[106] That was rejected on the facts by Wyn Williams J, who considered, first, that there was no evidence that an officer

100 In *B and others (former soldiers) v Chief Constable of Northern Ireland* [2015] EWHC 3691 (Admin), [2016] Crim LR 428 it was said that 'prompt and effective' had to be read conjunctively (paras 26–28).

101 Para 22.

102 [2019] EWHC 888 (QB).

103 Para 49.

104 [2011] EWCA Civ 911, [2012] 1 WLR 517 at para 42.

105 [2016] EWHC 1367 (QB).

106 Para 874.

had addressed the likelihood of the suspect attempting to walk out of the station during the course of his interview, and, second, 'the statutory provisions relating to the "necessity test" would be nullified if it was open to a police officer to say that arrest in advance of an interview under caution was always necessary to prevent the person being interviewed attempting to leave'.[107] Similarly, in *R (TL) v Chief Constable of Surrey* it was suggested that the court in *Hayes* was simply noting that there are disadvantages inherent in voluntary attendance, 'but whether these are decisive in any particular case must be fact-sensitive'.[108]

6.82 In *Hayes* the Court of Appeal also suggested that it would not be honest for an officer to invite a person to attend a voluntary interview if the officer intended to arrest the person the moment they elected to leave.[109] That, however, appears to be incorrect, as an officer inviting a suspect to a voluntary interview, knowing that the suspect might be arrested on electing to leave, is contemplated both by the PACE Code and, indeed, section 29 (considered at para 6.104 below).[110]

Arrest in order to utilise powers of search, entry and seizure

6.83 Arrest may be necessary in order to enable the officer to seize the person's phone or other electronic devices further to the powers in PACE ss18 and 32 to search a property and person on arrest.[111]

6.84 An alternative to arrest would be to invite the suspect to hand over the devices voluntarily. Whether that is a practical and effective alternative will be fact-specific. In *R (TL) v Chief Constable of Surrey* it was accepted that a request for the voluntary production of electronic devices would not have been effective. Even though the claimant had known he was under investigation and could already have deleted evidence if he had wished to do so, he did not know the precise allegations and it could 'not be inferred that the metaphorical horse had already bolted'.[112] A different approach was taken in *Commissioner of Police of the Metropolis v MR* in which the claimant had attended the police station voluntarily, at which point he was arrested. The court considered that the 'obvious alternative was to interview [the claimant], establish his identity and require that he hand over his phone' and any 'difficulties in this regard could have necessitated his arrest at that juncture, but not before'.[113] The same was accepted in *Rashid v Chief Constable of West Yorkshire*.[114] Ultimately, it will be open to the officer, instead of arresting the suspect, to ask the suspect to hand over the mobile telephone or other item of potential evidence which is

107 Para 877. Wyn Williams J did not consider that his analysis contradicted what was said in *Hayes*: see para 879. See, similarly, the reasoning of the first instance judge in *Commissioner of Police of the Metropolis v MR* [2019] EWHC 888 (QB) at para 14.

108 [2017] EWHC 129 (Admin), [2017] 1 WLR 2047 at para 47.

109 [2011] EWCA Civ 911, [2012] 1 WLR 517 at para 42.

110 See *Rashid v Chief Constable of West Yorkshire* [2020] EWHC 2522 (QB) at para 86.

111 See, for example, *Hayes v Chief Constable of Merseyside* [2011] EWCA Civ 911, [2012] 1 WLR 517 at para 42.

112 [2017] EWHC 129 (Admin), [2017] 1 WLR 2047 at para 65.

113 [2019] EWHC 888 (QB) at para 49.

114 [2020] EWHC 2522 (QB) at paras 88–91.

reasonably believed to be concealed on the suspect's person. Depending on the circumstances, making such a request may or may not be practicable.[115]

6.85 Some consideration has been given to whether it is lawful for the police to deploy the power of arrest so as to enable the police to use the power of entry and search after arrest pursuant to PACE s18 (as part of the 'prompt and effective investigation' which would justify and arrest for the purposes of PACE s24(5)(e)), rather than seek a warrant. On one view, deploying the power of arrest so as to avoid the procedural requirements of applying for a warrant subverts or circumvents the intention of parliament and the safeguards associated with applying for a warrant. In *R (TL) v Chief Constable of Surrey* the High Court was attracted by the argument that an intention to search premises following arrest could not be used to justify that arrest. But in the end the Court decided that it did not need to resolve the principle, noting that a holding 'that the police could never deploy section 18 considerations as the sole justification for an arrest under section 24(5)(e) would have far-ranging consequences',[116] and would mean, for example, that the Code G Code of Practice would need to be reviewed. However, on the facts of the case in *R (TL) v Chief Constable of Surrey* the court found that no reason had been provided for failing to apply for a warrant in advance of the arrest, and in those circumstances, at least, the intention to carry out a search (without a warrant and under PACE s18) could not be advanced as a reason to justify the necessity for the arrest.[117]

6.86 A warrant to search premises does not carry an implied authority to search any person. Where it is believed that the suspect, present at a search pursuant to warrant, may have items of evidential value concealed upon their person, then an arrest may be necessary in order to able to deploy the power of search upon arrest pursuant to PACE s32.[118]

Arrest in order to impose bail conditions

6.87 There has been some consideration as to the circumstances in which a desire to impose bail conditions upon the release of the suspect may meet the necessity reasons in PACE s24(5). For example, conditions of bail preventing contact with a complainant or witness may serve to protect a vulnerable person (in accordance with section 24(5)(d))[119] or prevent interference with witnesses, thereby allowing an effective investigation (in accordance with section 24(5)(e)).

6.88 In *Richardson v Chief Constable of the West Midlands*, Slade J considered that an arrest in order to impose bail conditions may be lawful.[120] The

115 As observed by Lavender J in *Rashid v Chief Constable of West Yorkshire* [2020] EWHC 2522 (QB) at para 40.

116 [2017] EWHC 129 (Admin), [2017] 1 WLR 2047 at para 71.

117 [2017] EWHC 129 (Admin), [2017] 1 WLR 2047 at para 73.

118 *Rashid v Chief Constable of West Yorkshire* [2020] EWHC 2522 (QB) at paras 44 and 88.

119 As to bail conditions seeking to prevent interference with a witness falling within PACE s24(5)(d), see *R (TL) v Chief Constable of Surrey* [2017] EWHC 129 (Admin), [2017] 1 WLR 2047 at paras 56–59.

120 [2011] EWHC 773 (QB), [2011] 2 Cr App R 1 at para 68.

courts have been conscious, however, that if the necessity for arrest can too readily be justified by a desire to impose bail conditions, then the protection afforded would be significantly lessened. Thus, in *R (TL) v Chief Constable of Surrey* Jay J accepted that bail conditions *could* meet the test for necessity, but only in the 'precise respect' that if there are reasonable grounds for believing that bail conditions are necessary to protect a witness from intimidation which 'would or might render the investigation substantially less effective' then the requirement of PACE s24(5)(e) would be satisfied.[121]

6.89 There must be some cogent basis to consider that bail conditions are both likely and necessary. In *B and others (former soldiers) v Chief Constable of Northern Ireland*[122] the court considered that the highest the arresting officer could put it, on the facts of that case, was 'to say that he would probably wish to consider the imposition of a condition or conditions' but that was not accepted to be a reasonable basis for considering that arrest is necessary to allow an effective investigation. The court observed that if a 'possible desire to impose bail conditions' was sufficient to meet the test of necessity then the protections afforded by the requirement 'would be swept away: arrest could in nearly every case be said to be necessary for this reason'.[123]

Arrest in domestic abuse cases

6.90 In cases where domestic abuse is alleged, the emphasis is on using the power of arrest as a part of the duty to take positive action to protect a victim of abuse. The guidance issued by the College of Policing (COP)[124] advises that:

> Where an offence has been committed in a domestic abuse case, arrest will normally be 'necessary' within the terms of the Police and Criminal Evidence Act 1984 (PACE) to protect a child or vulnerable person, prevent the suspect causing injury or criminal damage and/or allow for the prompt and effective investigation of the offence.
>
> ...
>
> The decision whether or not to arrest a suspect rests with the police officer, and officers should not ask victims whether they require an arrest to be made.

6.91 Given the positive duty on police to protect victims from further abuse (ECHR Articles 2 and 3 – see chapter 7) it is likely that the police will generally be able to justify an arrest where domestic abuse or violence is alleged.

6.92 That is not always so, and in *R (TL) v Chief Constable of Surrey* the suspect had allegedly raped his former partner, but the claimant had made clear that he would attend for voluntary interview and would not contact the complainant, and that was not doubted by the arresting officer.[125] That

121 [2017] EWHC 129 (Admin), [2017] 1 WLR 2047 at para 52.

122 [2015] EWHC 3691 (Admin), [2016] Crim LR 428.

123 [2015] EWHC 3691 (Admin), [2016] Crim LR 428 at para 64.

124 Stated in the COP's Authorised Professional Practice (APP) on Major investigation and public protection: Domestic abuse: Arrest and other positive approaches, available at: www.app.college.police.uk/app-content/major-investigation-and-public-protection/domestic-abuse/arrest-and-other-positive-approaches/.

125 [2017] EWHC 129 (Admin), [2017] 1 WLR 2047 at para 54.

was a 'somewhat unusual' case in which the claimant had known for some time that he was under investigation, was otherwise of good character and there was no evidence that he previously breached any assurance given. In the particular circumstances of that case, Jay J considered that the arrest had been made 'on general policy grounds rather than the particular circumstances of this claimant' and the arrest was unlawful.[126]

Arresting a child

6.93 PACE s24 does not contain any provisions designed to offer particular protection to a child. However, Children Act 2004 s11 requires every chief officer of police to make arrangements for ensuring that 'their functions are discharged having regard to the need to safeguard and promote the welfare of children'. That provision reflects at least the spirit of Article 3 of the UN Convention on the Rights of the Child (UNCRC) which requires that 'in all actions concerning children' taken by the state, the 'best interests of the child shall be a primary consideration'. Consistent with that, Article 37 of the UNCRC requires state signatories to ensure that 'arrest, detention or imprisonment of a child shall be in conformity with the law and shall be used only as a measure of last resort and for the shortest appropriate period of time'.

6.94 Those provisions were referred to in *ST v Chief Constable of Nottinghamshire*. Cotter J observed that:

> Proper recognition by those engaged within the criminal justice system of the need to consider the best interests, safeguarding and promotion of the welfare of children must begin with the first interaction, which, as regards a suspected offender, is usually within the investigation stage.[127]

Accordingly:[128]

> . . . the fact that the person to be arrested is a child requires specific consideration due to the need to have regard to the duty to safeguard and promote the welfare of children. Indeed it should be front and centre of the consideration of relevant circumstances and requires an assessment of whether a less intrusive step than arrest or detention is a practical alternative.

6.95 Age can be relevant not only to whether to arrest at all, but also to the timing of arrest. The relevance as to timing is specifically identified by the COP APP on 'Children and Young Persons', which describes that officers should 'pay particular regard to the timing of any necessary arrests of children and young people and ensure that they are detained for no longer than needed . . .'.[129] In *ST v Chief Constable of Nottinghamshire* a 14-year-old suspected of a robbery had been arrested at his home at 5.30am in the morning, primarily for the officer's convenience and the early morning being a good time to catch people at home. There had not been reasonable

126 [2017] EWHC 129 (Admin), [2017] 1 WLR 2047 at para 54.

127 [2022] EWHC 1280 (QB) at para 99.

128 [2022] EWHC 1280 (QB) at para 99.

129 See: www.college.police.uk/app/detention-and-custody/detainee-care/children-and-young-persons.

grounds for believing that arrest was necessary at the time that it took place, and the arrest was unlawful.[130]

Equality considerations

6.96 The necessity requirement should also be viewed in light of the requirement under Equality Act 2010 s20 to make reasonable adjustments in respect of those with disabilities so that where a suspect has a mental disability, the effect and impact of that condition should be taken into account. The relevant legal principles are considered in chapter 12.

Liability of a briefing officer

6.97 An officer who directs or procures an arrest to be effected by another officer, but does so without a proper basis, may have committed the tort of false imprisonment, for which the chief constable is vicariously liable. There is now a consistent line of cases supporting this proposition from *Davidson v Chief Constable of North Wales*[131] through to *Mouncher v Chief Constable of South Wales.*[132]

6.98 In *Davidson* a store detective reported to police seeing two friends steal a cassette and the two were arrested. The issue identified was whether the store detective had merely given the police information for them to act on or otherwise, or had caused or incited the arrest and imprisonment. On the facts, there was no evidence to suggest that the store detective was other than a giver of information. In the course of giving judgment, however, the court referred to the right of somebody wrongly arrested to a claim against the person who was responsible for causing the arrest.

6.99 In *R (Rawlinson and Hunter Trustees) v Central Criminal Court*[133] the Divisional Court dealt directly with both *O'Hara*[134] and *Davidson*. The appellant in *Rawlinson* argued that the court should recognise an exception to the principle in *O'Hara* where the arresting officer reasonably relied on information from another officer who knew or ought to have known that the information was misleading. That was rejected. In giving the judgment of the court, Sir John Thomas, President of the Queen's Bench, said that such an argument failed to take account of the decision in *Davidson*, in which the court was 'specifically considering the situation in which a person or body could be held liable for the acts of the arresting officer'.[135] The court referred to the right of somebody wrongly arrested to a claim against the person who was responsible for the arrest, by giving instructions to the police officer to arrest, or procuring, or directly encouraging the arrest.

130 [2022] EWHC 1280 (QB) at para 127.
131 [1984] 2 All ER 597, CA.
132 [2016] EWHC 1367 (QB).
133 [2012] EWHC 2254 (Admin), [2013] 1 WLR 1634.
134 *O'Hara v Chief Constable of the Royal Ulster Constabulary* [1997] AC 286, HL (Northern Ireland) and see para 6.71.
135 [2012] EWHC 2254 (Admin), [2013] 1 WLR 1634 at para 227.

6.100 A year later, the Court of Appeal, in *Commissioner of Police of the Metropolis v Copeland*,[136] was faced with the situation where it was alleged that one officer had lied to another officer when he told her that he had been assaulted by the appellant, Ms Copeland. Ms Copeland was arrested based on the information provided by an officer who had lied. The appellant succeeded at trial in a claim for false imprisonment and the Court of Appeal rejected an appeal by the Commissioner who argued that it was for the claimant to prove that an officer had lied to the arresting officer in order to procure an arrest, and not for the defendant to prove the officer was not lying. In the course of giving judgment, Moses LJ said that what mattered in this situation was not what was in the mind of the arresting officer, but whether the officer who had lied had done so deliberately,[137] and if that was the case then the arrest would be unlawful. In terms of the burden of proof, as is always the case, the court said it was for the Commissioner to prove the arrest was lawful. The Commissioner could not do so unless he could establish good faith in respect of the officer requesting the arresting officer to arrest Ms Copeland.[138] Reference was made to the dicta of Toulson LJ in *R (M) v Hackney LBC*[139] where he recognised the principle at common law that:

> There may be false imprisonment by A, although it was B who took the person into custody and B acted lawfully, provided that A directly caused B's act and that A's act was done without lawful justification.[140]

6.101 In the later case of *Mouncher v Chief Constable of South Wales*,[141] Wyn Williams J considered the scenario where a briefing to an arresting officer provides sufficient material to justify the arrest of the particular suspect, but omits material which would cause the arresting officer to conclude that no reasonable grounds existed to justify the arrest.[142] The judge reviewed the authorities, including *O'Hara*, and accepted, following the *Davidson*, *Copeland* and *Rawlinson* line of authority, that even if the conduct of the arresting officer is lawful, the chief officer may be vicariously liable for the actions of another officer who has instigated, promoted or incited the arrest, without appropriate justification.[143]

6.102 There is, however, earlier case-law that appears to conflict with the decision in *Mouncher*. In *Alford v Chief Constable of Cambridgeshire*,[144] a police officer was arrested for causing death by dangerous driving. At the time, the officer was involved in a high-speed pursuit. An initial report from a force different to that of the officer was critical of his driving and concluded that the pursuit should have been abandoned. There was then a subsequent report that found that his driving was of an acceptable standard. The arresting officer was only informed about the existence and

136 [2014] EWCA Civ 1014.

137 Para 18.

138 Para 21.

139 [2011] EWCA Civ 4, [2011] 1 WLR 2873 at paras 35–36.

140 *Copeland* at para 20.

141 [2016] EWHC 1367 (QB).

142 Para 429.

143 Para 433.

144 [2009] EWCA Civ 100.

findings of the first report. The Court of Appeal rejected an argument that the arrest was unlawful as the arresting officer had not been told of the subsequent report. In finding that the arresting officer had the required reasonable grounds to suspect, and that therefore the arrest was lawful, the court commented on the finding by the trial judge that the second report had not been deliberately withheld by the briefing officer. Knowledge of the report by the briefing officer (and senior officers) could not affect the lawfulness of the arrest carried out by the arresting officer. The case of *Alford* was referred to in the case of *Parker v Chief Constable of Essex* without any criticism.[145]

6.103 Another common situation involving information provided to the arresting officer that forms the basis of his or her reasonable grounds to suspect is where reliance is placed on information held on the PNC. If the arresting officer's information comes from an entry on the PNC, then it may only be sufficient to found reasonable suspicion if there is such urgency so as to make further enquiry impractical.[146] That may arise where, for example, the police receive the information during a stop and search of a person on the street or in a vehicle.

Voluntary attendance at a police station

6.104 Under PACE, someone who attends a police station voluntarily for the purpose of assisting with an investigation, without having been arrested, is entitled to leave at any time unless subsequently placed under arrest. There is no requirement on the police to tell a person who is attending voluntarily that they are free to leave, but PACE does make it clear that if a police officer decides to arrest a person, they must be informed immediately.[147] PACE *Code C: Code of practice for the detention, treatment and questioning of persons by police officers* (and see PACE ss28 and 37) states that if it is decided that an arrest is necessary then the person must be informed of the grounds and reasons for arrest and be brought before a custody officer who is then required to open a custody record and notify the detainee of their rights.[148] A failure to do so will make the detention thereafter unlawful.

6.105 An example of where detention during a voluntary attendance would become unlawful can be seen in the following example. A person agrees to go to a police station voluntarily to answer some questions. The officer questioning leaves the interview room to check on something that has been said, locking the door in the process so that the person cannot leave. There has here been a detention and a deprivation of liberty and as there has been no proper arrest the detention and loss of liberty is unlawful and the person can sue in tort for false imprisonment, and/or bring a claim for a breach of Article 5(1). Alternatively, if after a period of questioning the person decides that enough is enough and decides to leave and an officer

145 [2017] EWHC 2140 (QB) at para 23.

146 *Hough v Chief Constable of Staffordshire* [2001] EWCA Civ 39, (2001) Times, February 14.

147 PACE s29. Compare *R v Lemsatef* [1977] 2 All ER 835, CA and PACE Code C para 3.21.

148 PACE Code C para 3.21(a).

stops the person and says, 'You can't go, you're helping us with our enquiries', again, in the absence of a lawful arrest, the person could sue for false imprisonment and/or breach of Article 5(1).

6.106 Conversely, a person who is prepared to co-operate by, for example, voluntarily attending at the police station may have an action for false imprisonment or breach of Article 5(1) if the police decide, unnecessarily or in bad faith, so arbitrarily, to exercise their discretion to arrest the person.[149]

Power of arrest: terrorism

6.107 Terrorism Act (TA) 2000 s41 provides the power for a police officer to arrest a person whom they 'reasonably suspect' to be a terrorist – by which is meant a person who police reasonably suspect to have committed an offence contained in the Act, or a person who has been concerned in the commission, preparation or instigation of acts of terrorism. Acts of terrorism are defined in TA 2000 s1. A 'terrorist' will be a person who is, or is suspected to be, a member of or supports a proscribed organisation,[150] provides money or property to a proscribed organisation intending that it be used for the purposes of terrorism,[151] undertakes 'money laundering' of terrorist property,[152] provides weapon training,[153] or directs a terrorist organisation.[154]

6.108 If a person is arrested under this power, then the relevant rules that apply to their detention in respect of their treatment, the taking of samples, the duration of detention and review of their detention, are those set out in TA 2000 Sch 8.

6.109 Additional powers are granted to the police in respect of cordons being put in place where it is considered 'expedient' to do so for the purposes of a terrorist investigation.[155] These powers include ordering a person in a cordoned area to leave, and restricted access to a cordoned area.[156] These additional powers therefore provide further potential defences (justifications) to claims of false imprisonment and/or breach of Article 5.

6.110 A detailed discussion of police powers in respect of terrorism is beyond the scope of this book. For further discussion of anti-terrorist investigative powers and substantive terrorism offences, see Blackstone's Criminal Practice,[157] chapter B10.

149 See, for example, *Paul v Chief Constable of Humberside* [2004] EWCA Civ 308.
150 TA 2000 ss11 and 12.
151 TA 2000 s15.
152 TA 2000 s18.
153 TA 2000 s54.
154 TA 2000 s56.
155 TA 2000 s33.
156 TA 2000 s36.
157 Oxford University Press, annual publication.

Power of arrest: breach of the peace

Common law

6.111 The police may arrest without warrant a person committing a breach of the peace, a person who, it is reasonably apprehended, will imminently commit a breach of the peace,[158] or a person who, having committed a breach, is reasonably expected to be about to renew it.[159] In the leading case of *R v Howell*, Watkins LJ stated that a breach of the peace is committed:[160]

> . . . whenever harm is actually done or is likely to be done to a person or in his presence to his property or a person is in fear of being so harmed through an assault, an affray, a riot, unlawful assembly or other disturbance.

6.112 In *R (Laporte) v Chief Constable of Gloucestershire*[161] the House of Lords re-affirmed the requirement (where no breach of the peace is in progress) for there to be a reasonable apprehension of an imminent breach of the peace before the power of arrest arose. In that case, demonstrators had been prevented by the police from attending a demonstration. The coaches they were on had been searched by the police who determined that some of the protesters intended to cause a breach of the peace at the demonstration. The police then escorted the coaches back to London thus preventing the demonstrators from arriving at the demonstration that was to take place in Gloucestershire. No arrests were made, but the protesters were prevented from exercising their rights under ECHR Articles 10 and 11.[162] The House of Lords found there to be no evidence of an imminent breach of the peace and held that that the police could not take action short of arrest in circumstances that a breach of the peace was not sufficiently imminent to justify arrest. For further discussion of the *Laporte* case, see paras 10.33–10.34 and 10.67–10.69.

ECHR Article 5

6.113 In *McGrogan*,[163] the Court of Appeal described that the common law power to arrest had been given a 'clean bill of health' by the ECtHR in the case of *Steel v UK*[164] but noted the need, under the breach of the peace power, to comply with the requirement under Article 5(1)(c) to bring a lawfully

158 A police officer must 'honestly believe on reasonable grounds' that a breach of the peace is imminent for an arrest before the breach takes place to be lawful: Where the behaviour of a person is provocative but lawful behaviour the power to arrest must only be exercised in the clearest of circumstances that violence was imminent: *Foulkes v Chief Constable of Merseyside* [1998] 3 All ER 705, [1998] 2 FLR 789, CA; and see also *Maguire v Chief Constable of Cumbria* [2001] EWCA Civ 619.

159 The breach of the peace (actual or imminent) can occur in private or in public: *McConnell v Chief Constable of Greater Manchester* [1990] 1 WLR 364, CA. If in private it is not necessary that persons outside the property are affected, although this could be a highly relevant factor: *McQuade v Chief Constable of Humberside* [2001] EWCA Civ 1330, [2002] 1 WLR 1347.

160 [1982] QB 416 at p427, CA.

161 [2006] UKHL 55, [2007] 2 AC 105.

162 Freedom of expression and freedom of assembly.

163 *Chief Constable of Cleveland v McGrogan* [2002] EWCA Civ 86, [2002] 1 FLR 707.

164 (1999) 28 EHRR 603, [1998] Crim LR 893, ECtHR.

detained person before a court at the earliest opportunity.[165] Similarly, in *Ostendorf v Germany*,[166] it was held that detention to prevent a person from committing an offence could be justified under Article 5(1)(c),[167] but the arrest must also be effected for the purpose of bringing a person before a competent legal authority. Legislation and detention aimed exclusively at preventing and not at prosecuting offences could not be justified under Article 5(1)(c).

6.114 However, the Supreme Court had the opportunity to consider directly whether an anticipated breach of the peace, in essence a form of preventative detention, complies with Article 5(1)(c), in *R (Hicks) v Commissioner of Police of the Metropolis*.[168] The court concluded that detention in order to prevent a breach of the peace was lawful and did not breach Article 5(1)(c). The Supreme Court explicitly declined to follow the Strasburg case of *Ostendorf*.

6.115 The Grand Chamber of the ECtHR has now reversed its previous case-law, where from *Lawless v Ireland (No 3)*[169] through to *Ostendorf* it had established that preventative detention under Article 5(1)(c) had to be in the context of extant or anticipated criminal proceedings. In *S v Denmark*[170] the Grand Chamber decided that short-term preventative detention could be justified under Article 5(1)(c) even without an intention to pursue criminal proceedings.

6.116 While the Strasbourg court considers a breach of the peace to be 'a crime' for the purposes of Article 5, this is not the case domestically. In *Williamson v Chief Constable of the West Midlands*[171] the court confirmed that a breach of the peace was not a criminal offence within the meaning of PACE s34(1) as it was not capable of being subject to a charge leading to a conviction. The court found therefore that an arrest and detention for a breach of the peace is not subject to the protections provided for arrested persons in PACE. Although the court commented that the common law provides protection against arbitrary arrest and unreasonable detention.[172]

Arrest with a warrant

6.117 If a person is arrested under a warrant, they have no claim against the police officer who acts in obedience to the warrant.[173] Thus, it will generally be a defence to a claim for false imprisonment that a court has issued the warrant and that the police have executed it by taking the person into

165 For the purposes of the ECHR a breach of the peace counts as an offence, despite it not being classified as an offence under English law: *Steel v UK* (1998) 28 EHRR 603 at paras 46–49. As referred to in *R (Hicks) v Commissioner of Police of the Metropolis* [2017] UKSC 9.

166 [2013] 3 WLUK 193, (2013) 34 BHRC 738, ECtHR.

167 In *Ostendorf* the court did, however, find the detention to be lawful under Article 5(1)(b).

168 [2017] UKSC 9.

169 [1961] 7 WLUK 1, (1979–80) 1 EHRR 15, ECtHR.

170 [2018] 10 WLUK 776, (2019) 68 EHRR 17, ECtHR.

171 [2003] EWCA Civ 337, [2004] 1 WLR 14.

172 At para 19 per Dyson LJ.

173 Constables Protection Act 1750 s6.

custody. However, the police would not be protected if they did not act, in fact, comply with the warrant, for example, by arresting someone who was not named in the warrant,[174] or if the warrant was not signed or sealed. In *Horsfield v Brown*[175] Macnaghten J observed:

> If the constable acts in obedience to the warrant, then, though the warrant be an unlawful warrant, he is protected by the statute of 1750, but if the warrant be a lawful warrant, and he executes it in an unlawful way, then no action is maintainable against the magistrate, but an action is maintainable against the constable.

6.118 There are circumstances in which a constable will not be protected if the warrant is defective. While it has been held that an officer is protected in obeying a warrant that was 'invalid or unlawful' because it did not contain the form of words required,[176] it is doubtful whether the officer would be protected by a warrant that had a more substantial defect, such as the omission of the cause of arrest or the address at which it should be executed.[177] In *Bell v Chief Constable of Greater Manchester*,[178] Sir Mark Potter held that, when considering the issue of whether the defence under Constables Protection Act 1750 s6 had been negated, the issue was whether there was a formal defect on the face of the warrant sufficiently grave to invalidate it. The test was whether the defect relied upon was such as to raise a clear doubt as to whether an application had been lawfully made to, and granted by, the magistrates in the exercise of their jurisdiction (although Potter P observed that 'the law is by no means clear as to the level of grossness or obviousness which is necessary for the officer to lose his protection by reason of such defect',[179] which arguably remains the case).

Liability of informants for wrongful arrest

6.119 As above, a person may be liable in false imprisonment if that person directs or procures an arrest, and does so without lawful justification. As in *Copeland* (considered above at para 6.100) that may mean that a police officer is liable in tort for having caused another officer to arrest the claimant. It may also be that a member of the public is liable for having caused the arrest.

6.120 Two (albeit overlapping) questions arise. The first is whether the person instigated or actively promoted the arrest. As above, in *Davidson v Chief Constable of North Wales*[180] it was alleged that store detectives were liable in false imprisonment for having provided information to the police and the ensuing arrest. The Court of Appeal considered the question to be whether the store detective 'went beyond laying information before police officers for them to take such action as they thought fit and amounted to

174 *Hoye v Bush* (1840) 1 Man & G 775.

175 [1932] 1 KB 355 at p369, KBD; cited *in McGrath v Chief Constable of the Royal Ulster Constabulary* [2001] UKHL 39 at para 12.

176 *Horsfield v Brown* [1932] 1 KB 355 at p369, KBD.

177 See *Ward v Commissioner of Police of the Metropolis* [2003] EWCA Civ 1152 for discussion of the lawfulness of a 'sloppily drafted' warrant.

178 [2005] EWCA Civ 902.

179 At para 29.

180 [1994] 2 All ER 597, CA.

some direction, or procuring, or direct request, or direct encouragement, that they should act by way of arresting' the claimant.[181] On the facts of that case, the court found there to be no evidence that the store detective's actions went beyond the giving of information to the police officers for them to take such action as they thought fit, and that therefore it did not amount to a direction or direct request that the police should act by arresting the suspect. In *Commissioner of Police of the Metropolis v Copeland*, the court considered whether the person (in that case another officer) had 'procured or directly encouraged' the arrest.[182] The officer had done so by fabricating the allegation of having been assaulted by the claimant, without which allegation the claimant would not have been arrested.

6.121 The second question is whether, if the person instigated or actively promoted the arrest, there was some lawful justification for doing so. It is clear, as in *Copeland*, that there will be no lawful justification where arrest is procured by giving a deliberate falsehood to the arresting officer. In such circumstances, there may be an overlap with the tort of malicious procurement of an arrest, although the case-law tends to suggest that the tort only arises where the arrest is made pursuant to a warrant (see the discussion at paras 8.99–8.100). Procuring an arrest by way of a deliberate falsehood will likely give rise to liability irrespective of whether the defendant is a police officer or member of the public.

6.122 The absence of a lawful justification is not limited to dishonesty and cases of bad faith. In the different context of *R (M) v Hackney LBC*,[183] liability for false imprisonment arose where an approved mental health practitioner (AMHP) applied to detain the claimant, who in consequence of that application was detained by a hospital. The AMHP had honestly but mistakenly believed that the claimant's 'nearest relative' had lifted his objection. In fact, the 'nearest relative' had not done so and, further to the relevant statutory provisions, the detention was unlawful. The AMHP was liable for having procured the false imprisonment of the claimant, albeit that he had done so in good faith. Similarly, in the police context, Wyn Williams J in *Mouncher and others v Chief Constable of South Wales* contemplated liability arising in respect of a briefing officer who does not themselves having reasonable grounds for arrest, but provides information to the arresting officer that 'did justify an arrest albeit it was incomplete'.[184] There was no suggestion that the information being incomplete must be the product of dishonesty or bad faith. However, at least in respect of members of the public it seems unlikely that giving information in good faith that results in an arrest but transpires to be erroneous could give rise to liability for false imprisonment.

181 [1994] 2 All ER 597 at 602d, CA.
182 [2014] EWCA Civ 1014 at para 19.
183 [2011] EWCA Civ 4, [2011] 1 WLR 2873.
184 [2016] EWHC 1367 (QB) at para 433; see, also, para 429.

Stop and search

Overview

6.123 The police generally have no power to stop or detain a person to compulsorily question them. If an officer detains (without arresting) a person who walks away after refusing to answer questions, then it is likely this will amount to false imprisonment. In *Rice v Connelly*,[185] still arguably the foundational case on this point, it was held that:[186]

> . . . the whole basis of the common law is that right of the individual to refuse to answer questions put to him by persons in authority, and a refusal to accompany those in authority to any particular place, short, of course, of arrest.

6.124 There are now certain circumstances in which there is an obligation to answer questions. For example, it is now an offence for a person to refuse to provide their name and address when asked by a police officer who has reason to believe the person is acting in an anti-social manner.[187] Police officers also have some powers to require citizens to move from their location without arresting them, for example, giving dispersal directions under Anti-social Behaviour Act 2003 s30.

6.125 The police do, however, have various powers to carry out a stop and search of a person without a warrant and to detain the person for the purposes of the search. Two of the most commonly used powers are as follows:

- PACE s1: a police officer can search any person or vehicle for stolen or prohibited[188] articles and detain the person or vehicle to carry out that search, where there are reasonable grounds for suspecting that such items will be found.
- Misuse of Drugs Act (MDA) 1971 s23(2): a police officer may stop and search a person if there are reasonable grounds to suspect that the person is in possession of a controlled drug and the officer can detain the person for the purpose of searching him. This power to detain includes taking a person to a place where the search can properly be carried out.

6.126 The use of stop and search powers are governed by the *PACE Code of Practice A: Code of practice for the exercise by: police officers of statutory powers of stop and search; police officers and police staff of requirements to record public encounters*. There is also an APP manual,[189] which provides guidance for police on the use of stop and search powers, incorporating the provisions of PACE Code A. There is also government guidance on the 'Best use of stop and search scheme'.[190]

185 [1966] 3 WLR 17, CA.
186 At p419.
187 Police Reform Act 2002 s50.
188 Including offensive weapons, and tools used for burglary and theft: PACE s1(7).
189 Last updated on 29 September 2017, available on the COP website: www.app.college.police.uk/app-content/stop-and-search/.
190 Available at: www.gov.uk/government/publications/best-use-of-stop-and-search-scheme.

6.127 Guidance on what can amount to reasonable grounds to suspect for the purposes of carrying out a search is included in para 2.2 of the PACE Code A.[191]

6.128 Reasonable grounds for suspicion is the legal test which a police officer must satisfy before they can stop and detain individuals or vehicles to search them under powers such as PACE s1 (to find stolen or prohibited articles) and MDA 1971 s23 (to find controlled drugs). This test must be applied to the particular circumstances in each case and is in two parts:[192]

> (i) Firstly, the officer must have formed a genuine suspicion in their own mind that they will find the object for which the search power being exercised allows them to search (see Annex A, second column, for examples); and
> (ii) Secondly, the suspicion that the object will be found must be reasonable. This means that there must be an objective basis for that suspicion based on facts, information and/or intelligence which are relevant to the likelihood that the object in question will be found, so that a reasonable person would be entitled to reach the same conclusion based on the same facts and information and/or intelligence.
>
> Officers must therefore be able to explain the basis for their suspicion by reference to intelligence or information about, or some specific behaviour by, the person concerned . . .[193]

6.129 At PACE Code A para 2.2B it is made clear that the personal factors can never support a reasonable ground for suspicion:

> Reasonable suspicion can never be supported on the basis of personal factors. This means that unless the police have information or intelligence which provides a description of a person suspected of carrying an article for which there is a power to stop and search, the following cannot be used, alone or in combination with each other, or in combination with any other factor, as the reason for stopping and searching any individual, including any vehicle which they are driving or are being carried in:
> (a) A person's physical appearance with regard, for example, to any of the 'relevant protected characteristics' set out in the Equality Act 2010, section 149, which are age, disability, gender reassignment, pregnancy and maternity, race, religion or belief, sex and sexual orientation (see paragraph 1.1 and Note 1A), or the fact that the person is known to have a previous conviction; and
> (b) Generalisations or stereotypical images that certain groups or categories of people are more likely to be involved in criminal activity.

6.130 Despite these provisions of the Code, it is now well-documented that stop and search powers have disproportionately been used in respect of ethnic minority groups and black people in particular. An Equalities and Human Rights Commission paper from March 2010 reported that, since 1995, per head of population in England and Wales, recorded stops and searches of Asian people remained at between 1.5 and 2.5 times the rate for white people, and for black people between four and eight times the rate for

191 'Reasonable grounds to suspect' are also described in relation to arrest powers above at para 6.51.

192 PACE Code A para 2.2.

193 PACE Code A at paras 2.6B; 3.8; 4.6.

white people.[194] More recent figures reveal the disparity growing even wider, with black people becoming 9.5 times more likely than white people to be stopped in 2018/19.[195] A report by parliament's Joint Committee on Human Rights from November 2020 reported that 85 per cent of black people are not confident that they would be treated the same as a white person by the police.[196] (For further discussion of discrimination see chapter 12 below and, in particular, paras 12.10–12.14 regarding stop and search.) In April 2022 the Independent Office of Police Complaints (IOPC) published a 'National stop and search learning report' which sought to identify lessons to be learnt from recent IOPC investigations.[197] A number of thematic concerns were identified relating, for example, to the disproportionate stop and search of ethnic minorities, particularly black males; reliance on a smell of cannabis as a frequently asserted justification for stop and search; poor communication from officers resulting in an escalation; the routine use of handcuffs irrespective of whether a use of such force is necessary;[198] the lack of any consistent approach nationally to gathering and scrutinising data relating to stop and search; and vehicle stops perceived as being used as a 'fishing' power. The report noted complainants having described the 'lasting effect it can have, making them feel victimised, humiliated, and violated', and 'when the individual being stopped is a young child who may subsequently experience repeated stops and searches throughout their lifetime, the cumulative impact can be significant'.[199] A number of recommendations were made, including the development of new guidelines on safeguarding ethnic minorities from being stopped and searched because of decisions impacted by stereotypes and racial bias, and the commissioning of research into the trauma caused by the use of stop and search.

6.131 The powers to stop, search and detain are subject to the procedural requirements of PACE. Thus, a uniformed officer must tell the person it is proposed to search the officer's name and police station, the object of the proposed search, the grounds and the suspect's right to a record of the search.[200] In *Bonner v DPP*[201] it was accepted that plain clothes officers who had stopped and attempted to search a person had failed to comply with PACE s2(2) and (3) by failing to produce documentary evidence that

194 Stop and think: A critical review of the use of stop and search powers in England and Wales, EHRC, March 2010, available at: www.equalityhumanrights.com/sites/default/files/ehrc_stop_and_search_report.pdf .

195 Police powers and procedures: England and Wales, year ending 31 March 2019, Home Office, available at: https://assets.publishing.service.gov.uk/government/uploads/system/uploads/attachment_data/file/841408/police-powers-procedures-mar19-hosb2519.pdf.

196 Black people, racism and human rights, Joint Committee on Human Rights, 4 November 2020, available at: https://committees.parliament.uk/publications/3376/documents/32359/default/.

197 See: www.policeconduct.gov.uk/national-stop-and-search-learning-report-april-2022.

198 A report by HMICFRS, *Disproportionate use of police powers – A spotlight on stop and search and the use of force*, observed that black people were eight times more likely to be 'compliant handcuffed' (see pages 4-5).

199 See Part 31 of the Report.

200 PACE s2.

201 [2004] EWHC 2415 (Admin), [2005] ACD 56.

they were constables and by failing to state their names, their stations, the object of the proposed search and the grounds for making it. It is likely that failure to comply with these rules makes the search and detention unlawful.[202] The officer must make a record of the search with prescribed information included such as the object of the search and the ground.[203] Failure to record this information does not make the search and detention unlawful.[204]

6.132 The power to detain a person to carry out the search is for such period as is reasonably practicable for the search to take place, either at the place where the person is stopped or nearby.[205] This could include taking a person to a nearby police station to carry out the search. There is a specific requirement in PACE that a person to be searched should not be made to remove more than outer clothing in public.[206] Any such search must comply with ECHR Article 8.

Powers to stop and require information under road traffic laws

6.133 There are other powers that police have to stop and question members of the public which are not covered by PACE Code A or the COP APP guidance. These include wide-ranging powers under Road Traffic Act (RTA) 1988 s163 for uniformed or traffic officers to stop any vehicle driving on a road. Failure to stop amounts to a criminal offence for which a person can then be arrested. RTA 1988 s164(1)(a) provides further powers to require any person driving a motor vehicle on a road to provide personal information such as a driving license and, in prescribed circumstances, their date of birth. The section 163 power cannot be exercised by a plain-clothed officer, but such an officer would have a common law power to stop a vehicle.[207]

6.134 Neither statute nor guidance currently provides any limits as to the use of these powers and there is no requirement that the officer must have any suspicion of criminal activity. Concerns have arisen in recent years as to the use of these powers in connection with racial profiling, with a number of high-profile cases of black people having been stopped without apparent cause. As above, concern was expressed by the IOPC that section 163 is perceived as being used as a 'fishing' power. In 2020 the black British international sprinter Bianca Williams brought a claim alleging that she and her partner had been pulled over by the police on the grounds of their race, leading eventually to an IOPC investigation finding a case to answer for gross misconduct against five police officers (ongoing at the time of writing).

6.135 Section 163 is currently excluded from the scope of APP guidance and PACE Code A and the safeguards therein, including the requirement to

202 *O (a juvenile) v DPP* [1999] COD 446, QBD; *Bonner v DPP* [2004] EWHC 2415 (Admin), [2005] ACD 56; *R v Bristol* [2007] EWCA Crim 3214.

203 PACE s3.

204 *Basher v DPP* [1993] COD 372, DC.

205 PACE s2(8).

206 PACE s2(9).

207 *R (Rutherford) v Independent Police Complaints Commission* [2010] EWHC 2881 (Admin).

record the race of those subjected to stops, which enables proper monitoring of racial disparities and proportionality. This is of particular concern in the light of the figures showing significant racial disparities in relation to the use of general stop and search powers. It would be highly desirable that enforceable guidance is now produced to regulate the use of these prima-facie wide-ranging powers.[208] The IOPC in its April 2022 'National stop and search learning report' recommended that a standardised process be introduced to record data on the protected characteristics of those subjected to powers such as section 163, observing that the absence of recording in relation to section 163 results in a 'lack of transparency' which 'means that there is no opportunity for public scrutiny and accountability'.[209]

6.136 In the meantime, potential challenges to the lawfulness of stops and demands for personal data under road traffic powers may, in practice, only be brought where it can be shown that stops were not in good faith, or where there is 'malpractice, oppression, caprice or opprobrious behaviour'.[210] Claims might also be contemplated, although likely difficult, under ECHR Article 5 or 8 on the basis that the police action was disproportionate in the circumstances. (But see *Miller v Bell*[211] in which the High Court of the Justiciary in Scotland found that 'random checks' represented a necessary and proportionate response by society in attempting to prevent the commission of crime. In that case, the court considered that the 'randomness' of the stops would mitigate against police action being seen as motivated by 'whim or caprice'.) Discriminatory use of these powers may also be subject to challenge under Article 14 if evidence is available to support such a claim. (For further discussion of discrimination claims see chapter 12).

6.137 It should be noted that RTA 1988 ss163 and 164(1)(a) are unlikely to be exercisable once a person has completed their journey and is no longer driving on a road. In *Boyce v Absalom*[212] the court considered equivalent powers under Road Traffic Act 1972 ss161 and 162 which police had purported to exercise by approaching a man whom they had followed driving to his house and approached as he walked from his car to his front door. The court found that a police officer's powers under sections 161 and 162 ceased when the motorists' driving ceases. There was in this case no cause to believe the defendant had been committing any offence under the Road Traffic Act 1972 while driving, and the police had no power to stop and ask for details after he had parked and exited his car, despite the fact he had been driving on a road moments beforehand.

208 See, for example, Release, StopWatch and International Drug Policy Unit (based at the London School of Economics and Political Science) report: Michael Shiner, Zoe Carre, Rebekah Delsol and Niamh Eastwood, The colour of injustice: 'Race', drugs and law enforcement in England and Wales, 2018.

209 Part 21. Similar recommendations had been made by the HMIC in its March 2015, 'Stop and search powers 2: are the police using them effectively and fairly?' available at: www.justiceinspectorates.gov.uk/hmicfrs/wp-content/uploads/stop-and-search-powers-2.pdf.

210 *R (Beckett) v Aylesbury Crown Court* [2004] EWHC 100 (Admin) at, para 4.

211 2004 SCCR 534.

212 [1974] RTR 248, DC.

Special stop and search powers: public order

6.138 There are also controversial powers to stop and search a person without any requirement for reasonable grounds to suspect that the person is in possession of the prohibited items referred to above. Criminal Justice and Public Order Act (CJPOA) 1994 s60 gives a police inspector or above the power to authorise the stop and search of persons and vehicles within a locality where they have a reasonable belief that serious violent incidents may take place within that locality and believe it is expedient to make the authorisation to prevent their occurrence. The power also exists where there is a reasonable belief that there are persons in the area carrying offensive weapons without good reason. The authorisation is valid for up to 24 hours. Any officer then has the power to stop any pedestrian and search them for dangerous instruments or offensive weapons within that locality. Such a search can take place whether or not there are reasonable grounds for suspecting the individual person of carrying such weapons or articles. The powers in section 60 were found by the Supreme Court to be compatible with Article 5 in *R (Roberts) v Commissioner of Police of the Metropolis*.[213]

Special stop and search powers: terrorism

6.139 The TA 2000 provides for the power to stop and question and detain a person at a port or border where they 'appear to be' a terrorist.[214] This power is exercisable by an 'examining officer'. An examining officer includes a police officer, but also includes immigration officers and designated customs officers.[215] There is no need for the examining officer to have reasonable grounds to suspect of any offence, but merely that the person appears to the officer to be a terrorist. This power was found by the Court of Appeal to be incompatible with Article 10 where it applied to journalistic material; Laws LJ finding that the constraints on the exercise of the stop power in TA 2000 Sch 7 did not afford effective protection of journalists' Article 10 rights, and noting that, if journalists and their sources could have no expectation of confidentiality, they might decide against providing information on sensitive matters of public interest: see *R (Miranda) v Secretary of State for the Home Department*.[216]

6.140 A detailed discussion of police powers and terrorism is beyond the scope of this book. For more on the investigative anti-terrorism powers of police and a discussion of substantive terrorism offences see *Blackstone's Criminal Practice*, chapter B10.

Use of force to effect a search

6.141 PACE s117 (which allows a police officer to use reasonable force in carrying out functions under the Act) extends to detaining a person to allow a search under the Act to be effected. In *Thomas James Parry v James*

213 [2015] UKSC 79, [2016] 1 WLR 210.
214 As defined in TA 2000 s40(1)(b).
215 TA 2000 Sch 7 para 1(1).
216 [2016] EWCA Civ 6, [2016] 1 WLR 1505.

Sharples (sued as the Chief Constable of Merseyside Constabulary)[217] police officers detained a man at gun-point without giving any reasons while his house was searched under the authority of a warrant, but the Court of Appeal said that the 'controlling or restraining', which amounted to a wrongful arrest, was otherwise justified under PACE s117, which allows a police officer to use reasonable force in carrying out their duties under the Act. In *DPP v Meaden*,[218] the court confirmed that restricting the occupants of a house to one room while a lawful search was underway was also justified under PACE s117. This reasoning was applied in *Connor v Chief Constable of Merseyside*,[219] in which the court confirmed that there was, in principle, a power to take reasonable and necessary steps to detain the occupants of a house in the course of the execution of a search warrant – a conclusion which the court held was consistent with the principles of common law relating to the use of reasonable force and the principles embodied in the Criminal Law Act 1967 s3 and PACE s117. Further, a power could be implied which was necessary to ensure the safe and effective exercise of an express power.

Information to be provided upon arrest or stop and search

6.142 Even if an arrest, or indeed a stop and search, can be justified by the police, a claim for false imprisonment may still succeed if it can be shown that legal requirements at the time of arrest, or stop and search, have not been complied with.

6.143 The requirement that most often arises in civil actions involving an arrest is the necessity for the police to inform a person upon arrest of the fact of arrest and the grounds for the arrest, either at the time of the arrest or as soon as practicable afterwards. If the police fail to do either of these things, the arrest is unlawful.[220] PACE s28 states:

> (3) . . . no arrest is lawful unless the person arrested is informed of the ground for the arrest at the time of, or as soon as is practicable after, the arrest.
> (4) Where a person is arrested by a constable, subsection (3) above applies regardless of whether the ground for the arrest is obvious.

6.144 The Court of Appeal[221] has held that the best statement of the principles involved are to be found in the decision of the ECtHR in *Fox v UK*.[222] The ECtHR was considering, not PACE s28(3), but ECHR Article 5(2), which provides as follows: 'Everyone who is arrested shall be informed promptly, in a language which he understands, of the reasons for his arrest and of any charge against him.' The ECtHR said:

> Paragraph 2 of Article 5 contains the elementary safeguard that any person arrested should know why he is being deprived of his liberty. This provision

217 [1991] 7 WLUK 235, CA.
218 [2003] EWHC 3005 (Admin), [2004] 1 WLR 945.
219 [2006] EWCA Civ 1549.
220 PACE s28(1) and (3). The provisions enact the common law requirements as set out in *Christie v Leachinsky* [1947] AC 573, HL.
221 *Taylor v Chief Constable of Thames Valley* [2004] EWCA Civ 858, [2004] 3 All ER 503.
222 (1991) 13 EHRR 157 at para 40, ECtHR.

> is an integral part of the scheme of protection afforded by Article 5: by virtue of paragraph (2) any person arrested must be told, in simple, non-technical language that he can understand, the essential legal and factual grounds for his arrest, so as to be able, if he sees fit, to apply to a court to challenge its lawfulness in accordance with paragraph (4) . . . Whilst this information must be conveyed 'promptly' (in French: 'dans le plus court délai'), it need not be related in its entirety by the arresting officer at the very moment of the arrest. Whether the content and promptness of the information conveyed were sufficient is to be assessed in each case according to its special features.

6.145 Thus, it may not be necessary to specify a particular crime or to use precise and technical language if, by using commonplace language, it is clear to the suspect what type of offence he was being arrested for, so that he has an opportunity to volunteer information which would avoid the arrest.[223] For example, in *Clarke v Chief Constable of North Wales*, Sedley LJ said although no constable ever admits to saying 'You're nicked for handling this gear' or 'I'm having you for twoc-ing this motor', 'either will do and, I have no doubt, frequently does'.[224]

6.146 Whether sufficient information has been provided will include a consideration of the particular suspect (for example, if the suspect is a minor).[225] If the police have specific information about the alleged offence (such as when and where it occurred) it may be unlawful for this information not to be relayed to the arrested person at the time of the arrest.[226] However, in *Clarke*[227] the majority found that the police did not have to specify which class of controlled drugs a person was being arrested for, (although see the judgment of Sedley LJ for doubts about this approach). The obligation applies irrespective of whether the reason for the arrest is obvious.[228] In practice, however, the police are given some latitude by the courts in deciding what they are able to say to an arrested person, and when it can be said. For example, in *Walker v Commissioner of Police of the Metropolis*,[229] the Court of Appeal held that the claimant, who was told by a police officer simply that he was being arrested for 'public order', must have been fully aware that he was being arrested for his conduct, which was regarded by the officer as being a public order offence. Further, the court held that the particular legal label of a particular offence did not matter so much if the arrested person knew that he was being

223 *Abbassy v Commissioner of Police of the Metropolis* [1990] 1 All ER 193, CA; and see *Christie v Leachinsky* [1947] AC 573 , HL; *Ghafar v Chief Constable of the West Midlands* [2000] 5 WLUK 312, CA; *Clarke v Chief Constable of North Wales* [2000] 4 WLUK 102 at para 36, CA.

224 [2000] 4 WLUK 102 at para 36, CA. See also *Adler v Crown Prosecution Service* [2013] EWHC 1968 (Admin); *Walker v Commissioner of Police of the Metropolis* [2004] EWCA Civ 897.

225 *Taylor v Chief Constable of Thames Valley* [2004] EWCA Civ 858, [2004] 3 All ER 503.

226 *Wilson v Chief Constable of Lancashire* [2001] 2 WLR 302, CA; but see *Taylor v Chief Constable of Thames Valley* [2004] EWCA Civ 858, [2004] 3 All ER 503 where the Court of Appeal overturned the trial judge's finding that reference to throwing stones should have been made when arresting a person for public order offences at a demonstration.

227 *Clarke*, above.

228 PACE s28(3) and (4).

229 [2014] EWCA Civ 897, [2015] 1 WLR 312.

arrested for the conduct that he had immediately carried out in the face of the arresting officer.

6.147 It is not necessary for the arresting officer to provide the reasons themself, so long as these are provided by another officer.[230] It is lawful for the police to arrest a person and not provide them with the necessary information if it is not reasonably practicable to do so (for instance, if the person is struggling violently). The police still have a duty to inform the person that they are under arrest and the ground for the arrest as soon as it becomes practicable.[231] The arrest and detention will be lawful up to the time when it would have been practicable to have informed the person.[232]

6.148 Where it would have been practicable to inform a person of the reason for their arrest, but this was not done until sometime later, the arrest and the detention will be unlawful until those reasons are given.[233] In practice, this will usually happen when a person is taken before the custody officer at the police station and the circumstances of their arrest are recounted by the arresting officer in the presence of the person arrested and recorded on the custody record.

Excessive force and false imprisonment

6.149 The use of undue force in effecting an arrest (whether under a warrant or not) or using other powers to detain someone, will not make the arrest unlawful if the arrest was otherwise justified in law,[234] although the use of excessive force may amount to assault (see chapter 7).

Police detention

False imprisonment and detention after arrest

6.150 A detention precipitated by a lawful arrest can become unlawful if the police do not comply with the detailed rules set out in PACE. The custody officer at a police station is not under a duty to determine whether the initial arrest was lawfully made[235] but, equally, an unlawful arrest cannot be cured later by the custody sergeant.[236]

6.151 The custody officer has a duty to determine whether there is sufficient evidence to justify a charge against a suspect as soon as practicable after the suspect has arrived at the station.[237] If there is not sufficient evidence at this point, then the further detention of the suspect should only be

230 *Dhesi v Chief Constable of the West Midlands* (2000) Times, May 9, CA.

231 PACE s28(1) and (3).

232 *DPP v Hawkins* [1988] 1 WLR 1166, [1988] 3 All ER 673, QBD.

233 *Lewis v Chief Constable of South Wales* [1991] 1 All ER 206, CA.

234 *Simpson v Chief Constable of South Yorkshire* (1991) Times, March 7, (1991) Independent, March 14, CA.

235 *Clarke v Chief Constable of North Wales* [2000] 4 WLUK 102, CA.

236 *Richardson v Chief Constable of the West Midlands* [2011] EWHC 773 (QB), [2011] 2 Cr App R 1 at para 57; and *Lord Hanningfield of Chelmsford v Chief Constable of Essex* [2013] EWHC 243 (QB).

237 PACE s37(1) and (10).

authorised if there are 'reasonable grounds for believing that the person's detention without charge is necessary to secure or preserve evidence relating to an offence for which the person is under arrest or to obtain evidence by questioning the person'.[238] In *Wilding v Chief Constable of Lancashire* the Court of Appeal held that the word 'necessary' had to be construed in the light of all the circumstances and:[239]

> . . . In asking whether further detention was lawful or unlawful the court should ask itself whether the decision of the custody sergeant was unreasonable in the sense that no custody officer, acquainted with the ordinary use of language and applying his common sense to the competing considerations before him, could reasonably have reached that decision.

6.152 This approach to determining the lawfulness of the custody officer's decision to authorise detention was endorsed by the Court of Appeal in *Al-Fayed v Commissioner of Police of the Metropolis*.[240] An example of a case where the test of whether a detention was 'necessary' was not met is *ST v Chief Constable of Nottinghamshire* where the court found that the failure of a custody officer to consider the age of the detained person (who was fourteen) and to take into account information which should have been made available made the decision on decision 'unreasonable' in the sense described in *Wilding*.[241]

6.153 If the detention is not necessary, then a failure by custody officers can make the 'authorised' detention unlawful. Sedley LJ provided a practical explanation of the test in relation to when it will be lawful to detain a person for questioning in *Clarke v Chief Constable of North Wales*:[242]

> To detain a person for questioning in the hope that something incriminating will come out is clearly unlawful. To detain someone until they have been questioned about an offence which they are suspected on reasonable grounds of having committed is, by contrast, lawful so long as the suspicion has not meanwhile been dispelled and the questioning is not unnecessarily delayed.

6.154 The police may be liable for false imprisonment if other provisions of PACE are not complied with during detention. For instance, PACE requires that the detention should be reviewed at periodic intervals,[243] and consideration given to whether continued detention is necessary using a similar test to that applied when the original detention is authorised.[244] If the review is not properly carried out, then the detention from the time of the review will become unlawful. This is the case even if the police can argue that if the review had been carried out then further detention would have been authorised,[245] although there may be implications for the

238 PACE s37(2) and (3).

239 [1995] CA, transcript 574, 22 May 1995 per Beldam LJ at p10.

240 [2004] EWCA Civ 1579 at paras 96–98.

241 [2022] EWHC 1280 (QB) at para 143.

242 *Clarke* at para 43.

243 See PACE s40(3)(a) – first review within six hours, second within nine hours and every nine hours thereafter.

244 PACE s40.

245 *Roberts v Chief Constable of Cheshire* [1999] 2 All ER 326, CA.

amount of damages recoverable in such circumstances.[246] In *Mouncher v Chief Constable of South Wales* the defendant admitted that a failure to adhere to the requirement for reviews resulted in periods of time that the claimants were detained unlawfully, but the judge accepted that had the custody reviews taken plan timeously the detention of each of the claimants would have been authorised and they were entitled to nominal damages only.[247]

6.155 If, during a person's detention, it becomes clear that the reasonable grounds for suspecting them of an offence which justified the initial arrest have disappeared, then the grounds for continued detention also disappear and a custody officer must release the person immediately.[248] For example, if the suspected package found on a person turns out not to be an illegal drug then a person must be released. However, if a number of people are arrested for the same offence then it may be reasonable to detain them all until all have been interviewed about the offence.[249] If there is unreasonable delay[250] in investigating the case for which a person has been arrested, for example delay in carrying out an interview, then this delay may lead to a claim for a period of false imprisonment.[251]

6.156 In addition, if the police fail to follow the provisions enabling them to detain someone in excess of the statutory time limits (generally 24 hours in the first instance),[252] then the detention becomes unlawful. There is a positive duty to release a detainee or bring them before a magistrate within 36 hours of the start of the detention for the purpose of seeking a warrant of further detention and an action for false imprisonment should succeed if this is not done.[253] Even after the granting of a warrant of extended detention, the regime of reviews must be continued.[254]

6.157 Unless a person is released from police custody after being charged, the detention will be unlawful unless one or more of the limited grounds exist for keeping a person at the police station.[255]

6.158 Where a person is detained after arrest for breach of the peace, continued detention at the police station of the person is justified (for the purpose of bringing the person before a magistrates' court to obtain a bindover) where there is a reasonably held apprehension that the breach of the peace will be renewed within a short time but otherwise a person should be released.[256] Arrest and detention to bring before a court for a

246 See *R (Lumba) v Secretary of State for the Home Department* [2011] UKSC 12.

247 [2016] EWHC 1367 (QB) at paras 888–889.

248 PACE s34(2). See *Youssef v Home Office* [2004] EWHC 1884 (QB) for an example in the immigration detention context.

249 *Clarke*, above.

250 *Wilding v Chief Constable of Lancashire* [1995] CA transcript 574, 22 May 1995.

251 *Taylor v Chief Constable of Thames Valley* [2004] EWCA Civ 858, [2004] 1 WLR 3155 where the Court of Appeal referred to the 'relevant principles' relating to expedition set out in PACE Code C paras 1.1 and 1.1A.

252 PACE ss34 and 41–43.

253 See *R v Slough Justices ex p Stirling* [1987] Crim LR 576, DC; and PACE s43.

254 PACE s36; and see *Vince v Chief Constable of Dorset* [1993] 1 WLR 415, CA.

255 PACE s38; and see *Paul v Chief Constable of Humberside* [2004] EWCA Civ 308 at paras 53–59 for discussion of this area by Court of Appeal.

256 *Chief Constable of Cleveland v McGrogan* [2002] EWCA Civ 86, [2002] 1 FLR 707.

breach of the peace is a common law power and PACE does not apply.[257] However, the Court of Appeal has commented that it is 'good practice' for the police to treat any person detained for breach of the peace as if PACE applied to the detention, as that there is a need to regularly review the detention to ascertain if it remains justified.[258]

Detention for 'own protection'

6.159 PACE allows for the detention of a person at a police station for their own protection. PACE s38(1)(a)(vi) concerns arrested adults; and s38(1)(b)(ii), arrested juveniles. These allow for the detention of a person if the custody officer has 'reasonable grounds for believing that the detention of the person arrested is necessary for his own protection' (adults) or 'reasonable grounds for believing that he ought to be detained in his own interests' (juveniles).

6.160 A question arises as to whether this power is compatible with ECHR Article 5(1). Article 5 contains no equivalent lawful justification for the deprivation of liberty. In *Archer v Commissioner of Police of the Metropolis*[259] this question of compatibility arose in the context of juveniles. In that case, a 15-year-old had been detained in police custody, having been arrested for offences of violent disorder and possession of an offensive weapon. He was detained overnight, with bail being refused predominantly as there was a fear of reprisals from 'gang' members. Chamberlain J at first instance held that the post-charge power to detain a juvenile 'in his own interests' was compatible with Article 5. The matter was appealed to the Court of Appeal who upheld the decision.[260]

6.161 The Court of Appeal noted that a person could not be lawfully detained for their 'own protection' if none of the justifications in Article 5(1) apply. However, a person being detained on suspicion of having committed an offence with a view to being brought promptly before a court, but whose detention was regarded as necessary for his own protection, was still being detained 'for the purposes of bringing him before the competent legal authority' in accordance with Article 5(1)(c). That was so even if detention would have been unnecessary without the need to protect the person. The court found that there was nothing arbitrary about continuing to detain a suspect where they were being lawfully detained in order to be brought before a court, if releasing them put their life at serious risk.[261] It followed that PACE s38(1)(a)(vi) was not incompatible with Article 5. In reaching its judgment, the court noted the additional protections that applied to juveniles within the criminal justice system and the fact that children in police custody are particularly vulnerable. The best interests of the child had to be at the heart of any decision-making involving children. PACE s38 and Children Act 1989 s21 made it clear that there are very limited

257 *Williamson v Chief Constable of the West Midlands* [2003] EWCA Civ 337, [2004] 1 WLR 14.

258 *McGrogan* at para 44; and *Williamson* at para 23.

259 [2020] EWHC 1567 (QB), [2020] 1 WLR 3164.

260 [2021] EWCA Civ 1662.

261 *IA v France* [1998] HRCD 901, [1998] 9 WLUK 207, ECtHR; and *Buzadji v Moldova* [2016] 7 WLUK 76, 42 BHRC 398, ECtHR applied.

circumstances in which detention of children in police stations can be justified. Detention of juveniles for their own protection should be the exception, and not the rule.

Deterioration in conditions of detention

6.162 When a prisoner has been lawfully detained or committed to custody, a deterioration in the conditions of detention will not give rise to a claim for false imprisonment, but may give rise to a claim under the HRA 1998 for breach of Article 3 or 8, or possibly in the tort of negligence if the person suffers personal injury.

6.163 In two Court of Appeal cases the court had first, refused to strike out an action for false imprisonment by a convicted prisoner held overnight in a strip cell[262] and, second, suggested that an action for false imprisonment might be possible if the conditions of detention became unbearable.[263] On appeal to the House of Lords it was ruled that intolerable conditions of detention could not lead to a claim for false imprisonment.[264] In *Hague* Lord Bridge said:[265]

> I sympathise entirely with the view that the person lawfully held in custody who is subjected to intolerable conditions ought not to be left without a remedy against his custodian, but the proposition that the conditions of detention may render the detention itself unlawful raises formidable difficulties.

6.164 Lord Bridge went on to say that the logical solution was that if the conditions of an otherwise lawful detention are intolerable, the law ought to provide a remedy directly related to those conditions without characterising the fact of the detention itself as unlawful. A person detained or in custody is owed a duty of care in negligence and if kept in in conditions which cause physical pain or a degree of discomfort which can properly be described as intolerable, then this would be treated as a breach of the duty of care and damages owed.[266]

6.165 It is the case therefore that where conditions of detention are intolerable the remedy would be for a claim in negligence, or, under the HRA 1998. Conditions that are inhuman or degrading or unsafe may lead to an action under the HRA 1998 for breach of ECHR Article 3 and/or 8.[267] Articles 3 and 8 are considered in detail in chapter 7.

6.166 Additionally, if a person is held in conditions which breach *PACE Code C: Code of Practice for the detention, treatment and questioning of persons by police officers* (paras 8.1–8.88) then this may sound in increased compensatory or even exemplary damages (see chapter 17).

262 *Weldon v Home Office* [1990] 3 All ER 672, CA.

263 *R v Deputy Governor of Parkhurst Prison and others ex p Hague* [1992] 1 AC 58, HL.

264 *R v Deputy Governor of Parkhurst Prison and others ex p Hague* [1992] 1 AC 58, HL.

265 *R v Deputy Governor of Parkhurst Prison and others ex p Hague; Weldon v Home Office* [1992] 1 AC 58 at p165, HL.

266 *Hague* at pp165–166.

267 *Munjaz v Mersey Care NHS Trust* [2003] EWCA Civ 1036, [2004] QB 395; and see *R (BP) v Secretary of State for the Home Department* [2003] EWHC 1963 (Admin).

Detention after court proceedings

Overview

6.167 As a general principle, if someone is held after a court has ordered their confinement, there is no claim against the police for false imprisonment. Thus, any case against the police for false imprisonment will come to an end once the magistrates have decided to remand a person in custody. However, if there is a claim for malicious prosecution (see chapter 8) then damages can be claimed for any period spent in custody on remand.

6.168 Although a claim for false imprisonment against the police is generally precluded after a decision by the court to remand a defendant in custody, the police may still be liable under ECHR Article 5(3) if failings in an investigation and/or updating the court with relevant information causes a person to spend more time in prison that they should have done. See the discussion above, in particular regarding the case of *Zenati v Commissioner of Police of the Metropolis*,[268] at para 6.22.

Delays in effecting release

6.169 It is often the case that a prisoner may experience significant delays in being restored to freedom following a successful application for bail, an acquittal or receiving a sentence which amounts to an order for immediate release (for example, a suspended sentence, or a sentence of imprisonment amounting to time already served on remand). These delays appear, in many instances, to be the result of administrative processes put in place by security companies who are contracted by the Ministry of Justice to manage the transfer of prisoners between prisons and courts. Many have adopted procedures which involve contacting prison services after the court has ordered release to gain authorisation for the prisoner to be processed and released. In many cases, this process can take many hours, and can lead to prisoners being kept in custody overnight, or even longer.

6.170 The courts have yet to decide a case setting out the limits as to how long a prisoner can be held pursuant to administrative processes once the legal basis for their detention has abated, or been removed. It can reasonably be presumed that this will ultimately be a fact-specific enquiry, and subject to a proportionality or 'reasonableness' assessment. However, given the importance of the rights at stake, it is submitted that it is unlikely ever to be reasonable for detention to persist overnight where a court has ordered release.

'Kettling'

6.171 One of the most controversial forms of policing is the use of containment, or 'kettling'. This police tactic involves physically confining protestors within a relatively small space by deploying a police cordon. The technique can give rise to a false imprisonment and is considered in the chapter concerning protest at paras 10.70–10.78.

268 [2015] EWCA Civ 80, [2015] QB 758.

Negligence and imprisonment

6.172 As discussed in more detail in chapter 7, the Supreme Court has confirmed in *Robinson v Chief Constable of West Yorkshire*[269] that the police do not enjoy any immunity from suit in negligence in the conduct of their functions of the investigation and suppression of crime. Further, on a number of occasions it has been found that imprisonment is a type of damage which may found the tort of negligence, that is, that there can be a duty not to carelessly cause the claimant to suffer loss of liberty.[270] Thus, it may be that there are instances in which the tort of negligence affords a remedy to a claimant in respect of a period of imprisonment.

6.173 The sorts of circumstances in which a claim in negligence could be considered would be where an arrest results from an erroneous and carelessly placed PNC entry, or an imprisonment by a court results from the careless conduct of a 'field test' for drugs conducted by a police officer, or a detention is caused or prolonged by a failure to convey exculpatory information which would result in a court releasing the claimant.

6.174 The circumstances which will give rise to a duty of care not to carelessly inflict an imprisonment are not clear. In the immigration context, it has been held that the discharge of statutory duties in administrating immigration detention does not give rise to a duty of care. Thus, in *W v The Home Office*[271] the Court of Appeal rejected a claim by an asylum seeker that their detention was prolonged by carelessness in administration of the asylum application, in part on the basis that to impose a duty would create a potential conflict between the immigration officer's duty to the public, and due to the applicant. Similarly, in *Mohammed v Home Office*[272] a claim on similar facts was rejected, with the court finding that a failure to discharge a statutory power did not in itself give rise to a sufficient relationship of proximity between the immigration officer and the claimant. However, in *McCreaner v Ministry of Justice*[273] a prisoner was, further to administrative error, released about eight weeks after he became eligible for release on home detention curfew. Although his imprisonment remained authorised by a court order and, accordingly, lawful, a claim in negligence succeeded. Cranston J considered that the Ministry of Justice (MoJ) had assumed a responsibility on the facts to complete the administrative process allowing release, or alternatively that there was a sufficient relationship of proximity between the MoJ and the claimant so as to give rise to a duty of care.

6.175 There are examples of successful claims in the police context. In *Clarke v Crew and another*[274] the Court of Appeal allowed a claim in respect of a police officer negligently endorsing the warrant under which the prison authority imprisoned him which resulted in a miscalculation of his release

269 [2018] UKSC 4, [2018] AC 736.

270 See cases such as *W v Home Office* [1997] Imm AR 302, CA, citing *Everett v Griffiths (No 1)* [1920] 3 KB 163, CA.

271 [1997] Imm AR 302, CA.

272 [2011] EWCA Civ 351, [2011] 1 WLR 2862.

273 [2014] EWHC 569 (QB), [2015] 1 WLR 354.

274 [1999] 5 WLUK 460, [1999] Prison LR 59, CA.

date. It was only the prisoner and the police that had the information as to release date, and the prison authority was bound to rely upon the information provided by the police. In *Hough v Chief Constable of Staffordshire* Simon Brown LJ contemplated, obiter, that a negligence claim may lie against an officer who makes an errant entry on the Police National Computer resulting in an arrest.[275]

6.176 In *Welsh v Chief Constable of Merseyside and another*[276] the claimant claimed that the Chief Constable of Merseyside Police and the CPS had negligently failed to ensure that a magistrates' court, from which he was on bail for two offences of theft, was informed that the offences had subsequently been taken into consideration at the Crown Court. As a result of that failure, the magistrates' court issued a warrant for the claimant's arrest, and he was thereafter detained. The CPS (but not the Chief Constable) sought unsuccessfully to strike out the claim on the basis that no duty of care in negligence was owed. It was held that a duty was owed by the CPS in that particular case as the CPS had assumed a responsibility to the claimant by indicating to the police that it would note the file to the effect that offences would be taken into consideration in the Crown Court. The detention of the claimant could not be a false imprisonment, but he nevertheless had a remedy in negligence. Article 5 would likely also afford a remedy.[277]

6.177 It will not be the case that any investigative error resulting in a foreseeable imprisonment will give rise to a duty of care. First, the fact of a statutory duty or power in the discharge of police functions is not sufficient in itself to give rise to a duty. There must be particular features of the circumstances which give rise to sufficient proximity between the police officer and the claimant, or an assumption of responsibility. Second, the courts will be anxious not to impose duties of care which create a conflict of interest with police duties to the public (see the discussion of conflict of interest in the context of duty of care at paras 7.75–7.78). For example, a duty to put the correct rather than incorrect date on a warrant does not create any conflict with the officer's duty to the public, but that may not be the case with many other actions taken by the police.

Remedies

6.178 In theory there are three legal remedies for false imprisonment:

- self-help, ie escape;
- habeas corpus and judicial review;
- damages.

This chapter does not deal with damages available and quantum – these are dealt with in chapter 17 on damages.

275 [2001] EWCA Civ 39 at paras 18–19.

276 [1993] 1 All ER 692, QBD.

277 See the case of *Zenati v Commissioner of Police of the Metropolis* [2015] EWCA Civ 80, [2015] QB 758, considered earlier in the chapter.

Escape

6.179 In practice the dangers, both physical and legal, of attempting to escape from unlawful custody mean it should not be regarded as a 'remedy' at all. Its practical importance is rather as a defence if charged with a criminal offence of, say, assault with intent to resist arrest.[278]

Habeas corpus and judicial review

6.180 Habeas corpus can be used to bring a false imprisonment to an end, but is suitable only where there is no legal basis for the detention.[279] It is often used in conjunction with an application for judicial review challenging the lawfulness on public law grounds of a detention. Public funding can be obtained to apply to the High Court. There are procedural rules for applying for a writ of habeas corpus in Part 87 of the Civil Procedure Rules (CPR). Provisions relating to urgent applications to the Administrative Court are set out in Practice Direction (PD) 54B to CPR Part 54.

6.181 In some cases – where, for example, a detention at a police station is clearly unlawful – a telephone application to a judge for an injunction to order the release of the person may be possible. Such applications are unusual given the amount of time a person will usually be detained at a police station. The usual remedy is to sue for damages after the event.

6.182 The types of cases where it may be possible to bring a claim by way of judicial review, rather than a civil claim, would include those where the necessity of arrest is being challenged, as was the case in *R (TL) v Chief Constable of Surrey*,[280] or the lawfulness of a curfew or bail conditions, for example *R (Gedi) v Secretary of State for the Home Department*;[281] and *R (Jalloh) v Secretary of State for the Home Department*.[282]

6.183 Where there are complex and disputed facts it is unlikely that a challenge by way of judicial review will be appropriate.[283] There is of course also the much shorter time limit for bringing a claim by way of judicial review (within three months), and remedies are discretionary.

278 Offences Against the Person Act 1861 s38, as amended.
279 *R v Holmes ex p Sherman* [1981] 2 All ER 612, DC.
280 [2017] EWCA 129 (Admin).
281 [2016] EWCA Civ 409, [2016] 4 WLR 93.
282 [2018] EWCA Civ 1260, [2019] 1 WLR 394.
283 *Sher v Chief Constable of Greater Manchester* [2010] EWHC 1859 (Admin), [2011] 2 All ER 364.

CHAPTER 7

Personal injury, trespass to the person and failure to protect from harm

continued

Introduction

7.1 This chapter examines the civil claims that can arise when actions of a police officer directly cause death or personal injury or otherwise trespass to the person, as well as claims arising out of failures by the police to protect a person from harm caused by a third party. It considers:

- the causes of action of assault and battery; trespass ab initio; negligence; and intentionally causing psychiatric harm and harassment;
- claims for violation of Human Rights Act (HRA) 1998 Sch 1 Articles 2, 3, 4 and 8; and
- at the conclusion of the chapter, some consideration is given to the mechanisms for bringing a claim in respect of a death pursuant to the Fatal Accidents Act (FAA) 1976 and the Law Reform (Miscellaneous Provisions) Act (LRMPA) 1934.

7.2 Incidents of death and personal injury may also give rise to distinct claims of discrimination, for which see chapter 12.

Assault and battery

7.3 Assault and battery are two of the torts which constitute trespass to the person. The torts are sometimes referred to generically as 'assault', but they are different: an assault may be committed where the claimant is caused to fear the infliction of unlawful physical contact but no such contact in fact takes place – the actual infliction of unlawful physical contact is a battery.

Acts amounting to an assault or battery

Assault

7.4 An assault is an act causing the claimant to apprehend an imminent application of force. Something said may be capable of causing an apprehension of immediate personal violence and, accordingly, words alone may amount to an assault.[1] Although an assault may be committed without any physical contact in fact taking place, a mere threat of violence is not enough to constitute an assault unless there is also the means to carry out the threat. A person who with fists raised runs at another and would have hit that other if they had not been stopped, will probably have committed an assault.[2] However, persons shouting abuse at others on a bus whom they cannot reach do not commit an assault if they have no means of carrying out their threats.[3]

7.5 There is no need to show that the officer actually intended to use force, provided the claimant had a reasonable basis for believing that force was

1 See *R v Ireland* [1998] AC 147 at 162A, HL.

2 *Stephens v Myers* (1830) 4 C&P 349.

3 *Thomas v National Union of Mineworkers (South Wales Area)* [1986] Ch 20, ChD; compare *R v Ireland and Burstow* [1998] AC 147, HL.

to be used. Thus, in *Chief Constable of Thames Valley v Hepburn*[4] the claimant was assaulted where an officer who had no lawful basis to stop him leaving premises held out his baton as he tried to exit.

Battery

Overview

7.6 Although battery may often be associated with direct physical attacks causing personal injury, the tort may be perpetrated with minor touching. The fundamental principle of the tort is that a person's body is inviolate and even the slightest touching of another person may amount to a battery. The effect is 'that everyone is protected not only against physical injury but against any form of physical molestation'.[5] It is not necessary that the claimant suffers pain or physical injury as a result and anxiety and distress alone may be sufficient to found the tort and claim a remedy. Thus cutting hair,[6] taking fingerprints or a mouth swab,[7] and taking hold of the claimant's arm by a police officer in order to administer a caution[8] can all amount to battery.

7.7 That is not to say that any and all touching amounts to a battery. There may be limited circumstances in which the slightest touching of the sort that may reasonably occur between citizens in the course of ordinary life will not amount to a battery. In *Donnelly v Jackman*[9] an officer who had tapped a person twice on the shoulder to question him about an offence had not exceeded the bounds of acceptable conduct and had not therefore committed a battery. In *Collins v Wilcock*[10] the court explained that 'nobody can complain of the jostling which is inevitable from his presence in, for example a supermarket, an underground station or a busy street'.[11] Similarly, touching a person for the purpose of engaging his attention has 'long held to be acceptable' provided, of course, that there is 'no greater degree of physical contact than is reasonably necessary in the circumstances for that purpose.'[12]

7.8 A battery may equally be committed by use of something under the perpetrator's direct control, such as an officer's use of a baton, CS spray, or a police dog.

Consent

7.9 No battery will have been committed where the claimant has given consent. As a general principle of law, if a person consents to something that would otherwise be an infringement of rights, that person cannot later complain about it. Thus, if the police search someone in circumstances that there would otherwise be no lawful basis, but with that person's permission,

4 [2002] EWCA Civ 1841.
5 *Collins v Wilcock* [1984] 1 WLR 1172 at 1177, DC.
6 *Forde v Skinner* (1830) 4 C&P 239.
7 *Dumbell v Roberts* [1944] 1 All ER 326, CA; and *Commissioner of Police of the Metropolis v MR* [2019] EWHC 888 (QB).
8 *Collins v Wilcock* [1984] 1 WLR 1172, DC.
9 [1970] 1 WLR 562, DC.
10 [1984] 1 WLR 1172, DC.
11 [1984] 1 WLR 1172 at 1179, DC.
12 [1984] 1 WLR 1172 at 1177, DC.

then there is no battery. In *Freeman v Home Office (No 2)* the absence of consent was thought to be a matter to be proven by the claimant, although there is an argument that it is more properly considered a defence to be proven by the defendant.[13]

7.10 Difficulty may arise where a request is made by an officer, such as a request for a search, and the person feels pressure to agree, fearing consequences such as arrest. Has consent been given such that there has been no trespass? There is a general principle that:

> . . . a man cannot be said to be truly 'willing' unless he is in a position to choose freely, and freedom of choice predicates, not only full knowledge of the circumstances on which the exercise of choice is conditional, so that he may be able to choose wisely, but the absence of any feeling of constraint so that nothing shall interfere with the freedom of his will.[14]

7.11 Accordingly, if a person is arrested and asked to sign a form to consent to the taking of intimate body samples under threat of being kept at the station until the signature is given then the 'consent' would be invalid because it was obtained under duress and the person could sue for battery. However, while it is clear that an abuse of authority may negate apparent consent,[15] the mere fact that consent was obtained by a show of authority appears to be insufficient. In *Wainwright v Home Office*[16] the Court of Appeal held that consent to strip searching an inmate's visitors, obtained by prison officers indicating that the visit would not go ahead unless the searches were undertaken, was not vitiated by duress.

7.12 In practical terms, whether or not there has been consent in law will often turn on whether any express or implied 'threat' – or provision of information as to consequences of not consenting – is reasonable and in good faith. A person under arrest who is invited to comply with a request to enter a police vehicle else be forced to do so has simply been informed of the consequences of declining to consent and has not been placed under any inappropriate duress. However, if in the same scenario the officer knew there was no lawful power to use force then the warning of force would be inappropriate and would vitiate the consent given.

7.13 If, in the event, the force used extends beyond that to which the claimant gave consent then there will, of course, be a battery. In *Wainwright v Home Office* the defendants could not rely upon the claimants' consent because the searches had been conducted in breach of procedures, whereas the consent had been to searches carried out in the prescribed manner.

Intent

7.14 The physical contact must be intentional or reckless for it to amount to a battery. The conduct is intentional if the claimant shows that the officer deliberately used some physical force. There does not need to be any intention to cause the claimant injury or damage through the physical contact.

13 See *Freeman v Home Office (No 2)* [1984] QB 524, CA; and see the discussion in *Clerk & Lindsell on Torts*, Sweet & Maxwell, 23rd edn, para 14-93.

14 *Bowater v Rowley Regis Corp* [1944] KB 476 at 479, CA.

15 *Freeman v Home Office (No 2)* [1984] QB 524, CA.

16 [2001] EWCA Civ 2081, [2003] 3 All ER 943. The case went to the House of Lords on other grounds: [2003] UKHL 53, [2003] 4 All ER 969.

Nor does the extent of the claimant's injuries have to be foreseen.[17] Thus, the police may be liable for unintended, serious injuries resulting from a relatively minor but nonetheless deliberate act of force.[18]

7.15 A battery will also be established if the force is applied recklessly in the sense that the officer foresaw the risk of harm to the claimant but nonetheless proceeded to act and caused such harm.[19] If the act was neither intentional nor reckless there cannot be a battery, but there may still be a claim in negligence. The distinction is illustrated by the cases involving injuries caused to claimants by police dogs. If the dog is instructed by their police handler to attack the claimant and does so, the officer has committed a battery (subject to the defences discussed below). If the dog bites the claimant without the handler intending this or being reckless as to whether the dog would do so, the only available claim would be in negligence.[20]

7.16 The necessary intention in the application of force need not be specific to the claimant. If a police officer intends to commit a battery against one person but mistakenly strikes a second, then a battery has been committed against the second person. In the Northern Ireland case of *Livingston v Ministry of Defence*[21] a soldier shot a rioter while in fact aiming for another. It was no defence to battery that he shot the 'wrong' person in those circumstances.[22]

Defences

7.17 Once the claimant establishes a prima facie assault or battery the burden then shifts to the defendant to establish a defence. The defendant will generally have to prove that the act was committed in exercise of a lawful power, and that the extent of the force used was reasonable. Alternatively, a defence may be available under the Criminal Justice Act (CJA) 2003 s329 where the claimant has been convicted of an indictable offence arising out of the same incident.

Defences: in exercise of a lawful power

7.18 Generally, whether there is a defence to a claim for trespass will turn, firstly, on whether the prima facie assault or battery was committed by the officer in exercise of a lawful power. If not, then a trespass will have been committed irrespective of the extent of the force used. Second, even if there did exist some lawful power, the extent of the force used must nevertheless be reasonable.

7.19 The police have no general authority by virtue of their role as police officers to use force. Save where there exists some particular authority for

17 In contrast to the position in a negligence claim: see para 7.79.

18 See, eg, *Wilson v Commissioner of Police of the Metropolis* [2002] EWCA Civ 434 where the claimant sustained serious head injuries, for which the defendant was liable, as a result of an officer deliberately barging him to the ground.

19 *Haystead v Chief Constable of Derbyshire* [2000] 3 All ER 890, DC.

20 See *Pollard v Chief Constable of West Yorkshire* [1999] PIQR P219, CA; *Coles v Chief Constable of South Yorkshire* [1998] 10 WLUK 143.

21 [1984] 15 NIJB, CA.

22 *Livingston v Ministry of Defence* [1984] 15 NIJB, CA. See, in this jurisdiction, *Bici v Ministry of Defence* [2004] EWHC 786 (QB).

the use of force, a police officer accordingly has no greater right to use force than any member of the public. They may, of course, raise the same defences that members of the public can raise, such as self-defence. As addressed below, special provisions apply by virtue of CJA 2003 s329 where the claimant has been convicted of an indictable offence in the same incident arising out of which the claim for damages is made.

7.20 Pursuant to Criminal Law Act (CLA) 1967 s3, any member of the public, or a police officer, has a power to use such force as is reasonable 'in the prevention of crime, or in effecting or assisting in the lawful arrest of offenders or suspected offenders or of persons unlawfully at large'. Police have various powers of arrest and it will be for the police to identify the power that is prayed in aid as a defence. Significantly, the power provides a defence only in the case of 'lawful arrest'. Modest or otherwise reasonable force used in effecting an unlawful arrest will give rise to a trespass. Careful consideration is therefore required as the lawfulness or otherwise of the arrest, as to which see chapter 6 on deprivation of liberty.

7.21 Pursuant to Police and Criminal Evidence Act 1984 (PACE) s117 the police may use 'reasonable force', where necessary, in exercise of the powers arising under the Act. That includes not only the power of arrest pursuant to PACE s24, but also powers to stop and search, powers of entry and powers relating to persons detained in police custody. Again, PACE s117 will provide a defence to a claim only where the power under PACE is being exercised lawfully. Thus, in *Browne v Commissioner of Police of the Metropolis* the officer conducting a search pursuant to the Misuse of Drugs Act 1971 had failed, in breach of PACE s2, to provide the claimant with certain information before enforcing the carrying out of the search by force.[23] The force used was therefore a trespass.

7.22 An officer may rely upon powers arising under the Mental Health Act 1983 including, for example, the power pursuant to section 136 to remove a mental disordered person to a place of safety. It should be noted that, pursuant to section 139, no claim can be brought in respect of any act purporting to be done in pursuant to that Act save with permission of the court, sought and obtained in advance of issuing the claim.

Defences: reasonable force

Overview

7.23 Irrespective of whether the officer is purporting to act in self-defence, or pursuant to PACE s117 and/or CLA 1967 s3, the officer may only use force that is *reasonable* in all the circumstances.

7.24 The reasonableness or otherwise of the force used is fact-sensitive. Resolving the question of whether the force was reasonable may be assisted by the expert evidence of an independent expert on the use of force, although not necessarily so. Generally, the reasonableness of force used can be determined by a judge without expert evidence. Certainly, where the dispute as to the reasonableness of the force turns solely upon the resolution of a disputed fact(s), an expert will be unnecessary. It also may be assisted by reference to the relevant training manuals and the

23 [2014] EWHC 3999 (QB) at para 43.

national and internal guidelines as to the use of force and techniques of restraint. Such documents should generally be requested as part of pre-action disclosure. Where the force used occurred in the custodial context, it may be that the reasonableness or otherwise of the force used is informed by the PACE Codes of Practice.[24] The Codes are issued under PACE s67 and the Act specifically states that a failure on the part of a police to comply with a provision of the Code will not itself render the officer liable to civil proceedings. However, the Codes may inform whether or not any force used was reasonable.

7.25 Assessing reasonable force requires consideration of the following factors (discussed below):

- the minimum force required;
- mistaken belief in relevant facts;
- officer's knowledge of relevant matters;
- decision-making in stressful circumstances;
- reasonableness of the force and not the injury;
- the vulnerability of the claimant.

The minimum force required

7.26 The question of reasonableness of the force used will generally turn on whether it was the minimum required in all the circumstances and whether a lesser alternative was available. For example, in *Michael Gilchrist (by his mother and litigation friend, Novlyn Graham) v Chief Constable of Greater Manchester* it was unlawful to use a taser on a man who was being restrained on the ground by a number of officers as 'although he was struggling, there were sufficient officers at the scene' to restrain the claimant and the taser would have inflicted 'unnecessary pain.'[25] In *Minio-Paluello v Commissioner of Police of the Metropolis* it was unreasonable to lift a protester from the ground in a manner which caused a fracture to her arm.[26] It was unnecessary in the circumstances to use a technique which was not taught to officers and involved an obvious risk of injury. A defence is unlikely to be available where the claimant would have performed the relevant act voluntarily, making the use of force superfluous.[27]

Mistaken belief in relevant facts

7.27 Where the use of force is sought to be justified by reference to belief in relevant facts (such as, for example, the claimant being in possession of a gun) there must be an objectively reasonable basis for that belief. There will be no defence to the tort where an officer has an honest belief in a relevant fact for which there is no objectively reasonable basis. That is in contrast to the position of self-defence in criminal law and follows from the view of the House of Lords in *Ashley v Chief Constable of Sussex*[28] that to afford a defence in a civil claim to a defendant who not only mistakenly but unreasonably believed

24 The PACE Codes of Practice are available at: www.gov.uk/guidance/police-and-criminal-evidence-act-1984-pace-codes-of-practice.

25 [2019] EWHC 1233 (QB) at para 110.

26 [2011] EWHC 3411 (QB) at paras 68–69.

27 *Swales v Cox* [1981] 1 All ER 1115, QBD.

28 [2008] UKHL 25, [2008] 1 AC 962.

that he was about to be attacked would have insufficient regard to the right in principle of every person not to be subjected to physical harm by the intentional acts of another person. However, provided that the officer's belief had an objectively reasonable basis, whether or not it is in fact mistaken is irrelevant. In *Michael Alleyne v Commissioner of Police of the Metropolis* there was no assault where the officer had mistakenly but reasonably believed that the claimant was being non-compliant, although the claimant succeeded in a claim in negligence.[29]

7.28 The exception is that, pursuant to CJA 2003 s329, an honest but unreasonable belief may provide a defence where the claimant has been convicted of an offence arising out of the same incident (see below, paras 7.36–7.40).

Officer's knowledge of relevant matters

7.29 Reasonableness is determined only by what is known to the officer. The officer cannot be affixed with knowledge that the officer did not and could not reasonably be expected to have at the time. It might, however, be reasonable for the officer to have sought relevant information prior to using force, particularly if there was no necessity for the immediate use of force. For example, in *ZH v Commissioner of Police of the Metropolis* the officers confronted with an autistic child in difficulty at a swimming pool had 'ample opportunity . . . to have sought the advice and assistance of the carers as to the best way of safely removing' the child.[30]

7.30 Equally, errors made by persons other than the officer who uses force, such as those involved in the planning or briefing of an operation, are unlikely to be relevant. In *Farrell v Secretary of State for Defence*[31] the House of Lords considered the materially identical provision in Northern Ireland to CLA 1967 s3 and explained that it provides a defence at criminal law, and against being sued, to the person who uses force and 'defects . . . in the planning of the operation would not deprive them of that defence and render the force used unreasonable'.[32] In *Ashley v Chief Constable of Sussex*[33] a broader approach was considered, albeit obiter and no reference was made to *Farrell*. An attempt to follow the broader approach considered in *Ashley* was made in *NTC and others v Commissioner of Police of the Metropolis*[34] but the claimants were unable to distinguish *Farrell*.[35] Where an earlier mistake is made by an officer involved in the planning of the operation, a claim may arise alternatively in negligence against that officer, rather than a claim of assault against the officer who ultimately uses force. As was expressed in *Farrell*, 'Section 3(1) would provide no defence . . . in respect of a claim for negligence in the planning of the operation'.[36]

29 [2012] EWHC 3955 (QB) at paras 136–137.

30 [2012] EWHC 604 (QB) at para 90. The Commissioner appealed, unsuccessfully: [2013] EWCA Civ 69, [2013] 1 WLR 3021.

31 [1980] 1 WLR 172, HL.

32 At 178H–179B.

33 [2008] UKHL 25, [2008] 1 AC 962.

34 [2015] EWHC 1432 (QB).

35 In *NTC* permission to appeal was sought but refused: [2016] EWCA Civ 1396.

36 [1980] 1 WLR 172 at 179B, HL.

Decision-making in stressful circumstances

7.31 The courts will take into account the difficulty in making quick decisions in stressful circumstances. It is not always realistic to apply a consideration of all the theoretical options to a stressful situation and the courts have deprecated 'using jeweller's scales to measure reasonable force'.[37] As observed in *McCarthy v Chief Constable of Merseyside,* although police officers are trained, 'conditions on the street cannot be replicated in a training centre' and an officer considering the discharge of a taser is 'unlikely to have the luxury of mature reflection.' The officer 'may even freeze in a highly charged situation' and 'the courts must have regard not only to the rights of the person at the receiving end of the taser but also to the challenges facing a police officer endeavouring to maintain law and order in a volatile situation'.[38]

Reasonableness of the force and not the injury

7.32 The focus of the assessment of reasonableness should be upon the act itself, rather than its consequences and the seriousness of the injury suffered by the claimant. Plainly, an act which might foreseeably cause serious injury will require more by way of justification. Equally, a significant injury may be evidence of unreasonable force. However, a reasonable act which inadvertently results in serious injury is reasonable nonetheless,[39] and care should be taken not to place too much emphasis on the result of the force.[40]

The vulnerability of the claimant

7.33 Reasonableness may be influenced by the vulnerability of the claimant. A vulnerable person may cause just as much harm as someone who is not vulnerable and the use of force may be equally justified. However, it may be evident to the officer that a person who is suffering with a mental disorder or emotional distress is likely to be particularly distressed by the use of force. It may also mean that it is reasonable in the circumstances for additional or alternative tactics to be used in seeking to de-escalate the situation and avoid the need for the use of force. The College of Policing (COP) guidance explains that if officers are aware of information indicating a factor which may influence behaviour then the officers should take that into account when considering their approach. Consideration should be given to 'help create opportunities for the subject and officers to have more time and space to de-escalate the situation' and officers should consider being prepared 'to back off' and to 'give time and space if possible'.[41]

7.34 In *Michael Gilchrist (by his mother and litigation friend, Novlyn Graham) v Chief Constable of Greater Manchester*[42] the claimant was a man with

37 *Reed v Wastie* [1972] Crim LR 221.

38 [2016] EWCA Civ 1257 at para 19.

39 As in *Thompson v Chief Constable of Greater Manchester* [2020] EWCA Civ 739.

40 As in *McDonnell v Commissioner of Police of the Metropolis* [2015] EWCA Civ 573 per Bean LJ at paras 26–28.

41 COP Approved Professional Practice (APP) on Armed deployment, last updated April 2021, available at: www.app.college.police.uk/app-content/armed-policing/armed-deployment/.

42 [2019] EWHC 1233 (QB).

significant learning difficulties and autism. The police were called to respond to the claimant having appeared outside of his house in a distressed state and having broken a window and cut his hands. The court found that repeated use of a taser on the claimant was unreasonable, in part because there was no sign of an imminent attack. It was 'not a fast, dynamic situation' and there 'was time to step back, give him space and use persuasion to gain his co-operation'.[43] It was considered that the initial use of force was reasonable, but 'once [the officers] were appraised of his vulnerability as an autistic man, and his behaviour suggested that he was defensive rather than aggressive, a more cautious approach should have been adopted'.[44] A similar scenario was considered in *ZH v Commissioner of Police of the Metropolis*.[45]

7.35 Where officers have failed adequately to take into account the effect of a person's disability, there may be a separate claim to be brought pursuant to the Equality Act 2010 (as to which, see chapter 12).

Defences: Criminal Justice Act 2003 s329

7.36 Special provisions are imposed by CJA 2003 s329 where a claimant has been convicted of an indictable offence arising out of the same incident as that giving rise to the claim. In broad terms, it provides a defence to a claim wherever there is an honest (even if unreasonable) belief in the necessity of the force, and the force used is not 'grossly disproportionate'. The genesis of the provision was a desire to provide an element of protection from civil suit in so-called 'householder' cases in which, for example, a homeowner uses force to repel a burglar. However, in practice the provision has predominantly been relied upon by police forces defending force used in the execution of police functions.

7.37 Pursuant to CJA 2003 s329(1), the provision applies wherever a claim is brought that the defendant 'did an act amounting to trespass to the claimant's person' and 'the claimant has been convicted in the United Kingdom of an imprisonable offence committed on the same occasion as that on which the act is alleged to have been done'. It follows from the phrase 'an act amounting to trespass' that the section applies not only to claims of trespass, but also to any cause of action arising out of the same act.[46]

7.38 Proceedings to which the provisions apply may be brought only with the permission of the court.[47] As indicated by CJA 2003 s329(3) the court may give permission where 'there is evidence that', in effect, the defence set out in section 329(4) and (5) does not apply. That would appear to impose a relatively low threshold akin to a prima facie case. The Court of Appeal in *Adorian v Commissioner of Police of the Metropolis*[48] held that the requirement is procedural and directory rather than being one of

43 [2019] EWHC 1233 (QB) at para 106.

44 [2019] EWHC 1233 (QB) at para 117.

45 [2013] EWCA Civ 69, [2013] 1 WLR 3021.

46 See *Adorian v Commissioner of Police of the Metropolis* [2009] EWCA Civ 18 at para 43.

47 CJA 2002 s329(2).

48 [2009] EWCA Civ 18, [2009] 1 WLR 1859. The claim was given permission to proceed but subsequently failed at trial: see [2010] EWHC 3861 (QB).

jurisdiction. Accordingly, a failure to obtain permission can be remedied at any point on an application to the court, although a delay in seeking permission may have costs consequences.[49] The appropriate course is to first raise the matter in pre-action correspondence, and in *Adorian* Sedley LJ indicated that it 'will be a sensible use of initial correspondence for defendants to draw attention, where it potentially applies, to section 329 and to indicate whether they propose to take any point on it'.[50] Where permission is not to be resisted then parties may sensibly agree that permission is sought as part of issued proceedings. Otherwise, the better course, subject to considerations such as limitation, may be to make a pre-issue application for permission to bring proceedings.

7.39 Where permission is given, it is a defence pursuant to CJA 2003 s329(4) for the defendant to prove that the act was done for one of the purposes specified in section 329(5) *and* that 'in all the circumstances, his act was not grossly disproportionate'. The purposes specified in section 329(5) are, broadly, that the defendant did the act because they believed the claimant was about to commit or immediately beforehand had committed an offence; or the act was necessary to defend themself, another person or property, or to apprehend the claimant after they had committed an offence.

7.40 CJA 2003 s329 is not without controversy, and on one view it is surprising that a police officer may use disproportionate force in, say, effecting an arrest, perhaps causing significant injury, but have a defence on the basis that it was not grossly disproportionate. It is also striking that the use of section 329, predominantly in claims against police, has little to do with the parliamentary intention of protecting members of the public who are suddenly confronted with crime and respond with force. As Sedley LJ expressed in *Adorian*, 'There is nothing on the face of the section or in its shoulder-note which manifests an intention to afford the police a novel protection from claims by offenders for objectively unreasonable or unnecessarily violent arrests'.[51] Significantly, a question arises as to the manner in which it ought to be interpreted in order to comply with the HRA 1998 or, perhaps, whether the provision is incompatible. As below, Article 3 prohibits inhumane and degrading treatment which may include a battery by a police officer (see para 7.152 below). Arguably, CJA 2003 s329 operates to prevent a civil remedy, and therefore an effective remedy, where there has been a violation of Article 3 ECHR but the force is unreasonable rather than 'grossly disproportionate'. In *McDonnell v Commissioner of Police of the Metropolis* it was argued that the word 'grossly' in section 329(4) is otiose and adds a gloss to the word 'disproportionate' that is inconsistent with the appropriate approach under Article 3.[52] The Court of Appeal did not decide the point, instead resolving the appeal on other grounds.

49 That contrasts with the position in relation to the not dissimilar provision of Mental Health Act 1983 s138.

50 [2009] EWCA Civ 18, [2009] 1 WLR 1859 at para 42.

51 [2009] EWCA Civ 18, [2009] 1 WLR 1859 at para 6.

52 [2015] EWCA Civ 573 at para 18.

Trespass ab initio

7.41 If an officer uses lawful force but then goes on to use excessive and unlawful force, it is only the latter force that is a trespass. As expressed by Burnett LJ in *McCarthy v Chief Constable of Merseyside*:[53]

> A person fearing violence might reasonably have struck his assailant once, but not reasonably have done so repeatedly thereafter. If the first lawful blow could be demonstrated to have been responsible for a serious injury, it could hardly serve justice if compensation were paid for that injury on the basis that a subsequent strike, which did not materially contribute to the injury, was unlawful.

That dicta arose in the context of consideration of the doctrine of trespass ab initio and whether excessively prolonged use of a taser would necessarily render the entirety of the taser discharge as a trespass. The court considered that it did not.[54]

7.42 There may be circumstances, however, in which the doctrine does apply. The essence of the doctrine is that where a wrongful act is committed in furtherance of an abuse of power then the defendant is liable not only for those aspects which exceed the officer's authority, but for all that was done in exercise of the right. As expressed in *Clerk & Lindsell on Torts,* the perpetrator 'is said to be a trespasser ab initio, on the assumption that his subsequent misconduct evidences an intention from the first to commit unlawful acts under the colour of unlawful authority'.[55] Thus, an officer who sets about committing unlawful and excessive force will be liable for the entirety of it, even if aspects of the force used might conceivably be justified as lawful.

Burden of proof

7.43 As above, once a battery is established the burden of proof in a civil action shifts to the defendant to justify the battery.[56] In order to discharge that burden, it may be necessary for the defendant to provide explanation for injury suffered by the claimant. That is particularly so where the claimant suffered the injury in custody and under the defendant's responsibility. As explained in *Sheppard v Secretary of State for the Home Department*:[57]

> . . . there will be a powerful evidential burden resting upon the authorities to demonstrate that responsibility for the injury . . . does not lie at their door. It must be so as a matter of common sense . . . injury occurring when a person is in the custody of servants of the state plainly calls for an explanation. It does not follow, as I have said, that when it comes to a civil suit for damages the adjectival law relating to the burden of proof is changed; but the position is, of course, that a State defendant in such a case will virtually inevitably be required to put forward a substantial positive case on the facts if he is to avoid the conclusion that the claimant's case is proved.

53 [2016] EWCA Civ 1257 at para 48.

54 [2016] EWCA Civ 1257 at paras 47 and 51.

55 Sweet & Maxwell, 23rd edn, 2020, para 14-50.

56 *McCarthy v Chief Constable of Merseyside* [2016] EWCA Civ 1257 at para 6.

57 [2002] EWCA Civ 1921 at para 13.

7.44 A similar approach was taken outside of the custodial context in *Browne v Commissioner of Police of the Metropolis*.[58]

The claimant's behaviour

7.45 In claims for trespass, the liability of the defendant cannot be reduced further to any contributory negligence on the part of the claimant,[59] although the claimant's behaviour may be relevant to the question of whether aggravated damages are appropriate. However, the law will not permit a claimant to recover compensation where the claimant's cause of action is based upon their own criminal or immoral act, referred to either as the principle of ex turpi causa or, more recently, the illegality defence.[60] The principle can apply not only in the context of acts that are criminal, but also those that are immoral or 'quasi-criminal' and engage the public interest in the same way.[61]

7.46 The search for a clear and principled underpinning to the principle has been problematic and has been considered by the Supreme Court in a number of cases, including *Hounga v Allen*[62] and *Patel v Mirza*.[63] Significantly, it does not prevent a claimant from bringing a damages claim simply because they were engaged in criminal activity at the time of injury, and successful claims against the police for injuries sustained by excessive force used during a lawful arrest are commonplace. An example of the application of the principle is *B v Chief Constable of X*[64] in which an undercover police officer was retired and suffered psychiatric injury after it was discovered that he had been taking cocaine. The court considered that the true cause of the symptoms were the consequences of taking cocaine rather than any breach of duty by the chief constable, but that in any event the principle of ex turpi causa would apply.

7.47 Where a claimant has been convicted of a criminal offence, the rule against collateral challenge precludes a claim in the civil courts which effectively disputes the soundness of that conviction.[65] Convictions should be challenged directly by appeals within the criminal justice system seeking to have the conviction quashed, rather than by an indirect attack on the soundness of the conviction in a civil action. The courts are also concerned to prevent inconsistent decisions on the same issues arising between the criminal courts and the civil courts. However, the principle is only applied where the fact of the conviction necessarily precludes the case that the claimant seeks to raise in the civil claim. In *Simpson v Chief Constable of South Yorkshire*[66] the Court of Appeal refused to strike out a

58 [2014] EWHC 3999 (QB) at para 39.

59 See, for example, *McAleer v Chief Constable of the Police Service of Northern Ireland* [2014] NIQB 53.

60 Albeit that, rather than a defence, it is rule of judicial abstention *Les Laboratoires Servier and another v Apotex Inc and others* [2014] UKSC 55, [2015] AC 430 at para 23.

61 See Lord Sumption in *Les Laboratoires Servier and another v Apotex Inc and others* [2014] UKSC 55, [2015] AC 430 at paras 23–25.

62 [2014] UKSC 47.

63 [2016] UKSC 42, [2017] AC 467.

64 [2015] EWHC 13 (QB).

65 *Hunter v Chief Constable of the West Midlands* [1982] AC 529, HL.

66 (1991) 135 SJ 383, CA.

claim for battery against the police on the ground that the claimant had been convicted of crimes of violence in respect of the same incident, since the convictions did not, on the facts of the case, preclude the proposition that the claimant had also been assaulted by the police as he alleged. The doctrine can in principle apply to decisions made in courts other than the criminal courts.[67] A civil claim canvassing the same or similar issues to that previously determined by a different court but based on new evidence will not be an abuse of process.[68]

Negligence

Overview

7.48 In order to succeed in a claim for negligence, the claimant must establish that the defendant owed a duty of care; that the defendant breached that duty; and that the breach of duty caused the claimant foreseeable injury of a type recoverable in the tort of negligence.

7.49 The tort of negligence is of broad application, in that it imposes upon public authorities and private individuals alike liability for carelessly causing foreseeable injury. Two aspects of the tort, in particular, serve to keep the scope of the tort within reasonable bounds.

7.50 The first is the limits to circumstances in which the common law will impose a duty of care. Certainly following *Robinson v Chief Constable of West Yorkshire*[69] it is established that the police will generally owe such a duty not to carelessly cause the claimant, by their own positive acts, some foreseable personal injury. There are more limited circumstances in which the police may owe a duty of care to protect the claimant from harm caused by a third party.

7.51 The second aspect of the tort which limits its scope is the type of damage which may found the tort. The tort primarily arises where the claimant is caused physical injury, although a deprivation of liberty may also found the tort. Where physical injury is suffered, the claimant may also claim for consequential financial losses and also for recognised psychiatric illness. However, recovery for such losses absent physical injury – that is, in case of 'pure economic loss' or 'pure psychiatric injury' – is limited.

Duty of care

Duty not to carelessly cause foreseeable personal injury

Overview

7.52 Following the decision of the Supreme Court in *Robinson v Chief Constable of West Yorkshire*[70] the police are generally under a duty of care to avoid causing reasonably foreseeable personal injury. That applies irrespective

67 *Kamoka v Security Service* [2017] EWCA Civ 1665.
68 *Kamoka v Security Service* [2017] EWCA Civ 1665.
69 [2018] UKSC 4, [2018] AC 736.
70 [2018] UKSC 4, [2018] AC 736.

of whether, at the material time, the police are engaged in the investigation or suppression of crime.

7.53 The route to establishing that basic proposition was arduous, and care is needed when considering authorities pre-dating *Robinson*. The difficulty stems from the case of *Anns v Merton LBC*[71] and a long-held misunderstanding of the case of *Caparo Industries plc v Dickman*.[72] In *Anns* the court attempted to lay down a general approach to be applied in all circumstances in determining the existence of a duty of care. The approach entailed considering, first, whether there was a prima facie duty of care based on the foreseeability of harm; and second, consideration was to be given to whether there were reasons of public policy for excluding or restricting any such prima facie duty. Amid the almost infinite variety of circumstances in which harm may be foreseeable the setting of limits upon the broadening scope of the tort rested upon the courts in various cases deciding upon what 'public policy' best required. Subsequently, in *Caparo* the House of Lords placed emphasis on the need for a relationship of proximity between the claimant and defendant and referred to the ingredients of 1) foreseeability of damage; 2) a relationship characterised by one of proximity; and 3) it being 'fair, just and reasonable' to impose a duty. That was subsequently treated in many cases as being a tripartite test to be applied in all cases.

7.54 The result, particularly in the context of the tortious liability of public authorities, was the courts struggling to discern a principled and coherent basis to decide whether it was 'fair, just and reasonable' in any particular case to impose a duty. Often, reference was made to unevidenced ideas that the imposition of a duty of care may have a negative impact upon the discharge generally of the function of the public authority or would have unsatisfactory implications for public resources.

7.55 In the context of claims against the police, the landscape for negligence claims was, for the best part of three decades, set by *Hill v Chief Constable of West Yorkshire*.[73] That claim was brought by relatives of victims of Peter Sutcliffe, 'the Yorkshire Ripper', who contended that absent earlier failures Peter Sutcliffe would have been apprehended and the subsequent deaths avoided. Accordingly, the claims turned upon establishing that the police, in investigating and suppressing crime, owed a duty of care to future potential victims. The House of Lords held that no such duty existed. That was, and remains, entirely correct and is consistent generally with the limited circumstances in which the common law imposes a duty to protect from harm caused by third parties. What had a lasting and ultimately misleading affect was what was said by the House of Lords as to whether it would be 'fair, just and reasonable' to impose a duty of care on the police, often referred to subsequently as 'the *Hill* principle'. The court considered that the imposition of liability 'may lead to the exercise of a function being carried on in a detrimentally defensive frame of mind' and would result in 'a significant diversion of police manpower and attention

71 [1978] AC 728, HL.

72 [1990] 2 AC 605, HL.

73 [1989] AC 53, HL.

from their most important function, that of the suppression of crime'.[74] Similar concerns as to the consequences of imposing such liability upon the police were expressed by the House of Lords in *Brooks v Commissioner of Police of the Metropolis*.[75] In several subsequent cases it appeared that the police enjoyed something akin to an immunity when discharging their core functions of the investigation and suppression of crime.

7.56 The first significant step away from the *Hill* principle was by the Supreme Court in *Michael v Chief Constable of South Wales*.[76] That claim concerned alleged failures by the police to protect a woman whose partner had made a threat to kill her. Consistent with the outcome in *Hill v Chief Constable of West Yorkshire*, no duty of care was owed on the circumstances of the case to protect the woman from harm caused by a third party. However, the Supreme Court emphasised that the absence of a duty of care followed simply from well-established principles of the law of tort and did not involve any special protection from liability being afforded to the police.

7.57 That was followed by *Robinson v Chief Constable of West Yorkshire*[77] in which the claimant, a frail 76-year-old, was accidentally knocked into and injured by police officers seeking to arrest a suspected drug dealer in the street. The trial judge considered that, if a duty of care existed, then it had been breached, but considered that further to the *Hill* principle no such duty existed. The Court of Appeal agreed that there was no duty of care and considered that, applying both *Caparo* and *Hill*, there was a general principle that 'most claims against the police in negligence for their acts and omissions in the course of investigating and suppressing crime and apprehending offenders will fail the third stage of the *Caparo* test'.[78] Ms Robinson appealed successfully to the Supreme Court. The majority of the Supreme Court considered that the dicta in *Hill* as to whether it was fair, just and reasonable to impose a duty on the police did not give rise to any principle that the police will not generally owe a duty of care when discharging their core functions of investigating and suppressing crime. Indeed, as Lord Reed pointed out, Lord Keith had said in *Hill*, in terms, that:[79]

> There is no question that a police officer, like anyone else, may be liable in tort to a person who is injured as a direct result of his acts or omissions. So he may be liable in damages for assault, unlawful arrest, wrongful imprisonment and malicious prosecution, and also for negligence.

Further, the majority of the Supreme Court disapproved of the focus on whether a duty was 'fair, just and reasonable' to impose a duty. It was observed that although *Caparo* had often been cited as authority for a tripartite test to establishing a duty of care, the Lords had in fact set out a very different approach in which the common law developed not by applying a generic test, but incrementally and by applying established categories of

74 *Hill v Chief Constable of West Yorkshire* [1989] AC 53 per Lord Keith at 63D–H, HL.
75 [2005] UKHL 24, [2005] 1 WLR 1495 per Lord Steyn at para 30.
76 [2015] UKSC 2, [2015] AC 1732.
77 [2018] UKSC 4.
78 [2014] EWCA Civ 15, [2014] PIQR P14 per Hallett LJ at para 46.
79 *Hill* [1989] AC 53 at 59, HL, cited in *Robinson* [2018] AC 736 at 751D.

case.[80] Once a duty is established in any particular case, it will apply to all future cases of the same kind. It is 'unnecessary and inappropriate' to reconsider in each case whether it was fair, just and reasonable to impose a duty. Moreover, where a case did fall within an established category of case in which a duty of care is imposed, a duty could not be discarded further to considerations of policy or its 'broader merits'.[81] It is only where a claimant seeks to apply the law of negligence to a novel type of case that it is necessary to consider questions of policy and whether it is 'fair, just and reasonable' to impose a duty.[82]

7.58 Accordingly, the correct and first issue to consider was whether the circumstances of the claim in *Robinson* fell within an established category of case in which the common law already recognised a duty of care. At common law, public authorities are generally subject to the same liabilities in tort as private individuals. If conduct would be tortious if committed by a private person or body, it is generally equally tortious if committed by a public authority.[83] Accordingly, the police are subject to a duty not to carelessly cause foreseeable personal injury in accordance with the general law of tort.[84] Indeed, that is no less than an application of the principle of *Donoghue v Stevenson*.[85] In Ms Robinson's case, therefore, there was a duty of care: there was a reasonably foreseeable risk of injury to pedestrians close to the anticipated arrest and that was sufficient to impose upon the officers a duty of care towards those pedestrians.[86]

7.59 Notwithstanding the misapprehension in some authorities (at least prior to *Robinson*) that the police were generally immune from claims when performing their core functions of investigating and suppressing crime, there are various examples in which a duty not to carelessly cause personal injury, consistent with the approach in *Robinson*, has been imposed upon the police. An officer driving a vehicle will owe a duty of care to other road users irrespective of whether the officer is driving in hot pursuit of a suspect[87] or responding to an emergency call.[88] Duties of care have also been established in firing a CS gas canister into a gunsmith's shop when trying to apprehend an intruder;[89] in controlling a crowd during a football match;[90] and to the occupier of a home that was being searched pursuant to a warrant.[91] In *TBS v Commissioner of Police of the*

80 See *Robinson v Chief Constable of West Yorkshire* [2018] UKSC 4, [2018] AC 736 at 745D–746B.

81 [2018] UKSC 4, [2018] AC 736 at 746D–F.

82 [2018] UKSC 4, [2018] AC 736 at 746H–747G.

83 [2018] UKSC 4, [2018] AC 736 at 748C–F.

84 [2018] UKSC 4, [2018] AC 736 at 751E and 752E.

85 [1932] AC 562, HL (Scotland).

86 [2018] UKSC 4, [2018] AC 736 at 761E–G.

87 *Marshall v Osmond* [1983] QB 1034, CA.

88 *MacLeod v Commissioner of Police of the Metropolis* [2014] EWHC 977 (QB).

89 *Rigby v Chief Constable of Northamptonshire* [1985] 1 WLR 1242, QBD.

90 In *Alcock v Chief Constable of South Yorkshire Police* [1992] 1 AC 310, HL the House of Lords accepted that a duty of care was owed by the police when they were responsible for crowd control at a football match to persons who suffered psychiatric injuries as a result of deaths and injuries sustained by members of the crowd, subject to meeting the requirements of imposing liability for 'secondary victims' (see paras 7.82–7.84).

91 *Alleyne v Commissioner of Police of the Metropolis* [2012] EWHC 3955 (QB).

Metropolis[92] the High Court refused to strike out a claim in which it was alleged that the commissioner owed a duty of care in respect of psychiatric harm suffered by the claimant who was conceived in a relationship with an undercover officer during the course of a covert operation.

Distinguishing between acts and omissions

7.60 It is important to distinguish between cases in which the police by a positive act directly cause harm to the claimant, and cases in which the police by omission fail to protect the claimant from harm caused by the claimant themselves or a third party. As above, in the former the common law will generally impose a duty of care provided that the risk of harm is foreseeable. In the latter, the common law will not impose a duty, save in the limited circumstances described below.

7.61 Correctly identifying whether the claim involves an act or an omission is therefore important. It can also be challenging as any police response can on one view be characterised as an 'act'. For example, carelessly grading a call from a person in urgent need as requiring a non-urgent response is itself an act, but for the purposes of the tort it is more likely to be characterised as an omission to provide an urgent response. In *CN v Poole BC* Lord Reed described the distinction between acts and omissions as 'between causing harm (making things worse) and failing to confer a benefit (not making things better)'.[93] The person in urgent need has not been caused harm by the police, but the police failed to provide the benefit of an urgent response and make things better. Accordingly, it is likely an omissions case.

7.62 That the police themselves are the immediate cause of injury will be a good indicator of it being a positive act case, such as the police officer who carelessly knocked into the claimant in *Robinson*. However, that is not always so and there will be cases where although the immediate cause of the harm is a third party the police have nevertheless themselves caused harm or made 'things worse'. An example is *Knightley v Johns*[94] where a police officer attended the scene of a road accident and carelessly sent a vehicle the wrong way through a tunnel leading to an accident. The officer created unnecessary danger to the claimant and a duty was owed. Cases such as *Knightley v Johns* where the defendant creates or aggravates the source of danger are sometimes described as exceptions to the omissions principle, although on analysis it would appear that the reason the omissions principle does not apply is because they are positive act cases.

7.63 An example of the difficulty distinguishing between act and omission cases is *Tindall v Chief Constable of Thames Valley*.[95] In winter a portion of a road had frozen over with black ice further to a nearby water leak. A member of the public had taken it upon himself to warn traffic to slow down but ceased to do so when the police attended and erected a warning sign. The police left after a period without taking any steps to ensure notification of the hazard and shortly thereafter there was a fatal accident. The

92 [2017] EWHC 3094 (QB).
93 [2019] UKSC 25, [2020] AC 780 at para 28.
94 [1982] 1 WLR 349, CA.
95 [2022] EWCA Civ 25.

claimant argued that by removing the member of the public from the scene but not otherwise leaving the road safe the police had taken a positive step in that they had caused the warnings to other drivers to cease, themselves aggravating the risk to oncoming drivers. The claim was struck out, with the Court of Appeal considering it to be an example of a public authority responding ineffectually and failing to confer a benefit that might have resulted if they had acted more competently. It was therefore an omission or 'failure to confer a benefit' case.

7.64 A further example is *Chief Constable of Essex v Transport Arendonk BvBa*.[96] Officers had arrested a lorry driver and taken him to custody, stopped him from using two of his mobile phones, and left the lorry in a remote layby. The officers then did not speedily fulfil a promise to get the lorry operator's contact detail when it was known that there was a risk in the area of thefts from unattended lorries. The cargo was stolen. In declining to strike out, Laing J considered that the case shared features of both omission cases, and positive act cases. As it was not purely an omission case it was not considered to be unarguable that the police might owe a duty of care.[97] It might be thought that it was a case in which the harm had been caused by a third party, but that the police had themselves carelessly created an unnecessary danger by leaving the lorry vulnerable to theft, and accordingly akin to *Knightley v Johns*.[98]

Duty to protect against harm caused by third parties ('omissions' cases)

Overview

7.65 It is well-established that there is no general common law liability for omissions.[99] This means that private and public bodies alike will generally not owe a duty of care to protect individuals or their property against harm caused by the conduct of a third party. In *Robinson v Chief Constable of West Yorkshire*, Lord Reed underlined the distinction between 'careless acts causing personal injury . . . and careless omissions to prevent acts (by other agencies) causing personal injury'.[100] Thus, save for the well-defined exceptions, public authorities are generally under no duty to prevent the occurrence of harm, even if they have a statutory power or duty to do so.

7.66 In *Robinson*, Lord Reed cited an article by Tofaris and Steel entitled 'Negligence liability for omissions and the police'[101] which summarised the exceptions in this way:[102]

> In the tort of negligence, a person A is not under a duty to take care to prevent harm occurring to person B through a source of danger not created by A unless (i) A has assumed a responsibility to protect B from that danger,

96 [2020] EWHC 212 (QB).

97 [2020] EWHC 212 (QB) at para 88.

98 [1982] 1 WLR 349.

99 The focus here is liability for the conduct of third parties. It is well established that the police owe a duty to a detainee to take reasonable care to prevent suicide or self-harm (although the defence of contributory negligence may reduce damages): see *Reeves v Commissioner of Police of the Metropolis* [2000] 1 AC 360, HL.

100 At para 69.

101 [2016] CLJ 128.

102 [2018] UKSC 4, [2018] AC 736 at para 34.

(ii) A has done something which prevents another from protecting B from that danger, (iii) A has a special level of control over that source of danger, or (iv) A's status creates an obligation to protect B from that danger.

7.67 In *Michael v Chief Constable of South Wales*, the Supreme Court held that the police were not liable for failing to promptly respond to Ms Michael's call that her life was at risk from her former partner. The call operator carelessly failed to communicate the threat to the police with the result that, the police having failed to arrive in time, she was killed. The call operator had told Ms Michael that the police would want to call her back but had made no explicit communication that the police would arrive within a particular timeframe. The claimants, the victim's estate and her dependants, commenced proceedings against the two police forces involved, alleging negligence. Lord Toulson held that neither of the relevant exceptions to the third-party rule applied on the facts: the handler had given no assurance to the caller other than that she would pass on the call and no promise as to how quickly there would be a response. No advice or instruction had been provided. The court declined to create a new exception to the rule on omissions to encompass cases where the police were adverted to an imminent risk to life. Key to Lord Toulson's rationale for declining to impose a duty to protect against known risks of third party violence was the inevitable scope for misconstruction, possibly extending to threats against property and other types of less serious crime.[103]

7.68 In *CN v Poole BC*,[104] the Supreme Court robustly rejected the claim that the council's children's services had breached their duty of care to protect the claimants from the harassment of their neighbours. However, the claim floundered on its facts, not for 'policy' reasons. First, the case was argued primarily on the basis of the council's alleged failure to exercise its social welfare functions so as to protect the child claimants, including a failure to remove them from their mother's care. The court found that the mere existence of such statutory provisions did not of themselves impute an actionable duty at common law. Second, the alleged breach of duty had no possible basis. There were no grounds for removing the children from their mother, the harm suffered by the claimants being attributable solely to the conduct of the neighbouring family. Third, the council's relationship with the claimants lacked the necessary characteristics for an assumption of responsibility to arise. The council's investigation of the family's position did not involve the provision of a service to them on which reliance could be reasonably placed, nor could the claimants be said to have otherwise entrusted the council with their safety. It was in this context that Lord Reed sought to refine the central distinction as between causing harm ('making things worse') and failing to confer a benefit ('not making things better'), eschewing the more traditional 'act versus omission' terminology.

Exceptions

7.69 The exceptions can broadly be categorised under two headings (discussed below):

103 [2015] UKSC 2 at paras 119–120. See also *Griffiths v Chief Constable of Suffolk* [2018] EWHC 2538 (QB).

104 [2019] UKSC 25.

1) The first exception arises where the defendant has a special level of control over the source of a particular danger.
2) The second arises where the defendant assumes responsibility to safeguard the claimant.

Control over the source of danger

7.70 *Home Office v Dorset Yacht Co Ltd*[105] is the decisive case on the first exception, in which it was held that prison officers could be liable in negligence for allowing young offenders to escape and damage the plaintiff's yacht. This was premised on the fact that the offenders were under the officers' control at the time and on the 'special relationship' between the prison officers and the owners of the nearby yachts, who faced an exceptional risk of harm given their proximity to the detention site. In failing to effectively supervise the detainees, the officers had created a foreseeable risk of danger for this specific cohort, to be distinguished from the 'general risk of damage from criminal acts of others . . . [shared] with all members of the public'.[106] Insofar as it is founded on the *Dorset Yacht* case, there are two preconditions for the application of this exception to the third-party rule. A may be liable to B for loss suffered as a result of action by C if 1) A is responsible for controlling C's actions and 2) B is in a limited class of people who are exposed to a risk of particular damage which is different in its incidence from the risk of damage to the general public.[107]

Assumption of responsibility

7.71 Claims against the police for third party liability based on an 'assumption of responsibility' argument are likely to be more common than those based on the assertion of a 'special relationship' (as per *Dorset Yacht*). According to *Michael*, assumption of responsibility 'embraces the relationships in which a duty to take positive action typically arises: contract, fiduciary relationships, employer and employee, school and pupil, health professional and patient'.[108]

7.72 Whether or not an assumption of responsibility can be inferred will of course depend on the particular facts. It will generally be inferred from a specific representation by the police upon which reliance is placed by the claimant (as in *Sherratt* below). An assumption of responsibility will not be inferred simply from officers attending upon the claimant in the course of their duties,[109] or from the mere existence of a statutory duty, without something more.[110] In *CN v Poole BC,* Lord Reed cited the dicta in *Gorringe*[111] to reaffirm the principle that foresight of harm was not enough to establish an assumption of responsibility:[112]

105 [1970] AC 1004, HL.
106 At p1070D–E.
107 As per *Chief Constable of Essex v Transport Arendonk BvBa* [2020] EWHC 212 (QB) at para 34.
108 At para 100.
109 *Cowan v Chief Constable for Avon and Somerset Constabulary* [2000] 1 All ER 504.
110 *X v Hounslow LBC* [2009] EWCA Civ 286.
111 *Gorringe v Calderdale MBC* [2004] 1 WLR 1057.
112 *CN v Poole* [2019] UKSC 25 at para 32.

> Reasonable foreseeability of physical injury is the standard criterion for determining the duty of care owed by people who undertake an activity which carries a risk of injury to others. But it is insufficient to justify the imposition of liability upon someone who simply does nothing: who neither creates the risk nor undertakes to do anything to avert it.

7.73 In *Sherratt v Chief Constable of Greater Manchester*[113] a mother relied upon the police conducting a welfare check on her daughter. The police indicated to the mother that they would attend and conduct a welfare check, in consequence of which the mother did not do so herself (she did not live in close proximity). The police then failed to conduct an adequate welfare check. The police appealed a preliminary ruling in the claimant's favour on the question of whether a duty of care arose. In dismissing the appeal, the High Court distinguished *Michael* and applied *Kent v Griffiths,*[114] holding that it had been open to the Recorder to conclude on the agreed facts that the police call handler gave a specific assurance to the mother, in response to being told it was an emergency situation, that officers would be dispatched forthwith to the daughter's house to check on her wellbeing and that, if required, her transfer to hospital would be arranged by the police. The Recorder was justified in concluding that the mother detrimentally relied on these assurances, in not taking other action before it was too late to save her daughter and did not err in law in finding that the police had assumed responsibility for the welfare of the deceased.

7.74 In *Welsh v Chief Constable of Merseyside*[115] it was found to be arguable (on appeal from a strike out) that the Crown Prosecution Service (CPS) owed a duty of care to the plaintiff to ensure that the magistrates' court was informed that the offences for which he had been bailed had subsequently been taken into consideration by the Crown Court. The failure to do so resulted in the plaintiff's re-arrest and detention. The court found that there had been an additional assumption of responsibility for communicating this information to the Crown Court by a solicitor employed by the CPS. *Welsh* was distinguished in *Elguzouli-Daf v Commissioner of Police of the Metropolis*[116] where the Court of Appeal upheld a decision striking out actions for negligence brought by suspects who had been arrested in the context of investigations which were then discontinued. The Court of Appeal found that the CPS does not owe a general duty of care to the subjects of criminal investigations,[117] but recognised that there might be cases in which the CPS assumes by its conduct responsibility to a particular defendant. It emphasised

113 [2018] EWHC 1746 (QB).

114 [2001] QB 36, CA, where a duty of care was established when a doctor called 999 on behalf of an asthmatic patient and was given an assurance that an ambulance would arrive in minutes, and therefore did not take the claimant to hospital himself.

115 [1993] 1 All ER 692, QBD.

116 [1995] QB 335, CA.

117 At 349C–E.

that *Welsh* went no further than a finding that a duty of care was arguably owed and that it turned on its own special facts.[118]

Conflicting interests

7.75 The courts will be reluctant to impose a duty of care where the duty would conflict with the proper discharge of the defendants' responsibilities. Accordingly, in the context of a social services authority considering the removal of a child from a family further to child protection concerns a duty may be owed to the child, but not to the suspected abuser. A duty owed to the latter would conflict with the primary responsibility of the social workers for the welfare of the child.[119] In *Desmond v Chief Constable of Nottinghamshire* the Court of Appeal considered that a Chief Constable did not owe a duty of care to the subject of an enhanced criminal record certificate in circumstances that the alleged duty of care would conflict with the statutory purpose of protecting vulnerable persons.[120] In that case, the officer deciding whether to disclose that the claimant, who was a teacher, had been arrested on suspicion of an alleged sexual offence faced 'a delicate judgment' on whether it was appropriate to disclose that information, and it was important that an officer making that decision 'should not be inhibited by the possibility of proceedings for breach of a conflicting . . . duty of care'.[121]

7.76 In *SXH v Crown Prosecution Service* the Supreme Court held in relation to the Crown Prosecution Service (CPS) that its duty is to the public, not to the victim or suspect, and to recognise a duty of care towards victims or suspects would put the CPS in positions of potential conflict.[122]

7.77 Conflict of interests was also a significant consideration in the Supreme Court in *James-Bowen and others v Commissioner of Police of the Metropolis*[123] deciding that the Commissioner, in conducting litigation regarding the actions of officers, did not owe those officers a duty of care in protecting the officers' reputational and economic interests. In determining how the litigation was to be conducted there were stark differences between the interests of the commissioner and her employees which suggested that it would not be fair, just or reasonable to impose a duty.[124] Lord Lloyd-Jones observed in *James-Bowen* that the fact of potentially conflicting interests is not necessarily conclusive against the recognition of a duty of care and it was necessary to have regard to the competing underlying policy consideration when determining whether a duty of care may be imposed notwithstanding that it may give rise to a conflict of interest.[125]

7.78 Indeed, it might be said that in *Robinson* the duty of care to the claimant conflicted with the duty to supress crime, including by apprehending the

118 At 348G–349B.

119 *JD v East Berkshire Community Health NHS Trust* [2005] UKHL 23, [2005] 2 AC 373.

120 [2011] EWCA Civ 3, [2011] PTSR 1369 at 1389C–E.

121 [2011] EWCA Civ 3, [2011] PTSR 1369 at 1389D–E.

122 [2017] 1 WLR 1401 at para 38. See, similarly, *Elguzouli-Daf v Commissioner of Police of the Metropolis* [1995] QB 335, CA.

123 [2018] UKSC 40, [2018] 1 WLR 4021.

124 [2018] UKSC 40, [2018] 1 WLR 4021 at 4036D.

125 [2018] UKSC 40, [2018] 1 WLR 4021 at 4035D–G.

suspected drug dealer. However, the relevant authorities were considered in *Robinson* but the majority (at least impliedly) did not consider that there was such a conflict so as to render it inappropriate to impose a duty of care. However, there may be instances where the potential conflict is more acute so as to negate any duty of care. For example, decisions taken by a police officer as to whether or not to charge a suspect would appear to give rise to a similar conflict to that of the CPS in discharging its prosecutorial function.[126]

Foreseeability of harm

7.79 The duty of care will arise only where the risk of injury is foreseeable. The test is an objective on and is judged by reference to the facts the defendant knew or ought to have known at the time. There is no test based on a fixed point on the scale of probability, and the more severe the possible adverse consequences the less probable that eventuality will need to be to satisfy the reasonable foresight test.[127] There must be sufficient foreseeability such that a reasonable person would not ignore it or 'brush [it] aside as far-fetched'.[128]

Liability in respect of psychiatric injury

7.80 Damages for psychiatric injury will generally be recoverable where they result from physical injury caused by the claimant, or from the claimant having been physically imperilled by the defendant's conduct. What is relevant for the purposes of establishing a duty is the foreseeability of the physical injury or imperilment, and not the foreseeability of the psychiatric injury.[129]

7.81 There are some limited circumstances in which liability for 'pure psychiatric harm' (where the claimant has not suffered physically injury or imperilment) may be imposed. Examples include where a prisoner foreseeably suffers a psychiatric illness as a result of ill-treatment by officers which would appear to arise from the particular relationship between prison and prisoner.[130] Liability for pure psychiatric harm has also been imposed in stress at work cases.[131] In *Leach v Chief Constable of Gloucestershire*[132] the Court of Appeal declined to strike out a claim in respect of a failure

126 Such a case is *M v Commissioner of Police of the Metropolis* [2007] EWCA Civ 1361. Although it was decided on the basis of an overly broad understanding of the *Hill* principle which does not survive *Robinson v Chief Constable of West Yorkshire* [2018] UKSC 4, [2018] AC 736, the outcome is probably correct, and consistent with the principle that a duty of care would not be imposed that conflicts with the defendant's primary duty.

127 *Attorney-General of the British Virgin Islands v Hartwell* [2004] UKPC 12, [2004] 1 WLR 1273.

128 *Overseas Tankship (UK) Ltd v Miller Steamship Co Pty (The Wagon Mound No 2)* [1967] 1 AC 617 at 643.

129 *Page v Smith* [1996] AC 155, HL.

130 *R v Deputy Governor of Parkhurst Prison ex p Hague* [1992] 1 AC 58 at 165–166, HL.

131 Such as in *Barber v Somerset CC* [2004] UKHL 13, [2004] 1 WLR 1089. In *French v Chief Constable of Sussex* [2006] EWCA Civ 312 the claimant police officers were unsuccessful in arguing that the stress caused by negligently pursued disciplinary proceedings were analogous to 'stress at work' cases.

132 [1999] 1 WLR 1421, CA.

to provide counselling to a member of the public who suffered pure psychiatric injury having acted as an appropriate adult for the interviews of the serial killer Frederick West. In *Attia v British Gas plc* it was held that damages could be recovered in respect of psychiatric illness resulting from the claimant witnessing the destruction of her home by fire.[133]

7.82 A claimant who is physically imperilled and suffers resulting psychiatric injury is referred to as the 'primary victim.' A claimant who suffers psychiatric injury having witnessed another suffer physical injury or imperilment is a 'secondary victim'. The imposition of liability in respect of secondary victims is constrained by a number of policy limitations. In *Alcock v Chief Constable of South Yorkshire*[134] the House of Lords considered claims brought by relatives of those killed in the Hillsborough tragedy who had learnt of the circumstances after the incident or who were present at the stadium. The House of Lords considered that liability in respect of secondary victims would arise only where:

- the claimant had close ties of love and affection for the person injured or imperilled;
- the claimant was close to the incident in time and space; and
- the claimant directly perceived the incident rather than, for example, hearing about it from a third person.[135]

7.83 Applying those criteria, the claims failed. The House of Lords subsequently applied the same approach to deny claims by officers who assisted in the aftermath of the incident, stating that the criteria applied to bystanders and rescuers (unless sufficiently caught up in the events to qualify as a primary victim).[136] Thus, a partner or close relative who saw their loved one run over by a police car or shot by an officer or who saw the immediate aftermath of such events could qualify as a secondary victim (if they were not a primary victim), whereas a relative who was informed of these events some hours later and suffered trauma in consequence could not.

7.84 The *Alcock* criteria has given rise to a wealth of case-law and what has been described as a 'patchwork quilt of distinctions which are difficulty to justify'.[137] Full consideration of the law as it stands in relation to secondary victims is beyond the scope of this chapter, but see *Clerk & Lindsell on Torts* (23rd edn) at para 7-75 and the helpful discussion of the key authorities in *Paul (a child) v Royal Wolverhampton NHS Trust*.[138]

7.85 Cases of pure psychiatric injury may alternatively give rise to claims in the tort of intentionally causing psychiatric injury or harassment (considered below at para 7.94).

Standard of care and breach of duty

7.86 The question is whether the conduct of the defendant has fallen below what could reasonably be expected in the circumstances. The conduct will

133 [1988] QB 304, CA.
134 [1992] 1 AC 310, HL.
135 *Alcock v Chief Constable of South Yorkshire* [1992] 1 AC 310, HL.
136 *White v Chief Constable of South Yorkshire* [1999] 2 AC 455, HL.
137 *White v Chief Constable of South Yorkshire* [1999] 2 AC 455, HL, per Lord Steyn.
138 [2022] EWCA Civ 12.

be judged by reference to how a reasonable person of ordinary prudence would have acted in the particular circumstances. Where a person holds a particular post the adequacy of their conduct will be judged by reference to what would reasonably be expected of a person in that position. The acts will be judged by reference to what was known or ought to have been known of the claimant or any other relevant circumstances at the time.

7.87 As above, where the claim relates to injury sustained while in custody, a failure to follow the PACE Code of Practice will not itself give rise to any civil liability[139] but could be good evidence of a breach of duty. Similarly, failure to follow relevant force manuals, guidelines, training, etc, could be evidence of breach of duty in many instances of alleged negligence by officers, for example where police dogs were handled inappropriately, or carelessly discharging a weapon.

7.88 The seriousness of the risk involved may be relevant to what is required in order to discharge the duty of care.[140] An example is *Crooks v Ebanks*[141] where an armed police officer tripped and fell while chasing a robber and dropped the loaded gun he held in his hand, which discharged a bullet into the claimant's head.

7.89 As with the question of the reasonableness of the force used in the tort of battery, the standard of care imposed at common law takes account of the stress involved in the circumstances in question. In *Marshall v Osmond* it was emphasised that the duty is to take 'such care and skill as is reasonable in all the circumstances'. In that case, the police driver engaged in the pursuit of a suspect was operating in 'stressful circumstances' and although the officer had made an error of judgment the court was 'far from satisfied' that the officer had been negligent.[142] In *Costello v Chief Constable of Northumbria* it was said that 'liability should not turn on . . . shades of personal judgment and courage in the heat of the potentially dangerous moment'.[143] Those cases were cited in *Robinson*,[144] in which Lord Reed added that exposing the claimant to a risk of injury does not necessarily equate to a breach of duty. A duty of care 'is always a duty to take such care as is reasonable in the circumstances' and there 'may be circumstances which justify the taking of risks to the safety of members of the public which would not otherwise be justified'.[145] In *Thompson v Chief Constable of Greater Manchester*[146] an officer had caused a serious fracture to the arm of the claimant. The officer had applied a form of restraint which was inconsistent with the trained technique and posed a foreseeable risk to the claimant, but in the circumstances of a fast-moving incident there was still no breach of duty.

7.90 There may be circumstances that a court is willing to infer a breach of duty from the surrounding circumstances. In *Alleyne v Commissioner of*

139 PACE s67(10).

140 As in *Attorney-General of the British Virgin Islands v Hartwell* [2004] UKPC 12, [2004] 1 WLR 1273.

141 [1999] 1 WLR 1287, PC (Jamaica).

142 [1983] QB 1034 at 1038C–G, CA.

143 [1999] ICR 752 at, 767, CA.

144 [2018] UKSC 4, [2018] AC 736 at 762A–B.

145 [2018] UKSC 4, [2018] AC 736 at 762C–D.

146 [2020] EWCA Civ 739.

Police of the Metropolis[147] the claimant had suffered injury as officers executing a warrant at his home stepped over him whilst restrained on the floor. The judge considered that his injuries 'must have been sustained' by a want of care and a breach of duty was established.[148]

Causation

7.91 It is necessary for the claimant to demonstrate that the defendant's conduct did in fact cause the harm complained of. The courts ordinarily resort to the 'but for' test, that is, whether the claimant can prove on the balances of probabilities that but for the defendant's negligence that harm would not have been suffered. In some instances, primarily where there is scientific uncertainty as to the attribution between tortious and non-tortious causes, the courts have been willing to replace the 'but for' test with whether the defendant's negligence made a 'material contribution'.[149] However, if there are several causative factors and it is possible to identify the extent of the defendant's contribution, then the defendant is liable to that extent and no more.[150]

7.92 The material contribution test has frequently been of relevance in psychiatric injury cases where there may often be more than a single causative factor. For example, in *Page v Smith (No 2)* the claimant's pre-existing chronic fatigue syndrome had been in remission but had re-lapsed following a minor road traffic collision. As the collision had materially contributed to the syndrome causation was established. There has been some discussion as to whether given the inherent uncertainties in psychiatric injury cases it is appropriate to seek to identify the proportion of the injury attributable to the tortious act, although that may rest on the incorrect view that psychiatric injury is in principle always indivisible.[151]

7.93 Particular cases may also require consideration of whether there are intervening events, such as acts of the claimant or others, which 'break the chain of causation', as to which see *Clerk & Lindsell on Torts* (23rd edn), para 2-110 and following.

Threats, non-physical conduct causing psychiatric injury and harassment

Overview

7.94 There may be incidents in which the unreasonable conduct of a police officer causes a claimant distress or psychiatric injury but in circumstances where there is no actual or threatened physical contact. It might be, for example, that a police officer pesters a person in trying to provoke them, or makes an unjustified threat. In those circumstances, there will

147 [2012] EWHC 3955 (QB).

148 At 147.

149 See cases such as *Bonnington Castings Ltd v Wardlaw* [1956] AC 613, HL (Scotland) and *Bailey v Ministry of Defence* [2008] EWCA Civ 883, [2009] 1 WLR 1052.

150 *Thompson v Smiths Shiprepairers (North Shields) Ltd* [1984] QB 405, QBD.

151 [1996] 1 WLR 855, CA. See the discussion in *BAE Systems (Operations) v Konczak* [2017] EWCA Civ 1188.

not be any claim in battery or negligence. It might be that a claim arises for misfeasance in public office, which is considered in chapter 8 at para 8.103. There are also further torts which do not frequently arise in the context of claims against the police, but which may afford a remedy in such circumstances. A summary is provided of each.

Intentionally causing psychiatric injury

7.95 Intentionally causing psychiatric injury is a tort first recognised in *Wilkinson v Downton*[152] in which the claimant was falsely informed as a practical joke that her husband had been badly injured in a road accident. She suffered significant shock with lasting consequences. The court held that, notwithstanding that it had been intended as a practical joke, the defendant had plainly calculated to cause anxiety and distress and was liable to the claimant in tort. The tort succeeded again in *Janvier v Sweeney*[153] in which a man attended the claimant's home and falsely told her he was a detective from Scotland Yard and that she was wanted for corresponding with a German spy, in consequence of which she suffered nervous shock and a long period of illness.

7.96 With the broadening of the tort of negligence to permit recovery for psychiatric injury arising out of physical injury or the reasonable fear of immediate physical injury the tort has rarely been seen in reported cases, although more recently there have been a small number of cases arising in the context of harassment.[154]

7.97 The ingredients of the tort were considered by the Supreme Court in *O (a child) v Rhodes*.[155] It was considered that the tort has three elements:

1) a conduct element;
2) a mental element; and
3) a consequence element.

7.98 Taking the latter first, the *consequence* of the defendant's act must be that the claimant suffers physical harm or recognised psychiatric illness. Severe distress falling short of a recognised psychiatric illness is not sufficient to establish the tort.[156]

7.99 The *conduct* element requires 'words or conduct directed towards the claimant for which there is no justification or reasonable excuse, and the burden of proof is on the claimant'.[157] Given the relative paucity of authority the bounds of what may be 'justification or reasonable excuse' is not clearly defined. In *O (a child)*, a father could reasonably publish a book revealing a true and graphic account of abuse he had suffered as a child notwithstanding that the account might cause harm to his own child. In

152 [1897] 2 QB 57, QBD.

153 [1918–19] All ER 1056, CA.

154 As observed by Lady Hale and Lord Toulson in *O v Rhodes* [2015] UKSC 32, [2016] AC 219 at para 55, and see the cases cited therein.

155 [2015] UKSC 32, [2016] AC 219.

156 [2015] UKSC 32, [2016] AC 219 at para 73. The minority disagreed and considered that distress ought to be sufficient, per Lord Neuberger at para 119.

157 [2015] UKSC 32, [2016] AC 219 at para 74.

the context of police claims, there will likely be a reasonable excuse if the officer is acting in good faith and in execution of their police duties.

7.100 The *mental* element will be met where the defendant intends to cause physical harm or severe mental or emotional distress.[158] Recklessness on the part of the defendant as to whether harm will be suffered by the claimant is not sufficient. However, although the claimant must have suffered psychiatric injury in order to establish the tort, it will be sufficient if the defendant intends to cause severe mental or emotional distress. An example given by the Supreme Court was that of a hostage taker who intends to cause severe distress as the very means by which a payment is extracted but may have given no thought to whether psychiatric injury might be caused.

7.101 The courts will be anxious not to extend the tort into regulating or providing compensation simply for causing offence. A deliberately insulting remark designed to cause upset but not severe emotional distress will not be sufficient, even if the unintended consequences is psychiatric illness.[159] Lord Neuberger considered that 'given the importance of freedom of expression, which includes the need to avoid constraining ordinary (even much offensive) discourse, it is vital that the boundaries of the cause of action are relatively narrow'.[160]

7.102 Nonetheless, it is possible to conceive of circumstances in which the tort may arise in the context of claims against police, for example, where a police officer intends to cause distress by falsely asserting to a claimant that a family member has been arrested for a significant offence.

Harassment

Meaning

7.103 The Protection from Harassment Act (PHA) 1997 provides not only criminal sanction for harassment, but also a civil remedy for victims. Moreover, although the Act was brought in predominantly to provide criminal and civil liabilities for stalking, it covers a much wider scope of activity. PHA 1997 s1 prohibits a 'course of conduct' which 'amounts to harassment of another, and which he knows or ought to know amounts to harassment of the other'. The 'ought to know' aspect imposes an objective test and, by section 1(2) is judged from the perspective of 'a reasonable person in possession of the same information'. 'Harassment' is not defined in the Act, although it states that references to harassing a person 'include alarming the person or causing the person distress'.[161] In *Thomas v News Group Newspapers* harassment was described as a persistent and deliberate course of unreasonable and oppressive conduct, targeted at another person, which is calculated to and does cause that person alarm, fear or distress.[162] A 'course of conduct' can only be established where there has been at least two occasions on which there have been acts which together amount to harassment.

158 [2015] UKSC 32, [2016] AC 219 at para 87.
159 [2015] UKSC 32, [2016] AC 219 at para 86.
160 [2015] UKSC 32, [2016] AC 219 at para 104.
161 PHA 1997 s7(2).
162 [2001] EWCA Civ 1233, [2002] EMLR 4 at para 30.

Claims

7.104 A civil claim for damages and/or an injunction may be brought in relation to conduct that amounts to harassment as defined by the PHA 1997.[163] Damages may be awarded for anxiety caused by the harassment and for any resulting financial losses.[164] In contrast to the torts at common law, there is no requirement for a recognised psychiatric illness to be established – anxiety and upset is sufficient.

Defences

7.105 The PHA 1997 provides that there will be a defence to a claim if the defendant can show that the course of conduct:

- was pursued for the purpose of preventing or detecting crime;
- was pursued under any enactment or rule of law or to comply with any requirement imposed by any person under any enactment; or
- was reasonable in the particular circumstances.[165]

7.106 Notably, in respect of the first defence, it is sufficient that the course of conduct was pursued 'for the purpose' of preventing or detecting crime and there is no requirement that the conduct is reasonable. However, in *Hayes v Willoughby* the Supreme Court considered that a wholly subjective test would be problematic and that a defendant must at least be able to show that the acts were performed in good faith and at least some logical connection between the evidence and the ostensible reasons for the decision, and an absence of arbitrariness, of capricious reasoning so outrageous in its logic as to be perverse.[166] Accordingly:[167]

> Before an alleged harasser can be said to have had the purpose of preventing or detecting crime, he must have sufficiently applied his mind to the matter. He must have thought rationally about the material suggesting the possibility of criminality and formed the view that the conduct said to constitute harassment was appropriate for the purpose of preventing or detecting it. If he has done these things, then he has the relevant purpose.

Example

7.107 An example of a successful claim against a police officer for harassment is *KD v Chief Constable of Hampshire*.[168] A police officer was investigating an allegation that the claimant's former partner had sexually assaulted the claimant's daughter. In the course of his investigation, the officer required the claimant to answer questions in substantial and intimate detail about the claimant's life with her former partner, which the claimant contended had no relevance to the investigation. It was also alleged that the officer had visited her home and made telephone calls to her at home for personal discussions about their private life unrelated to the investigation; and that

163 PHA 1997 s3(1).
164 PHA 1997 s3(2).
165 PHA 1997 s1(3).
166 [2013] UKSC 17, [2013] 1 WLR 935 per Lord Sumption at para 14.
167 [2013] UKSC 17, [2013] 1 WLR 935 at para 15.
168 [2005] EWHC 2550 (QB).

he had touched her sexually, made sexual remarks to her, followed or stalked her in public places, and conducted himself in other respects in a manner which amounted to harassment or assault.

7.108 The judge considered that certain actions of the officer in obtaining detailed explicit information about the claimant's sexual conduct had been for his own gratification and was not for the purpose of preventing or detecting crime.[169]

Human Rights Act 1998

Introduction

7.109 Pursuant to HRA 1998 s6(1), it is unlawful for a public authority to act incompatibly with the rights under the European Convention on Human Rights (ECHR) set out at HRA 1998 Sch 1. HRA 1998 s7 provides a right to bring proceedings in vindication of violations of ECHR rights, and section 8 empowers a court to award damages in 'just satisfaction' of a claim. The ECHR rights of primary relevance to this chapter are:

- the right to life (Article 2);
- the prohibition of torture, inhumane or degrading treatment (Article 3);
- the prohibition of slavery, servitude and forced labour (including trafficking) (Article 4); and
- the right to respect for private and family life (Article 8).

7.110 Importantly, these rights not only prohibit public authorities from interfering with people's rights directly (the so called 'negative obligation') but can also require positive action to protect people from harm caused by third parties. These 'positive obligations' may be of a general nature or specific to one or more individuals. They also include a procedural obligation on the state to investigate apparent violations of the negative and positive obligations and credible allegations of harm caused by third parties where that harm results in death or treatment crossing the Articles 2, 3, 4 or 8 thresholds.

7.111 The negative and the positive obligations are discussed under each right below, although it should be kept in mind that the positive obligations in particular are very similar in content irrespective which of the specific ECHR rights is engaged.

Article 2: right to life

Overview

7.112 Article 2 provides that everyone's right to life 'shall be protected by law'. It prohibits the intentional taking of life save as provided in Article 2(2):

> Deprivation of life shall not be regarded as inflicted in contravention of this Article when it results from the use of force which is no more than absolutely necessary:

169 [2005] EWHC 2550 (QB) at paras 155 and 172.

(a) in defence of any person from unlawful violence;
(b) in order to effect a lawful arrest or to prevent the escape of a person lawfully detained;
(c) in action lawfully taken for the purpose of quelling a riot or insurrection.

7.113 Article 2 thus imposes a negative obligation upon the state not to deprive a person of their life, save as in accordance with Article 2(2). Article 2(2) also imposes a positive obligation to protect the lives of members of the public, including those in police custody, from the acts of third parties and other threats to life. The positive obligations to protect life are considered further below.

7.114 The European Court of Human Rights (ECtHR) has repeatedly stated that Article 2 ranks as one of the most fundamental provisions in the ECHR, which enshrines one of the basic values of the democratic societies making up the Council of Europe.[170] It has also explained that Article 2(2) does not define instances where it is permitted to intentionally kill an individual, but describes situations where it is permitted to use force which may result 'as an unintended outcome' in the deprivation of life.[171]

7.115 Article 2 may by violated not only by lethal force, but also by the infliction of force which puts the individual's life at risk.[172]

'no more than absolutely necessary'

7.116 The requirement that the use of force must be 'no more than absolutely necessary' is such that the use of force 'must be strictly proportionate in the circumstances' and the circumstances in which lethal force may be justified 'must be strictly construed'.[173] In *Nachova v Bulgaria* it was stated that the legitimate aim of effecting a lawful arrest:[174]

> . . . can only justify putting human life at risk in circumstances of absolute necessity

and:

> . . . there can be no such necessity where it is known that the person to be arrested poses no threat to life or limb and is not suspected of having committed a violent offence, even if a failure to use lethal force may result in the opportunity to arrest the fugitive being lost.

7.117 The national legal framework regulating arrest operations must make recourse to firearms dependent:[175]

> . . . on a careful assessment of the surrounding circumstances, and, in particular, on an evaluation of the nature of the offence committed by the fugitive and of the threat he or she posed.

170 *Giuliani v Italy* (2012) 54 EHRR 10 at para 174, ECtHR.
171 *Giuliani v Italy* (2012) 54 EHRR 10 at para 175, ECtHR.
172 *Makaratzis v Greece* (2005) 41 EHRR 49, ECtHR; *Davis v Commissioner of Police of the Metropolis* [2016] EWHC 38 (QB) at para 141.
173 *Nachova v Bulgaria* (2006) 42 EHRR 43 at para 94, ECtHR.
174 *Nachova v Bulgaria* (2006) 42 EHRR 43 at para 95, ECtHR.
175 *Nachova v Bulgaria* (2006) 42 EHRR 43 at para 96, ECtHR.

7.118 Moreover, law enforcement agents must be trained to assess whether or not there is an absolute necessity to use firearms:[176]

> . . . not only on the basis of the letter of the relevant regulations but also with due regard to the pre-eminence of respect for human life as a fundamental value . . .

7.119 In the case of operations to quell a riot or insurrection, the police should also be properly equipped so as to be able to conduct the operation while minimising the risk to life[177] – although, of course, the obligation must not be interpreted in such a way as to impose an impossible burden on authorities.[178]

7.120 Plainly, the force used will not be more than absolutely necessary if a lesser means of force can be used. A decision to open fire should, if possible, be preceded by warning shots.[179]

7.121 There is, however, a subjective element to the question of absolute necessity, with the ECtHR having recognised that it 'cannot substitute its own assessment of the situation for that of a law-enforcement officer who is required to react in the heat of the moment to avert an honestly perceived danger to his life'.[180] The use of force may be justified 'where it is based on an honest belief which is perceived, for good reasons, to be valid at the time but which subsequently turns out to be mistaken'.[181] In that respect, the test under Article 2 is no different to that in respect of trespass to the person.[182] In *Davis v Commissioner of Police of the Metropolis*[183] an officer mistakenly believed that the person shot had been pointing a gun at him. However, it was also an honest belief with an objectively reasonable basis and there was no violation of Article 2.

7.122 In a pre-planned operation, consideration as to compliance with Article 2 will extend to whether the operation was adequately planned and controlled so as to minimise the risk to life. There must be an analysis of all available information including consideration of the nature of the offence committed by the person to be arrested and the degree of danger they pose.[184] In that respect, Article 2 differs from the tort of trespass. There may be a violation of Article 2 arising out of deficiencies in the planning of an operation, irrespective of whether the officer who fired the shot did so lawfully and in self-defence. There must, however, be a causal connection between the failure in planning and the death.[185]

7.123 Compliance with Article 2 was considered in *Neville v Commissioner of Police of the Metropolis* which concerned a man who had died under police restraint. The court held that the restraint had been necessary, and when it became apparent that the man was unwell, medical assistance was

176 *Nachova v Bulgaria* (2006) 42 EHRR 43 at para 97, ECtHR.
177 *Gulec v Turkey*, (1999) 41 EHRR 49 at para 71, ECtHR.
178 *Makaratzis v Greece*, (2005) 41 EHRR 49 at para 69, ECtHR.
179 *Kallis and Adroulla Panayi v Turkey* [2009] ECHR 1662 at para 62, ECtHR.
180 *Giuliani v Italy* (2012) 53 EHRR 10 at para 179, ECtHR.
181 *McCann v UK* (1996) 21 EHRR 97 at para 200, ECtHR.
182 See *Bennett v UK* (2011) 52 EHRR SE7, ECtHR.
183 [2016] EWHC 38 (QB).
184 *Nachova v Bulgaria* (2006) 42 EHRR 43 at para 103, ECtHR.
185 *Davis v Commissioner of Police of the Metropolis* [2016] EWHC 38 (QB) at paras 149–151.

promptly sought. There was no violation of Article 2. The officers had been 'appropriately trained' and had 'reacted to a dynamic situation in which they found themselves in a way which they instinctively felt was best to assist the deceased and preserve his life'.[186]

Burden of proof

7.124 As with any civil claim, the burden of proof rests upon the claimant to establish that the death was unlawful for the purposes of Article 2. However, where the death occurs in custody, or otherwise in circumstances known wholly or partly to the state, there is an obligation upon the state to provide an explanation for the death or injury, and an inability to do so may well result in adverse inferences been drawn and the finding that the claimant's case is proven.[187]

The procedural duty to investigate deaths caused by agents of the state

7.125 It has also been held that Article 2 requires by implication that there should be some form of effective official investigation when individuals have been killed as a result of the use of force, the essential purpose of which is to secure the effective implementation of the domestic laws safeguarding the right to life. Moreover, in cases involving deaths caused by agents of the state, an effective investigation serves 'to ensure their accountability for deaths occurring under their responsibility'.[188]

7.126 For an investigation to be effective for the purposes of Article 2, the persons responsible for the investigation must be 'independent and impartial, in law and in practice'.[189] In *Ramashai v Netherlands* it was described that this means not only a lack of hierarchical or institutional connection, but also a 'practical independence'. The requirement of independence is important, as 'what is at stake here is nothing less than public confidence in the state's monopoly on the use of force'.[190] That said, it may be appropriate for an independent investigative body to rely on the investigative capabilities of a police force where the investigative task is 'technical and objective' in nature such that impartiality of the investigation is not adversely affected.[191]

7.127 The investigation must also be effective in the sense that it is capable of leading to the identification and punishment of those responsible. The authority must take 'the reasonable steps available to them to secure the evidence concerning the incident' and 'any deficiency in the investigation which undermines its ability to identify the perpetrator or perpetrators will risk falling foul of this standard'.[192] That can include the authorities obtaining eye

186 [2018] EWHC 20 (QB) at para 84.

187 See *Sheppard v Secretary of State for the Home Department* [2002] EWCA Civ 1921 at para 13.

188 *Nachova v Bulgaria* (2006) 42 EHRR 43 at para 110, ECtHR.

189 *Nachova v Bulgaria* (2006) 42 EHRR 43 at para 112, ECtHR. See, also, *In the matter of an application by Margaret McQuillan for judicial review (Northern Ireland) (Nos 1, 2 and 3)* [2021] UKSC 55 at paras 201 to 214.

190 *Ramashai v Netherlands* (2008) 46 EHRR 43 at para 325, ECtHR.

191 *Giuliani v Italy* (2012) 54 EHRR 10 at para 322, ECtHR.

192 *Ramashai v Netherlands* (2008) 46 EHRR 43 at para 324, ECtHR.

witness testimony, forensic evidence and, where appropriate, an autopsy which provides 'a complete and accurate record of injury and an objective analysis of the clinical findings, including the cause of death'.[193] Any deficiency in the investigation which undermines its ability to establish the cause of death or the person responsible will risk falling foul of this standard. Whether a deficiency in investigation will violate Article 2 depends on all the circumstances of the case and must be assessed 'on the basis of all relevant facts and with regard to the practical realities of investigation work'.[194]

7.128 The investigation must also be accessible to the victim's family to the extent necessary to safeguard their legitimate interests. There must also be a sufficient element of public scrutiny of the investigation, the degree of which may vary from case to case.[195] That does not necessarily preclude sensitive material being withheld, or officers being afforded anonymity having conducted a careful balancing of the competing interests.[196]

7.129 A requirement of promptness and reasonable expedition is implicit, and a prompt response is essential in maintaining public confidence in the adherence to the rule of law and in preventing any appearance of collusion in or tolerance of unlawful acts.[197]

7.130 Where there has been a death resulting from police use of force the investigative duty will generally be discharged by a combination of investigation by the Independent Office of Police Complaints (IOPC) and the inquest.

7.131 A particularly important part of the investigative process will often by at the very outset when initial accounts are yet to be taken, and at a stage when the extent of the IOPC's control of what is happening may be limited. One issue that can arise is the extent to which police colleagues who played a role in the operation resulting in lethal force might have opportunity to collude with one another as to the content of their accounts. Article 2 requires that 'appropriate steps' must be taken to reduce the risk of collusion. In *Ramashai v Netherlands* the two officers were not separated following the death and did not give a statement until three days later. There was no evidence that they had colluded, but 'the mere fact that appropriate steps were not taken to reduce the risk of such collusion amounts to a significant shortcoming in the adequacy of the investigation'.[198] However, whether officers having an opportunity to confer will violate Article 2 will depend upon all the circumstances, including other safeguards in place and the adequacy of the investigation considered as a whole.[199] In *Goodenough v Chief Constable of Thames Valley* the court found a violation of Article 2 in circumstances that the accounts from key officers had been given to all significant witnesses as part of a debrief, prior to giving their own accounts.[200] £5,000 was awarded to the

193 *Giuliani v Italy* (2012) 54 EHRR 10 at para 301, ECtHR.

194 *Giuliani v Italy* (2012) 54 EHRR 10 at para 302, ECtHR.

195 *Giuliani v Italy* (2012) 54 EHRR 10 at para 303, ECtHR.

196 *Bubbins v UK* (2005) 41 EHRR 24, ECtHR.

197 *Giuliani v Italy* (2012) 54 EHRR 10 at para 305, ECtHR; and *Maszepa v Russia* (2019) 68 EHRR 11, ECtHR.

198 At para 330.

199 See *R (Saunders) v Independent Police Complaints Commission* [2008] EWHC 2372 (Admin), [2009] 1 All ER 379 at paras 38–40; and *R (Delezuch) v Chief Constable of Leicestershire* [2014] EWCA Civ 1635 at para 55.

200 [2020] EWHC 1428 (QB) at paras 74–80.

mother and sister of the deceased, in recognition of the violation of the Article 2 investigative obligation.[201]

The Article 2 positive obligations to protect life

Overview

7.132 As is set out above, the Supreme Court has reaffirmed the limited circumstances in which the common law recognises a duty on the police and other public authorities to keep people safe from harm caused by third parties.[202] The court has also acknowledged that the ECHR confers somewhat broader obligations on the state in this respect.[203] This involves no contradiction for common law rights and those under the ECHR serve different purposes: 'Where civil actions are designed essentially to compensate claimants for their losses, Convention claims are intended rather to uphold minimum human rights standards and to vindicate those rights.'[204]

7.133 The positive obligations under Article 2 (and Articles 3, 4 and 8, in respect of which see below) consist of:

a) a general duty to the public (referred to as the 'systems obligation') and
b) an 'operational' duty specific to identifiable individuals or groups of individuals;
c) finally, there is also an 'investigative obligation' of the kind discussed above in the context of deaths caused by state agents.

In 'general, the first two positive obligations can be denoted as substantive, whereas the third aspect designates the States' (positive) procedural obligation'.[205]

7.134 The three positive obligations overlap to a significant extent, and are often engaged simultaneously. For example, systems failures may explain defects in investigations and obligations to protect people may arise during investigations into past treatment. This can influence the standards imposed in a particular case: for example, a 'requirement of promptness and reasonable expedition is implicit in all cases but where the possibility of removing the individual from the harmful situation is available, the investigation must be undertaken as a matter of urgency'.[206]

7.135 However, irrespective of which particular obligation or ECHR right is involved, the positive obligations are never absolute. The courts must bear clearly in mind 'the difficulties involved in policing modern societies, the

201 *Goodenough v Chief Constable of Thames Valley* [2020] EWHC 1428 (QB).

202 See the discussion in the negligence section above, paras 7.48–7.93.

203 In *Michael v Chief Constable of South Wales* [2015] UKSC 2, [2015] AC 1732 the Supreme Court dismissed both the claimants' appeal against the decision that the police did not owe a duty of care to a victim who called 999 alleging her partner had threatened her and the defendant's cross appeal that the Article 2 operational duty was potentially engaged by virtue of the same call.

204 *Van Colle v Chief Constable of Hertfordshire* [2008] UKHL 50, [2009] 1 AC 225 at para 138 referencing Lord Bingham in *R (Greenfield) v Secretary of State for the Home Department* [2005] UKHL 14, [2005] 1 WLR 673.

205 *SM v Croatia* (2021) 72 EHRR 1 at para 306, ECtHR.

206 *Rantsev v Cyprus* (2010) 51 EHRR 1 at para 288, ECtHR.

unpredictability of human conduct and the operational choices which must be made in terms of priorities and resources' and the need to interpret the duty 'in a way which does not impose an impossible or disproportionate burden on the authorities'.[207]

Breach and causation

7.136 In order to show a material breach of a positive obligation the claimant does not have to show that they suffered harm as a result of the breach, although a lack of harm might mean that there is no entitlement to damages.[208]

7.137 Where there has been harm the applicant need only show that there was a 'substantial chance' or 'real prospect' that without the violation the outcome and hence the harm would not have occurred.[209] This is a less stringent test than the 'but for' test under the common law discussed above. This difference is again attributable to the fact ECHR claims are concerned with correcting state action and vindicating rights rather than compensating for damage suffered.[210]

The 'general' or 'systems' obligation

7.138 The state must establish a framework of laws, procedures and systems of enforcement which will, to the greatest extent practicable, protect life and provide effective deterrence against threats to the right to life.[211] This applies in the context of any activity, whether public or not, in which the right to life may be at stake. The authorities are required to assess all the potential risks inherent in the relevant activity, and to take practical measures to ensure the effective protection of those whose lives might be endangered by those risks.[212]

7.139 Importantly, the duty is not limited to enacting a framework of laws, although that is obviously very important.[213] It extends to the systems deployed to enforce the law. Relevant aspects of the duty for the police are

207 *Osman v UK* [1999] 1 FLR 193 at para 116, ECtHR. This applies to all three obligations and irrespective of whether Articles 2, 3, 4 or 8 is involved (see *OOO v Commissioner of Police of the Metropolis* [2011] EWHC 1246 (QB) at para 156).

208 *R (CSM) v Secretary of State for the Home Department* [2021] EWHC 2175 (Admin) applying *Sarjantson v Chief Constable of Humberside* [2013] EWCA Civ 1252, [2014] QB 411.

209 *Van Colle v Chief Constable of Hertfordshire* [2008] UKHL 50, [2009] 1 AC 225 at para 138.

210 In *Van Colle v Chief Constable of Hertfordshire* [2008] UKHL 50, [2009] 1 AC 225 at para 138 it was said the difference in purpose seems 'to explain why a looser approach to causation is adopted under the Convention than in English tort law. Whereas the latter requires the claimant to establish on the balance of probabilities that, but for the claimant's negligence, he would not have suffered his claimed loss . . . under the Convention it appears sufficient generally to establish merely that he lost a substantial chance of this'.

211 *R (Amin) v Secretary of State for the Home Department* [2003] UKHL 51, [2004] 1 AC 653 at para 30; *Öneryildiz v Turkey (No 2)* (2005) 41 EHRR 20 at para 89, ECtHR.

212 *Öneryildiz v Turkey (No 2)* (2005) 41 EHRR 20 at para 71, ECtHR; *Kolyadenko v Russia* (2013) 56 EHRR 2 at paras 158, 166, ECtHR.

213 Although in *Griffiths v Chief Constable of Suffolk* [2018] EWHC 2538 (QB), [2019] Med LR 1 the court found that there had been no breach of the systems duty on the facts, it rejected the submission that the systems duty is limited to the relevant legislative framework (at para 572).

the employment and training of competent staff,[214] provision of adequate equipment[215] and implementing systems to detect and remedy individual failings and errors before harm is done, including errors at different organisational levels.[216] Breaches of the systems duty are evidenced by errors of practice that 'point to a systemic fault in the design or supervision of the system'.[217] As is set out above, these types of systemic issues will inform the requirements at a local level when the police are planning an operation that may result in the use of force. Similarly, the police will need to have systems in place to ensure police officers who are off duty are not able to abuse their equipment or powers to the detriment of other citizens.[218]

7.140 There may be a violation of the general obligation, for example by failure to have in place proper systems, even though no risk has been identified to a specified individual[219] and no harm has been suffered.[220] However, in practice alleged breaches of the systems duty are most often raised in the context of specific individuals and in connection with alleged breaches of the other positive obligations. For example, in *DSD v Commissioner of Police of the Metropolis*,[221] a case brought under Article 3, the court found that a number of systemic failings, which included failings over improper resource allocation, undermined the force's ability to protect women from a serial rapist.

The operational obligation

7.141 The police are under an operational duty to take preventative measures to protect an individual where they know, or ought to know, of the existence of a real and immediate risk to their life.[222] The duty is triggered if the risk concerns a specific named individual or a group of people or a sector of the public.[223] Similarly, the risk may emanate from an individual, a group of

214 *Savage v South Essex Partnership NHS Foundation Trust* [2008] UKHL 74, [2009] 1 AC 681 at paras 30, 45, 50, 97; *Mitchell v Glasgow City Council* [2009] UKHL 11, [2009] 1 AC 874 at para 66.

215 *Kakoulli v Turkey* (2007) 45 EHRR 12 at para 110, ECtHR.

216 *Öneryildiz v Turkey* (2005) 41 EHRR 20 at paras 89–95, ECtHR; *Kakoulli v Turkey* (2007) 45 EHRR 12 at para 106, ECtHR.

217 *R (Scarfe and others) v (1) Governor of HMP Woodhill and (2) Secretary of State for Justice* [2017] EWHC 1194 (Admin) at para 54.

218 In *Gorovenky and Bugara v Ukraine* (App Nos 36146/05 and 42418/05) 12 January 2012, at para 32, a killing by an off-duty police officer was not classified as state activity, but a breach of general obligation to protect public by allowing off-duty office to carry fire arms without proper assessment of risk.

219 *Savage v South Essex Partnership NHS Foundation Trust* [2008] UKHL 74, [2009] 1 AC 681 at para 31.

220 *R (CSM) v Secretary of State for the Home Department* [2021] EWHC 2175 (Admin) applying *Sarjantson v Chief Constable of Humberside* [2013] EWCA Civ 1252, [2014] QB 411.

221 [2014] EWHC 436 (QB). The findings of the High Court were upheld by the Supreme Court ([2018] UKSC 11, [2019] AC 196).

222 *Osman v UK* [1999] 1 FLR 193, ECtHR. A distinction should be drawn between evidence of a risk to life, and evidence of merely a risk of harm, which should not be equated with a risk to life with the benefit of hindsight (*R (Kent County Council) v HM Coroner for Kent (North-West District)* [2012] EWHC 2768 (Admin) at para 46). However, a risk of harm that meets the relevant thresholds in Articles 3, 4 and 8 may trigger the operational duty under those articles.

223 *Sarjanston v Chief Constable of Humberside* [2013] EWCA Civ 1252 at para 25.

individuals, self-harm[224] or even external factors like a need for medical treatment.[225] The information disclosing the risk might come to light in myriad different ways, for example police intelligence or a history of violence against the victim,[226] a complaint having been made or because the police are detaining a suspect with aggressive tendencies.[227]

7.142 A 'real' risk to life is one that is 'substantial or significant . . . and not . . . remote or fanciful'.[228] A risk of five per cent to 20 per cent is 'real' for these purposes.[229] An 'immediate' risk to life is one that is 'present and continuing'.[230] It is not necessary for the risk to be imminent just before death, provided that it exists at that moment, as opposed to a risk conditional on some event that may only arise at some point in the future.[231] In *Renolde v France*[232] the deceased had attempted suicide 18 days before his death and thereafter continued to show signs of worrying behaviour and although he had made no further attempts at self-harm the duty was engaged at the point of his death.

7.143 The operational duty is triggered not only where the police know of the relevant risk, but also where they ought to know. Bad judgment, lack of imagination and inertia do not afford an excuse to an authority which reasonably ought, in the light of what it knew or was told, to have made further inquiries or investigations. The authority is then to be treated as knowing what such further inquiries or investigations would have elicited.[233] It is not necessary that the failure to identify the risk to life should amount to gross negligence or willful disregard for there to be a violation of the operational obligation.[234]

7.144 Once triggered, the police must take such preventative measures within the scope of their powers which, judged reasonably, might be expected to avoid the risk.[235] The steps that it is reasonable for them to take depend on the circumstances of the case, the ease or difficulty of taking precautions, and the resources available.[236] The operational obligation does not amount to a requirement to prevent every possibility of violence and must be interpreted in a way which does not impose an impossible or disproportionate burden on the state.[237]

224 *Keenan v UK* (2001) 33 EHRR 38, ECtHR at para 92.

225 *R (CSM) v Secretary of State for the Home Department* [2021] EWHC 2175 (Admin).

226 *Opuz v Turkey* (2010) 50 EHRR 28, ECtHR.

227 *Edwards v UK* (2002) 35 EHRR 19, ECtHR at para 69.

228 *Rabone v Pennine Care NHS Foundation Trust* [2012] UKSC 2, [2012] 2 AC 72 at para 38.

229 *Rabone v Pennine Care NHS Foundation Trust* [2010] EWCA Civ 698 at paras 73 and 75. This conclusion was not varied or criticised by the Supreme Court in *Rabone v Pennine Care NHS Foundation Trust* [2012] 2 AC 72.

230 *Rabone v Pennine Care NHS Foundation Trust* [2012] UKSC 2, [2012] 2 AC 72 at paras 39–41.

231 *Rabone v Pennine Care NHS Foundation Trust* [2012] UKSC 2, [2012] 2 AC 72 at paras 39–40.

232 (2009) 48 EHRR 42, ECtHR.

233 *Van Colle v Chief Constable of Hertfordshire* [2008] UKHL 50, [2009] 1 AC 225 at para 34.

234 *Osman v UK* (2000) 29 EHRR 245 at para 116, ECtHR.

235 *Osman v UK* (2000) 29 EHRR 245 at para 116, ECtHR; and *Sarjantson v Chief Constable of Humberside* [2013] EWCA Civ 1252 at paras 26–29, 31.

236 *Re Officer L* [2007] UKHL 36, [2007] 1 WLR 2135 at para 21; *Rabone v Pennine Care NHS Trust* [2012] UKSC 2, [2012] 2 AC 72 at para 43.

237 *Osman v UK* (2000) 29 EHRR 245, ECtHR at para 116.

The procedural duty to investigate acts perpetrated by non-state actors

7.145 The extent of the police's obligation to investigate a death apparently or possibly caused by a third party is in principle no different from that discussed above in relation to deaths at the hands of state agents,[238] albeit that in the former scenario the investigation is not, necessarily at least, concerned with holding state entities accountable and therefore questions of independence are much less likely to arise. Always the investigation is to be carried out timeously and thoroughly and must be capable of identifying and punishing the perpetrator (although there is no right to a prosecution still less a conviction – the duty is not an obligation of result but of means[239]). It is no part of the court's role when considering the procedural duty to establish whether the deceased was in fact unlawfully killed or to determine the circumstances of the death (insofar as there is any doubt): it is solely concerned with the quality of the investigation.

7.146 Investigations into deaths caused by non-state actors may have to explore the contribution of public bodies to the extent that it is arguable that they failed in their substantive duties to protect the deceased.[240] To this end, the actions (or failures to act) by the police may be the subject of an Article 2 investigation by another police force, the IOPC or a coroner. The 'arguable' threshold in this context is not a high one.[241] The circumstances in which there must be an Article 2 compliant investigation into a death because of possible state complicity are not closed and may extend beyond situations where the police or another public service has assumed some form of relevant responsibility for the deceased, particularly if the deceased was especially vulnerable.[242]

Historic allegations and new evidence

7.147 New information regarding an historic investigation may come to light at a later stage. The court has held that where there is a credible new allegation, piece of evidence or item of information relevant to the killing, the authorities are under an obligation to take further investigative measures.[243] The nature and extent of any subsequent investigation will depend

238 Article 2 imposes a duty on that state to secure the right to life by putting in place effective criminal-law provisions to deter the commission of offences against the person, backed up by law-enforcement machinery for the prevention, suppression and punishment of breaches of such provisions. This obligation requires by implication that there should be some form of effective official investigation when there is reason to believe that an individual has sustained life threatening injuries in suspicious circumstances, even where the presumed perpetrator of the fatal attack is not a state agent: *Mustafa Tunç and Fecire Tunç v Turkey* [2015] 4 WLUK 150 at para 171, ECtHR.

239 *Jordan v UK* (2003) 37 EHRR 52 at para 107 ECtHR; *R (Amin) v Secretary of State for the Home Department* [2003] UKHL 51, [2004] 1 AC 653 at para 20(6).

240 *Jordan v UK* [2001] 37 EHRR 2 at paras 105–109, ECtHR; *R (Middleton) v West Somerset Coroner* [2004] UKHL 10, [2004] 2 AC 182, at paras 3, 19.

241 *R (AP) v HM Coroner for Worcestershire* [2011] EWHC 1453 (Admin) at para 60.

242 *Rabone v Pennine Care NHS Trust* [2012] UKSC 2, [2012] 2 AC 72 at paras 22–23.

243 *Brecknell v UK* (2008) 46 EHRR 42 at para 71, ECtHR.

on the circumstances of the particular case and may well differ from that to be expected immediately after the death has occurred.[244]

Victim status

7.148 By HRA 1998 s7(1), a person may bring a claim if they are 'a victim of the unlawful act' complained of, and by section 7(7) a person 'is a victim of an unlawful act only if he would be a victim for the purposes of Article 34 of the Convention if proceedings were brought in the [ECtHR] in respect of that act'. A relative of the deceased will often be recognised as an 'indirect victim' of the act relating to the death of the deceased. In *Daniel v St George's Healthcare NHS Trust*[245] it was observed that applications by indirect victims have been brought in two capacities. First, where the deceased next-of-kin is representing the estate or interests of the deceased. The second is where blood relatives, spouses or partners are claiming for their own pain, distress and bereavement at the treatment leading to their relative's death. Claims are generally brought by family members although a blood tie or marriage is not essential, with consideration being given to factors such as the nature and length of the relationship between the deceased and the claimant and the extent to which the alleged violation affected them personally.[246] Unmarried partners,[247] a fiancée[248] and foster parents[249] have been recognised as indirect victims.

Article 3: prohibition of torture, inhumane or degrading treatment

Overview

7.149 Article 3 prohibits torture and inhumane and degrading treatment. It is an absolute right, such that subjecting a person to inhumane and degrading treatment is incapable of lawful justification and will violate the person's rights. There may be instances, therefore, where there may be some lawful basis for a particular act whether pursuant to statute or common law, but there is nevertheless a violation of the person's rights protected by Article 3.

7.150 The treatment must be of a particular severity in order to engage the protection of Article 3. In *Price v UK* the court described that the assessment of the minimum level of severity is relative. It depends 'on all the circumstances of the case, such as the duration of the treatment, its physical and mental effects and, in some cases, the sex, age and state of health of the victim'.[250] It was also said that the court will take into account

244 *Harrison and others v UK* (2014) 59 EHRR SEI at paras 51 and 65, ECtHR. The standard of expedition in such cases is very different to the standard applicable in recent incidents where time is often of the essence (*Gurtekin and others v Cyprus* [2014] ECHR 519 at para 21), ECtHR.

245 [2016] EWHC 23 (QB), [2016] 4 WLR 32.

246 [2016] EWHC 23 (QB), [2016] 4 WLR 32 at paras 151–154.

247 *Velikova v Bulgaria* (App No 41488/98), 18 May 2000.

248 *Morgan v Ministry of Justice* [2010] EWHC 2248 (QB).

249 As in *Daniel v St George's Heathcare NHS Trust* [2016] EWHC 23 (QB), [2016] 4 WLR 32.

250 (2002) 34 EHRR 53 at para 24, ECtHR.

whether the object of the treatment is to humiliate and debase the person concerned, although the absence of any such purpose could not conclusively rule out a finding of violation of Article 3. In *Price* itself the applicant was a severely disabled woman who was detained for four days in circumstances that she was dangerously cold, she was at risk of developing bed sores, and unable to go to the toilet or keep clean without the greatest difficulty. There had been no intention to humiliate and debase, but there was nonetheless a violation of Article 3.

7.151 That a person is vulnerable further to a disability may also be relevant. In *MS v UK* the court emphasised that 'the mentally ill are in a position of particular vulnerability, and clear issues of respect for their fundamental human dignity arise whenever such persons are detained by the authorities'.[251] In *ZH v Commissioner of Police of the Metropolis* there had been a violation of Article 3 where a severely autistic 16-year-old boy had been lifted by officers from a swimming pool and placed in cuffs and leg restraints before being placed in the rear of a police van for about 25 minutes.[252]

7.152 That a person is detained will be relevant to whether the Article 3 threshold has been crossed. In *Bouyid v Belgium* the court explained that 'where an individual is deprived of his or her liberty or, more generally, is confronted with law-enforcement officers, any recourse to physical force which has not been made strictly necessary by the person's conduct diminishes human dignity and is in principle an infringement of the right set forth in article 3'.[253] In that case the court found a violation of Article 3 in relation to a law enforcement officer slapping a detained minor, noting the particularly humiliating nature of a slap to the face in the context of an officer flouting their duty against a person who is vulnerable by virtue of being detained.

7.153 In relation to age, the court in *Bouyid v Belgium* emphasised that it 'is vital for law-enforcement officers who are in contact with minors . . . to take due account of the vulnerability inherent in their young age' and police behaviour towards minors 'may be incompatible with the requirements of Article 3 of the Convention simply because they are minors, whereas it might be deemed acceptable in the case of adults'.[254]

7.154 On one view, the approach in *Bouyid* is surprising in indicating that any unnecessary physical force on a detained person, no matter how minor, violates Article 3. In *Yousif v Commissioner of Police of the Metropolis* Sir Brian Leveson characterised the facts of *Bouyid* as involving a campaign of deliberate police misbehaviour and warned of the potential adverse effects of lowering the level of severity required to establish a breach of Article 3.[255] In *Alseran v Ministry of Defence* Leggatt J described that warning as 'salutary' and expressed the view that it 'would not be consistent with the nature and status of Article 3 to treat any unlawful use of force by a state agent, however minor, as a violation of the right which it protects'.[256]

251 (2012) 55 EHRR 23 at para 39, ECtHR.
252 [2013] EWCA Civ 69, [2013] 1 WLR 3021.
253 (2016) 62 EHRR 32 at para 100, ECtHR.
254 (2016) 62 EHRR 32 at para 110, ECtHR.
255 [2016] EWCA Civ 364 at paras 59–60.
256 [2017] EWHC 3289 (QB) at para 231.

7.155 What is clear is that the suffering and humiliation of the detained person must 'go beyond the inevitable element of suffering or humiliation connected with a given form of legitimate treatment or punishment, as in, for example, measures depriving a person of their liberty'.[257] Thus, in *Archip v Romania* it was explained that the use of handcuffs and other instruments of restraint does not normally give rise to an issue under Article 3 where 'the measure has been imposed in connection with lawful detention and does not entail the use of force or public exposure exceeding what is reasonably considered necessary'.[258]

7.156 The severity threshold has been held to have been crossed in the case of a man being struck with a baton while resisting arrest causing heavy bruising causing him to be unable to work for five days;[259] an assault resulting in three broken ribs and a testicular haematoma;[260] and a blow to the head during arrest causing swelling and a bruise of 2cm.[261]

7.157 The severity threshold had not been crossed in *Yousif v Commissioner of Police of the Metropolis* where the claimant had been strip searched and moved cells whilst unclothed, primarily because both actions had been 'strictly necessary'. The court was not persuaded that breaches of the PACE Codes compelled the opposite conclusion.[262] Significant weight was placed on the officers acting on legitimate concerns and in good faith. There had not been any deliberate abuse of power, as in *Bouyid*.

7.158 Whether the treatment amounts to inhuman or degrading treatment, or to torture, is unlikely to be relevant to whether there has been a violation of Article 3 as all treatment which falls within Article 3 is prohibited absolutely. However, where the treatment amounts to torture the award of damages may be higher. In *El-Masri v Macedonia* the court described that a finding of torture will be reserved for 'deliberate inhuman treatment causing very serious and cruel suffering' and referred to the 'purposive element' of the intentional infliction of severe pain or suffering with the aim of obtaining information, inflicting punishment or intimidating.[263] In *Cestaro v Italy*[264] the court made a finding of torture in circumstances that the applicant had been attacked by police officers who kicked and hit him with wooden truncheons, causing multiple fractures and leaving him with permanent weakness in his right arm and leg.

The procedural duty to investigate Article 3 ill-treatment by agents of the state

7.159 A credible allegation of Article 3 ill-treatment by a police officer will trigger an investigative obligation. The Article 3 investigative duty has similar

257 *Wainwright v UK* (2007) 44 EHRR 40 at para 41, ECtHR.

258 *Archip v Romania* (App No 49608/08, 27 September 2011), ECtHR at para 52.

259 *Douet v France* (App No 16705/10, 3 October 2013), ECtHR (judgment in French only), cited in *Alseran v Ministry of Defence* [2019] QB 1251 at 925(i).

260 *Alberti v Italy* (App No 15397/11, 24 June 2014), ECtHR, (judgment in French only), cited in *Alseran v Ministry of Defence* [2019] QB 1251 at 925(ii).

261 *Samut Karabulut v Turkey* (App No 1699/04, 27 January 2009), ECtHR.

262 [2016] EWCA Civ 364.

263 (2013) 57 EHRR 25 at para 197.

264 App No 6884/11, 7 April 2015, ECtHR.

requirements to Article 2 in that it must be capable of leading to the identification and punishment of those responsible, it must be independent, it must be thorough and effective, and it must permit effective access for the complainant to the investigatory procedure.[265] However, in practical terms the manner in which the investigative duty may be discharged will often differ.

7.160 The nature of the Article 3 investigative duty was considered at some length in *R (MM) v Secretary of State for the Home Department*,[266] and summarised in *R (NM) v Secretary of State for Justice*.[267] See also, more recently, *MA v Secretary of State for the Home Department*.[268] There is a difference in emphasis as between the investigative duty imposed by Articles 2 and 3. In Article 2 the victim will have died and the only persons with knowledge of the circumstances of the death are officers of the state. In contrast, in Article 3 cases the victim is generally able to act on their own behalf and give evidence as to what happened. In Article 2 cases, particularly concerning deaths in state custody, there is likely to be 'especially grave concern' not only to ensure accountability but also to learn lessons from systemic mistakes.[269] Accordingly, the courts have considered that the alternatives of civil and criminal proceedings, and the possibility of ombudsman enquiries, will often be sufficient to discharge the Article 3 investigative duty. Moreover, in the absence of state complicity the essential obligation on the state is to provide a system under which civil wrongs may be remedied in litigation or criminal wrongs investigated and prosecuted.

7.161 Whether a broader 'human rights inquiry' is necessary is fact sensitive and the courts will inevitably be mindful of the potentially significant resource implications of imposing such an obligation.[270] In *MA v Secretary of State for the Home Department*[271] an inquiry with the ability to compel witnesses to give evidence in public hearings and with legal representation for the family was considered to be necessary in the context of egregious and systemic Article 3 ill-treatment at an immigration detention centre.

7.162 The effect is that in most instances of Article 3 ill-treatment by police officers the investigative duty can be discharged through a combination of the availability of civil proceedings and criminal investigation, and also by the IOPC. In the event of particular egregious and perhaps widespread violation of Article 3 by a particular unit or at a particular custody suite, a broader inquiry may be necessary.

265 *AM v Secretary of State for the Home Department* [2009] EWCA Civ 219, [2009] UKHRR 973.

266 [2012] EWCA Civ 668 at paras 12–28.

267 [2012] EWCA Civ 1182 at para 29.

268 [2019] EWHC 1523 (Admin) at paras 38–45.

269 [2012] EWCA Civ 1182 at para 29.

270 As in *R (P) v Secretary of State for Justice* [2009] EWCA Civ 701 at para 58.

271 [2019] EWHC 1523 (Admin).

The positive obligations

The general or 'systems' obligation

7.163 Article 3 requires the state to take measures to prevent the infliction of ill-treatment which breaches Article 3, including treatment inflicted by one private individual against another.[272] As part of its system obligation, the state is required to enact criminal law provisions to provide effective deterrence and punishment of violations of Article 3.[273] For example, in *MC v Bulgaria*[274] the domestic law appeared not to provide effective protection against rape and sexual abuse as only cases where there was evidence that the alleged victim had actively resisted were prosecuted and therefore the issue of consent was not investigated.

7.164 As with Article 2 (see above), the systems duty under Article 3 is broader than the obligation on the state to enact sufficient criminal law and will extend to the creation, funding and training of the institutions and infrastructure to implement and enforce the law. In the context of the police, this has particular relevance: for example, although analysed as part of the investigative duty, the failings that stymied the Metropolitan Police's ability to investigate the crimes of serial rapist John Worboys included systemic and not merely operational errors.[275]

The operational obligation

7.165 The operational duty applies to a real and immediate risk of Article 3 treatment of which the authorities know or ought to know.[276] The operational obligation under Article 3 mirrors the duty imposed by Article 2,[277] in respect of which see above and the discussion under Article 2 above.

The procedural duty to investigate Article 3 ill-treatment perpetrated by non-state actors

7.166 There is no doubt that the Article 3 investigative obligation applies to allegations of mistreatment by non-state actors.[278] The content of the duty is essentially the same as that which applies when the alleged perpetrators are agents of the state but, as with the Article 2 investigative duty, there are less likely to be concerns about independence of the investigator save where state complicity is alleged in the form of breaches of the substantive obligations to protect the victim.

7.167 The leading domestic case concerned the Metropolitan Police's failure to investigate serial rapist Jon Worboys.[279] In *DSD v Commissioner of Police*

272 *A v UK* (1999) 27 EHRR 611 at para 22, ECtHR.

273 *MC v Bulgaria* (2005) 40 EHRR 20 at paras 153, 166, ECtHR.

274 *MC v Bulgaria* (2005) 40 EHRR 20 at paras 153, 166, ECtHR.

275 *DSD v Commissioner of Police of the Metropolis* [2014] EWHC 436 (QB) at paras 243–313. The findings of the High Court were upheld by the Supreme Court [2018] UKSC 11, [2019] AC 196.

276 *Z v UK* (2001) 34 EHRR 3, at para 73, ECtHR; *Premininy v Russia* (2011) 31 BHRC 9, ECtHR.

277 *Rabone v Pennine Care NHS Foundation Trust* [2012] UKSC 2, [2012] 2 AC 72 at para 23.

278 *DSD v Commissioner of Police of the Metropolis* [2018] UKSC 11, [2019] AC 196 at paras 59–62.

279 *DSD v Commissioner of Police of the Metropolis* [2018] UKSC 11, [2019] AC 196.

of the Metropolis the Supreme Court upheld the findings made by the High Court that the police had made a number of significant failings when responding to credible allegations by Worboys' victims. The failings were both operational and systemic, including:

- a failure to train relevant officers in the intricacies of sexual assaults and, in particular, drug-facilitated sexual assaults;
- serious failures by senior officers properly to supervise investigations by more junior officers;
- serious failures in the collection and use of intelligence sources to cross-check complaints to see if there were linkages between them;
- a failure to maintain the confidence of victims in the integrity of the investigative process; and
- a failure to allocate proper resources to sexual assaults, including pressure from management to focus resources on other crimes.[280]

7.168 Not every failing in an investigation will breach the obligation. The Supreme Court followed the ECtHR and made it clear that Article 3 was not concerned with isolated mistakes or omissions.[281] Only 'obvious and significant shortcomings in the conduct of the police and prosecutorial investigation will give rise to the possibility of a claim', and the 'courts will . . . forestall challenges to police inquiries based on spurious or speculative claims'. [282]

7.169 It is not necessary for a claimant to prove as part of their claim under the HRA 1998 that they were in fact subjected to ill-treatment. All that is necessary is that there has been a credible allegation that they have been or at risk of being mistreated in a manner that would meet the Article 3 threshold. Relatedly, the court considering an alleged breach of the procedural duty need not (and cannot) decide on the alleged perpetrators' guilt.[283]

7.170 In *DSD* it was clear that the claimants had in fact suffered treatment reaching the high threshold in Article 3 because Worboys had been convicted of his crimes against them before they brought their claims. However, the fact convictions were ultimately secured did not nullify the significant defects and delay in the investigations such as to mean there was no breach of the investigative duty. Indeed, the fact the police force had already recognised and taken steps to remedy the systemic failings did not detract from the violations or the claimants' entitlement to compensation.[284]

280 *DSD v Commissioner of Police of the Metropolis* [2014] EWHC 436 (QB) at paras 243–313. The findings of the High Court were upheld by the Supreme Court [2018] UKSC 11, [2019] AC 196. For another example of where both operational and systemic errors lead to a breach of Article 3 in the context of serious sexual assault, see *C v Chief Constable of Northern Ireland* [2020] NIQB 3. For a case where the investigation passed the Article 3 test, see *R (AB) v Chief Constable of Hampshire* [2019] EWHC 3461 (Admin).

281 *MC v Bulgaria* (2005) 40 EHRR 20 at para 168, ECtHR.

282 Lord Kerr in *DSD v Commissioner of Police of the Metropolis* [2018] UKSC 11, [2019] AC 196 at para 72. See the discussion about the level of seriousness required in *R (Skelton) v HM Senior Coroner for West Sussex* [2020] EWHC 2813 (Admin) at paras 56–57.

283 *MC v Bulgaria* (2005) 40 EHRR 420 at para 168, ECtHR.

284 *DSD v Commissioner of Police of the Metropolis* [2014] EWHC 436 (QB) at para 13.

7.171 The 'credible allegations' test is not particularly demanding.[285] In particular, the police may not avoid the duty on the grounds that the allegation transpired not to be credible. In *CN v UK*, a case concerning Article 4, the court said that:[286]

> Although the Government have submitted that the applicant's account was not in fact credible, the Court observes that this was a conclusion reached following further investigation of her complaints. Indeed, the fact that the domestic authorities conducted any investigation into the applicant's complaints strongly indicates that, at least on their face, they were not inherently implausible. Consequently, the Court considers that the applicant's complaints did give rise to a credible suspicion ... which in turn placed the domestic authorities under an obligation to investigate those complaints.

7.172 Importantly, the allegation need not be made by or pursued by the alleged victim.[287] Once the matter has come to the attention of the police, they must act of their own motion.[288]

Article 4: prohibition of slavery, servitude and forced labour

Overview

7.173 Article 4 states:

> 1. No one shall be held in slavery or servitude.
> 2. No one shall be required to perform forced or compulsory labour.[289]

7.174 The police (or other agents of the state) are unlikely to infringe the negative obligation contained in Article 4 and hence it is not dealt with here.[290] The law regarding the content of Article 4 is set out briefly below.

7.175 The ECHR does not define slavery, servitude and forced or compulsory labour. In *R v K*[291] the Court of Appeal relied on several ECtHR cases to explain that 'slavery', 'servitude' and 'forced or compulsory labour' form a hierarchy of denial of personal autonomy:

285 Arguable means anything more than fanciful: *R (AP) v HM Coroner for Worcestershire* [2011] EWHC 1453 (Admin), [2011] BLGR 952.

286 (2013) 56 EHRR 24 at para 72, ECtHR.

287 *OOO v Commissioner of Police of the Metropolis* [2011] EWHC 1246 (QB).

288 See *Rantsev v Cyprus* (2010) 51 EHRR 1 at para 288, ECtHR. In *Chowdury and others v Greece* (App No 21884/15), 30 March 2017, ECtHR the court found that Greece had failed to comply with its positive obligations because the authorities, who knew through official reports and the media about the situation in which migrant workers found themselves well before the shooting incident involving the applicants, had failed to take adequate measures to prevent trafficking and to protect the applicants (at paras 111–115).

289 Article 4(3) states that 'forced or compulsory labour' does not include: '(a) any work required to be done in the ordinary course of detention imposed according to the provisions of Article 5 of [the] Convention or during conditional release from such detention; (b) any service of a military character or, in case of conscientious objectors in countries where they are recognised, service exacted instead of compulsory military service; (c) any service exacted in case of an emergency or calamity threatening the life or well-being of the community; (d) any work or service which forms part of normal civic obligations.'

290 *SM v Croatia* (2021) 72 EHRR 1 at para 304, ECtHR.

291 [2011] EWCA Crim 1691, [2011] 2 Cr App R 34.

- The essence of 'slavery' is treating someone as not belonging to oneself, by exercising power over that person as one might over an animal or an object.
- The essence of 'servitude' is one person's obligation to provide services to another, an obligation imposed by the use of coercion.
- The essence of 'forced or compulsory labour' is work exacted under the menace of a penalty and performed against the will of the person concerned, a concept which brings to mind the idea of either physical or mental constraint, the essential character of the work or service involved being work or service for which the person has not offered himself voluntarily. The court added that where 'forced or compulsory labour' is concerned, the menace of a penalty can be exerted in various ways. It can be direct or indirect and constraint may be mental or physical and can be imposed by force of circumstances. In *Siliadin v France*[292] the court found this element to be present where the applicant, an adolescent, had no right to be in France and lived in fear of arrest by the police.

7.176 In another case concerning young women who with the help of relatives in Europe escaped precarious circumstances only to find themselves working involuntarily without pay, *CN and V v France*,[293] the European Court of Human Rights said that work required of an individual under threat of a 'penalty' does not necessarily constitute 'forced or compulsory labor'; it is necessary to take into account, in particular, the nature and the volume of the activity in question in order to 'distinguish between "forced labor" and a helping hand which can reasonably be expected of other family members or people sharing accommodation'.[294] The court resorted to the concept of 'disproportionate burden' that was established in a previous case concerning a trainee lawyer who failed to establish that he was subject to compulsory labour when required to provide pro-bono work.[295]

7.177 In *CN and V v France* two sisters born in Burundi were brought to France by their aunt. They were accommodated in the basement of the house and were obliged to carry out all household and domestic chores, without remuneration or any days off. The applicants alleged that they lived in unhygienic conditions, were not allowed to share family meals and were subjected to daily physical and verbal harassment. Both applicants claimed that they were physically and verbally harassed on a daily basis by their aunt, who regularly threatened to send them back to Burundi. V went to school and obtained good results. When she returned from school she did her homework and then helped her sister with the domestic chores. In contrast, CN, the older child, did not go to school and had no days off or opportunity for leisure. The court found that the CN had been subjected to forced labour but that V had not. CN had been obliged to perform so much work that, without her help, the aunt would have been required to have recourse to a professional – and thus paid – employee. Moreover, CN, unlike V, had been in servitude because she had perceived herself to be trapped in the situation without hope of it ending.

292 (2006) 43 EHRR 16, ECtHR.

293 App No 67724/09, 11 October 2012, ECtHR.

294 *CN and V v France* (App No 67724/09) at para 74, ECtHR.

295 *Van der Mussele v Belgium* (1984) 6 EHRR 163, ECtHR.

7.178 It is clear that trafficking 'within the meaning of art.3(a) of the Palermo Protocol [ie the Protocol to Prevent, Suppress and Punish Trafficking in Persons, especially Women and Children] and art.4(a) of the Anti-Trafficking Convention [ie Council of Europe Convention on Action against Trafficking in Human Beings], falls within the scope of art.4 of the [ECHR]'.[296] It is not necessary to identify whether the trafficking constitutes 'slavery', 'servitude' or 'forced [or] compulsory labour'. However, it is imperative that the three components of trafficking are present, namely:

1) an action (the recruitment, transportation, transfer, harbouring or receipt of persons);
2) the means (threat or use of force or other forms of coercion, abduction, fraud, deception, abuse of power or of a position of vulnerability, or the giving or receiving of payments or benefits to achieve the consent of a person having control over another person); and
3) an exploitative purpose (including, at a minimum, the exploitation of the prostitution of others or other forms of sexual exploitation, forced labour or services, slavery or practices similar to slavery, servitude or the removal of organs).[297]

7.179 For Article 4, the concept of human trafficking relates to both national and transnational trafficking and irrespective of whether or not it is connected with organised crime.[298]

The positive obligations

7.180 There is no doubt that the positive obligations to protect and the investigative duty all arise in respect of conduct that engages Article 4.[299] In particular, states are required to put in place a legislative and administrative framework to prevent and punish trafficking and to protect victims.[300] For example, in *CN v UK*[301] the ECtHR held that the UK was in breach of the general systems obligation because forced labour and domestic servitude were at that time only outlawed in the context of trafficking.

7.181 As with ECHR Articles 2 and 3, Article 4 may, in certain circumstances, require a state to take operational measures to protect victims, or potential victims, of conduct including trafficking that violates Article 4. In order for such a positive obligation to arise in the circumstances of a particular case, it must be demonstrated that the state authorities were aware, or ought to have been aware, of circumstances giving rise to a credible suspicion that an identified individual had been, or was at real and immediate risk of being, trafficked or exploited within the meaning of Palermo Protocol

296 *Rantsev v Cyprus* (2010) 51 EHRR 1 at para 282, ECtHR.

297 *SM v Croatia* (2021) 72 EHRR 1 at paras 290 and 303, ECtHR. In the context of claims against local authorities in respect of trafficked children, see *R (TDT) v Secretary of State for the Home Department* [2018] EWCA Civ 1395, [2018] 1 WLR 4922 and *R (H) v Swindon Borough Council* [2021] EWCA Civ 1836.

298 *SM v Croatia* (2021) 72 EHRR 1 at paras 296 and 303, ECtHR.

299 *Rantsev v Cyprus* (2010) 51 EHRR 1 at paras 285–288, ECtHR; *MS (Pakistan) v Secretary of State for the Home Department* [2020] UKSC 9, [2020] 3 All ER 733.

300 *VCL and AN v UK* (App Nos 77587/12 and 74603/12), (2021) 73 EHRR 9, at para 151, ECtHR.

301 (2013) 56 EHRR 24, ECtHR.

Article 3(a) and Anti-Trafficking Convention Article 4(a). When this is the case, there will be a violation of Article 4 where the authorities fail to take appropriate measures within the scope of their powers to remove the individual from that situation or risk.[302]

7.182 The ECtHR has been influenced by the Anti-Trafficking Convention when considering the range of operational measures that might be required by Article 4. The convention stipulates that protection measures include facilitating the identification of victims by qualified persons and assisting victims in their physical, psychological and social recovery.[303] In the UK, these duties are largely co-ordinated by the Home Office through the National Referral Mechanism (NRM). The police play a vital role in identifying, referring and investigating possible cases of trafficking.

7.183 An issue perhaps unique to Article 4 is the prospect of alleged victims being prosecuted for transgressions of the law alleged to have been committed whilst trafficked. In *VCL and AN v UK* the ECtHR has observed that:[304]

> It is axiomatic that the prosecution of victims of trafficking would be injurious to their physical, psychological and social recovery and could potentially leave them vulnerable to being re-trafficked in future. Not only would they have to go through the ordeal of a criminal prosecution, but a criminal conviction could create an obstacle to their subsequent integration into society.

7.184 However, although it may do in individual cases, the existence of the positive obligation to protect victims of trafficking does not automatically prohibit a prosecution. In this respect, the court has held that early identification of victims of trafficking by a competent authority is of paramount importance and that any decision to prosecute should be taken after this assessment so that any subsequent prosecutorial decision would have to take that assessment into account. While the prosecutor might not be bound by the findings made in the course of such an assessment, the prosecutor would need to have clear reasons, consistent with the definition of trafficking contained in the aforementioned international instruments, for disagreeing with it.[305]

7.185 In *VCL and AN v UK* the ECtHR found that there had been a breach of Article 4 in respect of two young men who were convicted of drug offences despite the fact that their prosecutions and convictions had been upheld by the Court of Appeal. The ECtHR preferred the reasoning of the NRM, which had decided that the applicants were victims of trafficking, over that of the CPS and the Court of Appeal and held that there had been violations of Article 4 accordingly.[306]

7.186 As regards the investigative duty, the converging principles of the procedural obligation under Articles 2 and 3 ECHR have informed the requirements of the procedural obligation under Article 4.[307] In *CN v*

302 *Rantsev v Cyprus* [2010] 51 EHRR 1 at para 286, ECtHR.

303 *Chowdury v Greece* (App No 21884/15) 30 March 2017, at para 110, ECtHR.

304 *VCL and AN v UK* (App Nos 77587/12 and 74603/12), (2021) 73 EHRR 9 at 159, ECtHR.

305 *VCL and AN v UK* (App Nos 77587/12 and 74603/12), (2021) 73 EHRR 9 at 162, ECtHR.

306 *VCL and AN v UK* (App Nos 77587/12 and 74603/12), (2021) 73 EHRR 9 at para 175–183, ECtHR.

307 *SM v Croatia* (2021) 72 EHRR at 309, ECtHR.

UK[308] the applicant submitted that she was required to live with a couple, who demanded difficult care and needed her to be 'on call' 24 hours a day. She did so under coercion by a relative who had arranged for her illegal entry into the UK and received no notable remuneration. Her working hours and conditions, and the removal of her travel documents, were such as to render her unable to alter her own situation. The UK maintained that the circumstances did not amount to forced labour. The ECtHR declined to determine the issue; the facts gave rise to a 'credible suspicion' of forced labour and that was sufficient to trigger the investigative duty.

7.187 A similar approach was taken in a case concerning forced prostitution. As stated by the Grand Chamber:[309]

> . . . a conclusion as to whether the domestic authorities' procedural obligation arose has to be based on the circumstances prevailing at the time when the relevant allegations were made or when the prima facie evidence of treatment contrary to Article 4 was brought to the authorities' attention and not on a subsequent conclusion reached upon the completion of the investigation or the relevant proceedings . . . [i]ndeed, relying on such domestic findings and conclusions would entail a risk of creating a circular reasoning resulting in a case concerning an arguable claim or prima facie evidence of treatment contrary to Article 4 remaining outside the Court's scrutiny under the Convention.

In that case the unsuccessful prosecution of the alleged perpetrator had breached the procedural duty because the police had not contacted potential witnesses and neither had her social media been examined. Moreover, the police had relied too heavily on the applicant's inconsistent account (which the ECtHR recognised might have been a consequence of the deleterious effects of having been trafficked). The court confirmed that 'any action or lack of action on the part of the victim cannot justify a lack of action on the part of the prosecuting authorities'.[310]

Article 8: right to respect for private and family life

Overview

7.188 Article 8(1) protects the right to private and family life. However, the notion of private life is interpreted broadly and can include physical integrity. Thus, for example, searches (particularly intimate or strip searches), the taking of bodily samples, fingerprinting and photographing could all raise Article 8 issues.

7.189 However, Article 8 is not an absolute right and interferences with private and family life may be lawful in accordance with Article 8(2) which provides:

> There shall be no interference by a public authority with the exercise of this right except such as is in accordance with the law and is necessary in a democratic society in the interests of national security, public safety or the economic well-being of the country, for the prevention of disorder or crime,

308 (2013) 56 EHRR 24, ECtHR.
309 *SM v Croatia* (2021) 72 EHRR 1, ECtHR.
310 Para 336.

for the protection of health or morals, or for the protection of the rights and freedoms of others.

7.190 It follows, therefore, that an interference with physical integrity which is not 'in accordance with the law' will violate Article 8. Equally, there will be a violation where the interference is in accordance with the law, but is not 'necessary' for one of the specified purposes, such as for the prevention of disorder or crime. The question of necessity for Article 8 purposes ordinarily entails considering the proportionality of the interference.

7.191 Where the treatment of a person is not of a severity to amount to inhumane and degrading treatment for the purposes of Article 3, there may alternatively be an Article 8 claim. An example is *Wainwright v UK*[311] which concerned a mother and disabled son being strip-searched on visiting a relative in prison. The ECtHR considered that the manner in which the search was conducted and the importance of tackling an endemic drug problem in the prison was such that the treatment did not reach the minimum level of severity for the purposes of Article 3. However, the searches were nonetheless disproportionate to their legitimate aim and violated Article 8.

The positive obligations

7.192 The state's positive obligation under Article 8 to safeguard the individual's physical integrity may extend to questions relating to the effectiveness of a criminal investigation.[312] However, the courts have seldom considered in isolation the systems and operational duties inherent to Article 8 as they concern the acts of third parties. One such case is *Khadija Ismayilova v Azerbaijan*.[313] The court held that where the Article 8 interference took the form of threatening behaviour towards an investigative journalist highly critical of the government, it was of the utmost importance for the authorities to investigate whether the threat was connected to the applicant's professional activity and by whom it had been made.[314]

7.193 Article 8 is often pleaded alongside Articles 3[315] or 4,[316] and rarely is an applicant successful under Article 8 if the claim under Articles 3 or 4 fails.[317] The principle difference between Article 8 and Articles 2, 3 and 4 is that the latter rights are absolute and concern some of the most serious forms of mistreatment, whereas Article 8 is a qualified right and may be engaged by comparatively less serious conduct. As such, not all conduct that breaches Article 8 will necessarily be criminal: interferences with

311 (2007) 44 EHRR 40, ECtHR.

312 *Osman v UK* (2000) 29 EHRR 245 at para 128; *MC v Bulgaria* (2005) 40 EHRR 20 at para 150, ECtHR.

313 App No 65286/13, 10 January 2019, ECtHR.

314 App No 65286/13, 10 January 2019, ECtHR, at paras 117–120.

315 For example, *VC v Italy* (2019) 69 EHRR 13, ECtHR. The court has stated that when acts fall short of Article 3 treatment it may nevertheless fall foul of Article 8 (*Wainwright v UK* (2007) 44 EHRR 40 at para 43).

316 For example, see *SM v Croatia* (2021) 72 EHRR para 1, ECtHR.

317 In *SM v Croatia* the applicant relied on Articles 3 and 8 and did not initially raise Article 4. In the event, the Grand Chamber determined the claim under Article 4 pursuant to the jura novit curia principle and did not decide the Article 8 issue at all.

home, private and family life may only give rise to wrongs in civil law.[318] Therefore, when only Article 8 is engaged, the police are less likely to be involved in protecting people or carrying out investigations. One area where the court has made it clear that criminal sanction may be necessary even if the relevant conduct does not meet the high Article 3 threshold concerns domestic violence.[319] In *Buturugă v Romania*[320] the court emphasised the need to comprehensively address domestic violence in all its forms. The authorities in that case failed to take into consideration the various forms that domestic violence can take, including economic, emotional and psychological abuse. The state and therefore sometimes the police also has a positive responsibility to protect children from witnessing domestic violence in their homes.[321]

The mechanism for bringing claims in respect of death

Introduction

7.194 Where a claim is made in respect of a death, it is necessary to consider the appropriate mechanism to bring the claim. There is the LRMPA 1934, which allows the estate of the deceased to sue for any cause of action that the deceased would have had if they had not died. The FAA 1976 allows certain family members and equivalent individuals to sue for any loss they have suffered as a result of the death.[322] It is usual to see both Acts pleaded in the same claim. Different considerations arise in respect of any HRA 1998 claim in which a claim may be brought on behalf of the estate, or on behalf of family members as 'indirect victims' of the violation of Article 2 (see para 7.148 above).

7.195 Of some practical importance is that whereas a claim under the FAA 1976 may be brought by a single claimant on behalf of all those with a financial dependency on the deceased, all those bringing a claim as an

318 *Söderman v Sweden* (App No 5786/08) at 12 November 2013 at para 84, ECtHR. The applicant's stepfather had tried to secretly film her while naked when she was 14 years old. She contended successfully that the absence of any criminal sanction or civil remedy breached Article 8. It was clear, however, that criminal sanction was not the only way the state could fulfil its positive obligation under Article 8 and that an adequate civil remedy would have been sufficient (at 108).

319 *Bevacqua and S v Bulgaria* (App No 71127/01) at para 83, ECtHR. The other cases in which the ECtHR found that Article 8 required an effective application of criminal law mechanisms concerned: sexual abuse of a mentally handicapped individual (see *X and Y v Netherlands* (App No 8978/80) at para 27, ECtHR); allegations of physical attack against the applicant by three individuals during which she was kicked and thrown down the stairs (see *Sandra Jankovi ́c v Croatia* (App No 38478/05) at para 47, ECtHR); beating of a 13-year old by a grown-up man causing multiple physical injuries (see *Remetin v Croatia* (App No 7446/12) at para 91, ECtHR); beating of an individual causing a number of injuries to her head requiring hospitalisation (see *Isaković Vidović v Serbia* (App No 41694/07) at para 61, ECtHR); and serious instances of domestic violence (see *A v Croatia* (App No 55164/08) at para 67, ECtHR).

320 [2020] ECHR 136, ECtHR.

321 *Eremia v Republic of Moldova* (2014) 58 EHRR 2, ECtHR.

322 See, for instance, *Kirkham v Chief Constable of Greater Manchester* [1990] 2 QB 283, CA, where both procedures were pursued.

indirect victim for the purposes of an HRA 1998 claim must be listed as claimants.

7.196 The valuation of claims arising out of fatal accidents, particularly dependency claims under the FAA 1976, can give rise to fairly significant complexity and there will often be a need to seek specialist advice.

Law Reform (Miscellaneous Provisions) Act 1934

7.197 Pursuant to LRMPA 1934 s1(4), the estate of a person whose death has been caused by a tortious act can bring proceedings against the wrongdoer in respect of subsisting causes of action. The only exceptions to this are claims for defamation (which are extinguished at the moment of death)[323] and for bereavement damages under FAA 1976 s1A (which cannot be pursued under the LRMPA 1934 but which can be claimed by dependants of the deceased under the FAA 1976). The deceased's estate is also prevented from claiming exemplary damages.[324]

7.198 Under the LRMPA 1934, the estate can sue for reasonable funeral expenses incurred by the estate[325] and any losses suffered by the deceased before his/her death. Thus, the estate can claim for general damages for pain, suffering and loss of amenity suffered by the deceased before their death, as well as for special damages sustained by the deceased, including loss of earnings from the date of the accident to the date of death.[326] However, the estate is prevented from claiming for loss of potential income after the death.[327] The Act also does not allow for the recovery of any benefits consequent on the death (except funeral expenses, as mentioned above).[328]

7.199 Any claim under the LRMPA 1934 is additional to a claim by the deceased's dependants under the FAA 1976, as described below. The limitation period runs from the accrual of the cause of action,[329] except where the individual dies before the expiry of the cause of action, when limitation runs from the date of death. In cases involving personal injuries to the deceased person, the limitation period is three years from the date of the death or the date of the personal representative's knowledge of the facts supporting the action.[330]

Fatal Accidents Act 1976

Overview

7.200 The FAA 1976 allows dependants to claim for the losses they (as opposed to the deceased person) have suffered against anyone who causes death by their wrongful act, neglect, or default, provided that the deceased could

323 LRMPA 1934 s1(1).
324 LRMPA 1934 s1(2)(a).
325 LRMPA 1934 s1(2)(c).
326 LRMPA 1934 s1(4)
327 LRMPA 1934 s1(2)(a)(ii).
328 LRMPA 1934 s1(2)(c).
329 Limitation Act 1980 s11(4).
330 Limitation Act 1980 s11(5).

have made a claim if they had survived.[331] In other words, the act, neglect, or default must constitute a civil wrong. If the police would have had a good defence to the civil wrong, the dependants' claim for damages resulting from the death also fails.

Who can sue?

7.201 The FAA 1976 allows 'dependants' of the deceased to sue for losses resulting from the death, though the claim must be brought in the name of the executor or administrator of the deceased.[332] The list of dependants has been continuously expanded throughout the years to reflect evolutions in the definition of a family. Most recently, it was expanded to include civil partnerships, long-standing cohabitees of at least two years, and non-biological children/parents. The list of dependants in FAA 1976 s1(3) now comprises the following individuals:[333]

- spouse or civil partner;
- individuals living as the husband, wife, or civil partner of the deceased for two years before the date of death;
- former spouse or former civil partner (including those whose marriage or civil partnership has been annulled or declared void);[334]
- parents or other ascendants (including grandparents);
- individuals treated by the deceased as a child of the family in relation to any marriage or civil partnership of the deceased;
- children or other descendants (including grandchildren);
- individuals treated by the deceased as a parent; and
- siblings, uncles and aunts.

Wrongful act, neglect or default of the police

7.202 It must be shown that the wrongful act, neglect or default of the police caused the death.[335]

Damages

7.203 Damages awarded under the FAA 1976 are only for bereavement[336] and the loss of reasonable expectation of financial benefit.[337]

7.204 Damages for bereavement are of a fixed amount. On 1 May 2020, this sum was increased from £12,980 to £15,120 for deaths taking place on or after this date.[338] Such damages are awarded only to deceased's spouse, civil partner, or parent if the deceased was a child under the age of 18 and

331 FAA 1976 s1.

332 FAA 1976 s2(1), (2).

333 FAA 1976 s1(3) (as amended).

334 FAA 1976 s1(4)–(4A).

335 FAA 1976 s1(1) (as amended).

336 FAA 1976 s1A.

337 Consider the possible wider damages available for an action under the HRA 1998 for breach of Article 2.

338 Damages for Bereavement (Variation of Sum) (England and Wales) Order 2020 SI No 316.

did not have a spouse or civil partner.[339] The exclusion of unmarried cohabitees was found to be incompatible with Articles 8 and 14 ECHR (the rights to family life and non-discrimination) in the case of *Smith v Lancashire Teaching Hospitals NHS Foundation Trust and the Secretary of State for Justice*.[340] However, the law has not been changed since, and unmarried cohabitees remain excluded from the category of individuals who can claim a bereavement award.

7.205 Damages for the loss of reasonable expectation of financial benefit[341] can include such things as loss of a parent's financial support for a child (or vice versa), loss of a son's voluntary gifts during a period of employment[342] or loss of free services, where a wife who was killed acted as a housewife.[343] Children can claim for the loss of their mother's daily care,[344] although not for loss of love and affection.[345] However, if the person who died earned their income from a life of crime, the dependants are not allowed to claim for loss of the benefits of crime.[346]

339 FAA 1976 s1A(2).

340 [2017] EWCA Civ 1916.

341 For further details on the calculation of claims, see eg *Clerk & Lindsell on Torts*, 23rd edn, 2020, paras 29-94 to 29-113.

342 *Hetherington v North-Eastern Railway* (1882) 9 QBD 160, QBD.

343 *Berry v Humm & Co* [1915] 1 KB 627, QKBD.

344 *Hay v Hughes* [1975] QB 790, CA; *Regan v Williamson* [1976] 1 WLR 305, QBD.

345 *Hay v Hughes* [1975] QB 790, CA; *Regan v Williamson* [1976] 1 WLR 305, QBD.

346 *Burns v Edman* [1970] 2 QB 541, QBD.

CHAPTER 8

Abuse of power

continued

Introduction

8.1 This chapter focuses upon the common law torts most associated with deliberate abuse of police power: a) malicious prosecution and b) misfeasance in a public office. The scope and the elements of these torts are identified below, along with a discussion of the scenarios in which they are likely to arise in the context of police misconduct. The inter-relationship between the two torts and their respective advantages and disadvantages are considered, as is the principle of witness immunity as it may apply to misfeasance claims. Consideration is also given to the circumstances in which a prosecution may alternatively give rise to a claim pursuant to the Human Rights Act (HRA) 1998.

Malicious prosecution

Introduction

8.2 It is a tort maliciously and without reasonable and probable cause to initiate or maintain criminal proceedings against another person, which terminate in favour of that other and which result in damage to reputation, person, freedom or property.

8.3 The elements of the tort were identified by the courts in very different circumstances to modern policing and prosecutions. Until the creation of the first public police forces in the 1830s, almost all criminal prosecutions were private prosecutions brought by private individuals, usually the victims, who therefore had first-hand knowledge of the relevant circumstances. Application of the requirements of the tort to modern-day investigations and prosecutions can be problematic, as the discussion of its various elements and the related case-law below illustrates.

8.4 Nonetheless, claims in malicious prosecution have undergone a resurgence over the last two decades, particularly in the paradigm case of a prosecution based on fabricated accounts of the claimant's wrongdoing provided by police who were involved in the relevant events. Beyond that situation – for example, where police misconduct is involved in generating a prosecution based on false evidence from third parties – a claim in malicious prosecution may be trickier, but still have advantages over a claim in misfeasance in public office, for the reasons identified at paras 8.138–8.143 below (where the relationship between the two torts is considered).

8.5 In defining the requirements of the tort of malicious prosecution, the courts have been influenced by a number of competing policy considerations. On the one hand, the desirability of the tort providing a remedy for the serious damage that can result from a wrongful prosecution and the public interest in the dishonest manipulation of the legal process being categorised as tortious; on the other hand, a concern not to formulate the tort so widely as to deter proper law enforcement and/or inhibit citizens from reporting crime and the wish to discourage secondary litigation.[1]

8.6 The balance has been struck by the courts requiring a claimant to prove (among other matters) both that the prosecution was brought without reasonable and probable cause and that this was done maliciously. A prosecution brought in good faith will never be a malicious prosecution even if based on slender grounds or subsequently discredited material. Accordingly, although thousands of defendants in criminal proceedings are acquitted of the charges they are accused of every year, a relatively small proportion of them will have a viable case in malicious prosecution.

8.7 Also considered below is the extent to which an action in malicious prosecution may arise from damage caused by spurious civil or disciplinary proceedings; and the circumstances in which a claim of malicious process can be brought.[2]

The elements of the tort

8.8 To succeed in a claim for malicious prosecution, the claimant must show that they suffered 'damage' as a result of the following:[3]

- the claimant was prosecuted by the defendant;[4]
- the prosecution terminated in the claimant's favour;
- the prosecution was without reasonable and probable cause; and
- the defendant acted maliciously.

Procedural considerations

8.9 A malicious prosecution claim usually entitles the parties to choose trial by judge and jury, unless any of the prescribed exceptions apply.[5]

8.10 The six-year limitation period for commencing a claim runs from the date when the criminal proceedings terminated in the claimant's favour.[6]

Damage

8.11 Unlike some other causes of action (primarily assault, battery and false imprisonment), it is necessary to show that damage has been suffered by the claimant for the action to succeed. In practice, this requirement is

1 See Lord Steyn in *Gregory v Portsmouth City Council* [2000] 1 AC 419, HL at 426; and in *Crawford Adjusters (Cayman) Ltd v Sagicor General Insurance (Cayman) Ltd* [2013] UKPC 17, [2014] AC 366 at paras 43 and 49 (Lord Wilson), paras 82 and 84 (Baroness Hale), para 101 (Lord Kerr) and para 126 (Lord Sumption).

2 See paras 8.82–8.102.

3 *Martin v Watson* [1996] AC 74 at 80, HL.

4 References to 'the defendant' in this text include references to those for who the defendant is vicariously liable, as discussed at paras 2.28–2.30.

5 See Senior Courts Act 1981 s69 and County Courts Act 1984 s66, discussed in more detail at paras 15.77–15.89.

6 *Dunlop v HM Customs & Excise* [1998] 3 WLUK 241, CA.

sometimes overlooked, but historically only three types of damage fulfilled this criterion in a malicious prosecution claim, namely:

a) loss of reputation;
b) the risk of loss of 'life, limb or liberty'; and/or
c) financial loss caused by the costs of defending the charge.[7]

Loss of reputation

8.12 Loss of reputation is shown if the charge was 'necessarily and naturally' defamatory, that is to say, it was one that lowered the claimant in the estimation of right thinking members of society generally.[8] Accordingly, an alleged failure to pay a tram fare met the criterion as it involved an imputation of dishonesty.[9] On the other hand, an allegation of pulling a communication cord on a train without cause, did not convey a sufficiently discreditable reflection on the claimant.[10] Thus it will always depend upon the degree of moral stigma attached to the particular offence. For example, whereas some motoring offences such as drink driving or driving whilst disqualified will result in a loss of reputation, other motoring offences such as driving with a bald tyre or a defective light would be unlikely to suffice.

Loss of liberty

8.13 In respect of loss of liberty, it is enough if the offence for which the claimant is prosecuted is one punishable by imprisonment, so that the claimant is put in danger of losing their liberty; there need not be actual loss of liberty.[11]

Financial loss

8.14 Legal costs incurred in defending oneself against a malicious prosecution constitute sufficient damage to qualify as financial loss, even where the court grants an allowance towards those costs.[12]

8.15 It is sufficient for a claimant to prove that one of three forms of 'damage' discussed above resulted from the prosecution. If 'damage' in this sense is proved and the other elements necessary for liability are established, the claimant can then recover for all the consequences of the prosecution at the stage when compensation is assessed. Thus, distress and anxiety caused by the prosecution will be taken into account when the level of damages is determined. Distress was contemplated as part of the basic damages award in a successful malicious case in the guidelines issued by the Court of Appeal in *Thompson v Commissioner of Police of the Metropolis*.[13]

8.16 It has not been decided whether the requirement to show 'damage' could be satisfied by the claimant having suffered psychiatric injury; arguably this

7 *Savile v Roberts* (1698) 1 Ld Raym 374 at 378; *Manley v Commissioner of Police of the Metropolis* [2006] EWCA Civ 879, (2006) 150 SJLB 889 at para 26.

8 *Wiffen v Bailey & Romford UDC* [1915] 1 KB 600, CA.

9 *Rayson v South London Tramways Co* [1893] 2 QB 304, CA.

10 *Berry v British Transport Commission* [1962] 1 QB 306, [1961] 3 All ER 65, CA.

11 *Wiffen v Bailey & Romford UDC* [1915] 1 KN 600, CA; *Manley v Commissioner of Police of the Metropolis* [2006] EWCA Civ 879, (2006) 150 SJLB 889 at para 26.

12 *Berry v British Transport Commissioner* [1962] 1 QB 306, [1961] 3 All ER 65, CA.

13 [1998] QB 498, CA; see guideline (6).

could come within the concept of risk of injury to limb. However in practice, if psychiatric injury has resulted from the prosecution, it is likely that the charge involved damage to reputation and/or a risk of imprisonment, so that the prescribed criterion would be satisfied in any event. If 'damage' is established by one or more of these routes, then recovery for psychiatric injury will be permitted in addition.

8.17 In *Crawford Adjusters (Cayman) Ltd v Sagicor General Insurance (Cayman) Ltd*[14] the Privy Council held that the claimant could recover foreseeable economic loss suffered as a result of the earlier proceedings.

Prosecuted by the defendant

8.18 It must be shown both that the claimant was prosecuted *and* that the defendant was responsible for instituting and/or maintaining that prosecution.

A prosecution

8.19 A prosecution consists of 'setting a judicial officer in motion'.[15] Thus, there will only be a potential difficulty if an allegation is withdrawn at a very early stage, before the claimant is brought before a criminal court at all. However, the Supreme Court of Canada has held that laying an information before a magistrate is sufficient in itself to amount to a prosecution for these purposes.[16] Most criminal proceedings commence with a charge. If a summons is then issued, the commencement of the prosecution covers the laying of the information.[17] Clayton & Tomlinson submit that a prosecution will have begun if the claimant has been charged,[18] as this is the point from which damage to the claimant may result. On this basis, an action in malicious prosecution would lie even if the charge was then withdrawn before the case ever came before the court. However, the making of a complaint to a prosecuting authority, without more, cannot constitute a 'prosecution'[19] – neither can the fact of being interviewed and/or arrested.[20]

The prosecutor

8.20 Traditionally it was said that that prosecutor must be a person who was 'actively instrumental' in putting the law in motion.[21] Satisfaction of this requirement caused little difficulty in the days when the prosecution was brought by the alleged victim of the crime.[22] However, in a situation where those responsible for collating evidence and determining whether to charge have not been involved in the events that ground the prosecution,

14 [2013] UKPC 17, [2014] AC 366 at paras 77 and 78(i).
15 *Sewell v National Telephone Co* [1907] 1 KB 557, CA.
16 *Casey v Automobiles Rental Canada Ltd* (1965) 54 DLR (2d) 600, SC (Canada).
17 *Thorpe v Priestnall* [1897] 1 QB 159 at 162, QBD.
18 *Civil Actions Against the Police*, Sweet & Maxwell, 3rd edn, 2004, para 8-024.
19 *Mosley v Associated Newspapers Ltd* [2020] EWHC 3545 (QB), [2021] 4 WLR 29.
20 *CXZ v ZXC* [2020] EWHC 1684 (QB).
21 *Danby v Beardsley* (1880) 43 LT 603.
22 As discussed at para 8.3 above.

issues can arise as to the correct identity of the prosecutor(s). Difficulties stemming from the respective roles of complainant and investigator were compounded by the introduction of the Crown Prosecution Service (CPS)[23] and the increasing role played by the CPS in determining whether charges should be brought. Even if the charging decision is made by the police, it is now made by the custody officer (often after receiving advice from the CPS), rather than by a police officer involved in the incident itself or its investigation.[24]

8.21 In this context, defendants have sometimes argued that only the person who made the decision to charge (whether CPS lawyer or Custody Officer) can be 'the prosecutor' for the purposes of a malicious prosecution claim. If this proposition were correct it would effectively emasculate the tort as a remedy for abuse of power by the police, since the officer(s) said to have acted maliciously will be those involved in the events giving rise to the charge and/or the investigation and there will usually be little, if any, basis to suggest that the person remote from such matters making the formal charging decision has also acted in bad faith.

8.22 However, the courts have repeatedly rejected that approach in favour of examining the reality of the situation: 'The common law has not adopted the technical stance that the only person responsible is the person who actually made the charge'.[25] The issue has perhaps been laid to rest by the Court of Appeal's decision in *Copeland v Commissioner of Police of the Metropolis*.[26] *Copeland* confirms that the correct approach is to consider who 'in substance, is responsible for the prosecution having been brought'[27] and that this was the test identified by the House of Lords in *Martin v Watson*[28] and endorsed by the Court of Appeal in *AH v AB*[29] and in *Ministry of Justice v Scott*.[30]

8.23 It is suggested that this test provides a straightforward and practical approach that is fact-sensitive and adaptable to particular circumstances. It also means that it is possible for there to be more than one prosecutor in relation to a prosecution. In *Copeland* the Court of Appeal disapproved the distinction between simple cases and complex cases, proposed by Brooke LJ in *Mahon v Rahn (No 2)*,[31] as introducing unnecessary over-complication.[32]

8.24 The application of the test where the claimant alleges that they have been prosecuted on the basis of a false account given by one or more police officers is illustrated by *Copeland*.[33] The claimant was charged with assaulting Officer B in the execution of his duty after Officer B had made a statement describing the alleged assault. The decision to charge was made by

23 By the Prosecution of Offences Act 1985.

24 Police and Criminal Evidence Act 1984 (PACE) s37(1), (7), (7A) and s37B.

25 *Commercial Union Assurance v Lamont* [1989] 3 NZLR 187 at 193.

26 [2014] EWCA Civ 1014, [2015] 3 All ER 391.

27 [2014] EWCA Civ 1014, [2015] 3 All ER 391 at para 25.

28 [1996] 1 AC 74 at 86B, HL.

29 [2009] EWCA Civ 1092 at para 77.

30 [2009] EWCA Civ 1215 at paras 11, 14, 32, 39 and 51.

31 [2000] 1 WLR 2150 at paras 269–270, CA.

32 [2014] EWCA Civ 1014, [2015] 3 All ER 391, para 32.

33 [2014] EWCA Civ 1014, [2015] 3 All ER 391, para 32.

another officer who had not been present at the incident, after receiving advice from the CPS. At the trial of the malicious prosecution claim, the jury found that Officer B had fabricated his allegation of assault. The Court of Appeal agreed with the trial judge that in the circumstances, Officer B was in substance responsible for the prosecution having been brought and thus was the 'prosecutor'. The Court of Appeal rejected the defendant's submission that a complainant could only be 'the prosecutor' if the facts relating to the alleged offence were solely within their own knowledge, so that it was impossible for the person deciding whether to charge to exercise an independent discretion.[34] Accordingly, although there was some other evidence available to the charging officer, his decision making had been vitiated by the lies told by Officer B and on the facts found by the jury no conclusion other than that he was 'the prosecutor' could reasonably have been reached.[35]

8.25 *Ministry of Justice v Scott*[36] illustrates the application of the same test in the context of allegedly false accounts of assault and affray made by five prison officers in respect of the claimant, a serving prisoner. Police conducted a limited investigation before referring the matter to the CPS, who determined the claimant should be charged. Despite the availability of some additional evidence, the Court of Appeal agreed that the prison officers were capable of being the prosecutor and that the claim should not be struck out, since their accounts had procured the prosecution: 'The decision of the CPS was entirely predictable and the five complaining officers would have expected no other.'[37] The five prison officers were treated as one prosecutor for these purposes.[38]

8.26 A similar scenario may arise where the investigating officer, though not directly involved in nor having any direct knowledge the alleged offence as a victim or witness, has been involved in a manipulation of the evidence which is then concealed from the charging custody officer or the CPS. An example is *Rees v Commissioner of Police of the Metropolis*.[39] The investigating officer had prompted an unreliable witness to implicate the claimants in a murder and had done so to the extent of perverting the course of justice. The officer then failed to 'truthfully present the final report to the CPS' and thus deprived the CPS of the opportunity to 'exercise an independent judgment on the basis of evidence that [the officer] considered true and reliable'.[40] In those circumstances, 'an independent exercise of judgment by the CPS was impossible' and the officer was a prosecutor for the purpose of the malicious prosecution claim.[41] On the

34 The court clarified that in referring to this feature in *Martin v Watson* [1996] 1 AC 74 at 86H, HL, Lord Keith was identifying why the 'in substance' test was met in that instance and was not laying down a general rule: [2014] EWCA Civ 1014, [2015] 3 All ER 391 at para 30. A similar submission was also rejected by the Court of Appeal in *Ministry of Justice v Scott* [2009] EWCA Civ 1215 at paras 39 and 51.

35 [2014] EWCA Civ 1014, [2015] 3 All ER 391 at paras 33–34.

36 [2009] EWCA Civ 1215.

37 Pill LJ at para 42.

38 Pill LJ at para 44.

39 [2018] EWCA Civ 1587.

40 [2018] EWCA Civ 1587 at para 55.

41 [2018] EWCA Civ 1587 at para 55.

facts of that case, the Court of Appeal considered it inconceivable that with a full account from the officer the CPS would have charged the claimants. The Court of Appeal did consider that something more than the provision of false information was required, but in that case the CPS were 'deliberately manipulated . . . into taking a course which they would not otherwise have taken'.[42]

8.27 Occasionally an acquitted defendant may wish to contend that a civilian complainant is 'the prosecutor'. Satisfaction of the 'in substance' test is likely to be harder in these circumstances, as a false allegation made by a member of the public is unlikely to exert the same impact on the person deciding whether to charge as an allegation made by a police colleague or other officer involved in the criminal justice system. In this instance, the extent to which there is evidence additional to that from the complainant, enabling independent evaluation of their allegation, may well be decisive. In *Martin v Watson*[43] this was the key feature identified in a case where the claimant was prosecuted for a false complaint of indecent exposure that had been made by the defendant.

8.28 By contrast, in *AH v AB*[44] the defendant, who was alleged to have made an untrue complaint of rape, was found not to be 'the prosecutor'. The key features highlighted by the Court of Appeal were that she had not initiated the complaint to police, who had persuaded her to give evidence; and the CPS decided to charge the claimant after reviewing all the available evidence. Accordingly, she had done nothing to promote the prosecution and the CPS had made an independent decision after testing the evidence. The relative difficulty of establishing that a lay complainant is a prosecutor is also reflective of the courts' underlying concerns that victims and witnesses are not deterred from reporting crimes to the police.[45]

8.29 A defendant may be liable not only on the basis of their role in the institution of the prosecution (as discussed immediately above), but also if the defendant is actively instrumental in maintaining it – for example, by continuing a prosecution or causing it to be continued after becoming aware of the accused's innocence / sufficiently exculpatory material.[46] For example, in *Clifford v Chief Constable of Hertfordshire Constabulary*[47] Cranston J held that a police officer could still be 'the prosecutor' after charge and notwithstanding that the CPS were conducting the prosecution if he failed to forward to them evidence indicating the charge was baseless.[48]

42 [2018] EWCA Civ 1587, at para 58.

43 [1996] AC 74, HL.

44 [2009] EWCA Civ 1092.

45 See, for example, *Hunt v AB* [2009] EWCA Civ 1097, paras 58–59. In *Copeland v Commissioner of Police of the Metropolis* [2014] EWCA Civ 1014 at para 31, the court emphasised that the established test takes into account the concern that witnesses could be inhibited from coming forward.

46 *Tims v John Lewis & Co Ltd* [1951] 2 KB 459, CA (reversed on another point by the House of Lords: *John Lewis & Co Ltd v Tims* [1952] AC 676).

47 [2008] EWHC 3154 (QB).

48 [2008] EWHC 3154 (QB), paras 49–50 (although unsuccessful on the facts, the Court of Appeal overturned that decision: [2009] EWCA Civ 1259; and liability was subsequently established at the re-trial on the basis of the actions of the officer in determining to charge the claimant: [2011] EWHC 815 (QB)).

Termination of the prosecution in the claimant's favour

8.30 The criminal prosecution must have ended in favour of the person suing for malicious prosecution.[49] This can be achieved by an acquittal at trial or by the conviction being quashed on appeal.[50] An acquittal on a technicality or a discontinuance of proceedings is also sufficient for these purposes;[51] the termination may be unconnected to the strength of the prosecution case.[52] This is because the reason for the requirement is simply to avoid the possibility of conflict between the decision of a court trying the criminal charge and the court hearing the civil action and a collateral challenge to the former by the latter. Thus any termination of the criminal proceedings that does not result in conviction is one favourable to the claimant for these purposes: 'what the plaintiff requires for his action is not a judicial determination of his innocence, but merely the absence of any judicial determination of his guilt'.[53]

8.31 If offences are ordered to 'lie on the file' after a defendant has pleaded guilty to other charges, this may be treated as an adjournment of the proceedings, rather than a favourable termination – whereas proceedings that have been stayed as an abuse of process (for instance, because of the length of time it has taken to bring a prosecution) will probably be treated as a favourable termination, the crux being that the criminal proceedings are at an end and the claimant does not have to go further and show that no further criminal proceedings could be brought.

Outcomes involving acquittal and conviction

8.32 A favourable termination may exist where a trial concludes in a person being acquitted of some offences, but convicted of others; a malicious prosecution claim can be brought in relation to the charges that resulted in an acquittal, provided the other elements of the tort are satisfied and 'damage' in the sense discussed above results from those charges.[54] Similarly, a malicious prosecution claim may still be viable if there was only a conviction for a less serious offence than the one for which the person was charged.[55]

Bind-overs

8.33 Particular difficulties arise in relation to a defendant who was bound over to keep the peace and to be of good behaviour. If the claimant is bound over after the hearing of a 'complaint',[56] the case does not end in the

49 *Parker v Langley* (1713) 10 Mod 145 & 209.

50 *Herniman v Smith* [1939] AC 305, [1938] 1 All ER 1, HL; *Berry v British Transport Commission* [1961] 1 QB 306, [1961] 3 All ER 65, CA.

51 *Jones v Gwynn* (1712) 10 Mod 148 at 214; *Watkins v Lee* (1839) 5 M & W 270.

52 *Beckett v New South Wales* [2013] HCA 17 at para 50.

53 *Beckett v New South Wales* [2013] HCA 17 at para 6 citing in turn Salmond, *The Law of Torts*, 6th edn, 1924 at 595.

54 *Leibo v Buckman Ltd* [1952] 2 All ER 1057, CA.

55 *Boaler v Holder* (1887) 51 JP 277.

56 Pursuant to Magistrates' Courts Act 1980 s115.

claimant's favour and the claimant cannot sue.[57] More commonly, bind-overs are agreed to by the defence prior to the case being heard, in exchange for the prosecution offering no evidence on the charge before the court. In *Hourihane v Commissioner of Police of the Metropolis*[58] the police applied unsuccessfully to strike out a claim for malicious prosecution where the claimant had agreed to a bind-over, the CPS had offered no evidence, and the charges were duly dismissed. The Court of Appeal held that it was impossible to draw any inference that proceedings had terminated adversely to a defendant simply from the statement that the defendant was bound over to keep the peace. The court said there might be many reasons why a defendant would prefer to agree to be bound over rather than run the risk of conviction. However, although an action for malicious prosecution would not be precluded, in practice the credibility of the claim would be adversely affected in this kind of situation unless the claimant could convincingly explain why they accepted a bind-over in the circumstances.

Subsisting convictions

8.34 If there is a subsisting conviction, a claim for malicious prosecution cannot succeed, even if there is no further right of appeal and even if it can be proved that the conviction was obtained by fraud.[59] Where a dishonest abuse of authority can be shown, a claim might still arise in misfeasance.

The prosecution was without reasonable and probable cause

8.35 Reasonable and probable cause has been defined as:[60]

> . . . an honest belief in the guilt of the accused based upon a full conviction, founded upon reasonable grounds, of the existence of a state of circumstances, which, assuming them to be true, would reasonably lead any ordinary prudent and cautious man, placed in the position of the accuser to the conclusion that the person charged was probably guilty of the crime imputed.

8.36 The test involves a consideration of both the subjective state of mind of 'the prosecutor' at the time of the prosecutor's relevant actions and an objective assessment of the adequacy of the evidence at this juncture.[61] An absence of reasonable and probable cause can be established by reference to either (or both) of these evaluations. They are considered in turn below. However, it is worth emphasising that a claimant who is only able to show a lack of reasonable and probable cause in objective terms, is likely to struggle to establish bad faith on the part of the prosecutor, as required to

57 *Everett v Ribbands* [1952] 2 QB 198, [1952] 1 All ER 823, CA; *Bynoe v Bank of England* [1902] 1 KB 467, [1902] All ER 65, CA.

58 (1995) *Independent* 18 January, CA.

59 *Bassebe v Matthews* (1867) LR 2 CP 684.

60 *Hicks v Faulkner* (1878) 8 QBD 167 at 171, approved by the House of Lords in *Herniman v Smith* [1938] AC 305, HL.

61 *Glinski v McIver* [1962] AC 726, [1962] 1 All ER 696, HL; *Moulton v Chief Constable of the West Midlands* [2010] EWCA Civ 524 at para 25.

meet the requirement that the prosecutor acted maliciously (considered at para 8.64 below).

8.37 CPS advice on charging may often be relevant to the question of reasonable and probable and cause. The CPS may in principle assert privilege, although the Court of Appeal has questioned whether to do so is wise and consistent with the appropriate use of public funds.[62]

The subjective inquiry; the test and its application

8.38 In a trial by judge and jury, the factual assessment of the prosecutor's state of mind is an issue to be evaluated by the jury, provided there is some evidence to support the claimant's contention that police officers lacked an honest belief in the claimant's guilt.[63]

8.39 If the criminal prosecution is based on the accounts of police officers as eyewitnesses to events involving the claimant (for example, where the claimant is charged with assaulting an officer or obstructing an officer in the execution of their duty), the legal position is relatively straightforward. If the claimant gives a conflicting account of events and contends that the officers fabricated their statements in support of the criminal prosecution, the jury simply has to determine which party is giving the truthful version. If the jury find that the officers produced a concocted account of events, it follows that they lacked an honest belief in the claimant's guilt. The strength of the claimant's case in such circumstances is likely to depend upon evidential factors such as the credibility of the claimant's own account, whether the claimant has witnesses to the events in question, whether there are discrepancies between the officers' accounts and/or inconsistencies with contemporaneous documentation and/or inconsistencies with other known facts, such as injuries or lack of injuries sustained.

8.40 The position is more complicated if the evidence in support of the prosecution comes from a number of non-police sources and the relevant police officers did not witness the alleged offence. If the central evidence against the claimant comes from civilian witnesses or from expert forensic analysis or other third parties, in many circumstances it will be difficult to positively establish that police or CPS involved in the collation of evidence and/or the charging decision did not honestly believe in the prosecution at the time, however much the evidence may have been subsequently discredited at trial. In this context, it is important to consider what state of mind must be shown in order to establish that a prosecutor lacked the requisite honest belief.

8.41 References in the older cases to a lack of honest belief in the guilt of the accused need to be seen in the context described earlier, namely one where criminal proceedings were generally brought by those involved in the events, who would therefore have first-hand knowledge of the true circumstances.

8.42 However, more recent case-law decided in the context of a professional prosecutor (whether police, CPS or other prosecuting authority) has made

62 *Rees and others v Commissioner of Police of the Metropolis* [2018] EWCA Civ 1587 per Coulson LJ at paras 115–117.

63 *Herniman v Smith* [1938] AC 305, HL; *Dallison v Caffrey* [1965] 1 QB 348, [1964] 2 All ER 610, CA.

clear that the question is whether the prosecutor believed there is a proper case to go before the court / there is a fit case to be tried.[64] Thus, a police officer who planted incriminating evidence on a suspect or who falsified admissions would lack an honest belief in the prosecution case, irrespective of whether the officer personally believed that the person charged had committed the offence or not. Equally, a police officer or CPS lawyer who decided to charge a suspect knowing that in fact the evidence against them was groundless or discredited would lack an honest belief that there was a fit case to be tried.

8.43 This point is emphasised because defendants to malicious prosecution claims sometimes argue that irrespective of the pleaded allegations of wrongdoing, reasonable and probable cause is present simply because the officers in question genuinely believed that the claimant had committed the offence. However, recent authorities have confirmed that the focus is upon the sufficiency of the evidence said to support the prosecution and the defendant's knowledge of and honest belief in that.[65]

8.44 These kinds of issues were also the subject of a particularly detailed consideration by the High Court of Australia in *A v State of New South Wales* in the context of a police officer who decided to charge the claimant with sexual offences against children, where the only evidence available was the accounts of the two boys and the officer had expressed some doubt as to the reliability of their accounts.[66] The court concluded that in a case where the officer acted on material provided by third parties, the question was whether the prosecutor is shown not to have honestly concluded that the material was such as to warrant the setting of the processes of the criminal law in motion.[67]

8.45 It may be that the prosecutor is aware that aspects of the evidence are admissible and probative of the claimant's guilt, but also that other aspects of the evidence are tainted and not fit to go before the court. That scenario arose in *Rees v Commissioner of Police of the Metropolis* (see para 8.26 above). Significantly, in that case the trial judge considered that there *did* exist an objective reasonable and probable cause for the prosecution based on what admissible evidence existed at the time. However, the court still considered whether the officer had subjective reasonable and probable cause. The Court of Appeal addressed the apparently novel question of whether 'a prosecutor [can] have subjective reasonable and probable cause for a prosecution if he presents a case heavily reliant upon evidence which, because of his own misconduct, he knows is "certain or at least highly likely" to be ruled inadmissible by any trial judge?'[68] The Court of Appeal emphasised that the question is not whether the prosecutor had an honest belief in the guilt of the claimant, but whether the prosecutor had an honest belief that there was a fit case to be tried. Although there was an

64 *Glinski v McIver* [1962] AC 726, HL. Lord Denning at 758 and Lord Devlin at 770.

65 *Qema v News Group Newspapers Ltd* [2012] EWHC 1146 (QB) at paras 71–73; *Howarth v Chief Constable of Gwent* [2011] EWHC 2836 (QB) at para 14; and *Coudrat v Commissioners of Her Majesty's Revenue and Customs* [2005] EWCA Civ 616 at para 41.

66 [2007] HCA 10, (2007) 233 ALR 584, HC (Australia); see in particular the discussion at paras 48, 49, 62, 73 and 76.

67 [2007] HCA 10, (2007) 233 ALR 584 at paras 80–81, HC (Australia).

68 [2018] EWCA Civ 1587 at para 69.

objective reasonable and probable cause for the prosecution, the investigating officer was also perfectly aware that the case was not fit to be tried as it included evidence procured by the officer's own perverting of the course of justice. Accordingly, although on the facts there existed objective reasonable and probable cause, there was no subjective reasonable and probable cause.[69]

8.46 The extent to which such a scenario may arise in other cases will be a question of degree, dependent upon the importance of the tainted evidence to the prosecution case as a whole, as to whether the claimant can show that the prosecutor lacked an honest belief that the charge was warranted and there was a fit case to be tried.

Establishing a lack of subjective belief

8.47 A further aspect to consider is how a claimant raises sufficient evidence of a lack of honest belief for the case to be left to the jury on this issue, if the prosecutor was not present at the time of the relevant events and so does not have first-hand knowledge of the alleged wrongdoing. (As noted at para 8.39, where the claimant had direct involvement in the events and disputes the police officers' account, there is a straight conflict of fact for the jury to determine.)

8.48 Mere suspicion that officers concocted evidence or bullied potential prosecution witnesses will not suffice and some affirmative evidence of a want of honest belief is required for the trial judge to leave the issue to the jury.[70] However, the claimant may establish the necessary evidence by a process of inference, relying on features such as substantial inconsistencies in contemporaneous records or inexplicable changes in accounts given. A good example of this exercise is the decision of the Court of Appeal in *Paul v Chief Constable of Humberside*.[71] The court decided that the trial judge had erred in withdrawing claims in false imprisonment and malicious prosecution from the jury, as there was sufficient material to enable inferences to be drawn that the officers were not acting in good faith and that they had arrested and charged the claimant to deflect attention from their own potential culpability in relation to a related death in police custody, rather than because of a considered assessment of the evidence.

8.49 Less commonly, there may be direct evidence available – for example, from witnesses themselves that they were threatened or intimidated into falsely incriminating the claimant, or evidence from what officers themselves said at the time.

8.50 It has been said that it is impermissible to rely simply on the objectively weak nature of the prosecution case and contend from this that officers could not have honestly believed in the claimant's guilt.[72] However, it is suggested that this must be a question of degree; a striking absence of

69 [2018] EWCA Civ 1587 at para 75–76.

70 See *Howarth v Chief Constable of Gwent* [2011] EWHC 2836 (QB) at para 15 and the authorities cited therein.

71 [2004] EWCA Civ 308: the circumstances in which such issues may be left to the jury are also addressed in chapter 16 at para 16.66.

72 *Glinski v McIver* [1962] AC 726 at 754, HL.

any evidence supporting a charge could well indicate a lack of honest belief on the part of the prosecutor. In any event, there is no reason why the weakness of the case cannot be one factor that is considered, along with all others, when assessing whether inferences as to a lack of honest belief can be drawn.

8.51 It is well established that a lack of honest belief in the case cannot be inferred simply from proof that officers acted maliciously in the sense that they had an ulterior motive for the prosecution.[73] Thus, if police trigger a prosecution of an individual because the individual brought a previous complaint against one of their colleagues, but the charge was supported by sufficient, genuine evidence, the individual would not have a viable claim in malicious prosecution, despite the officers' improper motivation. However, the same facts can be used to support both a finding of malice and a finding of lack of reasonable and probable cause, if those facts point to officers lacking honest belief in the evidence put forward, for instance where evidence is fabricated.

8.52 In the relatively unusual event that the defendant fails to offer any explanation for the basis of the prosecution in circumstances that appear to call for one, the omission can be treated as evidence of a lack of reasonable and probable cause.[74]

8.53 Sometimes a defendant will seek to defend a contention of lack of honest belief on the basis that the prosecution was approved by the CPS and/or counsel and so, it will be said, police officers were simply following advice. However, this will not avail the defendant if officers withheld information from the lawyers or their decision was based on evidence that the officers knew to be concocted or otherwise substantially flawed. Supportive legal advice can only avail the defendant if the facts of the case were laid fairly before those lawyers.[75]

The objective inquiry: the test and its application

8.54 Even if the prosecutor honestly believed in the case put forward against the claimant, there will be a lack of reasonable and probable cause for the proceedings if, objectively judged, the evidence was too weak to properly support a case. The evidential situation is usually assessed at the point of charge (save where the conduct upon which the malicious prosecution claim is based occurs later, such as where the complaint is a failure to disclose subsequently obtained exculpatory evidence).

8.55 If the judge is sitting with a jury, the jury first decide any disputed facts that bear on this issue – for example, as to what information was known to the prosecutor at the time or as to the level and nature of enquiries that were actually made – and then the judge rules upon the objective question of whether there was sufficient evidence to support the prosecution.

73 *Glinski v McIver* [1962] AC 726 at 744 and 766, HL; *Matin v Commissioner of Police for the Metropolis* [2002] EWCA Civ 907.

74 *Gibbs v Rea* [1998] AC 786, [1998] 3 WLR 72, PC (Cayman Islands).

75 *Glinski v McIver* [1962] AC 726 at 745 and 759, HL; *Abbott v Refuge Assurance Co* [1962] 1 QB 432 at 448 and 450, CA and *Howarth v Chief Constable of Gwent Constabulary* [2011] EWHC 2836 (QB) at paras 19–20.

8.56 It has been said that there are a number of steps that an ordinarily prudent and cautious prosecutor would undertake – specifically the prosecutor would:

1) take reasonable steps to ascertain the true state of the case;
2) consider the matter on the basis of admissible evidence only; and
3) in all but plain cases, obtain legal advice as to whether a prosecution is justified and act upon that advice.[76]

8.57 When considering whether to charge a suspect, consideration should be given to each element of the offence and there must be prima facie admissible evidence of each element of that offence. It has been found that anything plainly inadmissible should be left out of account, but it is not necessary at that stage to consider the possibility that evidence might be excluded at trial after full legal argument.[77] More controversially, in the same case the Court of Appeal observed that account could be taken of evidence which the prosecutor believed would become available, but which had not yet crystallised in the form of a statement.[78]

8.58 The question is whether there was adequate material to place before the jury, not whether a conviction would be secured.[79] The objective evaluation of whether there was a lack of reasonable and probable cause does not entail the same test as the criteria in fact applied by police and lawyers pursuant to the Code for Crown Prosecutors,[80] which requires the decision-maker to consider whether there is a realistic prospect of conviction and whether it is in the public interest to proceed. Thus, circumstances may arise where the objective reasonable and probable cause test is met, although the prosecution should not have been brought – for example, because there were strong public interest considerations against doing so relating to the age or triviality of the charge or the accused's health.[81]

8.59 In seeking to establish a lack of reasonable and probable cause, it is not enough for a claimant to point to inconsistencies in the evidence, which might require explanation or clarification.[82] A prosecutor is not required to test every possible relevant fact before taking action: 'His duty is not to ascertain whether there is a defence but whether there is a reasonable and probable cause for the prosecution'.[83] However, it is possible that a lack of reasonable and probable cause could be established from a failure to

76 *Abbott v Refuge Assurance Co* [1962] 1 QB 432 at 454, CA.

77 *Coudrat v Commissioners of Her Majesty's Revenue and Customs* [2005] EWCA Civ 616 at para 42.

78 *Coudrat v Commissioners of Her Majesty's Revenue and Customs* [2005] EWCA Civ 616 at para 52.

79 *Howarth v Chief Constable of Gwent Constabulary* [2011] EWHC 2836 at para 16; *Qema v News Group Newspapers Ltd* [2012] EWHC 1146 (QB) at para 73.

80 Pursuant to the *Guidance on Charging to Police Officers and Crown Prosecutors* issued pursuant to PACE 1984 s37A.

81 This distinction is referred to in *Qema v News Group Newspapers Limited* [2012] EWHC 1146 (QB) at para 77.

82 *Moulton v Chief Constable of West Midlands Police* [2010] EWCA Civ 524 at para 26; *Howarth v Chief Constable of Gwent Constabulary* [2011] EWHC 2836 (QB) at para 17.

83 *Herniman v Smith* [1938] AC 305 at 319, HL; *Coudrat v Commissioners of Her Majesty's Revenue and Customs* [2005] EWCA Civ 616 at para 42.

follow obvious lines of enquiry, if doing so would have negated a viable case against the claimant.[84] It will always be a question of degree.

8.60 If the prosecutor was mistaken about a matter of fact which, if true, would have given sufficient basis for the prosecution, the issue is whether the mistake was a reasonable one to make.[85]

8.61 The significance of taking legal advice has been considered under the discussion of the subjective inquiry at para 8.53 above.

8.62 The fact that the claimant may have been convicted at trial is not treated as decisive of this issue, if the conviction is later quashed on appeal.[86] If when overturning a conviction the Court of Appeal expresses a view about the lack of evidence in support of the prosecution, it is unclear to what extent the claimant can rely upon this opinion in a subsequent civil action. Although no question of issue estoppel arises as the two parties to the litigation are not the same, one would expect considerable weight to be attached to the Court of Appeal's view.

8.63 As foreshadowed at para 8.36 above, if a claimant only shows a lack of reasonable and probable cause in objective terms, rather than establishing that the prosecutor did not honestly believe in the case put forward, it is likely to be difficult to show the further necessary ingredient of malice, unless there is clear evidence of a specific improper purpose, as discussed immediately below.

The prosecutor acted maliciously

The test

8.64 In order to prove that the prosecutor acted maliciously, it must be shown that the prosecutor's motive, or main motive, was something other than the desire to bring the claimant to justice.[87] In *A v State of New South Wales*[88] the High Court of Australia defined the requirement as: 'the dominant purpose of the prosecutor must be a purpose *other* than the proper invocation of the criminal law – an "illegitimate or oblique motive"'. Lord Kerr in *Crawford Adjusters (Cayman) Ltd v Sagicor General Insurance (Cayman) Ltd* described this as a 'good working definition'.[89]

8.65 In *Moulton v Chief Constable of the West Midlands*[90] the Court of Appeal rejected a submission that proving malice in this sense was an unduly onerous burden for a claimant, which ECHR Article 5 required to be reduced. Similarly, in *Keegan v Chief Constable of Merseyside*[91] the Court of Appeal rejected a submission that the requirement of malice in relation to a claim of maliciously procuring a search warrant (discussed at para 8.93)

84 For an example in a malicious process case, see *Keegan v Chief Constable of Merseyside* [2003] EWCA Civ 936, [2003] 1 WLR 2187, CA.

85 *Hicks v Faulkner* (1878) 8 QBD 167.

86 See, for example, *Herniman v Smith* [1938] AC 305, HL.

87 *Stevens v Midland Counties Railway* (1854) 10 Exch 352.

88 [2007] HCA 10, (2007) 233 ALR 584 at para 91, HC (Australia).

89 [2013] UKPC 17, [2014] AC 366 at para 109.

90 [2010] EWCA Civ 524 at paras 49–51.

91 [2003] EWCA Civ 936, (2003) 147 SJLB 869. The claim for violation of ECHR Article 8 is discussed at paras 9.81 and 17.172.

should be reformulated to equate to the broader concept of bad faith applied in the tort of misfeasance in a public office.

8.66 In circumstances where the claimant establishes that the prosecutor could not have believed the claimant was guilty because of the prosecutor's own knowledge that allegations were fabricated, there will be no difficulty in establishing malice. For example, in *Thompson v Commissioner of Police of the Metropolis*[92] police falsely alleged that the claimant had bitten an officer's finger and assaulted others in order to cover up their own brutality towards her as she was manhandled into a cell at the police station. In *Copeland v Commissioner of Police of the Metropolis* (discussed at para 8.22 above) the jury's finding that Officer B had fabricated his account of the assault, established both a subjective lack of reasonable and probable cause on his part and that he had acted maliciously.

8.67 Additionally, malice should be established without difficulty in the sorts of circumstances discussed at para 8.42 above where officers may have some general belief in the guilt of the claimant, but dishonestly and improperly procure or create a substantial part of the prosecution case. A desire to concoct evidence and/or to procure a conviction at any cost, affords evidence of malice. An example is that of *Rees v Commissioner of Police of the Metropolis* (discussed above at para 8.26) in which an officer who may have believed in the guilt of the claimants but knowingly put before the CPS a case which he knew was significantly tainted by his own wrongdoing and which he knew could not properly be presented in that form. The Court of Appeal considered that to find other than that to do so constituted malice would be 'a negation of the rule of law'.[93] Again, the court in *Rees* focused not on whether there was a belief in the guilt of the claimant, but on whether there was a belief in there being a fit case to be tried. If there is not, then a prosecution is not properly in the pursuit of justice and the prosecutor is acting maliciously.

8.68 Other examples of improper motives on the part of police include making false accusations to try to mask the officer's own misconduct; and punishing a claimant for an earlier complaint or civil action or for rudeness to officers. In *A v State of New South Wales*, the High Court of Australia accepted that charging in response to pressure from superiors in order to secure their favour / avoid their criticism could amount to malice.[94]

Inter-relationship between lack of reasonable and probable cause and malice

8.69 Although lack of reasonable and probable cause can never be inferred from malice (see para 8.51 above), a lack of reasonable and probable cause can provide evidence of malice.[95] However, the extent to which this is possible will depend upon the basis upon which a lack of reasonable and probable cause has been established. As already discussed, if it has been

92 [1988] QB 498, [1997] 2 All ER 762, CA.

93 [2018] EWCA Civ 1587 at para 91.

94 [2007] HCA 10, (2007) 233 ALR 584 at para 110, HC (Australia).

95 *Brown v Hawkes* [1891] 2 QB 718 at 722, CA.

shown that officers did not honestly believe in the charges brought, this will afford strong evidence of malice.[96]

8.70 However, establishing a lack of reasonable and probable cause by showing that objectively there was insufficient basis for the prosecution, does not generally provide evidence of malice as it is not inconsistent with the prosecutor acting out of the proper motive of seeking justice, but simply being careless or incompetent in assessing the evidence.[97] (Save, perhaps, where there is a very clear absence of evidence against the suspect.)[98]

8.71 In *Moulton v Chief Constable of the West Midlands*, in circumstances where it was accepted that the police officers involved had an honest belief in the case they put forward, the Court of Appeal emphasised that a poorly conducted and dilatory investigation into a rape allegation did not of itself provide evidence of malice, as opposed to a lack of proper management of the investigation and under-resourcing.[99]

> If the court holds that there was no honest belief in the validity of the prosecution, the court may well be ready to infer that the prosecutor has proceeded from some motive other than a legitimate desire to bring the accused to justice . . . It is axiomatic that it will be more difficult to prove malice in a case in which there was an honest but irrational belief in the validity of the allegation.[100]

8.72 The position is likely to be all the more difficult where a claim is contemplated against the CPS in respect of their pursuit of a weak prosecution. While the prosecutors may have been remiss in failing to appreciate this, there is unlikely to be evidence that they were acting for an ulterior motive and maliciously.[101]

8.73 Where the real problem is incompetence rather than malice, the claimant may be left without a civil law remedy, given the difficulty of showing the existence of a duty of care necessary for a claim in negligence.[102]

Roles of judge and jury

8.74 It is for the trial judge to assess whether there is some evidence of malice such that a jury could properly conclude that this element of the tort was proved. Whether or not, on that evidence, the motive was indeed

96 See also *Haddrick v Heslop and Raine* (1848) 12 QB 267; *Brown v Hawkes* [1891] 2 QB 718; and *Tempest v Snowdon* [1952] 1 KB 130, CA.

97 *Meering v Grahame White Aviation* (1919) 122 LT 44, HL; *Gibbs v Rea* [1998] AC 786, (Cayman 12 Lands) PC.

98 See *Coudrat v Commissioner of Her Majesty's Revenue and Customs* [2005] EWCA Civ 616 at para 55.

99 [2010] EWCA Civ 524 at paras 43, 48 and 52.

100 [2010] EWCA Civ 524 at para 52.

101 See, for example, *Thacker v Crown Prosecution Service*, 16 December 1997, CA, and the observation that 'an attempt to dress up a claim in respect of negligence or incompetence in the guise of malicious prosecution must fail'. See, more recently, *Young v Chief Constable of Warwickshire* [2021] EWHC 3453 (QB) at para 10, citing *Thacker*.

102 In *Moulton v Chief Constable of the West Midlands* [2010] EWCA Civ 524 at para 43, the Court of Appeal noted that case-law precluded a claim in negligence, despite the poor quality of the investigation and the consequential damage suffered by the claimant.

malicious is a question of fact for the jury to decide.[103] The respective roles of judge and jury are considered in more detail when we examine the course of the civil action trial.[104]

The claimant's innocence

8.75 The necessary elements of the tort of malicious prosecution discussed above do not entail requiring the claimant to prove innocence of the offence in question. The High Court of Australia has confirmed that the claimant's guilt or innocence of the charge is not an issue in a malicious prosecution action.[105] There are less clear statements in the domestic authorities – though the discussion by Sharp J in *Qema v News Group Newspapers Ltd* indicates that if the defendant proves the claimant's guilt, it could at least have a significant effect on damages.[106] It is suggested that this is the better view.

8.76 However, even if guilt does not preclude a finding of malicious prosecution, the reality is that strong evidence that the claimant in fact carried out the crime in question may well have a significant impact on the claimant's credibility and in turn on the merits of the claim.

Violations of the European Convention on Human Rights in respect of prosecution

Impact on malicious prosecution claims

8.77 Rights protected by the ECHR do not expand the circumstances in which the claimant can succeed in an action for malicious prosecution as such. Article 5(5) ECHR provides that everyone who has been detained in contravention of Article 5 shall have an enforceable right to compensation. However, a period of detention is regarded as lawful for these purposes if carried out pursuant to a court order, made within the court's jurisdiction, even if that order is subsequently quashed on appeal.[107] Accordingly, a violation of Article 5 does not arise from the sheer fact that a person spent time in custody prior to a trial at which they are acquitted or prior to a successful appeal against conviction.

8.78 As discussed at para 8.65 above, Article 5 ECHR does not require adaption of the ingredients of the tort of malicious prosecution.

103 *Hicks v Faulkner* (1878) 8 QBD 167; *Brown v Hawkes* [1891] 2 QB 718, CA; and *Dallison v Caffrey* [1965] 1 QB 348, CA.

104 See para 16.62.

105 *Beckett v New South Wales* [2013] HCA 17, HC (Australia) , confirming the general statement of principle in *Commonwealth Life Assurance Society Ltd v Smith* [1924] HCA 56, (1924) 35 CLR 275 (and overruling a previous exception under which innocence had to be proved if the prosecution had terminated by the entry of a nolle prosequi by the Attorney General).

106 [2012] EWHC 1146 (QB) at paras 91–92.

107 *Benham v UK* (1996) 22 EHRR 293, ECtHR.

Violations of ECHR Articles 5 and/or 8

8.79 However, there may be circumstances where an action for malicious prosecution would not succeed, in particular because malice and/or a lack of reasonable and probable cause cannot be established, but where a viable claim would arise for an ECHR violation, most notably in relation to Articles 5 and/or 8. There is also an instance of the European Court of Human Rights (ECtHR) finding that the prosecution of a journalist violated her Article 10 rights.[108] See para 10.4 for more on Article 10 ECHR.

8.80 The Court of Appeal's decision in *Zenati v Commissioner of Police of the Metropolis and the Crown Prosecution Service*[109] indicates that violations of ECHR Articles 5(1) and/or 5(3) may arise where a person suffers a protracted remand in custody as a result of police/CPS delay and/or incompetence, for example in relation to investigating potentially exculpatory material or bringing it to the criminal court's attention. The circumstances in *Zenati*, like the situation in *Moulton v Chief Constable of the West Midlands* where the malicious prosecution claim failed (see para 8.71 and 6.22, 6.29 and 6.168 above), involved delays by prosecutors in appreciating or actioning material that potentially exonerated the accused.

8.81 In *SXH v Crown Prosecution Service*[110] the Supreme Court rejected the proposition that Article 8 ECHR was engaged in the particular circumstances involving the claimant's prosecution for using false travel documents, which was discontinued after she was granted asylum and following her remand in custody. It is evident from the judgment that the scope for a finding of a violation of Article 8 in the context of a decision to prosecute is narrow. If the criminal offence itself is compatible with Article 8, then a decision to prosecute an individual for having perpetrated that offence will generally be lawful in accordance with Article 8(2).[111] That is, if the decision to prosecute engages Article 8(1) at all, as Lord Toulson considered that a decision to prosecute did not of itself involve any lack of respect for the autonomy of the defendant but placed the question of determining guilt or innocence before the court, which would also be responsible for deciding ancillary questions of bail or remand in custody.[112] The question of whether Article 8 might alternatively be engaged by the circumstances in which the CPS maintains (rather than instigates) a prosecution was left open.[113] In the Court of Appeal in *SXH*, Pitchford LJ considered that Article 8 could, exceptionally, be engaged by a decision to prosecute where the prosecutor was aware that the defendant had an unanswerable statutory defence, or where a decision to prosecute a dying woman may constitute a disproportionate interference with her private life.[114] It may be that such exceptional

108 *Pal v UK* (App No 44261/19), 30 November 2021, ECtHR; compare *Overd v Chief Constable of Avon and Somerset Constabulary* [2021] EWHC 3100 (QB).

109 [2015] EWCA Civ 80, [2015] 2 WLR 1563.

110 [2017] UKSC 30, [2017] 1 WLR 1401.

111 [2017] UKSC 30, [2017] 1 WLR 1401 at para 32 per Lord Toulson.

112 [2017] UKSC 30, [2017] 1 WLR 1401 at para 38 per Lord Toulson.

113 [2017] UKSC 30, [2017] 1 WLR 1401 at para 39 per Lord Toulson, and paras 41–48 per Lord Kerr.

114 *SXH v Crown Prosecution Service* [2014] EWCA Civ 90 at para 71.

circumstances would entail a violation of Article 8, notwithstanding the judgment of the Supreme Court. See para 7.189 for more on Article 8.

Malicious prosecution in relation to civil or disciplinary proceedings

8.82 Prior to the Privy Council's decision in *Crawford Adjusters (Cayman) Ltd v Sagicor General Insurance (Cayman) Ltd*,[115] the long established legal position was that there was no opportunity to bring a claim for malicious prosecution for damage suffered by a failed civil suit or disciplinary process that was brought maliciously. In *Gregory v Portsmouth City Council*[116] the House of Lords confirmed earlier authority from *Quartz Hill Consolidated Gold Mining Co v Eyre*[117] onwards to that effect.

8.83 The reasoning in *Quartz Hill Consolidated Gold Mining Co v Eyre*[118] was based on the proposition that none of the forms of damage identified in *Savile v Roberts*[119] would be incurred in respect of a maliciously brought *civil* claim; there would be no loss of liberty; damage to reputation would be avoided as false allegations could be corrected promptly; and consequential financial expense would be met by an award of costs. Thus, actions analogous to malicious prosecution were only permitted in a few discrete situations that were thought to involve potential prejudice to the victim at the outset of the proceedings that could not be put right immediately. These exceptions included malicious procurement of a bench warrant of arrest and malicious procurement of a search warrant.[120]

The Privy Council's decision in Crawford

8.84 In *Crawford Adjusters (Cayman) Ltd v Sagicor General Insurance (Cayman) Ltd*[121] the Privy Council decided by a 3:2 majority that a claim in malicious prosecution could be brought in respect of damage caused by an earlier civil claim, provided the usual ingredients of the tort were otherwise satisfied.[122]

8.85 The majority view was that the reasoning in *Quartz Hill Consolidated Gold Mining Co v Eyre* no longer held good given the potential damage to reputation from the public availability of pleadings and the period of time between pleadings and civil trial.[123] The majority was also influenced by the facts of the case before them and that absent a claim in malicious prosecution, there would be no recovery for the substantial losses suffered

115 [2013] UKPC 17, [2014] AC 366.
116 [2000] 1 AC 419 at 426–428 and 432–433, HL.
117 (1883) 11 QBD 674, CA.
118 (1883) 11 QBD 674, CA.
119 (1698) 1 Ld Raym 374; discussed at para 8.11 above.
120 These two exceptions are the most relevant to actions against the police and are discussed more fully at paras 8.93–8.102 below. For a list of the other exceptions, see *Crawford Adjusters (Cayman) Ltd v Sagicor General Insurance (Cayman) Ltd* [2013] UKPC 17, [2014] AC 366 at para 76 (Lord Wilson) and paras 143–144 (Lord Sumption).
121 [2013] UKPC 17, [2014] AC 366.
122 Those elements are summarised at para 8.8 above.
123 [2013] UKPC 17, [2014] AC 366 at para 61 (Lord Wilson)

by the claimants as a result of an earlier civil claim, for an alleged fraudulent conspiracy, which the trial judge had found to be bogus and aimed at putting the claimants out of business.[124] The minority disagreed, considering that there was a fundamental distinction between criminal and civil proceedings for these purposes and that developing the law in the way favoured by the majority was unprincipled and potentially very wide.[125]

The Supreme Court's decision in Willers

8.86 In *Willers v Joyce*[126] the Supreme Court was able to revisit the question of whether the tort of malicious prosecution existed in respect of maliciously pursued civil proceedings. The High Court had struck out a claim for malicious prosecution in respect of earlier civil claims for negligence and breach of fiduciary duty on the basis that it was bound by the doctrine of precedent to following the House of Lords decision in *Gregory v Portsmouth City Council* that no such tort arose in relation to maliciously brought civil proceedings. The judge granted a 'leapfrog' to the Supreme Court.

8.87 A Supreme Court constituted of nine judges decided by a majority of 5:4 that the approach in *Crawford* should be followed and it was held that the tort did exist in respect of maliciously pursued civil proceedings

8.88 With the parties having searched in vain for an answer in the origins of the tort and centuries old case law, the majority focused instead on the reasons of policy for and against permitting the tort. Ultimately, the majority considered that none of the countervailing policy factors outweighed the argument of 'simple justice' that it was 'unjust for a person to suffer injury as a result of the malicious prosecution of legal proceedings for which there is no reasonable ground, and yet not be entitled to compensation for the injury intentionally caused by the person responsible for instigating it.'[127] The claim was permitted to go to trial.

8.89 In theory, the availability of an action in malicious prosecution for earlier unsuccessful civil proceedings could be used by Chief Officers of Police with a view to deterring claimants from suing the police. However, it is suggested that the difficulties of proving that the earlier claim was brought without reasonable and probable cause and in bad faith and the small chance of recovering any damages from most such claimants would militate against such claims being brought or threatened save in the most exceptional circumstances.

Malicious defences in civil proceedings

8.90 In *Crawford*, the majority in the Privy Council flagged, without deciding, the possibility of a claim arising in respect of damage caused by a malicious *defence* of civil proceedings.[128] In *Energy Ventures v Malabu Oil & Gas Ltd*,

124 [2013] UKPC 17, [2014] AC 366 at para 39 (Lord Wilson) and paras 117–118 (Lord Kerr).

125 [2013] UKPC 17, [2014] AC 366 at paras 145–148 (Lord Sumption). An analysis in turn rejected by the majority: see paras 72–73 (Lord Wilson).

126 [2016] UKSC 43, [2018] AC 779.

127 [2016] UKSC 43, [2018] AC 779 at 802B–D, and 806D,

128 [2013] UKPC 17, [2014] AC 366 at para 78(g) (Lord Wilson) and paras 111–113 (Lord Kerr).

Males J accepted that there was an argument with a real prospect of success that the existence of a tort of malicious defence formed part of English law.[129] However, as was emphasised by the High Court in *Willers v Joyce*, his judgment was given in the context of an application for alternative service and he did not hear detailed submissions as to the effect of *Crawford*.[130]

8.91 Extending the opportunity to sue for damages in respect of losses caused by the malicious *defence* of civil proceedings would represent a much greater extension of the parameters of the tort of malicious prosecution and, as such, it is probably unlikely to find favour with the courts. Were it to do so, there might be circumstances in which it could avail litigants who had suffered damage as a result of a false defence of an earlier civil action against the police, though it could only apply where the earlier claim was ultimately successful (perhaps on appeal), but the bogus defence had nonetheless brought about damage.

Maliciously brought disciplinary proceedings

8.92 Given the number of circumstances that could give rise to claims that disciplinary action had been taken maliciously and the public interest in not deterring appropriate regulatory steps, it appears very unlikely that the approach of the majority of the Privy Council in *Crawford*, and now in the Supreme Court in *Willers*, would be extended this far. In Canada, the New Brunswick Court of Appeal has held that the tort of malicious prosecution should not be expanded to cover proceedings brought by self-regulating associations.[131]

Malicious process claims

8.93 This section briefly considers claims for malicious procurement of arrest warrants and search warrants.

The necessary elements

8.94 In relation to such warrants, there are four ingredients of the tort that the claimant must establish, namely:

1) a successful application for the warrant was made;
2) there was a lack of reasonable and probable cause for making the application;
3) it was made maliciously; and
4) there was resultant damage.[132]

8.95 In relation to proceedings that the claimant has no right to attend and which are conducted ex parte, such as applications for warrants, it need not be shown that they terminated in the claimant's favour.[133]

129 [2014] EWHC 1390 (Comm) at para 15.

130 *Willers v Gubay* [2015] EWHC 1315 (Ch) at paras 66–67.

131 *New Brunswick Real Estate Association v Estabrooks* [2014] NBCA 48.

132 *Roy v Prior* [1971] AC 470, HL; *Gibbs v Rea* [1998] AC 786 PC; and *Keegan v Chief Constable of Merseyside* [2003] 1 WLR 2187, CA.

133 *Gibbs v Rea* [1998] AC 786 PC; *Keegan v Chief Constable of Merseyside* [2003] 1 WLR 2187, CA.

Establishing a lack of reasonable and probable cause and malice

8.96 Proving a lack of reasonable and probable cause and proving malice have been described in detail under the preceding section on malicious prosecution claims.

8.97 In the absence of malice, a good claim for a violation of ECHR Article 8 could arise in respect of the procurement and execution of a search warrant on the claimant's home address if insufficient checks and investigations were first conducted, as illustrated by the ECtHR decision in *Keegan v UK*[134] (in circumstances where the domestic law claims for malicious procurement and negligence had been unsuccessful).[135] However, the Court of Appeal has rejected the suggestion that following the decision in *Keegan v UK* the issue of malice should be left to the jury, however slight the trial judge considered the supporting evidence to be.[136]

8.98 If the claimant cannot prove a lack of reasonable and probable cause and malice, in some circumstances an action in negligence may lie if the warrant was obtained on the basis of inaccurate information and potential difficulties with establishing a duty of care can be overcome.[137]

Involvement of a judicial process

8.99 A claim for malicious procurement of arrest can only arise in circumstances where the damage complained of by the claimant was brought about by the act of a judicial officer (typically a judge or magistrate issuing a warrant), as opposed to the ministerial act of, for example, a police officer. In the latter instance, if a claim lies, it is in the tort of false imprisonment. This distinction is reflective of one of the central policy objectives underlying the tort, namely to provide a remedy where the defendant has maliciously abused the court's powers.

8.100 However, this distinction has not always been kept in mind in the caselaw – see in particular *Sallows v Griffiths*, where the Court of Appeal upheld a claim for malicious procurement of arrest where the arrest was made as a result of false information given by the defendant to a police officer.[138] (In such circumstances, the correct cause of action is false imprisonment on the basis that the arrest was procured by the defendant, as explained in *Davidson v Chief Constable of North Wales*.[139])

134 (2007) 44 EHRR 33, ECtHR.

135 *Keegan v Chief Constable of Merseyside* [2003] 1 WLR 2187, CA.

136 *Connor v Chief Constable of Merseyside* [2006] EWCA Civ 1549, [2007] HRLR 6.

137 See, for example, *Hough v Chief Constable of Staffordshire* [2001] EWCA Civ 39 at para 18. There are a number of cases in which a duty of care has been imposed in connection with loss of liberty: see *McCreaner v Ministry of Justice* [2015] 1 WLR 354, *Welsh v Chief Constable of Merseyside Police* [1993] 1 All ER 692 and *Clarke v Crew* (unreported, 28 May 1999).

138 [2001] FSR 15, CA.

139 [1984] 2 All ER 597, CA at 602; applied for example in *Copeland v Commissioner of Police of the Metropolis* [2014] EWCA Civ 1014, see paras 19–21. This is discussed more fully in relation to claims in false imprisonment at paras 6.97-6.103.

Damage

8.101 'Damage' for these purposes is not as confined as under the tort of malicious prosecution (see para 8.11 above) and encompasses all forms of recognised damage.[140]

The Constables Protection Act 1750

8.102 If the ingredients of a malicious process claim are proved, the claimant will overcome the difficulty that otherwise arises because of the Constables Protection Act 1750 in suing in relation to arrests or searches undertaken in obedience to a warrant.[141]

Misfeasance in public office

Introduction

8.103 The tort of misfeasance in public office recognises that executive or administrative power may be exercised only for the public good and not for ulterior and improper purposes.

Elements

8.104 The elements of the tort were clarified by the House of Lords in *Three Rivers District Council v Bank of England (No 3) (Three Rivers (No 3))*.[142] They are:

1) the defendant must be a public officer;
2) the defendant must have acted in the purported performance of their public duty or must have exercised a power or opportunity made available to the defendant as a public officer;
3) the defendant must have acted unlawfully and with either targeted or untargeted malice;
4) the conduct must have caused the claimant material damage.

8.105 The principles of vicarious liability apply as much to misfeasance in public office as to any other tort involving malice, knowledge, or intention.[143]

8.106 The tort bears a resemblance to the criminal offence of misconduct in public office.[144]

140 See the discussion of what may amount to recoverable damage in, for example, the tort of negligence at para 7.51.

141 As discussed at paras 6.117–6.118.

142 [2001] UKHL 16, [2003] 2 AC 1.

143 [2001] UKHL 16, [2003] 2 AC 1 at 191D.

144 The elements of the criminal office of misconduct in public officer were set out in *Attorney General's Reference (No 3 of 2003)* [2004] EWCA Crim 868, [2005] QB 73. The Court of Appeal pointed to the difference between the crime and the tort as being that the former is committed upon an affront to the Crown and the public interest, whereas the tort requires a balancing of interests as between public officers and individual members of the public or organisations seeking private remedies having asserted a loss which must be proved (see para 48).

1) A public officer

8.107 In *Three Rivers (No 3)* Lord Steyn described the 'relatively wide sense' in which public office ought to be understood and gave the example of a local authority exercising private-law functions as a landlord as capable of being sued in misfeasance.[145] A police officer will certainly be considered a public officer.

8.108 A civilian employed by a police authority is also likely to be a public officer, as would any person privately contracted by a police authority to assist in the discharge of police functions. That would be consistent with the criminal offence of misconduct in public office in which it has been considered to embrace anyone appointed to discharge a public duty and who receives compensation for doing so.[146] In *R v Cosford and others*, the Court of Appeal considered that nurses employed by the prison service and working in a high security prison were public officers.[147] What was important was not so much the position held, but the 'nature of the duty undertaken' and:[148]

> . . . in particular, whether it is a public duty in the sense that it represents the fulfilment of one of the responsibilities of government such that the public have a significant interest in its discharge extending beyond an interest in anyone who might be directly affected by a serious failure in the performance of the duty.

In consequence, it is irrelevant whether, for example, a prison is run directly by the state or indirectly through a private company paid by the state as that 'does not alter the public nature of the duties of those undertaking the work: the responsibilities to the public are identical'.[149]

8.109 In the context of the criminal offence of misconduct in public office, those who have been held to be in public office have included a police officer in a period of suspension;[150] a retired police officer working as a civilian employee for a police force;[151] a police community support officer;[152] and a civilian call handler.[153]

8.110 A CPS prosecutor would also be a public officer to which liability in misfeasance could in principle attach.[154]

145 [2000] 2 WLR 1220 at 1230H. Such a claim was successfully made in *AA v Southwark LBC* [2014] EWHC 500 (QB).

146 *R v Bowden* [1996] 1 WLR 98 at 103, CA. Although remuneration is not an indispensable requirement for the holding of public office, as demonstrated in *R v Belton* [2011] QB 934, CA.

147 [2013] EWCA Crim 466, [2014] QB 81.

148 [2013] EWCA Crim 466, [2014] QB 81 at para 34.

149 [2013] EWCA Crim 466, [2014] QB 81 at para 37.

150 *Attorney General v Fraill* [2011] EWHC 1629 (Admin), [2011] 2 Cr App R 21.

151 *R v L (D)* [2011] EWCA Crim 1259, [2011] 2 Cr App R 159.

152 *R v Iqbal (Amar)* [2008] EWCA Crim 2066.

153 *R v Gallagher* [2010] EWCA Crim 3201.

154 *Elguzouli-DAF v Commissioner of Police of the Metropolis* [1995] QB 335, [1995] 2 WLR 173.

2) Acting in the purported performance of a public duty

8.111 The relevant act must be connected with the individual's functions as a public officer.

8.112 The tort can be constituted as an omission by a public officer to act, albeit Lord Hutton explained in *Three Rivers (No 3)* that the omission must be 'a deliberate one involving an actual decision and liability will not arise from injury suffered by mere inadvertence or oversight'.[155] Similarly, Lord Millett suggested that an omission could amount to misfeasance only where: a) the circumstances are such that the discretion whether to act can only be exercised in one way so that there is effectively a duty to act; b) the official appreciates this but nevertheless takes a conscious decision not to act; and c) the official does so with intent to injure the claimant or in the knowledge that such injury will be the natural and probable consequence of this failure to act.[156] To a significant extent, these requirements restate the requirement of malice (as below) rather than introduce any additional features required of a misfeasance claim directed to an omission rather than a positive act.

8.113 In *R v Dytham*[157] a police officer was successfully prosecuted for misconduct in public office where he had failed to intervene in an assault leading to the victim's death.

3) The state of mind of the officer: targeted and untargeted malice

8.114 What is generally referred to as targeted and untargeted malice comprise two distinct forms of the tort of misfeasance.

8.115 In both forms of the tort, the relevant act (or omission) must be unlawful. The test for unlawfulness is the same or similar to that used in judicial review[158] and, in general terms, may arise where the public officer has acted unreasonably, or has exceeded their powers, or used their powers for an improper purpose.

In *Eurasian Natural Resources Corporation Limited v Dechert LLP and others*,[159] failures by employees of the Serious Fraud Office to act in accordance with the duty to be independent, and the duty to properly record evidence, were considered to be unlawful acts for the purposes of a misfeasance claim.

Targeted malice

8.116 Targeted malice is the more straightforward form of the tort, albeit often the harder to prove. It arises where the officer specifically intends by the act or omission to injure the claimant.

Untargeted malice

8.117 Untargeted malice is more nuanced. As with targeted malice, bad faith is an essential element. In *Three Rivers (No 3)* Lord Steyn described 'the unifying element' between the two forms of the tort as 'conduct amounting to an

155 *Three Rivers (No 3)* [2000] 2 WLR 1220 at 1267B.
156 *Three Rivers (No 3)* [2003] 2 AC 1 at 237. See also Lord Hobhouse at 230C.
157 [1979] QB 722.
158 *Three Rivers (No 3)* [2003] 2 AC 1 at 230E.
159 [2022] EWHC 1138 (Comm).

abuse of power accompanied by subjective bad faith'[160] and the requirement of bad faith in the exercise of public powers as the raison d'être of the tort.[161] However, the inclusion of untargeted malice as a form of the tort recognises that subjective recklessness can be sufficient to establish bad faith and ground the tort. The underlying policy is that reckless indifference to consequences is as blameworthy as deliberately seeking such consequences.[162]

8.118 There are two elements to establish untargeted malice. First, the public officer must be shown to have known that they were acting unlawfully, or that they were subjectively reckless as to the lawfulness of their act.[163] Second, the public officer must either have known that the act would in the ordinary course of events cause damage to the claimant, or, was subjectively reckless as to whether such damage would be caused.[164] The second aspect is sometimes forgotten, but a pleading which fails to properly particularise both the damage and why the public officer must have foreseen it is deficient.[165]

Comparison

8.119 To take a practical example of the way in which targeted and untargeted malice may operate, consider the release by a police officer of a claimant's personal information to the claimant's employer. If the release was made unlawfully and with the specific purpose of causing the claimant to lose their job, targeted malice would be made out. If, alternatively, the release was made as a favour for the employer as a friend of the officer, and the officer had no interest in the outcome for the claimant but was recklessly indifferent to a serious risk that the claimant would be caused harm, it would be a case of untargeted malice.

Negligence never sufficient

8.120 It will not be sufficient to show simply that the public officer ought to have recognised the risk of unlawfulness of the act said to amount to misfeasance, or of damage to the claimant. The public officer must have appreciated the risk but disregarded it. Even gross negligence or bad misjudgement in the discharge of public duties will not suffice.[166] Lord Steyn described the necessary mental element as 'reckless indifference'.[167] Lord Hobhouse suggested that in relation to knowledge of the unlawfulness of the act the phrase 'without an honest belief' in the lawfulness of the conduct best conveyed the requisite state of mind covering both actual knowledge and dishonest disregard; as for knowledge of the consequences of the act for

160 *Three Rivers (No 3)* [2003] 2 AC 1 at 191.

161 *Three Rivers (No 3)* [2003] 2 AC 1 at 193C.

162 *Three Rivers (No 3)* [2003] 2 AC 1 at 192G per Lord Steyn.

163 *Three Rivers (No 3)* [2003] 2 AC 1 at 193C per Lord Steyn, and at 230F per Lord Hobhouse.

164 *Three Rivers (No 3)* [2003] 2 AC 1 at 196A per Lord Steyn, and at 230H-231C per Lord Hobhouse.

165 *Young v Chief Constable of Warwickshire Police* [2021] EWHC 3453 (QB) at para 10.

166 *Muuse v Secretary of State for the Home Department* [2010] EWCA Civ 453, para 77; *B v Reading DC* [2009] EWHC 998 (QB), para 75.

167 *Three Rivers (No 3)* [2003] 2 AC 1 at 193C.

the claimant, the phrase 'wilful disregard' best described the element of subjective recklessness.[168]

8.121 Although it may be possible to infer malice, if what is pleaded as giving rise to such an inference is equally consistent with mistake or negligence, then the pleading will be insufficient and will be liable to be struck out.[169] In *Young v Chief Constable of Warwickshire*, it was said in the context of failures in disclosure in a criminal prosecution that:[170]

> . . . in order for a case in misfeasance to get off the ground, it would be necessary for the material to have been of such a nature that no reasonable prosecutor . . . looking at it, could have said to himself anything other than that 'this needs to be disclosed to the defence immediately'.

Appreciation of a serious risk of harm to the claimant

8.122 It is not necessary to show that damage to the claimant inevitably flowed from the act done in bad faith. In *Three Rivers (No 3)* Lord Hope referred to awareness of a 'serious risk' that the claimant would suffer loss, although he declined to choose between the phrases 'probable loss', 'a serious risk of loss' and 'harm which is likely to ensure'.[171]

8.123 Neither is it necessary to show that the public officer knew that harm was likely to be caused to any particular individual. Instead, the intent required is directed at the harm complained of, or at least harm of the type suffered by the claimant.[172] The intent element is therefore made out where the officer is aware of or recklessly indifferent to a serious risk that harm will be suffered, irrespective of any knowledge or foresight of a particular victim. There is no requirement of proximity between the offending public officer and claimant, as there would be in a negligence claim.[173] Thus, as in *Akenzua v Secretary of State for the Home Department and another*, the release of a violent and dangerous criminal could in principle give rise to a claim in misfeasance notwithstanding that the identity of the persons likely to be harmed were unknown.[174] It is sufficient to plead that the harm in contemplation was to one or more victims who would be unknown unless and until the expected harm eventuated.[175]

Pleading bad faith

8.124 Misfeasance is a tort of personal bad faith and ultimately a claimant must establish bad faith on the part of a particular officer. However, it is not always necessary to identify the officer(s) at the outset if it is sufficiently

168 *Three Rivers (No 3)* [2003] 2 AC 1 at 231G.

169 *Young v Chief Constable of Warwickshire* [2021] EWHC 3453 (QB), at para 26.

170 At para 27.

171 *Three Rivers (No 3)* [2003] 2 AC 1 at 247C; see also 247F. In *Eurasian Natural Resources Corporation Limited v Dechert LLP and others* [2022] EWHC 1138 (Comm) it was said at para 186 that the defendant must act in the knowledge that the unlawful act is 'likely to cause damage to an individual' and that 'mere foreseeability of loss if therefore insufficient'.

172 *Three Rivers (No 3)* [2003] 2 AC 1 at 196A per Lord Steyn.

173 [2003] 2 AC 1 at 193G, per Lord Steyn.

174 [2002] EWCA Civ 1470, [2003] 1 WLR 741.

175 [2002] EWCA Civ 1470, [2003] 1 WLR 741 at para 20.

clear from the conduct pleaded by the claimant that bad faith on the part of individual officers was involved.[176]

4) Causation and material damage

Overview

8.125 It is necessary to show that the act or omission of the public officer caused the claimant 'special' or 'material' damage.[177] The tort is not, like some other intentional torts, actionable per se (ie without establishing damage).

8.126 In *Watkins v Home Office*[178] the claimant was a serving prisoner whose legal correspondence had been opened in breach of the prison rules and in bad faith. He had not suffered any particular injury other than a justifiable sense of outrage, but argued that he should have a civil remedy in the tort of misfeasance irrespective of whether he had suffered material damage. In the House of Lords, Lord Bingham, with whom the House agreed, recognised 'great force' in the submission that if a public officer knowingly and deliberately acted in breach of the officer's lawful duty the officer should be amenable to civil action at the suit of anyone who suffers at the officer's hands.[179] Lord Bingham described the 'obvious public interest in bringing public servants guilty of outrageous conduct to book'.[180] However, he ultimately found against the claimant, describing a consistent body of law which treated material damage as an essential ingredient of the tort.[181] He was not persuaded that it would be correct to develop the law by removing the requirement of material damage in order to allow the tort to be used as an instrument of punishment by the award of exemplary damages in cases where there was no material damage to compensate.[182] The primary role of the law of tort is to provide monetary compensation for those who have suffered material damage rather than to vindicate the rights of those who have not.[183] Thus, misfeasance in public office is 'never actionable without proof of material damage'.[184]

8.127 The question arises, then, as to the forms of loss that fall within material damage. In *Watkins* it was said to include 'financial loss or physical or mental injury', but not distress, injured feelings, indignation or annoyance.[185]

176 See *Chagos Islanders v Attorney General and others* [2003] EWHC 2222 (QB).

177 The case-law uses both expressions, but there is no distinction in this context between special and material damage: see *Karagozlu v Commissioner of Police of the Metropolis* [2006] EWCA Civ 1691, [2007] 1 WLR 1881 at para 44.

178 [2006] UKHL 17, [2006] 2 AC 395.

179 [2006] UKHL 17, [2006] 2 AC 395 at para 8.

180 [2006] UKHL 17, [2006] 2 AC 395 at para 8.

181 [2006] UKHL 17, [2006] 2 AC 395 at para 23.

182 [2006] UKHL 17, [2006] 2 AC 395 at para 26.

183 [2006] UKHL 17, [2006] 2 AC 395 at para 9.

184 [2006] UKHL 17, [2006] 2 AC 395 at para 27.

185 [2006] UKHL 17, [2006] 2 AC 395 at paras 1 and 7.

Mental injury

8.128 It is not clear whether, for the purpose of establishing material damage, mental injury is limited to a recognised psychiatric illness. In *Hussain v Chief Constable of West Mercia*[186] a taxi driver had called on the police for assistance on some 50 occasions and alleged that he had been responded to in a way that amounted to misfeasance. He relied on a psychiatric report which stated that the claimant experienced 'significant anxiety symptoms at stressful times, which he experiences . . . as irritability and physical discomfort' but did 'not have a current psychiatric diagnosis'.[187] The Court of Appeal found that the claim failed for want for material damage but the judges adopted different reasons.

8.129 Stanley Burton LJ considered the definition of material damage in *Watkins* to be the same as that in *McLoughlin v O'Brian*[188] and that it was necessary to demonstrate a recognised psychiatric illness.[189] Maurice Kay LJ considered that the damage of which the claimant complained was 'trifling' and insufficient to comprise material damage.[190] He did not, however, agree that it was necessary to show a recognised psychiatric injury. Noting that the tort was one of considerable gravity, he suggested it was important not to require too much by way of damage. Otherwise, there was:[191]

> . . . a risk that, in the hands of an average claimant, it would become a toothless tort, availing only commercial claimants who can show pecuniary loss and individual claimants with eggshell personalities who are tipped over the edge into recognized psychiatric illness. For my part, I would not wish to shut out a claimant who has the robustness to avert recognized psychiatric illness but who nevertheless foreseeably suffers a grievous non-physical reaction as a consequence of the misfeasance. It seems to me that what Lord Bridge was concerned to discount in *McLoughlin v O'Brien* . . . was 'normal human emotions', not significantly abnormal manifestations of non-physical sequelae. If my approach does not live easily with the established approach in cases of negligence resulting in personal injury, I would strive to treat misfeasance in public office exceptionally.

8.130 The Master of the Rolls declined to express a view as to which approach was correct, and thus there was no majority as to the correct approach in principle.[192]

8.131 Consistent with the approach advocated by Maurice Kay LJ in *Hussain*, the editors of *Clerk & Lindsell on Torts* suggest that as the tort is inherently concerned with abuse of power, it is at least arguable that the range of types of damage required for the tort to be actionable should be broader than the equivalent range of damage that will suffice for an action in negligence. They point to it already being established that purely economic

186 [2008] EWCA Civ 1205.
187 [2008] EWCA Civ 1205 at para 8.
188 [1983] 1 AC 410, [1982] 2 WLR 982.
189 [2008] EWCA Civ 1205 at paras 13–15.
190 [2008] EWCA Civ 1205 at para 19.
191 [2008] EWCA Civ 1205 at para 20.
192 [2008] EWCA Civ 1205 at para 21. Some consideration was given to *Hussain* in *Kimathi v Foreign and Commonwealth Office* [2018] EWHC 1305 (QB), but again, without deciding the point in the context of a misfeasance claim.

losses are more readily recoverable in an action for misfeasance that in an action for negligence.[193]

Loss of liberty

8.132 It is clear, however, that loss of liberty is sufficient to establish material damage. In *Karagozlu v Commissioner of Police of the Metropolis*[194] the claimant was a serving prisoner who had been transferred from open to closed prison conditions. The claimant alleged that the cause of the transfer was false information provided by a police officer and passed to the prison service maliciously with the intention of causing him damage. The Court of Appeal decided that loss of liberty was a form of material damage sufficient to support a claim for misfeasance in public office.[195] That was said to be consistent with Lord Bingham's definition of material damage in *Watkins* because 'loss of liberty, if not a form of physical injury, is at least akin to or analogous to physical injury'.[196] Moreover, in considering what constituted material damage, there was no reason to treat misfeasance differently to a claim in malicious prosecution, for which material or special damage is also a requirement.[197]

Damage to reputation

8.133 It may also be that injury to reputation is a sufficient loss to form material damage. It does not easily fall within Lord Bingham's definition in *Watkins* of financial loss and physical or mental injury. However, there was no issue in *Watkins* as to reputational damage. It is clear that damage to reputation is sufficient for a malicious prosecution claim (see para 8.12 above) and, adopting the approach of the Court of Appeal in *Karagozlu*, it might be argued there is no obvious reason why damage sufficient to establish a claim in malicious prosecution should not also be sufficient for misfeasance.

Exemplary damages

8.134 Exemplary damages may be awarded for a claim in misfeasance.[198]

Misfeasance in police cases

8.135 Many instances of police misconduct will fall within the more established torts such as false imprisonment in relation to a wrongful arrest. In those instances, a claim in misfeasance is usually superfluous. However, the tort of misfeasance may be of considerable assistance to claimants in circumstances going beyond arrest, detention and assault. Misfeasance in the context of criminal prosecutions is considered below.

193 23rd edn, Sweet & Maxwell, at 13-139. The issue came before the High Court in *N v Secretary of State for the Home Department* [2014] EWHC 3304 (QB), but Phillips J considered that on the facts of the case he did not need to determine whether the approach of Maurice Kay LJ was correct.

194 [2006] EWCA Civ 1691, [2007] 1 WLR 1881.

195 [2006] EWCA Civ 1691, [2007] 1 WLR 1881 at paras 29, 34.

196 [2006] EWCA Civ 1691, [2007] 1 WLR 1881 at para 39.

197 [2006] EWCA Civ 1691, [2007] 1 WLR 1881 at paras 34 and 42.

198 *Kuddus v Chief Constable of Leicestershire* [2001] UKHL 29, [2002] 2 AC 122.

8.136 Some examples of misfeasance claims in police actions include:

- Failing to properly conduct a disclosure exercise: *Chief Constable of South Wales v Daniels*.[199]
- Police officers developing sexual relationships with persons who were the subject of undercover operations: *DIL v Commissioner of Police of the Metropolis*[200] and *AKJ and others v Commissioner of Police of the Metropolis*.[201]
- An officer's deliberate failure to investigate a complaint of crime and forging related documentation: *Kuddus v Chief Constable of Leicestershire*.[202]
- Wrongful identification of the claimants as distributors of stolen imported vehicles, publicised by officers to customers of the business: *R Cruickshank Ltd v Chief Constable of Kent*.[203]
- Misuse of a known violent criminal as a paid police informant: *Akenzua v Secretary of State for the Home Department*.[204]

8.137 A significant advantage of this tort over a claim in negligence in police cases is the absence of a need to show that a duty of care arose, which can be problematic in relation to police investigations, as discussed in chapter 7. Misfeasance additionally offers the opportunity to recover aggravated and exemplary damages.

Differences between malicious prosecution and misfeasance

8.138 One important difference between the tort of malicious prosecution and that of misfeasance is that in the latter there is no requirement to demonstrate an absence of 'reasonable and probable' cause for the prosecution. In *Darker v Chief Constable of West Midlands*,[205] it was argued that the claim in misfeasance, said to arise from the earlier prosecution of the claimants, was an attempt to sidestep the requirements of the tort of malicious prosecution that should not be permitted.[206] The argument did not find favour with a majority of the House of Lords. Lords Cooke, Clyde and Hutton each rejected it (albeit Lord Clyde tentatively so).[207] In *Howarth v Chief Constable of Gwent and others*,[208] Eady J noted that their Lordships in *Darker* had not finally decided the point, but suggested there was no logical

199 [2015] EWCA Civ 680: compare *Young v Chief Constable of Warwickshire* [2021] EWHC 3453 (QB).

200 [2014] EWHC 2184 (QB).

201 [2013] EWCA Civ 1342, [2014] 1 WLR 285.

202 [2001] UKHL 29, [2001] 3 All ER 193. Liability was conceded and the case was contested on the issue of damages.

203 [2002] EWCA Civ 1840. The court accepted on a strike out application that the claim was arguable.

204 [2002] EWCA Civ 1470, [2003] 1 All ER 35.

205 [2001] 1 AC 435, HL.

206 [2001] 1 AC 435 at 456E per Lord Cooke, HL.

207 Lord Cooke at 456A–B, Lord Clyde at 456E, and Lord Hutton at 471D.

208 [2011] EWHC 2836 (QB).

reason why an inability to establish an absence of reasonable and probable cause should be a bar to a claim in misfeasance.[209]

8.139 It may appear, therefore, that claims in misfeasance may succeed in an array of circumstances in which a malicious prosecution claim may not. There are, however, two significant caveats.

8.140 First, in order to succeed in a claim for misfeasance in the context of a criminal prosecution, proving causation of damage will often turn on being able to prove that, absent the misfeasance, the prosecution would not have commenced or, perhaps, would have been discontinued. However, if there did exist reasonable and probable cause it may be difficult to prove that the prosecution would not have proceeded. Accordingly, whereas a malicious prosecution claim may fail for reasonable and probable cause, a misfeasance claimed pursued in the alternative may fail for causation. That is the rock upon which the claim in *Young v Chief Constable of Warwickshire* floundered.[210]

8.141 At first instance in *Rees v Commissioner of Police of the Metropolis*[211] the claimants argued, unsuccessfully, that it should be sufficient to establish that the misfeasance made a material contribution to the prosecution (rather than a 'but for' test) or that a claim could be made for the loss of chance of the prosecution not being pursued. The point was pursued on appeal but not decided by the Court of Appeal.[212]

8.142 Second, as discussed from para 8.144 below, a misfeasance claim will face the potentially significant barrier of witness immunity, whereas this doctrine does not apply at all to claims in malicious prosecution, which constitute an exception to it.

Limitation

8.143 Unlike in malicious prosecution where the time limit for bringing a civil claim runs from the date when the prosecution ended in the claimant's favour (see para 8.10), the limitation period for a misfeasance claim runs from the date of the misconduct relied upon, which may be substantially earlier.

Witness immunity

Introduction

8.144 The principle of witness immunity concerns evidence given in or for the purpose of any court proceedings and can arise in relation to a wide variety of torts and circumstances. It is considered here as, in the context of police misconduct, it can have particular relevance in misfeasance claims relating to criminal prosecutions.

209 [2011] EWHC 2836 (QB) at para 29.
210 [2021] EWHC 3453 (QB).
211 [2017] EWHC 273 (QB).
212 *Rees and others v Commissioner of Police of the Metropolis* [2018] EWCA Civ 1587 at para 101.

8.145 The core of the immunity is well-established and straightforward: a witness of fact enjoys immunity for anything said in the witness box in the course of court proceedings. Thus, the giving by a police officer of false evidence in the witness box cannot give rise to liability in misfeasance. It is also clear that written statements prepared for the purpose of court proceedings enjoy the same immunity.

Rationale for the immunity

8.146 In *Darker v Chief Constable of the West Midlands*[213] the House of Lords identified the justifications given for the immunity as:[214]

1) to protect witnesses who have given evidence in good faith from being harassed and vexed by unjustified claims;
2) to encourage honest and well-meaning persons to assist justice in the interest of establishing the truth and to secure that justice may be done;
3) to secure that the witness will speak freely and fearlessly; and
4) to avoid a multiplicity of actions in which the value or truth of the evidence of a witness would be tried all over again.

8.147 However, their Lordships also recognised that an immunity is in principle inconsistent with the rule of law and the imperative that a wrong ought not to be without a remedy.[215] Accordingly, the immunity only extends so far as is necessary to prevent it from being outflanked.[216] Generally, the position is that no immunity applies to actions of officers associated with their function as investigators, as opposed to their role as witnesses.

Scope of the immunity

8.148 In *Darker* it was confirmed that statements made by police officers and things said or done in the ordinary course of preparing reports to use in evidence where the functions they are performing can be said to be those of witnesses or potential witnesses attract immunity. However, as Lord Hope explained:[217]

> . . . there is no good reason on grounds of public policy to extend the immunity . . . to things done by [the officer] which cannot fairly be said to form part of their participation in the judicial process as witnesses. The purpose of the immunity is to protect witnesses against claims made against them for something said or done in the course of giving or preparing to give evidence. It is not to be used to shield the police from action for things done while they are acting as investigators.

213 [2001] 1 AC 435, HL.

214 This is how the Supreme Court in *Jones v Kaney* [2011] UKSC 13, [2011] 2 AC 398 summarised the justifications for the immunity identified in *Darker*: see Lord Phillips at 409A. In *Darker*, see Lord Hope at 446 and 447; Lord Hutton at 464; Lord Clyde at 460 and 461.

215 For example, Lord Hope in *Darker* at 446D, Lord Clyde at 456H, Lord Hutton at 468F.

216 See *Singh v Reading Borough Council* [2013] EWCA Civ 909, [2013] 1 WLR 3052, per Lewison LJ at para 66.

217 [2001] 1 AC 435 at 448D–E, HL.

8.149 Clearly, much of what is done in the course of a police investigation is done with a view to the presentation of evidence in court. The line between a self-standing investigative act which does not attract immunity, and the giving of evidence as a witness which does, can therefore be difficult to draw. Indeed, some activities which might be described as investigative, such as the preparation of reports with a view to these forming part of the evidence to be given in court, are likely to attract immunity.[218]

8.150 In *Darker*, Lord Hope approved the dicta of Sir Richard Scott V-C in *Bennett v Commissioner of Police of the Metropolis*[219] that the immunity extended to statements made or agreed to be made out of court 'if these were clearly and directly made in relation to the proceedings in court, for example, witnesses' proofs of evidence'. Lord Clyde suggested that in drawing the line in any particular case it may be necessary to study precisely what was being done and how closely it was linked with the proceedings in court: 'No immunity should attach to things said or done which would not form part of the evidence to be given in the judicial process.'[220]

Applications of the principle to policing situations

8.151 As an example, although a false statement made in evidence that a drug had been discovered in a property would attract immunity, the planting of a drug in the property would not. The point is that in the latter case the allegation relates not to the content of statements made in evidence, but to the doing of an act, namely, the creation or fabrication of evidence.[221] Moreover, the officer planting the drug would plainly have no intention of ever disclosing that fact in a statement or in oral evidence, thus it cannot be associated with any function as a witness.[222] Fabricating a written admission falsely stated to have been made by a defendant, or fabricating a written statement said to have been made by a witness, would not attract immunity for similar reasons.

8.152 On the very fringes of the immunity might be a dishonest entry by a police officer in a notebook purporting to record what the officer had witnessed. On one view, the written note is closely related to the officer's role in a prosecution as a witness; it is a statement made with a view to use in court proceedings. The better view, however, would be that the act comprises the fabrication of evidence (in the form of a contemporaneous note) such that the immunity does not apply. That would be consistent with Lord Hutton's view in *Darker* that the immunity does not extend to cover the wrongful fabrication of a note which will purport to be used to refresh the memory of the witness and give the impression to the jury that there is support for the witness's false statement.[223]

218 *Darker* [2001] 1 AC 435 at 459F, HL.
219 (1997) 10 Admin LR 245 at 252D–E, ChD.
220 [2001] 1 AC 435 at 460B.
221 See *Darker* [2001] 1 AC 435, HL, in particular Lord Hope at 449B-D, Lord Cooke at 453A, and Lord Clyde at 461.
222 *Darker* [2001] 1 AC 435 at 452E, HL, per Lord Mackay.
223 [2001] 1 AC 435 at 472A, HL; see also 471B.

8.153 The conduct of a disclosure exercise in the course of a criminal prosecution would not attract immunity, notwithstanding that the actions are closely connected with the giving of evidence, and that the disclosure officers would be required to make statements to court about the disclosure exercise. An argument to the opposite effect failed in *Chief Constable of South Wales Police v Daniels*,[224] the reason being that the substance of the complaint was not the content of any express or implied statements concerned with disclosure, but the way in which the disclosure exercise was performed. The fact that an activity may be intimately associated with the judicial phase of the criminal process, as distinct from the administrative or investigative function, does not, in itself, necessarily give rise to immunity.[225]

Whether the cause of action is based on the contents of a statement

8.154 It is important to consider whether the cause of action is based on the contents of a statement made as evidence. Where the gist of the cause of action is focused otherwise than on statements made in the course of the court proceedings the immunity is unlikely to apply. This was central to the court's reasoning in *Daniels*. In *Taylor v Director of the Serious Fraud Office* the immunity was said to be 'limited to actions in which the alleged statement constitutes the cause of action'.[226] It is for this reason that witness immunity does not bar a claim in malicious prosecution: it is the malicious abuse of process, not the making of the statement, that provides the cause of action.[227]

8.155 The principle explains *Singh v Reading BC and another*[228] in which a teacher brought a constructive dismissal claim in the employment tribunal alleging that a witness statement from the school business manager made in defence of her earlier discrimination claim contained false allegations about her which had been produced as a result of undue pressure from her then employer. The Court of Appeal decided that the immunity did not apply, as the gist of the cause of action was not the allegedly false statement itself but the improper conduct of the employer which had generated it and which was, for these purposes, a free-standing act, separate to the evidence.[229]

8.156 There was a different outcome in *CLG and others v Chief Constable of Merseyside*[230] in which a gun had been fired through the front door of the claimants' home. Despite some convictions, the claimants were still subjected to threats. Out of fear they refused to give evidence against the perpetrators and the Crown applied for a warrant for their arrest, but in

224 [2015] EWCA Civ 680.

225 See Lloyd-Jones LJ at para 42.

226 [1999] 2 AC 177 at 215, cited with approval by Lord Mackay in *Darker* [2001] 1 AC 435, HL at 450G.

227 *Taylor v Director of the Serious Fraud Office* [1999] 2 AC 177 at 219, HL, per Lord Hope.

228 [2013] Civ 909, [2013] 1 WLR 3052.

229 [2013] Civ 909, [2013] 1 WLR 3052, para 71.

230 [2015] EWCA Civ 836.

doing so released a police statement which revealed the claimants' new address. They suffered psychiatric injury and brought claims in negligence and under the Human Rights Act (HRA) 1998. The Court of Appeal recognised that the negligence claim was based not on the content of the officer's statement, but on what the CPS and the police subsequently did with it. Nonetheless, it considered that the immunity applied as the acts complained of were part and parcel of preparing for the officer to give evidence.[231] The decision appears to involve a surprisingly wide application of the immunity.

Acts subsequently the subject of evidence

8.157 Where the act complained of is one that does not itself attract the immunity, the position is unaffected by the fact that evidence is subsequently given about that act. For example, the officer who plants a drug does not benefit from immunity by presenting evidence about the discovery of the drug in court.[232]

Allegations of carelessness rather than fabrication

8.158 Their Lordships in *Darker* focused particularly on the fabrication of evidence, but Lord Mackay indicated that negligent conduct not reflected in a written report or statement would not attract immunity,[233] although Lord Hutton suggested to the contrary.[234] In *Smart v Forensic Science Ltd*[235] the claimant, who had been arrested on suspicion of possessing a live bullet, said he believed the bullet to be ornamental rather than live. The police obtained a forensic analysis from the defendant who reported that the bullet was live. As the offence was one of strict liability the claimant pleaded guilty. Some months later, the CPS identified that the bullet was not in fact live, and the conviction was set aside. The claimant brought a claim against the defendant alleging both deceit and negligence. The Court of Appeal refused to strike out the claim on the basis of witness immunity, reasoning that the claim founded in deceit comprised what their Lordships in *Darker* described as the fabrication of evidence which did not attract immunity. However, the court also held that some of the reasons given in *Darker*, including those of Lord Mackay, justified keeping the negligence claim alive.[236]

231 [2015] EWCA Civ 836, para 32. The negligence claim also failed on the basis that no duty of care was owed, see para 11.172.

232 See, for example, *Darker* [2001] 1 AC 435, HL Lord Hope at 449H and Lord Clyde at 461D. See, also, *Singh v Reading Borough Council* [2013] Civ 909, [2013] 1 WLR 3052 at para 59.

233 [2001] 1 AC 435 at 451G, HL.

234 [2001] 1 AC 435 at 472B, HL.

235 [2013] EWCA Civ 783, [2013] PNLR 32.

236 See Moses LJ at para 29 and Aikens LJ at para 36.

CHAPTER 9

Wrongful interference with land and goods

Introduction

9.1 This chapter will cover the wrongful interference with land and goods, under the following headings:

- trespass to land;
- interference with goods; and
- the European Convention on Human Rights (ECHR).

Trespass to land

Introduction

9.2 The right of individuals to be secure in their own homes and free from arbitrary searches is an ancient one that was guaranteed in important constitutional cases in the 18th century.[1] Today these rights are principally protected by the law of trespass.

9.3 Police officers commit trespass if, without permission or lawful authority, they enter or remain on land that the claimant possesses.

9.4 A claim can be brought for trespass to land without showing any actual damage.[2] However, the degree of loss will obviously affect the level of compensation awarded.[3]

'Land'

9.5 'Land' has a special meaning. It may include a person's home (whether a flat or a house, and including any garden), as well as business or other premises. It includes anything attached to the land or the structure of the home, such as a door or fitted cupboards. It also includes the air-space that is required for the ordinary use of the land.[4]

'Possession'

9.6 The claimant must 'possess' the land (ie must have a right to exclude other, including the defendant). A claimant who owns the freehold or leasehold or is a tenant (and, in any of these cases, has not sublet the property) certainly 'possesses' the land.

9.7 The position of licensees, such as lodgers, can be more complicated, given the relative nature of possession. A lodger in a private house does not have a right of exclusive possession of their room as against the landlord. However, a licensee may bring a claim in trespass against third parties – such as the police – where the terms of their licence include a

1 *Entick v Carrington* (1765) 19 St Tr 1030; *Wilkes v Wood* (1765) 19 St Tr 1153; see also *Attorney-General of Jamaica v Williams* [1998] AC 351 at 354–355, PC.

2 See, for example, *Stadium Capital Holdings (No 2) Ltd v St Marylebone Property Co plc* [2011] EWHC 2856 (Ch), [2012] 1 P&CR 7.

3 See chapter 14.

4 *Kelsen v Imperial Tobacco Co of Great Britain* [1957] 2 QB 334, QBD.

right to exclude third parties, expressly or impliedly (for example, if they are the key holder and have the right to bar other people from the room).[5]

9.8 There may similarly be difficulties if the person aggrieved lives with someone else who is the owner, for instance, a parent or partner (of whom they will be a licensee). Again, in such a case, they may be able to sue if they have the owner's authority to exclude strangers, but, if feasible, it is often preferable to sue in the name of the owner too.

9.9 It is also possible that a squatter who has actual possession of land, but no legal estate or other right in it, may sue for trespass,[6] although the limits of such a principle have not been tested.

9.10 Since the Human Rights Act (HRA) 1998 came into force, a claimant who does not have 'possession' of the land, may nonetheless be able to rely on an infringement of their rights under ECHR Article 8 (right to respect for private and family life) (as discussed later in this chapter).

'Entering or remaining on the land'

9.11 The slightest crossing of the boundary of land is capable of constituting a trespass: 'If the defendant place a part of his foot on the plaintiff's land unlawfully, it is in law as much a trespass as if he had walked half a mile on it'.[7]

9.12 The police can also be treated as 'entering' land if they have physical contact with the land – for instance, if a door or window is removed[8] or if a ladder is placed against a wall.[9] In such cases there is no need to show that the officers came any further into the home. Additionally, causing foreign matter to enter the land will be a trespass. This might include a police dog ordered to run on the land.[10]

9.13 There is no need to show that the police have used force in order to enter or remain on the land – although, if they have done so, it may be evidence that they did not have permission and it is likely to affect the amount of damages.

Defences to trespass to land

9.14 There are various bases on which police may enter premises. These include powers to enter to carry out an arrest and to conduct a search, either with or without a warrant. It is not possible here to describe all such powers, but reference will be made to those that are most commonly relied upon:

- licence to enter;
- entry under a search warrant;

5 *Marcroft Wagons Ltd v Smith* [1951] 2 KB 496 at 501, CA; *Hounslow LBC v Twickenham Garden Developments Ltd* [1971] Ch 233 at 257, ChD; *Manchester Airport plc v Dutton* [2000] QB 133 at 147, CA; *Mehta v Royal Bank of Scotland* (2000) 32 HLR 45, QBD. In the police context, see *Thomas v DPP* [2009] EWHC 3906 (Admin).

6 *Graham v Peat* (1801) 1 East 244.

7 *Ellis v Loftus Iron Co* (1874) LR 10 C&P 10 at 12.

8 *Lavender v Betts* [1942] 2 All ER 72.

9 *Westripp v Baldock* [1938] 2 All ER 779, [1939] 1 All ER 279, CA.

10 *Beckwith v Shordike* (1767) 4 Burr 2092; *Weir v Countryside Alliance Ltd* [2016] NIQB 16.

- entry other than under a search warrant;

The following issues will also be considered:

- 'trespass ab initio';
- mistake;
- presence of others.

Licence to enter

9.15 If the police are given permission to enter, then they have a licence to be on the land and are not trespassers. The person who gives the police the licence does not necessarily have to be the occupier, so long as it is someone acting under the occupier's authority. Once permission has been granted, it can be expressly revoked and if after a reasonable interval the police fail to leave they become trespassers.[11] In some circumstances, however, a licence granted by one co-occupier cannot be revoked unilaterally by another.[12]

9.16 Further, although the slightest entry onto land is a trespass, there is an implied permission for an officer to walk up the garden path to a house in order to ask for permission.[13] There is generally no implied permission to do anything else,[14] for instance to search the garden on the way to the front door. In some circumstances, however, where it is not possible for an officer to seek consent, they may nonetheless be entitled to assume that it would be given, for example to enter privately owned land over which a public right of way exists to cordon off a crime scene,[15] or when in 'hot pursuit' of a suspect.[16]

9.17 Officers may not be able to rely on consent to enter land which is not given freely or which is obtained by the provision of misleading information.[17]

Entry under a search warrant

9.18 A warrant to enter and search a property may be granted pursuant to a wide range of statutory powers. The most commonly used is that contained in Police and Criminal Evidence Act 1984 (PACE) s8 which enables officers to apply to a magistrate for a warrant to enter premises where there are reasonable grounds for believing the matters set out in section 8(1), namely that: a) an indictable offence has taken place; b) there is material on the premises likely to be of substantial value to the investigation of the offence; c) the material is likely to be relevant evidence (ie would be admissible at trial[18]); d) it does not include items subject to legal

11 *Minister of Health v Bellotti* [1944] KB 298, CA.

12 For example, *R v Thornley* (1981) 72 Cr App R 302, CA, in which the defendant could not revoke the permission granted to officers by his wife in the context of a domestic dispute.

13 *Robson v Hallett* [1967] 2 QB 939, QBD.

14 *Brunner v Williams* (1977) 73 LGR 266, DC.

15 *DPP v Morrison* [2003] EWHC 683 (Admin).

16 *Wiltshire v DPP* [2014] EWHC 4659 (Admin).

17 See the discussion on consent in the section on assault and battery at paras 7.9–7.13 above.

18 PACE s8(4).

privilege, excluded material or 'special procedure material';[19] and e) it would not be practicable to obtain access without a warrant.

9.19 'Material' is to be construed broadly and, although a container (for example, a filing cabinet) cannot be included in a warrant where only some of its contents would be relevant evidence,[20] the same does not apply to a computer.[21]

9.20 PACE s15 sets out various safeguards in relation to the process of application and the form of warrant itself.[22] They include:

- that the constable must state the grounds on which the application is made and various other matters;[23]
- that the application shall be supported by 'an information' in writing;[24]
- that the constable shall answer on oath any question that the court asks;[25]
- that the warrant shall authorise entry on one occasion only unless otherwise specified;[26]
- that the warrant shall specify various details;[27] and
- that two copies shall be made.[28]

In a straightforward case, where the information contains all of the information necessary to demonstrate that a warrant should be granted, the court may not necessarily need to record its reasons separately; although it should keep a record of any additional evidence given orally[29] and in more complex cases it will be necessary to record reasons separately.[30]

9.21 PACE s16 sets out various requirements in relation to the execution of warrants, including that:

- the warrant must be executed within three months of issue;[31]
- execution must be at a 'reasonable hour' unless the purpose of the search would be frustrated;[32]

19 In relation to which, see PACE ss9–14 and Sch 1.
20 Although see Criminal Justice and Police Act (CJPA) 2001 Part 2, below, in relation to seizure of such items.
21 *R (Faisaltex Ltd) v Preston Crown Court* [2008] EWHC 2832 (Admin), [2009] 1 WLR 1687 at paras 73–79.
22 Which must be satisfied by the warrant documents on their face, without reference to extraneous documents: *R (Van der Pijl) v Kingston Crown Court* [2012] EWHC 3745 (Admin), [2013] 1 WLR 2706.
23 PACE s15(2).
24 PACE s15(3).
25 PACE s15(4).
26 PACE s15(5).
27 PACE s15(6). As regards the level of specificity required, see for example *R (Superior Import/Export Ltd) v Commissioners for HMRC* [2017] EWHC 3172 (Admin) at paras 67–71 and the authorities cited therein.
28 PACE s15(7).
29 *R (Cronin) v Sheffield Justices* [2002] EWHC 2568 (Admin), [2003] 1 WLR 752.
30 *R (Rawlinson & Hunter Trustees) v Central Criminal Court* [2012] EWHC 2254 (Admin), [2013] 1 WLR 1634 at paras 202–208; *R (Newcastle United Football Club Ltd) v HMRC Commissioners* [2017] EWHC 2402 (Admin), [2017] 4 WLR 187 at paras 43–61.
31 PACE s16(3).
32 PACE s16(4).

- a copy of the warrant must be left with the occupier[33] or person in charge,[34] or failing this left 'in a prominent place on the premises';[35]
- the search and seizure must not exceed the terms of the warrant;[36]
- the warrant must be endorsed with the results of the search;[37] and
- it must thereafter be returned to the court[38] to be retained for 12 months.[39]

9.22 On the constable's application, the judge must be satisfied that the conditions in PACE s8 are made out. In *R (G) v Commissioner of Police of the Metropolis* Laws LJ stressed that:[40]

> There is a large body of authority which establishes three important propositions:
> 1. The issue of a search warrant or a warrant for seizure is a very serious interference with the liberty of the subject.
> 2. The officer applying for such a warrant must give full, complete and frank disclosure to the magistrate so as to enable the latter to base his decision on the fullest possible information.
> 3. The court itself must give the most mature and careful consideration to all the facts of the case . . .

9.23 However, it is important to bear in mind that the threshold for the granting of a warrant is only one of having 'reasonable grounds for believing' the matters in PACE s8(1) and that 'a likelihood [that material is likely to be of substantial value and relevant evidence] is less than a probability'.[41] Further, although the application should generally be provided to the suspect upon request[42] it is open to the judge to take into account material that cannot be disclosed to the suspect for reasons of public interest immunity (PII).[43]

9.24 Upon a challenge to the decision to issue a warrant by way of judicial review, the court will not consider the application afresh but simply whether the decision to grant a warrant was open to the judge on public law principles, as well as whether the warrant should be quashed on grounds of material non-disclosure by the police in making the application.[44] A

33 PACE s16(5).
34 PACE s16(6).
35 PACE s16(7).
36 PACE s16(8).
37 PACE s16(9).
38 PACE s16(10)–(10A).
39 PACE s16(11).
40 [2011] EWHC 3331 (Admin) at para 17. For further discussion see, for example, *R (Rawlinson & Hunter Trustees) v Central Criminal Court* [2012] EWHC 2254 (Admin), [2013] 1 WLR 1634 at paras 81–98; and *R (Chatwani) v National Crime Agency* [2015] EWHC 1283 (Admin) at para 103.
41 *R (Faisaltex) v Preston Crown Court* [2008] EWHC 2832 (Admin) at paras 30–31, citing *R v Chief Constable of Warwickshire ex p Fitzpatrick* [1999] 1 WLR 564, DC.
42 *R (Cronin) v Sheffield Justices* [2002] EWHC 2568 (Admin), [2003] 1 WLR 752.
43 *R (Haralambous) v St Albans Crown Court* [2018] UKSC 1, [2018] AC 236. For a recent summary of the principles to be applied in determining a PII claim, and the procedure to be followed in the substantive hearing where a PII claim is upheld, see *R (Jordan) v Chief Constable of Merseyside Police* [2020] EWHC 2274 (Admin).
44 See, for example, *R (Mills) v Sussex Police* [2014] EWHC 2523 (Admin), [2015] 1 WLR 2199.

warrant may be quashed where the information that should have been provided might reasonably have led the judge to refuse to issue the warrant.[45]

9.25 Even if the court quashes the warrant (which may be valuable, for example in terms of securing return of items seized under it), no claim in trespass will lie against the police in relation to things 'done in obedience' to the warrant, as the police will have defences under Constables Protection Act 1750 s6 and/or by way of lawful justification.[46] Section 6 envisages that a claim may be brought instead against the justice of the peace who granted the warrant, however, Courts Act 2003 s67E (providing that such a claim can only be brought if the justice granted the warrant outside their jurisdiction and in bad faith) means that this will almost never be feasible.

9.26 A claim for damages may lie against the police, however:

1) In trespass, if:
   a) 'there is a formal defect on the face of the warrant sufficiently grave to invalidate it'.[47] In *Bell,* Sir Mark Potter P noted that 'the law is by no means clear as to the level of grossness or obviousness which is necessary for the officer to lose his protection by reason of such defect',[48] but suggested that: 'The test . . . is directed to the question whether, the defect relied on is such as to raise a clear doubt as to whether an application has been lawfully made to, and granted by, the Justices in the exercise of their jurisdiction';[49]
   b) officers carry out a search that exceeds the terms or scope of the warrant, for example if they mistakenly enter an address that is not the one specified in the warrant.[50]
2) In the tort of malicious procurement, if the warrant was procured maliciously, without reasonable and probable cause, and damage resulted;[51] See also paras 8.93–8.101.
3) In negligence, in relation to damage caused as a result of a lack of reasonable care in executing the warrant.[52] See also paras 7.48ff above.
4) Under the HRA 1998 for a breach of ECHR Article 8, where reasonable and available precautions were not taken to ensure the application for the warrant was justified (even where malice is not shown).[53]

9.27 It has also been suggested that a failure by the police, on an application for a warrant, to disclose relevant information known to them may 'invalidate'

45 *R (Mills) v Sussex Police* [2014] EWHC 2523 (Admin) at para 55.

46 See, for example, *Bell v Chief Constable of Greater Manchester* [2005] EWCA Civ 902 at para 28; *R (C) v Nottingham and Newark Magistrates' Court* [2013] EWHC 3790 (Admin) at para 25.

47 *Bell v Chief Constable of Greater Manchester* [2005] EWCA Civ 902 at para 29.

48 Para 29.

49 Para 33.

50 *Hoye v Bush* (1840) 1 Man & G 775.

51 See, for example, *Gibbs v Rea* [1998] AC 786; and *Fitzpatrick v Commissioner of Police of the Metropolis* [2012] EWHC 12 (Admin), [2012] Lloyd's Rep FC 361 at para 142.

52 *Alleyne v Commissioner of Police of the Metropolis* [2012] EWHC 3955 (QB) at paras 136–143. For detailed discussion of negligence, in the context of personal injury and failure to protect, see paras 7.48–7.93, above.

53 See paras 9.79–9.83 below.

the warrant so as to give rise to a claim for damages.[54] However, it is not clear how, in the absence of malice or a breach of PACE s15 (discussed below), this is consistent with the Constables Protection Act 1750.[55]

9.28 PACE s15(1) provides that:

> This section and section 16 below have effect in relation to the issue to constables under any enactment, including an enactment contained in an Act passed after this Act, of warrants to enter and search premises; *and an entry on or search of premises under a warrant is unlawful unless it complies with this section and section 16 below* [emphasis added].

9.29 'It' here refers to the entry and search rather than simply the warrant, such that a breach of the requirements of section 16 will render the entire entry and search unlawful.[56] Thus section 15(1) provides important protection and it is vital to check that the requirements of sections 15 and 16 have been complied with in each case. There, are, however, a number of limitations to the application of section 15(1), for example:

- breaches of the requirements of sections 15 and 16 that are *de minimis* will not render the search unlawful;[57]
- PACE s15(1) applies only to requirements in relation to the *entry and search* and not, for example, the requirement in s16(9) that the warrant be endorsed with the results of the search[58] or that under s16(10) that the warrant be returned to the court thereafter;[59]
- similarly, excessive *seizure* during a search does not render the entire search unlawful by reason of PACE s16(8), so long as the extent of the *search* is within the scope of the warrant.[60]

9.30 Where it is thought that a warrant was unlawful and the claimant seeks a declaration to that effect so as to obtain the return of goods, the appropriate remedy will likely be judicial review. That may also include a claim for damages, if appropriate grounds exist, which can then subsequently be transferred to the county court or Queen's Bench Division

54 Professor Michael Zander QC, *Zander on PACE*, Sweet & Maxwell, 8th edn, 2018, at para 2–09, citing *R (Redknapp) v Commissioner of City of London Police* [2008] EWHC 1177 (Admin), [2009] 1 WLR 2091 at para 27 and *R (Mills) v Sussex Police* [2014] EWHC 2523 (Admin), [2015] 1 WLR 2199 at para 53. See also *R (Daly) v Commissioner of Police for the Metropolis* [2018] EWHC 438 (Admin), [2018] 1 WLR 2221 at paras 32–33.

55 It should be noted that none of the cases cited in the previous footnote expressly considered the effect of the 1750 Act. For a discussion of this point, see the submissions of the Serious Fraud Office in *Tchenguiz v Rawlinson & Hunter Trustees SA* [2013] EWHC 1578 (QB), [2013] Lloyd's Rep FC 535; and the decision of the Court of Appeal [2014] EWCA Civ 472, [2014] CP Rep 35; although the issues were never actually determined and the claim ultimately settled for £3 million.

56 *R (Bhatti) v Croydon Magistrates' Court* [2010] EWHC 522 (Admin), [2011] 1 WLR 948.

57 See, in relation to the requirement in s16(8), *R v Chief Constable of Warwickshire ex p Fitzpatrick* [1999] 1 WLR 564 at 575.

58 *R (Haly) v Chief Constable of West Midlands* [2016] EWHC 2932 (Admin) at para 17.

59 *R (Hicks) v Commissioner of Police of the Metropolis* [2012] EWHC 1947 (Admin) at para 247.

60 *R (Chaudhary) v Bristol Crown Court* [2014] EWHC 4096 (Admin), [2015] 1 Cr App R 18 at para 68, citing *R v Chesterfield Justices ex p Bramley* [2000] QB 576 at 497 and 587, doubting *Fitzpatrick*.

for determination;[61] however, it does *not* follow from a quashing of the warrant by the Administrative Court that liability can be established in tort.[62] Generally, where the concern of the claimant is to obtain damages, without any challenge to the validity of the warrant itself, the appropriate avenue will be a private law claim. Indeed, judicial review may be considered inappropriate if the court is required to determine questions of fact such as whether the seizure exceeded the scope of the warrant.[63]

9.31 Applications for search warrants and searches of premises are also governed by the provisions of Code B of the Codes of Practice issued under PACE.[64] A breach of the Code will not of itself give rise to a legal liability in respect of a search,[65] but such breaches may be relevant to whether the police are able to demonstrate that statutory conditions such as necessity are made out[66] and/or may well constitute an aggravating feature, thereby increasing the amount of damages that are awarded in relation to the search, if liability is established on other grounds.[67]

9.32 If the police have power to enter in a particular case, they may also use reasonable force, if necessary.[68] Obviously, force is not usually necessary if the occupier would have agreed to the police entering their home, if given the opportunity. For instance, if a person hears their doorbell ring and as they go to answer it, the door is kicked in and a number of police officers with a search warrant enter, the person may well have a good claim for trespass because they were not given the opportunity to consent. In *O'Loughlin v Chief Constable of Essex*[69] the Court of Appeal emphasised the 'severe burden' which an officer has to discharge when trying to prove that the use of force was really necessary. In that case, the defendant was unable to discharge the burden because officers failed to tell the occupier the real purpose of their visit before permission to enter was refused and force was employed. Where police have valid reason to suspect that the person in the property is armed or otherwise presents a danger to their safety, then use of force may well be justified in the circumstances.

Entry other than under a search warrant

9.33 The main statutory powers that enable officers to search premises without a search warrant are contained in PACE ss17, 18 and 32.

61 See, for example, *R (Bhatti) v Croydon Magistrates' Court* [2010] EWHC 522 (Admin), [2011] 1 WLR 948 at paras 24 and 32; *Tchenguiz v Rawlinson & Hunter Trustees SA* [2013] EWHC 1578 (QB).

62 See *Tchenguiz v Rawlinson & Hunter Trustees SA* [2013] EWHC 1578 (QB).

63 *Fitzpatrick* at 579; *R (Faisaltex Ltd) v Preston Crown Court* [2008] EWHC 2832 (Admin), [2009] 1 WLR 1687 at para 91.

64 *Code of Practice for searches of premises by police officers and the seizure of property found by police officers on person or premises*, 2013, available at: www.gov.uk/guidance/police-and-criminal-evidence-act-1984-pace-codes-of-practice.

65 PACE s67(10).

66 See, for example, *O'Loughlin v Chief Constable of Essex* [1998] 1 WLR 374; *Lineham v DPP* [2000] Crim LR 861.

67 Aggravated damages are discussed in chapter 17.

68 PACE s117. See discussion of this provision in relation to battery in chapter 6.

69 [1998] 1 WLR 374 at 383.

9.34 PACE s17 authorises officers to enter and search any premises for the purposes of:

a) arresting a person:
   i) under an arrest warrant; or
   ii) without warrant[70] for an indictable offence or certain other specified offences;
b) to recapture persons unlawfully at large; or
c) to save life and limb or prevent serious damage to property.[71]

Save in the latter instance, the power is only exercisable where the officer has reasonable grounds for believing that the person sought is on the premises. Belief imposes a higher threshold than suspicion.[72] Powers of search conferred by this section are limited to searches for the purpose that the power of entry was conferred.[73]

9.35 PACE s18 permits searches of premises occupied or controlled by a person under arrest for an indictable offence if an officer has reasonable grounds for suspecting that there is evidence on the premises, that is not subject to legal privilege, relating either to the offence for which the person was arrested or another indictable offence which is connected with or similar to that offence.[74] It should be noted that the person must actually occupy or control the premises: a reasonable, but mistaken, belief to this effect is not sufficient.[75] The extent of the search is limited to what is reasonably required to discover such evidence.[76] The search must be authorised in writing by an officer of at least inspector rank[77] unless it takes place before the person is taken to a police station and the person's presence at a place other than a police station is necessary for the effective investigation of the offence.[78] The officer who authorises the search, or is informed of a search carried out before the person was brought to the police station, must make a record in writing of the grounds for the search and the nature of the evidence sought,[79] however, failure to do so will not necessarily invalidate the search itself. [80]

9.36 PACE s32(2)(b) provides that, where a person is arrested for an indictable offence at a place other than a police station, an officer may search any

70 For discussion of arrest warrants and arrest without warrant see paras 6.38–6.96.

71 'Saving life or limb' can include saving a person from harming themselves (*Baker v Crown Prosecution Service* [2009] EWHC 299 (Admin)) but cannot include mere concern for a person's welfare (*Syed v DPP* [2010] EWHC 81 (Admin), [2010] 1 Cr App R 34). 'Serious damage to property' may include the death of an animal (*Marzan v RSPCA* [2016] EWHC 993 (Admin)).

72 As to the difference between 'belief' and 'suspicion', see *R v Hall* (1985) 81 Cr App R 260.

73 PACE s17(4).

74 PACE s18(1).

75 *Khan v Commissioner of Police of the Metropolis* [2008] EWCA Civ 723, [2008] PoLR 112.

76 PACE s18(3).

77 PACE s18(4). In *R v Badham* [1987] Crim LR 202 the Crown Court held that it was not sufficient for the authorising officer simply to make a record of authorisation in his notebook.

78 PACE s18(5)–(5A).

79 PACE s18(7).

80 *Krohn v DPP* [1997] COD 345.

premises in which the arrested person was when arrested / immediately before arrest for evidence relating to the offence for which the person was arrested. Unlike the power in PACE s17, this power does not require prior authorisation, nor does it require the constable to suspect that the arrested person constitutes a danger to himself or others for the purposes of section 32(1).[81] However, it must only be used 'to the extent that is reasonably required for the purpose of discovering ... any such evidence'[82] and requires the constable to have reasonable grounds for believing that such evidence is on the premises.[83]

9.37 Officers entering premises under PACE s17 or s18 should inform the occupier of the reason why the entry was required, unless circumstances make it impracticable to do so.[84]

9.38 All common law powers to enter premises for the purposes listed in PACE s17 are abolished, save the power to enter to deal with or prevent breaches of the peace.[85] PACE ss18 and 32, however, do not abolish the common law powers of search and seizure after arrest, which therefore remain relevant in relation to arrests falling outside the scope of those sections, for example in extradition cases.[86] The extent of the common law power is to be balanced with the principle that there should not be excessive intrusion into the homes of members of the public and has been held not to extend to searching the home of an acquaintance of a man arrested for the purposes of extradition.[87]

9.39 A question arises as to whether an officer may lawfully use powers of entry and search under PACE ss18 and 32 rather than seeking a warrant, thus avoiding the additional safeguards that such an application provides. The point was considered in *R (Virdee) v National Crime Agency*[88] and the general position is that there is no order of preference for the powers of entry under PACE, such that if the requirements for entry without warrant are made out then, in the absence of bad faith or improper motive, it will be lawful for the police to exercise that power rather than applying for a warrant. That, however, assumes that there is some justification for the arrest independent of the desire to search a premises. In *R (TL) v Chief Constable of Surrey*[89] it was argued that the power of arrest could not be used solely for the purpose of utilising the powers of search and seizure as section 18 is predicated upon their being some prior antecedent existence

81 *Hanningfield v Chief Constable of Essex* [2013] EWHC 243 (QB), [2013] 1 WLR 3632 per Eady J at paras 10–12.

82 PACE s32(3).

83 PACE s32(6).

84 *O'Loughlin v Chief Constable of Essex* [1998] 1 WLR 374; *Lineham v DPP*, [2000] Crim LR 861.

85 PACE s17(5) and (6). For an example of the latter, see *McLeod v Commissioner of Police of the Metropolis* [1994] 4 All ER 553 CA.

86 *R (Rottman) v Commissioner of Police of the Metropolis* [2002] UKHL 20, [2002] 2 AC 692 per Lord Rodger at paras 109–110.

87 See *Hewitson v Chief Constable of Dorset* [2003] EWHC 3296 (Admin) and the discussion on the common law powers of seizure below.

88 [2018] EWHC 1119 (Admin), [2018] 1 WLR 5073.

89 [2017] EWHC 129 (Admin).

of a lawful arrest and to do otherwise would undermine the statutory scheme. The court declined to decide the point.[90]

Other issues in relation to defences

'Trespass ab initio'

9.40 If the police enter land with lawful authority (rather than merely with the occupier's consent), and then commit a trespass, either to the person or to goods, this may nullify the lawful authority under which they first entered and make them trespassers from the initial moment of entry onwards. This common law doctrine is based on an old line of authority[91] and is known as 'trespass ab initio'. The ongoing relevance of the principle has been the subject of debate for some time: in *Chic Fashions etc Ltd v Jones*[92] Lord Denning described the doctrine as 'obsolete', although he subsequently went on to apply the principle in *Cinnamond v British Airports Authority*.[93] Certainly, not every transgression will render the police trespassers ab initio.[94] It has been suggested that the doctrine is 'best understood as an evidential one, rather than an absolute rule of law', in that the later transgression is simply evidence of the fact that the entry was never for the purposes intended by the authority.[95]

Mistake

9.41 Mistake is no defence to trespass. As long as the physical act of entry was intentional, the police cannot claim that they are not liable in trespass merely because they intended to enter another person's land and did not intend to interfere with the claimant's rights.[96] If, through negligence, the police unintentionally enter a person's land, that is likely also a trespass.[97]

Presence of others

9.42 If the police have hired video companies to film a search or invited the media to accompany them on a 'raid' such persons will not be covered by any search warrant and their presence, without consent, on a person's property would be a trespass. In *R v Marylebone Magistrates Court ex p Amdrell Ltd*[98] the Divisional Court strongly criticised the practices of media representatives accompanying the police on the execution of search warrants.

90 At paras 69–71.

91 See *Six Carpenters Case* (1610) 8 CoRep 146a.

92 [1968] 2 QB 299.

93 [1980] 1 WLR 582. For further discussion of the principle see *Clerk & Lindsell on Torts*, Sweet & Maxwell, 23rd edn, 2020, at para 18-39; *Winfield & Jolowicz on Tort*, 20th edn, 2020 at para 14-027.

94 For example if, during an otherwise lawful search, some items are seized by officers that fall outside the terms of their authority, there will be a case in trespass to goods in relation to those items, but the balance of the search remains lawful: *R v Chesterfield Justices ex p Bramley* [2000] QB 576.

95 *McCarthy v Chief Constable of Merseyside* [2016] EWCA Civ 1257 per Hallett LJ at para 46.

96 *Basely v Clarkson* (1681) 3 Lev 37.

97 *League Against Cruel Sports Ltd v Scott* [1986] QB 240.

98 (1998) 162 JP 719.

Further, such intrusion is likely to give rise to a breach of a suspect's right to respect for their home, private and/or family life under ECHR Article 8.[99]

Interference with goods

Introduction

9.43 If the police unlawfully damage or seize something that belongs to a person, for example, while searching the person in the street or searching their home, that person can seek damages and/or recovery of the goods, in a claim for 'trespass to goods' or 'conversion' (as well as some other causes of action which will be touched upon below).

9.44 There is a considerable overlap between trespass to goods and conversion. In many cases, it may be possible to sue either for one or the other or both. However, in general, a claim in conversion is appropriate in order to assert the right to the physical possession of something and in trespass to goods to assert the right to its physical condition. Conversion should therefore be used if the police have seized and retained something and its return or compensation for its value is required, and trespass to goods should be used if something has been damaged or altered or simply moved.

Conversion

The act of conversion

9.45 The most common form of conversion in relation to the police occurs when officers take items that they have no lawful authority to seize. However, claims also arise in circumstances where the original seizure of items was lawful, but the items continue to be retained after the authority to do so has been exhausted.[100] Retention of another's goods in circumstances which exclude that other from use and possession of them, coupled with an intention to keep them, amounts to a conversion.[101] To establish a conversion by retention it is not always necessary to show that the return of the goods has been demanded and that the request has been expressly / implicitly refused.[102] However, this is usually the easiest way to establish the criteria for this form of conversion and so it is advisable for such a demand to be made in writing and a negative response received before a claim is commenced. If goods are lawfully retained by the police, the fact that they are transferred temporarily to a third party for safe storage does not amount to a conversion.[103]

9.46 Strict liability applies to any act of conversion. Thus, provided the relevant conduct of the defendant was carried out voluntarily, it does not matter whether the defendant intended to interfere with another's goods or

99 *Richard v BBC* [2018] EWHC 1837 (Ch), [2019] Ch 169.

100 Officers' powers of retention are described below.

101 *Kuwait Airways Corp v Iraqi Airways Co (No 3)* [2002] UKHL 19, [2002] 2 AC 883.

102 *Kuwait Airways Corp* [2002] UKHL 19, [2002] 2 AC 883; *Martin v Chief Constable of Nottinghamshire Constabulary* [2003] EWCA 398.

103 *Martin v Chief Constable of Nottingham* [2003] EWCA Civ 398 at para 14.

whether, for example, the defendant genuinely and reasonably believed that the goods belonged to them.[104]

9.47 The claimant's consent to the taking / retention of the relevant items will negate any claim in conversion. However, officers may not rely on permission that is not given freely or which is obtained by the provision of misleading information.[105] Consent cannot be inferred if the claimant does not know of the relevant interference. Where a claimant's vehicle was wheel clamped when it was parked without authority on private land, the Court of Appeal held that consent to the trespass to goods (to the car) could not be inferred simply from the fact that the claimant was trespassing upon the defendant's land at the time; it had to be shown that the car owner was aware of the consequences of parking her car there.[106]

Who can sue?

9.48 To maintain an action in conversion, it must be proven that the claimant had actual possession of the goods or the immediate right to possession of the goods at the time when the tort was committed. Although the claimant will generally be the owner of the goods, ownership is not necessary to establish a claim in conversion.[107]

9.49 That the police believed the goods to relate to offences, for example suspected stolen goods or suspected proceeds of crime, will not in itself defeat a claim in conversion. If the possessor of the items is ultimately convicted of criminality, the courts will be able to make an order depriving the defendant of the goods in the majority of circumstances.[108] Otherwise, absent any statutory power to retain, the items must be returned to the previous possessor, who will have a better title to them than the police.[109] However, the rights of such a possessor may be fragile and can be defeated by anyone who can show a better title to the items, for example, in the case of a stolen car, the owner of the vehicle. Pursuant to the Torts (Interference with Goods) Act 1977 s8, the police can defend a claim in conversion by showing that someone other than the claimant has a superior title to the goods, provided they can point to a specific, identified individual.[110]

9.50 Pursuant to Police (Property) Act 1897 s1, a claimant whose property has been taken into the possession of the police in connection with the investigation of a suspected offence may apply to a magistrates' court for

104 *Kuwait Airways Corp* [2002] UKHL 19, [2002] 2 AC 883; though the speeches of Lords Nicholls, Hoffmann and Hope suggest that the defendant's degree of culpability will affect the extent of his/her liability for consequential losses.

105 See the discussion on consent in the section on assault and battery at paras 7.9–7.13 above.

106 *Vine v Waltham Forest LBC* [2000] 4 All ER 169.

107 For a general discussion of the circumstances where a claimant may have possession / a right to possession of the goods without being the owner, see *Clerk & Lindsell on Torts*, 23 edn, 2020 at paras 16-47 to 16-48.

108 For example pursuant to the Powers of Criminal Courts (Sentencing) Act 2000 s143.

109 *Costello v Chief Constable of Derbyshire Constabulary* [2001] EWCA Civ 381, [2001] 1 WLR 1437; *Gough v Chief Constable of the West Midlands Police* [2004] EWCA Civ 206.

110 *Costello, Verrechia v Commissioner of Police of the Metropolis* (2001) 15 March QBD.

an order requiring the delivery to them of the property. That right does not prevent the claimant from alternatively bringing a claim for conversion.[111]

Defences

9.51 It is for the police to demonstrate some lawful authority pursuant to statute or common law for the seizure or retention of the goods in question. The police have powers under various statutes to seize a wide range of specific items or types of evidence of particular offences. It is beyond the scope of this book to detail all such powers, however reference will be made to those most commonly employed: under PACE, the Criminal Justice and Police Act (CJPA) 2001 and the Limitation Act 1980.

PACE

9.52 Where a search warrant is granted pursuant to PACE s8, officers are empowered to seize and retain anything for which a search was authorised.[112] The legality of the seizure is therefore likely to depend upon issues equivalent to those discussed above in relation to search warrants and trespass to land, in particular, whether the scope of the seizure was authorised by the terms of the warrant, whether the search and seizure complied with PACE ss15–16 and whether the actions complained of were done in obedience to the warrant so that officers are protected by Constables Protection Act 1750 s6.

9.53 An officer is also empowered to seize anything that they may search for pursuant to PACE s18.[113]

9.54 Officers are also given a general power of seizure by PACE s19. The power is exercisable where an officer is lawfully on any premises and has reasonable grounds for believing that the relevant item has been obtained in consequence of the commission of an offence or that it is evidence in relation to an offence and that it is necessary to seize it to prevent it being concealed, lost, damaged, altered or destroyed.[114] This wide power extends to evidence of any crime and is not limited to material that is related to the offence currently under investigation. Thus the police could enter a home under a search warrant for, say, controlled drugs and instead lawfully seize goods which they reasonably suspect to be stolen. The power of seizure does not extend to an item that the officer has reasonable grounds for believing to be subject to legal privilege.[115] The powers of seizure contained in PACE s18(2) and s19 extend to the seizure of the whole premises where it is physically possible to seize and retain the premises in their totality, for example a caravan, vehicle or tent.[116]

9.55 The common law power of search and seizure where a person is arrested has been described earlier in relation to claims for trespass to land. There is also a common law power of seizure available to the police in the

111 *O'Leary International Ltd v Chief Constable of North Wales* [2012] EWHC 1516 (Admin), [2013] RTR 14.

112 PACE s8(2).

113 PACE s18(2). The scope of s18 is summarised above (under trespass to land).

114 PACE s19(2) and (3). For the power to retain such items, see CJPA 2001 s56.

115 PACE s19(6).

116 *Cowan v Commissioner of Police of the Metropolis* [1999] EWCA Civ 2031, [2000] 1 WLR 254.

absence of an arrest, if the criteria laid down by the Court of Appeal in *Ghani v Jones*[117] are satisfied. These are that the police have reasonable grounds for believing:

a) a serious offence has been committed;
b) the article in question is the fruit of the crime, the instrument by which it was committed or material evidence to prove commission of the crime;
c) the person in possession of the item committed the crime, was an accessory to it or their refusal to give the item to the officers is unreasonable.

The House of Lords confirmed that common law powers of seizure are additional to and are not impliedly repealed by the provisions of PACE.[118]

9.56 If the police lawfully seize items, they must supply a record of everything they have taken within a reasonable time of being asked for such a record.[119] They can be asked for the list at the time the items are taken or at any later time. A person can also ask for access to anything that has been seized, for example, to inspect it, or for anything that has been seized to be photographed or copied, provided that to do so would not prejudice police investigations or any later trial.[120]

9.57 Once something has been lawfully seized,[121] PACE s22(1) provides that the police are entitled to retain it for as long as is necessary in all the circumstances. For example, anything seized for the purposes of a criminal investigation can be retained for use as evidence in a trial or for investigation or forensic examination.[122] However, the police should return the original if a photograph or copy would be sufficient.[123] They can also retain anything in order to establish its lawful owner provided there are reasonable grounds to believe that the goods were obtained as the result of the commission of an offence.[124]

9.58 However, although the words of PACE s22(1) are general, it does not allow retention other than for law enforcement purposes related to the investigation and prosecution of offences.[125] Specifically, it does not provide a general power to retain items on the basis of public interest once any investigation has ended: see for example, *Webb v Chief Constable of the Merseyside*[126] in which the police were required to hand back money suspected to be the proceeds of drug dealing; *Costello v Chief Constable of*

117 [1970] QB 693.

118 *R (Rottman) v Commissioner of Police of the Metropolis* [2002] UKHL 20, [2002] 2 AC 692.

119 PACE s21(1), (2).

120 PACE s21(3), (4), (6), (8); see also *Arias v Commissioner of Police of the Metropolis* (1984) *Times* 1 August for the common law right to require the police to deliver up copies of documents that have been lawfully seized.

121 Whether under PACE ss19–20, which are expressly referred to in s22(1), or under s8: *Chief Constable of Wiltshire v McDonagh* [2008] EWHC 654 (QB).

122 PACE s22(2)(a).

123 PACE s22(4).

124 PACE s22(2)(b).

125 *Gough v Chief Constable of West Midlands* [2004] EWCA Civ 206 at para 35; *Chief Constable of Merseyside v Owens* [2012] EWHC 1515 (Admin) at paras 17–18.

126 [2000] QB 427.

Derbyshire[127] and *Gough v Chief Constable of West Midlands*[128] in which the police were required to return a car and car parts suspected to be stolen; and *Chief Constable of Merseyside v Owens*[129] in which the police were required to return CCTV footage of an arson attack on the claimant's garage even though they feared that he might use it to seek revenge. It has been suggested, however, that the position in the former cases may need to be revisited in light of Proceeds of Crime Act 2002 s329 which makes it an offence for anyone knowingly to acquire or possess criminal property.[130]

9.59 Nor can the police retain property solely in anticipation of a court making a compensation, forfeiture or restitution order against a person if s/he is later convicted of an offence.[131] However, they may be allowed a short period after expiry of the power under PACE s22 in order to decide whether to apply for re-seizure under the Proceeds of Crime Act 2002[132] or while a private prosecution is still being considered.[133]

9.60 If something is taken from a person while in police custody or detention on the ground that it might be used to cause physical injury to someone, to damage property, to interfere with evidence or to assist an escape, then it should be returned to them on release.[134] If it is not returned, the police can be sued in conversion.

9.61 If the police seize documents unlawfully – outside the scope of the relevant warrant or power, or in breach of the requirements in PACE ss15 and 16 – or the warrant under which they have seized them is quashed, the basic position is that they have no right to retain them and must return them (subject to statutory power to authorise retention, discussed below).[135] Nor can the unlawful seizure of items be cured by re-seizing them at the police station when the person has attended to collect them.[136]

Criminal Justice and Police Act 2001

9.62 The provisions of PACE are supplemented by CJPA 2001 Part 2.

9.63 CJPA 2000 s50 reversed the effect of *R v Chesterfield Justices ex p Bramley*.[137] The case was concerned with the situation where officers have to sift through large amounts of material (usually documentary) to establish whether and to what extent it contains items they are empowered to seize. The Divisional Court held that officers were not entitled to remove the material from the premises covered by the warrant in order to carry out this sift and that if they did so and the removed material contained items

127 [2001] EWCA Civ 381, [2001] 1 WLR 1437.
128 [2004] EWCA Civ 206.
129 [2012] EWHC 1515 (Admin).
130 *Clerk & Lindsell on Torts* at para 16-48.
131 *Malone v Commissioner of Police of the Metropolis* [1980] QB 49.
132 *Iqbal v South Bedfordshire Magistrates' Court* [2011] EWHC 705 (Admin).
133 *Scopelight Ltd v Chief Constable of Northumbria* [2009] EWCA Civ 1156, [2010] QB 438.
134 PACE s22(3).
135 See, for example, *R v Chief Constable of Lancashire ex p Parker* [1993] QB 577.
136 *R (Cook) v Serious Organised Crime Agency* [2010] EWHC 2119 (Admin), [2011] 1 WLR 144.
137 [2000] QB 576.

that fell outside the scope of their powers of seizure, a claim for trespass to goods would succeed. The position now, under CJPA 2001, is as follows:

- Section 50 provides that where an officer is lawfully on premises and finds anything which they have reasonable grounds to believe may be or may contain something which they are authorised to search for and would be subject to a power of seizure, if it is not reasonably practicable for the officer to determine whether what they have found is something that they are entitled to seize or the extent to which it contains something that they are entitled to seize, removal from the premises can occur to enable that determination to be carried out.[138]
- There is also an equivalent power of removal where the material that can be seized is comprised in something else that there would otherwise be no power to seize and it is not reasonably practicable to separate the two on the premises.[139] Officers are then obliged to carry out an initial examination of the property as soon as is reasonably practicable and to return items that are not within their original power of search or within the power of retention contained in section 56, save where it is not reasonably practicable to separate such items from the material they have taken.[140]

9.64 There are also obligations to return items subject to legal privilege and excluded and special procedure material[141] and further safeguards in relation to the powers in Part 2.[142]

9.65 In addition, CJPA 2001 s59 provides that where items have been seized 'in exercise, or purported exercise, of a relevant power of seizure'[143] (including the powers under PACE), any person with a relevant interest in the items may apply to the Crown Court for return of the items on the basis that a) there was no power to make the seizure or b) that property seized under certain of the CJPA 2001 powers is or contains privileged material, excluded material and/or special procedure material. If copies have been made, the court may order destruction of such copies.[144] On such application, however, the court may order that property that would otherwise fall to be returned may be retained if a warrant would now be granted to the person currently holding the property (ie the police) to seize it.[145]

Limitation Act 1980

9.66 Finally, it should be noted that once six years have elapsed since the date of seizure, the original owner's title will be extinguished under Limitation Act 1980 s3(2) and no action can be brought, either in conversion or under the Police (Property) Act 1897.[146]

138 CJPA 2001 s50(1).
139 CJPA 2001 s50(2).
140 CJPA 2001 s53(1)–(3).
141 CJPA 2001 ss54–55.
142 CJPA 2001 ss60–62.
143 Listed in CJPA 2001 Sch 1.
144 *R (Business Energy Solutions Ltd) v Crown Court at Preston* [2018] EWHC 1534 (Admin), [2018] 1 WLR 4887.
145 CJPA 2001 ss59(6)–(7).
146 *Commissioner of Police of the Metropolis v Meekey* [2021] EWHC 34 (Admin), [2021] QB 773.

Remedies

9.67 In theory, if the police have wrongfully taken goods out of a person's possession, the owner can lawfully resist the seizure and take them back again, and can use reasonable force against anyone who resists.[147] In practice, however, this right is principally relevant as a defence to a criminal charge, such as assault or obstruction, rather than as a 'remedy' which could ever be prudently recommended, as there is almost certain to be legal argument about whether the police were entitled to seize the goods.

9.68 If the case is straightforward and the person simply wants the goods back and is not concerned about claiming damages, an application to recover the property may be made in the magistrates' court under Magistrates' Courts Act 1980 s48 or the Police (Property) Act 1897. Similarly, where relevant an application may be made to the Crown Court under CJPA 2001 s59.[148]

9.69 However, as set out in relation to trespass to land above, any challenge to the validity of the warrant itself must be brought by way of a claim for judicial review.[149]

9.70 Otherwise, the lawfulness of the seizure may be tested by way of a civil claim – for damages, for an order for the return of the property, or both.[150] If the item is not returned, the claimant is entitled to compensation reflecting its value. Whether or not the item is returned, the claimant is entitled to damages for the loss of its use during the period of deprivation and for consequential losses occasioned by its absence.[151]

Trespass to goods

The act of trespass and other causes of action

9.71 If the police interfere with a person's belongings, there may be a claim for damages for trespass. The act of interference must be direct, such that if officers merely lock a room in the house, depriving the claimant of temporary access to his belongings inside, there is no claim in trespass to goods as the officer made no direct contact with the items.[152] The defendant's contact with the goods must also be deliberate rather than accidental.[153] However, it is unnecessary to show that the defendant appreciated at the time that the contact was unlawful.[154] It is also unnecessary for the claimant to show any physical damage to the item.[155] It has been suggested that, by analogy with

147 *Blades v Higgs* (1861) 10 CB (NS) 713.

148 See above, para 9.65.

149 For a discussion of the interaction between judicial review and CJPA 2001 s59–including the High Court's discretion, upon quashing a warrant, as to whether to allow the police to apply for retention under s59 – see *R (HS) v South Cheshire Magistrates' Court* [2015] EWHC 3415 (Admin), [2016] 4 WLR 74 at paras 61–66.

150 Torts (Interference with Goods) Act 1977 s3.

151 See chapter 7.

152 *Hartley v Moxham* (1842) 3 QB 701.

153 *National Coal Board v J E Evans & Co (Cardiff)* [1951] 2 KB 861.

154 *Wilson v Lombank Ltd* [1963] 1 WLR 1294.

155 *Transco Plc v United Utilities Water plc* [2005] EWHC 2784 (QB), in which the defendant turned off the claimant's gas valve, causing no physical damage but extensive financial loss.

trespass to the person,[156] no liability will lie where the defendant has not 'gone beyond generally acceptable standards of conduct'.[157]

9.72 To bring a claim in trespass to goods, the claimant must have been in possession of the goods at the time of the interference. Unlike in conversion, a right to possession is generally insufficient.[158]

9.73 Although the tort relates only to physical property, it has been suggested that manipulation of data on the claimant's computer is likely to fulfil this requirement.[159]

9.74 If a claim for trespass to goods succeeds, damages can be recovered for the costs of repair or replacement and for loss of use.

9.75 If the defendant handles or damages the claimant's goods carelessly rather than deliberately, the better view appears to be that the claim should be brought in negligence rather than trespass.

9.76 If a third party damages goods whilst they are in the defendant's custody, an action for negligence and/or breach of bailment may lie against the defendant if they were at fault in letting this happen. Although a detailed discussion of bailment is beyond the scope of this work,[160] it is worth noting a number of the potential advantages to a claim in breach of bailment, where this is available. First, where a bailee deviates from the terms of the bailment, they may become strictly liable for the goods as an 'insurer', such that they will be liable for any loss or damage regardless of fault.[161] Second, even where fault is required, the burden of proof in an action for breach of bailment will lie with the bailee, as opposed to the claimant in a claim for negligence. Third, because breach of bailment is considered to be a sui generis cause of action rather than a claim in tort (or contract), it would appear to fall outside the Torts (Interference with Goods) Act 1977 such that the bailee cannot avail themself of the defence under section 8 by identifying a third party with better title than the claimant.[162]

9.77 By way of example: if officers smash open a cupboard to access the contents during a search of the claimant's home, the usual cause of action would be *trespass to goods*. If an officer breaks a vase in the claimant's home by carelessly tripping and falling against it, the usual cause of action would be *negligence*. If there is any uncertainty as to whether the interference with an item was deliberate or careless, it would be advisable to bring the claim in *both trespass to goods and negligence* (see paras 7.48ff above). If officers seize the claimant's belongings and then leave them lying around the police station so that they are stolen by someone else, there would be a possible claim for *negligence and/or breach of bailment*. In *Sutcliffe v Chief Constable of West Yorkshire*[163] a claim for breach of bailment failed in relation to the claimant's car, which was damaged by vandals while in a police

156 Eg *Collins v Wilcock* [1984] 1 WLR 1172.

157 *Clerk & Lindsell* at para 16-133.

158 Certain exceptions are discussed in *Clerk & Lindsell* at para 16-138.

159 *Clerk & Lindsell* at para 16-135.

160 For a full discussion see, for example, *Palmer on Bailment*, Sweet & Maxwell, 3rd edn, 2009.

161 See, for example, *Mitchell v Ealing LBC* [1979] QB 1, *Shaw & Co v Symmons & Sons* [1917] 1 KB 799 and the cases cited therein.

162 See above in relation to conversion.

163 [1996] RTR 86.

compound, since the police had taken all reasonable precautions against such an eventuality.

Defences

9.78 As has already been seen, there are a number of powers under which the police may lawfully seize items, and where they have a power which can be exercised without consent, they can also use reasonable force if necessary to exercise the power.[164] For example, if they have power to search a home, they would also have power to break into a locked cabinet in order to search inside it, if this were both necessary and reasonable. However, this defence could be defeated if, for example, it could be shown that the plaintiff offered to unlock the cabinet, as the use of force would then be unnecessary (and unreasonable).

Action under HRA 1998 for breach of Convention rights

Article 8: right to respect for private and family life

9.79 ECHR Article 8(1) provides that 'everyone has the right to respect for his private and family life, his home and his correspondence'. Article 8(2) provides that there shall be no interference with this right except such as is in accordance with the law and is necessary in a democratic society in the interests of 'national security, public safety or the economic wellbeing of the country, for the prevention of disorder or crime, for the protection of health or morals, or for the protection of the rights and freedoms of others'.

9.80 It has been held that the statutory procedure for grant of a search warrant is generally compliant with the requirements of Article 8;[165] and with the requirements of Article 6 (right to a fair trial), even where not all of the material underlying the application can be provided to the suspect.[166]

9.81 However, as the Divisional Court recognised in *R (Cronin) v Sheffield Justices*,[167] any search of premises made without the consent of the occupier will automatically constitute an interference with Article 8(1). Thus the key question in each instance will be whether the police can show that the search was within the terms of Article 8(2). If the search was conducted in accordance with statutory and common law requirements, officers are likely to be able to establish that it was 'in accordance with the law' and that it pursued a legitimate aim (the prevention of disorder or crime and / or the protection of the rights of others). The more substantial question in most instances is likely to be whether the search was necessary in the sense that it was a proportionate means of pursuing the aim in question.[168] There may be instances where a search would otherwise be lawful under domestic law but where the police will be unable demonstrate that it was

164 PACE s117.

165 *Cronin v UK* (2004) 38 EHRR CD233.

166 *R (Haralambous) v St Albans Crown Court* [2018] UKSC 1, [2018] AC 236.

167 [2002] EWHC 2568 (Admin), [2003] 1 WLR 752.

168 For a discussion of the approach to proportionality under the ECHR see eg *Bank Mellat v HM Treasury* [2013] UKSC 39, [2014] AC 700.

a necessary response in the particular circumstances, particularly where adequate steps are not taken to ascertain the facts relevant to justification of the search.[169] In evaluating whether a search of premises was a proportionate response to the particular circumstances, courts are also likely to consider factors such as whether the relevant evidence could have been obtained by less intrusive means and whether the relevant legislation and practice afforded adequate and effective safeguards against abuse.[170]

9.82 In *Mouncher v Chief Constable of South Wales*[171] it was accepted, without argument on the point, that in light of the Constables Protection Act 1750 the quashing of a warrant is a necessary precondition to any claim for damages under the HRA 1998.[172] It is suggested that is incorrect. The 1750 Act affords protection in tort to individual officers acting in obedience to the warrant, for whom the relevant chief officer would otherwise be vicariously liable. On the other hand, the focus of HRA 1998 s6(1) is on the acts of the chief officer as a 'public authority' (albeit acting through their individual officers),[173] which may in any event include acts relating not only to the execution of the warrant (in obedience to it) but also to its procurement.[174]

9.83 Article 8 may also impose positive duties on the police to protect individuals from interference with their homes, for example by way of unlawful eviction of a tenant by their landlord – however, the law is so far relatively undeveloped in this regard.[175]

Article 1 of the First Protocol

9.84 Article 1 of the First Protocol to the ECHR (A1P1) provides that every person is entitled to the 'peaceful enjoyment of his possessions' and shall not be deprived of their possessions 'except in the public interest and subject to the conditions provided for by law'. So far, however, the application of A1P1 to the law on police interference with goods has remained largely undeveloped.[176]

169 See, for example, *McLeod v UK* [1999] 27 EHRR 493; *Keegan v UK* (2007) 44 EHRR 33.

170 *Funke v France* (1993) 16 EHRR 297.

171 [2016] EWHC 1367 (QB).

172 [2016] EWHC 1367 (QB) per Wyn Williams J at paras 452–453.

173 Indeed, see by analogy *Zenati v Commissioner of Police of the Metropolis* [2015] EWCA Civ 80, [2015] QB 758, in which the court considered that the relevant question was whether 'the state overall' had breached of Article 5 (right to liberty and security), notwithstanding that there was no false imprisonment at common law: per McCombe LJ at para 63.

174 *Keegan v UK* (2007) 44 EHRR 33.

175 See Nic Madge, 'Housing and human rights: lessons from Strasbourg: Part 5', JHL 2008, 11(5), 85–91; Daniel Clarke, 'An uncivil matter: unlawful eviction and the police', 3 June 2020, insights.doughtystreet.co.uk.

176 See *Scopelight Ltd v Chief Constable of Northumbria* [2009] EWCA Civ 1156, [2010] QB 438 at paras 55–57, in which the court held that A1P1 did not affect the approach that is required under PACE s22 in any event.

CHAPTER 10

Protest and freedom of speech

Introduction

10.1 This chapter will cover the right to protest and freedom of expression, enshrined in European Convention on Human Rights (ECHR) Articles 10 and 11; and the powers available to the police to restrict or prevent protest. This is an area of significant current political interest and legal development. The law, as discussed below, is current as at the date of publication. However, in May 2022 the Government introduced a new Public Order Bill, which is before Parliament at the time of writing. The Bill contains a range of new legal restrictions on the right to protest, including the introduction of a criminal offence of interfering with key national infrastructure, such as airports or railways, and the introduction of Serious Disruption Prevention Orders.

The right to protest and freedom of expression: ECHR Articles 10 and 11

Overview and background

10.2 Protest is deeply rooted in the history and culture of politics and law in England and Wales: Penn and Mead in the late 1600s; the Tolpuddle Martyrs in the 1830s; the Suffragettes in the early 20th century; the anti-Vietnam War and anti-apartheid protests in the 1960s and 1970s; the Miners' Strikes of the 1980s; the Iraq War and G20 protests in 2009; and the more recent 'Occupy' movement, Extinction Rebellion, Insulate Britain and the Black Lives Matter movements are just some of the high-profile instances of protest in British public life, all of which have involved the police and featured controversial policing practices.

10.3 The right to protest in domestic law was traditionally a negative right, simply allowing what was not prohibited:

> The approach of the English common law to freedom of expression and assembly was hesitant and negative, permitting that which was not prohibited . . . Dicey [wrote] 'it can hardly be said that our constitution knows of such a thing as any specific right of public meeting'.[1]

The enactment of the Human Rights Act (HRA) 1998 and its introduction of a positive right to assemble peacefully has been described as a 'constitutional shift' in the law of England and Wales.[2]

10.4 ECHR Articles 10 and 11 are enacted into domestic law by HRA 1998 Sch 1. The two articles are closely related, and will often be used together to protect the right to protest peacefully and express oneself freely.

10.5 Article 10 enshrines the right to freedom of expression:

> **Article 10: Freedom of expression**
> 1. Everyone has the right to freedom of expression. This right shall include freedom to hold opinions and to receive and impart information and ideas

1 *R (Laporte) v Chief Constable of Gloucestershire* [2006] UKHL 55, [2007] 2 AC 105 at para 34.

2 Sedley LJ in *Redmond-Bate v DPP* [1999] EWHC Admin 733, [2000] HRLR 249.

without interference by public authority and regardless of frontiers. This Article shall not prevent States from requiring the licensing of broadcasting, television or cinema enterprises.

2. The exercise of these freedoms, since it carries with it duties and responsibilities, may be subject to such formalities, conditions, restrictions or penalties as are prescribed by law and are necessary in a democratic society, in the interests of national security, territorial integrity or public safety, for the prevention of disorder or crime, for the protection of health or morals, for the protection of the reputation or rights of others, for preventing the disclosure of information received in confidence, or for maintaining the authority and impartiality of the judiciary.

10.6 Article 11 enshrines the right to peaceful assembly and free association:

Article 11: Freedom of assembly and association
1. Everyone has the right to freedom of peaceful assembly and to freedom of association with others, including the right to form and to join trade unions for the protection of his interests.

2. No restrictions shall be placed on the exercise of these rights other than such as are prescribed by law and are necessary in a democratic society in the interests of national security or public safety, for the prevention of disorder or crime, for the protection of health or morals or for the protection of the rights and freedoms of others. This Article shall not prevent the imposition of lawful restrictions on the exercise of these rights by members of the armed forces, of the police or of the administration of the State.

10.7 Both Articles 10 and 11 are 'qualified' rights. This means that they can be interfered with when the interference is prescribed by law, in pursuit of a legitimate aim, necessary in a democratic society and proportionate. By allowing lawful interference, the rights are concerned with balancing the competing interests of the individual and the community. The legitimate aims are those set out in Articles 10(2) and 11(2). The domestic and Strasbourg courts have recognised the fundamental importance of the rights to free expression and peaceful protest: they must be jealously guarded and any interference with them must be closely scrutinised.[3]

10.8 This section will focus on policing and protest, looking at the way human rights can be used in actions involving the police in this context.

Practical considerations

10.9 When considering whether to bring a claim against the police for breach of Articles 10 and/or 11 rights using the HRA 1998, it is important to make a realistic and practical assessment of the risks and benefits of doing so. In circumstances where concurrent or overlapping domestic torts are also available – for example, claims for false imprisonment and/or assault in cases of wrongful arrest at a protest or demonstration – it will often be sensible to focus on the domestic torts and to plead the context of the claimant's Articles 10 and/or 11 rights as relevant to the award of aggravated, or potentially exemplary, damages, rather than incurring the costs risk of pleading freestanding Articles 10 and/or 11 claims. From a

3 *R (Laporte) v Chief Constable of Gloncesteshire* [2006] UKHL 55, [2007] 2 AC 105 at 36–37; *Handyside v UK* (1979–80) 1 EHRR 737 at 49, ECtHR; *R v Secretary of State for the Home Department ex p Simms* [2000] 2 AC 115 at 126E–G, HL.

practical perspective, where there are good claims in domestic torts covering essentially the same loss, there is usually little to be gained in terms of additional damages by including freestanding claims for breaches of Articles 10 and/or 11, and there is a real risk that the court, especially in relatively low value county court claims, will find that the costs involved in addressing the additional legal arguments arising from freestanding, but overlapping, HRA 1998 claims are disproportionate.

10.10 The cases in which Articles 10 and 11 are likely to be of most use (beyond the context of aggravated damages) are those in which these rights can be relied on as a basis for challenging the legal certainty and/or proportionality of police measures which might otherwise be lawful under domestic law. This might arise, for example, in the context of applications for judicial review, or in civil actions where there is a challenge to the lawfulness of the statutory or common law powers under which the police purported to act or in criminal cases, when considering the scope of a 'lawful' or '"reasonable excuse" defence'.[4] At the time of writing, the circumstances in which human rights arguments can be relied on in defence to charges of criminal damage will be considered by the Court of Appeal following a reference by the Attorney General in the Colston Four case. Examples are discussed in the following passages.

Activities protected by Articles 10 and 11

10.11 Articles 10 and 11 protect free speech and peaceful protest. They are both interpreted widely. The European Court of Human Rights' (ECtHR's) guide to Article 10 and Article 11 provides a useful summary of the overarching principles and key Strasbourg case-law.[5]

Free speech

10.12 Article 10 protects political, artistic, academic and commercial speech, as well as ideas and opinions that may shock, disturb or offend the state or any sector of the population.[6] As expressed by the ECtHR in *Handyside v UK*: 'Such are the demands of . . . pluralism, tolerance and broadmindedness without which there is no "democratic society" '.[7] That an expression

4 See, for example, *R v Graham, Ponsford, Skuse and Willoughby* (2022), the case concerning the toppling of the statue of slave trader, Edward Colston, in Bristol during the Black Lives Matter protests in 2020.

5 *Guide on Article 10 of the European Convention on Human Rights: Freedom of assembly and association*, ECtHR, updated on 30 April 2021, available at https://www.echr.coe.int/documents/guide_Art_10_ENG.pdf. *Guide on Article 11 of the European Convention on Human Rights: Freedom of assembly and association*, ECtHR, updated on 31 December 2021, available at: www.echr.coe.int/Documents/Guide_Art_11_ENG.pdf. See also the Venice Commission's *Guidelines on freedom of peaceful assembly*, European Commission for Democracy Through Law (Venice Commission) and OSCE Office For Democratic Institutions And Human Rights (OSCE/ODIHR), 3rd edn, 8 July 2019, available at: www.venice.coe.int/webforms/documents/?pdf=CDL-AD(2019)017-e.

6 *R v Central Independent Television* [1994] Fam 192 at 532, CA. See also *O'Shea v MGN* [2001] EMLR 40, QBD; *Redmond-Bate v DPP* [1999] EWHC Admin 732, [2000] HRLR 249; *Handyside v UK* (1979–80) 1 EHRR 737.

7 *Handyside v UK* (1979–80) 1 EHRR 737 at 49.

is in 'opaque, profane or unsophisticated' terms, will not rob it of its protection.[8]

10.13 Different types of expression attract different levels of protection under Article 10 based on their perceived social and democratic value. For example, political and public interest expression is afforded a high level of protection under Article 10. Such expression has been held to include comment on police conduct[9] and corruption,[10] public health,[11] state corruption,[12] state economic activity[13] and state housing policy;[14] and criticism of political opposition.[15]

10.14 In *R (Miller) v College of Policing*[16] it was held that the police making a record of what is perceived by a complainant to be hate speech which did not amount to a crime was an interference with Article 10(1) which required justification. The Court of Appeal held that College of Policing guidance which required such recording with limited caveat had a 'chilling effect' on freedom of speech and was unlawful. In that case, the police had violated Article 10 in visiting the workplace of a member of the public who had sent tweets perceived by a complainant to be transphobic, and warning him that his tweets may escalate to a crime, notwithstanding the absence of any evidence that a crime had been or would be committed. Section 60 of the Police, Crime, Sentencing and Courts Act 2022, which is not in force at the time of writing, makes provision for the Secretary of State to issue a code of practice about the processing of personal data relating to non-criminal hate incidents.

Peaceful protest

10.15 Article 11 protects peaceful protests. It protects demonstrations that are irritating, contentious, heretical and eccentric,[17] including those that may annoy or give offence to people opposed to the ideas and claims that are being promoted.[18] An assembly will fall within the scope of Article 11 even where its aims and activities are wider than those of a traditional protest, such as providing education and seeking to raise public awareness.[19]

10.16 In *R (Countryside Alliance) v Attorney General*, Baroness Hale held that Article 11 must be read in the context of Articles 9 and 10 and as such it protects, 'the freedom to meet and band together with others in order to

8 *R (Miller) v College of Policing* [2021] EWCA Civ 1926 at para 38.

9 *Guja v Moldova* (2008) 53 EHRR 16, ECtHR; *Thorgeirson v Iceland* (1992) 14 EHRR 843, ECtHR.

10 *Flood v Times Newspapers Ltd* [2012] UKSC 11, [2012] 2 AC 273.

11 *Hertel v Switzerland* (1999) 28 EHRR 534, ECtHR.

12 *Marchenko v Ukraine* (2010) 51 EHRR 36, ECtHR.

13 *Uj v Hungary* (App No 23954/10), [2011] ECHR 1122, ECtHR.

14 *Lepojic v Serbia* (2007) 47 EHRR 1214.

15 *Faruk Temel v Turkey* (App No 16853/05), 1 November 2011.

16 [2021] EWCA Civ 1926.

17 *Redmond Bate v DPP* [1999] EWHC Admin 732, [2000] HRLR 249.

18 *Plattform 'Ärzte für das Leben' v Austria* (1988) 13 EHRR 204, ECtHR *Stankov and the United Macedonian Organisation Linden v Bulgaria* (2001) ECHR 2001-IX, ECtHR; *Alekseyev v Russia* (App Nos 4916/07, 25924/08, 14599/09), 21 October 2010, ECtHR.

19 See, for example, the characterisation of the 'Occupy' movement by Neuberger MR in *City of London Corporation v Samede* [2012] EWCA Civ 160, [2012] 2 All ER 1039 at 35.

share information and ideas and to give voice to them collectively', but not a right to assemble for recreational purposes such as fox hunting.[20] However, when this case was considered by the Strasbourg court, the ECtHR counselled against 'an unacceptably narrow interpretation' of Article 11 and observed that 'the Court is therefore prepared to assume that Article 11 may extend to the protection of an assembly of an essentially social character'. Nonetheless, the ECtHR went on to dismiss the application as manifestly unfounded on the basis that the ban on fox hunting only prevented gathering for the particular purpose of killing a wild mammal with hounds, it did not prevent huntsmen from associating with each other for alternative activities, such as drag or trail hunting. On that basis, while not rejecting the application of Article 11 in the way that Baroness Hale and Lord Hope had done, the ECtHR concluded that the prohibition on hunts culminating in the killing of a wild animal with hounds had not 'struck at the very essence of the right of assembly'.[21]

10.17 In general, assemblies for religious and cultural purposes will not be considered 'social' and as such are clearly protected under Article 11.[22] Article 11 protects participation in private and public meetings;[23] static and travelling marches; processions;[24] mass actions; demonstrations; 'sit-ins';[25] pickets and rallies;[26] campsites;[27] protests that cause disruption in certain circumstances;[28] and long-term protests.[29]

10.18 Where a demonstration is peaceful, the ECtHR has held that policing tactics must be tolerant and proportionate.[30] Article 11 can also protect illegal protests. For example, if a peaceful protest is organised in violation of the law that governs the use of the public highway, that protest will be unlawful under UK law – but the police must still respect the right to protest when dealing with it. This means that the measures the police take must be lawful, necessary and proportionate: it might be proportionate to disperse the protest after a few hours, but it might not be proportionate to use the fact that the protest was unlawful to prevent it from taking place altogether.

10.19 A significant feature in recent protest cases has been the distinction drawn, by both the domestic and Strasbourg courts, between a) protests which cause disruption as an inevitable side-effect of the protest activities and b) protests which are deliberately intended to cause disruption, for example by impeding activities of which the protestors disapprove. This issue has frequently arisen in the context of anti hydraulic fracturing

20 [2007] UKHL 52, [2008] 1 AC 719 at 118; see also the judgment of Lord Hope at 56.

21 *Friend v UK* (App No 16072/06, 24 November 2009, at 49).

22 *Stankov v Bulgaria* (App Nos 29221/95 and 29225/95, 2 October 2001) at 83–90, ECtHR.

23 *Rassemblement Jurassien and Unité Jurassienne v Switzerland* (1979) 17 DR 93, ECtHR.

24 *Christians Against Racism and Fascism v UK* (1980) 21 DR 138, ECtHR.

25 *G v Germany* (1989) 60 DR 256, ECtHR.

26 *Rai, Allmond and 'Negotiate Now' v UK* (1995) 19 EHRR CD93, ECtHR.

27 *City of London Corporation v Samede* [2012] EWCA Civ 160, [2012] 2 All ER 1039.

28 *G v Germany* (1989) 60 DR 256, ECtHR.

29 *Mayor of London (on behalf of the GLA) v Hall* [2010] EWCA Civ 817, [2011] 1 WLR 504, Neuberger MR at 38.

30 *Aldemir and others v Turkey* (App Nos 32124/02, 32126/02, 32129/02, 32133/02, 32137/02, 32138/02, 2 June 2008), ECtHR.

('fracking') protests, where the protest has taken the form of demonstrations outside the entrance to a fracking site, preventing vehicles from entering and exiting the site and, on occasion, slow walking in front of vehicles, or climbing or locking-on to vehicles. The Court of Appeal in *Cuadrilla Bowland Ltd v Persons unknown*[31] confirmed, in the context of appeals against suspended prison sentences for breach of civil injunctions, that protest actions which are deliberately intended to seriously disrupt activities carried out by others are 'not at the core' of the freedom of assembly protected by Article 11. However, the Supreme Court in *DPP v Ziegler and others* explained that deliberate disruption will not remove such a protest from the scope of the protection of Article 11 altogether – meaning that police action in relation to it must still meet the requirements of legality and proportionality.[32] In particular, there should be 'a certain degree of tolerance to disruption to ordinary life, including disruption to traffic, caused by the exercise of the right to freedom of expression or freedom of peaceful assembly'.[33] Where disruption is caused it is more likely that police action designed to bring the disruption to an end and/or to arrest and prosecute those who engaged in it, will be found to be lawful.[34] In *DPP v Ziegler* the Supreme Court upheld the decision of the District Judge that the actions of the defendants in causing a road to be closed in protest against an arms fair were protected by Articles 10 and 11, referring to matters such as the peaceful nature of the action, that the obstruction was aimed only at vehicles heading to the arms fair, that it was for a limited period, and the action related to a matter of general concern.

10.20 The courts have recognised that the manner, form and location of a protest can be an integral part of the message and therefore relevant to Articles 10 and 11 protection. For example, in *Mayor of London (on behalf of the GLA) v Hall*, the Court of Appeal recognised that protestors' desire to protest in Parliament Square was within the scope of Articles 10 and 11.[35] The same conclusion was reached in *Tabernacle v Secretary of State for Defence* where the Court of Appeal accepted that the 'Aldermaston Women's Peace Camp' that conducted a monthly weekend of vigils, meetings and demonstrations on land near an atomic weapons factory, was protected under Articles 10 and 11:[36]

> Some of those involved may have been steadfast participants the whole time. Others will have come and gone. But the camp has borne consistent, long-standing, and peaceful witness to the convictions of the women who have belonged to it. To them, and (it may fairly be assumed) to many who support them, and indeed to others who disapprove and oppose them, the 'manner and form' *is* the protest itself.

10.21 Article 11 will be engaged in respect of long-term or permanent protests as long as competing interests do not outweigh the protestors' rights. For

31 [2020] EWCA Civ 9, [2020] 4 WLR 29.

32 [2022] AC 408 at 70.

33 *DPP v Ziegler and others* [2021] 3 WLR 179 at 68.

34 See *Cuadrilla* at 43, 44 and 94. See also *Kudrevicius v Lithuania* 62 EHRR 34; *DPP v Ziegler* [2019] EWHC 71 (Admin), [2019] 2 WLR 1451; *Transocean Drilling UK Ltd v Greenpeace Ltd* [2020] CSOH 66, [2020] 7 WLUK 36.

35 [2010] EWCA Civ 817, [2011] 1 WLR 504.

36 *Tabernacle v Secretary of State for Defence* [2009] EWCA Civ 23.

example, in *Tabernacle*, the protest camp had been resident for one weekend each month for 23 years. The court found that attempts to restrict the protest were unlawful because they violated Article 11: the protestors were not infringing anyone else's human rights or freedoms, they were not significantly obstructing the highway and the fact that they had been protesting for 23 years without interruption suggested that there was no real justification for the sudden attempts to stop them.

10.22 By contrast, in *City of London Corporation v Samede*, the court considered whether the tents of the 'Occupy' protestors could lawfully be removed from St Paul's Cathedral churchyard in the City of London or whether this would breach their Articles 10 and 11 rights. The court held that the tents could be removed on the basis that the protest was obstructing the highway, causing a nuisance and interfering with other people's rights and freedoms, including the freedom to practise their religion under Article 9 by going to St Paul's Cathedral for worship.[37]

10.23 The same approach was taken in *R (Maria Gallastegui) v Westminster City Council* where Silber J held:[38]

> Indeed the area in which the claimant places her tent and makes her home is a public space which should belong to and should be accessible to all. It cannot be appropriated by any single person or group such as the claimant who has no proprietary rights in the area which she wishes to have as her home. The rights of the public to enjoy and use a place of such significant historical, political and cultural interest such as Parliament Square cannot be overridden by the claimant's right to take over part of that Square and use it as her home on an indefinite basis even as part of a protest.

10.24 In the Court of Appeal decision in the case (upholding Silber J's judgment), it was held that even if the legislation in question (the Police Reform and Social Responsibility Act 2011) amounted to a blanket ban from protesting with tents in Parliament Square, this was lawful, necessary and proportionate, particularly in light of the fact that parliament had given careful thought to the requirements of Articles 10 and 11 when passing the legislation and that the prohibition of tents did not materially undermine the ability to protest in the square.[39]

10.25 In *Lambeth LBC v Grant* a possession order made against occupiers of a camp on Clapham Common was held to be a justified interference with Articles 10 and 11 in circumstances that the occupiers had been able to express their views for almost a month, the common had no special significance for them, and the order would not prevent them from expressing their views in other ways.[40]

10.26 The Police, Crime, Sentencing and Courts Act 2022 received Royal Assent on 28 April 2022. Part 3 of the Act gives the police additional powers to impose conditions on public processions and assemblies, including noise-based conditions and increases the penalty for organisers who knowingly or recklessly fail to comply with conditions. Further, the

37 [2012] EWHC 34 (QB). The Court of Appeal upheld the High Court's decision: [2012] EWCA Civ 160, [2012] 2 All ER 1039.

38 [2012] EWHC 1123 (Admin) at 84.

39 [2013] EWCA Civ 28, [2013] 1 WLR 2377.

40 [2021] EWHC 1962 (QB).

test for 'serious disruption to the life of the community' in sections 12 and 14 of the Public Order Act 1986 has been broadened to include causing delay to the supply of time-sensitive products, and prolonged disruption to access to any essential goods or services. The non-exhaustive list of 'essential goods or services' is broadly drawn. Section 80 of the Act increases the maximum penalty for wilful obstruction of the highway to up to 51 weeks imprisonment. Part 4 of the Act increases the time for which a person must not return to land, having been given a direction under Criminal Justice and Public Order Act 1994 s61, from three months to twelve months.

Activities that are not protected by Articles 10 and 11

10.27 While Articles 10 and 11 protect activities that are sometimes unpopular, offensive and disruptive, they do not protect activities aimed at the destruction of any of the rights and freedoms contained in the ECHR.

Speech

10.28 Article 10, therefore, does not protect hate speech, including racism, xenophobia, anti-Semitism, aggressive nationalism and discrimination against minorities and immigrants.[41] It was out of a concern that such issues would be inflamed that the ECtHR upheld the lawfulness of the prohibition of marches about Northern Ireland in London in the 1990s.[42] This stance is mirrored in UK law by the prohibition of activities that incite hatred on the grounds of race or religion.[43]

Protest

10.29 Article 11 does not protect violent protests,[44] but, as noted above, a certain level of disruption arising out of a protest should be tolerated by the authorities.[45]

10.30 A violent protest is one where the organisers and participants have violent intentions that result in violent disorder.[46] To determine whether a demonstration is violent, the courts will look at the intention of the organisers and a distinction will be drawn between violence which is

41 See, for example, *Thomas v Newsgroup Newspapers* [2001] EWCA Civ 1233, [2002] EMLR 4; and *Norwood v DPP* [2003] EWHC 1564, [2003] Crim LR 888.

42 *Rai, Allmond and 'Negotiate Now' v UK* (1995) 19 EHRR CD93; *Christians against Racism and Fascism v UK* (1980) 21 DR 138.

43 The Racial and Religious Hatred Act 2006 and Public Order Act 1986 ss17–18 and ss29 A–29B. See, for example, *R v Malik* [1968] 1 All ER 582 (the trial of black rights activist Malcolm X for addressing a Black Power meeting in Reading).

44 *DPP v Ziegler and others* [2021] 3 WLR 179 at 69; *G v Germany; CS v Germany* (App No 13858/88), 6 March 1989, ECtHR; *Christians Against Racism and Fascism v UK* (1980) 21 DR 38; *Cisse v France* (App No 51346/99), 9 July 2002, ECtHR.

45 *Kudrevicius v Lithuania (GC)* (App No 37553/05), 15 October 2015, ECtHR; *Sergey Kuznetsov v Russia* (App No 10877/04), 23 January 2009, ECtHR; *Aldemir and others v Turkey; Oya Ataman v Turkey* (App No 74552/01), 5 March 2007, ECtHR; *Balcik v Turkey* (App No 25/02), 29 February 2008, ECtHR.

46 *G v Germany; CS v Germany* (App No 13858/88), 6 March 1989, ECtHR; *Christians Against Racism and Fascism v UK; Cisse v France* (App No 51346/99), 9 July 2002, ECtHR.

incidental to the assembly and violence which is intended by the organisers.[47] The burden of proving violent intentions on the part of the assembly organisers lies on the authorities[48]. Even if there is a real risk that an assembly might result in disorder as a result of developments outside the control of those organising it, it does not as such fall outside the scope of Article 11.[49]

The rights of peaceful protestors caught up in violence or suspected criminality

10.31 An individual does not lose the right to protest if they remain peaceful while others commit acts of violence or criminality in the course of the demonstration.[50] It follows that non-violent assemblies will retain their peaceful character notwithstanding the violent response of other demonstrators,[51] although the fact that individual peaceful protestors are unintentionally caught up in legitimate police attempts to prevent violence, may not amount to an interference with the peaceful protestors' rights under Articles 10 and 11.

10.32 This is demonstrated by the approach taken in *R (Parminder Singh and another) v Chief Constable of West Midlands*[52] where the Court of Appeal held that the police could lawfully use their dispersal powers under Anti-social Behaviour Act 2003 s30 in order to disband a group of protestors en masse. The court accepted that section 30 enabled a police officer to consider the presence or behaviour of any one or more of the persons in the group to be the presence or behaviour of the group and to give a direction to the whole group accordingly. Hallet LJ clarified this in her judgment, with which the other members of the court agreed:[53]

> . . . it is only when the behaviour of a group of people moves beyond legitimate protest and into the realms of behaviour that causes actual or likely intimidation, harassment, alarm and distress that an officer can use an authorisation to direct them to disperse.

10.33 By contrast, in *R (Laporte) v Chief Constable of Gloucestershire*,[54] the House of Lords considered the proportionality of police action that was directed at a small group of people but that impacted on a wider group. In that case, the police had escorted a bus, on which a group of would-be protesters were travelling, away from the site of a protest, because a small number of

47 *Christians Against Racism and Fascism v UK* (1980) 21 DR 38, ECtHR.

48 *Christian Democratic People's Party v Moldova (No 2)* (App No 25196/04), 2 February 2010 at 23, ECtHR.

49 *Schwabe and MG v Germany* (App Nos 8080/08 and 8577/08), 1 December 2011 at 103, ECtHR.

50 *Ezelin v France* (1991) 14 EHRR 362, ECtHR; *Ziliberberg v Moldova* (App No 61821/00), 1 February 2005, ECtHR.

51 *Christians Against Racism and Fascism v UK* (1980) 21 DR 38 at 'The law' para 4: 'the possibility of violent counter-demonstrations, or the possibility of extremists with violent intentions, [but] not members of the organising association, joining the demonstration cannot as such take away that right'.

52 [2006] EWCA Civ 1118, [2006] 1 WLR 3374.

53 At 89–92.

54 [2006] UKHL 55, [2007] 2 AC 105.

the passengers were suspected of being members of an anarchist group who were likely to engage in violence if they reached the site of the protest.

10.34 The police argued that their actions were necessary and proportionate even though they inevitably affected peaceful protestors as well as the small minority suspected of intending to commit violence. Ms Laporte argued that because the police action was premature, it was not possible for them to identify who (if anyone) was about to commit a breach of the peace. By taking action prematurely, 'the police were obliged to take action against the sheep as well as the goats'.[55] The House of Lords agreed: it was disproportionate for the police to interfere with the Articles 10 and 11 rights of those protestors who, like Ms Laporte, had done nothing to suggest they were other than peaceful, committed protestors simply because they were in the company of others, some of whom might, at some point in the future, commit a breach of the peace. This was particularly the case given that no crime had been committed and Ms Laporte was not suspected of having personally committed or of being about to commit any crime, or any breach of the peace.[56]

10.35 This is an important point of principle for police law practitioners, where it is not uncommon for the police to seek to justify the use of blanket measures that interfere with the rights of peaceful protestors on the basis that they are necessary to prevent a breach of the peace by a hardcore of violent individuals. However, the ultimate question is one of proportionality. There is no bright-line rule that prevents action from being taken against innocent third parties in order to address risks posed by those who threaten to breach the peace. In *Austin v Commissioner of the Police of the Metropolis*[57] the House of Lords held that the police can interfere with the rights of innocent third parties, but only if they have taken all other possible steps to prevent the breach of the peace and to protect the rights of third parties. This was a case involving kettling and the right to liberty under Article 5. However, the reasoning is highly relevant to protest cases given the frequent use of kettling (see further below at para 10.40) as a means of controlling public assemblies. When *Austin* was considered by the ECtHR, it also found that there was no violation of the rights of the innocent third parties caught up in the kettle, because the measures imposed had been rendered unavoidable by circumstances beyond the control of the authorities and were necessary in order to avert a real risk of serious injury or damage to property.[58]

10.36 The same approach was taken by the Court of Appeal in *McClure and Moos*,[59] where it emphasised that it was only where officers reasonably believed that there were no other means available to prevent an imminent breach of the peace that they could, as a matter of necessity, curtail the rights of innocent third parties. The court stressed that the containment of a crowd involved a serious intrusion on freedom of movement and that the test of necessity would only be met in extreme and exceptional

55 At 53.

56 At 55.

57 [2009] UKHL 5, [2009] 1 AC 564.

58 App Nos 39692/09, 40713/09 and 41008/0915, March 2012, [2012] 3 WLUK 484, (2012) 55 EHRR 14.

59 [2012] EWCA Civ 12.

circumstances. Where the police are considering using legal powers to prohibit a demonstration, they must start from the proposition that the rights to freedom of expression and assembly apply and conduct a rational and informed assessment as to whether the proposed interference with those rights is necessary and proportionate in pursuit of a legitimate aim.[60] Discussion of these cases in the context of false imprisonment and Article 5 ECHR can be found at paras 6.111–6.116 and 6.158.

Counter-protests

10.37 There is a duty on public authorities, including the police, to take reasonable and appropriate measures to enable lawful demonstrations to proceed peacefully.[61] Where conflicts between demonstrators and counter-demonstrators threaten to become violent, the police must balance the rights of the protestors to protest without interference from those who dislike their views, and the rights of the counter-protestors.

10.38 In *Laporte,* Lord Rodger gave the following guidance for dealing with situations where groups of protestors may clash:

1) Wherever it is possible to do so, preventative action must be directed at those who resort to or threaten violent action, and not at those to whom the violence is directed.
2) In cases where one group is making deliberately offensive remarks with the intention of provoking violence, they may be ordered to desist under the common law power to prevent a breach of the peace; and if they fail to do so, they may be arrested.
3) Even where it is not the intention of the provocative group to provoke violence, but nonetheless their behaviour is 'outrageous' in a 'way which is liable to produce such a reaction', then action may lawfully be taken against them if this is necessary to prevent a breach of the peace.
4) The difficult cases arise where the only way to prevent an imminent breach of the peace is to interfere with the Articles 10 and 11 rights of entirely innocent third parties who are in no way responsible for the violent reactions of others.

10.39 It will usually be considered a disproportionate interference for the authorities to ban a counter-protest where there is merely a risk of disorder and it may also be disproportionate for a counter-protest to be banned if allowing both demonstrations to proceed, but with a police presence to keep the peace, would have been possible.[62]

Protests on private property

10.40 There is currently no obligation under the ECHR for the authorities to require private individuals to allow peaceful assemblies by others to take

60 *Leigh v Commissioner of Police of the Metropolis* [2022] EWHC 527 (Admin).

61 *Plattform Arzte fur das Leben v Austria* (App No 10126/82), 21 June 1988 at 32; *The United Macedonian Organisation Ilinden and Ivanov v Bulgaria* (App No 44079/98), 20 October 2005 at 115.

62 *Öllinger v Austria* (2006) 46 EHRR 38.

place on their property.[63] This position is reflected domestically by the tort of trespass and aggravated trespass[64] and finds roots in the common law tradition that a landowner enjoys an absolute prerogative to determine who may enter or remain on his or her land and that every unauthorised entry onto private land is a trespass.[65] Accordingly, as a general principle, the landowner has an uncontrolled right to exclude any person from trespassing on private property. However, individuals engaging in peaceful protest on private property do not lose their rights under Articles 10 and 11 simply because they are committing a trespass. The court is still required to assess the necessity and proportionality of interfering with those rights.[66]

10.41 Nonetheless, recent domestic legislation has increased the number and type of locations at which trespass to land constitutes a criminal offence. The Serious Organised Crime and Police Act 2005 created a new offence of entering any protected site as a trespasser.[67] Protected sites include nuclear bases; military bases; the Palace of Westminster; 10 Downing Street; GCHQ; and other sites of royal or political significance.[68] Section 76 of the Police, Crime, Sentencing and Courts Act 2022 expands the geographical reach of 'controlled areas in the vicinity of the Palace of Westminster', for the purposes of Part 3 of the Police Reform and Social Responsibility Act 2011; and section 82 of the 2022 Act creates a new offence of residing on land without consent in or with a vehicle. This offence applies to all public land and is committed where a person over the age of 18 is residing or intending to reside on land with a vehicle and without the consent of the occupier of the land, has failed to leave, having been asked to do so, or re-enters the land within 12 months, and has either caused, or is likely to cause, significant damage, disruption or distress.

10.42 In *Appleby v UK*[69] a group of environmental campaigners sought to demonstrate in a privately owned shopping precinct. The ECtHR held that there was no right of entry to private property under Article 11, although it did recognise that where the bar on access to property would have the effect of destroying the essence of the rights under Articles 10 and 11, there may be a positive obligation on the authorities to regulate access to private property.

10.43 Another recent trend is the sharp increase in private companies seeking, and being granted, civil injunctions restraining protest activities

63 *Anderson v UK* (1998) EHRR 218, ECtHR; and *CIN Properties Ltd v Rawlins* [1995] 2 EGLR 130; *Appleby v UK* (2003) 37 EHRR 38, ECtHR.

64 Criminal Justice and Public Order Act 1994 ss61 and 69. These statutory provisions grew out of the medieval action for trespass quare clausum fregit – see, for example, *Semayne's Case* (1604) 5 Co Rep 91a.

65 *Entick v Carrington* (1765) 95 ER 807; *Coco v The Queen* (1994) 179 CLR 427; *R v Somerset County Council ex p Fewings* [1995] 1 WLR 1037.

66 *City of London Corporation v Samede* [2012] PTSR 1624 at paras 24–28; *Kuznetsov v Russia* (App No 10877/04), 23 October 2008, ECtHR.

67 Serious Organised Crime and Police Act 2005 s128, as amended by the Terrorism Act 2006.

68 Serious Organised Crime and Police Act 2005 (Designated Sites) Order 2005 SI No 3447; Serious Organised Crime and Police Act 2005 (Designated Sites under Section 128) Order 2007 SI No 930.

69 [2003] 37 EHRR 38, ECtHR.

at and in the vicinity of relevant company sites. This has particularly been a feature of action by companies involved in fracking, but injunctions have also been sought by numerous companies against animal rights and environmental campaigners. In 2018, prison sentences of 16 months, imposed on anti-fracking demonstrators, were overturned by the Court of Appeal in relation to breaches of civil injunctions, although the court refused to rule out prison sentences altogether in such cases.[70] In 2020, Greenpeace was fined £80,000 by the Scottish Court of Session for breach of an injunction providing for an exclusion zone around a mobile oil drilling rig.[71] There are recent examples of breaches of injunctions by campaigners resulting in custodial sentences[72] and also orders for costs.[73]

10.44 A number of recent guideline cases from the Court of Appeal clarify the parameters for the grant of such injunctions.[74] More detailed consideration of this type of injunction is outside the scope this publication, because, while they may ultimately result in sentences of imprisonment, if breached and a contempt of court is proved, they do not carry a power of arrest and the police should not ordinarily be involved in their enforcement. Nonetheless, it is important for practitioners working in this area to be aware of the parameters of civil injunctions against protestors, both because of the frequency with which they are now used by companies and local authorities to seek to restrain protest and also because of the frequent overlap between activities restrained under an injunction and offences which are commonly the subject of police action at a protest – for example, obstruction of the highway, contrary to Highways Act 1980 s137; 'watching and besetting', contrary to the Trade Union and Labour Relations (Consolidation) Act 1992 s241; and harassment, contrary to the Protection from Harassment Act 1997 ss1 and 2.

10.45 There are also a number of orders and powers akin to injunctions, which are available to the police, primarily under the Anti-social Behaviour, Crime and Policing Act (ASBCPA) 2014. These are considered further at paras 10.79–10.96 below.

Obligations imposed on the police by Articles 10 and 11

10.46 In *Laporte* Lord Bingham made it clear that the authorities are under a positive obligation to facilitate and protect the rights to peaceful protest and free speech. This means, for example, ensuring that there are sufficient numbers of police at a protest to protect peaceful protestors from violent disruptions by other protestors or counter-protestors. The

70 *R v Roberts (Richard)* [2018] EWCA Crim 2739, [2019] 1 WLR 2577; see also *Cuadrilla Bowland Ltd v Persons unknown* [2020] EWCA Civ 9.

71 *Transocean Drilling UK Ltd v Greenpeace Ltd* [2020] CSOH 66, [2020] GWD 23-300.

72 For example, *Cuciurean v Secretary of State for Transport and HS2* [2021] EWCA Civ 357; and *National Highways Ltd v Heyatawin and others* [2021] EWHC 3078 (QB).

73 *National Highways v Heyatawin* [2021] EWHC 3093 (QB).

74 *Barking and Dagenham LBC v Persons Unknown* [2022] EWCA Civ 13; *Canada Goose UK Retail Ltd v Person unknown* [2020] EWCA Civ 3030, [2020] 1 WLR 2802; *Cuadrilla Bowland Ltd v Persons unknown* [2020] EWCA Civ 9, [2020] 4 WLR 29; *Boyd v Ineos Upstream Ltd* [2019] EWCA Civ 515, [2019] 4 WLR 100.

importance of this obligation was described by the ECtHR in *Plattform 'Ärzte für das Leben' v Austria* as follows:[75]

> A demonstration may annoy or give offence to persons opposed to the ideas or claims that it is seeking to promote. The participants must, however, be able to hold the demonstration without having to fear that they will be subjected to physical violence by their opponents; such a fear would be liable to deter associations or other groups supporting common ideas or interests from openly expressing their opinions on highly controversial issues affecting the community.

10.47 The positive obligation to facilitate and protect the rights to peaceful protest and free speech must, of course, also be considered in the light of the obligation on public authorities under ECHR Article 14 to secure the enjoyment of ECHR rights without discrimination on any protected ground. Monitoring organisations such as Netpol[76] have observed little evidence of police forces taking steps to facilitate protest by those who would otherwise face barriers to doing so, for example on grounds of disability. Netpol have also raised concerns about the discriminatory and chilling effect on the right to peaceful protest of the disproportionate use of police powers against black and minority ethnic people in the context of public assemblies.

Police powers to restrict or prevent protest

Overview

10.48 Any restrictions on the right to protest will be closely scrutinised by the court. In *Ezelin v France* the ECtHR stated:[77]

> Freedom to take part in a peaceful assembly . . . is of such importance that it cannot be restricted in any way . . . so long as the person concerned does not himself commit any reprehensible act on such an occasion.

10.49 Where the police are justified in taking action to restrict a protest, the action must be the least restrictive option required to achieve the legitimate aim that the police are pursuing. This was emphasised in *Samede*, where the court stated: 'Action will not be proportionate unless it is the least intrusive means necessary to achieve the aim.'[78] This means that consideration should be given to the least intrusive or draconian measures when policing a protest, and the police must be able to show that the measures taken were justified under Articles 10(2) and 11(2). Typical examples of this might include extracting disruptive protestors while allowing peaceful ones to carry on protesting or preventing a protest from proceeding onto private land while diverting traffic so it could continue on a public highway.

75 (1988) 13 EHRR 204 at para 32.

76 The Network for Police Monitoring: 'Netpol seeks to monitor public order, protest and street policing, and to challenge and resist policing which is excessive, discriminatory or threatens civil rights', https://netpol.org/about/.

77 (1991) 14 EHRR 362 at 53.

78 *City of London Corporation v Samede* [2012] EWHC 34 (QB) at 99.

10.50 In considering the types of restriction that the police can use, the ECtHR has held that prior restraints on demonstrations on the basis of a possibility of minor incidents of violence are likely to be disproportionate, and any isolated outbreak of violence should be dealt with by way of subsequent arrest and prosecution rather than prior restraint.[79]

10.51 However, the ECtHR has also recognised that the police must be afforded a degree of discretion in taking operational decisions because such decisions are complicated and the police, who have access to information and intelligence not available to the general public, will usually be in the best position to make them.[80] Furthermore, the ECtHR has accepted that in the twenty-first century advances in communications technology have made it possible to mobilise protesters rapidly and covertly on a hitherto unknown scale and the ECHR should not be interpreted in such a way as to make it impracticable for the police to fulfil their duties of maintaining order and protecting the public.[81]

10.52 When considering whether restrictions on protests breach Articles 10 and 11, the courts have varied in their approach. In one case, the need to prevent graffiti and criminal damage to flowerbeds amounted to a legitimate reason for restricting demonstrations;[82] but in another, the Court of Appeal held that problems relating to traffic disruption and sanitation were merely issues of nuisance that were not sufficiently serious to justify interference with fundamental human rights.[83]

10.53 When considering whether a protest can be restricted lawfully, the Court of Appeal has held that the following factors should be considered:[84]

1) the extent to which the continuation of the protest would breach domestic law;
2) the importance of the precise location to the protesters;
3) the duration of the protest;
4) the degree to which the protesters occupy the land; and
5) the extent of the actual interference the protest causes to the rights of others, including the property rights of the owners of the land, and the rights of any members of the public.

10.54 There are a number of ways that the police can restrict the right to protest which may or may not be lawful, necessary and proportionate. For example, the right to protest may be affected or interfered with through such measures as:

79 *Stankov v Bulgaria*. But see the High Court's consideration of the use of pre-emptive measures in *R (Hicks) v Commissioner of Police for the Metropolis* [2014] EWCA Civ 3, [2014] HRLR 11, discussed below at para 10.69.

80 *PF and EF v UK* (App No 28326/09), 23 November 2010 at para 41; *Austin v UK* (2012) 55 EHRR 14 at para 55.

81 *Austin v UK* at para 56.

82 *Mayor of London (on behalf of the GLA) v Hall* [2010] EWCA Civ 817, [2011] 1 WLR 504, Lord Neuberger MR at 46. See also *R (Maria Gallastegui) v Westminster City Council* [2012] EWHC 1123 (Admin).

83 *Tabernacle v Secretary of State for Defence* [2009] EWCA Civ 23 at para 42.

84 *Mayor of London (on behalf of the GLA) v Hall* [2010] EWCA Civ 817, [2011] 1 WLR 504; *R (Maria Gallastegui) v Westminster City Council* [2012] EWHC 1123 (Admin); *City of London Corporation v Samede* [2012] EWHC 34 (QB).

- requirement for advance notice of protests under the Public Order Act (POA) 1986;
- use of preventive policing to prevent breach of the peace;
- kettling and cordons;
- the power of dispersal, civil injunctions, anti-social behaviour injunctions (ASBIs) and public spaces protection orders under the ASBCPA 2014;
- the power to stop and search and stop and account, and prosecute trespassers in a number of specific circumstances under the Criminal Justice and Public Order Act (CJPOA) 1994 and the Police Reform and Social Responsibility Act 2011.

10.55 There is not room in this section to detail all of the police powers to restrict or prevent protest, but some key issues that arise for police law practitioners are considered below.

Public Order Act 1986

10.56 POA 1986 s11 requires protestors to give the police advance notice of public processions. The notice must specify the date, time and route of the procession, as well as identifying the organiser. In *Bukta v Hungary* the ECtHR held that the requirement to give advance notice of a protest does not breach Article 11, although in circumstances where the protest has to take place urgently, it may be disproportionate for it to be dispersed by the police simply because of the failure to give notice.[85] Similarly, where there is no advance planning and/or no organisers, the House of Lords has held that POA 1986 s11 cannot apply.[86]

10.57 In *Blum and Others v DPP* the Divisional Court held that no individual proportionality assessment was required in respect of prosecutions for failure to comply with the requirements to obtain prior authorisation.[87] In its consideration of the case, the ECtHR upheld the Divisional Court's decision on the overall merits but stated that a proportionality assessment on a case-by-case basis was necessary, finding the following factors relevant to its decision that the prosecution was lawful on the facts of this case:[88]

1) the police ended the demonstration in a manner that was reasonable and calm;
2) the demonstration had not been an urgent response to a recent or imminent political event meaning that there was no time to comply with the prior authorisation procedures;
3) had the authorisation procedures been followed, it is unlikely that any conditions would have been imposed on the demonstration;

85 *Molnár v Hungary* (App No 10346/05), (2010) 5, EHRR 25, ECtHR.

86 *Kay v Commissioner of Police of the Metropolis* [2008] UKHL 69, at 22 and 69.

87 [2006] EWHC 3209 (Admin), [2007] UKHRR 233.

88 *Rai and Evans v UK* (App Nos 26258/07 and 26255/07), [2009] ECHR 1269, ECtHR. This proportionality assessment is applied by Neuberger MR in *Mayor of London (on behalf of the GLA) v Hall* [2010] EWCA Civ 817, (2011] 1 WLR 504 at 36.

4) the police had given the demonstrators an opportunity to disperse without the imposition of sanctions, but the demonstrators had refused; and
5) the sanctions imposed were not severe.

10.58 POA 1986 s12 provides the senior police officer present at the scene with the power to impose conditions on a public procession if certain criteria are met. Section 14 makes similar provision in respect of public assemblies. Any conditions that are imposed on either a procession under POA 1986 s12 or an assembly under section 14, such as prescribing the route, size or duration of the demonstration, must be both 'prescribed by law' and necessary and proportionate, or they will breach Articles 10 and 11.[89] The courts will be astute to ensure that any restriction meets the ECHR requirement of legality. In *R (Jones) v Commissioner of Police of the Metropolis*,[90] the Divisional Court held that a direction purportedly made under POA 1986 s14 restricting the location and duration of demonstrations forming part of the 2019 'Extinction Rebellion Autumn Uprising' was unlawful, because the various gatherings of protestors around central London did not fall within the definition of a single 'public assembly' for the purposes of POA 1986 s14. A 'public assembly' had to be in a particular location to which the public or any section of the public had access, which was wholly or partly open to the air, and which could fairly be described as a 'scene'. The location could not extend to the whole of central London – POA 1986 s14 did not therefore apply, and there was no power under that provision to impose restrictions on the multi-location protests.

10.59 POA 1986 ss13 and 14A empower the police to ban processions and trespassory assemblies, respectively, provided that specified conditions are met. These are draconian measures, and officers considering deploying them will need to address whether or not the decision to ban complies with the requirements of Articles 10(2) and 11(2). If it does not, the protestors who have been prevented from exercising their lawful rights may be able to bring a claim against the police under HRA 1998.

10.60 POA 1986 also creates statutory offences that are particularly relevant to protests. These include the offences of:

- riot (section 1);
- violent disorder (section 2);
- affray (section 3);
- causing fear or provocation of violence (section 4); and
- causing harassment, alarm or distress (section 5).

10.61 Police practitioners representing protestors will often find that their clients have been arrested and charged with one or more of these POA 1986 offences. In such circumstances it will be necessary to consider

89 For examples of the restrictions imposed on protestors see *Hall and others v Save Newchurch Guinea Pigs (Campaign) and others* [2005] EWHC 372, (QB); *University of Oxford and others v Broughton and others* [2006] EWHC 1233 (Admin); *Smithkline Beecham plc and others v Avery and others* [2007] EWHC 948, (QB) and [2009] EWHC 1488 (QB); *Heathrow Airport v Garman* [2007] EWHC 1957 (QB); *Huntingdon Life Sciences v Stop Huntingdon Animal Cruelty* [2007] EWHC 522 (QB); *Westminster City Council v Haw* [2002] EWHC 2073, (QB).

90 [2019] EWHC 2957 (Admin), [2020] 1 WLR 519.

whether the ingredients for the offence were made out and, if they were not, there may be grounds to bring a civil claim for unlawful arrest and detention. Where a protestor has been prosecuted and acquitted for an offence arising out of a protest and there are grounds to suggest that there was no reasonable or probable cause for bringing the prosecution and that the police acted maliciously, consideration should be given to bringing a malicious prosecution claim. If there is evidence to establish that police powers have been intentionally misused, there may be a basis for a claim in misfeasance (see chapter 8).

Breach of the peace and preventive policing

10.62 One tactic that arises in protest cases routinely is the use of preventive measures that the police seek to justify on the basis that they were necessary to prevent a breach of the peace.

10.63 A breach of the peace is a common law concept. It was defined in *R v Howell (Errol)* as follows:[91]

> We are emboldened to say that there is a breach of the peace whenever harm is actually done or is likely to be done to a person or in his presence to his property or a person is in fear of being so harmed through an assault, an affray, a riot, an unlawful assembly or other disturbance. It is for this breach of the peace when done in his presence or the reasonable apprehension of it taking place that a constable, or anyone else, may arrest an offender without warrant.

10.64 Committing a breach of the peace is not a crime: it can only give rise to a person being bound over to keep the peace see further para 6.111 above.

10.65 In *Steel v UK* the applicant argued that the definition of breach of the peace given in *Howell* was too broad and ill-defined to comply with the requirement that an arrest be made in accordance with the law under Article 10(2).[92] The ECtHR rejected this argument and the definition given in *Howell* was subsequently endorsed by the House of Lords in *Laporte*.

10.66 In *Foulkes v Chief Constable of Merseyside* the Court of Appeal gave further guidance on what constituted an imminent breach of the peace, such that an arrest could be justified by the police:[93]

> In my view the words used by Lord Diplock and in the other authorities show that where no breach of the peace has taken place in his presence but a constable exercises his power of arrest because he fears a [future] breach, such apprehended breach must be about to occur or be imminent . . . There must, I consider, be a sufficiently real and present threat to the peace to justify the extreme step of depriving of his liberty a citizen who is not at the time acting unlawfully.

10.67 The use of preventive public order policing in the context of an (allegedly) imminent breach of the peace came under scrutiny from the House of Lords in *Laporte*. It was held that the police had breached Ms Laporte's

91 [1982] QB 416, [1981] 3 All ER 383, CA.
92 (1999) 28 EHRR 603, ECtHR.
93 [1998] 3 All ER 705, CA.

Article 10 and 11 rights because their actions in diverting the coach in which she had been travelling from proceeding to the protest site and escorting it back to London had not been in accordance with the law, for the following reasons, among others:[94]

1) The POA 1986 conferred carefully defined powers on the police to control disorderly protests. It would be surprising if, alongside parliament's carefully drawn scheme, there existed a common law power to take other preventive measures solely on the basis that it was reasonable to do so, a condition that Lord Bingham described as 'uncertain and undefined'.
2) It is not enough to justify action that a breach of the peace is anticipated to be a real possibility.
3) Action short of arrest cannot be taken in circumstances where a breach of the peace is not sufficiently imminent to justify arrest.
4) Extension of police powers in the context of protests is a matter for Parliament and not the judiciary, given that Articles 10 and 11 are fundamental rights and any interference with them must be scrutinised with particular care. Lord Bingham reiterated the principle that, 'the Convention test of necessity does not require that a restriction be indispensable, but nor is it enough that it be useful, reasonable or desirable'.

10.68 The House of Lords distinguished Ms Laporte's case from the situation in *Moss v McLachlan* where members of one belligerent faction were less than five minutes away from confronting another belligerent faction and there was no police controlled area separate from the scene of the apprehended disorder.[95] In such circumstances it was plausible that a breach of the peace was about to be committed, albeit that was held to go to 'the furthermost limits of any acceptable view of imminence',[96] in contrast to the situation in *Laporte* where 120 protestors, by no means all of whom were members of the anarchist group known as the Wombles, were stopped five miles from the site of a heavily policed and lawful protest.

10.69 Since *Laporte*, the courts have considered whether the policing tactics used by the Metropolitan Police at the royal wedding in 2012 were compatible with Articles 10 and 11. The case of *Hicks* concerned a number of claimants, all of whom challenged aspects of the police tactics used at the royal wedding. A feature uniting all of the claims was that the individuals had been prevented from joining the wedding crowds in London when the police arrested them.[97] The claimants contended that the police had operated an unlawful policy of pre-emptively stopping and searching and arresting people who were considered likely to express anti-monarchist views, thereby operating an impermissibly low threshold of tolerance for public protest, contrary to Articles 10 and 11. The claimants also argued that the decision to arrest them was disproportionate under Articles 10(2)

94 *R (Laporte) v Chief Constable of Gloucestershire* [2006] UKHL 55 at 46–52.

95 [1985] IRLR 76, DC.

96 [2006] UKHL 55 at 118.

97 *R (Hicks) v Commissioner of Police of the Metropolis* [2014] EWCA Civ 3, [2014] HRLR 11.

and 11(2). They relied on the principle that the police should use the least restrictive option when interfering with fundamental rights. The claimants contended that the police could have moved them to locations where the expression of republican views was not deemed to be likely to cause a breach of the peace. However, the Divisional Court rejected those submissions as 'wholly unrealistic' and held that the arrests had been lawful and the interference with the claimants' Articles 10 and 11 rights had been proportionate in view of the reasonable apprehension on the part of the police of an imminent breach of the peace. See further discussion of this case in the context of Article 5 and subsequent appeal to the Supreme Court at paras 6.142–6.148.

Kettling and cordons

10.70 Another police tactic that is common in the context of protests, is the use of kettling, whereby protestors are held in a cordon, sometimes for a number of hours, in order to prevent a breach of the peace.

10.71 This practice was considered by the House of Lords and the ECtHR in *Austin* under Article 5 rather than Articles 10 and 11.[98] Nonetheless, it is relevant to protest cases, because of the frequency with which kettling is used. This case arose out of the May Day protests in central London in 2001, where approximately 3,000 protestors had gathered in the vicinity of Oxford Circus. In response to the situation, the police set up a cordon, which the claimant was prevented from leaving for around seven hours.

10.72 The House of Lords in *Austin* found that 'kettling' is lawful as long as the actions of the police are proportionate and reasonable, and any confinement is restricted to a reasonable minimum, as to discomfort and as to time, as is necessary for the relevant purpose, namely the prevention of serious disorder and violence:[99]

> . . . where there is a demonstration, particularly one attended by a justified expectation of substantial disorder and violence, the police must be expected, indeed sometimes required, to take steps to ensure that such disorder and violence do not occur, or, at least, are confined to a minimum. Such steps must often involve restraining the movement of the demonstrators, and sometimes of those members of the public unintentionally caught up in the demonstration. In some instances, that must involve people being confined to a relatively small space for some time.

10.73 The House of Lords placed considerable emphasis on the motives of the police in that case,[100] holding that where the police had genuinely intended to prevent injury and damage to property and maintain public order,[101] their actions were more likely to be lawful than if they had imposed the cordon in bad faith or for an improper motive.[102]

98 *Austin v Commissioner of Police of the Metropolis* [2009] UKHL 5, [2009] 1 AC 564; *Austin v UK* (2012) 55 EHRR 14, ECtHR.

99 At 59.

100 At 39 and 54. See also the Court of Appeal decision in *Austin* [2007] EWCA Civ 989 at 98–99 and 103–104.

101 The factual findings were that the intention behind the imposition of the cordon was to maintain public order, Lord Hope at 2.

102 At 63.

10.74 The Grand Chamber of the ECtHR upheld the House of Lords' approach, stating that the context in which state action is taken is an important factor to be taken into account when considering whether ECHR rights are engaged.[103] In this case, the conditions had been volatile and dangerous and in the circumstances the imposition of an absolute cordon was the least intrusive and most effective way to prevent serious injury and damage. However, the ECtHR went on to emphasise that measures of crowd control should not be used by the state directly or indirectly to stifle or discourage protest, and that 'kettling' would usually only be justified where necessary to prevent serious injury or damage. Where 'kettling' is used, its necessity should be kept under constant review by the authorities.[104]

10.75 The use of cordons was also considered in *R (McClure and Moos) v Commissioner of Police of the Metropolis*.[105] That case arose out of the G20 protests in London in 2009 and involved the police constructing a cordon at the 'Climate Camp' at Bishopsgate, even though the protestors there were largely peaceful. The police argued that the serious violence that had broken out at another protest a quarter of a mile from the Climate Camp justified their actions on the ground that there would be a breach of the peace if the violent protestors were allowed to join the Climate Camp protestors.

10.76 The Court of Appeal (overturning the decision of the Divisional Court, which had held that the cordon had been unlawful because a breach of the peace was not imminent)[106] held that the question for the court was whether, based on what they knew and perceived at the time, it was reasonable for the police to fear a breach of the peace. The court concluded that the officer in question had reasonably believed that there would be an imminent and serious breach of the peace. Furthermore, the court stated that the mere fact that a breach of the peace does not occur, is not an indication that the assessment that one was imminent was unreasonable. However, where (as in this case) the fear did materialise, namely protestors from the violent protest joining the Climate Camp, this did support the reasonableness of the assessment.[107]

10.77 In *R (Castle others) v Commissioner of Police of the Metropolis* the Divisional Court considered the obligations under the Children Act (ChA) 2004 that the police owed to children taking part in a protest.[108] The three claimants, aged between 14 and 16 years old, took part in a protest against university tuition fees during a school day. Believing that a breach of the peace was imminent, the police authorised the containment of 3,000 protestors on Whitehall, which included the claimants. They were held for several hours and not released until the early evening.

10.78 The claimants challenged the police's actions on the basis that they had failed to exercise their functions in a manner that complied with their

103 *Austin v UK* (2012) 55 EHRR 14 at para 59, ECtHR.
104 At 67–68.
105 [2012] EWCA Civ 12.
106 [2011] EWHC 957 (Admin), [2011] HRLR 24.
107 At 89.
108 [2011] EWHC 2317 (Admin), [2012] 1 All ER 953.

obligations to protect and promote the welfare of children under CA 2004 s11. The court accepted that the duty applied, but held that it had not been breached. While the claimants were not successful in their judicial review, this case is nevertheless important because it confirms that the duties under the CA 2004 have a direct application to police functions, including in the context of protests.

Anti-social Behaviour Crime and Policing Act 2014

10.79 The ASBCPA 2014 gives the police a number of coercive powers of relevance to the policing of protest. These include public spaces protection order, ASBIs and powers of dispersal.

Public spaces protection orders

10.80 The ASBCPA 2014 empowers local authorities to make a public spaces protection order under section 59, if satisfied on reasonable grounds that activities carried on in a public place within the authority's area, or which are likely to be carried on in such a place, have had, or are likely to have, a detrimental effect on the quality of life of those in the locality and the effect of those activities is, or is likely to be, persistent or continuing in nature; is, or is likely to be, such as to make the activities unreasonable; and justifies the restrictions imposed by the order. A public spaces protection order may prohibit specified things being done, or require specified things to be done by persons carrying on specified activities in the restricted area. Section 72 expressly requires a local authority in deciding whether to make a public spaces protection order and if so what it should include, to have particular regard to the rights of freedom of expression and freedom of assembly set out in ECHR Articles 10 and 11. Once such an order is made, ASBCPA 2014 s67 makes it a criminal offence to fail to comply with the order's requirements.

10.81 In *Dulgheriu v Ealing LBC*[109] the Court of Appeal considered the lawfulness of a PSPO made by the defendant local authority prohibiting abortion-related protest within a substantial 'safe zone' around a women's health clinic, save as to limited protest within a designated area 100 metres away from the clinic entrance. The Court of Appeal acknowledged that the protestors' rights under Article 9, as well as under Articles 10 and 11, were engaged. However, it held that the judge at first instance had been entitled to conclude, on the particular facts of the case, that the Article 8 rights of the service users visiting the clinic outweighed the Article 9, 10 and 11 rights of the protestors and that the terms of the PSPO were proportionate.

Anti-social behaviour injunctions

10.82 A separate and distinct power under the ASBCPA 2014 is the right of the police (and other specified public authorities) to apply to a court for an ASBI. Such an injunction may be granted where the court is satisfied, on the balance of probabilities, that the person to whom the injunction is directed has engaged or threatens to engage in anti-social behaviour and

109 [2019] EWCA Civ 1490, [2020] 1 WLR 609.

the court considers it just and convenient to grant the injunction for the purpose of preventing the respondent from engaging in anti-social behaviour. The significance of an ASBI over and above a regular civil injunction of the type considered in cases such as *Boyd v Ineos Upstream Ltd,*[110] *Cuadrilla Bowland Ltd v Persons unknown*[111] and *Canada Goose UK Retail Ltd v Persons unknown,*[112] is that ASBCPA 2014 s4 provides for the court to attach a power of arrest to the terms of the injunction. Injunctions of this type therefore engage the police – whether as applicants, or in the process of enforcement.

10.83 In *Birmingham City Council v Afsar,*[113] Warby J considered an application for an injunction under ASBCPA 2014 Part 1 against four named defendants and 'Persons Unknown seeking to express opinions about the teaching at Anderton Park Primary School'. The application was made by the local authority rather than the police, but the reasoning in the case is relevant as it applies equally to injunctions sought by the police under the Act. The purpose of Birmingham City Council in seeking the injunction was to constrain the frequent, regular and disruptive demonstrations that had been staged outside Anderton Park Primary school over a period of many months concerning the protestors' objections to the teaching of LGBT issues at the school. The named respondents contended that the provisions of the ASBCPA 2014 were not intended to be used to restrain or curb the exercise of Article 10 and 11 rights and that the power of the court to grant injunctions under ASBCPA 2014 Part 1 had to be read restrictively when conduct engaging those rights was in play. Warby J rejected this contention, finding that:[114]

> . . . there is no reason to doubt that in passing this legislation Parliament intended to confer power to seek and to grant injunctions to prohibit anti-social utterances and assemblies of all kinds, in any case where it is shown that this is necessary and proportionate in pursuit of one of the legitimate aims identified in Articles 10(2) and 11(2). The safeguards for the human rights of protestors lie in the Court's statutory duty under s6 of the HRA, and in the procedures of the Court. The Court can be relied on . . . to keep in mind the importance of freedom of expression and freedom of assembly. It can be trusted to avoid unwarranted interferences with these (and other) fundamental rights by insisting on compliance with the well-established principles, that any interference must correspond to a pressing social need, its necessity must be established by clear and compelling evidence, and it must not go further than is necessary.

10.84 He noted that:[115]

> Injunctions under the 2014 Act should not be lightly granted, and their terms should be carefully framed to ensure that they do not involve unnecessary or excessive interference with the rights of others. These considerations will be especially potent in the context of protests.

110 [2019] EWCA Civ 515, [2019] 4 WLR 100.
111 [2020] EWCA Civ 9, [2020] 4 WLR 29.
112 [2020] EWCA Civ 303, [2020] 1 WLR 2802.
113 [2019] EWHC 3217 (QB), [2020] 3 All ER 756.
114 At para 32.
115 At para 113.

10.85 However, on the facts of this case, Warby J was fully satisfied that the first three named respondents had engaged in or been party to a concerted course of conduct amounting to harassment, public nuisance and obstruction of the highway and that they would repeat such conduct if not restrained. In those circumstances he found an injunction under ASBCPA 2014 s1 to be a necessary and proportionate interference with the respondents' rights under Articles 10 and 11. In addition to granting the injunction against the first three named respondents, Warby J also indicated that he would grant an injunction against 'Persons unknown', but limited this to those persons who had been identified (anonymously) prior to the date of the hearing as participants in the protest and who had had notice of the proceedings.[116]

10.86 In *Barking and Dagenham LBC v Persons Unknown*,[117] the Court of Appeal reviewed the authorities on the granting of final injunctions against persons who are unknown and unidentified at the time of trial. Such persons are referred to as 'newcomers'. The Court of Appeal rejected the view, based on *Canada Goose UK Retail Ltd v Persons unknown*,[118] that final injunctions are limited to those who have become parties to the application prior to the date of the final order. At the time of writing this case, and the question of whether newcomers are caught by final injunctions, is subject to appeal to the Supreme Court.

Dispersal

10.87 The third significant power under the ASBCPA 2014 for the purposes of the policing of protest is the power of dispersal under Part 3. ASBCPA 2014 s34 empowers a police officer of at least the rank of inspector to authorise the use of dispersal powers in a specified locality, during a specified period of not more than 48 hours. Such authorisation may be given if the officer is satisfied on reasonable grounds that the use of those powers may be necessary for removing or reducing a) the likelihood of members of the public in the locality being harassed, alarmed or distressed, or b) the occurrence in the locality of crime or disorder. Section 34(3) requires the authorising officer to have particular regard to Article 10 and 11 rights when deciding whether to give an authorisation. Section 35 sets out the conditions on which a constable in uniform may exercise the powers of dispersal once an authorisation is in place.

10.88 The lawfulness of dispersal powers under the predecessor to ASBCPA 2014 Part 3, Anti-Social Behaviour Act 2003 s30, was considered by the Divisional Court in *R (Singh and another) v Chief Constable of West Midlands*,[119] discussed above at para 10.32.

116 *Birmungham City Council v Afsar* [2019] EWHC 3217 (QB), [2020] 3 All ER 756 at para 132.

117 [2022] EWCA Civ 13.

118 [2020] EWCA Civ 303, [2020] 1 WLR 2802.

119 [2006] EWCA Civ 1118, [2006] 1 WLR 3374.

Stop and search and stop and account

10.89 There are a number of statutory provisions which provide the police with powers to stop and search individuals and vehicles – these are addressed at paras 6.100–6.118. Such powers are often exercised in the context of the policing of protest. The police will maintain that this is justified either on the basis of reasonable suspicion that persons involved in the protest are in possession of offensive weapons or articles for use in causing criminal damage, or, where an authorisation is in place under CJPOA 1994 s60, searches can be conducted without the need for individual suspicion. The complaint from participants in demonstrations is that such powers are frequently used against protestors in a blanket and/or discriminatory fashion and are suspected of being intended by the police to have a chilling effect on the exercise of Article 10 and 11 rights, because would-be participants are deterred by the fear of being subjected to heavy-handed policing.

10.90 In *Howarth v Commissioner of Police of the Metropolis*,[120] the claimant challenged a stop and search conducted under Police and Criminal Evidence Act 1984 (PACE) s1, on the basis that the police had had no reasonable grounds to suspect him of being in possession of any prohibited articles and that the action had been an unlawful interference with his Article 10 and 11 (and 8) rights. The claimant had been on a train, travelling to attend a demonstration against the oil industry. An instruction had been given by a senior officer to search the protestors on the train on the basis of intelligence suggesting that some were in possession of chalk and molasses, to be used in direct action. Molasses and chalk had been used at previous similar demonstrations. The intelligence did not identify any individuals, but rather the intending protestors as a group. The claimant contended that the police actions in searching the entire group was intimidating and disproportionate, given the large number of people searched and the relatively low level of harm likely to be caused by the items sought. He also argued that the action was premature, because the protestors were still some way away from the site of the protest, so no criminal damage was imminent.

10.91 The Divisional Court rejected these submissions, finding that, having regard to the intelligence, the searching officer's suspicion that one or more protestors were carrying prohibited items was sufficient to establish reasonable grounds to search each member of the group, including the claimant. The court acknowledged that there would be limits to group searches, but that this would be bounded by the requirement of rationality:

> All will depend on the circumstances of each individual case. One can imagine that a search for a single item of technically offending material (for example, a paint spray) might not justify the searching of a very large group of demonstrators, but the search of such a group, in which one as yet unidentified individual is reasonably suspected of carrying a bomb, might be very different.[121]

10.92 On the facts of this case, the Divisional Court found that the officer's search had been reasonable and that the interference with the claimant's

120 [2011] EWHC 2818 (Admin).
121 At para 32.

rights had been proportionate to the legitimate aim of preventing crime. It is of note that, although the claimant in *Howarth* made complaint about the impact of the search on his Article 10 and 11 rights, it was not part of his case that the search had been conducted for an ulterior purpose (for example, to deter protestors from attending the demonstration).

10.93 Another common complaint raised by those attending demonstrations is of being required by police to give their names and addresses; and, on occasion being required to submit to being filmed doing so. This was the subject of challenge in *Mengesha v Commissioner of Police of the Metropolis.*[122] The claimant had been a legal observer at a trade union march, which had resulted in the police containing around 100 people, including the claimant, in a kettle. Police informed those held that everyone would be required to have their face photographed and their details taken as a condition of being released from the kettle. The claimant did not challenge the lawfulness of the kettle itself, nor the lawfulness of being searched pursuant to an authorisation that was in place under CJPOA 1994 s60. Her challenge was to the requirement to submit to being photographed and to provide her details.

10.94 In upholding her claim, the Divisional Court noted that there is a specific statutory power conferred by Police Reform Act 2002 s50 in relation to requiring a person to give their name and address where a constable in uniform reasonably believes that an individual has been or is acting in an anti-social manner. Further, PACE s64A confers power to take photographs for crime investigation purposes where a person is in a public place but under arrest. However, the conditions for the exercise of those powers were not met on the facts of this case and by the time of the hearing, the Commissioner was not seeking to rely on them as the basis for the questioning and filming of the claimant. The Divisional Court referred to the dicta of Lord Bingham in *Laporte* to the effect that where carefully defined powers have been conferred on police officers by statute:[123]

> It would . . . be surprising if, alongside those closely defined powers and duties, there existed a common law, power and duty . . . bounded only by an uncertain and undefined condition of reasonableness.

Applying this to the circumstances that arose in *Mengesha*, containment, or kettling, was only permissible as a measure of last resort for the purpose of averting an imminent breach of the peace – it could not lawfully be used for other purposes, such as enabling the police to obtain the personal details of everyone contained. Such action was unlawful.

10.95 The Divisional Court further confirmed the correctness of the decision in *Rice v Connolly*,[124] namely that there is no legal duty on a member of the public who is not under arrest to answer questions put by the police and a refusal to do so will not normally amount to obstructing the police unless the person being questioned supplies false evidence or is abusive or aggressive.[125]

122 [2013] EWHC 1695 (Admin).

123 Lord Bingham in *Laporte* at 52, cited by Moses LJ in *Mengesha* at 11.

124 [1966] 2 QB 414, DC.

125 Compare *Ricketts v Cox* (1982) 74 Cr App R 298, DC.

10.96 The ECtHR has also held that law-enforcement measures applied for a purpose other than that for which the powers in question were lawfully intended – for example, arrests for non-compliance with a lawful order of a police officer effected in order to deter or punish participation in an assembly – will not meet the ECHR requirement of lawfulness.[126]

126 *Hakobyan v Armenia* (App No 34320/04), [2012] ECHR 616, ECtHR; *Huseynli v Azerbaijan* (App No 67360/11), 11 February 2016, ECtHR.

CHAPTER 11

The police, information rights and data protection

continued

11.1 There has been a greatly increased focus over the last few years on the information collected, retained and used by the police in relation to individuals. From a position where there was little parliamentary or judicial interest in regulating this area, there is now a burgeoning amount of case-law and statutory oversight.

11.2 This chapter will look at the major categories of information held by the police on individuals and how it can be accessed. The various legal frameworks which permit the police to collect, retain and share information will be described, together with the detailed statutory guidance that has been developed in this area. Some of the mechanisms for challenging continued retention and requesting deletion will be examined.

11.3 The specific procedures whereby the police disclose information for the purposes of criminal record certificates and how to negotiate this are then set out. Next, police identification of informants and witnesses is discussed. The developing area of facial recognition technology is explored. The chapter ends with a description of the main causes of action that can be brought where retention or use of information is challenged, including actions under the Human Rights Act (HRA) 1998, the Data Protection Act (DPA) 2018, the tort of misuse of private information and defamation.

What information is held by the police

Introduction

11.4 Knowing what information is collected and retained by the police and where it is then stored is an important part of advising people who want to find out what information the police hold, with a view to making an application to have access to it, have it altered or have it destroyed. The following is a brief guide as to the sources of the information that is collected and held by the police.

11.5 There are four main national databases used by the police as follows:

1) the Police National Computer (PNC) is the main source of information for matters such as arrests, charges and convictions;
2) other information stored nationally is to be found on the Police National Database (PND);
3) fingerprint records are retained on a system known as IDENT1;
4) DNA profiles are kept on the National DNA Database (NDNAD) (although information associated with the profile including a person's name, address, descriptive details and relevant operational information, is held on the PNC).

11.6 Individual police forces will also retain local records which will not be found on the national databases and these will also be discussed.

Police National Computer

11.7 The PNC holds information concerning people and property, including convictions, wanted and missing people, stolen vehicles and other types of stolen property that can be electronically accessed by the police and other criminal justice agencies. The PNC Code of Practice (issued pursuant to

Police Act 1996 s39A), published by the National Centre for Policing Excellence in 2005, explains that the PNC is the only full-time, operational national police computer system routinely supported by data from all police forces. It is the prime source of information in relation to the nominal record of offenders processed by the police, and the courts. At the time of writing, consultation on a new Code of Practice has completed. The PNC will be phased out to be replaced by the Law Enforcement Data Service (LEDS) which will operate on a different platform. For a time, the two systems will operate side by side.[1] A record can be created on the PNC for a number of reasons, including where a person has been convicted of an offence but also where a person has been arrested, charged or reported for summons for the commission of, or involvement in, a recordable offence. The PNC will also say whether someone has failed to appear in court, is wanted for a specific offence or is disqualified from driving.

11.8 A PNC record also contains information about non-conviction outcomes including 'not guilty' adjudications, 'acquittals', 'discontinuances' and 'no further action' (NFA) disposals. The PNC will also contain personal information of a person if a DNA profile is retained by the police.

11.9 The PNC will be used in court to provide information about previous convictions. It is likely to be produced in a civil action against the police if a claimant has relevant convictions upon which the police wish to rely. It is possible to request a copy of the entries on the PNC through a subject access request (SAR) (see para 11.90).

11.10 As is explained below, there is a process for challenging entries on the PNC, either because they are inaccurate, or because it is disproportionate to continue to hold the information, although the grounds for success are highly restricted. It is very unlikely that records of convictions will ever be removed from a PNC record. The approach of the courts to entries on the PNC is reflected in the comments of Richards LJ in the case of *R (C) v Commissioner of the Police of the Metropolis*[2] where the claimant sought removal of non-conviction information on the PNC:

> . . . a PNC record that did not include the basic history of FJ's involvement with the police would be an incomplete and potentially misleading record. Moreover, if a similar allegation were made against FJ in the future, it would be profoundly unsatisfactory if it fell to be considered without knowledge of the earlier allegation and the arrest and investigation to which it gave rise. I am satisfied that retention of this kind of information in the PNC record is justified on any view.[3]

Police National Database

11.11 The PND is a national information management system used by the police to manage and share information with the purpose of preventing and detecting crime. The PND offers a capability for the police to share, access and search local information electronically, with other forces. The relevant

1 Code of Practice for the Police National Computer (PNC) and the Law Enforcement Data Service (LEDS) Consultation 2022 https://assets.college.police.uk/s3fs-public/2022-03/Code-of-Practice-for-PNC-and-LEDS-2022-consultation.pdf.

2 [2012] EWHC 1671 (Admin), [2012] 1 WLR 3007.

3 [2012] EWHC 1671 (Admin), [2012] 1 WLR 3007 at para 61.

code of practice[4] emphasises the importance of the police complying with the DPA 2018 and police policies on the management of police information (see below at para 11.61). The code sets out the relevant policing purposes for which data can be stored and shared on the PND as follows:

- protecting life and property;
- preserving order;
- preventing the commission of offences;
- bringing offenders to justice; and
- any duty or responsibility of the police arising from common or statute law.

11.12 The code sets out strategic priorities for the use of the PND while making it clear that it is up to chief officers to decide how to use it for policing purposes. This means that each police force will have its own policy as to what information it is recording. The strategic priorities include the protection of children and vulnerable people, understanding the threat of terrorism, and disrupting and preventing organised crime. Information obtained from the PND may be shared, provided the sharing is lawful (see below at para 11.161).

11.13 Although custody images (photographs taken by the police using Police and Criminal Evidence Act 1984 (PACE) powers on arrest) are retained on local systems, the police can also upload them from forces' local custody IT systems onto the PND. At the time of a government review into the retention of custody images, all but nine forces uploaded custody images onto PND. The review states that:

> As of July 2016, there were over 19 million custody images on PND, over 16 million of which had been enrolled in the facial recognition gallery making them searchable using facial recognition software. Many of these images are multiple images of the same individual. Recent advances in technology mean that it is now possible to search custody images on PND.[5]

Fingerprint database

11.14 The National Fingerprint Database and National Automated Fingerprint Identification System (NAFIS), now collectively referred to as IDENT1, was established in 1999 and holds fingerprint images obtained from persons and crime scenes by law enforcement agencies. It provides the ability to electronically store and search fingerprint images, for the purposes of comparing with fingerprints taken from scenes of crime. The police routinely take a set of fingerprints from all persons they arrest using powers under PACE.

11.15 Since 2012, the IDENT1 has been operated by the Home Office, but police forces have direct access to the system and they own the data they upload to it.

4 Code of Practice on the Operation and Use of the Police National Database, National Policing Improvement Agency, 2010, https://assets.publishing.service.gov.uk/government/uploads/system/uploads/attachment_data/file/243554/9999102808.pdf.

5 *Review of the use and retention of custody images*, Home Office, February 2017, para 1.5.

11.16 As at 31 March 2020, IDENT1 held 26,298,205 fingerprint forms relating to 8,397,761 individuals.[6]

National DNA Database

11.17 NDNAD is run by the Home Office on behalf of UK police forces. The *National DNA Database strategy board biennial report 2018–2020*[7] states that:

> NDNAD was established in 1995. It holds electronic records of deoxyribonucleic acid (DNA), known as profile records, taken from individuals and crime scenes, and provides the police with matches linking an individual to a crime scene or a crime scene to another crime scene.

11.18 The report states that between April 2001 and March 2020 the NDNAD produced 731,160 matches to unsolved crimes and in 2019/20 the NDNAD provided 22,916 routine matches including 601 to homicides and 555 to rapes and 219 urgent matches, including 58 to homicides and 56 to rapes.

11.19 The police can take a 'DNA sample' from every individual that they arrest (see para 11.41). This consists of their entire genome (the genetic material that every individual has in each of the cells of their body) and is usually taken by swabbing the inside of the cheek to collect some cells. It is useful to set out what the report says happens to the sample:

> The sample is then sent to an accredited laboratory, known as a 'forensic service provider' (FSP), which looks at discrete areas of the genome (which represent only a tiny fraction of that individual's DNA) plus the sex chromosomes (XX for women and XY for men) and use these to produce a 'subject' profile consisting of 16 pairs of numbers (which correspond to the 16 areas analysed) and a sex marker derived from the sex chromosomes. The profile is almost unique in unrelated individuals; the chance of two unrelated people having identical profile records is less than one in a billion. Aside from sex, a DNA profile does not reveal any other characteristics of the individual it is taken from such as their race or physical appearance.[8]

11.20 It is this profile which is loaded to the NDNAD where it can be searched against the DNA records recovered from crime scenes. As of 31 March 2020, the NDNAD estimates that it holds subject profile records of 5,604,185 individuals. There are circumstances where the police must automatically delete the DNA profiles of individuals (especially where they have been arrested but not charged or convicted) (see below para 11.122).

11.21 In 2019/20, 124,492 subject profile records were deleted from NDNAD.[9] This included 280 under the 'Deletion of Records from National Police Systems' guidance which provides for deletion earlier than the statutory requirement and which is explained in more detail below.

11.22 The police do not have direct access to the data held on NDNAD, but they will be informed of any matches it produces. Similarly, forensic service providers who undertake DNA profiling under contract to the

6 *NDNAD strategy board biennial report 2018–2020*, September 2020, para 2.2.1, www.gov.uk/government/publications/national-dna-database-biennial-report-2018-to-2020.

7 NDNAD Report, para 1.1.1.

8 NDNAD Report para 1.1.2.

9 NDNAD Report para 1.2.1.

police service, and submit the resulting crime scene and subject profile records for loading, do not have direct access to NDNAD.

Local records

11.23 As well as these national databases, each police force will keep local records about investigations of crime, arrests which have not resulted in charges, information and crime reports from the public, records of 999 calls. In the Metropolitan Police Service, for example, some of these records are kept with the Crime Reporting Information System (CRIS). The making, retention and use of these records is regulated by the law and practice detailed below in this chapter. How to access it by way of a SAR is described at para 11.90. The information retained can be important to individuals contemplating a civil action (see para 14.92). There may also be a sense of injustice that the police have retained information alleging criminal activity where no action has been taken, for example. All of the information retained is potentially available for disclosure on an enhanced criminal certificate (see below at para 11.150).

11.24 As part of this local record-keeping, the Home Office produces the *Home Office Counting Rules for Recorded Crime* (April 2021).[10] These rules indicate the very wide interpretation that police forces are expected to take when deciding to record a matter as a crime:

> 2.2 An incident will be recorded as a crime (notifiable offence) for 'victim related offences' if, on the balance of probability:
> (a) the circumstances of the victims report amount to a crime defined by law (the police will determine this, based on their knowledge of the law and counting rules); and
> (b) there is no credible evidence to the contrary immediately available.
> 2.3 A belief by the victim, or person reasonably assumed to be acting on behalf of the victim, (explained further at 3.6 ii), that a crime has occurred is usually sufficient to justify its recording. . . .
> 2.5 Once recorded, a crime will remain recorded unless additional verifiable information (AVI) is found and documented which determines that no notifiable crime has occurred or crimes are transferred or cancelled i.e. where crimes are created in error, or as a duplicate of an existing crime.

Sources of law relating to police retention and use of information

11.25 There are four main sources of statutory law which govern to the police taking retention and use of information:

1) European Convention on Human Rights (ECHR) Article 8 (as included in Schedule 1 to the Human Rights Act (HRA) 1998);
2) PACE;
3) DPA 2018;
4) Criminal Procedure and Investigations Act (CPIA) 1996, Code of Practice.

10 See: https://assets.publishing.service.gov.uk/government/uploads/system/uploads/attachment_data/file/992833/count-general-jun-2021.pdf.

Article 8 ECHR

11.26 The taking, retention and use of information relating to an individual's private life are issues which come within the ambit of ECHR Article 8 reads as follows:

> (1) Everyone has the right to respect for his private and family life, his home and his correspondence.
> (2) There shall be no interference by a public authority with the exercise of this right except such as in accordance with the law and is necessary in a democratic society in the interests of national security, public safety or the economic wellbeing of the country, for the prevention of disorder or crime, for the protection of health or morals or for the protection of the rights and freedoms of others.

The scope of Article 8(1) in data cases

11.27 The European Court of Human Rights (ECtHR) has stated that the concept of a private life is a broad term not susceptible to exhaustive definition. It has recognised that elements such as gender identification, name, sexual orientation and sexual life are important elements of the personal sphere protected by Article 8. It has also recognised that Article 8 protects a right to dignity and personal development and the right to establish and develop relationships with other human beings, including activities of a professional or a personal nature.

11.28 Article 8(1) has been successfully invoked by applicants in cases concerning traditional forms of covert surveillance such as telephone tapping[11] and the use of listening devices,[12] by the police, the Ministry of Defence[13] and by intelligence services.[14] The ECtHR considers the surveillance of legal consultations taking place in a police station to be analogous to the interception of a telephone call between a lawyer and client, given the need to ensure an enhanced degree of protection for that relationship and in particular for the confidentiality of the exchanges which characterise it.[15] The ECtHR has also found violations of Article 8 in relation to the storage of intercepted data concerning telephone, email and internet use, and retention of fingerprints, cellular samples and DNA profiles.[16] Article 8(1) is engaged where information relating to suspects and/or convicted offenders is disseminated, such as the criminal record information disclosure regime – which is discussed in detail at para 11.150 below.[17]

11.29 The ECtHR has been held that activities in a public context may in certain circumstances fall within the concept of a 'private life' and that in assessing this question, a person's reasonable expectations as to their

11 *Malone v UK* (1985) 7 EHRR 14, *Halford v UK* (1997) 24 EHRR 523, ECtHR.

12 *Khan v UK* (2001) 31 EHRR 45, ECtHR.

13 *Liberty and others v UK* (2009) 48 EHRR 1, ECtHR.

14 The actions of intelligence services fall beyond the remit of this chapter. See two cases on the (now repealed) Regulation of Investigatory Powers Act 2000: *Kennedy v UK* (2011) 52 EHRR 4 (regarding access to information) and *Big Brother Watch v UK* [2021] ECHR 58170/13 (regarding bulk interception).

15 *RE v UK* (2016) 63 EHRR 2 at para 131, ECtHR.

16 *S and Marper v UK* (2009) 48 EHRR 50.

17 *MM v UK* [2012] ECHR 24029/07, ECtHR.; *DS v UK* [2021] ECHR 70988/12, ECtHR.

privacy may be a significant, though, not necessarily conclusive, factor, as will be the extent to which a systematic or permanent record is made of material apparently in the public domain.[18] A person walking down the street expects to be observed by others, but may not expect their movements to become the subject of a permanent data record. Thus, the compilation of data by security services on particular individuals, even without the use of covert surveillance methods, can constitute an interference with their private lives.[19]

11.30 This aspect of the Article 8 protection is well illustrated by *Perry v UK*.[20] Police modified the operation of a security camera so as to take photographs of the applicant while he was in the custody suite and then inserted the footage into a montage of film of other persons for the purposes of showing to potential identification witnesses in relation to a robbery. The ECtHR held that an interference with the applicant's rights under Article 8(1) had occurred, as even if he expected to be filmed by security cameras in the custody suite, he would not have expected footage to be used as part of a subsequent identification procedure.[21]

The requirements of Article 8(2)

11.31 If the actions complained of are protected by Article 8(1), the court will then consider whether the circumstances fall within Article 8(2), so as justify the invasion of privacy. In other words, whether the interference was (i) in accordance with law, (ii) in pursuit of one or more legitimate aims and (iii) necessary in a democratic society to achieve those aims. (See paras 7.189 and 9.79 for application of Article 8(2) in cases involving physical treatment by police and execution of search warrants.)

In accordance with the law

11.32 The ECtHR requires the existence of a proper legislative framework for police use and disclosure of personal information and data. This largely involves a consideration of whether the use was sanctioned under domestic law.[22] 'The law' for this purpose comprises all relevant components: primary legislation, secondary legislation, statutory guidance and case-law. It is not enough merely for the power to be rooted in law; that law must attain the required quality. In other words, it must be compatible with the rule of law;[23] must provide adequate protection against arbitrary interference with ECHR rights; must be readily accessible; and those potentially affected by it must be able to foresee its consequences.

11.33 For example, in *MM v UK*[24] the ECtHR held that the retention and disclosure of caution data in police records in Northern Ireland in the

18 See, for example, *PG and JH v UK* [2001] ECHR 44787/98, ECtHR.

19 *Rotaru v Romania* [2000] ECHR 28341/95, ECtHR.

20 [2003] ECHR 63737/00, ECtHR.

21 The interference was not justified under Article 8(2) in that it was not 'in accordance with the law' as domestic procedures requiring identification processes were breached.

22 Intrusions upon private life used to fail this criteria on the basis that the activity was insufficiently regulated by domestic law, for example see *Malone v UK* (1985) 7 EHRR 64, and *Halford v UK* (1997) 24 EHRR 523, ECtHR.

23 *Big Brother Watch v UK* [2021] ECHR 58170/13 at 332–334, ECtHR.

24 [2012] ECHR 24029/07, ECtHR.

absence of regulation by a *statutory* system was not 'in accordance with law' and breached Article 8(2). In particular, the court reiterated that, in the context of the recording and communication of criminal record data, it was essential to have 'minimum safeguards concerning, *inter alia*, duration, storage, usage, access of third parties, procedures for preserving the integrity and confidentiality of data and procedures for their destruction [to provide] sufficient guarantees against the risk of abuse and arbitrariness'.[25]

Legitimate aim

11.34 The court must be satisfied that the intrusion pursued a legitimate aim, that is to say one of those specified in Article 8(2). For present purposes, the relevant aims are likely to be: 'the interests of national security', 'public safety', 'the prevention of disorder or crime' or 'the protection of rights and freedoms of others'. In the vast majority of instances, the police would have little difficulty in bringing the activity under challenge within one of those legitimate aims.

Necessary in a democratic society

11.35 The third element is likely to cause more difficulty. The court has to consider whether the interference is 'necessary in a democratic society', that is to say it meets a 'pressing social need' and the particular interference is proportionate to the legitimate aim being pursued. This will always depend upon an evaluation of the particular circumstances.

11.36 For example, in *Gaughran v UK*[26] the Strasbourg Court held that indefinite retention by the police of the applicant's biometric data and photograph on a local database was an interference that was disproportionate to the legitimate aim of prevention and detection of crime, notwithstanding that the applicant had been convicted of an offence. The decisive factor was the indiscriminate nature of the powers of retention – the data was held without any reference to the seriousness of the applicant's offence (driving with excess alcohol), without regard to any continuing need to retain that data, and in the absence of any real possibility of review. By contrast, the ECtHR recently held that the five-year retention of a photograph of a repeat offender with the possibility of review was necessary and proportionate.[27]

11.37 The proportionality of a particular interference must be considered at each stage of data processing: the collection, storage, use and communication of data. For example, in *Catt v UK*[28] the ECtHR recognised that there was a 'pressing social need' for the police to establish and maintain an 'Extremism database' that monitored protests of political activist groups whose past activities were known to be violent and potentially criminal. The court further held that the police were justified to *collect* the applicant's personal data given that he had publicly aligned himself with such a group (notwithstanding that the applicant was not himself suspected of criminal activities and had no previous convictions). However, there was no 'pressing social need' to *retain* the applicant's data in circumstances

25 At 195.
26 [2020] ECHR 45245/15.
27 *PN v Germany* [2020] ECHR, App No 74440/17 [2020] 2 WLUK 607, ECtHR.
28 (2019) 69 EHRR 7, ECtHR.

where the erasure of information was entirely reliant on the diligent application of highly flexible safeguards in a statutory code of practice and where, in effect, the applicant's data could be retained indefinitely.

Police and Criminal Evidence Act 1984

11.38 The key piece of legislation which empowers and regulates the police to obtain and record information about an individual is and the accompanying six statutory Codes of Practice (in particular Code D which provides guidance on the keeping of accurate and reliable criminal records).[29] Police powers arise at each stage of a criminal investigation and invariably involve information of a personal, sensitive and/or intimate nature, including as follows.

Stop and search, arrest and interview

11.39 The police have a duty to make records concerning searches and, where a person is arrested and taken to a police station, to ensure the record is made part of the person's custody record.[30] A person who is arrested may be photographed, including without their consent. That photograph may be used by, or disclosed to, any person for the prevention and detection of crime, and subsequently retained.[31] Any interview with a suspect must be audio-recorded.[32]

Entry, search and seizure

11.40 The police can obtain search warrants[33] which provide access to information about a suspect. In certain circumstances, a constable may apply for special provision for access records from which a living individual can be identified and which relate to that person's physical or mental health. In the course of executing a warrant, police officers have general powers of seizure covering anything (including computerised information) where (i) there are reasonable grounds to believe it is evidence in relation to an offence and (ii) it is necessary to do so in order to prevent the evidence being concealed, lost, alerted or destroyed. Seized material (or a photograph / copy thereof) may be retained as evidence so long as is necessary in all the circumstances.[34]

Detention

11.41 PACE also governs the ability of the police to collect and retain information of an intrinsically private character for the purpose of prevention and detection of criminal activity — including fingerprints,[35] impressions of

29 See: https://assets.publishing.service.gov.uk/government/uploads/system/uploads/attachment_data/file/903812/pace-code-d-2017.pdf.

30 PACE s3.

31 PACE s64A(1), (1B) and (4).

32 PACE s60.

33 PACE ss8–9, 12 and Sch 1.

34 PACE ss19–22.

35 PACE ss27 and 61.

footwear,[36] X-rays and ultrasounds,[37] 'intimate' DNA samples (eg urine)[38] and 'non-intimate' DNA samples (eg fingernail or mouth swab).[39] The provisions include safeguards both for the taking and retention of samples. For example, fingerprints can ordinarily only be taken with the written consent of the suspect.[40] Once taken, fingerprints are recorded on the person's custody record[41] and on police central records (see paras 11.14–11.16),[42] pending investigation or criminal proceedings.[43] In the event of a person's conviction for a 'recordable' (ie imprisonable) offence their fingerprints may be retained indefinitely.[44]

Data Protection Act 2018[45]

11.42 The DPA 2018 came into force on 25 May 2018, repealing the previous Data Protection Act 1998 and bringing the Law Enforcement Directive 2016/680/EU (LED) into UK law. The DPA 2018 was amended on 1 January 2021 by regulations under the European Union (Withdrawal) Act 2018, to reflect the UK's status outside the EU. The DPA 2018 comprises of three separate regimes.[46] The regime relevant for present purposes regulates law enforcement processing and is contained in DPA 2018 Part 3 (ss29–81).

11.43 Data protection legislation has been likened to a 'thicket' by the judiciary:[47] it is complex, technical and layers definitions upon definitions. It is not feasible to give a full summary of the provisions of Part 3 – what follows is necessarily an abbreviated overview.

The scope of the law enforcement regime: data, controllers and processing

11.44 DPA 2018 Part 3 applies to and regulates how data controllers process personal data for law enforcement purposes.[48] Each concept in that sentence needs defining and unpacking to understand the scope of the law enforcement regime.

36 PACE s61A.
37 PACE s55A.
38 PACE ss62, 65(1) and 65A.
39 PACE ss63, 65(1) and 65A.
40 PACE ss61(4) and 118.
41 PACE s8.
42 PACE s63AA.
43 PACE ss63D–63O.
44 PACE s63I(2); National Police Records (Recordable Offences) Regulations 2000 SI No 1139 reg 3 and Schedule.
45 For an outline of the provisions of the DPA 1998, please see the previous edition of this publication.
46 The general processing regime / the UK GDPR (DPA 2018 Part 2), the regime for law enforcement agencies (DPA 2018 Part 3) and the regime for the three intelligence services (DPA 2018 Part 4).
47 *Campbell v MGN Ltd* [2002] EWHC 499 (QB) at 77; and *Aven v Orbis Business Intelligence* [2020] EWHC 1812 (QB) at 12 (in relation to the DPA 1998).
48 This chapter focuses on data controllers, which will be the focus of the majority of claims. However, please note that regime also applies to data processors, ie 'any person who processes personal data on behalf of the controller (other than a person who is an employee of the controller)': DPA 2018 s32(3).

11.45 'Personal data' means any information relating to an identified or identifiable living individual.[49] This is a wide concept. An identifiable individual is any person:

> ... who can be identified, directly or indirectly, in particular by reference to–
> (a) an identifier such as a name, an identification number, location data or an online identifier, or
> (b) one or more factors specific to the physical, physiological, genetic, mental, economic, cultural or social identity of the individual.[50]

As such, personal data includes myriad information stored on police force databases, including fingerprints and other DNA information, as well as CCTV footage and photographs showing the individual.

11.46 'Processing' has a wide statutory definition and means any operation performed on data, including collection, recording, organisation, structuring, storage, adaption, alteration, retrieval, consultation, use, disclosure, restriction, erasure or destruction.[51] When processing personal data for any of the law enforcement purposes, a clear distinction must, where relevant and as far as possible, be made between personal data relating to different categories of data subject, such as (a) persons suspected of having committed or being about to commit a criminal offence; (b) persons convicted of a criminal offence; (c) persons who are or may be victims of a criminal offence; and (d) witnesses or other persons with information about offences.[52]

11.47 A 'data controller' means a 'competent authority' which determines the purposes and means of processing personal data, or has an obligation to process personal data imposed by an enactment.[53] 'Competent authorities' are persons listed in DPA 2018 Sch 7 and persons with a statutory functions for any of the law enforcement purposes.[54] This includes (but is not limited to) chief officers of police, prosecutorial agencies, other criminal justice agencies, and executive agencies such as HM Courts and Tribunals Service and HM Prison Service. A data controller can act alone or jointly with others. An example of data processed by 'joint controllers' is the PNC (see paras 11.7–11.110), which is managed on behalf of all police forces in the UK with individual chief constables jointly determining the purposes and meaning of processing of the personal data held on the database.

11.48 For the purposes of the DPA 2018, police officers and special constables (who are office holders rather than employees in the conventional sense) are treated as an extension of their chief officer – and, therefore, owe obligations to data subjects when processing their data.[55]

11.49 Finally, 'law enforcement purposes' are 'the purposes of prevention, investigation, detection or prosecution of criminal offences or the execution of criminal penalties, including the safeguarding against and the

49 DPA 2018 s3(1).
50 DPA 2018 s3(3).
51 DPA 2018 s3(4). See also DPA 2018 s29(1).
52 DPA 2018 s38(3).
53 DPA 2018 s32. See also s205 for the definition of 'enactment'.
54 DPA 2018 s30(1) and Sch 7.
55 DPA 2018 s33(2); Explanatory Notes 2018, para 176.

prevention of threats to public security'.[56] There is nothing in the DPA 2018 to suggest that the *sole* purpose of processing needs to be criminal law enforcement. However, any data processing carried out which is not for the *primary* purpose of criminal law enforcement (for example, when processing by the Human Resources department regarding police employees) will be covered by the general data processing regime under the UK General Data Protection Regulation (GDPR) (read with DPA 2018 Part 2).[57]

The data protection principles

11.50 The data controller is obligated to comply with the six data protection principles in relation to all personal data within their responsibility, as follows:[58]

1) The processing of personal data must be lawful and fair.
2) The purposes of processing personal data must be specified, explicit and legitimate.
3) Personal data must be adequate, relevant and not excessive for the law enforcement purpose for which it is processed.
4) Personal data must be accurate and, where necessary, kept up-to-date. Every reasonable step must be taken to ensure that personal data (in particular factual data) that is inaccurate is erased or rectified without delay.
5) Personal data must be kept for no longer than is necessary and must be reviewed periodically.
6) Personal data must be processed in an appropriately secure manner, using appropriate technical or organisational measures. This includes protection against unauthorised or unlawful processing and against accidental loss, destruction and damage.

11.51 The first data protection principle requires that in order for processing to be lawful it must be 'based on law' (be that statute, common law or the royal prerogative) *and* either carried out with the data subject's informed consent to processing or 'necessary' for a law enforcement purpose.[59] In this context, 'necessary' means 'reasonably', rather than absolutely or strictly necessary.[60] In other words, the processing needs to be a targeted and proportionate way of the competent authority achieving one of the law enforcement purposes.

11.52 Police cases often involve 'sensitive processing' – that is, the processing of personal data the reveals (among other things) a data subject's racial or

56 DPA 2018 s31.

57 *Guide to law enforcement processing*, Information Commissioner's Office (ICO), 15 April 2019, p4.

58 As summarised in DPA 2018 s34. See also ss35–41. Please note that the law enforcement data protection principles contain some differences to the data protection principles in DPA 2018 Part 2. For example, the first data protection principle has a 'transparency' requirement in Part 2, but has no such requirement in Part 3.

59 DPA 2018 s35(1)–(2).

60 *South Lanarkshire Council v Scottish Information Commissioner* [2013] UKSC 55, [2013] 1 WLR 2421, at 25–27. See also the *Guide to Law Enforcement Processing*, ICO, 15 April 2019, p12.

ethnic origin, political opinions, religious or philosophical beliefs, or trade union membership.[61] Such processing needs to be 'strictly necessary' for one of the specified purposes, including (but not limited to) performing a statutory function, protecting individuals' vital interests, safeguarding children and individuals at risk, and preventing fraud.[62] 'Strictly necessary' means that the processing has to relate to a pressing social need that cannot reasonably be achieved through less intrusive means. The police force must have an 'appropriate policy document' in place, explaining the procedures for ensuring compliance with the data protection principles and the policies on retention and erasure of data.[63]

The rights of data subjects

11.53 In addition to the first data protection principle, the data protection principles most likely to relate to police activity are the third, fourth, and fifth principles. Further, both the Information Commissioner's Office (ICO) *Guide to law enforcement processing* and section 6 of the National Police Chiefs' Council's *Data protection manual* provide useful commentary on each data protection principle.

11.54 DPA 2018 Part 3 confers rights on data subjects enforceable against data controllers, including:

1) the right of access;
2) the right to rectification;
3) the right to erasure;[64]
4) the right to restrict processing; and
5) the right against automated decisions.

The content and operation of access are summarised below at paras 11.93–11.104. The way in which data subjects can exercise their rights to rectification and erasure are summarised below at paras 11.119–11.160.

CPIA 1996 Code of Practice

11.55 Pursuant to CPIA 1996 s23, the secretary of state had a duty to prepare a code of practice containing provisions designed to ensure, among other things, that 'material' obtained in the course of a criminal investigation and that may be relevant to the investigation is recorded, retained and revealed to the prosecutor involved in any resultant criminal proceedings.[65] The most recent CPIA 1996 Code of Practice (also known as the 'Disclosure Code of Practice') was brought into force on 31 December 2020.

61 DPA 2018 ss35(3)–(5) and 42.

62 For the full list of specified purposes see DPA 2018 Sch 8.

63 DPA 2018 ss35(4)(b), (5)(c), 42(2). See the MPS policy document at www.met.police.uk/SysSiteAssets/foi-media/metropolitan-police/policies/mps-apd-law-enforcement-processing.

64 DPA 2018 ss43–48. In addition, data subjects have the right not to be subject to automated decision-making: DPA 2018 ss49–50.

65 See: https://assets.publishing.service.gov.uk/government/uploads/system/uploads/attachment_data/file/931173/Criminal-procedure-and-investigations-act-1996.pdf.

Duty to collect and record material

11.56 The code provides that in an investigation, police officers should pursue all reasonable lines of inquiry, whether these point towards or away from the suspect.[66] What is reasonable in each case will depend on the particular circumstances. Where information which may be relevant is obtained, it must be recorded at the time it is obtained or as soon as practicable after that time.[67]

Duty to retain material

11.57 The duty to retain material encompasses (insofar as it may be relevant to the investigation) crime reports and police officers' notebooks; custody records; records derived from tapes of telephone messages; final version of witness statements including any exhibits mentioned; interview records; communications between the police and experts such as forensic scientists; records of the first description of a suspect by each potential witness who purports to identify or describe the suspect; information provided by an accused person which indicates an explanation for the offence; and any material casting doubt on the reliability of a confession and/or on the reliability of a witness.[68]

11.58 All material which may be relevant to the investigation must be retained until a decision is taken whether to institute proceedings against a person for an offence. If a criminal investigation results in a prosecution, then all such material must be retained at least until the accused is acquitted or convicted, or the prosecutor decides not to proceed with the case. Where the defendant is convicted, the material must be retained at least six months from the date of conviction and/or (if longer and where applicable) until the convicted person is released from custody or discharged from hospital. If the defendant appeals against conviction, then the material must be retained until the appeal is determined or (where applicable) the Criminal Cases Review Commission decides not to refer the case.[69]

Duty to reveal material

11.59 The code sets out the manner in which material is revealed to the prosecutor by the police – and, in turn, disclosed to the defendant and their legal representative. In short, the code requires the revelation of all relevant material to the prosecutor and the listing of the irrelevant material in a schedule of unused or sensitive material.[70]

11.60 Notably, the failure of a police officer to comply with the code does not in and of itself render that officer liable to any criminal or civil proceedings. However, if it appears to a court or tribunal conducting criminal or civil proceedings that any failure is relevant to any question arising in the

66 Code of Practice, para 3.5.
67 Code of Practice, para 4.4.
68 Code of Practice, paras 5.4–5.5.
69 Code of Practice, paras 5.7–5.10.
70 Code of Practice, sections 6–10.

proceedings, then the court or tribunal will take it into account when deciding the question.[71]

Other codes of practice

Management of Police Information Code of Practice 2005[72]

11.61 This code is universally known as MOPI, and is a statutory code of practice issued by the Home Secretary pursuant to Police Act 1996 ss39 and 39A and a number of sections of the Police Act 1997.

11.62 The purpose of MOPI is to ensure that there is broad consistency between police forces in the way information is managed within the law, to ensure effective use of available information within and between individual police forces and other agencies, and to provide fair treatment to members of the public.[73]

11.63 The code emphasises that responsibility for the management and use of information within the police service rests with the chief officer of the police force which owns the information.[74]

11.64 Information is held by the police for 'policing purposes', and these are defined in the code as:

- protecting life and property;
- preserving order;
- preventing the commission of offences;
- bringing offenders to justice; and
- any duty or responsibility of the police arising from common or statute law.

11.65 MOPI sets out some broad principles in relation to the management of information by the police, which is then developed in detailed guidance sanctioned in MOPI (see below). The principles encompass obtaining and recording information, ensuring accuracy, whether it is necessary to retain information, sharing the information between forces and other agencies.

11.66 MOPI states that when information is recorded 'the source of the information, the nature of the source, any assessment of the reliability of the source, and any necessary restrictions on the use to be made of the information' should be recorded to permit later review, reassessment and audit.[75]

11.67 Importantly, MOPI states that information recorded must be 'reviewed at intervals to be prescribed in guidance under this Code, which may prescribe different intervals for different categories of information'.[76] The purpose of review is to consider whether information recorded for police

71 CPIA 1996 s26. See, for example, *R v Jackson (Christopher)* [2003] EWCA Crim 1793.

72 https://library.college.police.uk/docs/APPref/Management-of-Police-Information.pdf. At the time of writing a consultation into a new *Code of Practice for Information and Records Management* to replace the 2005 Code of Practice has been completed: https://assets.college.police.uk/s3fs-public/information-and-records-managementfurther-information.pdf.

73 MOPI para 1.1.4.

74 MOPI para 1.1.2.

75 MOPI para 4.3.2.

76 MOPI para 4.5.1.

purposes should be deleted or retained. At each review, the likelihood that the information will be used for police purposes should be taken into account.

11.68 MOPI explains that guidance may be issued which may specify a protocol for sharing information. In general the content and the assessment of the reliability of information recorded for police purposes should be made available to any other police force in England and Wales which requires the information for police purposes.[77]

11.69 In relation to sharing information with other agencies in England and Wales, the general approach (absent any statutory obligations) is said to be that the chief officer must be satisfied that it is reasonable and lawful to do so for the police purposes set out in MOPI.[78]

11.70 The guidance referred to in MOPI is found in an Authorised Professional Practice (APP) on 'Information Management / Management of Police Information / Retention, review and disposal' publication by the College of Policing.[79] The guidance covers collection and recording of information, evaluation, the need for common process, and the retention, review and disposal of information. It is this last which is often of most importance in this area: in what circumstances will the police decide to retain or dispose of information which has already been recorded.

11.71 The section of the APP which relates to collecting and recording information has detailed guidance as to the various purposes for which information is collected and recorded. Crime recording is perhaps the most likely area of interest for those wishing to challenge the information held by the police. The APP notes the National Crime Recording Standard (NCRS), which has three standard principles:

1) The police register an incident report for all reports of incidents (whether from victims, witnesses or third parties and whether crime related or not).
2) An incident is recorded as a crime (notifiable offence) if, on the balance of probability:
   - the circumstances as reported amount to a crime defined by law; and
   - there is no credible evidence to the contrary.
3) Once recorded, a crime remains so unless there is additional verifiable information to disprove it.

11.72 The APP discusses other systems under which information can be recorded, such as custody systems which retain a person's personal and arrest details, the reports of any incidents reported to the police and more specialised purposes for retaining information such as the national firearms licensing management system.

11.73 Under whatever format or area the information is held, the APP states that certain principles must be considered. As well as ensuring that a record is only created for a policing purpose (see para 11.11) and complies

77 MOPI para 4.7.

78 MOPI para 4.8.

79 See: www.college.police.uk/app/information-management/management-police-information/retention-review-and-disposal. Updated 23 November 2021.

with data protection principles, there are more practical principles designed to ensure there is an audit trail, that duplication is avoided and that there are links made with other relevant information held about a person, and where appropriate, the source of the information should be recorded.

11.74 The APP notes that the relevant data protection principles are reflected in DPA 2018 Part 3 Chapter 2 at ss37–39, and include requirements for the information held to be accurate, adequate and relevant. A police force is required to have an Information Charter (or privacy notice) to inform individuals of the types of personal data they process, the purposes for which they are processed, and any recipients it may be disclosed to.[80]

11.75 The requirement for common process is essentially a requirement for information to be held in a format which allows sharing with other forces. This is especially important in situations where public protection is engaged. The APP states:

> *Common processes for managing police information*
>
> **Public protection**
>
> In this context, public protection refers to offenders who have been convicted of serious sexual or violent offences and who are the subject of extended supervision or registration arrangements. Public protection also includes potentially dangerous people who may not have been convicted of serious offences, but whose behaviour causes significant concern about their risk of serious offending in the future.

11.76 Certain types of information are highlighted:

- Information relating to all offenders who have been managed under multi-agency public protection arrangements (MAPPA).
- Information relating to individuals who have been convicted, acquitted, arrested, questioned, charged or implicated in relation to murder, a serious offence as specified in the Criminal Justice Act 2003, or historical offences that would be charged as such if committed today.
- Potentially dangerous people, ie, those who have not been convicted of, or cautioned for, any offence of a sexual or violent nature and who do not fall within any of the MAPPA categories. Their behaviour, however, gives reasonable grounds for believing that there is a real likelihood of them committing an offence or offences likely to cause serious harm.

11.77 Advisers concerned with how a particular force applies the APP in practice should note that each force must have an information management strategy (IMS) as required by the Code of Practice which sets out the principles for information management within a force. It should also be made publicly available.

11.78 Retention, review and disposal of information held by the police is a key element of the information management regime. As the APP states:

> Retaining information relating to offending behaviour helps forces to prevent and detect crime and to protect the public. However, retaining

80 For example, the Metropolitan Police privacy notice is at: www.met.police.uk/privacy-notice/.

every piece of information collected is impractical and unlawful. Consideration must be given to the types of information that need to be retained, the length of that retention and the practical implications of storing these records in their various formats.[81]

11.79 The APP recognises the large number of statutory obligations and standards against which processing of information has to be considered, all of which have been referred to in this book. The full list made is as follows:

- MOPI Code of Practice 2005;
- DPA 2018;
- HRA 1998;
- CPIA 1996;
- Protection of Freedoms Act 2012;
- Regulation of Investigatory Powers Act 2000;
- Freedom of Information Act (FOIA) 2000;
- other codes, such as the code of practice on the management of records issued under FOIA 2000 s46; and the Surveillance Camera Code of Practice 2013.

11.80 These are the statutes which underpin police decisions on whether to retain or dispose of information which is held. These decisions are made as part of a review process in which National Retention Assessment Criteria (NRAC) are applied. The NRAC asks a series of questions focused on potential risk factors, to enable reasonable conclusions to be reached about the risk of harm presented by a person, and to decide whether the retention of the record is necessary and proportionate for the purpose for which it is retained. The NRAC questions are as follows:

- Is there evidence of a capacity to inflict serious harm?
- Are there any concerns in relation to children or vulnerable adults?
- Did the behaviour involve a breach of trust?
- Is there evidence of established links or associations which might increase the risk of harm?
- Are there concerns in relation to substance misuse?
- Are there concerns that an individual's mental state might exacerbate risk?
- Are there any other issues that impact on the level of risk the individual presents?
- Could this individual be of interest to ongoing public inquires?[82]

11.81 The APP advises that where the answer to any of these questions is 'yes' and the risks are still current, then information about the person should be retained and considered at scheduled reviews, but with the safeguard that the records should be up to date and adequate.

11.82 However, when completing a NRAC template for retaining information, the APP also states that there are other key points to consider as follows:

- The infringement of an individual's privacy caused by retaining their personal information must satisfy the proportionality test.

81 APP under 'Retention'.

82 APP under 'National retention assessment criteria'.

- Records that are accurate, relevant, up to date and necessary for policing purposes are held for the minimum period designated by the appropriate MOPI group. This helps to ensure that forces have sufficient information to identify offending patterns over time, and to guard against individuals' efforts to avoid detection for lengthy periods.

11.83 The guidance also says that if information is to be kept beyond a designated period (see below), 'there is a requirement to review whether it is still necessary to keep the record for a policing purpose'.[83]

11.84 After the initial decision to retain information, there are two kinds of review in relation to the retention of information (other than information and records held on the PNC: see below para 11.123 for the process of applying for PNC deletions other than court convictions).

11.85 A 'triggered' review[84] will take place where there are concerns about the adequacy, relevance or accuracy of a record that have surfaced during, for example, Disclosure and Barring Service (DBS) checks (see 11.150), FOI checks, subject access requests (SAR) (see para 11.90) or requests for deletion of information. The APP states that:

> Basic checks should be conducted prior to disclosure to ensure that the information being provided is accurate, relevant and of sufficient quality. ... any significant issues identified should instigate a triggered review of the record and any updates must be adequately documented for audit purposes.

Thus if the SAR reveals information which a person believes should no longer be retained by the police, then it should be checked that a triggered review has been, or will be, carried out by the police.[85]

11.86 A 'scheduled' review is one which will take place from time to time depending into which of the four groups defined in the APP the information falls. The review schedules apply to information related to people convicted, acquitted, charged, arrested, questioned or implicated with an offence within the relevant group:[86]

1) Group 1 contains the most serious offences and public protection matters where the information will be retained until the person has reached 100 years of age, although there will be a review every 10 years to ensure adequacy and necessity and that retention is justified.
2) Group 2 contains information relating to sexual, violent or serious offences that are not listed as serious specified offences in the Criminal Justice Act 2003 and can be retained only for as long as the offender or suspected offender continues to be assessed as posing a risk of harm, using the NRAC (see above at para 11.80). After every 10-year clear period, these records should be reviewed and a risk-based decision should be made on whether they should be disposed of or retained.
3) Group 3 contains records relating to people who are convicted, acquitted, charged, arrested, questioned or implicated for offending behaviour that does not fall within group 1 or group 2. These records are

83 APP under 'National retention assessment criteria'.
84 APP under 'Triggered reviews'.
85 APP under 'Triggered reviews'.
86 APP under 'Management of Police Information groups'.

retained for an initial six-year clear period, followed by subsequent five-year clear period reviews.

11.87 A clear period is defined in the APP as 'the length of time since a person last came to the attention of the criminal justice system as an offender or suspected offender for behaviour that can be considered a relevant risk factor'.[87]

11.88 For advisers wanting to be sure that the necessary reviews have been carried out and the reasons for continued retention of information, there is a requirement for the review process (triggered or scheduled) to be documented through a template which sets out the NRAC criteria. If data is retained, then a record must be kept as to how the individual in question meets the outlined risk criteria.

Finding out what information is held

11.89 Requests for information under the DPA 2018 and FOIA 2000 are a valuable tool for building a civil claim, of any of the kinds described in this book. Both mechanisms for accessing information allow a prospective claimant and their legal representatives to obtain information that otherwise might not be available until after issue of proceedings or by way of Part 18 requests for further information.

11.90 A request under the DPA 2018 (commonly known as a 'subject access request' or SAR) is particularly useful. The data subject has a right to obtain confirmation that a police force is processing their data and, if so, to request access to that data.[88] As such, a well targeted request can bolster the accuracy of advice to a prospective claimant on the merits of their claim, for example by revealing at an early stage the extent to which a claimant's case is supported by the records held by the police about the claimant. In turn, this can assist the prospective claimant's legal representatives in assessing whether the prospective claim is suitable for public funding from the Legal Aid Agency (LAA) (see chapter 14) or by way of a conditional fee arrangement (CFA).

11.91 In addition, if the claimant is concerned about the accuracy or amount of the information held by the police or the use to which it might be put, then securing access to personal data under the DPA 2018 is often the essential first step enabling the data subject to subsequently exercise their other rights to rectification, erasure or restriction on processing.

11.92 Both the DPA 2018 and FOIA 2000 are technical and complex pieces of legislation. What follows is, therefore, a summary overview of the key provisions.

87 APP under 'Clear periods'.

88 DPA 2018 ss43 and 45. Please note the right does not encompass 'personal data contained in a judicial decision or in other documents relating to an investigation or proceedings created by or on behalf of a court of other judicial authority': s43(4).

Data Protection Act 2018

The right of access

11.93 A right to access data is of little use if the data subject does not know that their personal data is being processed by the data controller. To combat this, the DPA 2018 places an obligation on the data controller (eg the relevant police force) to make certain information 'generally available to the public', for example as a page on the data controller's website – including the identity and the contact details of the controller and the contact details of the data protection officer.[89]

11.94 The right of access by a data subject is contained in DPA 2018 s45, and can only be exercised against a data controller. In short, the data subject is entitled to obtain from the controller a) confirmation as to whether or not personal data concerning them is being processed and b) if so, access to the personal data and the following information:

- the purposes of and legal basis of the processing;
- the type of personal data concerned;
- the recipients or categories of recipients to whom the personal data has been disclosed (including third countries or international organisations);
- the period for which it is envisaged that the personal data will be stored or, where that is not possible, the criteria used to determine that period;
- the existence of the data subject's right of rectification of personal data and right of erasure or personal data or restriction of its processing;
- the existence of the data subject's right to lodge a complaint with the Information Commissioner and the contact details of the Commissioner; and
- the communication of the personal data undergoing processing and of any available information as to its origin.

Restrictions on the right of access

11.95 Both the obligation on data controllers to inform data subjects of their rights and a data subject's right to access are not absolute. The obligation and right can be wholly or partially restricted where (in the view of the data controller) it is a 'necessary and proportionate'[90] measure to:

- avoid obstructing an official or legal inquiry, investigation or procedure;
- avoid prejudicing the prevention, detection, investigation or prosecution of criminal offences or the execution of criminal penalties;
- protect public security or national security; or
- protect the rights and freedoms of others.

11.96 In making this assessment, the data controller must have regard to the fundamental rights and legitimate interests of the data subject.[91] As a matter of reality, therefore, the police have considerable discretion to limit

89 DPA 2018 s44(1)–(2).

90 DPA 2018 ss44(4), 45(4).

91 For a case where these respective issues were considered in a police case, see *Zaw Lin v Commissioner of Police of the Metropolis* [2015] EWHC 2484 (QB).

a data subject's access to information, especially, for example, if there is an ongoing criminal investigation.

11.97 This is somewhat mitigated by the obligation on a data controller to inform the data subject in writing and without undue delay that the provision of information or rights of the data subject have been restricted and the reasons for that restriction. This obligation applies unless the provision of the information would undermine the purpose of the restriction,[92] in which case the data subject would receive a 'neither confirm nor deny' response as to whether the information is held or not. As a safeguard, the data controller must inform the data subject of i) their right to ask the Information Commissioner to review whether the restriction imposed by the controller was lawful; ii) the data subject's right to lodge a complaint with the Information Commissioner;[93] and iii) the data subject's right to apply to a court for an order requiring the data controller to provide further information.[94]

11.98 In addition, where a data controller considers that a request is 'manifestly unfounded or excessive',[95] then the controller can charge a 'reasonable fee'[96] for dealing with it or, even, refuse the request altogether. Both 'manifestly unfounded' and 'excessive' are undefined in the statute. DPA 2018 s53(2) provides one example of a potentially excessive request, namely one that 'merely repeats the substance of previous requests'. The threshold for a 'manifestly ill-founded or excessive' claim is high and the burden rests on the data controller to demonstrate that the threshold has been met when refusing a request on that basis.[97]

Making a data subject request

11.99 It follows that a legal representative will be concerned with formulating the SAR in such a way as to reduce the likelihood of the data controller restricting the data subject's access to information and/or rejecting the request outright. The DPA 2018 does not stipulate any formalities for making a subject access request. However, legal representatives should anticipate any potential objections from the data controller by:

- putting the request in writing and expressly stating that the request is being made pursuant to DPA 2018 s45;

92 For example, where unbeknown to the data subject they are under investigation by the law enforcement agency and in the latter's view to disclose the fact of processing would prejudice that investigation.

93 DPA 2018 s51.

94 DPA 2018 s167. The data controller must record the reasons for a decision to restrict (whether wholly or partly) the provision of information to a data subject and/or the rights of a data subject and, if requested to do so by the Commissioner, make that record available to the Commissioner for scrutiny.

95 DPA 2018 s53.

96 A 'reasonable fee' is one that takes into account the administrative costs of providing the information (eg the cost of reproducing any document containing the information or postage fees): see Freedom of Information and Data Protection (Appropriate Limit and Fees) Regulations 2004 SI No 3244 reg 6.

97 For example, in the event the data subject challenges the data controller's refusal of their request on this basis and requests the Information Commissioner reviews the decision.

- providing detailed identification information (eg full name, date of birth and residency address) and, if the data subject is willing, copies of supporting documents as proof of identification and address (eg passport, driving licence, bills from the last three months); this should prevent delay to the deadline in which the data controller must respond (see below);
- where possible, focussing the data request (eg by time period, specific criminal investigation or specific police database) to mitigate the risk that the data controller will consider the request 'excessive';
- offering to pay a reasonable fee, if it is otherwise likely that the data controller will consider the request 'excessive';
- requesting a specific method of communication by which the data subject wishes to receive a response and, where applicable, providing the relevant postal and/or email address;[98]
- where applicable, the data subject could also ask for the communication in a particular format that takes into consideration any disability they may have – for instance, a partially sighted data subject may wish to ask for data in an electronic format enlarged to a particular font size and/or for the information to be provided orally.

11.100 Although these are all useful factors to take into account, it is very likely that the police force concerned will have a specific SAR form which can be completed online.[99] If a data subject wishes to know what information is held by the police on national police records, like the PNC, then the application needs to be made to the Criminal Records Office (known as ACRO) which has its own application form.[100]

The data controller's response

11.101 When a data controller accepts and provides personal data in response to a request, then it must take reasonable steps to ensure it is in a concise, intelligible and easily accessible form, using clear and plain language.[101] A data controller must respond to a request for access to information within one month beginning from the date upon which the controller received the request.[102] In the event the controller requests further information to verify a data subject's identity and/or a fee, then the one month time

98 DPA 2018 s52(2)–(3) provides that the response may be provided in any form, including electronically and, where it is practicable to do so, the data controller must also provide the information in the same form as the request.

99 See, for example, the Metropolitan Police form which can be accessed at: www.met.police.uk/rqo/request/ri/request-information/rso/request-information-about-yourself-or-someone-else/id-like-to-request-information-about-myself/?lid=&cid=&rid=11230&stepid=1-1.

100 See: www.acro.police.uk/Subject-access#:~:text=You%20have%20the%20right%20to,contact%20the%20relevant%20force%20directly.

101 DPA 2018 s52.

102 DPA 2018 s54.

period begins from the date upon which that information or fee was received.[103]

Enforcement

11.102 Where a data subject is dissatisfied with the response of the data controller – for example, where the request has been deemed 'manifestly unfounded or excessive', or where the data subject is informed that the right to access has been wholly or partially restricted – then they may request that the Information Commissioner checks that the refusal or restriction was lawful. The Information Commissioner has statutory powers to a) require that a data controller provides the Commissioner with information reasonably needed for the purposes of investigating the data subject's request (known as an 'information notice') and b) permits the Commissioner to carry out an on-site assessment, during which the data controller must, among other things, direct the Commissioner to relevant documents (known as an 'assessment notice').[104]

11.103 If the Commissioner determines that the refusal or restriction was unlawful, then they have a suite of powers available under DPA 2018 Part 6, including enforcement notices requiring the data controller to take specified steps (ie to provide the information requested by the data subject) and monetary penalties.

11.104 If the Commissioner determines that the refusal or restriction was lawful, then the data subject can appeal that decision to the First-tier Tribunal within 28 calendar days. The data subject can also apply to the First-tier Tribunal if the Information Commissioner does not respond to their complaint or has not provided the data subject with information about the progress of the complaint within three months.[105]

Freedom of Information Act 2000

11.105 FOIA 2000 s1 confers an entitlement on any person making a request for information to a public authority to be informed in writing by the public authority whether it holds the information in the description specified in the request ('the duty to confirm or deny') and, if that is the case, to have that information communicated. This provision applies to all criminal justice bodies including a police and crime commissioner, the Mayor's Office for Policing and Crime, a chief officer of a police force in England or Wales, the British Transport Police, the Ministry of Defence Police and the Independent Office for Police Conduct (IOPC).[106] The entitlement

103 Please note that the one month time limit was accurate at the date of publication. The DPA 2018 contains provision for the secretary of state to make regulations specifying a period of up to three months. Therefore, legal representatives must check the current time limit when advising clients.

104 See of the DPA 2018 ss142–145 (regarding information notices) and ss146–147 (regarding assessment notices).

105 DPA 2018 s166.

106 FOIA 2000 Parts V and VI, Sch 1.

applies to information held by public authority at the time when the request is received.[107]

11.106 Where the information that is sought by an individual is personal data in relation to the individual, the material is exempt from the access requirements of the FOIA 2000.[108] The intention is that access to personal information relating to the applicant is governed by the DPA 2018 rather than the FOIA 2000; the latter is intended to cover information that is not personal in nature to the requester.

11.107 The FOIA 2000 will also have limited applicability where the information required relates directly to other individuals. Information will be exempt from the rights of access conferred by the FOIA 2000 if it constitutes personal data relating to a person other than the applicant and to disclose it to the applicant would contravene the DPA 2018 principles; or where the information would be covered by an exemption provision of the DPA 2018,[109] or where the subject of the information has objected to the processing of their data.[110] The rationale for this provision is to restrict the circumstances in which an individual may use the FOIA 2000 to obtain information about others – a balance has to be struck between rights of access and third parties' rights of privacy.

11.108 Information relating to policing that would not be caught by the personal data exemptions from the FOIA 2000 (discussed above) could include, for example, material concerning:

- force policies, plans and priorities;
- statistical information, for example concerning detection rates, personpower or costings;
- police officers and employees, provided the information related to their public activities;
- organisation of the police force;
- individuals no longer alive; and
- minutes and accompanying documentation of certain meetings.

Exemptions

11.109 There are two bases upon which a public authority can refuse to engage with a request. First, FOIA 2000 s12 permits a public authority to refuse any request which would cost more than £450 to process, calculated at a rate of £25p/h for 18 hours' work.[111] The section is best understood as 'a guillotine' designed to prevent the 'burden of the public authority from becoming too onerous under the Act'.[112] That fee *does not* include the cost

107 Subject to any amendments or deletions that would have occurred between the date of the receipt of the request and the date upon which the information is communicated, irrespective of the receipt of the FOIA 2000 request.

108 FOIA 2000 s40.

109 FOIA 2000 s40.

110 FOIA 2000 s40(3B) and UK GDPR Article 21.

111 Accurate on the date of publication. See Freedom of Information and Data Protection (Appropriate Limit and Fees) Regulations 2004 SI No 3244 reg 3.

112 *Quinn v Information Commissioner*, EA/2006/0010 at 50. The cost estimate must be 'sensible, realistic and supported by cogent evidence': *Randall v Information Commissioner* EA/2007/004 at 12. See also *Kirkham v Information Commissioner* [2018] UKUT (ACC) at 26.

of redaction of names (FOIA 2000 s4(3)(d)), but *does* include the costs that the public authority has incurred for not collating or storing information efficiently.[113] The local authority must consider separately the cost of the duty to confirm or deny, and the cost of the provision of information (with the latter more likely to exceed the £450 limit, than the former). This means that any requests should be as focused and specific as possible.

11.110 Second, FOIA 2000 s14 allows the public authority to refuse 'vexatious or repeated requests'[114] and is generally used by public authorities which have been overburdened with requests about a particular subject matter.

11.111 In addition, there are 23 types of 'exempt information' which may fall outside the applicant's entitlement to request information. These exemptions fall into two broad categories: a) absolute exemptions and b) qualified exemptions.[115] In short, where an absolute exemption applies the public authority can automatically withhold information.[116] Where a qualified exemption applies, then the public authority must apply a 'public interest test' before deciding whether to disclose the information.

11.112 In this context and put simply, the public interest test requires the public authority to weigh the public interest in maintaining the exemption against the public interest in disclosure. The public authority must consider the public interest test separately in relation to the duty to confirm or deny and to the disclosure of the requested information. The Information Commissioner's Office publishes on its website a detailed and useful guidance document entitled *The public interest test* setting out how the test operates, which should be consulted when making a request and/or challenging a public authority's refusal to disclose information.[117]

11.113 For the purposes of this chapter it is not possible to explore all 23 exemptions. However, the exemptions likely to be most relevant to the policing context are the two interlinked[118] exemptions contained in FOIA 2000 ss30 and 31.[119] The exemptions are both qualified[120] and so require consideration of the public interest test by the public authority. By way of brief summary, the exemptions provide the following:

- *The investigations and proceedings conducted by public authorities' exemption.* FOIA 2000 s30 is concerned with information obtained or

113 *Commissioner of Police of the Metropolis v Information Commissioner* [2014] UKUT 479 (ACC) at 37.

114 *Dransfield v Information Commissioner* [2015] EWCA Civ 454, see para 68 and Annex.

115 See FOIA 2000 s2 for a complete list of the exemptions and which category they fall under.

116 For example, information supplied to the public authority by specified security agencies: FOIA 2000 s23.

117 At: https://ico.org.uk/media/for-organisations/documents/1183/the_public_interest_test.pdf.

118 For an exposition of the differences between the two exemptions, see *England v Bexley LBC and The Information Commissioner,* [2007] UKIT EA/2006/0060, 10 May 2007 at 23–27.

119 FOIA 2000 Part II should be consulted in its entirety when advising a person considering an information request. Other potentially relevant exemptions include s21 (information accessible to the applicant by other means), s24 (national security), s32 (court records), s38 (health and safety) and s40 (personal information).

120 FOIA 2000 s36 is absolute only insofar as it relates to information held by the House of Commons or House of Lords, which is not relevant for present purposes.

recorded by the public authority for the purpose of a *specific* investigation or criminal proceedings conducted by it, or that relates to the obtaining of information from confidential sources. Section 30(1) exempts information held by the public authority *at any time* for the purposes of: a) any investigation which it has a duty to carry out with a view to it being ascertained whether a person should be charged with or is guilty of an offence; b) an investigation which may lead to a decision to institute criminal proceedings; or c) for the conduct of criminal proceedings. Section 30(2) also exempts, among other things, information obtained for civil proceedings and that relates to confidential sources. Section 30 is a class-based exemption, which means that the local authority does not need to demonstrate that disclosure would prejudice the investigation or proceedings in order to satisfy the public interest test and rely on the exemption. In other words and by way of example, the exemption can apply despite the police having decided years previously not to prosecute or refer to the CPS for a charging decision.[121]

- *The law enforcement exemption.* FOIA 2000 s31(1) exempts information where disclosure would, or would be likely to, prejudice the prevention or detection of crime; the apprehension or prosecution of offenders; the administration of justice; the assessment or collection of any tax or duty; the operation of immigration controls; the maintenance of 'security and good order' in prison or other detention institutions; or the exercise by any public authority of functions for ten specified purposes or civil proceedings brought for the same ten specified purposes.[122]

Making an information request

11.114 In contrast to the DPA 2018, the FOIA 2000 specifies how a person should make a request for information. Pursuant to FOIA 2000 s8, a request must be in writing (by email or post), state the name of the applicant and an address for correspondence, and describe the information requested. Many people make their request through the WhatDoTheyKnow website which provides links to the public authorities covered by the FOIA 2000.[123] In addition:

- Where possible, an applicant should focus the request for information (eg by time period, specific criminal investigation or specific police database) to mitigate the risk that the public authority will consider that the cost of compliance would exceed the appropriate limit and/or that the request is 'vexatious'.
- An applicant may wish to invite the public authority to exercise its duty under FOIA 2000 s16 to 'provide [reasonable] advice and assistance' in formulating the request. Including this invitation can be particularly

121 See *Prince v Information Commissioner and Devon CC* [2017] UKFTT 2017/0066 (GRC) at 17.

122 The specified purposes are set out in FOIA 2000 s31(2). The purposes are broad, including, for instance, ascertaining whether any person 'has failed to comply with the law' or 'is responsible for any conduct which is improper'.

123 See: www.whatdotheyknow.com/.

useful when the applicant lacks sufficient information to narrow their request.

- If possible and/or appropriate in the particular case, an applicant can offer to pay a reasonable fee – again to mitigate the risk that the public authority will consider the cost of compliance would exceed the appropriate limit and/or in a case where the public authority is likely to request a fee.[124]
- The applicant can express a preference for communication by one of the following means: a) a copy of the information in a specific form (permanent or otherwise); b) the provision of a reasonable opportunity to inspect the record containing the information; or c) the provision of a digest or summary in a specific form (permanent or otherwise).[125] FOIA 2000 s11 provides that where an applicant expresses one of these preferences, then the public authority 'shall so far as reasonably practicable give effect to that preference'.[126]
- The applicant can request that specific documents are provided. While the entitlements conferred by FOIA 2000 are in relation to 'information' 'recorded in any form', rather than 'documents' or 'records',[127] the Court of Appeal has recognised that 'information' must be broadly construed and that there will be cases where a public authority needs to provide a copy of a document in order to comply with a request for information.[128]

The public authority's response

11.115 As a general rule, the public authority must comply with a request for information promptly and in any event not later than the twentieth working day following the date of receipt.[129] However, in the event the public authority reasonably requires and requests further information to identify and locate the information,[130] then the time limit begins from the date upon which that information as received. Where the public authority charges a fee to the applicant, the period between the fee notice being given and the fee being paid are disregarded for the purposes of

124 The public authority may charge a fee for the disclosure of information, by giving the applicant a written 'fees notice' specifying the amount to be charged. There is no statutory cap on a 'maximum fee'. The public authority can take into account the reasonable administrative costs of providing the information (eg the cost of reproducing any document containing the information or postage fees): see Freedom of Information and Data Protection (Appropriate Limit and Fees) Regulations 2004 SI No 3244 reg 6.

125 The right to express a preference for a particular '*form*' of communication extends to selecting the particular software format (eg Excel files): *Innes v Information Commissioner* [2014] EWCA Civ 1086, [2015] 2 All ER 560 at 37.

126 If the local authority determines it is not reasonably practicable, then it is obliged to notify the applicant of the reasons for that determination.

127 Sections 1 and 84.

128 *Independent Parliamentary Standards Authority v The Information Commissioner and Ben Leapman* [2015] EWCA Civ 388 at paras 32–48.

129 This is accurate at the time of publication. However, please note that FOIA 2000 s10(4) confers a power on the Minister for the Cabinet Officer to extend this period by regulations up to the sixtieth working day.

130 FOIA 2000 s1(3) read with s10.

calculating the time limit.[131] Where the public authority relies upon a qualified exemption, then the time limit is extended 'until such a time as is reasonable in the circumstances' for the purpose of conducting the public interest balancing exercise.[132]

11.116 Where the public authority refuses a request for information it must provide its justifications in a 'section 17 notice'.[133] That notice varies depending on which exemption(s) the public authority relies upon. However, it must, among other things, a) contain reasons for reliance on certain FOIA 2000 exemptions; b) contain details of any complaint procedure (or state that it does not have one); and c) contain details of the right to complain to the Information Commissioner. If the public authority fails to provide this information, then the applicant should send a letter requesting the required information as soon as possible.

Enforcement

11.117 Where a request for information has been refused by a public authority, there are four main options available:

1. *Offer to pay for the FOI request to be processed.* This is applicable if not already done so in the request itself and the local authority relies on FOIA 2000 s12.
2. *Refine the FOI request and/or make a second request.* Some public authorities may seek to rely on FOIA 2000 s14 in response, which does not oblige a public authority to comply with a request for information which is identical or substantially similar to a previous request (see above). However, properly construed, section 14 is a narrow provision that should not be used to 'prevent a requester from narrowing the focus of a second request in order to pursue a particular line of enquiry'.[134]
3. *Request an internal review by the public authority.* The Freedom of Information Code of Practice issued by the Minister for the Cabinet Office states that it is best practice for public authorities to provide 'internal review' procedures for dealing with disputes about the handling by them of requests for information.[135] It is usual practice to accept a request for an internal review made within 40 working days from the date a public authority has issued an initial response to a request and public authorities are not obliged to accept internal reviews after this date. Requests for internal review should be acknowledged and the applicant informed of the target date for responding. This should normally be within twenty working days of receipt – although it can take considerably longer. The internal review should be undertaken by a different person to the individual(s) who initially handled the request and should 're-evaluate' the request, including any public interest decision. The outcome of the review will be communicated to the applicant in writing. If the reviewer decides that the request was

131 FOIA 2000 s10(2).

132 *Prior v Information Commissioner*, [2006] UKIT EA/2005/0017.

133 FOIA 2000 s17.

134 *Thackeray v Information Commissioner's Office*, [2012] UKFFT EA/2011/0082 (GRC) at 26.

135 Freedom of Information Code of Practice, 4 July 2018, pp21–22. Available at:www.gov.uk/government/publications/freedom-of-information-code-of-practice.

wrongly rejected and, accordingly, that the information should be disclosed, then that information should normally be provided at the same time as the applicant is informed of the outcome of the review.

4. *Complain to the Information Commissioner.* If the internal review is unsuccessful, then the applicant can complain to the Information Commissioner.[136] The Information Commissioner will consider the merits of a request for information and any reliance on the public interest. In so doing, the Information Commissioner is entitled to make their own enquiries and to formulate a case on behalf of the applicant. At the end of the process, the Information Commissioner will publish a decision notice on the ICO website (www.ico.org.uk) and can require the public authority to disclose information, usually within 35 days. If the local authority does not comply, then the Information Commissioner has the power to issue an enforcement notice (a notice requiring positive action with a deadline for doing so backed by the sanctions of monetary penalties and/or High Court contempt proceedings). If the Information Commissioner decides in favour of the public authority, then an appeal to the First-Tier Tribunal can be considered (which can conduct a further full merits assessment). It is worth noting that a public authority is entitled to invoke any exemption not previously relied upon in reaching its decision, including that processing the request would exceed the cost limit.[137]

11.118 The first three options can be pursued concurrently. The fourth option can only be pursued once any internal complaints procedure has been exhausted.

Applying to delete or amend information held by the police

Retention

11.119 The powers for the police to retain information are sometimes set out in statute. Thus, police powers to take and retain DNA samples and fingerprints are set out in PACE. The most common circumstance for taking DNA and fingerprints is when a person is arrested.

11.120 PACE also includes the requirement for the DNA *sample* obtained by the police to be immediately destroyed once the DNA *profile* has been obtained and no later than six months after it was taken, except in cases where the sample is needed as evidence for court. PACE allows the police to indefinitely retain the biometric information of individuals convicted of a recordable offence.[138] An exception is made for persons under 18 where certain provisions are met.

11.121 In most cases where a person is not convicted, PACE states that police cannot retain the biometric information (DNA samples and fingerprints). This applies to people who are charged but not convicted of a minor

136 FOIA 2000 s50.

137 *DEFRA v Information Commissioner* [2011] EWCA Civ 1606.

138 However, the ECtHR judgment in the case of *Gaughran v UK* App 45245/15 (2020) Times, 22 April indicates that the blanket use of this power is unlawful.

offence or arrested but not charged with a qualifying offence. The biometric information to be immediately deleted unless, in respect of the latter, an application to retain the information is made to the Biometrics Commissioner under PACE s63G.

11.122 Code D of the PACE Codes of Practice provides a table which explains the statutory retention periods for fingerprints and DNA,[139] reproduced below. The retention period depends on the outcome of the investigation of the recordable offence in connection with which the fingerprints and DNA samples was taken, the age of the person at the time the offence was committed and whether the recordable offence is a qualifying offence and whether it is an excluded offence.[140] A 'recordable' offence is one for which the police are required to keep a record. Generally speaking, these are imprisonable offences; however, it also includes a number of non-imprisonable offences such as begging and taxi touting. A 'qualifying' offence is one listed under PACE s65A (the list comprises sexual, violent, terrorism and burglary offences). An 'excluded' offence is a recordable offence which is not a qualifying offence, was committed when the individual was under 18, for which they received a sentence of fewer than 5 years imprisonment and is the only recordable offence for which the person has been convicted.

Table – Retention periods

(a) Convictions

Age when offence committed	Outcome	Retention period
Any age	Convicted or given a caution or youth caution for a recordable offence which is also a qualifying offence	INDEFINITE
18 or over	Convicted or given a caution for a recordable offence which is NOT a qualifying offence	INDEFINITE
Under 18	Convicted or given a youth caution for a recordable offence which is NOT a qualifying offence	1st conviction or youth caution – 5 years plus length of any prison sentence. Indefinite if prison sentence 5 years or more. 2nd conviction or youth caution: Indefinite

139 PACE Code D, pp49–50.

140 See PACE ss63D–63L for full details.

(b) Non-convictions

Age when offence committed	Outcome	Retention period
Any age	Charged but not convicted of a recordable qualifying offence	3 years plus a 2 year extension if granted by a District Judge (or indefinite if the individual has a previous conviction for a recordable offence which is not excluded)
Any age	Arrested for, but not charged with, a recordable qualifying offence	3 years if granted by the Biometrics Commissioner plus a 2 year extension if granted by a District Judge (or indefinite if the individual has a previous conviction for a recordable offence which is not excluded)
Any age	Arrested for or charged with a recordable offence which is not a qualifying offence.	Indefinite if the person has a previous conviction for a recordable offence which is not excluded otherwise NO RETENTION)
18 or over	Given Penalty Notice for Disorder for recordable offence	2 years

11.123 The National Police Chiefs' Council (NPCC) has issued guidance entitled *Deletion of records from national police systems* which outlines the national process for record deletion in respect of records held on the PNC, the NDNAD and the National Fingerprints Database (IDENT1)[141] with the purpose of ensuring that police forces take a consistent approach to applications for deletions under these three national police systems.

11.124 The guidance has an unusual statutory status as it constitutes statutory guidance issued by the National DNA Database Strategy Board in relation to the destruction of DNA profiles, pursuant to PACE s63AB(2), but also covers, on a non-statutory basis, the deletion of DNA samples, fingerprints and PNC records. The guidance only covers records held on these national databases, and does not cover locally held records, custody photographs[142] (see below at para 11.136) or records held on the PND.

11.125 In effect, the guidance outlines circumstances in which the police should consider the deletion of data held in central records in circumstances where they would otherwise have the power to retain it. For example, as explained at para 11.127, there are set periods for the retention of biometric data but it is possible, nevertheless, to make an application for deletion before that period comes to an end.

11.126 The general approach in relation to PNC records is explained as follows:

> 1.5.5 Under this Guidance, PNC records are retained until a person is deemed to have reached 100 years of age. However, Chief Officers can exercise their discretion, in exceptional circumstances, to delete conviction records, specifically those relating to non-court disposals e.g. adult simple cautions and conditional cautions as well as any 'Event History' owned by

141 *Deletion of records from national police systems (PNC/NDNAD/IDENT1)*, 2018, www.acro.police.uk/ACRO/media/ACRO-Library/Deletion-of-Records-from-National-Police-Systems-(Guidance)-v2-1-April-2020.pdf.

142 Although the guidance says the deletion of custody photographs will be considered if there is a request for other records covered by the guidance.

them on the PNC but only where the grounds for so doing have been examined and agreed.

11.127 The guidance goes on to say that court convictions are not eligible for record deletion under the process set out in the guidance.[143] This includes conditional and absolute discharges.[144] In *R (QSA) v National Police Chiefs' Council*,[145] the Division Court decided that the importance of keeping a comprehensive record of convictions, was sufficiently important to the criminal justice system and other public services to justify interference with Article 8 rights by the application of the 100-year rule to a person's convictions. Convictions will only be removed if there is a successful appeal in the criminal courts. Applications for deletion are not considered if there is an ongoing investigation or prosecution.

11.128 In relation to biometric information, the guidance emphasises that there are statutory duties to delete information where it has been obtained as a result of an unlawful arrest, where the arrest was as a result of mistaken identity, or where a person was not arrested at the time the biometric information was taken.[146] In these circumstances, the guidance points out that deletion should be automatic and a request should not be necessary. It should be noted that where biometric information is deleted it may still be necessary to apply to have the associated PNC entry deleted, as otherwise it will be retained.

11.129 Although the national records are held and processed by local chief constables, and chief constables are the final decision-makers in relation to the retention and deletion of information and biometric records, any application for deletion should be sent to ACRO (the ACPO Criminal Records Office), and the Retention and Deletion Unit (RDU) at ACRO provides recommendations on applications to chief constables to seek to ensure that a consistent approach is applied to decision making across the various police forces.

11.130 In making an application for deletion, it is important to note that the guidance contains a list of examples where deletion should be considered.[147] Although the list is not exhaustive, it is very likely that an application on other grounds (outside any statutory requirements) will be refused.

11.131 As well as circumstances where it can be shown that biometric information was unlawfully taken, or there was a proven case of mistaken identity or it has been shown that an arrest was unlawful, there is a very limited list of examples. This includes where it has been established that there was 'no crime' (where, perhaps, a suspicious death is shown to be a death by natural causes), or where it has been shown that there was a malicious or false allegation. Where a person's status is unclear at the time of the arrest, and it transpires, for example, they were a victim and not a suspect, then deletion will be considered as will circumstances where a person can

143 Para 1.5.6.

144 Para 5.1.3.

145 [2021] EWHC 272 (Admin), [2021] 1 WLR 2962; and see *Chief Constable of Humberside v Information Commissioner (Secretary of State for the Home Department intervening)* [2009] EWCA Civ 1079, [2010] 1 WLR 1136.

146 See PACE ss63D and 63R.

147 Annex B.

establish an alibi, or where another person has been convicted of the offence.

11.132 If a case is found to have been disposed of incorrectly by administrative error or, for example, where a caution is reviewed and withdrawn, then a deletion application will be appropriate, and deletion must be considered where this is recommended by a court.

11.133 Finally, there is more of a 'catch-all' example, where deletion would be in the wider public interest, where matters such as the seriousness of the offence, level of culpability, and age of the offender are taken into account, although the public interest in deletion will be balanced against the usual approach of the police to retain national records.

11.134 Essentially, then, a successful applicant will most often need to show, with positive evidence, that they did not commit the offence for which they were arrested before deletion of biometric data and PNC records outside the statutory requirements in PACE will be considered. It is not enough simply to have been found not guilty of an offence, or for the file to be marked for 'no further action' (NFA), on the basis that there may be myriad reasons why such an outcome has occurred. Retention of information on the PNC in such circumstances can be in accordance with the DPA 2018 and also not breach a person's rights under ECHR Article 8.[148]

11.135 If an application is refused, then the guidance sets out provision for further representations to be made and considered.[149] If that is unsuccessful then an application can be made for judicial review, although the case law indicates a strong preference for retaining a full record of information on the PNC, other than in the examples set out in the guidance.

Custody photographs

11.136 PACE s64A provides police with the power to take facial photographs (known as 'custody images') of anyone who is detained following arrest. There are no statutory provisions which deal with the retention of custody images whether a person is charged with an offence or not and whether or not a charged person is then acquitted.

11.137 In 2012, the Divisional Court ruled that the retention of images from unconvicted individuals under the Metropolitan Police Service's then policy for the retention of custody images, which followed the Code of Practice on the Management of Police Information and accompanying guidance (MOPI), was unlawful.[150] Essentially, the policy allowed for potentially indefinite retention of these custody images and the court held that this constituted an unjustified breach of Article 8 rights of people who had not been convicted of any offence. The court granted a declaration to this effect on the basis that the policy of the police was under review.

11.138 In response to this judgment, the government commissioned a review of the current framework for the acquisition, retention and deletion of

148 *R(YZ) v Chief Constable of South Wales* [2022] EWCA Civ 1083; *R (CL) v Chief Constable of Greater Manchester* [2018] EWHC 3333 (Admin).

149 Para 8.1.2.

150 *R (C) v Commissioner of Police of the Metropolis and Secretary of State for the Home Department* [2012] EWHC 1681 (Admin), [2012] 1 WLR 3007.

custody images as well as their operational uses and governance arrangements (the Custody Image Review).[151] This reported as follows:

> 1.7 . . . this review proposes giving individuals the facility (if they have *not* been convicted of the offence(s) in relation to which the custody image was taken . . . to apply to chief officers of police forces to have their custody image deleted. . . . Where such an application is made it is recommended that there should be a presumption in favour of deletion, with chief officers having the discretion to retain an image where this is necessary for a policing purpose *and* there is an exceptional reason to do so. . . .

11.139 The recommendations of the review have not led to any change in the law. However, the College of Policing has included guidance as part of the MOPI APP (referred to earlier in this chapter) which is said to 'support' the review.[152]

11.140 This confirms that a person may request deletion of a custody image in circumstances where the person was:

- arrested but not charged;
- not convicted of the offence for which the image was taken;
- convicted and a predetermined time (group 3 deletion) has elapsed since the conviction.

11.141 The APP emphasises the presumption in favour of deletion where a person has not been convicted, and that retention should only be considered for a law enforcement reason where there is 'an exceptional reason to do so'. The APP provides an example of where a person is 'considered to pose a substantial risk of harm'. The APP explains that it is only custody images which will be considered as part of the process. This reflects the approach of the review that its ambit:[153]

> . . . expressly excludes images which were primarily gathered as intelligence and/or are held as evidence. This is because such images are held as police information or evidence in relation to specific events, rather than for verifying the identity of an individual who is already known to the police.

11.142 The APP explains that it is important to check for multiple copies of the custody photograph subject to the application and ensure that these are all deleted as well, and that copies may be held in both local and national systems. Advisers should remember to raise this point when assisting with an application. Where a custody image is deleted, a system record will be completed to note the date of deletion and who authorised it.

Local police records

11.143 As has been explained earlier in this chapter, police forces retain a lot of information which does not find its way into national police records, but is available for use and retention. This chapter has explained how to apply

151 *Review of the use and retention of custody images*, Home Office, February 2017, www.gov.uk/government/publications/custody-images-review-of-their-use-and-retention (emphasis in original).

152 *Retention, review and disposal*, updated 23 November 2021, www.college.police.uk/app/information-management/management-police-information/retention-review-and-disposal.

153 Custody Image Review, fn 3.

to see what information is held, (see para 11.90) and explained how the information can be used, for example, in an enhanced criminal record certificate (ECRC) (see para 11.150). How long the information can be retained for is governed by MOPI and accompanying practice guidance already referred to (see para 11.86). Ultimately, though, whether the information is lawfully retained will depend on the application of the principles in the DPA 2018 and whether retention and use is proportionate for the purpose of ECHR Article 8, and whether the continued retention of the information is reviewed appropriately from time to time. The ECtHR in *Catt v UK*[154] set out the interrelationships between the common law, the DPA 2018, MOPI and ECHR Article 8 in deciding whether retention of information on local police records was lawful and proportionate.

Police disclosure for criminal record certificates

11.144 There is a complicated system governing the disclosure of information relating to a person's criminal record and other information held by the police. Sometimes the procedures require a person to disclose information for the purposes of employment or volunteering, but there are situations where the police are called upon to disclose information, especially if a person is applying for a position working with vulnerable people or children, or which has other sensitivities.

11.145 The Rehabilitation of Offenders Act (ROA) 1974 sets out the scheme for when employees can avoid disclosure of criminal records to would-be employers, and the Police Act (PA) 1997 with associated statutory instruments deals largely with the basic and enhanced certificates applied for by employees when required for particular kinds of employment.

11.146 The Rehabilitation of Offenders Act (ROA) 1974 sets out periods of time when convictions or cautions for individuals become 'spent' so that there is no requirement to disclose these when asked for most kinds of employment (although some serious convictions never become spent). However, even when convictions or convictions are usually to be treated as spent, there are circumstances, governed by the ROA 1974 (Exceptions) Order 1975 where these protections are removed.[155] In general, these are situations where a position is applying for certain kinds of professional job or position, or where there will be involvement working with children or vulnerable adults.

11.147 Both the ROA 1974 and the PA 1997 have faced a number of challenges in the higher courts (including the Supreme Court[156]) on the basis that their disclosure provisions are either 'not in accordance with the law' or amount to a disproportionate interference with ECHR Article 8 right to respect for privacy (or both). This section will deal mainly with the scheme under the PA 1997, which has the greater input from the police, but the two statutes are linked.

11.148 Under the PA 1997, the Disclosure and Barring Service (DBS) has the responsibility for issuing criminal conviction certificates (CCCs) when

154 (2019) 69 EHRR 7, ECtHR.

155 SI No 1023. See articles 3 and 4 and Sch 1.

156 See *R (T) v Chief Constable of Greater Manchester* [2013] EWCA Civ 25, [2013] 1 WLR 2515 and *R(P) v Secretary of State for the Home Department* [2020] AC 185.

requested by an individual,[157] and criminal record certificates (CRCs)[158] or Enhanced Criminal Record Certificates (ECRCs)[159] if an application is made by a person whose application is countersigned by a registered person (see below).

11.149 A CCC simply sets out all 'unspent' convictions and cautions. A CRC is issued when a person applies for one of the exempt positions under the ROA 1974 (which includes for example solicitors, barristers and accountants),[160] when most unspent convictions, cautions, warnings and reprimands held on the PNC will be disclosed. Even here there are exceptions which rule out some convictions and cautions being disclosable, taking into account the nature of the offence, when it was committed, and whether there is more than one conviction/caution.[161] The exact list in the PA 1997 can be amended by Order.[162]

11.150 The Police Act 1997 (Criminal Records) Regulations 2002[163] prescribe the purposes for which an ECRC might be required.[164] They included a range of matters, starting with various categories of work with children and with vulnerable adults, and extending to such matters as obtaining licences under the Gambling Act 2005 or the National Lottery etc Act 1993, and assessing suitability for employment related to national security, and suitability to obtain a taxi driver licence. When an ECRC is applied for, the same information provided for a CRC will be relevant. In addition information held on the DBS barred lists (maintained under the Safeguarding Vulnerable Groups Act 2006) will be included, together with relevant non-conviction information from the police (see below at para 11.152).

11.151 In all but the application for an ECRC, the role of the police is limited. Records of convictions, cautions and other formal adverse disposals in the criminal justice system will be disclosed as required by the relevant legislation, and these are not dealt with in further detail in this chapter. Where a person believes that the information disclosed is incorrect, there is a right of review through the DBS website where the information will be checked and reviewed with the police force.

11.152 However, when an ECRC is applied for, there is a discretion placed in the hands of the police, to decide what, if any, 'non-conviction' information is disclosed for the purposes of an ECRC. PA 1997 s113B(4) currently states that:

> Before issuing an enhanced criminal record certificate the Secretary of State must request any relevant chief officer to provide any information which–
> (a) the chief officer reasonably believes to be relevant for the purpose described in the statement under subsection (2), and
> (b) in the chief officer's opinion, ought to be included in the certificate.

157 PA 1997 s112.

158 PA 1997 s113.

159 PA 1997 s115.

160 See the full list in Exemption Order 1975 Sch 1.

161 PA 1997 s113A(6)–(6E).

162 The most recent is the Police Act 1997 (Criminal Record Certificates: Relevant Matters) (Amendment) (England and Wales) Order 2013 SI No 1200.

163 SI No 233.

164 Reg 5A.

11.153 As indicated, before the police consider disclosing such information, there has to be a statement by the registered person (usually an employer) that the certificate is required for the purposes of an exempted question asked for a prescribed purpose.[165] An 'exempted question' is a reference to matters excluded from the protections of the ROA 1974.[166]

11.154 The first key point here is that 'any information' can be provided by the police. This means that the police can look at all its records, local and national, to see if there is anything that could be disclosed. This might include intelligence received about someone, complaints from others, or records about investigations which have not led to conviction or charge. It might be that the person asking for the certificate has no idea that the information is held by the police (which is why it is sometimes sensible to make a SAR (see above at para 11.90)) prior to an application for an ECRC. However, the police can only disclose information for the purposes of an ECRC if it is 'reasonably believed to be relevant'.

11.155 In effect, a police force is usually considering an application for an ECRC from an applicant whose employer or potential employer wishes to employ that person in one of a range of potentially sensitive posts, and then has to decide whether any information at all that the police hold about that person should be disclosed to the employer.

11.156 Under earlier versions of the scheme each police force took its own approach as to what information 'ought to be disclosed'. However, statutory guidance has been issued pursuant to PA 1997 s113B(4A) which includes principles to assist the police and to which they must have regard,[167] and which reflect the approach of the courts in earlier cases.[168] The most important points for the police to take into account from this are:

- Whether the information is 'relevant' is to be given its natural meaning. For example, what may be relevant to an application connected with caring for children or vulnerable adults may not be relevant when a person is seeking a licence under the gaming legislation, and vice versa.
- The information should be of 'sufficient gravity to justify its inclusion'. Information that is trivial or which simply demonstrates poor behaviour, would not fall under this category.
- The information must be 'sufficiently current'. It also must be 'sufficiently credible'. This means assessing whether the information came from a credible source and whether it is more likely than not to be true.[169]
- Whether information ought to be included is to be read and given effect in a way which is compatible with the applicant's right to respect for private and family life under ECHR Article 8, because disclosure

165 PA 1997 s113B(2).

166 PA 1997 s113A(6).

167 *Statutory disclosure guidance*, Home Office, third edition, November 2021, www.gov.uk/government/publications/statutory-disclosure-guidance.

168 See, for example, *R (L) v Commissioner of Police of the Metropolis* [2010] 1 AC 410.

169 Guidance paras 18–19.

will 'in virtually every case, involve an interference with the applicant's private life'.[170]

- Thus, disclosure must be necessary to pursue a legitimate aim including consideration of whether there are any other realistic and practical options to pursue that aim.
- The chief officer should consider whether the applicant should be afforded the opportunity to make representations before a decision on disclosure is made, especially where there is uncertainty about disclosure because of its source, reliability; or because of the potential effect of disclosure on the person's private life.
- The reasons for disclosure should be clearly set out, to show that balancing of the various factors has been carried out.

11.157 The guidance continues to explain that information about the mental health of a person which is held by the police will not usually, in itself, be appropriate for disclosure unless there are specific concerns raised for example, about potential harm to other people.[171]

11.158 In practice, any dispute about the disclosure must be first raised with the DBS who will explore the issue with the police.[172] Following that a person who is dissatisfied by the disclosure decision can now apply for a review to an Independent Monitor if it is believed that the information provided is not relevant or ought not to be included.[173] The Independent Monitor must also follow the statutory guidance issued to the police. The most recent figures show that in 2019 the total number of disputed disclosure cases received by the Independent Monitor was 139 and in 2020, the figure was 87. In 2019 the Independent Monitor upheld the disclosure decision of the police in only 35 cases, and in 2020 in 32 cases.[174] Thus there is a high proportion of cases where the Independent Monitor does not agree with the disclosure proposed by the police, even following a review by the DBS.

11.159 A person who disagrees with the result of the review by the Independent Monitor can apply for judicial review.[175] The Supreme Court recently decided that, on judicial review, it was the role of the judge to form their own view on whether disclosure was proportionate while giving weight to the view of the primary decision-maker as the person with the relevant statutory authority and institutional competence.[176] That case considered the particularly contentious disclosure of information relating to an acquittal: the Supreme Court decided that, on the facts of the case, disclosure was not unlawful, but was concerned about the lack of guidance about

170 Guidance para 26.

171 Guidance para 42.

172 See: www.gov.uk/report-problem-criminal-record-certificate/dispute-a-mistake.

173 PA 1997 s117A.

174 *Independent Monitor Annual Report 2020*, https://assets.publishing.service.gov.uk/government/uploads/system/uploads/attachment_data/file/1005799/IMR_2020_-_21.07.2021.pdf .

175 See, for example, *LG v Independent Monitor* [2017] EWHC 3327 (Admin); *R (LK) v Independent Monitor* [2016] EWHC 1629 9 (Admin); *R (MS) v Independent Monitor* [2016] 4 WLR 88.

176 *R (R) v Chief Constable of Greater Manchester* [2018] UKSC 47, [2018] 1 WLR 4079.

when and how information about criminal proceedings not leading to a conviction should lead to disclosure.

11.160 Advisers in this area will first of all need to check whether an ECRC is necessary. When looking at the information disclosed by the police, advisers should consider the guidance to the police and whether it has been followed. The inclusion of additional information on the ECRC has been described as often being a killer blow to the job prospects of the applicant.[177] In many cases (see the Independent Monitor review figures above at para 11.158), representations will lead to the information being withdrawn or at least a less harmful form of words being used in the certificate, if the information can be shown to be inaccurate, unreliable or not relevant to the job applied for.

Police sharing and disclosure of information

The Data Sharing Code of Practice

11.161 The Information Commissioner publishes a statutory code containing practical guidance in relation to the sharing of personal data,[178] the Data Sharing Code of Practice, which sets out both the statutory requirements under the DPA 2018 and also promotes good practice in the sharing of personal data.[179] The first Data Sharing Code was published in 2011 and, at the time of publication, the most recent version was published in October 2021.[180] The Code recognises and highlights the benefits of sharing data between organisations, with one of its express aims being to clear up misconceptions about data sharing and barriers to sharing.[181] In particular, the Code recognises 'compelling reasons' why data sharing is needed in law enforcement purposes.[182]

APP Guidance

11.162 The College of Policing published APP guidance on information sharing to aid forces with their statutory duties under the UK GDPR, DPA 2018 and HRA 1998.[183] The APP defines 'information sharing' as disclosing information for a policing purpose either to a third-party organisation or between different parts of an organisation, on a one-off or ongoing basis. The APP contains guidance on both the types of agreement that enable information exchange – for example, data processing contract, memorandum of understanding, service level agreement and information sharing agreement – and

177 Lord Neuberger in *R(L) v Commissioner of Police of the Metropolis* [2010] 1 AC 410 at para 83.

178 DPA 2018 s121.

179 DPA 2018 s121(1) and (5).

180 Data Sharing Code of Practice, Information Commissioner's Office, 5 October 2021, available at: https://ico.org.uk/for-organisations/guide-to-data-protection/ico-codes-of-practice/data-sharing-a-code-of-practice/. In particular, see 'Law enforcement processing' (pp53–58).

181 Data Sharing Code of Practice, 'Common misconceptions about data sharing' (p13).

182 Data Sharing Code of Practice, 'Law enforcement processing' (p53).

183 College of Policing, APP 'Information management', available online at: www.college.police.uk/app/information-management.

the necessary requirements for such an agreement to be effective. The APP also provides forces with an overview of their obligations and powers to share information with third parties under the data protection regime (as discussed above at para 11.161), including in situations which are not covered by a formal information sharing agreement. Finally, the APP provides a list of factors that forces should consider when deciding whether to enter into an information sharing agreement and signposts forces to a national Information Sharing Agreement template and to the ICO's statutory guidance.

11.163 The requirements police must fulfil when sharing information vary depending on the recipient of that information. Broadly speaking, recipients fall into four categories:

1) data processors;
2) other competent authorities;
3) domestic recipients who are not competent authorities; and
4) third countries and international organisations.

Data processors

11.164 When the police share information with a processor to manage data on their behalf, then that relationship must be governed by prior written contract. Further, the data processor must provide guarantees to implement appropriate technical and organisational measures and must maintain a record of the processing activities carried out.[184]

Competent authorities

11.165 Police can share information with a different police force and/or other competent authorities, provided that the sharing of information is primarily for one of the law enforcement purposes. Both the sender and recipient of information will need to comply with the data protection principles and additional conditions for the processing of sensitive personal data (as outlined above at para 11.52).

Recipients that are not competent authorities

11.166 The police are able to share information to a recipient that is not a competent authority or to a competent authority for a non-law enforcement purpose (as defined in DPA 2018 s31), provided that 'the processing is authorised by law'.[185] The Data Sharing Code of Practice notes that in the absence of an obvious statute or code of practice providing authorisation, common law may be the natural basis for police forces to rely upon.[186] For example, prior to the Domestic Abuse Act 2021, the Domestic Violence Disclosure Scheme relied on the police's common law power to disclose information where it is necessary to do so to prevent crime.

11.167 In *R(M) v Chief Constable of Sussex*[187] the claimant was a vulnerable child with convictions for shoplifting and assault. The police force shared

184 DPA 2018 ss59 and 61–62.

185 DPA 2018 s36(4).

186 See also the College or Policing's APP on 'Information sharing' available at: www.app.college.police.uk/app-content/information-management

187 [2021] EWCA Civ 42.

M's name, date of birth, photograph and bail conditions with a local business crime reduction partnership (BCRP), as part of an information sharing agreement. The BCRP's function was to manage an exclusion notice scheme which prohibited persons from entering its members' commercial premises. As a result of receiving the information, the BCRP made an exclusion order in relation to M. The Court of Appeal held that an information sharing agreement between the police and BCRP did not breach the DPA 2018 – in particular, that there was no requirement for 'specific safeguards' in respect of data relating to children.[188]

International transfers

11.168 The DPA 2018 contains special provisions relating to the transfer of personal data to third countries and international organisations.[189] In brief, there are three general conditions.[190] First, the transfer must be necessary for any of the law enforcement purposes. Second, the transfer must be based on 'adequacy regulations'[191] or, alternatively, must be based on appropriate safeguards or fulfil specified 'special circumstances'.[192] Third, the intended third-party recipient must be a relevant authority or meet additional conditions.[193]

11.169 In *Elgizouli v Secretary of State for the Home Department*[194] the transfer of personal data regarding two British members of an Islamic State cell (known as 'the Beatles') to the US for use in capital criminal proceedings lacked the necessary 'adequacy decision'[195] or appropriate safeguards. Accordingly, the Supreme Court held that the transfer was unlawful.

Police identification of informants and witnesses

11.170 The courts have accepted that a duty of confidence and/or an assumption of responsibility in negligence may be owed to informants, ie people who provide information to the police in the expectation that their identity will not be revealed to those who are the subject of the intelligence.

11.171 In *Swinney v Chief Constable of Northumbria*[196] the Court of Appeal held that it was arguable that such a duty arose in relation to the claimant who had passed information to officers in the belief that it would be used on an

188 See also *Cooper v National Crime Agency* [2019] EWCA Civ 16 regarding information sharing practices between law enforcement agencies under the DPA 1998 and, in particular, the use of such data in disciplinary proceedings.

189 DPA 2018 ss72–78.

190 DPA 2018 s73.

191 DPA 2018 ss74A–74B.

192 DPA 2018 s76.

193 DPA 2018 s77.

194 [2020] UKSC 10, [2021] AC 937.

195 Following the UK's withdrawal from the EC 'adequacy decisions' have been replaced with domestic 'adequacy regulations'.

196 [1996] 3 All ER 449, CA.

anonymous basis.[197] In *Donnelly v Chief Constable of Lincolnshire*[198] it was accepted that officers owed a duty of care in negligence to a participant informer involved in providing information on drug smuggling and the case was not argued on the basis of breach of confidence.[199] In *X and Y v Chief Constable of Greater Manchester Police*[200] the claimants had received assurances of anonymity from the police when they agreed to supply information relating to a murder, but the Crown Prosecution Service (CPS) divulged their role and identity to the defendants at the criminal trial. Liability for breach of confidence and negligence was conceded and the hearing involved an assessment of damages. Compensation was awarded to reflect consequential psychiatric trauma, disruption to the claimants' previous life and loss of earnings. In *An Informer v A Chief Constable*[201] the Court of Appeal accepted that the police owed a duty of care in negligence to protect the claimant from risks to which he was potentially exposed as a result of his activities as a covert human intelligence source. The duty encompassed the claimant's physical safety and wellbeing, but did not extend to protecting him from pure economic loss or from investigation of suspected criminal conduct on his part.

11.172 The situation of witnesses differs from that of informants. In *CLG v Chief Constable of Merseyside Police*[202] the Court of Appeal held that there was no assumption of responsibility in circumstances where the police inadvertently disclosed the residential address of two summonsed witnesses to the defendant. The witnesses had not disclosed their address to the police on a confidential basis and, accordingly, their situation was not analogous to that of an informant. In any event, the information was provided in witness evidence and, accordingly, was protected by witness immunity.[203]

11.173 In summary, in the case of an informant (whether used on a casual or a formalised basis) it will probably be relatively straightforward to establish the existence of a duty of confidence and/or a duty of care in negligence owed by the officers involved. The more difficult issue is likely to be whether the duty was breached in the particular circumstances. This will depend, among other factors, upon the claimant's reasonable expectation, in turn based on any assurances given at the time, the degree of the threat posed and the extent to which disclosure of the material is required in any criminal trial process.

197 At trial the action proceeded in relation to the negligence claim, where no breach was established on the facts: *Swinney v Chief Constable of Northumbria (No 2)* (1999) Admin LR 811, QBD.

198 [2001] 9 WLUK 164, QBD.

199 The court found that the duty of care had not been breached on the facts.

200 [2004] EWHC 764 (QB).

201 [2012] EWCA Civ 197.

202 [2015] EWCA Civ 836.

203 See also: *A & B v Chief Constable of Hampshire* [2012] EWHC 1517 (QB).

Facial recognition technology

Overview

11.174 As society's technology has advanced, so too has police surveillance technology.

11.175 Perhaps one of the most talked about police surveillance technology is automated facial recognition technology (AFR). It is an overt technology, but does not require the police to interact with an individual in order to capture their data.

11.176 AFR can refer to two different kinds of facial recognition technology which are labelled as: AFR Locate and AFR Identify. AFR Locate refers to what is known as 'live' facial recognition technology, which matches images of people walking past facial recognition cameras against images on a 'watch list'.[204] AFR Identify matches still images against a watch list. 'AFR' in this chapter will refer to AFR Locate.

11.177 When AFR is deployed, it indiscriminately scans and takes a digital photograph of distinct points on the faces of passers-by. AFR uses these points to create a unique biometric map that is encoded and then compared against corresponding coded images from people on police watch lists.[205] A full description of the technical operation of AFR was outlined by the Divisional Court in *R (Bridges) v Chief Constable of South Wales*:[206]

> (1) *Compiling/using an existing database of images.* AFR requires a database of existing facial images (referred to in this case as 'a watchlist') against which to compare facial images and the biometrics contained therein. In order for such images to be used for AFR, they are processed so that the 'facial features' associated with their subjects are extracted and expressed as numerical values.
> (2) *Facial image acquisition.* A CCTV camera (which could be mounted on e.g., a van, lamp post or contained in a handheld device) takes digital pictures of facial images in real time. This may be done by (i) taking a static photograph in a 'controlled' environment (for example where an individual has her photograph taken at a border gate when presenting a passport); or (ii) capturing a moving image when a person passes into the camera's field of view, using a live feed. This case is concerned with the latter, i.e. the use of AFR cameras in real time, in a 'live' context.
> (3) *Face detection.* Once a CCTV camera used in a live context captures footage, the software (i) detects human faces and then (ii) isolates individual faces.
> (4) *Feature extraction.* Taking the faces identified and isolated through 'face detection', the software automatically extracts unique facial features from the image of each face, the resulting biometric template being unique to that image.
> (5) *Face comparison.* The AFR software compares the extracted facial features with those contained in the facial images held on the watchlist.
> (6) *Matching.* When facial features from two images are compared, the AFR software generates a 'similarity score'. This is a numerical value indicating

204 *Liberty's briefing on police use of live facial recognition technology*, Liberty, November 2019.

205 *Liberty's briefing on police use of live facial recognition technology*, Liberty, November 2019.

206 [2019] EWHC 2341 (Admin), [2020] 1 WLR 672 at 24.

the likelihood that the faces match, with a higher number indicating a greater likelihood of a positive match between the two faces. A threshold value is fixed to determine when the software will indicate that a match has occurred. Fixing this value too low or too high can, respectively, create risks of a high 'false alarm rate' (i.e. the percentage of incorrect matches identified by the software) or a high 'false reject rate' (i.e. the percentage of true matches that are not in fact matched by the software). The threshold value is generally suggested by the manufacturer, and depends on the intended use of the AFR system. It is common to suggest setting the threshold value so that the False Alarm Rate is 0.1%, 0.01% or 0.001%. Most AFR systems, however, allow the end user to change the threshold value to whatever they choose. However, operators of AFR systems are able to amend the 'threshold [of similarity] value', above which a similarity score is taken to indicate a potential match.

11.178 There is no statutory framework for the operation of AFR. The legality of its use was broadly stated to be in line with the Police's common law powers of 'use, retention and disclosure of imagery of individuals for the purposes of preventing and detecting crime',[207] emanating from the power to prevent and detect crime.[208] However, the common law offers little protection in relation to collection, storage and use by the state of personal data.[209]

Bridges

Overview

11.179 In *R (Bridges) v Chief Constable of South Wales*, the claimant stated that he had been scanned by AFR on two occasions and challenged South Wales Police's use of the technology on four grounds:

1) its use was incompatible with ECHR Article 8 – primarily on the basis that it is not 'in accordance with the law' but also because it was not necessary or proportionate as required by Article 8(2) (see paras 11.27–11.33);
2) its use breached the DPA 1998 (now the DPA 2018) (see paras 11.42–11.60);
3) South Wales Police failed to comply with its obligation to undertake a lawful 'data protection impact assessment'; and
4) South Wales Police failed to discharge the 'public sector equality duty' (PSED) as set out in the Equality Act (EqA) 2010 (see chapter 12).

11.180 The Divisional Court rejected all four grounds. The claimant appealed to the Court of Appeal, which found that South Wales Police's deployment of AFR on the two occasions complained of:

a) was not 'in accordance with the law' as required by ECHR Article 8(2) (see paras 11.32–11.33);

207 *R (Wood) v Commissioner of Police of the Metropolis* [2009] EWCA Civ 414, [2010] 1 WLR 123, the police took and retained photographs of the claimant in the street for the purpose of gathering evidence about possible disorder and criminal conduct. Laws LJ and Lord Collins held that this was lawful (see paras 50–55 and 98–100 respectively).

208 *Rice v Connolly* [1966] 2 QB 414 at 419B–C per Lord Parker CJ.

209 See Lord Reed's observations in *R (T) v Chief Constable of Greater Manchester* [2014] UKSC 35, [2015] AC 49 at 88.

b) South Wales Police had failed to comply with its obligation to undertake a lawful data protection impact assessment (a consequence of the breach of Article 8); and
c) South Wales Police failed to discharge the PSED (see paras 12.94–12.97).[210]

11.181 The court dismissed the challenge that the use of AFR was not necessary or proportionate under ECHR Article 8 (as it did not arise once its use was not 'in accordance with the law') and its use was held not to be in breach of the DPA 1998 or DPA 2018.

Principles of the decision

11.182 While the court accepted that *Bridges* was only concerned with the use of AFR by South Wales Police and did not necessarily concern the future use of AFR by another force or nationally,[211] it is plain that police forces using AFR will need to bear in mind the principles derived from *Bridges*.

11.183 Therefore, the important practicalities of the decision for practitioners are as follows.

1) Between two poles

11.184 First, despite the biometric and intrusive nature of the images taken by AFR, the court held that it was not akin to fingerprints.[212] The court also rejected the argument that it was analogous to the taking of photographs or the use of CCTV cameras.[213] It was held that the technology fell between these two 'poles' of the indiscriminate and blanket retention of DNA profiles and fingerprints of individuals not convicted of any offence on the one hand,[214] and the police's retention of personal information on a national database of people attending public protests on the other.[215]

2) Targeting and deployment

11.185 Second, the court rejected the argument that the technology was 'in accordance with the law', as the framework had two fundamental deficiencies: it lacked specificity and objective criteria as to:

i) who was being targeted; and
ii) where the technology was being deployed.[216]

The combination of DPA 2018, the Surveillance Camera Code of Practice and South Wales Police's own policies were not adequate, in this particular case, to amount to a 'sufficient legal framework' to meet the requirement of ECHR Article 8(2) of 'in accordance with the law'.[217]

210 *R (Bridges) v Chief Constable of South Wales* [2020] EWCA Civ 1058, [2020] 1 WLR 5037.
211 *Bridges*, para 61.
212 *Bridges*, para 65.
213 *Bridges*, para 85.
214 *S v UK* (2008) 48 EHRR 50, GC.
215 *R (Catt) v Association of Chief Police Officers of England, Wales and Northern Ireland* [2015] AC 1065.
216 *Bridges*, para 91.
217 *Bridges*, para 91.

Who the technology targets

11.186 South Wales Police Privacy Impact Assessment stated that the watch list could by populated with 'persons wanted on suspicion for an offence, wanted on warrant, vulnerable persons and other persons where intelligence is required'.[218] The last category was of particular concern to the Court. Such a category left 'too broad a discretion vested in the individual police officer to decide who should go onto the watchlist';[219] it lacked objective criteria against which this could be adjudged.

Where the technology was to be deployed

11.187 Much less consideration was given to the question of the circumstances in which the 'where' question would be 'in accordance with the law'. South Wales Police's Privacy Impact assessment stated that: 'As we are testing the technology South Wales Police have deployed in all event types ranging from high volume music and sporting events to indoor arenas.'[220] The court held that this underlined their concern as i) it was merely a 'descriptive statement and does not lay down any normative requirement as to where deployment can properly take place'; and ii) 'the range is very broad and without apparent limits'.[221] The court noted that there was no requirement that the location be one that the police had reasonable grounds for believing that people on the watchlist will be present.[222]

11.188 The court stated that the automatic and instantaneous deletion of data of anyone who does not match with a person on the watchlist should be a legal requirement for an adequate legal framework.[223]

11.189 As the case was concerned only with the two instances of deployment of AFR by South Wales Police, the Court of Appeal did not examine any further the question of whether facial recognition technology was a necessary and proportionate tool in any great detail. Instead, it stated that the question would have been whether a fair balance had been struck between the interests of the claimant against the community at large.[224]

3) Public sector equality duty

11.190 Third, the court found that the police force had failed to discharge the PSED. The court was unable to adjudicate whether the technology deployed by South Wales Police was biased on the grounds of race or sex. However, the fact that South Wales Police 'never sought to satisfy themselves, either directly or by way of independent verification, that the software program in this case does not have an unacceptable bias on grounds of race or sex',[225] was enough to find that the PSED was breached (see paras 12.94–12.97 for more detail on the PSED).

11.191 The background of PSED was emphasised by the court:[226]

218 *Bridges*, para 123.
219 *Bridges*, para 124.
220 *Bridges*, para 130.
221 *Bridges*, para 130.
222 *Bridges*, para 96.
223 *Bridges*, para 93.
224 *Bridges*, para 140.
225 *Bridges*, para 199.
226 *Bridges*, para 177.

That background is to be found in the Stephen Lawrence Inquiry Report in 1999, which led to the Race Relations (Amendment) Act 2000. That Act introduced a new section 71 into the Race Relations Act 1976, to replace an earlier version which had applied only to local authorities. The provision has since been expanded to embrace other protected characteristics and now finds its place in section 149 of the Equality Act 2010.

What happened next

11.192 Following the judgment, South Wales Police stated they would not appeal. The ICO[227] and Biometrics Commissioner[228] repeated their calls for a nationwide legal framework and statutory code of practice for AFR.[229]

11.193 In relation to the PSED, the Biometrics Commissioner since emphasised:

> To fully meet the PSED obligations, forces will have to consider any discriminatory effects of the algorithms that they are proposing to use and whether any such possible effects will exacerbate any discrimination that may have taken place prior to the deployment of the software. For example, if there is evidence that there may be discrimination in a police force's use of their arrest powers, then that may feed through to the database from which a watch list is drawn up for use in an AFR deployment. If the protected characteristic which had been discriminated against in the exercise of arrest powers was the same characteristic that the evidence suggested was discriminated against by the AFR software, then that would have a compounding discriminatory effect or vice versa. This is simply to recognise that any discrimination in the criminal justice system cannot be examined as an isolated event but instead for its systemic consequences.[230]

Surveillance Commissioner's Code

11.194 The Surveillance Camera Commissioner's Code of Practice (SCCP) regulating the use of AFR has been revised and should be a starting point for any practitioner when considering whether any particular deployment is

227 See: https://ico.org.uk/about-the-ico/news-and-events/news-and-blogs/2020/08/ico-statement-on-the-court-of-appeal-judgment/.

228 *Interim Report by the Commissioner for the Retention and use of Biometric Material*, https://assets.publishing.service.gov.uk/government/uploads/system/uploads/attachment_data/file/942155/Commissioner_for_the_retention_and_use_of_biometric_material_-_Interim_Report_December_2020__002_.pdf.

229 The new government gave a manifesto commitment to provide a strict legal framework to govern the future police use of biometrics and artificial intelligence: www.gov.uk/government/news/response-to-announcement-on-live-facial-recognition; https://assets-global.website-files.com/5da42e2cae7ebd3f8bde353c/5dda924905da587992a064ba_Conservative%202019%20Manifesto.pdf.

230 *Interim Report by the Commissioner for the Retention and use of Biometric Material*, para 28.

'in accordance with the law' or its location and timing gives rise to concern.[231]

11.195 In considering where to deploy facial recognition, the SCCP emphasises:[232]

> . . . appropriate consideration should be made as to the impact upon the fundamental rights and freedoms of people within that location, regardless as to whether they are on the relevant police watchlist. In particular members of the public may be discouraged or inhibited from otherwise exercising their legitimate rights in the vicinity of where the LFR cameras are located, (usually referred to as the 'chilling effect'). For example, citizen's rights such as the right of privacy, freedom of religion, freedom of expression, freedom of assembly may be inhibited for example where LFR is deployed proximate to places of religious worship, at schools where children or parents gather or at lawful protests. There may be additional considerations which apply where deployments are considered in areas where there are vulnerable communities or community tensions are high.

11.196 Importantly, the SCCP notes that use should be 'timebound' with a clear start and finish and that rationality grounds may be raised when considering when to deploy AFR:[233]

> . . . it may be less justifiable to deploy LFR at particular locations to search for individuals, simply on the basis that a large volume of people frequent or pass through the area and it is hoped that a person on a watchlist may be amongst the crowds. Rather, the police should be able to demonstrate that decisions as to when and where they look for persons who they seek by means of LFR, are based upon reasonable grounds.

11.197 It is emphasised that when considering proportionality that:[234]

> Where determining the proportionality of use of LFR, the seriousness of the circumstances to be addressed and intended outcomes being pursued should be balanced against the risk of intrusion on the rights of citizens. Any deployment should not be allowed to continue longer than is necessary to achieve the intended outcomes.
>
> Proportionality is not only about balancing the effectiveness of LFR over other methods but of explaining why the particular technique or tactic is the least intrusive necessary to achieve the desired aim . . .

APP guidance

11.198 The College of Policing has subsequently produced APP guidance on the use of Live Facial Recognition.[235] The guidance sets out that:

231 *Facing the camera, good practice and guidance for the police use of overt surveillance camera systems incorporating facial recognition technology to locate persons on a watchlist, in public places in England & Wales, The Protection of Freedoms Act 2012 & The Surveillance Camera Code of Practice. Issued by the Surveillance Camera Commissioner by virtue of section 34(2)(c) Protection of Freedoms Act 2012 and the Surveillance Camera Code of Practice*, November 2020, www.gov.uk/government/publications/police-use-of-automated-facial-recognition-technology-with-surveillance-camera-systems.

232 SCCP, para 3.52.

233 SCCP, para 3.46.

234 SCCP, paras 3.78, 3.79.

235 See: www.college.police.uk/app/live-facial-recognition?s=.

- live facial recognition technology should be used in a responsible, transparent, fair and ethical way and only when other, less intrusive methods would not achieve the same results;
- all use of the technology has to be targeted, based on intelligence and have a set time for use to start and end;
- images placed on the predetermined database must meet a proportionality and necessity criteria and be reviewed before every deployment;
- police forces should give notice about the use of live facial recognition, making use of social media and their website, unless there is a critical threat that makes this impractical;
- chief officers should involve their elected police and crime commissioner to provide oversight.

Causes of action

11.199 There are five main causes of action available to a prospective claimant in relation to information and/or data held, used or disclosed by the police. These are:

1) judicial review;
2) actions under the DPA 2018;
3) an action for a breach of ECHR Article 8;
4) an action for misuse of private information; and
5) defamation.

This section focuses on the procedure for bringing a claim in each cause of action. The substantive law for the latter two causes of action is not covered elsewhere in this chapter and, therefore, is outlined in brief below.

Judicial review

11.200 An action for judicial review in the High Court can be a remedy against public bodies in data rights cases. As will be seen in this book, police forces and other bodies linked with the criminal justice system are public bodies whose decisions can be subject to judicial review (see para 14.5).

11.201 Judicial review claims are traditionally brought under one or a combination of the three conventional heads of review: illegality / ultra vires, irrationality (*Wednesbury* unreasonableness) and procedural unfairness. A public authority (which includes police bodies when exercising public functions) that acts incompatibly with a ECHR right unlawfully breaches its statutory duty under HRA 1998 s6 (unless acting in accordance with primary legislation which it is not 'possible' to interpret compatibly with the ECHR). Where Article 8 is relied upon, the claimant must satisfy the 'victim' test in HRA 1998 s7 and ECHR Article 34 (ie the claimant must be an individual directly affected, as opposed to an non-governmental organisation (NGO) or other entity).

11.202 In the information and data rights sphere, judicial review can be used as a mechanism for challenging policing decisions at a policy level. For example, challenging a pilot project for the use of automated facial recognition technology, a statutory scheme for police disclosure of spent convictions to potential employers, or the retention period of biometric data associated with persons no longer suspected of a criminal offence.[236] Judicial review is often also used where the police have retained or disclosed information where it is argued that this is in breach of policies already in place. Some examples have already been discussed in the section above on enhanced criminal record certificates (see para 11.159).

11.203 It is important to note that judicial review is described as a remedy of last resort where alternative remedies should usually be exhausted before taking a case to the High Court. Thus while neither statutory regime for the DPA 2018 and FOIA 2000 contains a provision expressly excluding judicial review both statutes contain court and tribunal remedies which should be considered first. For example, in *R (Hussain) v Secretary of State for Justice*,[237] a remedy in judicial review was refused because of the right to apply to the court for a disclosure order under the DPA 1998. Judicial review may be granted where there is a gap in the statutory regime, which would leave the claimant without a route of appeal: for example, *R (Evans) v Attorney-General*.[238] Such gaps are rare in both statutory regimes.[239] It is also sometimes possible to argue that judicial review is the more effective remedy for the issue raised (for example because of the delay in the alternative remedies, or because wider public interest matters are in issue), and there are cases where the application of the DPA 2018 (such as the *Bridges* case[240]) has been argued in judicial review cases alongside other grounds. Specialist advice should be obtained before embarking on such a route.

11.204 Preliminary issues, including limitation periods, for commencing an application for judicial review are discussed in chapter 14.

Data Protection Act 2018

11.205 In addition to the Information Commissioner and First-tier Tribunal remedies outlined above, a data subject can apply for judicial remedy by bringing a claim for breach of a statutory duty in the High Court or (more

236 These examples reflect the claims in *R (Bridges) v Chief Constable of South Wales* [2018] EWCA Civ 1058, *R (P) v Secretary of State for Justice* [2019] UKSC 3 and *R (GC) v Commissioner of Police of the Metropolis* [2011] UKSC 21.

237 [2016] EWCA Civ 1111.

238 [2015] UKSC 21.

239 For an analysis of the appeal gaps in the two regimes see *Information Rights*, Philip Coppel QC, Vol 1, pp1123–1123 (as regards the FOIA 2000) and pp1189–1190 (as regards the DPA 2018).

240 [2018] EWCA Civ 1058.

frequently) the county court.[241] If the court is satisfied that the data subject has been unlawfully denied one of their rights under the data protection regime, then it can make a compliance order requiring the data controller to take specified steps (ie to provide the information requested by the data subject) and/or pay compensatory damages.[242] The limitation period is three years (in personal injury cases) or six years from the date upon which the cause of action accrued or the date of knowledge of the person injured.[243]

Article 8

11.206 The elements of the ECHR Article 8 right to respect for private life have been discussed elsewhere in the book and in this chapter at paras 11.26–11.37. Pursuant to HRA 1998 s7(1), a claimant can rely on Article 8 as part of a head of claim in a judicial review (see above at para 11.203) or as a stand-alone claim against a public authority that has acted unlawfully. Such an action can result in an award of damages, if necessary to afford 'just satisfaction' to the claimant. Some examples of awards under Article 8 for misuse of information are included at para 17.170.

Misuse of private information

11.207 In many cases a claim for misuse of private information offers an alternative or a complementary cause of action to a claim under the data protection regime. The tort developed from the law of breach of confidence in order to comply with public authorities' Article 8 obligations under the HRA 1998,[244] and the two causes of action are often concurrently pleaded, along with a claim under the DPA 2018.[245]

11.208 It should be noted that, in contrast to breach of confidence, the tort of misuse of private information (and pursuant to the HRA 1998 and the DPA 2018) can give rise to damages for 'distress' and it is not necessary to establish personal injury or other loss caused by the misuse of information. Some guidance about the level of damages available for this tort can be found in *Gulati v MGM*[246] and *TLT v Secretary of State for the Home Department*.[247]

11.209 The tort of misuse of private information has been successfully relied upon by claimants in a range of situations. The 'misuse' is two-pronged, encompassing both the unlawful access to private information and some positive wrongful action taken in relation to the information in question

241 Applying the usual guidelines in Civil Procedure Rules (CPR) 1998 SI No 3132 Practice Direction (PD) 7A.

242 See DPA 2018 ss167 and 169.

243 Limitation Act 1980 ss2 and 11.

244 See the summary in *Murray v Express Newspapers* [2008] EWCA Civ 446 at 24–28.

245 The action for breach of confidence is not covered in this chapter. The essential elements are: 1) the information must have the necessary quality of confidence about it; 2) the information must have been imparted in circumstances importing an obligation or confidence; and 3) there must be an unauthorised use of that information to the detriment of the party communicating it.

246 [2015] EWCA Civ 1291.

247 [2016] EWHC 2217 (QB).

(typically, disclosing it to a third party). The wrongful action can be intentional or accidental. For example, in *TLT* the defendant uploaded a spreadsheet containing personal details of lead asylum applicants to the UKBA website in error.

11.210 A claim in misuse of private information involves a two stage test.[248] The first question is whether the claimant had a 'reasonable expectation of privacy' in relation to the information in question. In other words, is ECHR Article 8 engaged? That determination will consider to what extent the information is already in the public domain, as well as whether the information is anodyne and/or trivial. If the first question is answered in the affirmative, then the second question arises: whether, in all the circumstances, the interference with the claimant's Article 8 rights (by the police or other body) was justified?[249] Both stages are highly fact sensitive and an assessment may change with the passage of time.

11.211 By way of example, a prospective claimant would ordinarily have no reasonable expectation of privacy in respect of a criminal charge at the time of their prosecution, conviction or sentencing for that offence; however, once a sufficient period of time has passed following conviction the autonomy of the individual and the public interest in their reintegration into society may require the fact and details of prior criminal convictions to remain private.[250] Similarly, a person arrested for an offence may seek to argue that they had a reasonable expectation of privacy in relation to their arrest if the police published their name in a press release prior to charge and absent any proper operational reason for doing so.[251]

11.212 A claim in misuse for private information can be brought in the County Court or High Court. The usual considerations contained in CPR PD 7A apply when considering which court to issue in. Any High Court claim for misuse of private information must be issued in the Media and Communications List in the Queen's Bench Division. Before bringing a claim, the prospective claimant should follow the Pre-Action Protocol for Media and Communications Claims. When a decision has been made to bring a claim, then PD 53B needs to be consulted and adhered to, which sets out mandatory requirements for statements of case.

Defamation

11.213 Successful claims in defamation have been brought in the policing context where an officer or force has made ill-considered and indiscriminate disclosure of defamatory factual statements to third parties (for example, by way of circulars, guidance or correspondence), which have no proper

248 *McKennitt v Ash* [2006] EWCA Civ 1714 at para 11.

249 *Re JR38 's application for judicial review* [2015] UKSC 42, [2016] AC 1131, at 66.

250 There is considerable jurisprudence on this issue. See, by way of example, *NT1 and NT2 v Google LLC* [2018] EWHC 799 (QB) (directly considering misuse of private information) and *R (L) v Commissioner of Police of the Metropolis* [2009] UKSC 3, [2010] 1 AC 410 (considering the proportionality of an interference of Article 8).

251 See *ZXC v Bloomberg Media LLP* [2022] UKSC 5; *Sir Cliff Richard v BBC and Chief Constable of South Yorkshire* [2018] EWHC 1837 (Ch). The police defendant accepted liability and paid the claimant damages of £400,000 and legal fees.

connection to the police's duty to detect and prevent crime and protect potential victims of crime.[252]

11.214 There are two separate civil actions in defamation: an action for libel which is concerned with the publication of a defamatory statement in writing or some other permanent form (including a recording) and an action for slander which is concerned with the publication of a defamatory statement by word of mouth.

11.215 The essential elements that a claimant needs to prove to bring an action in defamation (libel or slander) are:

1) that the statement complained of referred to the claimant;
2) that the statement bore a meaning that was defamatory of the claimant; and
3) that the defendant published the statement or was otherwise responsible for its publication.

Where the claimant seeks to bring a claim in respect of multiple statements, each element needs to be satisfied in respect of each individual statement.

11.216 In addition, a claimant in an action in slander must prove special damages, unless the statement imputes that the claimant committed a criminal offence punishable by imprisonment or the words are calculated to disparage the claimant in any office, profession, calling, trade or business.[253] These extra requirements coupled with the difficulty of pleading and proving the precise words used in a slander claim mean that the majority of defamation actions are libel claims. As such, the remainder of this section solely addresses libel claims.

11.217 In most libel cases involving police records and documentation, the first and third elements explained above should be relatively straightforwardly established. However, the second element will require careful consideration. In order to prove that a statement was defamatory there are two requirements the claimant must satisfy. First, that the statement bore a meaning that was defamatory of the claimant at common law. A classic formulation of a defamatory statement is one that 'would tend to lower [the claimant] in the estimation of right-thinking members of society generally, or be likely to affect a person adversely in the estimation of reasonable people generally'.[254] Whether a statement is defamatory at common law is therefore considered objectively (hence the reference to right-thinking and reasonable people) and subject to evolution (for example, a statement that was defamatory fifty years ago will not necessarily be defamatory today). Secondly, by Defamation Act 2013 s1(1): 'A statement is not defamatory unless its publication has caused or is likely to cause serious harm to the reputation of the claimant.' The effect of this provision is that a claimant must prove not only that the statement had an

252 See *Wood v Chief Constable of the West Midlands* [2004] EWCA Civ 1638, [2005] EMLR 20 where a Detective Chief Inspector sent three letters to third parties involved in the insurance industry about the claimant's alleged offending.

253 Defamation Act 1952 s2.

254 *Skuse v Granada Television* [1996] EMLR 278 at para 286, CA; *Allen v Times Newspaper Ltd* [2019] EWHC 1235 (QB) at 19.

inherent tendency to cause substantial harm to their reputation, but also that it did as a matter of fact cause such harm.[255]

11.218 Where a claimant satisfies the elements of a libel claim, the Defamation Act 2013 offers three main defences to a defendant: truth (section 2), honest opinion (section 3) and public interest (section 4).[256] However, in the policing context, the most common defence in cases of limited or targeted publication (as opposed to, for example, press releases) is the qualified privilege defence, which applies where a statement is made on 'an occasion where the person who makes a communication has an interest or duty, legal, social or moral, to make it to the person who whom it is made, and the person to whom it is so made has a corresponding [ie a reciprocal] interest or duty to receive it'.[257] Where a privileged occasion is established by the defendant the defence can only be defeated if the claimant proves malice. This defence has been successfully relied upon where, for instance, a police officer made disclosures of the claimant's alleged assault against a minor in a series of child protection conferences.[258]

11.219 In a libel case, the court will decide at a preliminary hearing the 'single meaning' of each statement. In so doing, the court will determine the level of meaning – for example 1) an imputation of guilt; 2) an imputation of reasonable grounds to suspect; and 3) an imputation that there were grounds to investigate.[259] The court will also often determine at the same time: i) whether the meaning is defamatory of the claimant at common law; and ii) whether the statement is one of fact or opinion, or a mixed statement of both. The level of meaning and characterisation of the statement is crucially important to the claimant's prospect of success in the claim, as it affects which defences the defendant can rely upon, determine what the defendant needs to prove and can even affect the evidence that is required to satisfy the civil standard of proof. For example, it is much harder for a defendant to establish the truth of a factual statement that a person is guilty of murder[260] (an allegation of serious criminality for which clear evidence would be required) than for a defendant to establish an

255 *Lachaux v Independent Print Ltd* [2019] UKSC 27 at 14.

256 For an authoritative overview of these defences see *Duncan and Neill on Defamation and Other Media and Communications Claims*, 5th edn, LexisNexis, 2020, chapters 1–14.

257 *Adam v Ward* [1917] AC 309, HL; see also *Kearns v General Council of the Bar* [2003] EWCA Civ 331.

258 *H v Chief Constable of H* [2003] EWCA Civ 102.

259 *Chase v News Group Newspapers* [2002] EWCA Civ 1772 at 45. These 'Chase levels' are used as helpful shorthand in many cases, but they are by no means the only levels of meaning available and the spectrum of possible meanings in any given case may be much broader.

260 This example is based on *Bento v Chief Constable of Bedfordshire* [2012] EWHC 1525 (QB). In that case, the defendant issued a press release with the meaning that '(a) a jury had already found that the Claimant had murdered [the victim]; (b) the evidence as it stood . . . showed that he probably killed her, which was sufficient to justify proceeding with [a] retrial; (c) the CPS decision to offer no evidence was therefore wrong' (para 10). The defendant did not seek to rely on a defence of truth, but instead unsuccessfully sought to rely on a defence of qualified privilege.

honest belief in an opinion statement contained in a press release regarding the claimant, for example, being 'an extreme hate speaker'.[261]

11.220 The limitation period for a claim in defamation is one year from the date of publication. Defamation proceedings must be started in the High Court, unless the parties agree in writing that they should be started in the county court.[262] As with misuse of private information, any High Court claim for libel must be issued in the Media and Communications List in the Queen's Bench Division. Before bringing a claim the prospective claimant should follow the Pre-Action Protocol for Media and Communications Claims. When a decision has been made to bring a claim, then CPR PD 53B needs to be consulted and adhered to, which sets out mandatory requirements for statements of case.

11.221 Defamation is a highly technical area of law and legal proceedings are costly, both objectively and relative to other causes of action discussed above. As such, it is essential that any person considering bringing a claim obtains advice from lawyers with specialist knowledge.

261 This example is taken from *Butt v Secretary of State for the Home Department* [2019] EWCA Civ 933.

262 County Courts Act 1984 ss15(2)(c) and 18.

CHAPTER 12

Discrimination claims against the police

continued

Introduction

12.1 The Macpherson Report arising out of the investigation into the 1993 racially motivated murder of Stephen Lawrence,[1] published in February 1999, was a turning point in race relations in the UK, setting out 70 recommendations aimed at addressing institutional racism within the police. The Black Lives Matter campaign and the apparently discriminatory impact of the policing of the COVID-19 pandemic have continued to raise serious questions about racism within the police service in the UK and abroad. In addition, the abduction, rape and murder of Sarah Everard by a serving police officer in March 2021 and several other controversies have led to robust public debate about the issue of alleged sex discrimination within police forces.

12.2 Complex, but different, issues call for consideration in respect of other minority groups' experiences of policing.

12.3 Complaints against the police can be brought in relation to discrimination: the Standards of Professional Behaviour contained in Police (Conduct) Regulations 2012[2] Sch 2 require that police officers 'act with fairness and impartiality' and 'do not discriminate unlawfully or unfairly'. The Independent Police Complaints Commission (IPCC – now the Independent Office for Police Conduct (IOPC)) produced comprehensive guidance on the investigation of such complaints.[3] Further detail on police complaints can be found in chapters 3 and 4.

12.4 This chapter provides an overview of some of the main concerns with respect to discrimination by the police. It then describes the main ways of challenging discriminatory policing – through claims under the Equality Act (EqA) 2010 and the Human Rights Act (HRA) 1998. It concludes with a summary of the specific procedural issues that apply in litigating these sorts of claims.

Background and context

The Macpherson Report and its implementation

12.5 The 70 recommendations of the Macpherson Report addressed issues ranging from the definition of a racist incident, the prosecution of racist crime and the treatment of victims and witnesses, to stop and search and the recruitment, retention, training and discipline of police officers.

12.6 Since the report's publication, there have been efforts to foster policies that meet these recommendations.

12.7 However, it is clear that many challenges remain. In 2017, the Lammy Review highlighted that members of black and minority ethnic groups

1 *The Inquiry into the matters arising from the death of Stephen Lawrence* Cm 4262-I, TSO, 1999.

2 SI No 2632.

3 *IPCC guidelines for handling allegations of discrimination*, IPCC, 2015, available at: www.policeconduct.gov.uk/sites/default/files/Documents/research-learning/guidelines_for_handling_allegations_of_discrimination.pdf. See further paras 4.36–4.42 above.

continue to be disproportionately represented throughout the criminal justice system, from stop and search, to imprisonment, to deaths in custody as well as being more likely to have force used against them.[4]

12.8 In July 2021, the House of Commons Home Affairs Committee conducted a detailed inquiry into progress of the Macpherson recommendations 22 years on.[5] It found that since the Macpherson Report was published, there have been important positive developments in policing including significant improvements in the policing of racist crimes, in the commitments made to promoting equality and diversity and in good examples of local community policing. However, the inquiry identified 'persistent, deep rooted and unjustified racial disparities' in key areas.[6] The report stated:[7]

> The failure to make sufficient progress on BME recruitment, retention and progression, troubling race disparities in the police misconduct system, unjustified inequalities in the use of key police powers such as stop and search and a worrying decline in confidence and trust in the police among some BME communities point to structural problems which disadvantage BME groups.

It proposed urgent action in those areas.

Diversity in police forces

12.9 There have been some improvements in the diversity of police forces: as at 2021, 3.1 per cent of officers were Asian, 1.3 per cent were black, and 2.2 per cent were of a 'mixed' racial/ethnic background (an increase from, respectively 1.5 per cent, 1 per cent and 1 per cent in 2007).[8] However, police forces still do not reflect the diversity of the UK population as a whole;[9] there is significant geographical variation with respect to these figures;[10] and black and minority ethnic officers are disproportionately concentrated in the lower ranks of the police. In July 2021, the House of Commons Home Affairs Committee described as 'inexcusable' the fact that on current rates of progress, police forces will not be representative of their communities for another twenty years. It recommended that new minimum targets for current recruitment be set immediately, so that all forces in England and Wales reflect the ethnic diversity of their local populations and a national target of at least 14 per cent is met by 2030.[11]

4 *The Lammy Review: An independent review into the treatment of, and outcomes for, Black, Asian and Minority Ethnic individuals in the Criminal Justice System*, September 2017.

5 *The Macpherson Report: Twenty-two years on*, House of Commons, Home Affairs Select Committee, 21 July 2021.

6 At p4.

7 At para 552.

8 *Ethnicity facts and figures: Police workforce*, 29 January 2021.

9 The 2011 census recorded 6.8 per cent of people as Asian, 3.3 per cent black and 2.2 per cent as mixed: *Ethnicity and national identity in England and Wales: 2011*, Office for National Statistics (ONS).

10 In London, for example, in the 2011 census, 40.2 per cent of residents identified with either the Asian, Black, Mixed or Other ethnic group: *Ethnicity facts and figures: Regional ethnic diversity*, 1 August 2018.

11 *The Macpherson Report: Twenty-two years on*, pp6–7 and chapter 4.

Stop and search and arrest

12.10 The Macpherson Report made four recommendations focused on the use of stop and search powers. While there is now better reporting and transparency in regard to stop and search, there are still deep concerns about its use. In 2017, the Criminal Justice Alliance reported that three-quarters of the Black, Asian and minority ethnic young people aged 16–30 polled for the report thought that they and their communities were unfairly targeted by stop and search.[12] Home Office statistics from February 2021 confirm that between April 2020 and March 2021, there were 52.6 stops and searches for every 1,000 black people, compared to 7.5 for every 1,000 white people.[13] This means that black people are seven times more likely to be stopped and searched than white people.

12.11 The picture is similar for arrests: as at September 2020, there were 29 arrests for every 1,000 black people, and nine arrests for every 1,000 white people;[14] meaning that black people are over three times as likely to be arrested as white people.

12.12 Evidence suggests that these patterns with respect to race were exacerbated further during the COVID-19 'lockdown' in the spring and early summer of 2020: research by Liberty found that nationally, people of colour were over 50 per cent more likely than white people to be fined for breaching the lockdown; and that some forces were nearly seven times more likely to fine people of colour than white people.[15] During the three-month period between March and June 2020 when lockdown measures were in place, the Metropolitan Police Service recorded 98,280 stop and searches, with 79 per cent of those stopped being issued with a 'no further action' disposal and only ten per cent leading to an arrest.[16]

12.13 In its July 2021 report, the House of Commons Home Affairs Committee concluded that:[17]

> . . . no evidence to this inquiry has adequately explained or justified the nature and scale of the disproportionality in the use of stop and search powers . . .
>
> Given that the majority of people stopped and searched are not found to be committing any crime, stops should be initiated in a respectful and appropriate manner, with care taken to manage conflict and de-escalate encounters where necessary. Stop and search must always be used in a focused and targeted way.

The Committee was critical of the fact that recent 'sensible' recommendations from Her Majesty's Inspectorate of Constabulary and Fire and

12 *No respect: young BAME men, the police and stop and search*, Criminal Justice Alliance, 2017.

13 *Ethnicity facts and figures: Stop and search*, 27 May 2022.

14 *Ethnicity facts and figures: Arrests*, 12 May 2022.

15 Liberty Investigates, *BAME people disproportionately targeted by coronavirus fines*, May 2020.

16 Across the period of March 2020 to March 2022 the figures indicate only a slightly higher arrest rate (11.7%), with the overwhelming majority of stops and searches leading to no further action (75.5%). *Stop and search dashboard*, Metropolitan Police, accessed 5 May 2022, available at: www.met.police.uk/sd/stats-and-data/met/stop-and-search-dashboard/.

17 At p8.

Rescue Services (HMICFRS) had still not been widely implemented or sustained, and called for further reforms, including recording the ethnicity of those who are subject to road traffic stops, additional training for police officers and staff on communication, conflict management and de-escalation, and full use of body worn video, with internal reviews and external community oversight.[18]

12.14 Shortly after publication of the Committee's report, the government proposed a permanent relaxation of 'section 60' police powers: these powers (derived from the Criminal Justice and Public Order Act 1994 s60) enable police search to anyone for a weapon if they have 'reasonable grounds' to think they are involved in crime. They were restricted in 2014 so they could only be used if police believed there was an immediate violent threat, during a limited number of hours. Those restrictions were eased in 2019 to allow police to carry out searches 24 hours a day and on grounds of possible violence. In July 2021 the government proposed to make the changes permanent. Later that year, Liberty and StopWatch threatened legal action, in response to which the Government admitted that the equality impact assessment on the policy decision was flawed. However, in May 2022 the Home Secretary confirmed that restrictions would be permanently lifted. [19]

The use of force

12.15 There are continued concerns that police officers use force disproportionately against those perceived to be from black and ethnic groups. Home Office data for police forces other than the Metropolitan Police indicates that from April 2020 to March 2021 use of force tactics, including handcuffing, ground restraint, use of batons, tasers and firearms were applied to people perceived as being from a black ethnic group at a rate five times higher than those perceived as being from a white ethnic group.[20] In the Metropolitan Police area, the rate was four times higher. Tasers (known as conducted energy devices or CEDs) were used 6.5 times more often against those perceived as being from a black ethnic group than those perceived as being from a white ethnic group (albeit the rate is five times higher in the Metropolitan Police area).[21]

Deaths in custody

12.16 In 2020/21, the IOPC recorded deaths during or following police contact including 25 road traffic fatalities, one fatal police shooting, 19 deaths in or following police custody, 54 apparent suicides following police custody,

18 Chapter 6.

19 https://www.gov.uk/government/news/home-secretary-backs-police-to-increase-stop-and-search.

20 *Police use of force statistics, England and Wales: April 2020 to March 2021*, Home Office, para 4.6.

21 At para 6.4. See also *The Macpherson Report: Twenty-two years on*, paras 401–418.

and 92 other deaths following police contact that were independently investigated by the IOPC.

12.17 Of the 19 deaths in or following police custody, 17 of those who died were white and two were black; 12 were identified as having 'mental health concerns'; 14 were known to have a link to alcohol/or drugs; and two were people detained under the Mental Health Act 1983.

12.18 Further, of the 54 apparent suicides, three people had been in mental health detention and 38 had known 'mental health concerns'.[22]

12.19 INQUEST – which provides expertise on state-related deaths and their investigation to bereaved people, lawyers, advice and support agencies, the media and parliamentarians – has regularly expressed concern that black men are disproportionately represented in deaths in custody and that there are complex links between deaths and mental ill health, intoxication and restraint.[23]

Women and girls in the criminal justice system

12.20 Violence against women and girls includes rape and sexual abuse, sexual harassment, stalking, coercive and controlling behaviour, trafficking, gang violence, female genital mutilation, forced marriage and issues relating to the production of pornography and prostitution. A large proportion of the women detained in prisons, mental health institutions and immigration centres have suffered sexual abuse and domestic violence. The Centre for Women's Justice was established in the UK in 2016 due to ongoing concerns that women as victims, defendants and witnesses suffer very significant disadvantage in the criminal justice system, including levels of sexism within the police service that at times appears institutionalised.[24]

12.21 One particular area of concern has been the undercharging of cases involving violence against women. In December 2019 Her Majesty's Crown Prosecution Service Inspectorate (HMCPSI) reported that since 2016, the number of cases prosecuted by the CPS has fallen by 52%, despite the fact that there had been a 43% rise in the number of rape allegations to the police. There had been a 23% fall in the number of cases referred to the CPS for a decision by the police. This means that while reports of rape to the police had nearly doubled, a significant number of these cases had not been referred to the CPS. Inspectors concluded that more work was needed to investigate the discrepancy between the number of cases reported and the number of cases prosecuted by the CPS.[25] In June 2021, the government published its End-to-End Rape Review Report on Findings and Actions, setting out an action plan for improving the criminal justice system's response to rape in England and Wales.[26] Further issues on which the Centre for Women's Justice has worked include the

22 *Deaths during or following police contact: Statistics for England and Wales 2020/21*, IOPC, July 2021.

23 *BAME deaths in police custody*, available at: www.inquest.org.uk/.

24 See: https://www.centreforwomensjustice.org.uk/why-we-exist/.

25 HMCPSI, *2019 rape inspection: A thematic review of rape cases by HM Crown Prosecution Service Inspectorate.*

26 *HM Government, End-to-End Rape Review Report on Findings and Actions (June 2021),*

circumstances in which the police may lawfully ask a victim or witness to provide material from their digital devices in the course of a criminal investigation, the consequences of police officers entering into long-term sexual relationships with women while undercover and the increase in domestic violence and the restriction of services for victims during the Covid-19 pandemic.[27]

12.22 Several controversies have placed the question of institutionalised sexism within the police service firmly on the national agenda in recent years.[28] In June 2020, sisters Bibaa Henry and Nicole Smallman were stabbed to death. The IOPC found that Metropolitan Police officers did not properly investigate reports from the sisters' family that they were missing[29] and that several officers had taken and shared photos of the sisters' bodies through a private WhatsApp group.[30] In March 2021, Sarah Everard was abducted, raped and murdered by a serving police officer. Clashes with police followed at the vigil held after her death on Clapham Common and members of Reclaim These Streets succeeded in a judicial review of the Metropolitan Police's decision to withdraw permission for the vigil to go ahead.[31] In September 2021 Sabina Nessa was murdered, leading to criticism of the police advice to women to keep themselves safe.[32] In January 2022 the Independent Office of Police Conduct published its report on Operation Hotton, a series of investigations into the conduct of officers primarily based at Charing Cross police station. The report referred to messages between officers that included misogynist, racist, anti-Semitic and other discriminatory language and led to a series of recommendations aimed at addressing racism, misogyny, bullying and harassment in the Metropolitan Police.[33] The Metropolitan Police has announced a review into its culture and standards of behaviour, an examination into all ongoing investigations of sexual and domestic abuse allegations against officers and staff and the publication of a new action plan for tackling violence against women and girls.[34] The Angiolini Inquiry has also been established, in order to explore the circumstances in which an off-duty Metropolitan police officer was able to abduct, rape and murder Sarah Everard.[35]

27 See: https://www.centreforwomensjustice.org.uk/.

28 For a summary of these issues, see https://researchbriefings.files.parliament.uk/documents/CDP-2022-0046/CDP-2022-0046.pdf.

29 See: https://www.policeconduct.gov.uk/news/failings-identified-how-mps-handled-missingpersons-reports-murdered-sisters.

30 See: https://www.policeconduct.gov.uk/news/investigation-update-regarding-inappropriatephotographs-taken-murder-scene-wembley.

31 *Leigh v Commissioner for the Police of the Metropolis* [2022] EWHC 527, Times, May 9, 2022

32 See, for example, https://www.bbc.co.uk/news/uk-england-london-58665603.

33 See:https://www.policeconduct.gov.uk/sites/default/files/Operation%20Hotton%20Learning%20report%20-%20January%202022.pdf

34 See: https://www.met.police.uk/notices/met/our-response-to-issues-raised-by-the-crimes-of-waynecouzens/.

35 See: https://www.angiolini.independent-inquiry.uk/.

Gender identity and sexual orientation issues

12.23 Between February and April 2017, 5,375 lesbian, gay, bi and trans (LGBT) people across England, Scotland and Wales completed an online questionnaire about their life in Britain today, which was administered by data analytics firm YouGov on behalf of LGBT charity Stonewall. The survey found that two in five trans people (41 per cent) and three in ten non-binary people (31 per cent) had experienced a hate crime or incident because of their gender identity in the previous 12 months. The figure was even higher for younger trans adults, of whom 53 per cent reported such experiences. The research also indicated that hate crime against trans people is significantly underreported – four in five trans people (79 per cent) indicated that they had not reported incidents to the police and some of those who had reported a hate crime did not feel supported by the police or even that they experienced further discrimination by the police. More than two in five trans people (44 per cent) reported avoiding certain streets altogether because they did feel safe there as an LGBT person.[36]

12.24 The Metropolitan Police has also faced allegations that its investigations into the deaths of four young men in Barking (who had been murdered by the serial killer Stephen Port) were influenced by the fact that his victims were young, gay men.[37] Although the Coroner withdrew the issue of 'prejudice' from the jury considering the deaths of the men,[38] in her Preventing Further Deaths report, she agreed with the Independent Office for Police Conduct's view that 'the possibility of assumptions being made about the lifestyle of young gay men and the potential vulnerability of men cannot be ignored, and may reveal that intersectionality was present in policing in 2014/2015, and may still be'.[39] MPs have also called for an inquiry into alleged homophobia within the Metropolitan Police.[40]

Disability and crime

12.25 In 2020/21, there was an increase in disability hate crimes by nine per cent. In October 2020, Home Office figures showed that the number of disability hate crimes recorded by police forces in England and Wales had continued to climb.[41] However, Crown Prosecution Service (CPS) statistics suggest that the number of prosecutions for such cases dropped by

36 *LGBT in Britain: Trans report,* YouGov and Stonewall, 2018.

37 See, for example, G Wilford, 'Stephen Port: Police missed Grindr serial killer because victims were gay, families say in lawsuit', *Independent,* 3 June 2017, www.independent.co.uk/news/uk/crime/grindr-stephen-port-scotland-yard-met-police-homophobia-serial-killer-a7734031.html.

38 See the Coroner's ruling, paragraphs 11-28, at https://webarchive.nationalarchives.gov.uk/ukgwa/20220429151131mp_/https://www.eastlondoninqu ests.org.uk/wp-content/uploads/2021/12/10.-ELI-Ruling-following-submissions-on-29-November-2021-FINAL__-100471033_1.pdf/.

39 See the Coroner's Preventing Further Deaths report, paragraph 65: at https://webarchive.nationalarchives.gov.uk/ukgwa/20220429150932mp_/https://www.eastlondoninqu ests.org.uk/wp-content/uploads/2022/01/ELI-PFD-Report-with-Annexes-FINAL.pdf/.

40 See: https://www.bbc.co.uk/news/uk-england-london-59644779/.

41 *Home Office official statistics, Hate Crime, England and Wales, 2020 to 2021.*

nearly 40 per cent in a year (from 579 prosecutions in 2018/19 to 360 in 2019/20), the third year in which the figures had fallen. This was said to be as a result of a steep reduction in the number of cases referred to prosecutors by police forces. One positive figure in the CPS report was that its conviction rate for disability hate crime offences rose from 72.4 per cent in 2018/19 to 81.1 per cent in 2019/20.[42] Nevertheless, the overall picture led disability rights campaigners to argue that the police services across England and Wales were failing disabled people.[43] In October 2021 the charity Leonard Cheshire reported, based on police statistics, that online disability hate crime had increased by over 50% on the previous year's figures.[44]

Crimes against older people

12.26 The population of England and Wales is ageing. While older people are generally less at risk of crime, some types of crimes – those linked to physical, mental, or financial abuse – disproportionately affect older people. Some older people are especially at risk, because perpetrators target them or because their circumstances (for example, if they are bereaved, lonely or living with dementia) makes them vulnerable. Some older people are socially isolated and so do not have established support mechanisms to help them recover if they become victims.[45]

12.27 In 2017, the Home Secretary commissioned an inspection to establish the nature and extent of problems affecting older people within the criminal justice system, and how well these are understood by police forces and the CPS. In their joint report published in July 2019, HMICFRS and HMCPSI praised the work of police officers in their initial dealings with older victims of crime, including attending promptly to reports of crime from older victims. However, the report found that afterwards, officers struggled to deal with some of the complex needs of older people. It concluded that generally the police have only a 'superficial understanding' of the nature and extent of crimes against older people, which often results in a poorer service to older victims. This meant that older people were not always properly safeguarded, referral to victim support services for older people was too inconsistent and older people were not always offered the support of intermediaries, or helped to give their best evidence, for example by video-recording their evidence or using hearing loops. As a result of the inspection, HMICFRS and HMCPSI made a series of recommendations aimed at improving responses to older victims of crime and vulnerable adults more generally.[46]

42 *CPS official statistics: Hate crime England and Wales 2019–2020*, October 2020.

43 See, for example, the comments of Anne Novis, Chair of Inclusion, on the Disability News Service, 15 October 2020.

44 See: https://www.leonardcheshire.org/about-us/our-news/press-releases/lockdowns-trigger-surgedisability-hate-crime/.

45 Domestic abuse prevalence and victim characteristics, November 2021: https://www.ons.gov.uk/peoplepopulationandcommunity/crimeandjustice/datasets/domesticabuse prevalenceandvictimcharacteristicsappendixtables/.

46 *The poor relation: The police and CPS response to crimes against older people*, HMCPSI and HMICFRS, July 2019.

Overview of the legal framework

12.28 The primary route by which claimants can bring a private law damages claim against the police for discrimination is the EqA 2010. Claimants can also rely on a police force's failure to comply with the public sector equality duty (PSED), set out in the EqA 2010, in private law claims or in judicial review proceedings.

12.29 In some cases the HRA 1998 offers an alternative or additional cause of action (see further paras 12.98–12.05).

12.30 Finally, in damages claims for common law torts such as assault or false imprisonment, claimants can argue that an award of aggravated damages should be increased to reflect the fact that police actions towards them were influenced by their race, sex or gender or one of the other 'protected characteristics' (see further paras 12.133–12.136 and 17.18–17.33).

Discrimination claims against the police under the Equality Act 2010

Overview

12.31 Prior to the passage of the EqA 2010, advisers had to grapple with a patchwork of primary and secondary legislation that applied to the bringing of discrimination claims against the police. Different legislation, and different levels of protection, applied to each of the 'protected characteristics' (explained below at paras 12.41–12.57). This confusing picture was replaced in October 2010 with the composite EqA 2010. This took a much more consistent approach across all the protected characteristics, and expanded the circumstances in which claimants can sue the police for discriminatory conduct.

12.32 In order to bring a claim for discrimination under the EqA 2010, a claimant needs to ensure that three key elements are satisfied:

1) the conduct being challenged falls within the scope of the EqA 2010;
2) the act complained of amounts to one or more type of prohibited conduct under the EA 2010; and
3) the claimant is covered by one or more of the relevant protected characteristics.

These elements are addressed in turn.

Scope: applicability of the Equality Act 2010 to police cases

12.33 Prior to the Macpherson Report (see para 12.5), there were significant legal difficulties in suing the police for race discrimination under the Race Relations Act (RRA) 1976.

12.34 One of these difficulties was that the only applicable section of the RRA 1976 was section 20 which related to the provision of 'services'. In *Farah v Commissioner of Police of the Metropolis,*[47] it was made clear that this section

47 [1998] QB 65, CA.

applied to those parts of police officers' duties involving 'assistance to or protection of members of the public'. Further, in *Brooks v Commissioner of Police of the Metropolis and others*,[48] the Court of Appeal permitted 'services' claims arising from the handling of the investigation into the death of Stephen Lawrence to proceed to trial. However, in *Farah*, the Court of Appeal indicated that those police acts which a private person would never do (such as gaining forcible entry to a property) would not be covered by section 20. It was therefore generally understood that police powers of stop and search, arrest etc would not amount to the provision of a service for the purposes of section 20.

12.35 The Macpherson Report sought to fill this gap, by recommending that 'the full force of the Race Relations legislation should apply to all police officers'.[49] This was achieved by adding a new section 19B to the RRA 1976, covering general 'public functions', which had the effect of bringing police functions such as stop and search and arrest, within the scope of the RRA 1976.

12.36 The key provision for practitioners is now EqA 2010 s29, which covers both services and public functions. In practical terms, the effect of section 29(6) is that claimants need to consider whether the act by the police of which they complain can properly be characterised as a 'service', and if not whether it is a 'public function'.

12.37 'Public function' has the same meaning in the EqA 2010 as 'function of a public nature' for the purposes of the HRA 1998 (see para 7.109). In relation to private or voluntary organisations, this would cover activities carried out on behalf of the state and which are not similar in kind to services that could be performed by private persons.[50] The vast majority of police acts which are likely to generate claims of discrimination – such as stop and search, arrest, detention and searches of property – will fall under this part of section 29.

12.38 The definition of 'service' is a broad one. It includes permitting access to and use of any place which members of the public are permitted to enter, and the provision of goods and facilities, whether or not for payment.[51]

12.39 The net result of the above is that most police acts will be either a public function or a service. However, the same act cannot be both, because section 29(6) refers to 'the exercise of a public function that is *not* the provision of a service' (emphasis added).

12.40 EqA 2010 s29 is subject to some limitations:

- Along with the remainder of EqA 2010 Part 3, it does not extend to the protected characteristics of age (so far as relating to persons who have not attained the age of 18) or marriage and civil partnership.

48 [2002] EWCA Civ 407.

49 The Commission of Racial Equality's Third Review of the Act had contained a similar recommendation (April 1988).

50 *Statutory code of practice on services, public functions and associations*, Equality and Human Rights Commission (EHRC), para 11.15; available at: www.equalityhumanrights.com/en/publication-download/services-public-functions-and-associations-statutory-code-practice.

51 *Statutory code of practice on services, public functions and associations*, EHRC, paras 11.3–11.4.

- Further, for the purposes of EqA 2010 s26(3) and (6) claims of harassment, neither religion or belief or sexual orientation is considered a relevant protected characteristic.
- Section 29 does not apply to parliamentary, legislative or judicial functions and certain acts of the armed forces and security services.[52]

The protected characteristics in discrimination claims against the police

Overview

12.41 EqA 2010 Part 2 Chapter 1 sets out the following protected characteristics which may apply to discrimination claims against the police:

- race (section 9);
- religion or belief (section 10);
- sex, pregnancy and maternity (sections 11 and 17);
- sexual orientation (section 12);
- gender reassignment (section 7);
- disability (section 6);
- age (section 5).

Race

12.42 The EqA 2010 defines 'race' as including colour, nationality and ethnic or national origins.[53] A person has the protected characteristic of race if they fall within a particular 'racial group'.[54] 'Racial group' means a group of persons defined by reference to race (including colour, nationality and ethnic or national origins). A racial group can be made up of two or more distinct attributes.[55] The Explanatory Notes to the EqA 2010 give the example of 'black Britons' which is a racial group encompassing those people who are both black and who are British citizens.[56]

12.43 Frequently a claimant will be unable to tell, particularly at an early stage of proceedings, whether their adverse treatment was because of their colour or because of their ethnic or national origins. For example, a young man may have been stopped by the police because he is black (colour) or because he is Afro-Caribbean (national origins). When there is any doubt, it is advisable to make or plead any claim in the alternative.

52 EqA 2010 Sch 3 Part 1. Section 29 is subject to further limitations outside of the policing context such as with respect to education, health/care, immigration and other matters: EqA 2010 Sch 3 Parts 2–10. Along with the remainder of EqA 2010 Part 3, it does not extend to the protected characteristics of age (so far as relating to persons who have not attained the age of 18) or marriage and civil partnership (EqA 2010 s28(1)). Further, for the purposes of sections 26(3) and 26(6) claims of harassment, neither religion or belief or sexual orientation is considered a relevant protected characteristic (EqA 2010 s29(8)).

53 EqA 2010 s9(1).

54 EqA 2010 s9(2).

55 EqA 2010 s9(4).

56 EqA 2010 Explanatory Notes, at 50.

Religion or belief

12.44 The protected characteristic of religion or belief includes any religion and any religious or philosophical belief.[57] The meaning of religion and belief in the EqA 2010 is broad and is intended to be consistent with European Convention on Human Rights (ECHR) Article 9 (which guarantees freedom of thought, conscience and religion).[58] The main limitation for the purposes of Article 9 is that the religion must have a clear structure and belief system. The EqA 2010 therefore protects religions such as Christianity, Judaism, Islam and Hinduism, as well as others such as Baha'i, Jainism, Rastafarianism and Zoroastrianism. A religion need not be mainstream or well-known to be protected under the Act. In addition, denominations or systems of belief within religions, such as Methodism or Sabbatarianism within Christianity, or Sunni or Shia within Islam, are likely to be religions for the purposes of the Act. The EqA 2010 also protects a *lack of* any such religion or belief. This means that people without a religion, such as atheists, humanists and secularists, are protected under the Act. It also means that a person who has a particular religion will be protected if they are discriminated against because they lack another, different religion.[59]

12.45 The Explanatory Notes to the EqA 2010 further set out criteria for determining a 'philosophical belief': it must be genuinely held; be a belief and not an opinion or viewpoint based on the present state of information available; be a belief as to a weighty and substantial aspect of human life and behaviour; attain a certain level of cogency, seriousness, cohesion and importance; and be worthy of respect in a democratic society, compatible with human dignity and not conflict with the fundamental rights of others. Beliefs such as humanism, pacifism, vegetarianism and the belief in man-made climate change are all protected, but beliefs such as Holocaust denial, or a belief in racial superiority, would not be.[60]

Sex, pregnancy and maternity

12.46 'Sex' refers to a male or a female of any age. In relation to a group of people, it refers to either men and/or boys, or women and/or girls.[61] A claim might arise, for example, if male officers treated a female victim of crime in an abusive and derogatory way, because of her sex. Specific prohibitions on discrimination against women due to pregnancy, childbirth and breast feeding are set out in EqA 2010 s17.

Sexual orientation

12.47 For the purposes of the EqA 2010, 'sexual orientation' means a person's sexual orientation towards persons of the same sex; persons of the opposite sex; or persons of either sex.[62] Claims may arise in circumstances where

57 EqA 2010 s10(1) and (2).
58 EqA 2010 Explanatory Notes, at 51.
59 *Religion or belief: a guide to the law*, EHRC, 2016, p4.
60 *Religion or belief: a guide to the law*, EHRC, 2016, p5.
61 EqA 2010 ss11 and 212(1).
62 EqA 2010 s12(1).

an individual reports homophobic abuse to the police that is then not adequately investigated, if there is a basis for arguing that the reason for the inadequate investigation is the orientation of the victim.[63]

Gender reassignment

12.48 A person has the protected characteristic of 'gender reassignment' for the purposes of the EqA 2010 if the person is proposing to undergo, is undergoing or has undergone a process (or part of a process) for the purpose of reassigning the person's sex by changing physiological or other attributes of sex.[64] Under EqA 2010 s7(2), a person who has the protected characteristic of gender reassignment is referred to as a 'transsexual' person, which is generally considered an outdated phrase.

12.49 On its face, the protected characteristic of gender reassignment under the EqA 2010 focuses on those trans individuals who are contemplating or have undergone medical treatment to reassign their sex. Many gender fluid and non-binary people would not be in this situation. However in *Taylor v Jaguar Land Rover Ltd*,[65] an employment tribunal took an expansive approach to this provision in holding that a gender fluid engineer who suffered abuse and harassment at work was protected by the EqA 2010. Jaguar Land Rover had argued that being 'gender fluid or non-binary' did not fall within the definition of the protected characteristic of 'gender reassignment' under the EqA 2010, but the tribunal ruled that it was 'clear . . . that gender is a spectrum' and that it was 'beyond any doubt' that being non-binary or gender fluid was covered by the protected characteristic of 'gender reassignment' under the EqA 2021.

Disability

12.50 A person has a 'disability' for the purposes of the EqA 2010 if they have a physical or mental impairment and the impairment has a substantial and long-term adverse effect on their ability to carry out normal day-to-day activities.[66] 'Substantial' is defined as more than minor or trivial.[67] 'Long-term' means that the impairment has lasted or is likely to last for at least 12 months or for the rest of the affected person's life.[68] EqA 2010 Sch 1 contains further provisions on how to determine who is a disabled person for the purposes of the Act and sets out certain conditions that are to be treated as a disability in their own right.

12.51 In most circumstances, a person will have the protected characteristic of disability if they have had a disability in the past, even if they no longer have the disability.[69] Save in the most obvious of cases, expert evidence establishing that a claimant has a disability as defined by these provisions will be required.

63 This was the subject of the original claim in *Cary v Commissioner of Police of Metropolis* [2014] EWCA Civ 987, although the judgment was limited to the issue of assessors.

64 EqA 2010 s7(1).

65 *Taylor v Jaguar Land Rover Ltd* [2020] ET/1304471/2018, 14 September.

66 EqA 2010 s6(1).

67 EqA 2010 s212(1).

68 EqA 2010 Sch 1 para 2.

69 EqA 2010 s6(4).

12.52 Claims may arise if officers failed to treat seriously a crime reported by a person with hearing and speech difficulties and/or failed to take the necessary steps to appreciate the allegations they were making. The EqA 2010 may also require the police to make reasonable adjustments to their provision of services or exercise of public function, for example by providing a sign language interpreter when conducting a house search,[70] or adjusting the force and physical restraint used on a disabled person[71] (see further 'duty to make reasonable adjustments' below at paras 12.79–12.83).

12.53 Another issue that can arise is where police officers arrest and detain an individual for behaviour which is in fact caused by a disability. This can lead to questions about whether the police officers should have modified their usual policing tactics to take account of the person's disability, and potentially there may be a claim if they have not done so.

Age

12.54 For the purposes of the EqA 2010, 'age' means a person belonging to a particular age group.[72] A reference to an age group is a reference to a group of persons defined by reference to age, whether by reference to a particular age or to a range of ages.[73] 'Age group' is not further defined, and it can potentially be very broad, for example 'over fifties'.[74] The EqA 2010 protects all ages groups except those aged 18 and under, for whom there is no protection under this section in relation to the provision of goods, facilities and services and in the exercise of public functions.[75] For example, a pensioner who believed that the investigation into a crime they had reported had been influenced by their age could bring a claim under these provisions.

Combined/intersectional discrimination

12.55 Some people face discrimination because of a combination of protected characteristics. For example, a black woman may suffer prejudice or harassment that a black man or white woman would not experience. This problem was designed to be addressed by EqA 2010 s14, which prohibits direct discrimination because of a combination of two protected characteristics, but this section has not yet come into force. However, there is some ability to bring such claims under the HRA 1998 (see below at paras 12.98–12.107).

The prohibited conduct

12.56 The forms of discrimination prohibited by the EqA 2010 are:

- direct discrimination;

70 *Finnigan v Chief Constable of Northumbria* [2013] EWCA Civ 1191, [2014] 1 WLR 445.
71 See, for example, *Commissioner of Police of the Metropolis v ZH* [2013] EWCA Civ 69, [2013] 1 WLR 3021.
72 EqA 2010 s5(1).
73 EqA 2010 s5(2).
74 EqA 2010 Explanatory Notes, at 36.
75 EqA 2010 s28(1).

- indirect discrimination;
- discrimination arising from a disability;
- breach of a duty to make reasonable adjustments;
- harassment;
- victimisation.

Direct discrimination

Main form

12.57 Direct discrimination is established where a person is treated less favourably than somebody else because of their protected characteristic.[76] Two elements must be proved: 1) that the alleged discrimination has treated the person less favourably than it treats or would treat others; and 2) that the difference in treatment is because of a protected characteristic.

Less favourable treatment

12.58 There is no definition of less favourable treatment in the EA 2010. It essentially means being treated *differently* or *worse*. It is not necessary to show actual harm. Although the test posed by the legislation is an objective one, the person's perception of the effect of treatment on them is likely to influence the court's conclusion as to whether, objectively, the treatment was less favourable.[77] A 'comparator' is used to shed light on the reason for the treatment.

12.59 The most straightforward comparator will demonstrate that someone without the person's protected characteristic was not treated in the same way (ie unfavourably). For example two 16-year-old boys leave a train station together. One is black and one is white. Only the black boy is stopped and searched by officers under the Misuse of Drugs Act 1971. He believes there was no good reason for the stop and search.[78] In this scenario, the black boy can point to his white friend as a 'real' comparator.

12.60 If no real comparator is available, a hypothetical comparator can be constructed, to show that someone without the person's protected characteristic would not have been treated in the same way (ie unfavourably). It is important that the comparator is someone in the same or not materially different circumstances from the claimant, which may often be a point of dispute. For example, a Muslim man makes a series of requests arising from his religious needs while he was detained in police custody. He describes the custody sergeant making offensive comments to him. The sergeant admits that he may have grumbled about having to respond to the requests made by the man, but says that this was because the man was making so many requests and it was a busy night, not because of his race or religion. The CCTV footage for the custody suite shows that the man did make considerably more requests than the other detainees, but also

76 EqA 2010 s13(1). The wording is similar to that used in the previous equality legislation such as the Sex Discrimination Act 1975 and the Race Relations Act (RRA) 1976 (both now repealed) and incorporates many of the same elements necessary for finding direct discrimination. The case-law under that regime therefore remains relevant, for example in relation to the meaning of 'less favourable treatment'.

77 *Chief Constable of West Yorkshire Police v Khan* [2001] UKHL 48, [2001] 1 WLR 1947.

78 *IPCC guidelines for handling allegations of discrimination*, p4.

shows that the requests made by the other detainees, who were all white, were responded to without any negative remarks. There is no actual comparator, but the different treatment of the white detainees can be used to construct a hypothetical comparator to help assess how a white detainee who made a similar number of requests to the claimant would likely have been treated.[79]

12.61 An exception to the need for a comparison is where it is clear that the alleged behaviour is discriminatory even without making a comparison – for example, the use of discriminatory language.

Because of a protected characteristic

12.62 A complaint of direct discrimination will only succeed where the court finds that the protected characteristic was the reason for the claimant's less favourable treatment. Whilst showing direct discrimination will usually involve an analysis of the stated reasons for the differential treatment, it is not necessary for a claimant to show that the alleged discriminator discriminated consciously.[80] Direct discrimination cannot be justified, unless the claim is one of direct age discrimination, in which case the court will scrutinise the reasons for the less favourable treatment with care.[81]

Additional forms

12.63 There are two further forms of direct discrimination.

- **Discrimination by association.** Direct discrimination can also occur when an individual is treated less favourably because of a protected characteristic that the claimant does not personally possess, but because of their association with someone who does possess it. This form of discrimination can occur in various ways, for example where the victim is a relative or partner of someone with a protected characteristic or where someone has campaigned to help someone with a particular protected characteristic. A well-known example of associative discrimination was *EBR Attridge Law LLP (formerly Attridge Law) v Coleman* in which the claimant alleged she had been treated less favourably because she had a disabled son. Following a ruling from the European Court of Justice, the Employment Appeal Tribunal held that the Disability Discrimination Act 1995 could be interpreted so as to enable her to bring direct discrimination and harassment claims.[82]
- **Discrimination by perception.** Discrimination because of a person's perceived characteristic is also proscribed by EqA 2010 s13. For example, in *Chief Constable of Norfolk v Coffey*,[83] a police officer succeeded in proving that she had been discriminated against because of perceptions about the extent of her hearing loss. If a police officer discriminates against someone because they perceive them to be gay or

79 *IPCC guidelines for handling allegations of discrimination*, p45.

80 *Glasgow City Council v Zafar* [1997] 1 WLR 1659 at 1664, HL (Scotland).

81 EqA 2010 s13(2). In such cases, the discriminatory treatment must be a 'proportionate means of achieving a legitimate aim'.

82 [2007] ICR 654.

83 [2020] 2 All ER 490, [2020] ICR 145.

transgender (but they are not in fact either), this would amount to discrimination by perception.

Indirect discrimination

Overview

12.64 Indirect discrimination has been described as 'an attempt to level the playing field by subjecting to scrutiny requirements which look neutral on their face but in reality work to the comparative disadvantage of people with a particular protected characteristic'.[84] In other words, it occurs where a policy or practice is applied equally across all groups, but the result is still that a particular protected group are put at a disadvantage, and where the policy or practice cannot be objectively justified.[85]

12.65 The elements of an indirect discrimination claim against the police are that:

1) The police force applies (or would apply) a provision, criterion or practice (PCP) equally to everyone within the relevant group, including the claimant.
2) The PCP puts (or would put) people who share the claimant's protected characteristic at a particular disadvantage when compared with people who do not have that characteristic.
3) The PCP puts (or would put) the claimant at that disadvantage.
4) The police force cannot show that the PCP is justified as a proportionate means of achieving a legitimate aim.

The PCP

12.66 The function of the PCP in an indirect discrimination (and reasonable adjustment) claim is to identify what it was about the conduct of the police that caused substantial disadvantage to the victim. The concept of the PCP has been given a broad interpretation by the courts. It can include criteria, policies, informal practices, one-off decisions and decisions to do something in the future, such as a policy that has not yet come into force.[86] An example would be a police practice or policy of treating disabled persons in the same way as non-disabled persons, even though the two groups have different physical or mental limitations.

Pool for comparison

12.67 In establishing whether a PCP places persons of a protected characteristic at a particular disadvantage, the starting point is to look at the impact on people within a defined 'pool' for comparison. The pool in a particular case may consist (for example, in the context of policing) of a single street, neighbourhood, or the population within the local catchment area of an arrest. One method for doing so is to consider whether persons within a

84 *Homer v Chief Constable of West Yorkshire* [2012] UKSC 15, [2012] 3 All ER 1237 at para 17.

85 EqA 2010 s19; *IPCC guidelines for handling allegations of discrimination*, p5.

86 See *Ishola v Transport for London* [2020] 2 WLUK 47 at 27–38, where the Court of Appeal held that a one-off act or decision could amount to a 'practice' in certain circumstances. A 'real risk' is capable of being a disadvantage within the meaning of the EqA 2010 s19(2)(b): *Commissioner of Police of the Metropolis v Keohane* [2014] 3 WLUK 58, [2014] ICR 1073, EAT.

selected 'pool' who share the relevant protected characteristic are more likely to fall at the hurdle of the PCP than those who do not possess the characteristic.

Particular disadvantage

12.68 The PCP that puts members of a protected group at a 'particular disadvantage' must also put the claimant at that disadvantage. It is not enough for the claimant to establish their membership of the protected group.[87] However, the wording of the provision is broad enough to protect those who are deterred from using a service because they knew that a PCP would prevent them from being successful, or PCPs which have not yet been applied but would have a discriminatory effect if they were.

12.69 In contrast to direct discrimination, indirect discrimination does not require a causal link between the conduct (the PCP) and the protected characteristic. Instead, it requires a causal link between the PCP and the disadvantage suffered by the group or individual.[88] However, there is no requirement that a PCP must put every member of the group with a particular protected characteristic at a disadvantage.[89]

Justification

12.70 A PCP can be justified if it is a 'proportionate means of achieving a legitimate aim'. The burden would fall to the police force to prove the justification, and it would be for the court to conduct a detailed analysis of the practices involved so as to determine whether the treatment was justified. The approach generally taken by the court or tribunal is to split the justification issue into two questions: 1) Can the respondent establish that it was pursuing a legitimate aim? 2) If so, can the respondent establish that the measures taken to achieve that aim were appropriate and proportionate?[90]

12.71 A legitimate aim must be a real, objective consideration and not in itself discriminatory. Examples of legitimate aims are provided in the EHRC's *Statutory code of practice on services, public functions and associations*, and include economic efficiency, ensuring that services and benefits are targeted at those who most need them, the fair exercise of powers, ensuring health and safety, preventing fraud or other forms of abuse or inappropriate use of services, ensuring the wellbeing and dignity of service users.[91] The prevention of crime is likely to be a legitimate aim for these purposes. Avoiding costs is unlikely to be regarded, on its own, as a legitimate aim.[92] In cases where a public authority is seeking to justify indirect

87 *Boon v Chief Constable of Lancashire* ET/1900473/13; see also *Keane v Investigo and others* UKEAT/0389/09.

88 *Gray v Mulberry Company (Design) Ltd* [2019] EWCA Civ 1720.

89 *Essop v Home Office (UK Border Agency); Naeem v Secretary of State for Justice* [2017] UKSC 27, per Lady Hale.

90 *Hardys & Hansons plc v Lax* [2005] EWCA Civ 846, [2005] ICR 1565.

91 *Statutory code of practice on services, public functions and associations*, EHRC, para 5.30.

92 In *Heskett v Secretary of State for Justice* [2020] EWCA Civ 1487, [2021] ICR 110 at para 89, it was held that the saving or avoidance of costs could not, without more, amount to the achieving of a legitimate aim for the purpose of the defence of justification in a discrimination claim; but that an employer's need to reduce its expenditure, and specifically its staff costs, in order to balance its books could constitute a legitimate aim for that purpose.

discrimination, courts and tribunals will have regard to the extent that the respondent has complied with their public sector equality duty[93] (see below 12.94–12.97).

12.72 In order to determine whether the measures taken were 'appropriate and proportionate', the court will perform a balancing exercise to assess whether the aims relied upon by the respondent were sufficient to outweigh the impact of the measures in question on the protected group generally and on the claimant in particularly. The measures taken will likely not be considered appropriate and proportionate if the respondent could have used less discriminatory means to achieve the same objective.

12.73 For example, a policy that all detainees remove hats or headgear when entering police custody will disproportionately affect Sikh men who wear turbans and Jewish men who wear skullcaps. If such a policy was challenged, the court would look carefully at the police force's reasons for having in place such a policy. If the reasons given did not justify the adverse impacts on particular groups, and the men question, they would have been indirectly discriminated against.[94]

Discrimination arising from disability

12.74 This form of discrimination is established where someone is treated unfavourably because of something arising from their disability; and there is no objective justification for treating them this way.[95] This form of discrimination is different to direct discrimination because that form of discrimination, in the context of disability, addresses less favourable treatment due to the disability itself: this form of discrimination is about unfavourable treatment arising from something linked with the disability.

12.75 There is no statutory definition of 'unfavourable' treatment. However, the Supreme Court has held that a 'relatively low threshold of disadvantage' is sufficient.[96]

12.76 The 'consequences' of a disability include anything which is the result, effect, or outcome of a disabled persons' disability,[97] such as an inability to comprehend or follow instructions, a need for particular type of communication, additional physical and psychological support, medical needs, difficulties in using public transport. The case law indicates that a loose causal connection between the claimant's disability and the unfavourable treatment will be sufficient in some cases.[98] Further, the court may infer the reason for the unfavourable treatment.[99]

12.77 In practice, many claims based on EqA 2010 s15 will depend on the issue of justification. The same defence is available in an indirect

93 *Statutory code of practice on services, public functions and associations*, EHRC, para5.36.

94 *IPCC guidelines for handling allegations of discrimination*, p6.

95 EqA 2010 s15(1)(a), (b).

96 *Williams v Trustees of Swansea University Pension and Assurance Scheme* [2018] UKSC 65, [2019] 1 WLR 93 at 27.

97 *Statutory code of practice on services, public functions and associations*, EHRC, para 5.9.

98 *Hall v Chief Constable of West Yorkshire* [2015] IRLR 893 at para 35, EAT.

99 *Pnaiser v NHS England* [2016] IRLR 170, EAT.

discrimination claim and it is reasonable to suppose that the same principles apply to both tests.

12.78 For example, an officer arrests a young woman for allegedly anti-social behaviour which arises from her autism. If the officer knows or should have known she was disabled, the arrest will amount to discrimination arising from disability if the police force cannot prove that the arrest was objectively justified.

Breach of a duty to make reasonable adjustments for those with disabilities

12.79 Police forces can be liable for failing to comply with the duty to make reasonable adjustments. There are three elements to the duty:

1) a duty to take reasonable steps to avoid substantial disadvantage caused by the application of a PCP;[100]
2) a duty to take reasonable steps to avoid substantial disadvantage caused by a physical feature;[101] and
3) a duty to take reasonable steps to provide an auxiliary aid to avoid putting a disabled person at a substantial disadvantage.[102]

12.80 For the duty to arise, the claimant must be placed at a 'substantial disadvantage' in comparison with persons who are not disabled. Whether a person is placed at a substantial disadvantage is an objective question. 'Substantial' is defined as 'more than minor or trivial'.[103]

12.81 In deciding whether the adjustments made are 'reasonable', the court applies an objective test based on the type of service provided; the nature of the service provider its size and resources; and the effect of the disability on the individual disabled person.[104] The EHRC's *Statutory code of practice on services, public functions and associations* sets out a non-exhaustive list of factors which might be taken into account when assessing reasonableness:

- Would the step effectively overcome the substantial disadvantage?
- Is it practicable for the service provider to take the steps?
- What are the financial or other costs of making the adjustment?[105]
- Would taking the step cause any disruption?

100 EqA 2010 s20(3). This requirement might involve, for example, the modification of the terms of a general policy or practice for the provision of services.

101 EqA 2010 s20(4). This requirement covers modifications that may have to be made to the built (ie physical) environment, such as the installation of an entrance ramp to aid access by wheelchair users.

102 EqA 2010 s20(5). 'Auxiliary aid' includes a reference to an auxiliary service: s20(11). This requirement might involve, for example, the provision of special computer software or the services of a sign language interpreter.

103 EqA 2010 s212(1).

104 *Smith v Churchills Stairlifts plc* [2005] EWCA Civ 1220, [2006] ICR 524.

105 If the adjustment is reasonable, then the service provider must pay for it. The service provider cannot require the disabled person to pay for, or contribute towards the cost of, reasonable adjustments (EqA 2010 s20(7); and *Statutory code of practice on services, public functions and associations*, EHRC, para 7.40).

- What are the service provider's financial and other resources?[106]
- How much of the service provider's resources have already been spent on making adjustments?
- Is there any financial or other assistance available?

12.82 An adjustment might be reasonable, and therefore required, where there is a 'prospect' that it will succeed,[107] or where there adjustment only partially removes the disabled person's disadvantage.[108]

12.83 For example, a deaf and non-verbal man has experienced a number of instances of disability hate crime from his neighbours. He is able to use British Sign Language (BSL) to communicate, but he finds it difficult to get access to an interpreter in order to report crimes to the police. He prefers to communicate in writing where possible. He has repeatedly sent written evidence of the disability hate crimes that he has been victim to, but he is unhappy about the limited action taken. He complains that officers have failed to properly consider this written evidence because it is not accompanied by oral explanations. The court would look carefully at whether the police force had made reasonable adjustments to their usual means of receiving oral evidence from complainants, given the difficulties the man had faced in getting access to a BSL interpreter to report the crimes.[109]

Harassment

12.84 There are three types of harassment included within the EqA 2010 – one which is of general application and two of which only relate to sexual harassment.

12.85 The general definition of harassment incorporates three elements:

1) unwanted conduct;
2) which relates to a relevant protected characteristic; and
3) which violates a person's dignity or creates a degrading, humiliating, or offensive environment for them.[110]

12.86 Looking at these components in detail:

- 'Unwanted' in this context means essentially 'unwelcome' or 'uninvited'. Conduct that is clearly offensive or obviously violates a claimant's dignity will likely be automatically regarded as unwanted. The victim need not have made the perpetrator aware that the conduct was

106 It is more likely to be reasonable for a service provider with substantial financial resources to have to make an adjustment with a significant cost than for a service provider with fewer resources (*Statutory code of practice on services, public functions and associations*, EHRC, para 7.31). An organisation's resources must be looked at across the whole organisation, not just for the branch or section that provides the particular service (EHRC, p78).

107 *Griffiths v Secretary of State for Work and Pensions* [2017] ICR 160.

108 *Noor v Foreign and Commonwealth Office* [2011] ICR 695, EAT.

109 *IPCC guidelines for handling allegations of discrimination*, p65.

110 EqA 2010 s26(1). The relevant protected characteristics are: age; disability; gender reassignment; race; religion or belief; sex; and sexual orientation: EA 2010 s26(5).

unwanted. The victim's perception will strongly influence the court's assessment of whether the conduct was unwanted.[111]

- The test of conduct 'related to' a protected characteristic is wider than the test for direct discrimination, which requires treatment 'because of' a protected characteristic.
- In deciding whether the conduct violates a person's dignity or creates a degrading, humiliating, or offensive environment for the claimant, the court will consider the perception of the victim, the other circumstances of the case and whether it is reasonable for the conduct to have that effect.[112]

12.87 The first specific type of sexual harassment is established where the perpetrator engages in unwanted 'conduct of a sexual nature' and the conduct has the purpose or effect set out in the general definition.[113] The second is established where someone is treated less favourably, either by the perpetrator or a third party, because of their rejection or submission to conduct of a sexual nature.[114]

12.88 Harassment can include making offensive comments, jokes or insulting gestures that relate to relevant protected characteristic even if they are not specifically directed at the complainant themselves. For example, a woman complains that while she was detained in police custody she overheard a group of police officers making rude and sexually suggestive comments about another female detainee. She complains that she found this upsetting and that it made her more uneasy and fearful about being held in custody. The comments were not directed at the woman. However, the conduct complained about relates to a relevant protected characteristic and the woman has said that the officers' actions were both unwanted and created an offensive and even intimidating environment. This raises the potential for a claim of harassment.[115]

12.89 Another example would be where a trans woman was stopped by police and they kept calling her 'sir' and 'he' when speaking to her and arresting her, despite her complaining about it.

111 See *Reed v Stedman* [1999] IRLR 299; and *Insitu Cleaning Co v Heads* [1995] IRLR 4. For examples of such conduct, see the Equality and Human Rights Commission's Technical Guidance on Sexual Harassment and Harassment at Work, section 2.8: https://www.equalityhumanrights.com/sites/default/files/sexual_harassment_and_harassment_at_work.pdf

112 EA 2010 s26(4)(a)–(c); and *Pemberton v Inwood* [2018] EWCA Civ 564, [2018] ICR 1291. Relevant circumstances may include the victim's personal circumstances, such as their health, including mental health; mental capacity; cultural norms; or previous experience of harassment; and also the environment in which the conduct takes place: *Statutory code of practice on services, public functions and associations*, EHRC, para 8.2.1(b).

113 EqA 2010 s26(2).

114 EqA 2010 s26(3).

115 *IPCC guidelines for handling allegations of discrimination*, p5.

12.90 Harassment claims can also be brought under the Protection from Harassment Act 1997.[116]

Victimisation

12.91 Victimisation is established under the EqA 2010 where someone is subjected to a detriment because either the victim has done a 'protected act', such as bringing a discrimination claim, complaining about harassment, or assisting another claimant's discrimination complaint (such as by giving evidence)[117] or the victimiser believes that the victim has done, or may do, a protected act (even if that belief is wrong).[118] False statements made in bad faith are not protected.[119] A claimant in a victimisation claim does not need to show that they have been treated less favourably than someone who did not do the protected act: they need only show that they have been subjected to a detriment because of a protected act. The test for detriment in victimisation cases is the same as that in discrimination cases, so a detriment is made out if the claimant might reasonably consider that it changed their position or put them at a disadvantage.[120]

12.92 As with direct discrimination, victimisation need not be consciously motivated.[121] If, therefore, a police officer repeatedly stops and searches someone without good reason, because they have brought a previous civil claim against the police, this is likely to amount to victimisation.

Aiding discrimination

12.93 It is unlawful for someone (A) to knowingly aid another (B) in committing an act that contravenes EqA 2010 Part 3 (which includes s29).[122] In *Hallam v Avery*[123] the House of Lords held that the requirement that the assistance is provided 'knowingly' means that the aiding party must know that the 'primary' discriminator is treating, is about to treat or is contemplating treating the claimant in a discriminatory way. Thus if a defendant does not know that this will occur, or only suspects that it will happen, no liability will arise under this section. This approach meant that in *Hallam*, a police force was found not to have unlawfully aided a local authority to discriminate against travellers. The police had advised the council to

116 Protection from Harassment Act 1997 s1(2). In contrast to a harassment claim under the EqA 2010 which can potentially be brought in relation to a single incident, the 1997 Act only applies where there is a 'course of conduct'. A further difference is that, whereas the EqA 2010 only covers harassment that is related to a relevant protected characteristic, the 1997 Act can encompass conduct that is non-discriminatory.

117 The protected acts are listed in EqA 2010 s27(2).

118 *Thompson v London Central Bus Co Ltd* [2016] IRLR 9, EAT.

119 EqA 2010 s27(3). Just because the evidence, information, or allegation was false does not mean that it was given or made in bad faith. It is for the respondent to establish bad faith: *Lucas v Chichester Diocesan Housing Association Ltd* [2005] 2 WLUK 141, EAT.

120 *Statutory code of practice on services, public functions and associations*, EHRC, para 9.7.

121 *Statutory code of practice on services, public functions and associations*, EHRC, para 9.10; see also *Nagarajan v London Regional Transport and others* [2000] 1 AC 501, HL.

122 EqA 2010 s112(1).

123 [2001] UKHL 15, [2001] 1 WLR 655.

impose additional conditions on the hire of one of its rooms on the grounds that the event was to be a 'gypsy wedding' but had not been a party to or involved in the making of the decision, and the council could have responded to the information in a number of lawful ways.

The public sector equality duty

12.94 EqA 2010 s149(1) sets out the PSED. It requires police forces as public authorities[124] to have 'due regard' to the need to eliminate discriminatory conduct prohibited by the Act, advance equality of opportunity and foster good relations between those with a protected characteristic and those without. In section 149(3) there is a non-exhaustive list of factors to which the public authority must have particular regard. They are the need to:

a) remove or minimise disadvantages suffered by persons who share a relevant protected characteristic that are connected to that characteristic;
b) take steps to meet the needs of persons who share a relevant protected characteristic that are different from the needs of persons who do not share it; and
c) encourage persons who share a relevant protected characteristic to participate in public life or in any other activity in which participation by such persons is disproportionately low.

12.95 The approach to be taken to compliance with the PSED was summarised by Aikens LJ, giving the judgment of the Divisional Court, in *R (Brown) v Secretary of State for Work and Pensions*,[125] as follows:

1) The public authority decision-maker must be aware of the duty to have 'due regard' to the relevant matters.
2) The duty must be fulfilled before and at the time when a particular policy is being considered.
3) The duty must be 'exercised in substance, with rigour and with an open mind'. It is not a question of 'ticking boxes'.
4) While there is no duty to make express reference to the regard paid to the relevant duty, reference to it and to the relevant criteria reduces the scope for argument.
5) The duty is non-delegable.
6) The duty is a continuing one.
7) It is good practice for a decision-maker to keep records demonstrating consideration of the duty.

There is a clear inter-relationship between the EqA 2010 s149 duty and substantive obligations under section 29(7). In the absence of demonstrated compliance with the section 149 duty, the public authority may be in no position to demonstrate compliance with its substantive non-discrimination obligations: *Coll v Secretary of State for Justice*.[126]

12.96 The government's Explanatory Notes to the Bill that preceded the EA 2010 gave several examples of how the PSED might operate in practice. These included that the duty could lead a police authority to review its

124 EqA 2010 Sch 19 Part 1 para 1.
125 [2008] EWHC 3158 (Admin), [2009] PTSR 1506 at paras 90–96.
126 [2017] UKSC 40, [2017] 1 WLR 2093 at 2108C–D.

recruitment procedures to ensure that they did not unintentionally deter applicants from ethnic minorities, with the aim of eliminating unlawful discrimination; and that the duty could lead a local authority to provide funding for a black women's refuge for victims of domestic violence, with the aim of advancing equality of opportunity for women and in particular meeting the different needs of women from different racial groups.

12.97 In *R (Bridges) v Chief Constable of South Wales*,[127] the Court of Appeal found a breach of the PSED by South Wales Police when it had adopted a trial of cameras using automated facial recognition (AFR) software in a variety of public spaces throughout Cardiff including train stations football stadiums and an arms fair. The court found that the police had never investigated whether AFR had an unacceptable bias on grounds of race or gender in accordance with the PSED. The potential for racial bias in AFR software with a risk of disproportionately false identifications in the case of people from black, Asian and other minority ethnic backgrounds should have been considered properly by the police. The court traced the origin of the PSED back to the Macpherson Report and commented that public concern about the relationship between the police and black, Asian and other minority ethnic communities has not diminished in the intervening years. The court stressed that the reason why the PSED is so important is that it requires a public authority to give thought to the potential impact of a new policy that may appear to it to be neutral but that may turn out in fact to have a disproportionate impact on certain sections of the population. This case is further discussed at paras 11.179–11.191.

Discrimination claims against the police under the Human Rights Act 1998

Introduction

12.98 The HRA 1998 offers an alternative or additional route to bringing a claim against the police for discrimination.

12.99 Discrimination claims under the HRA 1998 rely on ECHR Article 14 (prohibition of discrimination), incorporated into domestic law via HRA 1998 Sch 1, which provides that:

> The enjoyment of the rights and freedoms set forth in this Convention shall be secured without discrimination on any ground such as sex, race, colour, language, religion, political or other opinion, national or social origin, association with a national minority, property, birth or other status.

12.100 The issues that need to be considered by the courts in assessing whether an infringement of Article 14 has been established are as follows:

1) Do the facts fall within the ambit of one or more of the ECHR rights?
2) If so, was there a difference in treatment in respect of that right between the claimant and those put forward for comparison?
3) If so, was the difference in treatment on one or more of the proscribed grounds protected by Article 14?

127 [2020] EWCA Civ 1058, [2020] 1 WLR 5037; Police misconduct update, November 2020 *Legal Action* 29.

4) If so, were the others relied upon for comparison in an analogous situation?
5) If so, was the difference in treatment objectively justifiable in the sense that it had a legitimate aim and bore a reasonable relationship of proportionality to that aim?[128]

Facts within the ambit of a ECHR right

12.101 ECHR Article 14 does not provide a 'free standing' right to claim for unlawful discrimination. As its wording makes clear, Article 14 affords protection against discrimination in the exercise of the other rights protected by the ECHR. Thus, a discrimination claim cannot be brought in reliance on Article 14 if the conduct in question is unrelated to any of the substantive rights protected by the ECHR. However, the claimant does not need to show that the conduct amounted to a breach of any of the other rights guaranteed by the ECHR. It is sufficient if the claimant shows that the treatment complained of falls within the 'ambit' or the 'subject matter' protected by another ECHR right.[129] This is a fairly broad concept and the relationship between the conduct complained of and the protection afforded by another article of the ECHR may be a loose one. A discrimination claim under Article 14 against the police might therefore arise as a result of:

- an inadequate investigation into a death in custody – conduct potentially falling within the ambit of Article 2 (see paras 7.112–7.115);
- a failure to take due care of a suspect in custody – conduct potentially falling within the ambit of Article 2 (see paras 7.149–7.158);
- strip searching or other actions capable of seriously humiliating the claimant – conduct potentially falling within the ambit of Article 3;
- arrest or detention – conduct potentially falling within the ambit of Article 5 (see chapter 8);
- failures to act to prevent foreseeable attacks – conduct potentially falling within Articles 2, 3 and/or 8 (see paras 7.163–7.172);
- restrictions on prisoners' access to family visits – conduct potentially falling within the ambit of Article 8;
- refusal to provide detainees of a certain religion with prayer facilities – conduct potentially falling within the ambit of Article 9.[130]

A difference in treatment

12.102 As with claims under the EqA 2010, claimants can rely on real or hypothetical comparators to show a difference in treatment – in other words they can point to someone who was actually treated differently in the same

128 *Wandsworth LBC v Michalak* [2002] EWCA Civ 271, [2003] 1 WLR 617 at para 20, as amplified in *R (Carson) v Secretary of State for Work and Pensions* [2003] EWCA Civ 797 at para 52 and approved in *R (Marper) v Chief Constable of South Yorkshire* [2004] UKHL 39, [2004] 1 WLR 2196.

129 *Rasmussen v Denmark* (1998) 7 EHRR 371; *Abdulaziz, Cabales & Balkandali v UK* (1985) 7 EHRR 471, ECtHR.

130 Discussed above at para 12.44.

circumstances, or 'construct' a comparator and argue that such a person would have been treated differently.

Treatment on a prohibited ground

12.103 Article 14 itself lists a number of grounds upon which discrimination is prohibited by the ECHR, namely: sex; race; colour; language; religion; political or other opinion; national or social origin; association with a minority; property; and birth. However, this list is not exhaustive as the words 'such as' and 'other status' in Article 14 make clear. By way of example, 'other status' has been held to include discrimination on the grounds of sexual orientation, age and poverty.[131] Article 14 claims can also be 'combined' in the sense of being on the ground of more than one status: *R (A) v Secretary of State for Health*,[132] quoting a Strasbourg case, *BS v Spain*, in which a) a woman who was b) black and c) a prostitute established a ground of discrimination contrary to Article 14 by reference to the interaction of all three factors.[133]

An analogous situation

12.104 Additionally, it is necessary to show a difference of treatment in comparison to other persons in an analogous or relevantly similar situation. For example, the European Court of Human Rights has found that remand prisoners were in a comparable position to convicted prisoners as regards long-term visits[134] and that men and women were in a comparable situation as regards prison sentencing policy[135] and deferral of prison sentences.[136]

Justification

12.105 Unlike in relation to claims of direct discrimination under the EqA 2010, discrimination claims based on Article 14 can be defended by the alleged discriminator showing that the treatment complained of was justifiable in the circumstances. The burden of proof in relation to the first four issues listed above at para 12.100 is on the claimant; the burden then shifts to the defendant to establish justification. The defendant has to show both that the treatment complained of pursues a legitimate aim and that it is a proportionate response to the aim in question, when balanced against the discriminatory effects involved.[137]

131 See, respectively, *Dudgeon v UK* (1982) 4 EHRR 149, ECtHR; *N v UK* (App No 11077/84), 49 DR 170, ECtHR; and *Airey v Ireland* (1979–1980) 2 EHRR 305, ECtHR.

132 [2017] UKSC 41, [2017] 1 WLR 2492 at para 27.

133 (App 47159/08) (2012) ECHR 1904.

134 *Chaldayev v Russia* (App No 33172/16), 2019, ECtHR.

135 *Khamtokhu and Aksenchik v Russia* (App No 60367/08 and 961/11), (2017) 65 EHRR 6, ECtHR.

136 *Enache v Romania* (2017) 65 EHRR 6, ECtHR.

137 *Belgian Linguistic* (1979–80) 1 EHRR 252, ECtHR; see for example from the domestic courts, *R(L) v Manchester City Council and another case* [2001] EWCA Civ 707, [2001] 9 WLUK 415.

Litigating a private law discrimination claim against the police

12.106 This section sets out some of the specific procedural features that apply to discrimination claims against the police.

Vicarious liability and the reasonable steps defence

Vicarious liability

12.107 Prior to the enactment of the Race Relations (Amendment) Act (RRAA) 2000, chief officers of police were not vicariously liable for the discriminatory acts of their officers, as the Court of Appeal had decided that the provision in the Police Act 1964 which usually renders the chief officer of police liable for the torts of individual officers did not apply to the RRA 1976.[138] Suing individual officers was impractical, cumbersome and frequently unlikely to yield any compensation if the individual officer defendant had limited assets. The RRAA 2000 made chief police officers vicariously liable for their officers' acts and made provision for payment from police funds of awards and settlements of such claims.[139] These changes effectively meant that police officers were deemed to be employees for the purposes of the RRA 1976. The relevant provision is now found in the EqA 2010 s42.

12.108 In general, in cases where an employee carries out an act or acts of discrimination, it is necessary to establish whether the employer is vicariously liable for the employee's actions. The same now applies to police officers by virtue of section 42. Thus, under the EqA 2010, anything done by a person 'in the course of . . . [their] employment must be treated as also done by the employer'.[140] The statute clarifies that 'it does not matter whether that thing is done with the employer's or principal's knowledge or approval'.[141] Advisers will therefore need to have regard to case-law on the vicarious liability concept, which will determine whether the act has been done in 'the course of . . . employment'. The Supreme Court recently considered this issue in *WM Morrison Supermarkets plc v Various claimants*[142] and *Barclays Bank plc v Various claimants*.[143] Vicarious liability in actions against the police is further discussed at paras 14.120–14.128.

The reasonable steps defence

12.109 Chief police officers can be protected from discrimination claims if they can show that they took 'all reasonable steps to prevent' the perpetrator from doing the discriminatory act or 'anything of that description'.[144] If the defence is raised, the court will assess whether the police force has

138 *Farah v Commissioner of Police of the Metropolis* [1998] QB 65, CA.
139 RRAA ss76A and 76B.
140 EqA 2010 s109(2).
141 EqA 2010 s109(3).
142 [2020] UKSC 12, [2020] 2 AC 989.
143 [2020] UKSC 13, [2020] 2 AC 973.
144 EqA 2010 s109(4).

comprehensive policies and practices in place for eliminating discrimination by its officers: for example, whether effective training, guidance and supervision is given to officers, whether discriminatory conduct is robustly challenged and whether complaints relating to discrimination are adequately dealt with.

Limitation

Limitation under the Equality Act 2010

12.110 The primary rule is that claims brought under the EqA 2010 in the civil courts must be brought within six months less one day from the date of the act complained of.[145] Where the unlawful act is a failure to act, time starts to run from the date on which the person in question decided upon it.[146]

12.111 The court has discretion to extend time under EqA 2010 s118 where it considers that it is just and equitable to do so.[147] Section 118 does not specify any factors to which a court is instructed to have regard when considering whether it is just and equitable to extend time. It has been held that parliament chose to give courts the 'widest possible discretion' when applying section 118, which only requires consideration of all material factors.[148] The Court of Appeal has provided some guidance on the application of the discretion in the context of EqA 2010 claims made in the employment tribunal, holding that the two factors that will almost always be relevant are a) the length of, and reasons for, the delay and b) whether the delay has prejudiced the defendant.[149]

12.112 If a claimant shows that the act complained of is in fact a series of related acts constituting 'conduct extending over a period', then time runs from the end of that period of discriminatory conduct.[150] In *Commissioner of Police of the Metropolis v Hendricks*[151] (a race discrimination claim brought under the RRA 1976) the Court of Appeal adopted a broad interpretation of what amounted to an act extending over a period and held that the claim involving more than 50 officers and 100 incidents over 11 years in different police stations constituted a continuing act for the purpose of the RRA 1976. The Court of Appeal held that the crucial distinction was between events that were linked by, for example, a discriminatory practice and events that were unconnected or isolated.

12.113 A similar example would be if a claimant was harassed by a number of different officers over a period of several years, but the harassment all stemmed from a racially prejudiced entry about the claimant on the force's computer, or from the fact that the claimant had earlier made a complaint of race discrimination against one of the officers involved. In those

145 EqA 2010 s118(1)(a).

146 EqA 2010 s118(6)(b).

147 EqA 2010 s118(1)(b).

148 *Hewlett v Chief Constable of Hampshire* [2018] EWHC 3927 (QB) at 30–31.

149 *Abertawe Bro Morgannwg University Local Health Board v Morgan* [2018] EWCA Civ 640 at para 19.

150 EqA 2010 s118(6)(a).

151 [2002] EWCA Civ 1686.

circumstances 'the act extending over a period test' would arguably be met.

12.114 In any event, acts that are time barred can still form part of the evidence in the case from which inferences of discrimination may be drawn. In other words, the court can consider evidence in relation to 'out of time' incidents to inform its analysis of the incidents within the claim.

Limitation under the HRA 1998

12.115 Proceedings under the HRA 1998 should usually be commenced within 'one year beginning with the date on which the act complained of took place'[152] although the court has the power to extend this time limit if it considers it equitable having regard to all the circumstances.[153]

12.116 Unlike the EqA 2010, there is no 'continuing act' provision in the HRA 1998. However, the Supreme Court has confirmed that where there is a single continuing act of alleged incompatibility with the ECHR, the one-year limitation period prescribed by HRA 1998 s7(5)(a) runs from when the continuing act ceased, rather than when it began.[154]

Forum and mode of trial

County court jurisdiction

12.117 Claims against the police for a breach of EqA 2010 s29 can be the subject of civil proceedings like other claims in tort. However such claims must be brought in the county court.[155]

The appointment of assessors

12.118 In discrimination claims againt the police in the county court, a judge must exercise the power under County Courts Act 1984 s63(1) to appoint a lay assessor to sit with the judge unless the judge is satisfied that there are good reasons for not doing so.[156] This marks a change from the position under the RRA 1976, which provided that a judge must sit with assessors unless the parties consented to the judge sitting without them. An assessor appointed to assist the court in a discrimination claim made under the EqA 2010 should be a person 'of skill and experience in the matter to which the proceedings relate'.[157] However, assessors do not need to have special skills relating to the particular protected characteristic at issue.[158] Given the relatively small number of EqA 2010 claims determined in the county courts, many circuit judges will have very little or no exposure to such cases and so assessors have a potentially important role to play. The county courts may have limited experience of appointing assessors, and parties may need to be proactive in identifying potential candidates

152 HRA 1998 s7(5)(a).
153 HRA 1998 s7(5)(b). Discussion as to how this applies can be found at para 14.28.
154 *O'Connor v Bar Standards Board* [2017] UKSC 78, [2017] 1 WLR 4833.
155 EqA 2010 s114(1).
156 EqA 2010 s114(7).
157 County Courts Act 1984 s63(1).
158 *Cary v Commissioner of Police of the Metropolis* [2014] EWCA Civ 987 at para 46.

(such as lawyers with experience of discrimination issues or public sector equality professionals) and proposing the same to the court at an early stage.

The role of assessors and the relationship with juries

12.119 In cases where claims are brought under both the EqA 2010 and for false imprisonment and/or malicious prosecution, difficulties may arise in relation to mode of trial as the common law claims will usually entitle the parties to a jury trial, if either party so chooses.[159]

12.120 The Court of Appeal has confirmed that assessors' functions are wide and their role extends to assisting the judge with making findings of fact.[160] Accordingly, it is hard to envisage how one trial could take place involving both a jury and assessors because their respective fact-finding roles would overlap with each other although this sometimes happens.

12.121 The holding of two separate trials would generally be considered undesirable in principle because of the risk of different factual findings being made on the same facts.

12.122 Accordingly, in cases were a jury and assessors are an option, advisers will need to compare the relative merits of a trial before a jury with a trial before a judge and an experienced discrimination assessor and agree a forum, or invite the court to determine the issue. If, for example, the case turned primarily on an assessment of the credibility of witnesses, a jury may be preferable. In such cases the parties may agree, or the court may find, that the role of the jury was a good reason for not appointing an assessor. If the case involved a complex indirect discrimination claim where fairly subtle effects of a particular policy or rule would have to be assessed or where a court was being asked to consider questions relating to the implementation of positive duties, a judge and assessor may be more suitable.

Proving discrimination

12.123 A two-stage approach to the burden of proof applies in discrimination claims.[161] The first stage is that the claimant must show 'prima facie evidence' from which the tribunal could conclude, in the absence of any other explanation, that the service provider committed an act of discrimination. If the claimant satisfies the first stage, then the burden shifts to the defendant, who must show that it did not discriminate. If the defendant cannot provide a sufficient explanation, then the court is required to uphold the claim.[162] The Court of Appeal gave guidance on the operation of the burden of proof provisions in *Igen Ltd v Wong*.[163]

12.124 The guidance recognises that it is unusual to find direct evidence of discrimination. It is often therefore necessary to draw appropriate

159 See chapter 16 on jury trials in common law claims.

160 *Ahmed v Governing Body of Oxford University* [2002] EWCA Civ 1907, [2003] 1 WLR 995, at 32.

161 EqA 2010 s136(1).

162 *Ayodele v Citylink Ltd* [2017] EWCA Civ 1913, [2018] ICR 748 at 93.

163 [2005] IRLR 258.

inferences from the findings of fact on the evidence. For example, in *Durrant v Chief Constable of Avon and Somerset*,[164] it was held (under the RRA 1976) that the judge failed to consider the two-stage analysis in holding that a dual-heritage woman had not been subjected to race discrimination following her arrest for assault. The facts had satisfied the threshold test for the first stage, and it had therefore been incumbent on the police to prove that there was an innocent, non-racial ground for her treatment.

Remedies

Remedies under the Equality Act 2010

Overview

12.125 Although county court judges hearing discrimination claims under the EqA 2010 have the power to grant any remedy that the High Court can grant in proceedings in tort or in a claim for judicial review,[165] in practice the main remedies available in county court discrimination claims are damages (including compensation for injuries to feelings); and a declaration that the claimant's rights have been violated

12.126 Damages in claims under the EqA 2010 are awarded in much the same way as any other claim in tort for breach of statutory duty: a claimant may claim compensation for the consequences of the discriminatory act. Unlike the position in relation to personal injuries arising out of negligence, the claimant does not have to show that any injury relied upon was the reasonably foreseeable result of the wrongdoing provided that it was the natural and direct consequence of it.[166]

Damages for psychiatric injury

12.127 Guidance as to the level of damages for psychiatric injury can be found in the Judicial College's *Guidelines for the assessment of general damages in personal injury cases*. Where a psychiatric injury is modest and effectively merged with the injury to feelings, the court may sometimes elect to make a single, global award.[167] Medical evidence is generally needed to support a claim for damages for psychiatric injury. A letter from a GP detailing the claimant's symptoms and medical treatment may suffice in less serious cases. In serious cases, formal expert evidence is likely to be needed, and this should specifically address the causative link between the symptoms and the act(s) of discrimination. See also paras 17.13–17.15.

Damages for injury to feelings

12.128 Damages may also be awarded for injury to feelings, whether or not any claim for personal injury is made out.[168] Quantum for injury to feelings is assessed by reference to the bands set out in *Vento v Chief Constable of West*

164 [2017] EWCA Civ 1808, [2018] IRLR 263.
165 EqA 2010 s119(1).
166 *Essa v Laing Ltd* [2004] IRLR 313, CA.
167 *Martins v Choudhary* [2007] EWCA Civ 1379, [2008] 1 WLR 617.
168 *Richardson v Howie* [2004] EWCA Civ 1127, [2005] PIQR Q3.

Yorkshire.[169] These bands are regularly uprated in guidance from the Presidents of the Employment Tribunal. The most recent guidance from 6 April 2022 provides:[170]

> 2. In respect of claims presented on or after 6 April 2022, the Vento bands shall be as follows: a lower band of £990 to £9,900 (less serious cases); a middle band of £9,900 to £29,600 (cases that do not merit an award in the upper band); and an upper band of £29,600 to £49,300 (the most serious cases), with the most exceptional cases capable of exceeding £49,300.

12.129 In general terms, the court will have regard to the following matters when deciding the appropriate measure of damages to award:

1) The seriousness of the discrimination itself. Relevant factors will include what was said or done and how it was said or done, including whether it was in public or private.
2) The evidence of the victim of discrimination, including the impact of the discrimination on them.
3) Any medical evidence of the effect the discrimination had on the individual.

12.130 The claimant's evidence about the impact of the discrimination on their feelings is therefore extremely important, and where possible should cover:

- how the incident made the claimant feel when it occurred and immediately afterwards;
- for how long it affected them;
- whether it caused them to become upset about particular things as opposed to a general feeling of being upset or disappointed; and
- whether it stopped them from doing things that they might otherwise have done, and if so, for how long.

12.131 In *Durrant v Chief Constable of Avon and Somerset*[171] the claimant's race discrimination complaint focussed on her arrest, handcuffing and a significant delay in allowing her to go to the toilet at the police station, with the result that she was obliged to urinate on the floor in front of a group of male officers. It was found that the unlawful conduct occurred as a result of unconscious bias on the part of two police officers. The court considered that her case fell towards the lower end of the middle *Vento* band in terms of seriousness. She recovered £14,000 in damages for injury to feelings in November 2017 (an award which would need to be uprated in line with inflation to give its present value).

Other losses

12.132 Other losses, such as loss of earnings or other 'special damages', are calculated on normal tortious compensation principles.

169 [2002] EWCA Civ 1871, [2003] ICR 318.

170 *Presidential Guidance: Employment Tribunal awards for injury to feelings and psychiatric injury following De Souza v Vinci Construction (UK) Ltd [2017] EWCA Civ 879. Fifth Addendum To Presidential Guidance originally issued on 5 September 2017*, 28 March 2022, available at: www.judiciary.uk/wp-content/uploads/2013/08/Vento-bands-presidential-guidance-April-2022-addendum-1.pdf.

171 [2017] EWCA Civ 1808, [2018] IRLR 263.

Aggravated damages

12.133 Aggravated damages may also be awarded in circumstances similar to those referred to in *Thompson and Hsu v Commissioner of Police for the Metropolis*,[172] namely where 'there are aggravating features about the case which would result in the [claimant] not receiving sufficient compensation for the injury suffered if the award were restricted to a basic award'. Such aggravating features can include humiliating circumstances at the time of arrest or any conduct of those responsible for the arrest or the prosecution which shows that they had behaved in a high handed, insulting, malicious or oppressive manner either in relation to the arrest or imprisonment or in conducting the prosecution. Aggravating features can also include the way the litigation and trial are conducted.[173]

12.134 In *Richardson v Howie*,[174] the court suggested that aggravated damages should not be awarded in addition to basic damages for injury to feelings. However, it has been suggested that the decision 'is, fortunately, being generally ignored'.[175]

Exemplary damages

12.135 Exemplary damages are payable in exceptional cases where:[176]

> . . . there has been conduct, including oppressive or arbitrary behaviour, by police officers which deserves the exceptional remedy of exemplary damages . . . exemplary damages should be awarded if, but only if, [the court considers] that the compensation awarded by way of basic and aggravated damages is in the circumstances an inadequate punishment for the defendants.

In *Kuddus v Chief Constable of Leicestershire Constabulary*,[177] the House of Lords established that exemplary damages could be awarded under the RRA 1976.

12.136 In an indirect discrimination claim, if the court is satisfied that the provision, criterion or practice was not applied with the intention of discriminating against the claimant, the county court must not make an award of damages unless it first considers whether to make any other disposal.[178]

12.137 The county court must not grant a remedy other than an award of damages or the making of a declaration unless satisfied that no criminal matter would be prejudiced by doing so.[179]

172 [1998] QB 498, CA, beginning at p514. See chapter 17 on damages.

173 *Thompson and Hsu* guidance at para (8). For an example of aggravated damages due to the conduct of litigation, see *Zaiwalla & Co v Walia* [2002] IRLR 697, EAT.

174 [2004] EWCA Civ 1127, [2005] PIQR Q3.

175 *McGregor on Damages*, Sweet & Maxwell, 20th edn, at para 42-007. However, see further discussion in chapter 17 on damages.

176 *Thompson and Hsu* guidance at para (12)(b) and see further chapter 17.

177 [2001] 3 All ER 193.

178 EqA 2010 s119(5) and (6).

179 EqA 2010 s119(7).

Remedies under the Human Rights Act 1998

12.138 If a court concludes that a public authority has acted unlawfully contrary to the HRA 1998, it may grant such relief or remedy, or make such order, within its powers as it considers just and appropriate.[180] However, no award of damages is to be made unless, taking account of all the circumstances of the case, including a) any other relief or remedy granted, or order made, in relation to the act in question (by that or any other court); and b) the consequences of any decision (of that or any other court) in respect of that act, the court is satisfied that the award is necessary to afford just satisfaction to the person in whose favour it is made'.[181]

12.139 In deciding whether to award damages and if so the amount, the court must take into account the principles applied by the European Court of Human Rights in relation to the award of compensation under ECHR Article 41.[182]

180 HRA 1998 s8(1).

181 HRA 1998 s8(3).

182 HRA 1998 s8(4). See chapter 17 on damages under the HRA 1998.

CHAPTER 13

Prosecution decisions involving the police

Introduction

13.1 The decision to prosecute, or not to prosecute, is one with far-reaching implications for both the complainant and for the accused. This chapter will examine the legal and procedural framework within which such decisions are made, as well as the relevant routes available to challenge such decisions.

13.2 There are two contexts in which prosecutorial decisions are important. The first is in relation to decisions to prosecute police officers suspected of criminal offences. This can happen when there has been a police complaint or where a recordable conduct matter has been investigated by a police force or the Independent Office for Police Conduct (IOPC). The circumstances in which a case must be referred to the Crown Prosecution Service (CPS) are dealt with at paras 4.105–4.108. There may be circumstances where a complainant is dissatisfied with the decision taken in such a situation.

13.3 The second is where the police are involved in a decision to prosecute, and a victim of crime (for example) is dissatisfied with the decision made not to prosecute. It is also the case that those charged with criminal offences may feel aggrieved that this has happened, but normally such grievances will need to be explored during the criminal justice process itself (and then through the police complaints system or a claim for malicious prosecution, if later there is an acquittal) (see chapters 3, 4 and 8).

13.4 This chapter will cover the decision to prosecute; the prosecutorial test; the Threshold Test; the Victim's Right to Review (VRR); and judicial review of decisions in this area.

The decision to prosecute

13.5 As explained below, there are provisions which set out whether an offence is to be charged by the police (through the custody officer) or the CPS. The decision to prosecute is governed by the following relevant materials:

- Police and Criminal Evidence Act 1984 (PACE) ss37, 37A and 37B;
- *The Code for Crown Prosecutors* ('the Code'),[1] issued by the Director of Public Prosecutions (DPP) under Prosecution of Offences Act 1985 s10; and
- The DPP's guidance on charging (known as 'the Director's Guidance'),[2] issued pursuant to PACE s37A.
- Part of the CPS Legal Guidance entitled 'Police: Guidance on the handling of allegations of criminal offences against the police'.[3]

1 Issued 26 October 2018, available at: www.cps.gov.uk/publication/code-crown-prosecutors.

2 *Charging (The Director's Guidance)*, sixth edn, December 2020, available at: www.cps.gov.uk/legal-guidance/charging-directors-guidance-sixth-edition-december-2020.

3 Available at: www.cps.gov.uk/legal-guidance/police-guidance-handling-allegations-criminal-offences-against-police.

13.6 When the decision to charge falls to the police, it is the custody officer who is responsible for making the decision.[4]

13.7 CPS prosecutors make charging decisions in all cases not allocated to the police. In cases where more than one offence is under consideration for charging, and one such offence is an offence which must be referred to a CPS prosecutor, then all related offences in the case will also be referred to consider which should be charged.[5]

13.8 When the police are deciding whether a person should be charged with an offence, it is the Director's Guidance which has to be followed either in deciding whether to charge or what information should be sent to the CPS by the police, if it is the CPS which has to make the charging decision.

13.9 Thus, the custody officer must review the available evidence, disclosable material and any other relevant material or information and assess whether there is sufficient evidence to meet the appropriate Code Test (Full Code or Threshold) (see paras 13.16 and 13.33 below).[6] If it is decided that there is sufficient evidence to pass the evidential stage, and that prosecution is in the public interest, the appropriate Code Test will be met, and the case can proceed to a charging decision.[7]

13.10 The Director's Guidance contains a list of cases where the police are permitted to charge. These include any summary-only offence, irrespective of plea; shoplifting cases (provided it is suitable for sentence in the magistrates' court); and an either way offence anticipated as a guilty plea and suitable for sentence in the magistrates' court.[8]

13.11 There are exceptions to this list contained in the guidance – for example:[9]

- a case requiring the consent to prosecute of the DPP or Law Officer;
- a case involving a death;
- connected with terrorist activity or official secrets;
- a case classified as Hate Crime or Domestic Abuse under CPS Policies;
- a case of harassment or stalking;
- an offence of Violent Disorder or Affray;
- causing Grievous Bodily Harm or Wounding, or Actual Bodily Harm;
- a Sexual Offences Act offence committed by or upon a person under 18;
- an offence under the Licensing Act 2003.

13.12 The CPS will review all police charged cases prior to the first hearing in accordance with their duty under the Code. As the Director's Guidance says:[10]

> An offence charged by the police in circumstances not permitted by this Guidance may amount to a breach of PACE. The decision may be subject to legal challenge and may give rise to civil liability, especially if a suspect has been detained in custody.

4 PACE s37(7).
5 PACE s37(7).
6 Director's Guidance, para 4.1.
7 Director's Guidance, para 4.2.
8 Director's Guidance, Annex 1.
9 Director's Guidance, Annex 1, para 1.
10 Director's Guidance, para 4.10.

13.13 The CPS have powers to take over an investigation in such circumstances, and also to discontinue a prosecution if the CPS disagrees that the Full Code Test or Threshold Test is met.[11]

13.14 In all other cases not covered by Annex 1 to the Director's Guidance, the case must be referred by the police to the CPS for a charging decision where it is considered that the Full Code Test or Threshold Test is met, together with the relevant information about the case as set out in Annex 3 to the Director's Guidance.

The prosecutorial test

Overview

13.15 Thus, at the heart of the charging process when considering whether to bring a prosecution is the Full Code Test, as defined by the Code for Crown Prosecutors,[12] which has to be considered by the police when deciding to charge or to refer the case to the CPS, and by the CPS when making charging decisions.

13.16 The Full Code Test encompasses two tests:

- whether there is a realistic prospect of conviction; and
- the interests of justice.

13.17 A prosecution must only be commenced or continued when a case has passed both stages of the Full Code Test. The only exception to this is where the Threshold Test applies (as set out below). The Full Code Test is to be applied when all outstanding reasonable lines of inquiry have been pursued or, if the lines of inquiry have not yet been completed, if a prosecutor is satisfied that any further evidence or material is unlikely to affect the application of the Full Code Test, whether that be in favour of or against a prosecution.[13]

The evidential stage

13.18 The question to be considered at the evidential stage is whether there is sufficient evidence to provide a realistic prospect of conviction. If there is not enough evidence to secure a realistic prospect of conviction, then the case cannot proceed, no matter how strong the public interest in prosecuting might be.[14]

13.19 The question of whether a realistic prospect of conviction exists is an objective test, to be considered on the balance of probabilities. Any prosecutorial decision is required to have regard to the impact of any potential defence and any other information that the suspect has put forward or upon which they might rely. The test assumes an impartial and reasonable tribunal, properly directed and acting in accordance with the law.[15] The

11 Director's Guidance, paras 4.11–4.12.
12 Code for Crown Prosecutors, section 4.
13 Code for Crown Prosecutors, para 4.3.
14 Code for Crown Prosecutors, para 4.6.
15 Code for Crown Prosecutors, para 4.7.

impact of this is particularly relevant in cases of, for example, alleged sexual assault. The requirement to assume such a tribunal should provide a safeguard against a prosecution not being commenced because the decision-maker fears a jury would disbelieve a complainant on the grounds of any of the many stereotypes that have been historically pervasive in such cases.

13.20 It is also important in potential prosecutions brought against police officers, as it means that what should not be taken into account is any perceived unreasonable prejudice likely against the complainant or in favour of the police officer.

13.21 When considering the sufficiency of evidence, prosecutors should take into consideration the admissibility of evidence including the likely success of any application to exclude certain evidence, and the importance of any such evidence to the case as a whole. They should also consider the reliability/credibility of the evidence, and whether there is any other material that might affect the sufficiency of the evidence, including unexamined as well as examined material already acquired by police during the course of their investigation, and any further material that might be obtained through further reasonable lines of inquiry.[16]

13.22 The approach to the evidential standard was considered in *R (B) v DPP*[17] In that case, the claimant applied for judicial review of the decision of the CPS to discontinue a prosecution against his alleged assailant, essentially because his mental health problems set out in a medical report could make him an unreliable witness. The court found that, on the facts of the case, the contents of the medical report were insufficient for the prosecution to decide that the claimant's identification of his assailant was more likely than not to be as a result of hallucinations. The court also found that the decision to terminate the prosecution on the eve of the trial of a serious assault added 'insult to injury' and amounted to a breach of the positive duty under the European Convention on Human Rights (ECHR) Article 3 to provide protection through the legal system by bringing to justice those who commit serious acts of violence against others (see further on this in chapter 7). The claimant was awarded £8,000 damages under HRA 1998.

13.23 The case is an important reminder of victims' rights and the need for prosecutors to properly consider the Code when deciding how to proceed with a prosecution. Again, this might be especially important when consideration is being given to whether to prosecute police officers, in circumstances where there may be doubts about a complainant's reliability. The centrality of the objective merits test (as opposed to what has been a bookmaker's test which considers a case predictively based on the experience of juries) was underlined in *R (End Violence Against Women Coalition) v DPP*,[18] an unsuccessful challenge to what was thought to be a change in CPS policy: the Court of Appeal confirmed that the Full Code Test simply sets out a merits approach.

13.24 The CPS Legal Guidance section 'Police: Guidance on the handling of allegations of criminal offences against the police' provides advice which

16 Code for Crown Prosecutors, para 4.8.

17 [2009] EWHC 106 (Admin), [2009] 1 WLR 2072.

18 [2021] EWCA Civ 350.

suggests that the CPS should be wary of those who have been arrested who make allegations against police officers. If advisers are urging the CPS to bring prosecutions against police officers in these circumstances, it may be important to address any such potential concerns:

> Some defendants may see an advantage in making allegations to discredit officers involved in the case against them. It is important to consider whether there is evidence to suggest that a complainant or other witness has a motive for not telling the truth in an objective assessment of the evidence. However, care must be taken not to dismiss the evidence of complainants simply because they themselves face criminal allegations or have previous convictions. All the evidence must be carefully weighed under the Code for Crown Prosecutors.

13.25 The advice points out that a police officer will often rely on use of their legal powers as a defence to a possible prosecution. In deciding whether the evidential test is passed the guidance states that 'careful analysis' of the following is required:

- the extent of the relevant power;
- conditions which need to be satisfied before the power may be exercised;
- the way in which the officers exercised any discretion;
- the degree of force used in exercising the power.

13.26 It is also noted that if a case proceeds, the prosecution must adduce sufficient evidence to satisfy a jury beyond reasonable doubt that the officer was not acting in accordance with their legal powers. Where force is alleged to have been used in the prevention of crime or arrest, the Guidance says that the following factors must be considered when considering the lawfulness of an officer's actions:

- the nature and degree of force used;
- the seriousness of the offence which is being prevented or in respect of which an arrest is being made;
- the nature and degree of any force used against an officer by a person resisting arrest.

The public interest stage

13.27 The standard practice is to consider the evidential stage before moving on to consider the public interest stage. However, there are cases where the public interest is so overwhelmingly against a prosecution that a decision-maker might consider the public interest test immediately, without having fully reviewed the evidential stage. The evidential step should only be leapfrogged where there is sufficient information on criminality for a fully-informed decision about public interest to be made.[19]

13.28 In most cases, therefore, if a prosecutor is satisfied that there is a realistic prospect of conviction, they must then go on to consider the public interest test. The question of whether a prosecution is in the public interest or not is, like the evidential stage, to be determined objectively on the balance of probabilities: that is, whether a prosecutor is satisfied (or not)

19 Code for Crown Prosecutors, paras 4.4, 4.5.

that there are public interest factors tending in favour of prosecution which outweigh those tending against [20] At this point, the prosecutor will also consider whether an out-of-court disposal in lieu of prosecution, might satisfy the public interest.[21]

13.29 Paragraph 4.14 of the Code for Crown Prosecutors sets out a series of questions for a prosecutor to consider when deciding whether or a not a prosecution is in the public interest. It is a non-exhaustive list, and it is acknowledged that not all questions will be relevant to each prosecution: prosecutors are required to consider the questions in tandem with any public interest factors set out in relevant guidance or policy issued by the DPP. The weight given to each question will vary according to the facts and merits of the case in question.

13.30 Under paragraph 4.14 of the Code, a prosecutor should consider a range of factors, and the following is a summary:

a) *How serious is the offence committed?*
b) *What is the suspect's level of culpability?* The higher the level of culpability, the more likely it is that prosecution is required. The question of culpability is likely to include questions relating to:
   i) the suspect's level of involvement;
   ii) the degree of planning;
   iii) the level of benefit received by the suspect;
   iv) the suspect's previous criminal history;
   v) the likelihood of further offences being committed;
   vi) the suspect's age and maturity (see below);
   vi) any coercion or exploitation of the suspect; and
   vii) any personal circumstances of the suspect (eg significant mental or physical ill-health).
c) *The circumstances of the victim, and any harm caused to them.* This is likely to include:
   i) the victim's vulnerability;
   ii) any relationship of trust;
   iii) any suggestion that the offence is motivated by any form of prejudice;
   iv) the impact of the prosecution on the victim; and
   v) the views of the victim.
d) *What was the suspect's age and maturity at the time of the offence?* This evaluation is likely to include an assessment of the best interests and welfare of the child if the suspect is under 18, having regard to the principal aim of the youth justice system, which is to prevent offending.
e) *The impact on the community of a prosecution.* This criterion engages not just a physical community in terms of location, but can include people who share certain characteristics, experiences or backgrounds, including an occupational group.
f) *Whether prosecution is a proportionate response.* This factor will include an assessment of the cost of prosecution and effective case management.

20 Code for Crown Prosecutors, para 4.9.
21 Code for Crown Prosecutors, para 4.10.

g) *In cases where public interest immunity does not apply, whether sources of information require protecting*. Examples include where a prosecution might harm an ongoing investigation, international relations, or national security.

13.31 The CPS Legal Guidance in relation to the prosecution of police officers states that prosecutors should take into consideration likely or actual disciplinary outcomes when considering whether criminal prosecutions should be pursued against an officer. If the CPS decide not to prosecute, it is still possible for disciplinary proceedings to be brought.[22]

13.32 The Legal Guidance reminds prosecutors that it is important for the maintenance of public and police confidence that a different standard is not allowed to develop in prosecution cases against police officers, and the fact that there has been a complaint against the police should not influence the decision.

The Threshold Test

13.33 Where the Full Code Test is not met, the Threshold Test can be applied to charge a suspect, albeit in limited circumstances. The Threshold Test applies when the seriousness or circumstances of the case justifies the making of an immediate charging decision, and there are substantial grounds to object to bail.[23]

13.34 The Threshold Test must only be applied when necessary. It requires a rigorous examination of five conditions, all of which must be met, to ensure a case is not charged prematurely.[24] There must be:

1) reasonable grounds to suspect that the person to be charged has committed the offence;
2) and further evidence can be obtained to provide a realistic prospect of conviction, within a reasonable period;
3) the seriousness of the circumstances of the case must justify the making of an immediate charging decision;
4) there must be continuing substantial grounds to object to bail; and
5) it must be in the public interest to charge the suspect, applying the public interest section of the Full Code Test based on the information available at the time.

13.35 Any decision to charge under the Threshold Test must be kept under review. A prosecutor must be proactive in securing from the police outstanding evidence or other material in accordance with an agreed timetable. Evidence must be regularly assessed to ensure the charge is still appropriate and that continued objection to bail is justified. The Full Code Test must be applied as soon as the anticipated further evidence or

22 *R v Chief Constable of Thames Valley ex p Police Complaints Authority* [1996] COD 324 DC and chapter 5.

23 Code for Crown Prosecutors, section 5.

24 Code for Crown Prosecutors, para 5.2.

material is received and, in any event, in Crown Court cases, usually before the formal service of the prosecution case.[25]

The Victim's Right to Review

13.36 The Victim's Right to Review (VRR) of prosecution decisions is relevant in two ways in relation to the police. There is a right of review of CPS prosecution decisions which will be relevant where the CPS is considering whether to prosecute a police officer. There is also a right to review when the police are making decisions about prosecutions in the circumstances set out above.

The CPS and the Victim's Right to Review

13.37 The VRR was introduced in 2013 following the case of *R v Killick*[26] when the Court of Appeal encouraged the DPP to produce a clear procedure for a victim to seek a review of a prosecution decision.

13.38 The VRR scheme provides victims of crime with a specific process to seek a review of a CPS decision not to prosecute, to deal with an offence by way of an out of court disposal, or to discontinue an existing prosecution. It is listed as an entitlement in the *Code of Practice for Victims of Crime* (Victim's Code).[27]

13.39 The CPS Legal Guidance sets out details of how the VRR will work in practice. Where an investigator is responsible for notifying a victim of a decision not to bring proceedings, the investigator will advise the victim of their right to review on behalf of the CPS. This notification will include information about the nature of the decision (not to charge or to discontinue proceedings) and whether the decision was made on evidential or public interest or other grounds.

13.40 A request for a review should ordinarily be made within ten working days of the date of the decision letter informing a victim of a decision not to prosecute. Requests may be submitted after ten working days, although a delay may impact negatively on the outcome of the decision-making process. The Guidance states that requests made more than three months after the qualifying decision was communicated are unlikely to be accepted unless there are exceptional circumstances.

13.41 The CPS should usually complete the review process in six weeks, victims are entitled to request a meeting with their local CPS office to discuss a decision, before requesting a review under the VRR scheme. The VRR scheme can include two stages of review. First, there can be a local resolution stage where reviews are conducted by a new prosecutor at the appropriate local CPS office where the original decision was made. Second, (if the original decision not to prosecute is upheld), if eligible, a

25 Code for Crown Prosecutors, para 5.11.

26 [2011] EWCA Crim 1608.

27 Last updated 21 April 2021, available at: www.gov.uk/government/publications/the-code-of-practice-for-victims-of-crime.

review independent from the local CPS office where the original decision was made, can be carried out.

13.42 Examples of when the CPS might overturn a decision not to prosecute are listed in the policy document *Reconsidering a prosecution decision*[28] and include the following, which will be of interest to advisers considering applying for a review:

- cases where a review of the original decision shows that it was wrong, and it is important to bring a prosecution to maintain confidence in the criminal justice system;
- cases that have been stopped to allow for the collection of further anticipated evidence;
- cases that were originally not prosecuted or discontinued for lack of evidence, but where significant evidence is later discovered;
- cases involving a death in which a new review following an inquest finds that a prosecution should be brought;
- cases which are either not prosecuted or in which a prosecution is stopped as a result of the prosecutor not being satisfied that the Full Code Test can be applied, owing to outstanding inquiries, information or material that the prosecutor has requested. Such cases might be reinstituted when the inquiries are completed or the information or material is received.

13.43 The legal process for reinstituting proceedings following a successful review is found at Prosecution of Offences Act (POA) 1985 s23(3). By POA 1985 s23(9), the DPP has an unqualified right to reinstitute proceedings in respect of the same offence, subject only to the right of the defendant to revive the proceedings under POA s23(7). POA 1985 s23A(5) allows the DPP to reinstitute proceedings in respect of the same offence, in the Crown Court.

13.44 As will have been seen in chapter 4, the Independent Office for Police Conduct (IOPC) has a role in deciding whether a case of a police officer will be referred to the CPS following a managed or directed investigation of a complaint by the IOPC.[29] In relation to this decision, the IOPC has also introduced a VRR, as set out in its *Victims' Right to Review policy*.[30]

The police and the Victim's Right to Review

13.45 Where the police are responsible for the charging decision, there is also a policy in place, pursuant to the *National Policing Guidelines on Police Victim Right to Review*[31] ('VRR Guidelines'), issued by the Association of Chief Police Offices (ACPO) in 2015 (although each police force will have its own scheme based on the VRR Guidelines). Part 7 of the Guidelines deals with the process of review itself:

28 As updated February 2021, available at: www.cps.gov.uk/legal-guidance/reconsidering-prosecution-decision.

29 Police Reform Act 2002 Sch 3 para 23(2).

30 December 2020, available at: https://policeconduct.gov.uk/sites/default/files/Documents/appeal_forms/IOPC_victims_right_to_review_policy.pdf.

31 Available at: http://operationresolve.co.uk/media/1370/np_guidance_on_police_victim_right_to_review_feb_2.pdf.

> 7.4 The reviewing officer must approach the case afresh and reach their own conclusion regarding whether a prosecution should be brought, whether the matter should be referred to the CPS, whether further enquiries are necessary or that no further action should be taken.
> 7.5 The reviewing officer's decision takes precedence over the original decision.
> ...
> 7.8 Factors that might be regarded as leading to a determination that the original decision was 'wrong' include:
> - An unreasonable decision to disregard compelling evidence;
> - A significant misinterpretation of the evidence;
> - A failure to consider, or an unreasonable decision to ignore, relevant policy;
> - An incorrect application of the law.
>
> 7.9 The outcome of the review and the rationale for the reviewing officer's decision should be recorded in writing. The rationale should clearly set out why the original decision was wrong, considering the factors in paragraph 7.8. This is important if the decision is subsequently challenged through judicial review.

Judicial review

13.46 Following the conclusion of the VRR process, there is no scope for any further review by the CPS, the IOPC or the police (depending on who has carried out the VRR). If a victim remains dissatisfied with the decision, and/or wishes to challenge it further, then all the schemes advise that an application for judicial review will be the next step. It should be noted that there is likely to be an expectation that a review under the VRR scheme will have been exercised before any judicial review of a decision is commenced. Judicial review law and practice is not set out in detail in this book, but see Civil Procedure Rules (CPR) Part 54 for procedural rules and, in particular, the respective time limits for bringing cases: see also paras 14.4–14.7 below.

13.47 Successful judicial review challenges to a decision not to prosecute following a VRR referral will be rare. In *L v DPP and another*[32] the High Court noted:[33]

> It is highly likely that where a review has taken place, and the review can be seen to be careful and thorough, proceedings for judicial review to challenge the decision will be the more difficult to advance ...
>
> ... if there has been a review in accordance with this procedure, then, it seems to me, that the prospect of success will, as I have said, be very small.

13.48 This reflects the general approach of the High Court in any event that interventions in prosecutorial decision-making will only be appropriate in rare circumstances. This has been variously expressed by the High Court as follows, and as summarised by the CPS legal guidance:[34]

32 [2013] EWHC 1752 (Admin).

33 At paras 10 and 13.

34 CPS Legal Guidance: *Appeals: Judicial review of CPS prosecuting decisions*, 27 September 2019, available at: www.cps.gov.uk/legal-guidance/appeals-judicial-review-cps-prosecuting-decisions.

- 'only in very rare cases' (*S v Crown Prosecution Service*);[35]
- 'very rarely' (*R (Birmingham) v Director of the Serious Fraud Office*);[36]
- 'highly exceptional remedy' (*Sharma v Browne-Antoine*);[37]
- 'very rare indeed' (*R (Pepushi) v Crown Prosecution Service*);[38]
- 'sparingly exercised' (*R v DPP ex p C*).[39]

13.49 It is recognised that different prosecutors might reach different conclusions having reviewed the same material.[40] As such, provided the reviewing prosecutor has asked themselves the appropriate questions and considered relevant policies and all of the evidence, the court will be unlikely to interfere.

13.50 Although the courts are reluctant to uphold challenges of prosecutorial decisions, it is also recognised that:[41]

> . . . the standard of review should not be set too high, since judicial review is the only means by which the citizen can seek redress against a decision not to prosecute and if the test were too exacting an effective remedy would be denied.

13.51 In *Torpey v DPP*, the High Court did uphold a challenge to a CPS decision not to prosecute a police officer for causing death by dangerous driving. The High Court found that the CPS had interpreted the law on causation too narrowly and that 'the interpretation of the criminal law lies within the expertise of this court and does not usurp any constitutional independence of the CPS'.[42] In that case, the High Court also upheld the challenge to the decision on the basis of an absence of identification of the evidence considered and relied upon, by the reviewing CPS lawyer.

13.52 For a case where the prosecutor failed to comply with relevant CPS policy, see *R v DPP*.[43] There may, however, be circumstances where a departure from CPS policy is justified: see *A v R*;[44] *R (Kebilene) v DPP*.[45] For an example of a prosecution found to be irrational, see *R (Purvis) v DPP*.[46]

13.53 For a more recent summary of the case-law, see the case of *R (Canham) v DPP*,[47] a case which also held that the engagement of Article 2 ECHR in a case where someone has died in the care of the state does not require a different approach to judicial review by the court to that set out in the case-law above.

35 [2015] EWHC 2868 (Admin).
36 [2006] EWHC 200 (Admin), [2007] 2 WLR 635.
37 [2006] UKPC 57, [2007] 1 WLR 780.
38 [2004] EWHC 798 (Admin), [2004] Imm Ar 549.
39 [1995] 1 Cr App R 136, QBD.
40 See *R (Manning) v DPP* [2001] QB 330; *R (B) v DPP* [2009] EWHC 106 (Admin), [2009] 1 WLR 2072.
41 *Manning*, para 23.
42 [2019] EWHC 1804 (Admin) at para 52.
43 [1995] 1 Cr App R 136, QBD.
44 [2012] EWCA Crim 434.
45 [2000] 2 AC 326, HL.
46 [2018] EWHC 1844 (Admin).
47 [2021] EWHC 3361 (Admin) at paras 32–40.

13.54 Finally, for persons, who feel they have been wrongly charged by the CPS, the court of appeal considered the question of the remedy of judicial review in *A v R*.[48] The Lord Chief Justice said:[49]

> As to judicial review, there can, we suggest, be very few occasions indeed when an application for permission by or on behalf of a defendant should not be refused at the outset on the basis that an alternative remedy is available in the Crown Court. This is the appropriate tribunal for dealing with these questions on the rare occasions on which they may arise. Precisely the same considerations apply to a case involving summary trial.

13.55 The 'alternative remedy' discussed would of course include the right to make a submission of no case to answer or abuse of process in the criminal trial process, and to appeal any conviction to the Court of Appeal.

48 [2012] EWCA Crim 434.

49 At para 81.

CHAPTER 14

Bringing a claim against the police: pre-issue considerations

continued

Introduction

14.1 Bringing civil claim against the police is a specialist area of law. Lawyers involved in this area will need to be familiar with the issues of evidence, practice and procedure that are likely to arise. These considerations are explored in this and the following two chapters, which span pre-issue preparation to the conclusion of the civil trial and any appeal.

14.2 Claimants often will have had their confidence in authority badly shaken by their experiences with the police. Accordingly, a client-centred approach is essential when preparing for and conducting this specialist litigation. The first step is to meet with the claimant to listen to their experience with the police, to understand their objectives in instructing a lawyer and to provide sensitive but realistic advice on the prospects of achieving those objectives. Those objectives will vary depending on the claimant and the case, but can range from seeking an explanation to seeking a criminal prosecution of a police officer.

14.3 This chapter will discuss the initial consideration of whether a public law or private law cause of action is most appropriate in the circumstances; the necessity for permission in some private law actions; civil claims and police complaints; protecting the claimant's position in relation to limitation; preliminary issues in civil actions; pre-action disclosure; the relationship between a police complaint and a civil action; suing after a criminal prosecution and after other disposals; whom to sue; and finally, the Criminal Injuries Compensation Scheme.

Private or public law cause of action?

14.4 The focus of this chapter is upon what are called 'private law' actions against the police, where the usual remedy will be the award of damages. This can encompass torts such as false imprisonment, assault and battery, and malicious prosecution. It can include cases brought under the Human Rights Act (HRA) 1998, the Data Protection Act (DPA) 2018 and the Equality Act (EqA) 2010.

14.5 However, in many cases against the police, a private law action for damages will not be the appropriate way of proceeding. In many chapters of this book relating to various causes of action, reference has been made to an application for judicial review, where 'public law' remedies are available to quash decisions made by the police and other bodies such as the Crown Prosecution Service (CPS), the Independent Office of Police Conduct (IOPC) and government departments. Specific references to possible judicial review cases in this book are as follows, although this is by no means a definitive list of the kinds of cases that can be brought:

- chapter 2 – failure of police and crime commissioners and chief officers to discharge their duties (paras 2.76 and 2.89), possible unlawfulness of police guidance (para 2.104);
- chapters 3 and 4 – judicial review of unlawfulness in the police complaints system: failure to record a complaint (para 3.70), decisions about suspension of officers (para 3.147), to apply 'special procedures'

(para 4.14), referring a case to the CPS (para 4.107), the decision of the IOPC in independent investigations (para 4.116), the outcome of a review of a police complaint decision (para 4.135);

- chapter 5 – various decisions in the disciplinary process (paras 5.15, 5.32, 5.50 and 5.109);
- chapter 6 – challenging the lawfulness of arrest and detention (paras 6.23 and 6.183);
- chapter 9 – challenging the legality of a search warrant (paras 9.24, 9.30 and 9.69);
- chapter 10 – challenging police policies and decisions in relation to protests (para 10.78);
- chapter 11 – challenging decisions and policies relating to data processing (paras 11.135, 11.159 and 11.200–11.204);
- chapter 12 – challenging decisions and policies relating to discrimination matters (paras 12.28 and 12.125); and
- chapter 13 – challenging prosecution decisions (paras 13.22, 13.46–13.54).

14.6 Consideration will therefore need to be given at an early stage as to whether the most appropriate means of achieving the claimant's objectives is via public law or private law proceedings. Examples of when the public law route will be appropriate include where a claimant is seeking to challenge a police policy or to quash a policing decision where no right of appeal is available (for example, a decision to impose a caution, or not to prosecute someone, or to impose restrictions on protests). Specialist advice will often be necessary in deciding whether judicial review is the right course for a claimant, and what tactics should be adopted to pursue such a claim. It will often be necessary to exhaust 'alternative remedies' such as statutory reviews or complaints processes before bringing a judicial review case.

14.7 This chapter does not deal in detail with judicial review practice and procedure. It is important to note, though, that judicial review claims must usually be brought very promptly, and in any event within three months, and so expedition in bringing a claim is very important (see para 14.23). Limitation periods for private law actions are described below, and they are often much longer.

Necessity for permission in some private law actions

14.8 For the vast majority of private law actions, there is no necessity to seek permission to bring a civil claim from the court, but it is important to flag up two situations where it is necessary:

1) First, as set out in paras 7.38–7.40 above, where a claimant wishes to take a claim for trespass to the person (ie assault, battery or false imprisonment) arising out of precisely the same events that they were found guilty of an imprisonable offence, they will first need the court's permission to issue the claim pursuant to Criminal Justice Act (CJA) 2003 s329. This can arise, for example, where a claimant suffered injury during an arrest but where the claimant was also convicted of

assaulting a police officer during the same arrest. The court will require evidence that the defendant's act was grossly disproportionate[1] or that the defendant was *not* acting only because they believed that the claimant was in the process of committing an offence and they believed it was necessary to defend themself and/or their property or to prevent crime or apprehend a criminal.[2] The Court of Appeal held in *Adorian v The Commissioner of Police of the Metropolis*[3] that a failure to make an application for permission pre-issue was a procedural irregularity that could be potentially be cured by an application post-issue at the discretion of the court. Clearly it is much safer to ensure that any necessary application is made prior to issue, so as to avoid the need to apply for relief from sanctions (see para 15.74).

2) Second, Mental Health Act (MHA) 1983 s139 requires a claimant to apply for permission – specifically from a High Court judge – before a private law claim is issued in the county court or High Court in respect of any act purporting to be done in pursuance of the MHA 1983. This requirement does not apply where the intended defendant is the Secretary of State for Health, a health authority, a health trust or a clinical commissioning group (CCG).[4] This is because MHA 1983 s139 is primarily designed to prevent individual mental health care professionals being subject to unwarranted litigation from those in their care. Permission is, however, required in any claim against the police arising in this context, including where a chief officer is being sued vicariously, for example where police officers acted unlawfully when removing a claimant to a place of safety pursuant to MHA 1983 s136.

14.9 MHA 1983 s139 is the easier of these two permission hurdles to vault as the requirement under section 139 is to prove the defendant's act was done in bad faith or without reasonable care, whereas CJA 2003 s329 requires a claimant to prove that the defendant's act was grossly disproportionate or not in self-defence etc. MHA 1983 s139, is however, much stricter in its application, such that the House of Lords struck out a claim in *Seal v Chief Constable of South Wales*[5] purely on the basis that permission had not been obtained prior to issuing proceedings. This was despite the fact that had the claimant applied for permission for pre-issue it would have been granted on the facts, and notwithstanding that it was no longer open to the claimant to apply for permission in order to issue a fresh claim as limitation had expired.

Civil claims and police complaints

14.10 Another important consideration at an early stage will be whether it is advisable for the claimant to make a formal police complaint in respect of the index events, and how this might affect the timing and pursuit of a

1 CJA 2003 s329(3)(b).
2 CJA 2003 s329(5).
3 [2009] EWCA Civ 18, [2009] 1 WLR 1859. See also discussion at para 7.38.
4 MHA 1983 s139(4).
5 [2007] UKHL 31, [2007] 1 WLR 1910.

civil claim. The framework for the investigation of police complaints is discussed in chapters 3 and 4 of this book.

14.11 There are a number of factors which may inform a claimant's decision about whether to make or proceed with a police complaint. Chief among those is the client's objective, bearing in mind that a complaint investigation is the primary means by which police officers might be held individually accountable for their actions via criminal or disciplinary proceedings. Where a civil claim is envisaged, the following additional features of the police complaints system are also relevant to arriving at a decision as to whether to pursue a complaint on a case-by-case basis:

1) The police complaint investigation may generate evidence that is of use and benefit in a civil claim. For example, the officers may be required to provide their account of events in writing, at interview and/or at a hearing. The complaint investigators may also have greater access to witnesses, expert evidence and the power to seize evidence (such as police officers' mobile phones).[6]
2) The claimant will usually have to provide some form of account to the complaints investigation (see paras 4.23–4.24). This can be problematic where the claimant does not have access to the available evidence, such as CCTV.
3) The complaint investigation and any subsequent disciplinary/criminal proceedings can cause delay to civil claims in some circumstances.
4) While not necessarily admissible in civil proceedings, complaint findings that are critical of the officers can assist to encourage settlement in the civil proceedings.

14.12 The inter-relationship between civil proceedings, criminal proceedings and the police complaint system are further discussed later in this chapter (see paras 14.101–14.115).

Limitation

14.13 Upon being instructed to take a claim against the police, one of the immediate priorities will be to protect the claimant's position in relation to limitation periods, and so this issue is dealt with in detail at an early point in this chapter.

14.14 There is an increasing range of potential causes of action which have been utilised in actions against the police, and calculating the correct limitation periods and protecting the claimant's position in that regard can be challenging.

14.15 The end-point for the applicable limitation periods can depend on the type of proceeding or cause of action. Similarly, the starting-point for the applicable limitation periods will depend on the cause of action. For example, the limitation period begins to run in a claim for false imprisonment from the point of the claimant's confinement or detention (see paras 6.10–6.13), but in a claim for malicious prosecution from the date of the favourable outcome for the claimant (such as discontinuance of

6 Police Reform Act (PRA) 2002 Sch 3 para 1 and see chapter 4.

the prosecution or an acquittal, either at trial or on appeal). See paras 8.30–8.31 above.

14.16 Accordingly, if a claimant instructs lawyers soon after the favourable conclusion of criminal proceedings lasting in excess of six years, that might mean the limitation period has expired in respect of a claim for false imprisonment, even though the limitation period for malicious prosecution has only just begun to run.

14.17 Similarly, when a claim is brought for misfeasance in public office, the limitation period runs from the point when the misfeasance occurred and damage was suffered (where damage is required to complete the cause of action, as discussed at paras 8.125–8.127 above). Therefore, in a situation where a claimant was acquitted on appeal some years after officers fabricated evidence to support the conviction, the limitation period in relation to a claim in misfeasance would expire some considerable time before an action for malicious prosecution became statute barred.

14.18 Different rules also apply depending on the statute which governs the limitation period for the cause of action in question. The Limitation Act (LA) 1980 governs the limitation periods pertaining to common law claims (eg trespass to person, malicious prosecution, negligence, breach of confidence, misuse of private information) and causes of action which derive from statues that contain no discrete rules on limitation (eg DPA 1998/2018). Of those causes of action governed by the LA 1980, there are also different rules where a claim for personal injury (PI) is involved (discussed below at paras 14.25–14.26).

14.19 The EqA 2010 and the HRA 1998 each contain distinct rules on limitation periods for causes of action arising under each of those statutes.

14.20 The limitation periods for claims commonly taken against the police include the following:

- Judicial review: promptly and no later than[7] three months from when the grounds for the claim first arose.[8]
- EqA 2010: within six months from the discriminatory act/omission.[9]
- HRA 1998: within one year of the act complained of.[10]
- Battery: three years from the date of injury.[11]
- False imprisonment: three years from the date of confinement if PI claimed, six years if not.[12]
- Malicious prosecution: three years from the date of the favourable outcome of the prosecution if PI claimed, six years if not.[13]
- Misfeasance in public office: three years from the misfeasant act and/or date the claimed damage ended (if applicable) if PI is claimed, six years if not.[14]

7 The time limit cannot be extended by agreement between the parties.
8 Civil Procedure Rules 1998 SI No 3132 (CPR) 54.5(1)(a)–(b).
9 EqA 2010 s118(1).
10 HRA 1998 s7(5).
11 LA 1980 s11; *A v Hoare and others* [2008] UKHL 6.
12 LA 1980 ss2, 11; *A v Hoare and others* [2008] UKHL 6.
13 LA 1980 s11; *A v Hoare and others* [2008] UKHL 6.
14 LA 1980 s11; *A v Hoare and others* [2008] UKHL 6.

- DPA 2018: three years from the data breach if PI is claimed, six years if not.[15]
- Negligence causing PI/death: three years from date of injury/death.[16]
- Negligence not causing PI: six years from date of damage.[17]

Limitation periods are referred to in several other places in this book. The most substantive references are as follows:

- chapter 6 – limitation periods compared for Article 5 and false imprisonment claims (para 6.31);
- chapter 7 – limitation periods for claims under the Fatal Accidents Act 1976 and the Law Reform (Miscellaneous Provisions) Act 1934 (para 7.199);
- chapter 8 – limitation periods for malicious prosecution and misfeasance claims (paras 8.10 and 8.143);
- chapter 9 – limitation periods in interference with goods cases (para 9.66);
- chapter 11 – limitation periods in Data Protection Act 2018 case (para 11.205), limitation periods in defamation claims (para 11.220);
- chapter 12 – limitation periods in discrimination cases (paras 12.110–12.116).

14.21 These general rules operate with some qualifications. For example, the EqA 2010 provides that conduct extending over a period is to be treated as done at the end of the period. Thus, if the discriminatory conduct is a continuing act, that might allow some flexibility as to when the six-month limitation period begins to run.[18] A similar argument might be made in relation to breaches of rights under the European Convention on Human Rights (ECHR) which are ongoing for more than a year, although there is no express provision to that effect in the HRA 1998.[19] Time for a continuing act will only start to run from the date when the continuing act ceased, not when it began.[20] It is also worth noting that the date 'of the act complained of' from which limitation begins to run under the HRA 1998, will usually be the public authority's causative breach of the ECHR right.[21] In addition there is discretion to extend the limitation period in cases under HRA 1998, EqA 2010 and for judicial review: see paras 14.28–14.30.

14.22 The LA 1980 also provides for various exceptions to the general rule for those causes of actions under its remit. For example, where the claimant is under 18 years of age, the limitation period does not begin to run until their 18th birthday.[22] Similarly, the relevant limitation period under the LA 1980 does not begin to run against a claimant who lacks capacity to conduct legal proceedings at the time the cause of action accrues because of an 'impairment of, or a disturbance in the functioning of, the mind or brain'

15 LA 1980 s9.

16 LA 1980 s11(4), (5)

17 LA 1980 s2.

18 EqA 2010 s118(6)–(7).

19 *O'Connor v Bar Standards Board* [2017] UKSC 78; *R (G) v Secretary of State for Justice* [2010] EWHC 3407 (Admin).

20 *O'Connor v Bar Standards Board* [2017] UKSC 78 para 30.

21 *D v Commissioner of the Police of the Metropolis* [2012] EWHC 309 (QB).

22 LA 1980 s28(1).

for as long as that claimant lacks capacity.[23] This means that where a claimant has an ongoing lack of capacity throughout the time from which the cause of action accrued, the limitation period will not start to run. Once capacity is regained, the limitation period will start to run and will continue to run even if the claimant loses capacity again.[24] It must not be forgotten, however, that there no similar provisions under the HRA 1998 relating to minors or those with capacity.

14.23 Of particular relevance to police actions, limitation periods under the LA 1980 also do not begin to run where 'any fact relevant to the claimant's right of action has been deliberately concealed from him by the defendant'. In these circumstances, the period runs from the time when the claimant discovers the concealment or from the point when they could have discovered it by using reasonable diligence.[25] A deliberate breach of duty in circumstances where it is unlikely to be discovered for some time amounts to deliberate concealment for these purposes.[26] Deliberate concealment therefore covers intentional wrongdoing that, by its nature, is unlikely to be discovered for a considerable period of time, if the wrongdoer does nothing to draw it to the claimant's attention.[27] Accordingly, this concept could cover police misconduct that was not readily apparent to the claimant at the time but emerges subsequently, for example if officers pressurised or induced a third party to falsely incriminate the claimant. In this instance, the claimant would know from the outset that the testimony incriminating them was false, but they would not necessarily appreciate that this stemmed from improper police behaviour. The deliberate concealment must relate to a fact that forms part of the 'right of action', as opposed to those which simply strengthen an existing case.[28]

14.24 As such, it may be difficult for the claimant to obtain an advantage from this statutory provision in a false imprisonment claim, as the cause of action is treated as complete when the detention occurs and any subsequently discovered facts would bolster an existing claim, rather than create a fresh cause of action.[29] In contrast, in a malicious prosecution claim, a lack of reasonable and probable cause for the prosecution and malice on the part of the wrongdoer are intrinsic elements of the cause of action.[30] Thus, subsequently discovered police misconduct relating to those issues may well amount to facts relevant to the right of action, so that the running of the limitation period is postponed and in some circumstances the limitation period may only begin to run once the misconduct has come to light.

23 LA 1980 ss2, 28(1) and (2) and 38(2), as amended. Section 38(2) imports the definition of lack of capacity from Mental Capacity Act 2005 s2(1), which states that 'a person lacks capacity in relation to a matter if at the material time he is unable to make a decision for himself in relation to the matter because of an impairment of, or a disturbance in the functioning of, the mind or brain'.

24 *Prideaux v Webber* (1660) 1 Lev 31.

25 LA 1980 s32(1).

26 LA 1980 s32(2).

27 *Cave v Robinson* [2002] UKHL 18, [2002] 2 All ER 641.

28 *Johnson v Chief Constable of Surrey* (1992) *Times*, November 23, CA.

29 As is illustrated by the decision in *Johnson v Chief Constable of Surrey*.

30 See the section on malicious prosecution in chapter 8.

14.25 For claims in respect of personal injuries arising from causes of action governed by the LA 1980, the primary limitation period is three years from the date when the cause of action is complete (usually the date of the incident itself).[31] However, the three-year period can run from a subsequent point if the 'date of knowledge' is later. The date of knowledge is the time when the potential claimant / personal representative first had knowledge:

- that the injury in question was significant;
- that the injury/death was attributable in whole or in part to the act/omission relied upon;
- of the identity of the defendant and (if different) the identity of the person responsible for the act/omission relied on.[32]

14.26 An injury is treated as being significant for these purposes if the person in question would reasonably have considered it sufficiently serious to justify instituting proceedings against a defendant who did not dispute liability and who was able to satisfy judgment.[33] Knowledge is judged not only by reference to what the potential claimant actually knew, but also by reference to the information the claimant might reasonably be expected to acquire, including with the help of experts,[34] such as solicitors or doctors. If the potential claimant knows of the relevant factual matters necessary to make out a case, it is irrelevant that they do not appreciate that as a matter of law a claim exists (for example, because they have never heard of the tort of negligence). Lack of awareness of the relevant law, does not affect the date of knowledge.[35]

14.27 It is important to note that the above exceptions, which defer the start date of limitation periods for causes of actions governed by the LA 1980, do not apply to claims under the EqA 2010, HRA 1998 or in judicial review. For example, the limitation period for an EqA 2010 claim on behalf of a claimant without capacity starts to run from the date of the discriminatory act, not from the date when the claimant regains capacity.[36] Limitation periods in discrimination claim are discussed in more detail at paras 12.110–12.114.

14.28 In some circumstances it is possible to ask the court to extend the end-point of a limitation period. The applicable rules again vary depending on the cause of action. Under the EqA 2010, the court can be asked to allow a claim issued outside the usual six-month limitation period to proceed if there are 'just and equitable' grounds.[37] The HRA 1998 also provides for a claim issued outside the usual one year limitation period if there are 'equitable' grounds.[38]

14.29 Under the LA 1980, it is not possible to extend the end-point of the six-year limitation period that applies to non-PI claims under any circumstances; however, it is possible to extend the three-year limitation period

31 LA 1980 s11(4).
32 LA 1980 s14(1).
33 LA 1980 s14(2).
34 LA 1980 s14(3).
35 LA 1980 s14(1).
36 *AP v Tameside MBC* [2017] EWHC 65 (QB).
37 EqA 2010 s118(1); *Hewlett v Chief Constable of Hampshire* [2018] EWHC 3927 (QB).
38 HRA 1998 s7(5); *Rabone v Pennine NHS Trust* [2012] UKSC 2, [2012] 2 AC 72 at para 75; *Hackney LBC v Williams* [2017] EWCA Civ 26.

that applies to PI claims in certain circumstances.[39] The court will consider whether it is 'equitable' to allow such a claim to proceed. In determining this issue, the court will have regard to:

- the length of and the reasons for the delay;
- the extent to which any relevant evidence has been rendered less cogent by the delay;
- the conduct of the claimant, for example, the extent to which they sought to obtain expert advice and the nature of any advice received and the extent to which they acted promptly once they were aware of the need to issue proceedings;
- the conduct of the defendant in so far as that was responsible for any of the delay incurred.[40]

14.30 In public law proceedings, if a claimant wishes to issue judicial review proceedings outside the three-month limitation end stop imposed by CPR 54.5(1)(b), the claimant must make an application when issuing the judicial review claim form to extend that time limit pursuant to CPR 3.1(2). The judicial review claim form has a section providing for such applications. The court has a discretion to extend time for good reason.

14.31 In contrast, in private law proceedings any limitation defence is first raised by a defendant in the defence. A claimant then responds to that limitation defence in the reply, including to set out any arguments as to a) why the proceedings were in fact issued within limitation; or b) if not, why it is equitable for the court to allow the claim to proceed notwithstanding that it was issued outside limitation. It is then a matter for the court to determine the limitation defence as a preliminary issue before or at the trial of the claim.

14.32 Prior to issuing private law proceedings (though not in judicial review cases[41]), it is open to a claimant to consider entering into an agreement with a defendant to 'standstill' the applicable limitation periods until an agreed point in the future. This prevents the defendant from raising a limitation defence if a claim is not issued at court during the standstill period. With the advent of causes of action with short limitation periods, these agreements can be useful. For example, where instructions are received from a claimant close to the expiry of limitation and time is needed to explore the letter of claim procedure prior to issuing proceedings, or where related criminal proceedings are ongoing. Defendants are often amenable to this way forward in the hope that it will ultimately lead to proceedings not being issued against them. It is important that a standstill agreement is in writing,[42] carefully drafted[43] and that the parties comply with its terms.[44]

14.33 The alternative to entering into a limitation standstill agreement is to issue a claim form at court which immediately stops the limitation clock from running and provides a four-month period before service of proceed-

39 LA 1980 s33.

40 LA 1980 s33(3).

41 CPR 54.5(2).

42 *Thomas v Home Office* [2006] EWCA Civ 1355, [2007] 1 WLR 230.

43 *Russell v Stone* [2017] EWHC 1555 (TCC).

44 *Muduroglu v Stephenson Harwood* [2017] EWHC 29 (Ch).

ings needs to be despatched.[45] If further time is needed beyond that date, it is usually possible to agree a consent order with the defendant whereby the claim form is served in compliance with CPR 7.5(1) and time for service of Particulars extended to an agreed point in the future. A consent order has the added benefit of the court's approval to the agreed extensions of time.

14.34 While not formal limitation periods, other time frames to be aware of in this area of law include the deadline for making an application to the Criminal Injuries Compensation Authority (CICA) within two years of suffering an injury as a victim of violent crime[46] (discussed later in this chapter).

14.35 It will clearly be important to diarise the limitation periods for all applicable causes of action in all cases as a matter of priority post-instruction.

Preliminary issues in civil actions

14.36 Preliminary issues in civil actions include:

1) preserving and gathering evidence;
2) obtaining public funding if the claimant is eligible or establishing another basis upon which a retainer might be entered into;
3) taking a proof of evidence from the claimant;
4) complying with the pre-action protocols and exploring the letter of claim procedure.

Preserving evidence

14.37 It is important to preserve and gather at the earliest possible stage all available relevant evidence. This can sometimes involve urgently contacting a CCTV operator, eyewitness or writing to the police to prevent a particular item of evidence becoming lost or deleted. Suggested documents/evidence to request/preserve immediately following the first meeting with a claimant will include:

- body worn videos and CCTV;
- eye witness accounts;
- custody record;[47]
- police radio records;
- subject access requests (SARs) pursuant to the DPA 2018 (police, CPS etc) (see chapter 11);

45 CPR 7.5(1).

46 *The Criminal Injuries Compensation Scheme 2012*, Ministry of Justice, made on 13 November 2012, and as amended on 13 June 2019, para 87 (available at: www.gov.uk/government/publications/criminal-injuries-compensation-scheme-2012).

47 *Police and Criminal Evidence Act 1984 (PACE): Code C – Revised – Code of Practice for the detention, treatment and questioning of persons by Police Officers*, Home Office, 2019, para 2.4A (available at: www.gov.uk/guidance/police-and-criminal-evidence-act-1984-pace-codes-of-practice): 'When a detainee leaves police detention or is taken before a court they, their legal representative or appropriate adult shall be given, on request, a copy of the custody record as soon as practicable. This entitlement lasts for 12 months after release.'

- court records: memorandum of acquittal; the register entry (which lists all the claimant's attendances at court); magistrates' clerk's notes of hearing, Crown Court's notes of appeal;
- full file from the claimant's criminal defence solicitor, including the duty solicitor who attended the police station (who might be from a separate firm);[48]
- medical records (eg ambulance, A&E, GP, counsellor etc);
- report from any treating GP or hospital;
- police surgeon / forensic medical examiner / custody nurse's personal clinical note of attending on the client in custody, which is distinct from their clinical entry on police records. This is obtained either by writing to the defendant, or by writing directly to the medical professional if you can establish their contact details (their name should be on the custody record).

Funding a case

Public funding

14.38 Civil legal aid is administered by the Legal Aid Agency (LAA), an executive agency of the Ministry of Justice (MOJ) and largely via their online portal, the Client and Cost Management System (CCMS). The scheme is governed by the Legal Aid, Sentencing and Punishment of Offenders Act 2012 (LASPO) and its supporting Regulations.

14.39 The Standard Civil Contract 2018[49] brought cases that were previously known as 'AAP etc' (ie 'actions against the police' and other related claims) into a category called 'claims against public authorities' (CAPA) ie claims against 'a public authority with the power to prosecute, detain or imprison and the claim arises out of, or is closely related to, the exercise of such a power'; and/or 'where the claim is for PI based on allegations of deliberate abuse of a person while in the care of a public authority or other institution, or the failure of such a body to take a person into care'.[50] The CAPA category therefore permits claims against the police, CPS, prisons, those who detain under immigration or mental health powers, and to private companies carrying out detention and escort functions. Fatal Accidents Act 1976 claims are specifically included. Private law claims under HRA 1998 will be covered.

14.40 The CAPA category also encompasses 'abuse of a child or a vulnerable adult'. 'Abuse' and 'vulnerable adult' are defined in LASPO Sch 1 Part 1 para 3(5) as 'physical or mental abuse, including (a) sexual abuse, and (b) abuse in the form of violence, neglect, maltreatment and exploitation'. A 'vulnerable adult' means 'a person aged 18 or over whose ability to protect himself or herself from abuse is significantly impaired through physical or

48 Much of the contents of the criminal defence solicitors' file will attract legal professional privilege and so should be filed separately.

49 LAA, 2018, available at: www.gov.uk/government/publications/standard-civil-contract-2018.

50 See: https://assets.publishing.service.gov.uk/government/uploads/system/uploads/attachment_data/file/10 21134/2018_Standard_Civil_Contract_Category_Definitions__September_2021_.pdf/.

mental disability or illness, through old age or otherwise'. Sexual offences are also included (as described in LASPO Sch 1 Part 1 para 39).

14.41 There are two levels of CAPA funding: Legal Help and Legal Representation (also called certificated funding). Financial eligibility criteria apply to both.

Legal Help

14.42 This type of legal aid is controlled and administered by practitioners under the terms of their Standard Civil Contract with the LAA. It is also called Controlled Work. Before they can start work under the scheme, providers must ensure that their client satisfies the financial eligibility test, that they have provided adequate evidence of their means, and that a form CW1 has been completed. The evidence requirements apply equally to those in receipt of passported benefits. The LAA publishes guidance on determining financial eligibility for Controlled Work.

14.43 Legal Help can be used to cover the costs of assessing merits and then applying for a certificate of Legal Representation, or it can be used to cover the legal costs of acting in other matters which will not come before a court, such as police complaints. Disbursements can be claimed under Legal Help, including for court transcripts and medical reports.

14.44 Legal Help is paid on a fixed fee[51] basis unless the level of profit costs exceeds the relevant threshold, in which case costs are paid by reference to the applicable hourly rate. These are submitted as 'Escape Fee Cases'.

Legal Representation

14.45 Legal Representation can take the form of either Full or Investigative Representation:

- Investigative Representation may be applied for where it is not possible without further investigation to estimate prospects of success. Claimants with a certificate of Investigative Representation can apply for a full certificate once the merits become clearer. Sometimes, a certificate of Full Representation will be refused and a certificate of Investigative Representation granted instead.
- Full Representation funding permits proceedings to be commenced and pursued, where Investigative Representation generally does not.

Scope

14.46 To qualify for a certificate of public funding, the case must firstly be 'in scope'. Scope is defined in LASPO Sch 1 Part 1 paras 21 and 22:

- Paragraph 21 provides that funding is available for claims against a public authority which constitute an abuse of its position or powers where the act or omission is deliberate or dishonest; and results in harm to a person or property that was reasonably foreseeable. Intentional torts are deliberate by definition, and issues of dishonesty

51 Civil Legal Aid (Remuneration) Regulations ('Remuneration Regs') 2013 SI No 422 Sch 1 Part 1.

will be very much fact-specific.[52] It is also not necessary to show that all losses resulting from an unlawful act are foreseeable in order to attract funding; merely that 'harm to a person or property' was foreseeable. By way of example, false imprisonment always results in loss of liberty and can result in psychiatric injury: it will be sufficient for this aspect of paragraph 21 if just the loss of liberty was reasonably foreseeable.

- Paragraph 22 provides public funding for claims in tort or judicial review in respect of an act or omission by a public authority that involves a significant breach of ECHR rights. The Lord Chancellor's guidance under section 4 of LASPO[53] defines 'significant' as bearing its natural meaning, and identifies relevant factors as including the severity of the violation, whether the breach was deliberate, and 'whether the individual has suffered a significant disadvantage taking account of both the applicant's subjective perceptions and what is objectively at stake in a particular case'.[54]

14.47 LASPO Sch 1 Part 2 specifically excludes from funding claims for false imprisonment, assault/battery, PI/death, negligence, trespass to land/goods, damage to property and breach of statutory duty 'except to the extent that Part 1 of this Schedule provides otherwise' – which returns the question to paragraphs 21 and 22 set out above. Claims for clinical negligence are specifically excluded by paragraph 21(3).

Means test and a merits test

14.48 If a claim is in scope, applicants for certificated funding for legal representation must then satisfy both a means test and a merits test.

14.49 The detailed rules on means assessment are set out in the LAA's *Lord Chancellor's guidance on determining financial eligibility for certified work*,[55] and their *Means assessment guidance*. The LAA also offers an online 'eligibility calculator'. The Civil Legal Aid (Procedure) Regulations 2012 and the Civil Legal Aid (Financial Resources and Payment for Services) Regulations 2013 prescribe the process for evidencing and calculating financial eligibility.

14.50 The calculation of financial eligibility requires the assembly of all financial information relevant to both the applicant and their partner, including bank statements for all accounts, wage slips or confirmation of benefits, proof of housing costs if those figures are not clear from the bank statements, business accounts for the self-employed etc. At the time of writing, the gross income limit is £2,657 per month, the disposable income limit is £733 and the capital threshold is £8,000. The disregard for mortgages/loans on a client's home is capped at £100,000 and a further £100,000 disregard is applied to the client's share of equity in the property.

52 *R (Sisangia) v Director of Legal Aid Casework* [2016] EWCA Civ 24, [2016] 1 WLR 1373 .

53 *Lord Chancellor's guidance under section 4 of the Legal Aid, Sentencing and Punishment of Offenders Act 2012*, August 2021, available at: www.gov.uk/guidance/funding-and-costs-assessment-for-civil-and-crime-matters.

54 Para 11.2(b).

55 See: https://assets.publishing.service.gov.uk/government/uploads/system/uploads/attachment_data/file/1045682/Lord_Chancellor_s_guidance_on.pdf and: www.gov.uk/guidance/civil-legal-aid-means-testing.

The LAA will collect contributions where disposable income exceeds £315 per month and/or where capital exceeds £3,000.

14.51 The Civil Legal Aid (Merits Criteria) Regulations ('Merits Regs') 2013[56] set out the parameters for an assessment of merits. The following are the key provisions:

- Merits Regs 2013 reg 5 defines 'prospects of success' using the following measures:
  - very good (80 per cent or higher);
  - good (60–80 per cent)
  - moderate (50–60 per cent)
  - borderline (where it is not possible by reason of disputed law, fact or expert evidence to decide that the chances of success are 50 per cent or more or classify prospects as poor);
  - marginal (45–50 per cent);
  - poor (less than 45 per cent prospect of succeeding);
  - unclear – there must be identifiable preliminary investigations that can be undertaken after which it should be possible to assess prospects as within one of the other categories
- Merits Regs 2013 reg 8 defines the 'proportionality test' as met 'if the Director is satisfied that the likely benefits of the proceedings to the individual and others justify the likely costs, having regard to the prospects of success and all the other circumstances of the case'. The reference to 'benefits' usually means the level of damages that would be awarded in a successful claim.
- Merits Regs 2013 reg 39 sets out the standard funding criteria. These are that the applicant does not have access to other funding, a conditional fee agreement (CFA) is not suitable, other avenues for a resolution have been exhausted, and having regard to the complexity etc of the pleadings. If prospects of success are assessed at 60 per cent or more, then it will need to be explained why a CFA is not suitable, for example if the client cannot afford disbursements or if after-the-event (ATE) insurance is not available. 'Other avenues' should not ordinarily be taken to include the police complaints process, on the basis that this does not usually assist with liability and does not permit active participation by the applicant. See further paras 14.61 and 14.71.
- In the context of judicial review proceedings, Merits Regs 2013 reg 39 requires confirmation that the applicant is the most appropriate party to bring the proceedings, and the other avenues to be exhausted will include appeals processes as appropriate to the circumstances.
- Merits Regs 2013 reg 42 defines the cost-benefit criteria that will ordinarily apply by reference to the measures in reg 5 and applies the 'reasonable private paying individual test' to claims that are not primarily about damages and do not disclose a significant wider public interest.[57]
- Merits Regs 2013 reg 43 makes clear that only cases that fall within the 'very good' to 'moderate' bracket will be considered for funding, and that cases that are 'borderline' or 'marginal' will only be so considered

56 SI No 104.

57 'Significant wider public interest' is defined in Merits Regs 2013 reg 6.

if they disclose a wider public interest or are of overwhelming importance to the client.

- Merits Regs 2013 regs 53–56A apply specifically to public law claims. The decision to be challenged must be susceptible to challenge and the proposed defendant must have been notified of the proposed challenge and been given time to respond if practicable. Merits Regs 2013 reg 56(3) makes clear that prospects of success in a prospective challenge must be 50 per cent or higher unless the case is of significant wider public interest, of overwhelming importance to the individual or relates to a Convention breach, in which case the LAA will consider cases with borderline or marginal prospects of success. The proportionality test must be met.
- Merits Regs 2013 regs 57–59 applies specifically to CAPA claims, and it dis-applies the usual cost/benefit criteria in reg 42 and reg 43. Instead, applications for full representation under LASPO Sch 1 Part 1 paras 21 and 22 may be granted where: a) the proportionality test is met; and b) the LAA is satisfied that the prospects of success fall between 'very good' and 'moderate'.

14.52 The Lord Chancellor's guidance under section 4 of LASPO offers further assistance in applying the Merits Regs 2013 in CAPA cases. In particular:

- Guidance, para 4.2.4 confirms that 'likely costs' should be an estimate of costs up to the *disposal* of the proceedings. Therefore, this can be likely costs up to settlement, taking into account the stage at which it is anticipated the claim may settle, and not necessarily to trial.
- Guidance, para 4.2.7 addresses the proportionality test, invoking CPR 44.3(5) and inviting a consideration of whether the likely costs:

  . . . bear a reasonable relationship to:

  a) The sums in issue in the proceedings;
  b) The value of any non-monetary relief in issue in the proceedings; and
  c) Any wider factors involved in the proceedings, such as reputation or public importance.
- Guidance, para 4.2.8 addresses cases not possessing a significant wider public interest, and makes clear that:

  . . . the proportionality test is, however, intended as a less stringent test than the prospects of success, damages, costs matrix or the reasonable private paying individual test because of the higher priority of the proceedings to which it is applied. Accordingly, for any claim that is primarily for damages or other sums of money, the proportionality test will be considered to be satisfied pursuant to CPR 44.3(5)(a) if the appropriate damages (or other sums) to costs ratio is met. For other claims, the test will be considered satisfied having regard to CPR 44.3(5)(b), if the reasonable private individual test is met.
- Guidance, para 4.2.9 gives additional guidance on what should be considered when looking at 'all the circumstances of the case' in reg 8, noting that it will be necessary to consider:

  (i) the importance of the issues raised by the case pursuant to CPR 44.3(5)(e): for example how serious is the abuse of power alleged in a claim against a public authority?
  (ii) how far short of the appropriate damages/costs ratio or the reasonable private paying individual the case falls. The less cost effective the case

appears to be, the more serious must be the issues raised by the case to justify the provision of services.

- Guidance, para 7.38 addresses the circumstances in which the LAA will be satisfied that the usual appeal route in respect of a public law decision does not need to be pursued before funding for a challenge is granted ie when the alternative will provide only a partial remedy, or where the alternative cannot be pursued in time to provide an effective remedy.
- Guidance, para 7.41 and 7.42 offer guidance in respect of the requirement to notify the prospective defendant in a public law challenge, ie that this will not be necessary if this would create 'a significant risk of prejudice to the prospects of ultimately bring a successful challenge'. The CPR *Pre-action protocol for judicial review* should be followed (see paras 14.75–14.82).

Submitting the application

14.53 All submissions for funding are made through the CCMS online portal. There is useful guidance on how to use this software in the LAA's CCMS Quick Guides.

14.54 CCMS will require costs information to be entered for each cause of action and for separate estimates for each cause of action that that is being applied for to be provided to include on the certificate, broken down by profit costs, disbursements, expert fees and counsel's fees.

14.55 The 'merits interview' on CCMS requires that details are given of previous legal aid (including costs), and about the options of ATE insurance, pursuing the case via a CFA, whether alternative dispute resolution (ADR) has been pursued, and about cost-benefit. Details of the different proceedings to be included in the certificate will be requested and separate estimates for each cause of action of prospects of success, damages and costs to trial or other disposal including by reference to basic, aggravated, exemplary and/or special damages will need to be given. Explanation will be required if it is like by the care will settle before trial. CCMS will calculate the cost-benefit ratio for each cause of action based on this information, and by reference to the statutory criteria and guidance above.

14.56 A detailed statement of case, can be uploaded in which to give relevant background, but this is also an opportunity to further explain how the case falls within LASPO Sch 1 Part 1 paras 21 and/or 22, and how it satisfies the Merits Regs 2013, referencing as appropriate the Lord Chancellor's guidance. Other supporting documents, such as evidence of means, pleadings, correspondence etc can also be uploaded.

14.57 Once all the relevant information concerning scope, means and merits has been entered, the means and merits declarations for the client to sign will need to be printed. Application cannot be submitted until it is possible until to confirm that those signatures have been obtained. In circumstances where it is not possible to obtain a signed declaration prior to submitting the CCMS application – for example, where the client is in hospital or otherwise unable to attend the office or it is an emergency application – the LAA has procedures which means that a client does not have to immediately sign the application.

Assessment

14.58 The LAA will assess financial eligibility before reviewing the merits of the application. Once granted, it is possible to amend the case or client, or extend the costs limitation via the CCMS portal. Most certificates are granted with a scope limitation that leads to the exchange of witness statements. Funding refusals can also be appealed through CCMS.

14.59 At the time of writing, it is possible to exercise delegated functions to grant an Emergency Certificate of public funding or to amend a Substantive Certificate. If sufficient financial information is available the provider can apply for a Substantive certificate in the same way as above, save that the use of delegated functions must be recorded in the application. If full financial information is not available, the provider should select 'Emergency' as the application type and then follow the steps above. A substantive amendment must be submitted within 7 days of the notification that an Emergency Certificate has been granted.

Alternative sources of funding

14.60 Clients who are not eligible for legal aid can opt to pay privately for legal services if they are able to, although without insurance or other support (see below) they will be at risk in respect of paying the legal costs of opponents if the case is lost. There are other options for funding, as follows.

Conditional fee agreements (CFAs)

14.61 CFAs formalise an agreement between client and solicitor whereby the solicitor agrees that they will not be paid their costs if a case does not succeed. Clients will often pay their own disbursements under a CFA. The decision as to whether to offer a CFA will very much depend on the solicitor's assessment of risk, and of their likely total exposure in the event of an unsuccessful claim. A discounted CFA might instead be offered, under which the client pays a reduced hourly rate, with the remainder of the hourly fee being conditional upon success.

14.62 Success fees can be applied as part of a CFA, but these will come out of client damages. As CAPA damages are often modest, this may be prohibitive.

14.63 CFAs of course do not offer any protection in respect of adverse costs. Care should be taken in the drafting of CFAs, and the Law Society provides a template[58] which should address the possible pitfalls.

Qualified one-way cost shifting

14.64 The qualified one-way cost shifting (QOCS) scheme was introduced by LASPO to CPR 44.13–44.17 and can offer adverse costs protection to CAPA claimants. Where QOCS applies, this makes any order for costs against the claimant unenforceable beyond any damages awarded, so the claimant is not putting their personal assets at risk by embarking on litigation. QOCS applies to proceedings which include a claim for damages:

58 *Model conditional fee agreement*, Law Society, July 2021, available at: www.lawsociety.org.uk/en/topics/civil-litigation/model-conditional-fee-agreement.

- for PI;
- under the Fatal Accidents Act 1976;
- for the estate of a deceased person under the Law Reform (Miscellaneous Provisions) Act 1934 arising out of death or PI.

14.65 There are exceptions to QOCS, to be found in CPR 44.15 and 44.16, which automatically apply where the claim has been struck out on the grounds that:

- there are no reasonable grounds for bringing the claim;
- there has been an abuse of process; or
- the conduct of a claimant or representative is likely to obstruct justice.

14.66 There are further exceptions where the permission of the court is required to trigger their application, ie where:

- the claim is found to have been fundamentally dishonest;
- there is also a claim for the benefit of a person other than the claimant;
- there is a claim brought by the claimant to which the QOCS provisions do not apply (such as a claim other than a personal injury claim).

14.67 It is the final of these exceptions which chiefly concerns CAPA lawyers, as it appears to invoke what has become known as 'mixed claims' ie consisting of PI and non-PI elements. This is described in the case-law as 'the CPR 44.16(2)(b) exception'. It is likely that the majority of CAPA claims will include non-PI elements, for example a claim for damages for false imprisonment. At present, the position is that QOCS protection does not apply to non-PI elements, although there may be some limited scope for arguing the point if the case could fairly be described as a PI claim in the round[59] such as in the case of an assault causing physical injury, or a relatively clear false imprisonment causing extensive psychiatric injury where that becomes the dominant focus of the claim. The extent of the costs protection in mixed claims will not, however, become apparent until the conclusion of the proceedings because there is no mechanism for determining if QOCS applies until after the trial has concluded.

Before-the-event insurance

14.68 Prior to making a legal aid application or entering into a CFA consideration must be given to whether the client has the benefit of a before-the-event (BTE) insurance policy. These are most commonly available as part of a home contents insurance policy. It is rare for such policies to cover the types of claims that CAPA lawyers will pursue. Many are limited to PI claims, or exclude intentional torts or claims against public authorities.

14.69 Where the policy does provide cover, the client will generally have to request permission to use a solicitor of their choice rather than a solicitor chosen by the insurer, and will have to persuade the insurer of the merits of the case. Such policies may be limited to a specified sum which covers both own solicitor costs and adverse costs orders.

14.70 It is important to consider any insurance policies that clients hold and to check the small print for any potential cover.

59 *Brown v Commissioner of Police of the Metropolis* [2019] EWCA Civ 1724.

After-the-event insurance (ATE)

14.71 ATE insurance is a policy entered into to provide adverse costs cover after an incident has occurred. Post-LASPO, ATE premiums in CAPA cases are no longer recoverable from defendants,[60] and are therefore payable out of claimant damages. Pre-LASPO premiums could reach tens of thousands of pounds. This has led to the virtual elimination of ATE insurance in CAPA cases as insurers have withdrawn from the market. ATE premiums are, though, still recoverable in claims for publication and privacy proceedings (eg misuse of private information).[61]

Other potential sources of funding

14.72 Some other potential sources of funding include the following:

- Trades union will sometimes underwrite legal proceedings brought by members – but this is often limited to employment matters or to instructing solicitors used by the union. The existence of this type of funding will need to be ruled out before entering into a CFA.
- Damages-based agreements (DBAs) are similar in operation to CFAs, but where fees are linked to the amount of damages awarded. These are very rare in CAPA cases, unsurprisingly perhaps given that damages can be modest. Practitioners should refer to the Damages-Based Agreements Regulations 2013[62] for guidance.
- The Equality and Human Rights Commission (EHRC) will sometimes support individual cases of discrimination through their legal support scheme.
- Crowdfunding has developed as an alternative source of funding, through websites such as CrowdJustice. Success will inevitably depend on the nature of the case, with campaigns tending to attract more funding than individuals.

Proof of evidence

14.73 If requests for documents are made from the various sources around the same time as any application for certificated funding is submitted to the LAA, ideally the documents should arrive around the same time as any public funding certificate. This is a good stage to obtain a full proof of evidence from the claimant, including their comments on the documents gathered to date. As the credibility of a claimant is often central to the success of a police action, a clear and comprehensive record of the claimant's memory of the index events is important to capture at an early stage. This will include a claimant's comments on any previous accounts they have provided about the index events, including comments to:

- the police (eg any comments, statements or complaints made by the claimant in response to being arrested, detained, interviewed or charged);
- any complaint investigators;

60 LASPO s46.
61 LASPO s46.
62 SI No 609.

- previous solicitors (which may be subject to legal professional privilege (LPP));
- medical professionals;
- the media (including social media); and/or
- the courts (at trial or on appeal).

14.74 This proof, which is protected from disclosure by LPP, can then be updated as the disclosure process continues to unfold. Its contents will inform the preparation of documents to be served such as any complaint statement, letter of claim, statement of case, and witness statement for exchange in civil proceedings.

Pre-action protocols

14.75 The purpose of pre-action protocols is to facilitate early exchange of information between parties, with a view to encouraging settlement of their dispute without the need for litigation, and, failing which, to prepare the ground for expeditious conduct of proceedings.[63]

14.76 Currently 18 pre-action protocols have been approved by the Master of the Rolls for different types of claims.[64] Some of those protocols may apply to an action against the police depending on the nature of the claim – for example, the PI, clinical disputes, judicial review or media and communication protocols. Attempts to agree a specific pre-action protocol for actions against the police have not proved successful to date. In those circumstances, and where none of the other 18 protocols applies on the facts, the Practice Direction (PD) on Protocols applies.[65]

14.77 The PD on Protocols sets out the steps the parties are expected to take prior to the issue of litigation where there is no applicable protocol. The court will expect substantial compliance with the steps set out in in the PD. Failure to follow those steps may be taken into account when case management directions are given, and costs orders are made.[66] Failure to comply can result in sanctions, including penalties on costs, interest and/or a stay on proceedings pending compliance by the errant party.[67]

14.78 The PD on Protocols provides for the following steps:

1) The claimant writes a letter of claim to the defendant explaining a summary of the facts, the basis on which the claim is made, what the claimant wants from the defendant and disclosing key documents.
2) The defendant responds within a reasonable period of time – 14 days in a straightforward case and no more than three months in a very complex one. The reply should confirm whether the claim is accepted, if not, why not and explain any facts or parts of the claim in dispute. Key documents should be disclosed relevant to the issues in dispute.[68]

63 *Practice direction – pre-action conduct and protocols* ('PD on Protocols'), para 3 (available at: www.justice.gov.uk/courts/procedure-rules/civil/rules/pd_pre-action_conduct).
64 Available at: www.justice.gov.uk/courts/procedure-rules/civil/protocol.
65 PD on Protocols, para 2.
66 PD on Protocols, paras 13–14.
67 PD on Protocols, paras 15–16.
68 PD on Protocols, para 6.

3) The parties should consider whether negotiation or some other form of Alternative Dispute Resolution (ADR) might enable them to settle their dispute. A party's silence in response to an invitation to participate in ADR, or a refusal to participate, might be considered unreasonable by the court and could lead to costs penalties.[69] Litigation should be a last resort.
4) After taking the above steps, the parties should each undertake a 'stocktake' to see if proceedings can be avoided or at least to narrow the issues in dispute.[70]

14.79 If expert evidence is required, the PD on Protocols states that the parties should consider using a single joint expert, particularly in low-value claims.[71] This still leaves open the possibility of each party instructing their own expert depending on the nature of the claim.

14.80 Actions against the police requiring expert evidence will often be claims for personal injury, to which the *Pre-action protocol for personal injury claims* ('PI Protocol')[72] applies. The PI Protocol expressly provides the option for each party to instruct their own expert in multi-track cases and sets out the procedure to be followed in that regard,[73] as does the *Pre-action protocol for the resolution of clinical disputes* ('Clinical Disputes Protocol').[74]

14.81 The *Pre-action protocol for judicial review* ('JR Protocol')[75] recognises the urgency that can attach to claims for judicial review due to the nature of the relief sought, for example an injunction, and due to the requirement to commence judicial review proceedings promptly (discussed above). Accordingly, the JR Protocol expects a defendant to respond to a letter before claim within 14 days,[76] and acknowledges that in very urgent cases there may not be time to send a letter before claim prior to issuing proceedings.[77]

14.82 The *Pre-action protocol for media and communications claims* ('Media and Communications Protocol')[78] covers claims in defamation, misuse of private information, data protection law or harassment by publication, and claims in breach of confidence and malicious falsehood. Claims for misuse of private information, breach of confidence and breach of data protection law are increasingly common in actions against the police. The period for responding to a letter of claim under this protocol is 14 days due to the reputational issues that are often involved, for example, in defamation claims.

69 PD on Protocols, paras 8–11.
70 PD on Protocols, para 12.
71 PD on Protocols, para 7.
72 Available at: www.justice.gov.uk/courts/procedure-rules/civil/protocol/prot_pic.
73 PI Protocol, para 7.
74 Clinical Disputes Protocol, para 4 (available at: www.justice.gov.uk/courts/procedure-rules/civil/protocol/prot_rcd).
75 Available at: www.justice.gov.uk/courts/procedure-rules/civil/protocol/prot_jrv.
76 JR Protocol, para 20.
77 JR Protocol, para 6.
78 Available at: www.justice.gov.uk/courts/procedure-rules/civil/protocol/prot_def.

Letter of claim

14.83 The letter of claim[79] is a key means of trying to achieve ADR and avoid litigation. It is an opportunity to inform and influence the defendant's assessment of the nature, merit and value of the claimant's claim. If it is not successful in achieving ADR, it may at least assist in narrowing the issues in dispute. Its content forms part of an open document, on which the claimant can be cross-examined at trial. Although letters of claim do not need to include a statement of truth and do not have the same status as a statement of case,[80] any person who knowingly makes a false statement in a pre-action protocol letter may be subject to proceedings for contempt of court.[81] For all these reasons, careful preparation of the letter of claim is vital.

14.84 The PD and the applicable protocols set out the information that should be included in a letter of claim.[82] The PI Protocol and the JR Protocol each append a suggested proforma.[83] In preparing a summary of the facts, it will be necessary to consider documents including:

- the claimant's proof of evidence;
- the claimant's comments on the documentary evidence;
- any previous accounts (eg complaint statement, police interview, court testimony, account provided to medical professionals, media etc);
- any other witness evidence and any audio-visual evidence (eg CCTV, body worn video (BWV)).

If this kind of evidence is not yet available, consideration should be given to whether the letter of claim can be deferred until the relevant evidence is secured, failing which sending a less detailed letter of claim might be advisable. It is usually possible to engage in further correspondence once the defendant has provided any documentary disclosure with the protocol response.

14.85 The letter of claim should set out the claimant's case on liability under each head of claim and explain the remedies sought, for example, admission of liability, apology, deletion/correction of data, damages (basic, aggravated, exemplary and/or special damages) etc. See chapter 11 in relation to 'data' remedies and chapter 17 for damages. The level of detail deployed will vary depending on the case strategy. It will usually be helpful to highlight the strengths of the proposed claim and to identify factors relevant to the remedies sought. For example, if aggravated and/or exemplary damages are claimed, the letter should explain the basis for claiming those heads of damage. If the claimant is already in receipt of expert evidence that is supportive of the claim and that evidence is ready to be disclosed, consideration should be given to enclosing it with the letter of claim. However a claimant may wish to put the defendant to proof in a claim where the defendant bears the burden of proving their officers' actions were lawful and to defer some detail until the defendant has addressed those issues. For

79 Pre-action protocol letter in judicial review proceedings.
80 Eg JR Protocol, para 5.7.
81 PD on Protocols, para 2.
82 PD on Protocols, para 6(a); Media and Communications Protocol, para 3.1 onwards.
83 PI Protocol, Annex B1; JR Protocol, Annex A.

example, in false imprisonment cases, the burden of proof is on the police to prove that detention is lawful (see chapter 6).

14.86 If there are documents relevant to the claim that are likely to be in the possession of the defendant, a list of those documents should be included in the letter of claim. These might include:

- CCTV/BWV;
- stop-and-search records;
- documents generated by a criminal investigation or prosecution of the claimant;
- custody record;
- documents generated by the investigation of the claimant's police complaint; and/or
- relevant policy guidance.

14.87 As the letter of claim is communicated in open correspondence, it would usually not be appropriate to discuss any issues relating to litigation risk in that document. Similarly, neither the PD nor the protocols envisage the letter of claim addressing the level of quantum sought in any detail. It will usually be more appropriate to discuss such matters in 'without prejudice' correspondence, possibly after receiving the defendant's open response to the letter of claim.

14.88 The PD and the applicable protocols set out the information that should be included in the defendant's open response to a letter of claim.[84] The PI Protocol and the JR Protocol each append a suggested proforma.[85] The commentary in the White Book provides that the defendant's response should be detailed and not simply deny the claim. If a defendant is prepared to admit liability, the letter should say so clearly. According to the commentary, a response in which a defendant does not address liability but just encourages settlement negotiations is not within the spirit of the CPR.[86] This commentary is useful to cite to defendants who fail to provide an open response to a letter of claim confirming whether liability is admitted or denied with reasons.

14.89 The parties are encouraged by the PD and the protocols to actively consider ADR and a letter of claim should make clear that the claimant is open to that prospect; however, there is no requirement on the parties to make settlement offers as part of the letter of claim procedure. A claimant will usually wish to consider a defendant's response to a letter of claim before deciding on an appropriate ADR strategy; however, in some private law cases it is worth considering sending a CPR Part 36 liability-only offer along with the letter of claim. Offering to settle for a high percentage of liability (eg 90 per cent or above of the entire claim) can carry potential benefits in terms of cost protection in some cases. This decision will be fact-sensitive. It is always safest to use the court form 242A: offers to settle when making Part 36 offers.

14.90 In a claim for PI, the parties should consider as early as possible whether the claimant has reasonable needs arising that could be met by

84 PD on Protocols, para 6(b); Media and Communication Protocol, para 3.6.
85 PI Protocol, Annex B2; JR Protocol, Annex B.
86 White Book 2022, Sweet & Maxwell, Vol 1, Section C, para C1A-005, p2660.

medical treatment or other rehabilitation measures. If so, a suggested procedure is set out in the PI Protocol.[87]

14.91 If the claimant has the benefit of a public funding certificate or if QOCS applies (discussed above at para 14.64), this should be explained in the letter of claim, including as it may encourage the defendant to settle the claim. If the claimant has an ATE insurance premium the cost of which is potentially recoverable for the defendant (for example in a claim for misuse of private information), the defendant must be informed of that fact in the letter of claim (see para 14.71).[88]

Pre-action disclosure

14.92 Much of the material which will inform the preparation of a letter of claim will be obtained from the criminal defence lawyers instructed by the claimant in any preceding criminal investigation or prosecution and/or subject access request (SAR) pursuant to the DPA 2018, to the relevant police forces or other organisations. Police forces and local authorities tend to require the completion of a specific form and their requirements in terms of proof of identity and address can be onerous. Material that should be disclosed by the police in response to a SAR – sometimes in redacted form – includes BWV footage and contemporaneous police records such as computer-aided despatch (CAD) logs and crime reports. Custody records are disclosable without the need for a SAR by writing to the relevant police station pursuant to PACE Code C, para 2.4A.

14.93 The DPA 2018 expects a response to a SAR within one month of receipt, although this can be extended to up to three months if the request is complex. DPA 2018 s45(4) allows restrictions on disclosure in certain circumstances including to 'avoid obstructing an official or legal inquiry, investigation or procedure' and to 'avoid prejudicing the prevention, detection, investigation or prosecution of criminal offences'. The withholding of disclosure for those reasons must, however, a) balance those concerns against the fundamental rights and legitimate interests of the data subject; b) be necessary and proportionate; and c) be for no longer than necessary. A blanket refusal to disclose can and should be challenged on these bases where appropriate.

14.94 Disclosure under the DPA 2018 should consist of all recorded information relevant to the request and this should mean copies of original documents rather than transcripts or summaries. More detailed information about making a SAR can be found at paras 11.89–11.100.

14.95 It will also assist to secure comprehensive early disclosure if a clear list of outstanding documents is requested in the letter of claim. It is important to consider all the likely forms of data capture relevant to the index event and cite reference numbers from crime reports where possible.

14.96 If, notwithstanding efforts made to obtain information from these sources and/or via the letter of claim procedure, the proposed defendant still does not provide sufficient pre-action disclosure to allow an assessment

87 PI Protocol, para 4.

88 PD on Protocols, para 9.3.

of the risks of issuing proceedings, the prospects of success and/or to allow the claim to properly be pleaded, an application for pre-action disclosure may be appropriate.

14.97 CPR 31.16 codifies the process for obtaining disclosure before proceedings are started, pursuant to Senior Courts Act 1981 s33 and County Courts Act 1984 s52. The court can only make an order for pre-action disclosure where:

- the respondent and applicant are both likely to be parties to subsequent proceedings;
- if the proceedings had started, the documents sought would be within the ambit of 'standard disclosure' within the meaning of CPR 31.6;[89]
- disclosure before proceedings have started is desirable to dispose fairly of the anticipated proceedings, assist the dispute to be resolved without proceedings, or to save costs.[90]

14.98 Disclosure will evidently be 'desirable' if it enables the applicant to effectively assess the merits of a claim before incurring the cost of issuing and pleading a claim. It is not necessary to show that the initiation of proceedings is itself likely.[91]

14.99 Applications should be made in accordance with CPR Part 23.[92] The application must be supported by evidence. This would usually be in the form of a witness statement from the claimant's solicitor, addressing each of the criteria summarised above. The application should be confined to documents which are 'strictly necessary' for the purpose of assessing merits and preparing pleadings.[93] The court will not look kindly upon 'fishing expeditions'.[94] BWV footage of the index events is one good example of material that is likely to be necessary to assess the merits of issuing proceedings, if a relevant incident has been captured.

14.100 An order is unlikely to be granted unless voluntary disclosure of the documentation has first been sought and refused and the costs of a pre-action disclosure application are usually borne by the applicant in any event, unless there is evidence of unreasonable conduct on the part of the respondent. Sending a careful application to the proposed respondent pre-issue can often lead to voluntary disclosure.

The relationship between a police complaint and a civil action

14.101 When someone seeks advice after they have been ill-treated by the police, they often wish to establish the prospects of the police officer(s) in question being disciplined and/or criminally prosecuted. Those prospects will inevitably be highly fact-specific – however, twenty years after the PRA

89 See chapter 15 for a discussion of the ambits of standard disclosure.

90 CPR 31.16(3).

91 *Black v Sumitomo Corporation* [2001] EWCA Civ 18, [2003] 3 All ER 643.

92 See paras 15.94–15.104.

93 *Willow Sports Ltd v Sportslocker24.com Ltd and another* [2021] EWHC 2524 (Ch).

94 *Taylor Wimpey UK Ltd v Harron Homes Ltd* [2020] EWHC 1190 (TCC).

2002 brought the (then) Independent Police Complaints Commission (IPCC – now the IOPC) into being, it remains the case that only a very small proportion of complaints are upheld, and a smaller proportion still lead to any kind of action being taken against an impugned officer (for links to the IOPC's statistical information, see para 3.15 above). It is incumbent on advisers to ensure that clients are aware of this situation to allow clients to make an informed choice as to whether to make or to proceed with a police complaint or not. Despite perceived shortcomings of the complaints system, for example the vast majority of complaints are still investigated by the police themselves, many clients decide to complain nonetheless, including in recognition of the fact that it is their hard-won civil right to do so, in the hope that the system will be improved if enough complainants insist upon better outcomes, and because their complaint will remain on the officer's record which might assist another potential complainant. The various pros and cons of lodging a complaint are discussed at para 14.11 above, and the procedure for pursuing a complaint is discussed in chapters 3 and 4.

14.102 If a complaint is initiated, an adviser will often assist a client to prepare a complaint statement, rather than a client being interviewed by the investigator of the complaint. This is to remove any potential hostages to fortune by ensuring that that the client's account is comprehensive and accurate. Increasingly, complaints are being investigated without the investigator taking a detailed account from the complainant, such that proving a statement can ensure this happens. In complaint investigations where there is a good prospect of an officer being subject to criminal proceedings, it is usually preferable for the client to be interviewed by the investigator as this is the usual means of obtaining a victim's witness evidence for criminal proceedings. See para 4.24 above for further discussion on these points.

14.103 If a client decides not to lodge a police complaint but raises a 'conduct matter' is raised during related civil proceedings (eg in a letter of claim), the police are under a duty to consider investigating that issue whether or not the client has lodged a complaint regarding that matter.[95] If the police decide to investigate it as a conduct matter, it can be advisable to ask for it to be also investigated as a complaint so that the client can apply for a review of the outcome of the investigation (as discussed in chapter 4 on complaints).

14.104 Many clients decide to pursue a civil claim against the police as well as lodging a complaint against an individual officer(s) in order to maximise their prospect of securing some form of positive outcome. It is therefore important to understand how both remedies can be pursued in tandem.

14.105 When a complaint investigation is ongoing at the time a defendant is required to provide a response to the civil claim (eg to a letter before action or particulars of claim), defendants tend to suggest a limitation standstill (see para 14.32) or to apply for stay of the civil proceedings until the complaints process is finally determined. In some cases, that way forward can be to a claimant's advantage – for example, where a claimant has no costs protection in the civil claim and is keen to flush out the police account via the complaint investigation without incurring a costs risk. However, in

95 PRA 2002 Sch 3 para 10. Conduct matters are discussed further at paras 4.43–4.53.

many other cases, this way forward will be a recipe for delay in the civil claim, as complaint investigations frequently become protracted.

14.106 It is also important to be clear that unless a criminal trial (or in some cases disciplinary proceedings) emanating from a police complaint is due to take place imminently there is no legal bar on a police complaint process and a civil claim proceeding in tandem.

14.107 Defendants seeking to stay proceedings pending the outcome of a complaint where disciplinary or criminal proceedings are *not* imminent, can be referred to the line of authorities emanating from *Jefferson Ltd v Bhetcha;*[96] *DPR Futures Ltd;*[97] *Guinness v Saunders;*[98] *Secretary of State for Health v Norton Healthcare Ltd and others;*[99] and most recently *FM Conway Ltd v Suggett.*[100] The thrust of those cases is reflected in the county court decision in *Abraham and another v Commissioner of Police of the Metropolis*[101] where it was held that:

> . . . the burden is on the defendant, [to show] that there is some real prejudice to the defendant that if I do not stay the proceedings it is going to prejudice the defendants in the way the disciplinary proceedings are to proceed. My fundamental point is this: there are no current disciplinary proceedings or criminal proceedings and it is at the moment pure speculation . . .

14.108 In essence, civil proceedings should not be stayed unless there is a real risk of prejudice to imminent criminal or disciplinary proceedings which cannot be otherwise addressed with appropriate case management directions.

14.109 An argument occasionally still made by defendants is that if the chief officer were to decide a position on liability in the civil claim prior to the resolution of the complaint process, the officers under investigation might mount an abuse of process argument in any eventuating disciplinary proceedings against them, on the basis that the chief officer had prejudged the question of guilt by deciding on liability. This argument arose out of the 'dual role' the chief officer previously played as defendant in the civil claim and arbiter of guilt in the disciplinary proceedings, which fell away with the introduction of independent legal chairs in January 2016.[102] That principle has less force now that disciplinary hearings are chaired by an independent, legally qualified chair rather than a senior police officer. This is confirmed by the Administrative Court's decision in *Chief Constable of Thames Valley Police v Police Misconduct Panel*[103] which considered whether a chief officer could judicially review a disciplinary panel. It held that in disciplinary proceedings where there is a legally qualified chair, 'the Panel appointed is sufficiently separate from and independent of the Chief Constable to enable him to bring such a challenge by way of judicial

96 [1979] 1 WLR 898, CA.

97 [1989] 1 WLR 778 ChD.

98 CA, 17 October 1998.

99 [2003] EWHC 1905 (Ch), *The Times*, 26 August 2003.

100 [2019] EWHC 3173 (QB).

101 [2004] 1 WLUK 539, County Court.

102 Police (Conduct) (Amendment) Regulations 2015 SI No 626. Now see Police (Conduct) Regulations 2020.

103 [2017] EWHC 923 (Admin).

review'.[104] It must follow that a chief officer no longer has that 'dual role'. See paras 5.16–5.18 for more on the role of the legal chair.

14.110 If a defendant refuses to provide a response to, say, a letter of claim, and the claimant decides that they wish to proceed with the claim, the next step will be to serve a claim form and particulars of claim. This will force the defendant to serve a defence, or to apply for a stay pending the resolution of the complaint investigation, which can be resisted relying on the matters set out above (subject to the usual costs risks of objecting to any application).

Suing after a criminal prosecution

14.111 Those with a claim against the police will sometimes have been charged with criminal offences relating to the index events. It will usually be wise to wait and see how the criminal trial turns out before making a final decision on whether to sue the police, provided limitation periods allow for this approach. For example, if there is a potential claim under the EqA 2010 or HRA 1998 and the criminal process is likely to take more than six or 12 months to conclude, it may be necessary to arrange a limitation standstill agreement (see para 4.32) or, failing which to issue a claim form. (Limitation issues are discussed above at paras 14.13–14.35.)

14.112 As described in chapter 8, claims for malicious prosecution can only be brought where the criminal process concluded in favour of the accused claimant. An acquittal can also be supportive of the claimant's credibility more generally. Conversely, a conviction will make any claim for malicious prosecution impossible and may be detrimental to the claimant's wider credibility. Where a claimant has been criminally convicted but succeeds in a civil claim in relation to the same index events – for example, in a false imprisonment on the basis of excessive detention – the damages awarded are also likely to be lower as both judges and juries may feel that the claimant is less deserving and certainly not entitled to aggravated or exemplary damages (see paras 17.18–17.59). However, the false imprisonment claim cannot be struck out simply on the ground that the person had committed the offence for which they were arrested, since the bare fact of a conviction is not enough to establish that their arrest and detention was necessarily lawful in such circumstances.[105]

14.113 Accordingly, there is no general rule that the police cannot be sued for something that arose out of an incident which led to a conviction. Another example is where someone has been arrested for an offence which they committed but the police have used an unreasonable degree of force in making the arrest. In those circumstances, the arrested person still has a potential claim for assault. This may be the case even though the claimant has been convicted of a crime of violence arising out of the same incident. The conviction does not necessarily mean that the police did not assault the claimant as claimed[106] – however, the claimant may first need to apply

104 At para 31.

105 *Hill v Chief Constable of South Yorkshire* [1990] 1 All ER 1046, CA.

106 *Simpson v Chief Constable of South Yorkshire* (1991) *The Times*, 7 March, CA.

to obtain permission to issue the claim for trespass to person in these circumstances (as discussed above at paras 7.38 and 14.8).[107]

14.114 However, a doctrine called the 'rule against collateral challenge' prevents a claimant from bringing a civil claim where establishing the ingredients of the tort relied upon would necessarily involve disputing the basis of a criminal conviction. This could arise, for example, if the claimant alleged that police assaulted them to try and obtain a confession, but the confession had already been accepted as valid in the criminal proceedings.[108] The rule against collateral challenge is discussed in detail at para 7.47.

14.115 Subject to the important exceptions discussed above, a claimant can – in theory at least – seek to prove that although they were convicted of an offence relied on by the defendant, they did not in fact commit that offence. If a defendant pleads the conviction in the defence, the claimant can seek to show their innocence on a balance of probabilities.[109] The obstacles to achieving this in practice will clearly be formidable, especially as a claimant may not have access to the witnesses or other evidence on which the conviction was based.

Suing after other disposals

14.116 As an alternative to criminal prosecution, claimants are sometimes offered and accept a police caution, of which there are two types: a simple caution and a conditional caution.[110] As a police caution is not a prosecution, the tort of malicious prosecution cannot be claimed in respect of the administration of a police caution. The same applies to other disposals intended as alternatives to criminal prosecution such as fixed penalty notices.

14.117 A pre-requisite of accepting a police caution is that the claimant must first accept responsibility for the offence alleged against them. There is no procedural bar to a claimant subsequently resiling from that admission in related civil proceedings; however, this contradiction may prove injurious to their wider credibility. In those circumstances, it therefore will be important for the claimant to explain in the ensuing private law claim the reason for their earlier admission – for example, because they were placed under improper pressure by the police to admit and/or were desperate to get out of custody. In some cases, a claimant may decide instead, or in addition, to seek the removal of the caution via an application to the Criminal Records Office[111] and/or judicial review proceedings.

14.118 In *Abraham v Commissioner of Police of the Metropolis*,[112] the claimant had accepted a caution after she admitted a police version of facts which she subsequently said represented a gross exaggeration of the circumstances that led to her arrest. Her arrest had been in respect of disorderly

107 CJA 2003 s329; *Adorian v Commissioner of Police of the Metropolis* [2009] EWCA Civ 18, [2009] 1 WLR 1859.

108 See *Hunter v Chief Constable of West Midlands* [1982] AC 529, HL.

109 Civil Evidence Act 1968 s11(2)(a).

110 CJA 2003.

111 See: www.acro.police.uk. See further, chapter 11.

112 [2001] 1 WLR 1257, CA.

conduct.[113] The defendant was successful in striking out the claimant's case for false imprisonment as an abuse of process on the basis that in accepting the caution she had admitted the police's version of the events, which would have justified the arrest. The Court of Appeal allowed the claimant's appeal on the basis that the rule against collateral challenge did not apply in relation to cautions, as opposed to convictions. The Court of Appeal held that the similarities between a caution and a conviction were not sufficiently strong to engage that rule. The court was mindful that:[114]

> . . . on the assumed facts,[115] a lady of previous good character had been brought to the police station under arrest on a false pretext. She must have been anxious about her two children from whom . . . she had been separated. Her admission was to an account of events which both she and [the Police Sergeant] knew to be false. True she had the advice of a solicitor but her admission was contributed to, if not caused, by the unlawful arrest and false recounting of events.[116]

14.119 This will apply with even greater force to disposals such as a fixed penalty notice, which do not require any admission of guilt by a claimant prior to acceptance. The position in relation to bind-overs to keep the peace is considered in para 8.33.

Whom to sue

Vicarious liability

14.120 The principle of vicarious liability – which holds employers jointly liable with employees for their employees' wrongful acts committed in the course of their employment – does not apply at common law to members of a police force, because constables are not employees of the police authority (see chapter 2). Statute has, however, extended the principle of vicarious liability to include the police service by statute through the Police Act 1996.[117] Accordingly, a chief officer of police is liable for any unlawful conduct committed by police officers, including special constables and Police Community Safety Officers (PCSOs), acting 'under his[/her] direction and control in the performance or purported performance of their functions' in the same manner as an employer is liable in respect of unlawful conduct of its employees in the course of their employment. A chief officer is therefore, in the case of a tort, treated as a joint tortfeasor.

14.121 A chief officer can therefore be sued, and in practice will usually be sued, alone. While it is possible to sue individual officers either alone or with their chief officer, there can be serious disadvantages in doing so. For

113 Contrary to Public Order Act 1986 s5.

114 At para 19.

115 The facts had to be assumed in the claimant's favour at this point, as the defendant was seeking to strike out the claim on a preliminary basis.

116 The duty solicitor had told her that accepting a caution would not preclude a future civil claim.

117 Police Act 1996 s88(1), as amended by PRA 2002 which replaced references to 'torts' with 'unlawful conduct' thus including conduct that is unlawful, for example, because it is contrary to the HRA 1998.

example, chief officers may be more inclined to settle out of court, whereas individual officers may wish to hold out for their day in court, causing delay and an increased cost risk. A greater sum in damages cannot be won by suing individual officers in addition to their chief officer, as any damages are apportioned between the various defendants, and the individual officers may be impecunious.

14.122 In addition, if individual officers are joined as defendants, they have the right to attend all of the trial to hear the entirety of the evidence. Whereas if they attend trial as witnesses, rather than as a party to the proceedings, the claimant can apply to the judge for them to be excluded from the courtroom up until the point they testify. There is no general rule that witnesses should be kept out of court until they have given their evidence in civil proceedings; however, judges are sometimes willing to grant these applications in trials which turn on the credibility of competing witness accounts (see para 16.12 which deals with this in more detail).

14.123 Generally it is therefore only necessary to consider adding individual officers as defendants to a claim if there is a possibility that the chief officer might deny liability on the basis that the individual officers were not acting in the performance or purported performance of their functions at the relevant time. In those circumstances the case might be lost against the chief officer but still succeed against the individual officers. In practice, it is sometimes possible (subject to limitation periods) to wait and see if the chief officer denies liability on this ground and then to join the individual officers to the action if necessary. Very occasionally it may be necessary to join individual officers as defendants to proceedings under the EqA 2010, essentially where a chief officer seeks to defend the claim on the basis that the police force did all it could to prevent the individual officers acting in the manner alleged by the claimant. It is very rare for chief officers to take this approval to individual officers.[118]

14.124 There is a two-stage test for the existence of vicarious liability.[119] The first limb requires an assessment of the relationship between the defendant and the perpetrator of the act complained of; and the second limb assesses whether the connection between that relationship and the act complained of was so close as to give rise to legal liability.

14.125 The question of whether this test is met is highly fact specific. In *Lister v Hesley Hall Ltd*[120] the House of Lords held that a children's home was liable to victims of child sexual abuse because the abuser was employed by them as a warden in the home. In contrast, in *TVZ and others v Manchester City Football Club*[121] the defendant was held not to be liable for sexual abuse by a youth coach who had held himself out as a scout for the defendant but who was not directly employed by the club.

14.126 In *Barclays Bank plc v Various claimants*,[122] 126 claimants were sexually assaulted by a doctor employed by the bank to conduct medical examina-

118 EqA 2010 ss109(4), 110(1)–(2).

119 *Various claimants v Catholic Child Welfare Society* [2012] UKSC 56; *Cox v Ministry of Justice* [2016] UKSC 10; and *Mohamud v WM Morrison Supermarkets plc* [2016] UKSC 11.

120 [2002] 1 AC 215.

121 [2022] EWHC 7 (QB).

122 [2020] UKSC 13, [2020] AC 973.

tions. Barclays argued that the doctor was an independent contractor, but both the High Court and the Court of Appeal found the bank to be vicariously liable for the doctor. The Supreme Court overturned those judgments on the basis that that there was no relationship between the bank and the doctor akin to employment. Baroness Hale suggested that such a relationship might arise if the perpetrator had been acting under the direction and control of the business, and within its employment structures, in order to further the objectives of the business and/or if the perpetrator's role was integral to the business. Those factors will be worth reviewing if the perpetrator of the index event was not directly employed by a defendant, for example, in the case of civilian detention officers in a police station.

14.127 There will also be cases involving a direct employee, or indeed a police officer, where a defendant will argue that vicarious liability does not apply because the officer was 'on a frolic of their own', whether on or off duty. Vicarious liability will not apply in those circumstances where the conduct of the perpetrator was so far outside of the scope of their relationship with the defendant as to belie legal responsibility. In the policing context, it would arise where the actions of an officer were not purported to be policing functions, as illustrated by the following decisions:

- In *N v Chief Constable of Merseyside*,[123] an off-duty police officer used his uniform and warrant card to abduct and rape a woman. Vicarious liability was not attributed to the chief constable on the basis that the officer in that question was not 'purporting to perform a police function such as arrest, or enforcing police authority'.[124] Rather, he had simply used the fact of his office to reassure his victim into getting into his car.
- Similarly, in *Makanjuola v Commissioner of the Police of the Metropolis*[125] it was held that the commissioner could not be held liable for an officer who allegedly demanded sexual favours in return for not reporting a suspect's immigration 'irregularities' because the alleged misconduct was so extreme that it could not even *purportedly* have been done in the performance of a police function.
- In *Weir v Bettison (Chief Constable of Merseyside)*[126] the Court of Appeal held that the chief constable was liable for an assault on a member of the public by an off-duty constable. The officer believed that the claimant had interfered with his girlfriend's belongings and manhandled him down a flight of stairs, slapping him hard. The officer had told the claimant that he was a police officer and that he was going to take him to the police station. The Court of Appeal held that as the officer had purported to act in his capacity as an officer at the time, vicarious liability was established. The court held that the powers of a police officer are conferred by law, by virtue of the office of constable, such that there is no necessity for any authorisation given by a superior officer. In that sense, the vicarious liability owed by a chief officer is wider than that of employers.

123 [2006] EWHC 3041 (QB).
124 At para 35.
125 [1989] 7 WLUK 405, (1990) Admin LR 214.
126 [2003] EWCA Civ 111, [2003] ICR 708.

- In *Bernard v Attorney-General of Jamaica*[127] the Privy Council held that the defendant was vicariously liable for the unlawful shooting of the claimant by a police officer of the Jamaica Constabulary Force. The claimant was using a public telephone when the officer intervened saying he was 'police' and demanding to use the phone immediately. The claimant refused to let go of the telephone and the officer assaulted the claimant, before shooting him in the head with his service revolver. There were some factual uncertainties over the circumstances of the shooting. The Privy Council assumed in the defendant's favour that the constable was not on duty at the time of the shooting and that his indication of needing to use the phone for police business was a pretext to get his own way, rather than due to a genuine police emergency. The Privy Council decided that vicarious liability was nonetheless established, as the shooting had arisen from the officer's purported assertion of police authority to which the claimant refused to yield. In addition, the officer had subsequently arrested the claimant for assaulting him in the execution of his duty. Although the arrest was entirely bogus in the circumstances, the arrest for this alleged offence underscored that the constable was purporting to act as a policeman immediately before he shot the claimant. The Privy Council also took into account the risk created by the fact that the police authorities routinely permitted constables to take loaded service revolvers home and to carry them while off duty. The latter factor would not have been enough in itself to establish vicarious liability; however, it reinforced the court's conclusion in the circumstances.

14.128 Accordingly, the mere fact that a person who is behaving badly happens to be an off-duty police officer is insufficient to make a chief officer liable for the person's acts. However, if a police officer seeks to gain some improper advantage in their private life when engaged in a confrontation with a member of the public, by purporting to acting as a constable, they invoke their office and therefore the potential liability of their chief officer. It should also be noted that the *Home Office guidance: conduct efficiency and effectiveness*[128] makes clear that where an off-duty officer's conduct suggests that they are acting in their capacity as a police officer, they are considered to have put themselves on duty.[129]

Mutual aid, collaborative agreements and temporary service

14.129 The Police Act 1996 allows chief officers to put in place arrangements to place their officers or civilian employees under the direction and control of another chief officer, where this is in the interests of efficiency and effective policing. Where a police officer is provided to another force under such a mutual aid arrangement they are treated as being under the direction and control of the receiving chief officer, making the chief officer of the

127 [2004] UKPC 47.

128 February 2020, available at: https://assets.publishing.service.gov.uk/government/uploads/system/uploads/attachment_data/file/863820/Home_Office_Statutory_Guidance_0502.pdf/.

129 At para 2.21.

receiving force statutorily vicariously liable for the officer's unlawful conduct.[130] Analogous arrangements apply for cross-border aid between forces in England and Wales, Scotland and Northern Ireland.[131]

14.130 Police forces can also collaborate with each other in terms of sharing staff, legal services, premises, equipment, skills etc, for example, those performed by Underwater Search Units.[132] The legislation is silent on the question of whether an officer from one force is under the direction and control of the chief officer in whose area they are operating under such an agreement. It may therefore be necessary to establish the question of direction and control as a matter of fact rather than simply assume that the officer is operating under a mutual or cross-border aid arrangement.

14.131 Police officers who are seconded to undertake certain 'relevant services' on a temporary basis outside their own force are treated as remaining members of their original police force for certain purposes of the Police Act 1996. However, the Home Secretary is vicariously liable for any unlawful conduct committed by such officers in the performance or purported performance of their functions and in the case of a tort is treated for all purposes as a joint tortfeasor.[133] 'Relevant services' includes such matters as duties at police training colleges, forensic science laboratories and staff officers to inspectors of constabulary.

Cadets

14.132 A police cadet is not a constable or a member of a police force, but is treated as being a person undergoing training with a view to becoming a member of a police force. For the purposes of vicarious liability, the chief officer is treated as the cadet's employer and vicariously liable.[134]

Special police forces

14.133 There are three special police forces whose officers are warranted in like fashion to police officers: British Transport Police (BTP), the Civil Nuclear Constabulary (CNC) and the Ministry of Defence Police (MDP). The BTP and CNC are overseen by dedicated policing authorities which report to the Department for Transport, while the MDP is overseen by a committee which reports to the secretary of state. Civil actions concerning officers deployed by these forces can be brought against chief officers.

14.134 Civil actions concerning officers in other independent police forces, such as harbours or airport police, may usually be brought against the employing body or the individual or both, subject to any local or private Act of Parliament governing the force.[135]

130 Police Act 1996 s24(3).
131 Police Act 1996 s98.
132 Police Act 1996 s23.
133 Police Act 1996 s97(9).
134 Police Act 1996 s28.
135 See Halsbury's Laws, Police and Investigatory Powers, Vol 84 (2019, Lexis Nexis) para 29.

Special constables and police community support officers

14.135 A chief officer is liable for the wrongful acts of special constables and PCSOs under the chief officer's control in the same way as with regular members of a police force. The main difference between special constables and regular members of a police force in the context of misconduct cases lies in the extent of their geographical jurisdiction. A person who is a special constable and who purports to act as a police officer outside an area in which they have jurisdiction is in the same position as an ordinary member of the public. This presumably also applies to a PCSO who acts outside their jurisdiction.

14.136 For further information on special constables, see para 2.36.

Civilian employees

14.137 A great many policing functions are now carried out by civilians employed by the relevant police force – for example, control room staff, front desk staff, scenes of crime officers and the handling and transportation of prisoners. Sometimes staff employed by private suppliers or agencies are deployed in a policing context – for example, detention officers employed by G4S within a custody suite. It will be necessary to establish who directly employs a civilian employee, and the usual rules on vicarious liability will apply to that relationship.

14.138 For further information on civilian employees, see paras 2.39–2.50.

Community safety accreditation schemes

14.139 Community safety accreditation schemes were introduced by the PRA 2002 to contribute to community safety and security and (in co-operation with the police) to combat crime disorder, public nuisance and other forms of anti-social behaviour. In relation to the accredited persons, it is the employer who is vicariously liable.[136]

National Crime Agency

14.140 In 2013 the National Crime Agency (NCA) brought together the functions previously carried out by the National Criminal Intelligence Service (NCIS), the National Crime Squad (NCS), the Child Exploitation and Online Protection Centre (CEOP), the National Policing Improvement Agency (NPIA), the Serious Organised Crime Agency (SOCA), as well as some functions of the former UK Border Agency (UKBA). It is intended to take a strategic oversight role in the detection and prevention of serious crime across the UK. It is also the conduit for inquiries from law enforcement agencies outside the UK, including Interpol and Europol. See further on the NCA at paras 2.60–2.63.

14.141 The head of the NCA is a Director General who holds the rank of chief officer and reports to the Home Secretary. The NCA as an entity is liable 'in the same manner as an employer is liable in respect of unlawful conduct of

136 PRA 2002 s42(10).

employees in the course of their employment'[137] for unlawful conduct by a constable or other person carrying out or purporting to carry out the functions of the agency, including where that person is a member of an NCA-led international joint investigation team or carrying out surveillance under Regulation of Investigatory Powers Act 2000 s76A. In tortious claims, the NCA will be considered a joint tortfeasor with the constable or employee.[138]

Media strategy

14.142 Complaints and civil actions against the police will often merit and engage the public interest. If so, it will be important to advise a claimant on a media strategy along with a litigation strategy. In so doing, it is vital not to prejudice any ongoing legal proceedings, especially if they involve a jury. Claimants will need advice against engaging with the media, including social media, until any jury trial or inquest has concluded, for fear of 'trial by media' creating a potential abuse of process and even requiring those hearings to start afresh with a new jury.

14.143 If a client's reasons for bringing a case were to clear their name or to see the police being held accountable in public for their misconduct, an effective media strategy will be key. It is important to avoid winning the case in court but losing in the court of public opinion.

14.144 Once the jury has delivered its verdict or conclusion, or potentially at an earlier stage in a non-jury case, the claimant will benefit from advice on how best to set the narrative in any media coverage. This can include briefing appropriate journalists, issuing a carefully prepared media release via the Press Association and social media, providing interviews to the media and so on. The media will often request photographs of those involved to enhance an article or broadcast.

14.145 Media scrutiny can lead to the police, the IOPC and/or CPS taking the claimant's case more seriously; however, media coverage can also lead to a claimant receiving unwelcome attention from the tabloid press or being trolled on social media. Defendants also increasingly search social media posts made by a claimant for pre-trial cross-examination material.

14.146 In some cases it can be particularly important to protect clients from unwanted publicity. For example, a claimant whose claim arises from their status as a victim of sexual offences in criminal proceedings is entitled to anonymity.[139]

14.147 Claimants will wish to be prepared for the fact that most hearings in legal or disciplinary proceedings (see chapter 5) are open to the public and therefore the media. Subject to any reporting restrictions, journalists will therefore usually be free to publish and/or broadcast the evidence that is heard from witnesses in open court while the hearing progresses.

14.148 In a non-jury case, if a claimant does engage with the media before they have given evidence at trial, great care should be taken to ensure that nothing is said that could provide the defendant with material for cross-

137 Crime and Courts Act 2013 Sch 4 para 2(1).

138 Crime and Courts Act 2013 Sch 4 para 2(5).

139 Sexual Offences (Amendment) Act 1992 ss1, 2.

examination, such as inconsistencies or exaggeration in the claimant's account. If the claimant decides to engage with the media at this stage, it may well be advisable to confine the discussion to background and/or overall impact of the index events.

14.149 Any media release should ideally be sent to the Press Association ('the wire'), in addition to named journalists, often home affairs or legal correspondents. In cases where publicity can be shown to be particularly important, such as in a test case, the time spent on press work may be allowed on the costs assessment.

14.150 As many civil actions against the police and related inquests are heard before juries, the closer the case gets to a final hearing, the more caution should be exercised in speaking publicly about the case, so as not to fall foul of the laws of contempt of court and the laws against perverting the course of justice.

Criminal Injuries Compensation Scheme

14.151 The Criminal Injuries Compensation Scheme[140] allows for payments to be made to victims of crimes of violence. A person assaulted by the police can be as much the victim of a crime as of a civil wrong. A victim of a police crime of violence is therefore as free as the next person to make a claim. The scheme can be used for claims arising out of crimes of violence that result in death.

14.152 A claim for damages in the civil courts is almost always preferable to a claim under the scheme. Court procedures are designed to allow the evidence to be tested and for all the issues to be thoroughly explored. The procedures under the Scheme do not anticipate that the 'criminal' will participate and deny the crime, although this has happened in claims to the scheme alleging police violence. Furthermore, as will be seen below, the level of compensation awarded can be lower than that in the courts.

14.153 The main advantage of the scheme is that it is designed to be accessible without legal representation. It is usually most appropriate if a person does not qualify for public funding, cannot afford a lawyer and/or the merits of a civil claim are uncertain.

14.154 The scheme is administered by the Criminal Injuries Compensation Authority (CICA).[141] Broadly speaking, the scheme allows financial awards to be made:

- to recognise physical and mental injuries caused by violent crimes;
- in certain circumstances, to compensate for past or future lost earnings or special expenses caused by a violent crime; and
- for the death of a close relative as a result of a violent crime, including, in some cases, compensation for the loss of earnings for the person who was killed.

140 *The Criminal Injuries Compensation Scheme 2012*, Ministry of Justice, made on 13 November 2012, and as amended on 13 June 2019 – referred to in this chapter as the 'scheme', available at: www.gov.uk/government/publications/criminal-injuries-compensation-scheme-2012.

141 Criminal Injuries Compensation Authority, Alexander Bain House, Atlantic Quay, 15 York Street, Glasgow, G2 8JQ (www.gov.uk/government/organisations/criminal-injuries-compensation-authority).

14.155 In 1996, a tariff of fixed compensation payments for specific types of injury was introduced. The current scheme applies to all applications received on or after 27 November 2012 and continues to use a tariff of injuries.[142] Applicants do not need legal advice or representation to apply for compensation. The scheme specifically provides that where an applicant is legally represented, the cost of the representation will not be met by the ClCA.[143]

14.156 Compensation can be paid under the scheme to an applicant who:

- has sustained a criminal injury on or after 1 August 1964;[144]
- is ordinarily resident in the UK;[145] and
- was in Great Britain when injured.[146]

14.157 Criminal injury means an injury which appears in Part A or B of the tariff in Annex E[147] that is directly attributable to a crime of violence.[148] This includes physical injury (including a fatal injury), mental injury and disease. Where a person has sustained a mental injury as a result of a sexual assault, they will be entitled to an injury payment for whichever of the sexual assault or the mental injury would give rise to the highest payment under the tariff.[149]

14.158 The CICA can refuse or reduce an award due to:

- the applicant's failure to report the incident giving rise to the criminal injury to the police as soon as reasonably practicable;[150]
- the applicant's failure to co-operate in attempting to bring the assailant to justice;[151]
- the applicant's failure to give reasonable assistance to the CICA;[152]
- the applicant's conduct, criminal record or character.[153]

14.159 The applicant should also have sent the CICA their application as soon as reasonably practicable and no later than two years after of the date of the incident which caused the injury.[154] The CICA may still accept the

142 2012 Scheme, Annex E.

143 2012 Scheme, para 93; and *C v Secretary of State for the Home Department* (2003) 22 May, QBD, Mitting J, unreported, which held that a claimant's rights under the ECHR were not breached by the CICA's refusal to pay the claimant's cost of representation.

144 2012 Scheme, para 17.

145 2012 Scheme, para 10(a). Paragraphs 10(b)–(c) provide limited exceptions to this requirement, including if the victim was an asylum-seeker or had been referred to a competent authority as a potential victim of human trafficking.

146 2012 Scheme, para 8. If an applicant was not injured in Great Britain, they may still be eligible for compensation if they meet any of the five circumstances listed in Annex C of the scheme.

147 2012 Scheme, Annex A.

148 2012 Scheme, para 4. See also Annex B for the definition of 'crime of violence'. The introduction of Annex B means that the decision in *Jones (by Caldwell) v First Tier Tribunal and CICA* [2013] UKSC 19 on the interpretation of the term 'crime of violence' will no longer apply to applications made under the 2012 Scheme.

149 2012 Scheme, Table 34.

150 2012 Scheme, para 22.

151 2012 Scheme, para 23.

152 2012 Scheme, para 24.

153 2012 Scheme, paras 25–27.

154 2012 Scheme, para 87.

application if the applicant can show good reasons why they have not met this condition.[155]

14.160 Once the CICA receives the application and its enquiries show that the applicant is entitled to an award, the CICA assesses the size of any award by using the tariff of injuries.[156] In certain circumstances, where no provision is made for an injury in the tariff, the CICA may refer that injury to the secretary of state for inclusion in the tariff, if it considers the injury is sufficient degree of seriousness.[157]

14.161 The applicant may also get additional compensation if, as a result of a violent crime, they have lost earnings or the ability to earn for longer than 28 weeks.[158]

14.162 An applicant may also be eligible for compensation if they were a dependant or a close relative of a victim of violent crime who has since died. To be eligible under this provision, a claimant needs to be either:[159]

a) The spouse or civil partner of the deceased, who was living with the deceased in the same household;
b) the partner of the deceased (other than a spouse or civil partner) who was living with them in the same household and had done so for a continuous period of at least two years immediately before the date of death;
c) a person who would satisfy sub-paragraph (a) or (b) but who did not live with the deceased because of either person's ill-health or infirmity;
d) the spouse or civil partner, or a former spouse or civil partner, of the deceased who was financially dependent on the deceased;
e) a parent of the deceased; or
f) a child of the deceased.

14.163 Applications for compensation can be submitted online.[160] The following information may be required:

- the date and location of the crime;
- the name of the police station where the crime was reported;
- crime reference number;
- GP details;
- details of any previous applications you have made to CICA; and
- details of any unspent criminal convictions.

14.164 An applicant should be aware that by signing the application form, they are giving permission to the CICA to receive all the records, evidence and other information about the applicant and the circumstance of the injury. This includes information about the applicant's medical condition and the evidence that they may have given to the police as well as information about the applicant's income, tax and benefits situation (if the claim is being made for loss of earnings or expenses).

155 2012 Scheme, para 89.
156 2012 Scheme, para 33.
157 2012 Scheme, para 38.
158 2012 Scheme, para 44.
159 2012 Scheme, para 59.
160 At: www.gov.uk/claim-compensation-criminal-injury/make-claim.

14.165 Claims officers in the claims assessment section of the CICA determine claims for compensation in accordance with the scheme.[161]

14.166 The length of time needed to assess a claim will vary depending on its complexity. Applicants can expect to wait up to 12 months to receive payment of their claim.[162]

14.167 If an applicant disagrees with a decision of the claims assessment section, they are entitled to ask for a more senior officer within the authority to review the decision. CICA must receive the application for review within 56 days after the date of the written notice of determination by the original claims officer.[163]

14.168 If applicants wish to appeal against the reviewed decision, an appeal is made to the First-tier Tribunal (Criminal Injuries Compensation), formerly known as the Criminal Injuries Appeals Panel, which is independent of the authority.[164] The application must be made in accordance with Tribunal Procedure Rules. The tribunal must receive the appeal form within 90 days of the date of the review decision. The tribunal will send a copy of the appeal from to CICA, who will usually respond to the tribunal and applicant within six weeks.[165]

14.169 The tribunal will decide whether to decide the appeal using the paperwork provided to them or via an oral hearing. The applicant may request an oral hearing, which will be attended by two or three tribunal members, a clerk, a CICA representative and any witnesses. The applicant does not have to have a legal representative to the hearing, but a legal adviser may assist in presenting their case. The cost of representation will not be met by CICA or the tribunal. There is no right to appeal the tribunal's decision, but an applicant may be entitled to ask for a judicial review of the tribunal's decision in certain circumstances.[166]

14.170 There is nothing to prevent a claimant making an application to the scheme and a civil claim in respect of the same injury; however, any award made under the scheme will usually be deducted from any damages received via a civil claim for that injury to avoid double recovery.[167] A live topic, yet to be resolved by case-law, is whether CICA should offset civil damages awarded in respect of personal injury from a CICA award but not damages awarded for other purposes, for example to vindicate a claimant's human rights by way of just satisfaction. Currently CICA tends to off-set both types of damages, which is the subject of several ongoing appeals.

14.171 If an award is made under the scheme to a claimant with a public funding certificate for a civil claim which is ongoing, that award must be declared to the LAA as capital received by the claimant and can lead to the public funding certificate for the civil claim being withdrawn if the amount exceeds LAA capital thresholds.

161 2012 Scheme, para 86.

162 *Criminal injuries compensation: a guide*, CICA and MOJ, 26 March 2014, last updated 15 February 2022, available at: www.gov.uk/guidance/criminal-injuries-compensation-a-guide.

163 2012 Scheme, para 101.

164 2012 Scheme, para 125.

165 See: www.gov.uk/criminal-injuries-compensation-tribunal.

166 See: www.gov.uk/criminal-injuries-compensation-tribunal.

167 2012 Scheme, para 85.

CHAPTER 15

Bringing the action – from issue of proceedings to exchange of witness statements

continued

Introduction

15.1 This chapter provides an overview of the stages of bringing an action against the police. It concentrates on the main procedural points which arise in private law cases for damages for tort actions and cases involving the Human Rights Act (HRA) 1998, Equality Act (EqA) 2010 and Data Protection Act (DPA) 2018. Further points are made in the specific chapters which deal with all these causes of action in paragraphs 6–12, which should also be consulted. This chapter does not apply to cases brought for judicial review. Limitation issues for judicial review cases are set out in chapter 14, together with a list of references to possible judicial review cases referred to elsewhere in the book (see para 14.5). Specialist advice should be sought on judicial review practice and procedure, but a useful overview is provided in the Administrative Court publication *Judicial Review Guide 2021*[1] which is updated from time to time. Thus, in relation to private law actions, this chapter covers the following:

- funding, costs and rules;
- starting a claim, including the claim form;
- alternative dispute resolution (ADR);
- striking out the claim;
- summary judgment;
- allocation;
- case and costs management hearings;
- costs budgets;
- relief from sanctions;
- pre-trial case management;
- jury trial;
- anonymity;
- disclosure;
- exchange of witness statements;
- hearsay notices;
- offers to settle and payments into court;
- expert evidence.

Funding and rules

Extension of public funding

15.2 Chapter 14 dealt in detail with applying for public funding. Many civil claims against the police are funded by the Legal Aid Agency (LAA) under the Legal Aid, Sentencing and Punishment of Offenders Act 2012 (LASPO).[2] The initial certificate of public funding granted by the LAA usually has a limitation attached to it, such as: 'limited to obtaining external counsel's opinion or the opinion of an external solicitor with higher court

1 https://assets.publishing.service.gov.uk/government/uploads/system/uploads/attachment_data/file/1022369/HMCTS_Administrative_Court_Guide_2021_Final_Web.pdf/.

2 LASPO Sch 1 para 21.

advocacy rights, particularly with regard to merits and quantum'. In these circumstances, the terms of the certificate will need to be extended before proceedings can be issued.

15.3 This will normally involve the solicitor completing a CLS APP 8 form; enclosing a positive opinion from counsel; and addressing merits, quantum and the prescribed criteria for funding.[3] Practitioners will also need to check that the scope of the certificate includes all the causes of action now contemplated.

The overriding objective

15.4 It is important for practitioners to be well versed in the rules that govern litigation. The Civil Procedure Rules 1998[4] (CPR) substantially changed the way civil cases were handled by the courts, and also reinforced procedural rules which, although acknowledged in the past, were not always put into effect. Most parts of the CPR are supplemented by practice directions.

15.5 The courts must give effect to the overriding objective when exercising any powers conferred by the CPR[5] and the parties are required to help the court in furthering the overriding objective.[6] The overriding objective is described as follows:[7]

15.6 (1) These rules are a new procedural code with the overriding objective of enabling the Court to deal with cases justly and at proportionate cost.

(2) Dealing with a case justly and at proportionate cost includes, so far as is practicable–
- (a) ensuring that the parties are on an equal footing and can participate fully in proceedings, and that parties and witnesses can give their best evidence;
- (b) saving expense;
- (c) dealing with the case in ways which are proportionate–
  - (i) to the amount of money involved;
  - (ii) to the importance of the case;
  - (iii) to the complexity of the issues; and
  - (iv) to the financial position of each party;
- (d) ensuring that it is dealt with expeditiously and fairly;
- (e) allotting to it an appropriate share of the court's resources, while taking into account the need to allot resources to other cases; and
- (f) enforcing compliance with rules, practice directions and orders.

3 The latter is discussed in chapter 14.
4 Available at: www.justice.gov.uk/courts/procedure-rules/civil/rules.
5 CPR 1.2(a).
6 CPR 1.3
7 CPR 1.1.

Starting a claim

15.7 CPR Part 7 sets out how to start proceedings. Part 7 introduces the 'claim form'. This is a single form of originating process for all claims in the High Court and the county court.

High Court or county court?

15.8 If the proceedings include a claim for damages in respect of personal injury, they can only be commenced in the High Court if the financial value of the claim is £50,000 or more.[8] Accordingly, if a claimant in a civil action against the police seeks damages for personal injury, it is mandatory to start proceedings in the county court whenever the overall damages are unlikely to exceed £50,000.

15.9 In cases that do not include a claim for consequential personal injuries, the claim may only be started in the High Court if the value of the claim is more than £100,000.[9] The High Court has power to transfer the case to the county court (and vice versa) if that is considered the more appropriate forum.[10] Factors that will be taken into account in determining whether transfer is appropriate include:

- the financial value of the claim (and the amount in dispute, if different);
- the availability of a specialist judge;
- whether the facts, legal issues, remedies and/or procedure are straightforward or complex;
- the importance of the outcome to the general public;
- the adequacy of the court facilities available, particularly in relation to disabilities, special measures for witnesses or disabilities.[11]

15.10 A case with a value of less than £50,000 will generally be heard in the county court, whereas a case with a value of more than £100,000 will usually be heard in the High Court.[12] Where a case has a value of under £100,000 but is issued in the High Court, it will usually be transferred to the county court unless it is of a specified kind, including claims for malicious prosecution or false imprisonment and actions against the police.[13] Nonetheless, even these types of cases can still be transferred where the issues appear straightforward and thus county court trial appropriate.

15.11 Aside from the possibility of transfer, if a case is commenced in the wrong court, there is a power to reduce the costs that would otherwise be

8 High Court and County Courts Jurisdiction Order 1991 SI No 724 art 5; and see CPR Practice Direction (PD) 7A, para 2.2.

9 High Court and County Courts Jurisdiction Order 1991 SI No 724 art 4A; and see CPR PD 7A, para 2.1.

10 County Courts Act 1984 ss40(2), 41(1) and 42(1).

11 CPR 30.3(2).

12 High Court and County Courts Jurisdiction Order 1991 SI No 724 art 7(5); and CPR PD 29 para 2.2.

13 CPR PD 29 paras 2.2 and 2.6.

awarded by a figure of up to 25 per cent, if the High Court considers that proceedings should have been brought in the county court.[14]

15.12 The High Court also has a power to simply strike out a case if it considers that it should have been brought in the county court, and the person bringing the proceedings knew or ought to have known of that requirement.[15]

15.13 In practice, most police cases are commenced in the county court unless there are particularly serious allegations involved and / or quantum is particularly large.

The claim form

15.14 Proceedings are started when the court issues a claim form at the request of the claimant. It is important to distinguish what the claim form must contain from what the particulars of claim must contain. Essentially, the claim form contains a brief summary of the claimant's causes of action and the particulars of claim gives the details of these.

15.15 There are three possible ways of dealing with the particulars of claim:

1) The claimant can include their particulars of claim on the claim form itself.
2) The claimant may prepare their particulars of claim as a separate document and serve them with the claim form.
3) The claimant may prepare their particulars of claim as a separate document and serve them within 14 days of the service of the claim form or by the latest time for serving the claim form (if this is a subsequent date).[16]

15.16 If the adviser has been instructed in the case from the outset and has carried out the pre-action considerations referred to in chapter 14, option 2 (above) will be the most common and preferred option. Option 3 is used where the claim form has to be issued quickly, for example, because otherwise a difficulty with limitation would arise (see further paras 14.13–14.35).

15.17 The claim form must contain a concise statement of the nature of the claim and specify the remedy which the claimant seeks. Where the claimant is making a claim for money, it must contain a statement of value in accordance with CPR 16.3; and contain such other matters as may be set out in the practice direction.[17] CPR PD 22 requires the claim form to be verified by a statement of truth in the following form:

> [I believe] [The claimant believes] that the facts stated in the claim form are true. [I understand] [The claimant understands] that proceedings for contempt of court may be brought against anyone who makes, or causes to be made, a false statement in a document verified by a statement of truth without an honest belief in its truth.[18]

14 Senior Courts Act 1981 s51(8), (9).
15 County Courts Act s40(1).
16 CPR 7.4.
17 CPR 16.2.
18 CPR PD 22 para 2.1.

15.18 A claimant may apply for an order extending the period within which a claim form may be served or the parties may extend the period by agreement in writing.[19] The general rule is that the claim form should be served within its initial period of validity (generally, four months).[20] If it is not so served, an application to extend its validity should be made within the same initial period (or any agreed extension). In those circumstances an extension of time will usually be granted if good reason is shown. However, if no such application has been made during the four-month period, and an application is subsequently made to extend time, the court can only grant the extension if:

- the court has failed serve the claim form; or
- the claimant has taken all reasonable steps to serve the claim form but has been unable to do so; and
- in either case, the claimant has acted promptly in making an application.

15.19 Most of the cases in relation to extensions of time for serving the claim form have concerned what amounts to taking 'reasonable steps' to effect service.[21]

15.20 The court also has a power to authorise retrospectively steps that have already been taken to bring the claim form to the attention of the defendants, where there is good reason to do so.[22] Relevant factors include: a) whether the claimant has taken reasonable steps to effect service in accordance with the rules; b) whether the defendant or their solicitor was aware of the contents of the claim form at the time when it expired; and c) what if any prejudice the defendant would suffer by the retrospective validation of a non-compliant service of the claim form, bearing in mind what the defendant knew about its contents.[23]

The particulars of claim

15.21 Particulars of claim that are not included in the claim form must be verified by a statement of truth in the form that has been set out above. Practitioners need to warn their clients that proceedings for contempt of court can be brought against the maker of a false statement, if it is verified by a statement of truth made without an honest belief in its truth.[24]

15.22 The particulars of claim must include a statement of the facts on which the claimant relies. Save where the claim is a very straightforward one, particulars of claim are usually drafted by counsel. In cases where the facts and / or appropriate causes of action are complex, it may be useful for the claimant to have a conference with counsel before the pleading is prepared or finalised. Aside from specific rules as to what the particulars of claim

19 CPR 2.11.

20 CPR 7.5.

21 *Boxwood Leisure Ltd v Gleeson Construction Services Ltd and another* [2021] EWHC 947 (TCC); *Qatar Investment and Projects Holding Co and another v Phoenix Ancient Art SA* [2021] EWHC 2243 (QB).

22 CPR 6.15(2).

23 *Barton v Wright Hassall LLP* [2018] UKSC 12, [2018] 1 WLR 1119 at para 10.

24 CPR 32.14.

should contain (summarised below), it is generally to the claimant's advantage to set out the case in some detail in the pleading, emphasising factors that assist in establishing liability and summarising all elements relevant to the quantum of the damages sought. Such an approach is likely to assist with facilitating an early settlement of the claim in circumstances where the claimant has a strong case. To the extent that it is possible, the particulars of claim should be factually consistent with what has been set out in the letter before action (see paras 14.83–14.89) as any inconsistencies can form the basis for cross-examination at trial (see chapter 16).

15.23 If the claimant is seeking aggravated damages or exemplary damages (see chapter 17), a statement to that effect and the grounds for claiming them must be included. A statement confirming that the claimant is seeking interest should also be included, if that is the case.[25]

15.24 In personal injury claims, the particulars of claim must set out the claimant's date of birth and give brief details of the injuries sustained.[26] The claimant must attach to their particulars of claim a schedule of any past and future expenses and losses that are claimed.[27] Where the claimant is relying on the evidence of a medical practitioner in support of a claim for personal injuries, their report must be served with the particulars of claim (see chapter 14)[28] (if it has not already been served with the letter of claim, prior to the issue of proceedings: see chapter 14). However, in *Mark v Universal Coatings*, the court held that the failure to serve a complete schedule of loss and/or medical report does not carry an express or implied sanction that would require an application for relief from sanctions (see further below).[29] In some cases, there may be good reasons why a medical report or detailed schedule of loss cannot be served with the particulars of claim, for example where the claimant's prognosis is uncertain. In those cases, directions can be sought at the first costs and case management conference (CCMC) to deal with the service of experts' reports and schedules and counter-schedule of loss.

15.25 The elements of the various torts for which claims can be made, are set out in chapters 6–12. It is important for each of the elements to be pleaded in the particulars of claim. The following is a brief reminder of some of the main points.

15.26 In actions for assault and battery, the intentional nature of the acts relied upon should be specified if this is not already apparent from the conduct described.

15.27 In actions for false imprisonment, as the burden of proof is on the police to prove that a detention is lawful, strictly speaking, the claimant need only state that the detention was unlawful. However, in practice, it is usually desirable to set out more fully the nature of the unlawfulness alleged, so that the police are required to address all the relevant allegations in their defence. For example, if the false imprisonment is alleged to stem from an officer's failure to comply with a specific duty – such as

25 CPR 16.4.
26 CPR PD 16 para 4.1.
27 CPR PD 16 para 4.2.
28 CPR PD 16 para 4.3.
29 [2018] EWHC 3206 (QB).

giving prescribed information on arrest[30] – this should be specifically pleaded, so that the claimant's case is clear. There will generally be an obligation upon the claimant to put points upon which reliance is placed, irrespective of whether the burden of proof rests upon the defendant.[31]

15.28 In actions for malicious prosecution, all five elements required to prove malicious prosecution must be specifically pleaded. These are:

1) that there was a prosecution which was initiated or continued by the defendants; and
2) that the prosecution was terminated in the claimant's favour; and
3) that the prosecution was brought without reasonable or probable cause; and
4) that the officers acted maliciously; and
5) that the prosecution caused the claimant loss or damage.[32]

15.29 In actions for trespass to land, the claimant needs to plead their entitlement to possession of the land in question and the acts of the defendant which are alleged to constitute trespass (see chapter 9). In an action for misfeasance in a public office, all the ingredients which make up the tort will need to be specially pleaded. If a claimant wishes to rely on evidence under Civil Evidence Act 1968 s11 of a conviction for an offence, this must be specifically pleaded in the particulars of claim.[33]

Acknowledgement of service and defence

15.30 CPR Parts 9, 10, and 15 deal with the response a defendant is required to make to the claim form served upon them.

15.31 Where the defendant is served with a claim form which states that the particulars of claim are to follow, the defendant must file an acknowledgement of service 14 days after service of the particulars of claim. In any other case, the acknowledgement of service must be filed 14 days after service of the claim form.[34]

15.32 On receipt of an acknowledgement of service, the court notifies the claimant in writing. The acknowledgement of service is a standard form that must be enclosed by the claimant in the documents served upon the defendant. The acknowledgement of service needs to be signed by the defendant or their legal representative.

15.33 It is possible for the claimant to apply for judgment without trial (called a 'default judgment') where a defendant has failed to file an acknowledgement of service or has failed to file a defence.[35] The grounds for setting aside or varying a default judgment are contained in CPR Part 13. Clearly,

30 See Police and Criminal Evidence Act 1984 (PACE) s28(3), discussed in the section on false imprisonment in chapter 6.

31 By way of example, see *Magee v Chief Constable of Derbyshire* [2020] EWHC 3569 (QB) at para 54.

32 These elements are discussed in detail in chapter 8.

33 CPR PD 16 para 8.1. This practice direction also sets out the other matters which must be included in the particulars of claim, if relied on.

34 CPR 10.3.

35 CPR Part 12.

if there would be grounds to set aside the judgment, then it may not be wise to increase costs and delay matters by applying for a default judgment.

15.34 A defendant who wishes to defend all or part of a claim must file a defence. The general rule is that the period for filing a defence is 14 days after service of the particulars of claim or if the defendant files an acknowledgement of service under CPR Part 10, 28 days after service of the particulars of claim.[36] The CPR provides that the defendant and the claimant may agree that the period for filing a defence specified be extended by up to 28 days.[37] If agreement is reached for the extension of time, the defendant must notify the court in writing to this effect.[38]

15.35 If the defendant requests an extension of time, the claimant's adviser should consider the defendant's justification for doing so. Very often, it will be unreasonable to refuse a short extension of, say, two to three weeks. If agreement is not reached, the defendants can apply to the court for an extension of time. If an extension is to be resisted, it is important for the claimant's solicitors to prepare a chronology for the court showing that the defendant has already had sufficient time to prepare a defence, including that the claimant complied with the pre-action protocol. Chapter 14 at paras 14.105–14.110 discusses this scenario where a police complaint investigation is outstanding.

15.36 A defence must be verified with a statement of truth. The form of the statement of truth is the same as that required in the particulars of claim.[39]

15.37 Just as the particulars of claim must contain certain matters to avoid an application being made for it to be struck out, similarly, a defence must include certain matters to avoid an application being made by the claimant for judgment. The defendant must state which of the allegations in the particulars of claim are denied; which are admitted; and which cannot be admitted or denied and the claimant must prove. If the defendant denies an allegation the defence must state the reasons for doing so and must set out any alternative version of events that the defendant intends to put forward.[40] Where the burden of proof is on the defendant, for example to explain why detention is lawful in a false imprisonment case, this must be fully set out in a defence.

15.38 Where the claim is for personal injury and the claimant has attached a medical report in respect of the claimant's related injuries, the defence should state whether the defendant agrees, dispute or neither agree nor dispute but has no knowledge of the matters contained in the medical report. Where any part of the medical report is disputed, reasons need to be given for doing so. Where the defendant has obtained a medical report on which reliance is intended to be placed, this needs to be attached to the defence. Similarly, if a schedule of past and future expenses and losses has been served, the defendant needs to set out a response in a counter-schedule.[41]

36 CPR 15.4.
37 CPR 15.5.
38 CPR 15.5.
39 CPR PD 22.
40 CPR 16.5.
41 CPR PD 16 para 12.

15.39 The defence must also give details of other matters upon which the defendant intends to rely. For example, if the defendant is taking a point on the limitation period, details must be provided in the defence.[42]

15.40 In practice, the police are likely to deny anything that can be denied, or to require the claimant to prove anything that is outside of the police's knowledge.

15.41 It is usually helpful for the claimant to be interviewed in person to obtain instructions on the defence, and a statement drawn up expressing those instructions.

Reply

15.42 A claimant is entitled to file and serve a reply to the defence. This must be done when filing the allocation questionnaire.[43]

15.43 A reply is not compulsory. A reply can be served if the claimant wishes to respond to any matters raised in the defence. For example, if the police have set out in the defence that they intend to rely on the conviction of the claimant, then, if the claimant intends to deny the conviction or allege that it was erroneous, this must be pleaded and the reply would be the most appropriate time to do this.

15.44 A reply must not contradict or be inconsistent with the particulars of claim, and should only be used to allege facts in answer to the defence which were not included in the original claim form. In practice, a reply is occasionally used to clarify the legal basis for the claim, or to state a response to matters pleaded in the defence. For example, if a chief constable denied vicarious liability, it may be helpful to state a response, both to clarify the issues between the parties and, potentially, to strengthen the claimant's position in negotiating a settlement. Other examples would include a reply to any legal basis set out to justify detention, or where reliance is placed on a limitation period by the defendant. However, a reply should not stray into setting out submissions on the law and facts which should be reserved for trial.

15.45 As with any statement of case, it should be accompanied by a statement of truth.

Further information

15.46 CPR Part 18 sets out the basis on which an application for further information can be made. Before making an application for an order under Part 18, the party seeking clarification or information should first serve on the party from whom it is sought a written request for the clarification or information, stating a date by which the response to the request should be served. The date must allow a reasonable time to respond.

15.47 A request should be concise and strictly confined to matters which are reasonably necessary and proportionate to enable the party making the request to prepare their own case or to understand the case that has to be met.[44] A request may be made by letter if the text of the request is brief and

42 CPR PD 16 para 13.1.

43 CPR 15.8.

44 CPR PD 18 para 1.2.

the reply is likely to be brief. Otherwise the request should be made in a separate document.

15.48 CPR Part 18 and the associated practice direction explain the procedure for requesting and providing further information. The response to a request for further information should be verified by a statement of truth. Should the responding party refuse to provide further information voluntarily then an application can be made to the court.

Alternative dispute resolution

15.49 The courts are increasingly encouraging parties to explore ADR, such as mediation, where possible.[45] A request can be made for the court to stay proceedings to allow time for alternative dispute resolution.[46] The court can also stay the case on its own initiative if considered appropriate, and refer the parties to a mediation service.[47]

15.50 The parties may meet in a 'roundtable meeting' (often called a RTM) to discuss the issues in the case and seek to agree a compromise or settlement of the claim. The discussion will generally be led by the legal representatives, although the lay client(s) may be present and have an opportunity to contribute. An alternative is a more formal mediation using an independent mediator. All parties meet with a mediator who helps the parties to communicate with each other and to try to reach an agreement to the dispute. The obvious advantages of mediation are the speed within which a case can be resolved, as well as the freedom for the parties to reach their own agreed solution. For example, an apology can be forthcoming from a defendant police force as one of the terms of a settlement reached via mediation. Sometimes an apology is more important to the claimant than the level of compensation recovered. If the claimant is in receipt of public funding, then the reasonable costs of the RTM or mediation can be claimed from the LAA.

15.51 Mediation is less likely to succeed if there is a stark contrast between the versions of events given by the claimant and the police. Similarly, if there is a point of law involved which can only be resolved by a court, then mediation may not be productive.

15.52 If a party unreasonably refuses to engage in mediation, then the court can make an adverse costs order against that party, regardless of the outcome of the litigation.[48] Relevant factors can include: the nature of the dispute; the merits of the case; the extent to which other settlement methods were attempted; whether the costs of mediation would be disproportionately high; whether mediation would involve significant and prejudicial delay; and whether the mediation had a reasonable prospect of success.

45 See, for example, *Thakkar v Patel* [2017] EWCA Civ 117, [2017] 2 Costs LR 233; *Marsh v Ministry of Justice* [2017] EWHC 3185 (QB); *R (Essex CC) v Secretary of State for Education* [2016] EWHC 1724 (Admin).

46 CPR 24.6.

47 CPR 24.6A.

48 *Halsey v Milton Keynes General NHS Trust* [2004] EWCA Civ 576; *Buchell v Bullard* [2005] EWCA Civ 358; [2005] CP Rep 36.

Striking out the claim

15.53 The court may strike out all or part of a statement of case if it appears to the court:

- that it discloses no reasonable grounds for bringing or defending the claim; and/or
- that the statement of case is an abuse of the court's process or is otherwise likely to obstruct the just disposal of the proceedings; and/or
- that there has been a failure to comply with a rule, practice direction or court order.[49]

15.54 Defendants to civil actions against the police tend to apply to strike out the claim if they contend that it is unsustainable in law, even on the facts that the claimant alleges. A common example of this is where the claim is brought in negligence and the defendant alleges that no duty of care exists.[50]

Summary judgment

Overview

15.55 The court may give summary judgment against a claimant or a defendant on the whole of a claim or in relation to a particular issue.

15.56 In order to succeed in an application for summary judgment, the applicant has to show that the other party has no real prospect of establishing liability / defending the claim or winning on the relevant issue and that there is no other compelling reason why the case or issue should be disposed of at trial.[51] In order to defeat the application for summary judgment, it is sufficient for the respondent to show that the claim has a 'realistic' as opposed to 'fanciful' prospect of success. The courts have held that a 'realistic' claim is one that carries some degree of conviction, in other words it is more than merely arguable. However, the respondent is not required to show that their case will probably succeed a trial.[52] The court at the summary judgment application will consider the merits of the respondent's case only to the extent necessary to determine whether it has sufficient merit to proceed to trial. Although the application notice for a summary judgment will include an identification of the written evidence on which the applicant relies, and why the order is being sought,[53] the application is not a mini trial.[54]

15.57 Most applications for summary judgment are made at the close of pleadings and before witness statements have been exchanged; although an application can also be made after witness statements have been served.

49 CPR 3.4.
50 See the section on negligence in chapter 6.
51 CPR 24.2.
52 *AC Ward & Sons Ltd v Catlin (Five) Ltd* [2009] EWCA Civ 1098 at para 24.
53 CPR 24.4.
54 *Swain v Hillman* [2001] All ER 91.

Resisting an application for summary judgment

15.58 A claimant may be able to resist an application for summary judgment by showing that resolution of the claim or issue will depend upon the findings made at trial in relation to disputes of fact between the parties. Many actions against the police involve the claimant and defendant putting forward starkly different versions of the same incident. Accordingly, issues relating to liability will often be incapable of resolution until the facts have been established and this can only be done when the disputed testimony is heard and evaluated at trial. Some civil actions against the police are heard by a judge sitting with a jury, rather than by a judge alone (as is discussed below at paras 15.77–15.89).

15.59 In *Safeways plc v Tate*[55] the Court of Appeal suggested that where a claim involved causes of action that conferred a right to jury trial, a judge was precluded from usurping the role of the jury and entering summary judgment, if this involved assessing any issues of fact. However, the Court of Appeal then re-considered this point in *Alexander v Arts Council*[56] and concluded that summary judgment could be entered in a case involving claims that would be heard by a jury, if the judge found that the evidence when taken at its highest was such that a properly directed jury could not find in favour of the party seeking to resist the application. This process does not involve the judge in deciding where the truth lies between rival accounts, but in seeing if the party resisting the application could succeed if all the disputed facts are assumed in their favour. For example, a judge might decide that even if all points in dispute were found in favour of a claimant, a claim for misfeasance should be struck out because there was insufficient material to support an inference that an officer was acting in bad faith. This approach mirrors the role that a judge has at trial – the judge can withdraw issues from the jury if the factual evidence is incapable of supporting them.[57]

Appropriateness and implications

15.60 Advisers will need to consider when it is appropriate to make an application for summary judgment against a defendant. For example, if the detention is clearly unlawful in a case where the claim is for false imprisonment (see chapter 7) on the basis of a legal point that does not rely on disputed facts and can even be established on the version of events given by the defendants, it may be worth making such an application. The application, if well founded, can also put pressure on the police to settle a claim.

15.61 Advisers should, however, bear in mind the implications should the application for summary judgment be unsuccessful – the claimant will have to pay the defendant's costs of the application as well as their own. (For claimants who are publicly funded, this will have an impact on the statutory charge: see chapter 14, which deals with public funding).

55 [2001] 4 All ER 193, CA.

56 [2001] 1 WLR 840, CA.

57 This is discussed in more detail in chapter 16.

Allocation

15.62 Once the defence (and any reply) has been filed, the court will provisionally allocate the claim to a track and serve on the parties a notice of proposed allocation requiring them to file directions questionnaires.[58] A final decision on allocation will be made after filing of questionnaires, if necessary after a hearing.

15.63 There are three tracks:[59]

1) The small claims track is the normal track for claims that are worth £10,000 or less, where the value for any claim for damages for personal injuries is £1,000 or less.
2) The fast track is the normal track for any claim that is not in the small claims track and has a value of £25,000 or less, and where the trial is likely to last no longer than one day and oral expert evidence is likely to be limited to one expert per party in up to two fields.
3) The multi-track is the normal track for all other claims.

15.64 When deciding what track to allocate to, the court will have regard to a range of factors including the financial value of the claim, the nature of the remedy sought, the likely complexity of the facts, law or evidence, the number of parties, the amount of oral evidence which may be required, the importance of the claim to others and the views and circumstances of the parties.

15.65 Police defendants may argue that a case should be allocated to the small claims or fast track based solely on the value of the claim. However, the value of the claim should not be the only determining factor and in most cases the small claims track will not be appropriate for police disputes. The small claims track is intended for 'straightforward' claims that do not require substantial preparation and can be conducted by a litigant in person without legal representation. Examples given in the practice direction include consumer disputes; accident claims; disputes about the ownership of goods; and most financial disputes between landlords and tenants – none of which are analogous to a claim for battery, misfeasance or false imprisonment.[60]

15.66 Similarly, although a claim may be worth less than £25,000, the multi-track will be the appropriate track if the factual and/or legal issues are complex and/or the trial is likely to take longer than a day. Many claims against the police include issues under the Human Rights Act (HRA) 1998, or multiple defendants, or claimants with particular vulnerabilities, all of which will be factors pointing towards the multi-track. It is also worth pointing out that actions against the police can be tried before a jury (see below paras 15.77–15.89) and/or are in principle appropriate for case management and trial in the High Court, again indicating that the multi-track is more appropriate.[61]

58 CPR 26.3.
59 CPR 26.6.
60 CPR PD 26 para 8.1.
61 CPR PD 29 para 2.6.

Case and costs management hearings

15.67 If the court allocates a case to the multi-track, it will usually fix a CCMC, for the parties to attend, at which directions relating to the management of the case to trial will be made.

15.68 To avoid a hearing, the parties can agree directions and costs budgets (see further para 15.72) by consent and send to the court agreed directions when the allocation questionnaire is filed.

15.69 If a claim involves false imprisonment or malicious prosecution, thereby entitling a claimant to a trial by jury (see paras 15.77–15.89), then an application for a jury trial should be made within 28 days of service of the defence.[62]

15.70 As well as mode of trial, directions will address matters such as disclosure, exchange of witness statements and expert evidence (all of which are considered in detail at paras 15.93, 15.127 and 15.147). Directions will also provide, where appropriate, for photographs and/or plans to be admitted in evidence at trial (and for them to be agreed, if possible). Where the court clerk's notes of evidence or a transcript of the evidence given at earlier criminal proceedings is relied upon,[63] a direction is usually made to the effect that the notes or transcript is to be admissible at the trial without the maker being required to give evidence.

15.71 The first CCMC in a claim is likely to be allocated between 30 minutes and two hours. The parties should endeavour to try and agree the necessary directions in advance. The person attending the CCMC should be someone who is familiar with the case and who has sufficient authority to deal with any issues that are likely to arise.[64] There are provisions in the CPR to allow for the variation of a case management timetable, by applying to the court[65] or in some circumstances by agreement between the parties.[66]

Costs budgets

15.72 Most claims in the multi-track are now subject to a process of prospective costs management, through costs budgeting and costs management orders.[67] The parties are expected to file and exchange costs budgets at least 21 days prior to the first case management conference setting out their estimated costs for each 'phase' of the proceedings. If a budget is not agreed, the other party must file a discussion report setting out the areas of dispute. If a party fails to file a costs budget on time, they will be treated as having filed a budget comprising only the applicable court fees.[68]

62 CPR 26.11.
63 As discussed in chapter 14.
64 CPR 29.3.
65 CPR 29.5.
66 CPR 2.11.
67 CPR 3.12–3.18.
68 CPR 3.15.

Preparing a costs budget is often a skilled task carried out with the assistance of a costs draftsperson and consultation with counsel's clerk.

15.73 At the CCMC, the court will decide on a proportionate budget for each phase that is not agreed in each party's budget. It is important to get the budgeting process right at the outset: unless the budgets are subsequently varied on account of significant developments, the court is likely to restrict the winning party to the costs in their approved budget.[69]

Relief from sanctions

15.74 Since the introduction of procedural reforms in 2013 following recommendations by Lord Justice Jackson (often called the 'Jackson Reforms'), the courts now take a much stricter approach to compliance with procedure rules and directions.[70] A party who fails to keep to the timetable fixed by the court or who fails to apply for an extension before expiry of the deadline, is in real jeopardy of court orders imposing severe sanctions upon them, including striking out the whole or part of their statement of case and/or costs penalties.

15.75 In considering whether to grant relief from sanctions, the court must have regard to the need to ensure litigation is conducted at proportionate cost and to ensure compliance with rules, practice directions and orders.[71] Unless the breach is neither serious nor significant, or there is good reason for the breach, the court will be unlikely to grant relief. Merely overlooking the deadline due to the pressure of work or other reasons is unlikely to be a good reason to justify a breach.

Pre-trial case management

15.76 In the run-up to trial, the court will send the parties a pre-trial checklist (listing questionnaire) for completion and return by a date specified in the directions given at the case management conference, unless it considers that the claim can proceed to trial without a checklist being completed.[72] Due to the limited number of trial centres that are able to facilitate a trial by jury, often the longest delay in litigation is caused by waiting for the trial date. To avoid this unnecessary delay, it is important for the court to be provided with dates to avoid for counsel, witnesses and experts as soon as possible. The court will endeavour to set a trial timetable and fix a trial date as soon as it has all the information before it.

69 CPR 44.4.

70 *Mitchell v News Group Newspapers Ltd* [2013] EWCA Civ 1537; *Denton v TH White Ltd and another* [2014] EWCA Civ 906.

71 CPR 3.9.

72 CPR 29.6.

Jury trial

15.77 The rules governing entitlement to trial by jury are contained in Senior Courts Act 1981 s69 and County Courts Act 1984 s66 (which are in similar terms). If an application for a jury trial is duly made to the court in a claim in respect of malicious prosecution or false imprisonment the court 'shall' order trial with a jury, *unless* the court is of the opinion that the trial 'requires any prolonged examination of documents or accounts or any scientific or local investigation which cannot conveniently be made with a jury'.[73]

15.78 As discussed in the section above concerning directions, an application for a claim to be tried by a jury should be made within 28 days of the service of the defence,[74] but the court has a power to extend this period in appropriate cases.[75]

15.79 Often, an action which involves a claim for either false imprisonment and/or malicious prosecution will also include other torts such as assault, battery, trespass etc. These other torts do not entitle a claimant to a jury trial. However, once a claimant has a tort for which for which there is a jury trial as of right, then at trial the jury will usually be asked to also consider questions of fact in relation to the other torts. However, that is not always so, and the judge can determine those issues rather than the jury.[76] It may be appropriate for the judge to do so when those issues are largely comprised of issues of law which are for the judge in any event. The court can even split the trial into a part heard with the jury, and without, although to do so is unusual.[77]

15.80 Claimants sometimes prefer a trial before a judge and jury rather than one with a judge only. A claimant may well find more comfort in disputed factual issues being determined by a jury, and may feel that the presence of a jury is consistent with the importance of the claim. However, it is important that advisers fully explain to them the advantages and disadvantages of a jury trial and a judge-only trial.

15.81 A jury trial will inevitably take longer than a judge-only trial. If funds are limited, then a judge only trial may be preferable. Additionally, where the claim is one which involves a claimant and/or issues that may be unpopular, then it may be desirable to avoid trial by one's peers. In such circumstances, the jury may be unduly swayed by prejudicial material. Juries may also be influenced sometimes by general negative media reporting of the 'compensation culture', 'police officers only trying to do their job', 'greedy claimants', 'abuse of legal aid' etc. In addition, if the case relies on a close study of documents and inferences to be drawn from them, legal arguments about police powers or it is a case where it is necessary to highlight a departure from usual police practice, it may be desirable to opt for a judge-only trial rather than a jury trial.

73 County Courts Act 1984 s66(3) and Senior Courts Act 1981 s69(1).
74 CPR 26.11.
75 CPR 3.1.
76 *Hutt v Commissioner of Police of the Metropolis* [2003] EWCA Civ 1911 at para 27.
77 *Natalie Quinn v Chief Constable of Thames Valley* [2017] EWCA Civ 390.

15.82 Against this, however, it must be remembered that many claimants who have been acquitted by their peers after a jury trial in the Crown Court will have a huge amount of confidence in the ability of their peers to decide upon liability and quantum in a civil action. Further, jurors in some city areas, who may be ethnically diverse and younger, will have experience of contact with the police and will be able to use their common sense and experiences to assess the credibility of both the claimant's and the defendant's witnesses.

15.83 In respect of false imprisonment claims following arrest without warrant, the question of whether an officer held an honest suspicion of the claimant having committed an offence is a question of fact which may be left to a jury, but the question of whether there is an objectively reasonable basis for that suspicion is a question of law (subject to the resolution of any disputed underlying facts) for a judge. Accordingly, if the claim is focused exclusively on the question of objective reasonableness, further to undisputed facts, there may be little purpose in a trial by jury.

15.84 Where a right to a jury trial applies, either party can take advantage of it. Accordingly, although it is more frequently a claimant who seeks a jury trial, there may be cases where the defendant considers that a jury trial is in its interests and applies for one, against the claimant's wishes.

15.85 As above, even in cases of false imprisonment and malicious prosecution, the court has a discretion not to order trial by jury where the trial 'requires any prolonged examination of documents or accounts or any scientific or local investigation which cannot conveniently be made with a jury'.[78] Where a party objects to a trial by jury on that basis, the court should ask:[79]

1) Will the trial involve a prolonged examination of documents or a scientific investigation?
2) If so, can it conveniently be made with a jury?
3) If not, should it nonetheless exercise its discretion to order trial with a jury?

15.86 Even if the case involves a prolonged examination of documents or a scientific investigation, the right to jury trial is not lost if this can be undertaken conveniently with a jury. It is only if there is a 'substantial difficulty' in conducting this exercise with a jury, as compared to with a judge alone, that the exception to the right to a jury trial can be made out.[80] However, this involves a consideration of the effect of a jury trial on the length of the case and the costs of the litigation, as well as an assessment of a jury's ability to resolve the particular issue(s).[81]

15.87 In cases where it can be established that a trial does involve the prolonged examination of documents or a scientific investigation, and it cannot conveniently be made with a jury, the court still needs to consider whether it should exercise its discretion to order trial with a jury. If the case turns on substantial disputes of fact between the parties and/or involves

78 County Courts Act 1984 s66(3) and Senior Courts Act 1981 s69(1).

79 *Taylor v Anderton* [1995] 1 WLR 447, CA, *Aitken v Preston* [1997] EMLR 415, CA; and *Phillips v Commissioner of Police of the Metropolis* [2003] EWCA Civ 382

80 *Aitken v Preston* [1997] EMLR 415, CA.

81 See *Taylor*; *Aitken*; *Phillips* in fn 79 above.

serious wrongdoing, the claimant may be able to persuade the court that the case is nonetheless suitable for jury trial.

15.88 Where the material alleged to make the trial too complicated to be heard by a jury relates to quantum only, rather than liability, then a possible solution is to have a 'split trial' with a jury determining questions of fact relevant to liability and a judge alone subsequently assessing damages, if the claimant makes out all or some of the claims.[82] However, where the objection to a jury trial is based on the alleged complexity of medical evidence, the defendant will often persuade the court that the material is relevant to liability as well as to quantum if it impacts also on the claimant's credibility.

15.89 The court has a broader power to order trial by jury in any claim even where the action does not include claims in false imprisonment or malicious prosecution.[83] However, this power is rarely exercised in favour of granting a jury trial in practice,[84] even if the action includes claims in assault or misfeasance, where it might be said that some issues analogous to the disputes of fact that arise in false imprisonment or malicious prosecution cases are present.

Anonymity

15.90 The general rule in civil proceedings is that hearings must be held in public in accordance with the fundamental principle of open justice.[85] This extends to pleadings, judgments and orders, copies of which can be requested by members of the public.[86] However, the court may order that the name of a party or witness is not to be disclosed if non-disclosure is necessary to secure the administration of justice or in order to protect the interests of that party or witness.[87] Derogations from the principle of open justice are usually only justified in exceptional circumstances.[88]

15.91 It may, for example, be necessary to apply for an anonymity order to protect the interests of a child or person lacking capacity,[89] or to protect the claimant or a witness from violence.[90] There is an automatic ban on the publication of material identifying the victims of sexual offences.[91] Anonymity is unlikely to be granted, however, merely to protect the reputation of a party or witness who has been accused (but not convicted) of a

82 *Conlon v Chief Constable of Northumbria* [2000] 3 WLUK 51, CA.
83 Senior Courts Act 1981 s69(3); County Courts Act 1984 s66(2).
84 *H v Ministry of Defence* [1991] 2 QB 103, CA.
85 CPR 39.2.
86 CPR 5.4C.
87 CPR 39.2(4).
88 *Various Claimants v Independent Parliamentary Standards Authority* [2021] EWHC 2020 (QB) at para 34; Practice Guidance: Interim Non-Disclosure Orders [2012] 1 WLR 1003.
89 CPR 31.2(3)(d). For the approach adopted in approval hearings for children or protected parties, see *JX MX v Dartford and Gravesham NHS Trust* [2015] EWCA Civ 96.
90 *Secretary of State for the Home Department v AP (No 2)* [2010] UKSC 26, [2010] 1 WLR 1652, at para 14.
91 Sexual Offences (Amendment) Act 1992.

criminal offence.[92] In each case, the court will balance the fundamental interests of open justice against the private and family rights of the applicant seeking anonymity under European Convention on Human Rights (ECHR) Article 8.[93]

15.92 An application for anonymity can be made with the claim form or at any time during the proceedings. It is usually preferable to make an application either at the time of issue or as soon as possible afterwards and certainly before trial, to prevent any inadvertent disclosure or prejudice to other parties.

Disclosure

Overview

15.93 CPR Part 31 deals with disclosure of documents. Disclosure is defined as 'stating that a document exists or has existed'.[94] In claims in the multi-track which do not include a claim for personal injuries, the parties must file a report briefly describing the relevant documents 14 days before the first case management conference. In all other cases, disclosure is dealt with in directions, usually set at the first case management conference, unless an application is made by a party. (Chapter 14 deals with pre-application disclosure.)

Standard disclosure

15.94 The normal direction made by the court is for the parties to give standard disclosure.[95] Standard disclosure is defined as encompassing:[96]

a) documents upon which a party relies;
b) documents which adversely affect their own case or adversely affect another parties case or which support another parties case; and
c) documents of which disclosure is required by a relevant practice direction.

15.95 The rules require that a reasonable search should be made in respect of documents referred to under b) and c) above.[97] CPR Part 31 applies to all claims except claims on the small claims track. If the claimant is aware of a document that has not been disclosed then consideration should be given to making an application for specific disclosure (see para 15.105 below).

15.96 A 'document' means anything in which information of any description is recorded.[98] A party's duty of disclosure is limited to documents which are or have been in their 'control', which includes documents held by third parties, over which the party has a right to request to inspect or take

92 *Khuja v Times Newspapers Ltd* [2017] UKSC 49, [2019] AC 161.
93 *Khuja v Times Newspapers Ltd* [2017] UKSC 49, [2019] AC 161.
94 CPR 31.2.
95 CPR 31.5.
96 CPR 31.6.
97 CPR 31.7.
98 CPR 31.4.

copies.[99] A defendant may be required, for example, to disclose work-related messages and emails stored on an employee or officer's personal electronic devices.[100]

15.97 The rules provide that there is a right to inspect a disclosed document unless it is no longer in the control of the disclosing party, or that party has a right to withhold inspection or it will be disproportionate to the issues in the case to permit inspection.[101] Ordinarily, inspection is carried out by the provision of photocopies of documents or electronic disclosure, on agreement to paying reasonable costs.[102] However, an inspection of original documents should be arranged where there is any issue over their authenticity.

15.98 The procedure for standard disclosure is that each party must make, and serve on every other party, a list of documents using form N265. The list must identify the documents in a convenient order and manner and as concisely as possible. A list should be in chronological date order with the earliest date first and the most recent document last. The list must indicate those documents in respect of which the party claims a right or duty to withhold inspection and those documents that are no longer in the parties' control. The list must state what has happened to documents that come within the latter category.

15.99 The list must include a disclosure statement made by the party disclosing the documents. This should indicate the extent of the search that has been made to locate the documents which the disclosing party is required to disclose and certify that they understand the duty to disclose documents and that to the best of their knowledge they have carried out that duty.[103]

15.100 The parties may agree in writing to disclose documents without making a list and to disclose documents without the disclosing party making a disclosure statement.[104]

15.101 The duty of disclosure continues during the proceedings. This means that if documents to which the duty extends come to a party's notice at any time during the proceedings, the party must immediately notify any other party. This is particularly relevant where claims are issued before the Independent Office for Police Conduct (IOPC) has completed the investigation into a claimant's complaint. Other situations where the ongoing duty is relevant would be where there is an ongoing linked criminal case or complaint. An additional matter which may be the subject of the continuing duty to disclose is if the claimant or any of the claimant's witnesses are convicted in relation to a different or separate matter. Similarly, if a police officer is disciplined in relation to a different and separate matter, this will also form part of the continuing duty of disclosure.

15.102 A party may also inspect a document mentioned in a statement of case, a witness statement, a witness summary or an affidavit.[105] A party may also

99 CPR 31.8.
100 *Phones 4U Ltd (in administration) v EE Ltd and others* [2021] EWCA Civ 116.
101 CPR 31.3.
102 CPR PDs 31A and 31B.
103 CPR 31.10.
104 CPR 31.10(A).
105 CPR 31.14(1).

apply for an order of inspection of any document mentioned in an expert's report which has not already been disclosed in the proceedings.[106] With this in mind, it is important to read statements and reports carefully.

15.103 A party may not rely at trial on any document which the party fails to disclose or in respect of which does not permit inspection, unless the court gives permission.[107]

15.104 A party to whom a document has been disclosed may only use the disclosed document for the purposes of the proceedings in which it is disclosed.[108] There are exceptions to this where the documents have been read to or by the court or referred to at the hearing (so long as it was held in public), or where the court gives permission or the party who disclosed the document and the owners of the document agree.[109]

Specific disclosure

15.105 If a party believes that the disclosure of documents given by the other side is inadequate, an application may be made for an order for specific disclosure. [110]

15.106 It is sensible to write the police first if it is thought that there is anything additional which should be disclosed. An application needs to be made to the court in accordance with CPR Part 23. The application notice must specify the order that the applicant intends to ask the court to make and must be supported by evidence. An order for specific disclosure is an order that a party must do one of the following things:

1) disclose documents or classes of document specified in the order; or
2) carry out a search to the extent stated in the order; or
3) disclose any documents located as a result of that search.

15.107 In deciding whether or not make an order for specific disclosure, the court will take into account all the circumstances of the case and, in particular, the overriding objective. If disclosure is objected to on the basis that the documents contain personal information, the court must balance the ECHR Article 6(1) right to a fair hearing against the other party's Article 8 right to respect for private life.[111] The more relevant the document is to the issues in dispute in the claim; the more likely it is that the court will order disclosure.

15.108 Chapter 14 sets out many of the standard police documents that should be made available on disclosure, if they relate to issues in the case.

The claimant's documents

15.109 In most cases against the police, the claimant will have few documents to disclose (and most of these are likely to be copies of documents, such as the custody record, received from the police).[112]

106 CPR 31.14(2).
107 CPR 31.21.
108 CPR 31.22.
109 CPR 31.22.
110 CPR 31.12.
111 *Nayler v-Beard* [2001] EWCA Civ 1201, [2001] 2 FLR 1346.
112 See chapter 2.

15.110 It is important for solicitors to inform their clients as soon as possible of the need to preserve all documents that may be relevant, whether they assist the client's case or not. As disclosure also has to be given of documents created after the action has commenced, no new non-privileged documents should be generated without legal advice.

15.111 Where financial losses are claimed supporting documents should be disclosed for example, in relation to loss of earnings documents such as wage slips, employers letters and benefit details.

15.112 Where there is a claim for personal injuries medical records will need to be disclosed.

Disclosure from third parties

15.113 The claimant or the defendant can make an application for disclosure against a person who is not a party to the action. The court may make an order for disclosure against the third party only where:

- the documents of which disclosure is sought are likely to support the case of the applicant or adversely affect the case of one of the other parties to proceedings; and
- disclosure is necessary in order to dispose fairly of the claim or to save costs.[113]

15.114 An example of where the police were ordered to give third party disclosure occurred in an action by a prisoner against the Home Office for alleged assaults by prison officers. The Court of Appeal held that disclosure by the police of prison officers' statements made under caution to the police when they were investigating the assaults should be ordered. Strict conditions were attached by the court on the extent and manner of the disclosure.[114]

Documents concerning previous misconduct

15.115 Claimants will be anxious to discover any documents that link the defendant police officers with previous incidents of police misconduct, whether similar in kind, or not. The admissibility of such material as similar fact evidence and/or as relevant to a witness's credit is discussed in depth at paras 16.29–16.37. Where evidence of past misconduct is purely admissible in relation to issues of credit, disclosure will not be ordered.[115] Where the material can amount to similar fact evidence, disclosure may be required.[116] Advisers should be conscious that it will be preferable to resolve any dispute as to the disclosure and admissibility in advance of trial. Opportunities to do so may be at the CCMC, a separate hearing to deal specifically with the application, or at a pre-trial review.

113 CPR 31.17.

114 *Frankson and others v Secretary of State for the Home Department* [2003] EWCA Civ 655, [2003] 1 WLR 1952, CA.

115 *Thorpe v Chief Constable of Greater Manchester* [1989] 2 All ER 827, CA.

116 *Steele v Commissioner of Police of the Metropolis* (1993) 18 February, CA.

15.116 Any certificates of convictions in the criminal courts are admissible under Civil Evidence Act 1968 s11 and are therefore disclosable.

Documents exempt from inspection

15.117 There are a number of grounds on which the police (or the claimant) may or must refuse to permit inspection of a document which is relevant and material to the determination of issues involved in the civil proceedings. If a privilege or immunity is claimed in respect of a document, then it must still be identified in the list of documents but it need not actually be produced, unless a court orders that the document is not exempt from production. Those documents for which immunity or privilege is claimed should be listed separately in the list of documents.

Legal professional privilege

15.118 Legal professional privilege can be claimed for confidential communications with lawyers for the purpose of seeking or giving legal advice or for use in actual or contemplated litigation. The courts will look at the dominant purpose for which the document was prepared in cases where it appears that there was more than one purpose.[117] Legal professional immunity can be waived expressly or impliedly.

Public interest immunity

15.119 A party may refuse to produce documents on the grounds of the harm that would be occasioned to the national or public interest.[118] This principle has become known as 'public interest immunity' (PII). A claim to PII can only be justified if the public interest in preserving the confidentiality of a document outweighs the public interest in securing justice by determining the action on the basis of all relevant, available documentation. Each case must be taken on its own merits, and the court will carry out a balancing exercise between the two competing interests. In appropriate cases, the court may inspect the documents first.[119]

15.120 There are two kinds of claims to PII: class claims and contents claims. The first applies where it is said that a document should not be disclosed because of the type of document that it is, regardless of the content. The second kind applies where it is said that a document contains information that it would prejudice the public interest to disclose. In each case, the court must carry out the balancing exercise referred to above.[120]

15.121 Historically, 'class' PII was thought to attach to all documents generated during a police complaints investigation, on the basis that it was necessary for witnesses to be confident that statements made by them to the investigators would not be disclosed in civil proceedings.[121] However,

117 *Three Rivers District Council v Bank of England (No 6)* [2004] UKHL 48, [2005] 1 AC 610.

118 *Conway v Rimmer* [1968] 1 All ER 874, HL.

119 *R v Chief Constable of West Midlands ex p Wiley* [1995] 1 AC 275, HL; *Al Rawi v Security Service* [2011] UKSC 34, [2012] 1 AC 531.

120 *Toombs v Commissioner of Police of the Metropolis* (2000) 15 November, QBD.

121 *Neilson v Laugharne* [1981] QB 736, CA.

in *R v Chief Constable of West Midlands ex p Wiley*[122] the House of Lords held that a 'class' immunity extending to all the documents generated by the investigation of a complaint against the police was not justified. As explained in more detail in chapter 4, there is now a presumption that documents generated by a complaints investigation will be disclosed to the complainant during the assessment of the complaint. PII has been held to cover communications with informants[123] and between the police and the Crown Prosecution Service (CPS).[124]

15.122 The court will first ask itself whether a document is sufficiently relevant and material to require disclosure in the interests of justice. If a document is relevant and material, then it must be disclosed unless it is confidential, and a breach of confidentiality will cause harm to the public interest which outweighs the harm to the interests of justice caused by non-disclosure.[125]

15.123 The police may well claim public interest immunity in relation to documents that relate to sensitive policing operations and/or to police informers. As indicated above, in those circumstances the court will have to weigh up the public interest in withholding the information against its potential value to the party who seeks to make use of it in the litigation.[126] However, the police cannot rely on a 'neither confirm nor deny' policy to protect the confidentiality of operational methods that are no longer in use or are arguably illegitimate, or to protect the anonymity of undercover officers whose names are already in the public domain.[127]

15.124 In some cases it may be possible to argue that part at least of the material sought should be disclosed or that the document(s) in issue should be provided in a redacted form. Alternatively, a summary or reformulation of the document can be provided without causing harm to the public interest, a process which is sometimes called 'gisting'.[128] As Lord Woolf said in *ex p Wiley*:

> There is usually a spectrum of action which can be taken if the parties are sensible which will mean that any prejudice due to non disclosure of documents is reduced to a minimum.

Privilege against self-incrimination

15.125 The heads of claim in a civil action against the police may well, in effect, allege that a criminal offence has been committed. The most common example of this will be assault. People in civil proceedings alleged to have committed a criminal offence are granted, by the common law, a privilege against self-incrimination if there is reasonable likelihood that they will be charged as a result of disclosing the information. Thus a police officer

122 [1995] 1 AC 274, HL.

123 *D v NSPCC* [1978] AC 171, HL; *Commissioner of Police of the Metropolis v Bangs* [2014] EWHC 546 (Admin).

124 *Goodridge v Chief Constable of Hampshire* [1999] 1 WLR 1558, QBD.

125 *Ex p Wiley* per Lord Templeman at 280H–281H; *R (AIG) v Commissioner of Police of the Metropolis and another* [2021] EWHC 584 (Admin) at para 4.

126 For example, see in relation to informers the approach of the Court of Appeal in *Chief Constable of Greater Manchester v McNally* [2002] EWCA Civ 14, [2002] 2 Cr App R 37.

127 *DIL v Commissioner of Police of the Metropolis* [2014] EWHC 2184 (QB).

128 *R (AIG) v Commissioner of the Police of the Metropolis* [2021] EWHC 584 (Admin) at para 15.

could refuse to disclose information to the claimant which indicates that a criminal offence has been committed by the officer. However, that privilege is enjoyed by the officer, and not the chief constable. Accordingly, a chief constable when sued as being vicariously liable for actions committed by officers under the chief constable's control (chapter 14) cannot claim the privilege in relation to documents which incriminate those officers.

15.126 In many civil actions against the police, the CPS will have already considered whether to prefer charges against police officers, as part of the complaints and discipline machinery (see chapters 4 and 5) and, in the vast majority of cases, will have decided not to prosecute. In such cases, a claim of privilege against self-incrimination is less likely to succeed.

Exchange of witness statements

15.127 In all cases (jury and non-jury), exchange of witness statements is compulsory. Witness statements contain the factual accounts of the witnesses that the party intends to adduce as evidence at the trial.

15.128 A party who is required to serve a witness statement for use at trial but is unable to obtain one – for example, because a potential witness is currently untraceable or uncooperative – may apply without notice, for permission to serve a witness summary instead. A witness summary must include the name and address of the intended witness. It must also be served in the period in which a witness statement would have had to be served.[129]

15.129 A witness statement should be in the witness's own words and should be restricted to matters of which the witness has personal knowledge.[130] It should contain evidence that the witness would be allowed to give evidence orally and should not include opinion evidence (save where necessary to provide a full and coherent explanation and factual account). It should not quote at length from documents or include legal argument.[131]

15.130 The witness statement should be headed with the title of the proceedings. At the top right-hand corner of the first page there should be clearly written the party on whose behalf it is made, the initial and surname of the witness, the number of the statement in relation to that witness, the identifying initials and number of each exhibit referred to, the date it was made and the date of any translation.[132] The witness statement should be expressed in the first person and should also state the full name of the witness; the witness's place of residence or if the witness is making the statement in their professional business, or other occupational capacity; the address at which the witness works; the position held; and the name of the employer.

15.131 The importance of a full and accurate witness statement should not be underestimated. Save in trial by jury, the statement will generally stand as

129 CPR 32.9.

130 CPR PD 32 para 18; and *Alex Lawrie Factors Ltd v Morgan* (1999) *Times*, August 18, CA.

131 CPR PD 57A; *JD Weatherspoon plc v Harris* [2013] EWHC 1088 (Ch); *Blue Manchester Ltd v (1) Bug-Alu Technic GmbH and another* [2021] EWHC 3095 (TCC).

132 CPD PD 32 para 17.

the claimant's evidence-in-chief. Therefore, it is the sole opportunity to give unrestricted evidence to the court of the claimant's account. A court may not permit a witness to adduce evidence not in the statement, unless it relates to an issue that has arisen since the statement was served (for example, as a result of the other party's witness evidence). Further, stating matters for the first time at trial may look less credible and will likely be the focus of cross-examination. Statements of all witnesses to be called must be exchanged, as it will be unusual for the court to allow a witness whose statement has not been exchanged to give evidence at court.

15.132 By the time witness statements come to be exchanged, the claimant's version of events is likely to have been given already on several occasions of which the defendant is aware. The claimant's statement in support of a police complaint, the letter of claim, the particulars of claim and medical reports and records will all need to be carefully examined to ensure that as far as is possible there are no discrepancies between the claimant's account as set out in these documents and the account given in the witness statement. Where there are inconsistencies between various accounts, it can be helpful for those to be addressed 'upfront' in the statement.

15.133 It is common for counsel to be instructed to advise upon draft witness statements before they are exchanged. Some solicitors find that this is a good time to have a conference with counsel to review the evidence and to seek advice for the purposes of removing any limitation placed on the certificate of public funding, and to consider making an offer of settlement.

15.134 CPR PD 32 indicates the form that witness statements should take. An exhibit used in conjunction with the witness statement should be verified and identified by the witness and remain separate from the witness statement. Where a witness refers to an exhibit, or exhibits, they should state: 'I refer to (description of exhibits) marked "............." '.[133] A witness statement must be verified by a statement of truth, the form of which is set out above in relation to particulars of claim (see para 15.17).

15.135 If a witness statement or a witness summary is not served in respect of an intended witness within the time specified by the court, the witness may not be called to give evidence unless the court gives permission.[134]

15.136 The claimant and the claimant's witnesses need to be advised of the implication of providing a witness statement. Proceedings for contempt of court may be brought against a person who makes, or causes to be made, a false statement in a document verified by a statement of truth without an honest belief in its truth.[135]

15.137 The aim of the exchange of witness statements is to effect a fair and speedy trial of the issues and to save costs. It is thought that when all parties 'have their cards on the table' there will be a greater incentive to settle the case. Thus when the witness statements are received from the police, they should be carefully studied to see if their contents affect the assessment of the strengths and weaknesses of the case and examined for areas of agreement and lines of potential cross-examination.

133 CPR PD 32 para 18.
134 CPR 32.10.
135 CPR 32.14.

Hearsay notices

15.138 'Hearsay' is defined as a statement made otherwise than by a person while giving oral evidence in proceedings which is tended as evidence of the 'matter stated and references to hearsay include hearsay of whatever degree'.[136] Where a party intends to rely on hearsay evidence at the trial, a hearsay notice must be served no later than the latest date for serving witness statements.[137] The hearsay notice must:

- identify the hearsay evidence;
- state that the party serving the notice proposes to rely on that hearsay evidence at the trial; and
- give the reasons why the witness will not be called.

Offers to settle and payments into court

Overview

15.139 Offers to settle made in accordance with the provisions of CPR Part 36 are called 'Part 36 offers'. There is no prohibition against a party making an offer to settle in any way the party chooses, but if the offer made does not comply with provision of this Part, the consequences specified do not flow unless the court so orders. The costs consequences of refusing an offer vary depending on a number of factors, including which party made the offer and when it was made.

15.140 A Part 36 offer of settlement must be in writing and must contain prescribed information.[138] This can be achieved by completing form N242A. The offer can relate to the whole or to part of the claim. A Part 36 offer will remain open for acceptance until trial unless its terms provide for it to automatically expire on a given date or it is formally withdrawn by the offeror. However, if the offer is not accepted within 21 days, then costs consequences can apply.

15.141 There are certain instances where the court's permission is required before a Part 36 offer can be accepted, for example within 21 days of trial.[139] Where a Part 36 offer is accepted without needing the permission of the court, the claimant will be entitled to their costs of the proceedings up to the date of serving the notice of acceptance, including recoverable pre-action costs.[140] The cost will be on a standard basis if not agreed.

15.142 Where a claimant rejects the defendant's Part 36 offer but then fails to do better at trial, the court will order the claimant to pay the defendant's costs from the latest date upon which the payment or offer could have been accepted, unless the court considers it unjust to do so.[141] The effect of such an order will usually mean that any damages awarded to the

136 CPR 33.1.
137 Civil Evidence Act 1995 s2(1)(a); and CPR 33.2.
138 CPR 36.5–36.6.
139 CPR 36.11.
140 CPR 36.13, 36.14.
141 CPR 36.17.

claimant will be off-set against costs owed to the defendant and/or to the LAA by way of the statutory charge and the claimant will be left with no tangible benefit. If a claimant has unwisely rejected a reasonable offer, it will usually be difficult to persuade the judge that it would be unjust to make the usual order for costs.

15.143 Where the claimant makes a Part 36 offer that the defendant rejects, beneficial provisions relating to costs and interest apply if the claimant does better than the Part 36 offer or at least as well at trial.[142] Unless the court considers it unjust to do so, it should award the claimant interest at a rate not exceeding ten per cent above base rate for some or all of the period starting with the latest date on which the defendant could have accepted the offer, costs on an indemnity basis from the same date and an additional sum usually amounting to ten per cent of the damages awarded.

15.144 The fact that a Part 36 offer has been made cannot be revealed to the trial judge or jury until the question of costs comes to be decided at the end of the case.

Specific issues in civil actions against the police

15.145 In many cases, the claimant is not interested so much in the financial aspect of the case but in vindication in court and making the police accountable for their actions. Very often, then, clients are reluctant to accept a settlement. However, in publicly funded cases, such an offer or payment may have ramifications for the continuation of public funding if it is rejected. The offer will need to reported to the LAA and funding may be withdrawn if a reasonable offer has been refused. Thus, unless an offer or payment is clearly unreasonable, it is usually prudent to obtain counsel's advice upon whether it would constitute a reasonable settlement before a decision is made to accept or reject it. The difficulty is compounded by the fact that it can be hard to predict the level of damages that a jury will award at trial if the claim succeeds.

15.146 On the other hand, the Part 36 procedure for making offers can be useful for claimants who want to take the initiative in obtaining a settlement of the claim – for example, if there are likely to be funding difficulties in the future or if the claimant does not want to go to trial and give evidence. Equally, if it is apparent that the defendant is unlikely to want to settle the claim, a Part 36 offer pitched at just below what the claimant is likely to recover at trial, may lead to the award of enhanced interest and costs at trial, as discussed above. It is possible for a claimant to make a Part 36 offer for 'nil' damages if the police accept liability.[143]

Expert evidence

15.147 Examples of expert evidence are reports from medical experts, forensic experts, handwriting experts, accountants or employment consultants.

142 CPR 36.17.

143 *MR v Commissioner of Police of the Metropolis* [2019] EWHC 1970 (QB), [2019] Costs LR 1441.

The experts most commonly used in actions against the police will be medical experts, as claims for consequential personal injury are frequently made. The instruction of medical experts is considered in chapter 2, including the issue of when the claimant can instruct their own medical expert and when they should seek to agree instruction of a joint expert with the defendant.[144] However, depending on the facts of the case, other experts might be relevant, including experts on restraint techniques; dog handling; firearm and CS gas use; and crowd control.

15.148 The parties are asked in the allocation questionnaire to state whether they will be seeking to adduce expert evidence and if so, the name and other details of the expert whom the party wishes to use and whether any progress has been towards the preparation of single reports by experts or the instruction of a joint expert.[145]

15.149 Expert evidence can only be relied upon at trial with the court's permission. Usually, where expert evidence is appropriate, the court will initially give permission, for the evidence to be given by way of written report. A direction to this effect is usually considered at the first case management conference. Specific permission is required for a party to call an expert to give oral evidence at trial.[146] This issue is usually considered once the extent of the dispute between the parties' experts has been clarified, as is explained below.

15.150 An expert's report must be disclosed to the other party, whether or not the expert is to give oral evidence. A party may put written questions about an expert's report to an expert instructed by another party.[147] Written questions may be put only once (without the court's permission) and must be put within 28 days of receipt of the expert's report. Where a party sends written questions or questions direct to an expert, a copy of the questions should, at the same time, be sent to the other party's solicitors.[148]

15.151 When permission is given by the court to rely on written expert evidence the court will usually give directions for there to be a discussion between the experts for the opposing parties, in order to narrow the issues, to identify the extent of agreement and disagreement between them and the reasons for any disagreement.[149] The directions will provide for a statement of the areas of agreement and disagreement and the reasons for the latter to be prepared and agreed by the experts. However, the content of the discussions between the experts may not be referred to in court unless the parties expressly agree. Advisers should ensure that experts are fully briefed as to the relevant issues in the case and have all material documentation, before they enter into these discussions.

15.152 Once the experts' statement of areas of agreement and disagreement is available, the court will be able to decide whether oral expert evidence should be given at the trial.

144 Even where a joint expert is used, the parties may each prepare their own instructions for them: CPR 35.8.

145 CPR 35.7.

146 CPR 35.5.

147 CPR 35.6.

148 CPR PD 35 para 4.2.

149 CPR 35.12.

CHAPTER 16

Trial and appeals

continued

Introduction

16.1 This chapter addresses the key framework for and principles of the conduct of trials and appeals in police claims. Police claims are one of the few areas of civil law in which claims can be determined by juries, and it is on trial by jury[1] which the chapter primarily focuses, although trial by judge alone will also be addressed. This chapter will begin by discussing pre-trial preparation; it will then outline the principles of evidence; next it will give a detailed overview of the course of the trial; and finally it will explain appeals from the outcome of the trial to higher courts.

Pre-trial preparation

Costs and case management conference

16.2 At least by the time of the costs case management conference (CCMC) (see paras 15.67–15.74), some careful thought would have been given to the conduct of the trial. Issues such as whether there should be a 'split trial' on liability and quantum should already have been considered. A split trial may be appropriate where there are complex factual issues relating to quantum of damages, distinct from those at issue in relation to liability, which might sensibly be postponed until liability is determined. Any contemplated applications for disclosure (See paras 15.93–15.108) should be made well in advance of trial, and preferably either at the case management conference, or directions sought at that stage to facilitate such issues being resolved. In any Equality Act (EqA) 2010 claim, consideration is required as to the need for assessors, as to which see paras 12.118–12.122.

The pre-trial review

16.3 As already discussed, in advance of trial, the court will send out a pre-trial checklist (see para 1576). The purpose is to check that there has been compliance with court directions and also to result in a firm listing for trial. Parties are encouraged (albeit not required) to exchange copies of the checklist before filing so as to avoid the court being given conflicting or incomplete information. Failure to file the checklist within the directed timeframe will result in an 'unless order' striking out the claim.

16.4 Where the trial is complex or lengthy, the court will generally require a pre-trial review. Such a review is generally warranted in a jury trial. It is an opportunity to ensure that the trial will proceed efficiently, and that particular areas of dispute may be identified and narrowed. If a review has not previously been directed as part of the case management directions, it may be directed following filing of the pre-trial checklist. Standard directions for a pre-trial review require the claimant to serve (if possible) agreed draft directions, chronology, statement of the issues, case summary, and trial timetable. It is generally far better, if at all possible, to have instructed trial counsel at a pre-trial review. At the very least, Civil Procedure Rules 1998

1 For the provisions on trial by jury, see paras 15.77–15.89.

(CPR) 29.3(2) requires the legal representative to be familiar with the case and 'with sufficient authority to deal with any issues that are likely to arise'.

16.5 There is no requisite list of matters that might be considered as part of a pre-trial review, but could include:

a) practical arrangements for trial, such as the court having the means to play video footage;
b) the timetable for the trial;
c) whether the court has appropriate time for pre-reading;
d) directions for skeleton arguments and authorities;
e) contents of the trial bundle and jury bundle;
f) narrowing the issues in dispute
g) the extent to which oral expert evidence remains necessary;
h) whether any witness statements can be read;
i) whether witnesses of fact are to be present in court during the evidence of other witnesses;
j) any special measures for witnesses, such as attendance by video-link.

A number of these matters are considered below.

Timetable

16.6 In respect of the trial timetable, expectations as to the level of detail can vary. It is generally unnecessary to descend into the precise time each witness is expected to take, and it is difficult to do so with accuracy. However, the timetable does need to be sufficiently detailed to enable proper and fair management of the trial. It should set out the anticipated time for opening and closing submissions and the order of witnesses with an estimate as to how it is envisaged that the witness evidence will progress. Unless the complexity will likely necessitate a reserved judgment, it should also include time for judgment.

Directions

16.7 It is worth noting that although the trial will generally be conducted in accordance with any directions made at a case management conference or pre-trial review, the trial judge may ultimately direct otherwise.[2]

The trial bundle

16.8 Unless directed otherwise, the claimant must file a trial bundle not more than seven days and not less than three days before the start of the trial.[3] CPR Practice Direction (PD) 32 para 27.5 provides a list of documents that should be included in the trial bundle, which includes:

- the claim form and all pleadings;
- a case summary and/or chronology;
- all witness statements and summaries;
- any notices of intention of rely on hearsay evidence;

2 CPR 29.9.
3 CPR 39.5(2).

- any notices of intention to rely on evidence (such as a plan, photograph etc) which is not contained in a statement;
- any medical and expert reports;
- any order giving directions as to the trial; and
- 'any other necessary documents'.

16.9 Regard should be had to rules CPR PD 32 paras 27.7–27.11 as to the form of the bundle. The bundle should be agreed where possible.[4] A copy should also be produced for use not only by the court, but also by the witness. A bundle of authorities should be agreed and prepared separately by counsel.

16.10 Significantly, CPR PD 32 para 27.2 provides that all documents contained in bundles which have been agreed for use at a hearing are admissible as evidence of their contents, unless the court orders otherwise or 'a party gives written notice of objection to the admissibility of particular documents'. Care must therefore be taken when agreeing a trial bundle as to whether the documents therein are properly admissible. Similarly, although perhaps in slight tension with CPR PD 32 para 27.2, the PD states at para 27.12 that the parties should seek to agree that the documents in the bundle may be treated as evidence of the facts stated in them 'even if a notice under the Civil Evidence Act (CEA) 1995 has not been served'.

The jury bundle

16.11 The jury will not be provided with a copy of the trial bundle. There is no specific authority governing what the jury should be given and the matter is ultimately one for the discretion of the trial judge (albeit the bundle should be prepared by the claimant). The jury bundle usually comprises documentation that has a visual element or which is otherwise sufficiently complex that the jurors would have difficulty following the evidence without sight of it. Thus, the most common materials included in jury bundles are photographs (eg of the claimant's injuries, or of the scene etc), plans, and the custody record. Pleadings and exchanged witness statements are never included in the bundles. Occasionally witness statements from the criminal trial, expert reports, or medical records are included, if the jury would have difficulty comprehending the evidence without this documentation.

Presence of witnesses in court

Overview

16.12 The respective credibility of the parties' accounts is often central to the success or failure of a civil action. Accordingly, both parties are usually concerned about the prospect of witnesses tailoring their evidence to fit with other testimony already given. Witnesses who are also parties to the action cannot be excluded from the courtroom, but other witnesses can be (save for expert witnesses), albeit in most types of civil cases, witnesses will remain in court throughout the trial. One option in police claims, is

4 CPR PD 32 para 27.12.

for the police witnesses to be permitted to listen to the claimant's counsel opening the case and to the claimant's evidence, so that they are fully aware of the case against them, and for them then to be excluded from the court room until their evidence has been given. Equally, any witnesses of fact that the claimant proposes to call are usually expected to remain outside court while the claimant and the claimant's witnesses give evidence, until they are called to give evidence.

Compelling the attendance of witnesses

16.13 An unwilling witness may be summonsed to give evidence, the procedure for which is now largely set out in CPR Part 34. A summons will generally be considered unnecessary unless the witness would otherwise fail to attend.

16.14 It can sometimes happen in police cases that the police force declines to put forward as a witness an officer who has been critical of the actions of the police (for example, in the course of and revealed by the police complaints process). A claimant may be anxious that the court hears from such a witness. One possibility would be to rely on an earlier account given by the officer as hearsay. More likely, and if the evidence is controversial, it should be indicate to the chief constable that if the witness is not put forward as a witness then a summons will be sought.

Principles of evidence

16.15 A full exploration of the principles relating to evidence is beyond the scope of this book, and practitioners would be well advised to utilise a text such as *Phipson on evidence*.[5] However, of frequent importance in police claims are issues of hearsay; the admissibility of police complaint and Independent Office for Police Conduct (IOPC) reports; and similar fact and bad character evidence. Those issues are considered below.

The admission of hearsay evidence[6]

16.16 Hearsay is a statement made otherwise than by a person while giving oral evidence which is tendered as evidence of the matters stated.[7] Thus, any written statement tendered as evidence is hearsay. 'Statement' includes any representation of fact or opinion, however made, and thus also covers statements made in different media such as audio or video recording.[8] Where a witness gives oral evidence as to matters stated by another, whether it is hearsay depends upon whether the matter stated is relied upon as going to the truth of what is stated. For example, evidence that a person has said 'I'm going to punch you', is not hearsay; it is tendered as evidence of the fact of what was said, rather than the truth of its contents. In contrast, evidence that a person had said ' "Mr Smith" told me he is

5 Sweet & Maxwell, 20th edn, 2021.

6 For a fuller consideration of the law relating to hearsay in civil proceedings, see chapter 29 of *Phipson on evidence*, 20th edn.

7 CEA 1995 s1(2).

8 *Hijazi v Yaxley-Lennon* [2021] EWHC 2008 (QB).

going to punch you', would be hearsay if it is tendered as evidence that Mr Smith had indeed made that threat.

16.17 The current approach to hearsay evidence, as reflected primarily in the CEA 1995, is to seek to ensure that relevant evidence is before the court, and increasingly the fact that evidence may be hearsay goes to the weight to be given to it rather than to whether it is admissible at all. Thus, CEA 1995 s1(1) states the general rule that in civil proceedings evidence shall not be excluded on the ground that it is hearsay.

16.18 The court then has a broad discretion as to the matters to which regard may be had, and a non-exhaustive list of considerations is given at CEA 1995 s4(2). The trial judge has a broad discretion as to how and in what order questions regarding admissibility and weight of evidence are addressed.[9]

16.19 The admission of written statements as hearsay is not necessarily limited to circumstances in which the matters stated are agreed or uncontroversial. However, in practice statements adduced as hearsay should generally be reserved for uncontroversial matters. Written rather than oral evidence should remain the exception rather than the rule and caution should be exercised before tendering important evidence through hearsay statements.[10]

16.20 The requirement for serving a hearsay notice has been addressed at para 15.138. Where no hearsay notice has been served, the statement will nevertheless be admissible if it forms part of the agreed bundle, pursuant to CPR PD 32 para 27.2 as described above. If its presence in the bundle is agreed then a formal hearsay notice should not be required.[11] Further, a failure to give notice does not in fact affect the admissibility of the evidence, but it may be taken into account by the court in respect of costs and the weight to be given to the evidence.[12]

16.21 Where the statement of a witness who is to be called to give oral evidence itself contains hearsay evidence, the notice requirement is complied with by the fact of serving the witness statement.[13] However, where the witness is not to be called to give oral evidence, the party relying on the statement is required to inform the other parties of that fact and give reasons as to why the witness is not being called.[14]

Admissibility of complaint and IOPC reports

16.22 In police claims, consideration is often required as to the admissibility and relevance of complaint reports produced either internally by the police force, and/or by the IOPC.

16.23 Such reports may be admissible and relevant in two distinct respects. The first is as evidence of fact. For example, such reports may include accounts given by the police officers and other witnesses involved. Such

9 *Shagang Shipping Ltd v HNA Group Company Ltd* [2020] UKSC 34, [2020] 1 WLR 3549 at para 58.

10 *Gubarev v Orbis Business Intelligence Ltd* [2020] EWHC 2912 (QB) at para 115(2).

11 *Charnock v Rowan* [2012] EWCA Civ 2.

12 CEA 1995 s2(4).

13 CPR 33.2.

14 CPR 33.2(2).

evidence, adduced as evidence of the truth or otherwise of the matters stated, should be admissible and relevant.

16.24 More difficult is the extent to which either party may place reliance upon any opinion expressed in the reports of the investigators. For example, if a report concludes with the opinion that the force used was unreasonable, may that be relied upon in the civil trial? Expert opinion evidence at a civil trial is ordinarily restricted to that obtained pursuant to the provisions of CPR Part 35.

16.25 A helpful analysis can be found in in *Rogers v Hoyle*[15] which concerned a claim against a pilot in respect of a fatal accident. It was claimed that he had performed a manoeuvre for which he had insufficient training and experience. The Court of Appeal held that a report produced by the Department for Transport's Air Accident Investigation Branch (AAIB), the authors of which were neither identified nor called to give evidence, was both admissible and of probative value, both as evidence of fact and as expert opinion evidence. The following principles are evident from the judgment:

a) Pursuant to CEA 1995 s1, such a report should not be excluded on the ground that it is hearsay. Insofar as the report consists of statements or reported statements of fact, it is, prima facie, admissible.[16]
b) Expert opinion is admissible because it is the product of a special expertise which the trial judge is unlikely to possess and which, even if the judge did, it is not the judge's function to apply. The bar to be surmounted in order to count as an expert 'is not particularly high, the degree of expertise going largely to the weight to be given to the evidence rather than its admissibility'. In that case, the court had little difficult in inferring that the authors of the report could be treated as experts in their respective fields.[17]
c) If an expert opined on matters that required no expertise to evaluate, it is inadmissible, but it was unnecessary to exclude opinions in this category. Instead, the judge can take into account those matters which reflect an expertise.[18]
d) CPR Part 35 seeks to govern the instruction of experts within the proceedings. However, it is not a comprehensive and exclusive code for the admission of opinion evidence.[19]

16.26 In that case, the court noted that the authors of the report were 'experienced and expert individuals fulfilling a public duty' and 'a non-lawyer would be astonished' that such a report 'was not something to which a court could even have regard'.[20]

16.27 Insofar as the opinion of the author of the report is largely premised on resolving disputed facts it is difficult to see why any such opinion should be admissible. In resolving disputed facts the author will have no more expertise than the trial judge, and the trial judge will likely have the benefit

15 [2014] EWCA Civ 257, [2015] QB 265.
16 [2014] EWCA Civ 257, [2015] QB 265 at para 31.
17 [2014] EWCA Civ 257, [2015] QB 265 at paras 41–43.
18 [2014] EWCA Civ 257, [2015] QB 265 at paras 53–54.
19 [2014] EWCA Civ 257, [2015] QB 265 at para 63.
20 [2014] EWCA Civ 257, [2015] QB 265 at para 29.

of further evidence cross-examination. However, where the opinion is premised upon judgment informed by expertise and experience as a police officer and/or IOPC investigator it may be admissible, albeit the weight to be attached to it may be limited. The extent to which the investigator is independent will be relevant.

16.28 In a judge-only trial, there may be a greater willingness for such evidence to be admitted, with the confidence that the judge can, ultimately, give the report negligible or no weight at all if that is warranted. There should be greater caution in putting opinion evidence of questionable value before a jury, but that will be a question for the judge to decide in the absence of the jury.

Similar fact evidence

16.29 'Similar fact evidence' refers to evidence of circumstances not directly concerning the matter in issue at trial, but which are nonetheless probative, ordinarily because it is said to go to the propensity or likelihood of the claimant or defendant having acted in the manner alleged. Such evidence can often arise in police claims, either relating to the past criminal behaviour of the claimant, or past misconduct of the police officers involved.

16.30 The leading authority on the admissibility and use of such evidence is that of the House of Lords in *O'Brien v Chief Constable of South Wales*.[21] There is a two-stage approach. The first stage is to consider whether the similar fact evidence is relevant. It is relevant if it 'is logically probative or disprobative of some matter which requires proof", and accordingly makes the matter which requires proof 'more or less probable'.[22] It is recognised that the past actions of a party on similar facts can be relevant. As expressed by Lord Bingham in *O'Brien*, that 'evidence of what happened on an earlier occasion may make the occurrence of what happened on the occasion in question more or less probable can scarcely be denied'.[23] If similar fact evidence is probative, then it is relevant and legally admissible.

16.31 If the evidence is probative and therefore legally admissible, the judge must proceed to the second stage of considering whether in exercise of the court's case management powers it nevertheless should not be admitted. The primary factor will be the extent to which the evidence is probative. Against that the judge must balance the extent to which such evidence may be prejudicial. It should not be admitted if it is 'likely to give rise to irrational prejudice which outweighs the probative effect that the evidence has in logic'.[24] The consideration is recognised to carry particular weight where the decision maker is a jury 'whose members are not experienced as are judges in putting aside irrational prejudice'.[25] Lord Bingham suggested that unless the probative value outweighs its prejudicial effect 'by a considerable margin'

21 [2005] UKHL 26, [2005] 2 AC 534.

22 [2005] UKHL 26, [2005] 2 AC 534, per Lord Bingham at para 3, citing *R v Kilbourne* [1973] AC 729 at 756, HL.

23 [2005] UKHL 26, [2005] 2 AC 534 at para 4.

24 [2005] UKHL 26, [2005] 2 AC 534, per Lord Phillips at para 11.

25 [2005] UKHL 26, [2005] 2 AC 534, per Lord Phillips at para 11, and per Lord Bingham at para 6.

then the evidence is likely to be excluded.[26] The court will also consider the extent to which admission of the evidence will result in a lengthening of the trial and escalation in terms of time and cost. In police cases there are, additionally, considerations as to 'the public interest in exposing official misfeasance' and the need for 'the public righting of public wrongs'.[27]

16.32 Where there are a number of previous convictions or complaints, there will need to be a careful evaluation of the probative and prejudicial value of each incident. *Hegazy and others v Commissioner of Police of the Metropolis*[28] is an example of the court considering a number of complaints against the same officers, but giving careful consideration in relation to each complaint as to the extent to which each is probative, prejudicial, and may lengthen the trial, and ultimately taking a view in relation to each as to whether it should be admitted.

16.33 Where the similar fact evidence comprises a significant volume of documentation, the extent to which the trial will be lengthened will be mitigated where the trial is by judge only and the material can, to an extent, be covered by reading out of court.[29]

16.34 Where the similar fact evidence is itself contentious, then it is less likely to be admitted. It will be of more limited probative value and its admission may invite a 'trial within a trial'. Thus, in *Mahboob v Chief Constable of the West Midlands*[30] the Court of Appeal considered that the trial judge had been correct to refuse to admit, in a jury trial, a witness statement tendered in an unsuccessful civil claim against the same officer. It would have distracted the jury from the core issues.

16.35 Nonetheless, unsubstantiated complaints against an officer, at least in circumstances which bear a similarity to what is alleged in the claim, *can* be of probative value and should at least be disclosed. Indeed, in *Murphy v Commissioner of Police of the Metropolis*[31] the court considered that in considering the first stage identified in *O'Brien* of relevance – which is also the test for disclosure – there should be no distinction between allegations that had been substantiated and those that had not. It ought not to be assumed that unsubstantiated complaints were of no probative value, and the court observed that a finding that the complaint was unsubstantiated was not necessarily a finding that it was wholly without merit. Such an unsubstantiated complaint was admitted in *Alleyne v Commissioner of Police of the Metropolis*, with one relevant factor being that the complaint had resulted in a civil claim for which damages had been paid by the police force without offering a substantive defence.[32]

16.36 In *O'Brien* itself, the claimant was pursuing a claim in misfeasance and malicious prosecution. Central to his claim was the allegation that the investigation officers used operational methods which were oppressive, dishonest and unprofessional. He contended, successfully, that evidence as to the

26 [2005] UKHL 26, [2005] 2 AC 534, per Lord Bingham at para 6.
27 [2005] UKHL 26, [2005] 2 AC 534, per Lord Bingham at para 5.
28 [2014] EWHC 235 (QB).
29 As observed in *Hegazy v Commissioner of Police of the Metropolis* at para 13.
30 [2010] EWCA Civ 1509.
31 [2012] EWHC 4123 (QB).
32 [2012] EWHC 4406 (QB).

same officers using the same or similar methods in two earlier cases should be admitted. In *McPherson v Chief Constable of Nottinghamshire*[33] the issue at trial was whether the police had assaulted the claimant, or whether the claimant had assaulted an officer. The Court of Appeal considered that the trial judge had been correct to admit those of the claimant's criminal convictions which indicated a propensity for violence or dishonesty, not least as the claimant's 'credibility and his propensity to lose his temper and to lash out were at the heart of the jury's deliberations'.[34] Convictions for offences of criminal damage and breach of a non-molestation order were considered to be probative as, although not directly concerning violence, were probative of a propensity to act in an aggressive or violent way.

16.37 That a conviction is 'spent' does not necessarily mean that it cannot be adduced as similar fact evidence. The Rehabilitation of Offenders Act 1974 s4(1) provides that spent convictions are prima facie admissible unless they fall within an exception, such as section 7(3) where the court is satisfied that justice cannot be done except by admitting them. Section 7(3) calls for an exercise of judgment and the overriding requirement is that justice shall be done which in the context of civil proceedings includes taking into account the interests of both parties, and that justice requires that there should be a fair trial between them.[35] A single and historic offence may not be probative. Where there is a pattern of offences over a longer period, that some convictions are spent is less likely to be relevant.[36]

The course of the trial

16.38 The following discussion of the course of the trial will encompass:

- the skeleton argument;
- empanelling the jury;
- the claimant's opening speech;
- the claimant's evidence;
- submission of no case to answer;
- the defendant's case;
- obtaining a verdict on liability in a jury trial;
- closing speeches;
- the summing-up;
- the jury's decision on liability;
- the jury's decision on quantum;
- costs.

The skeleton argument

16.39 A skeleton argument for trial can often be relatively short. It should set out the key issues and the relevant legal principles. It might assist the judge

33 [2016] EWCA Civ 6.
34 [2016] EWCA Civ 6 at para 15.
35 *Thomas v Commissioner of Police of the Metropolis* [1997] QB 813, CA.
36 As in *McPherson v Chief Constable of Nottinghamshire* [2016] EWCA Civ 6 at para 16.

on what is anticipated in terms of the trial timetable, the order of witnesses, and so on.

16.40 In a jury case, it should say little, if anything, of the facts. It may usefully address the questions that are to be asked of the jury on the issue of bias and connections with any of the parties (see para 16.44).

16.41 In a judge-only trial, there is a strategic call to be made as to the use to which a skeleton argument may be put. Addressing the facts can be the first opportunity to persuade the trial judge, and it can be particularly useful in a document heavy case in which the judge may be assisted by navigating the key documents. However, detailed argument also forewarns the opposing side and its witnesses of likely areas of focus in cross-examination.

Empanelling the jury

16.42 The jurors are selected from a panel by ballot in open court.[37] In a High Court trial there are 12 jurors,[38] and in the county court there are eight.[39] The grounds for challenging jurors are limited. A challenge to the whole jury could only be made in the extremely unlikely event that it could be shown that the officer appointed to summon the jurors was biased or had acted improperly.[40] An individual juror can be challenged for bias. However, in practice this is only likely to arise if the juror is known by one of the parties or their witnesses, since members of the jury cannot be questioned to discover their opinions.

16.43 Before jurors are sworn in, it is good practice for them to be informed of the names of the parties and their witnesses, so as to avoid a situation where a juror recognises a witness and realises that they cannot continue to sit on the case once it is underway. Where a potential juror knows a party or witness, that juror should be discharged. The purpose is to avoid the perception of bias, which is necessary both at common law and as a means of compliance with Human Rights Act (HRA) 1998 Sch 1 Article 6 (the right to a fair trial). The test in relation to the composition of a jury is well established: a person should be tried by an independent and impartial tribunal and that justice would not be seen to be done if, on the particular facts of the case, a fair minded and informed observer would conclude that there was a real possibility of jury bias, whether conscious or unconscious.[41]

16.44 In most civil actions, the trial judge will ask the potential jury members a question along the lines of whether they or any close relatives are serving police officers or employees of the defendant police force, although practice varies. It is sometimes disputed, and issues can arise as to the breadth of the question and whether, for example, it should encompass a connection with any police force nationally, or just of the force in question.

37 Juries Act 1974 s11.

38 Juries Act 1974 s17.

39 County Courts Act 1984 s67.

40 A jury cannot be challenged on the basis of its racial composition: *R v Ford* [1989] 3 WLR 762, CA.

41 *R v Abdroikov and others* [2007] UKHL 37, [2007] 1 WLR 2679.

16.45 By definition, a jury in a civil claim against the police will be determining disputes of fact in which the evidence of police officers will be central, and the jury should not include a juror who is or is closely connected to a police officer.

16.46 In criminal cases, the question of whether the inclusion of a police officer on the jury would meet the test for apparent bias is decided taking into account the circumstances of the particular case, including the extent to which the case in question turns on a contest between the evidence of the police and the evidence of the defendant.[42]

The claimant's opening speech

16.47 Many civil actions, the burden of proving contested issues will be shared between the parties, since the police will bear the burden of proving the lawfulness of any arrest and detention and the claimant will have to prove allegations of assault and malicious prosecution. However, even if the burden of proof falls largely on the defendant, it is usual for the claimant to begin and there may, in any event, be damages to be proved , which will be necessary to establish a cause of action for some torts.

16.48 The claimant's case commences by their counsel making an opening speech to the jury. Counsel should:

- explain to the jury the difference between a civil and a criminal case;
- outline the torts (the civil wrongs) that the police are accused of;
- summarise the parties' rival accounts so that the jury can appreciate the main factual issues in dispute;
- indicate to the jury the role that they will play in deciding liability and quantum;
- go through the documents that they have in their bundles; and
- explain the nature of other documents, such as pleadings, that they may hear reference to during the evidence.

16.49 Legal jargon should be avoided as much as possible. It is a matter of tactical judgment whether and to what extent counsel emphasises factual points in the claimant's favour at this stage. On the one hand it is important to engage the jury's attention; on the other hand, it is advisable not to alert the police to lines of attack that they may not yet have anticipated, nor to promise the jury evidential outcomes that may not be delivered.

The claimant's evidence

16.50 The claimant will be the first witness to give evidence. In a jury trial, evidence will be given in chief, as the jury will not have seen the witness's statement and will need to hear the whole of the claimant's evidence from the witness box. In a judge-only trial, the ordinary position is that a witness statement shall stand as the evidence-in-chief and the witness will be cross-examined on it.[43] The court will only give permission for a witness

42 See *R v Abdroikov and others* [2007] UKHL 37, [2007] 1 WLR 2679 and *R v Khan and others* [2008] EWCA Crim 531, [2008] 3 All ER 502 at para 29.

43 CPR 32.5.

to amplify their statement and give evidence on new matters only if there is 'good reason not to confine the evidence of the witness to the contents of his witness statement'.[44]

16.51 The way in which the claimant responds to cross-examination is frequently vital to the success of the claim. Advisers should have in mind that 'witness coaching' is prohibited.[45] Nonetheless, in a civil claim the witness can be assisted in having a familiarity with the evidence before the court and in particular the contents of their own witness statement. Claimants should expect to be cross-examined on all aspects of their accounts. In particular, questions will be asked of any departure in evidence in chief from the account in the exchanged witness statement or in earlier 'on record' accounts such as that given at the criminal trial or for the purposes of a complaint against the police. It is also commonplace for defence counsel for the police to cross-examine on inconsistencies between the account given in evidence and that recorded by medical experts or other health care professionals who have had dealings with the claimant. Any apparent divergence between the allegations made and the degree of injury suffered will also be highlighted and counsel for the defendant will be astute to emphasise any apparent exaggeration in the damages claim. Cross-examination should be anticipated on past convictions and on any damaging material in disclosed medical records. All witnesses can be re-examined in relation to matters arising out of cross-examination.

16.52 Once the claimant has given evidence, any supporting witnesses of fact will be called. Once again in a jury trial, the jury will not have seen the witness statement and evidence will have to be given in chief. If their evidence is of importance to the case, they can also expect a sustained challenge to their credibility in cross-examination.

16.53 Although the jury will be asked to consider liability and quantum separately (see paras 16.76–16.81), it is usual for the evidence relating to both to be given at the same time, not least because evidence relating to injuries and other aspects of quantum may have a direct bearing upon credibility.

16.54 The claimant may be calling evidence from a medical expert. Where both parties are calling an expert, it is advisable for the experts to be present in court when the other gives evidence so that the expert giving evidence second can comment on the other's evidence. For this reason, in most trials the parties agree to interpose the expert evidence so that it is heard sequentially, either at the end of the claimant's case or after all the witnesses of fact have testified. Dependent upon the circumstances it may be helpful for the experts to hear the claimant's evidence.

Submission of no case to answer

16.55 At the end of the claimant's evidence, the police may submit that there is no case to answer and the claim should be dismissed. This submission is not made in the majority of civil action trials, as many cases include a

44 CPR 32.5(3)–(4).

45 See *Ultraframe (UK) Ltd v Fielding* [2005] EWHC 1638 (Ch), referring to the fact that a witness' evidence should be 'his honest and independent recollection, expressed in his own words' (para 25). The rule is also reflected in the professional obligations of both solicitors and barristers.

claim for false imprisonment where the burden of justifying the detention lies on the police and the evidence they propose to give on that aspect of the case is usually closely interlinked with the other causes of action. However, in a case where the burden of proof lies exclusively on the claimant, for example where malicious prosecution alone is alleged, the submission is sometimes made. Such applications should be rare, however, and the ordinary course should be for any strike out application to be made and determined well in advance of trial.[46] The occasion for a mid-trial strike out application should generally be limited to where there has been a significant and material change in the state of the evidence.

16.56 If the defendant raises the issue, two preliminary points arise: 1) should the defendant be required to elect to call no evidence if the submission fails? and/or 2) what is the proper time for making the submission? A defendant should rarely be permitted to make a submission of no case to answer without first being put to their election subject to what is said below in relation to the position in a jury trial.[47] The two main reasons given for this approach are, first, that it is generally undesirable for the trier of fact to express a view on the facts until all material evidence has been heard; and second, if the submission succeeds, but the claimant overturns that decision on appeal, there will be need for a re-trial if all material evidence has not been heard.[48]

16.57 In jury cases, the position has always been more flexible; the first stated reason can have no application, and the second applies with lesser force, given that in some instances the Court of Appeal will have little choice but to order a re-trial even if all the evidence has been given, to enable a jury to deliver its verdict on the facts. Accordingly, it has been held that in a civil jury trial the court has a discretion whether to require the defendant to elect before the submission of no case to answer is made.[49] In *Payne v Harrison*[50] the Court of Appeal emphasised that in a civil jury trial a judge is not bound to rule upon a submission of no case to answer at the close of the claimant's evidence and may postpone a determination of whether there is a case to go to the jury until after all the evidence has been heard. This approach may commend itself to the court; once the judge has heard all the evidence, a clearer view can be formed of the merits of the submission and the risk reduced of an erroneous decision being made, which ultimately requires a re-trial.

16.58 From a claimant's perspective, it is likely to be advantageous for any such ruling to be postponed until after the police evidence has been heard, since material may arise in cross-examination of officers that provides support for the claimant's case. Insofar as the claimant needs to establish malicious motivation on the part of the officers, the evidence may well come from their evidence, in particular responses to matters put to them in cross-examination. Thus the interests of justice and of affording a fair

46 See *National Westminster Bank plc v Rabobank Nederland* [2006] EWHC 2959 (Comm), [2007] 1 All ER (Comm) 975 and chapter 16.

47 *Benham Ltd v Kythira Investments Ltd* [2003] EWCA Civ 1794 at para 32.

48 See *Boyce v Wyatt Engineering* [2001] EWCA Civ 692.

49 *Young v Rank* [1950] 2 All ER 166, KBD; *Payne v Harrison* [1961] 2 All ER 873, CA.

50 [1961] 2 All ER 873, CA.

trial tend to point to the desirability of the ruling being made after all the evidence has been heard. If, however, the trial judge is persuaded to make a ruling at the end of the claimant's case in a jury trial, the judge should ask whether on the evidence adduced by the claimant the claim has a real prospect of success.[51] If the evidence fails to meet this threshold, the claim will be dismissed; if the ruling is in the claimant's favour, the police will normally proceed to call their evidence. In a case where the submission has been made after the defendant has been required to elect not to call evidence, the judge will determine whether there is a sufficient case to go to the jury on the evidence adduced. It is not for the judge to assess whether the claimant has proved their case on a balance of probabilities, unless this can be resolved purely by a ruling on the law; in any case involving disputed facts this would be to trespass into the jury's fact finding role (discussed at para 16.65 onwards).

The defendant's case

16.59 The defence may or may not choose to open the defence with an opening statement, although generally do not do so. The defendant's evidence is usually comprised wholly or mainly of police officers' evidence. In giving their evidence-in-chief, officers can refresh their memory from any contemporaneous note made of events and are, in that respect, at an advantage over the claimant's witnesses. Officers are likely to be cross-examined about any significant discrepancies between their account and the accounts given by other officers; any discrepancies between their current account and earlier 'on record' accounts that they made or what can be seen on CCTV or body-worn video; lack of supporting injuries (where relevant) and any failure to employ or adhere to their powers.

16.60 Although in cases of false imprisonment the burden of proving a lawful justification rests upon the police, where a point is to be taken that an aspect is not proven, it should be put by the claimant's counsel to the relevant officer(s) in evidence. It is generally not open to a claimant to remain silent, and then complain that the defendant has not discharged its burden.[52]

16.61 Where there is a matter in issue going to the state of the mind of the officer, it is not necessarily the case that the defendant needs to call direct evidence from the officer. In *Magee v Chief Constable of Derbyshire* the question of whether the custody officer held the requisite belief that detention was necessary to secure or preserve evidence was left to the jury notwithstanding that the custody officer was not called to give evidence. The jury were entitled to consider what was stated on the custody record and evidence as to the surrounding circumstances. Inferences may be drawn, provided that there is a 'core basic factual foundation' for the drawing of such an inference.[53]

51 *Benham Ltd v Kythira Investments Ltd* at para 27.

52 *Magee v Chief Constable of Derbyshire* [2020] EWHC 3569 (QB) at para 54.

53 [2020] EWHC 3569 (QB) at para 113. See, similarly, *Rashid v Chief Constable of West Yorkshire* [2020] EWHC 2522 (QB), [2020] EWHC 2522 (QB) at paras 75–76.

Obtaining a verdict on liability in a jury trial

16.62 The key role of the jury in a civil trial is to resolve the main disputed issues of fact. The jury indicates its decision by answering questions provided to it in the affirmative or in the negative. The trial judge then uses these answers to determine whether as a matter of law the claim succeeds or fails. The general approach to be adopted was set out by the Court of Appeal in *Dallison v Caffery*.[54] It is for the judge to rule which issues of fact should go to the jury. The jury does not need to resolve every area of disputed fact; rather it needs to determine those disputes of fact that will enable the judge to rule on the claims. Thus, with the assistance of counsel, the judge must decide which issues the jury should be asked about. It is very well-established that for reasons of legal policy the judge and not the jury should decide the objective issues that arise in relation to false imprisonment and malicious prosecution claims, that is whether there were reasonable grounds to suspect the claimant of the relevant offence and whether there was reasonable and probable cause for the prosecution.[55] Thus, any attempt to ask the jury whether the arresting officer had reasonable (as opposed to honestly held) grounds to suspect that the claimant had committed the offence for which the claimant was arrested is a fundamental error of law that will lead to the decision being quashed even where the question had been agreed by counsel.[56] The judge rules upon these objective questions once the jury has resolved any disputed facts that may bear on the issue, for example if there is a dispute over the information that the officer had at the time of the arrest. Thus, in *Banjo v Chief Constable of Greater Manchester*,[57] Lord Woolf explained:

> The question . . . as to whether or not there are reasonable grounds for suspicion will depend upon the evidence which is before the fact finding tribunal. A Judge can only rule, as a matter of law, that the officers had, or did not have, reasonable grounds for suspicion when the factual evidence, including that which is and is not in dispute, establishes that to be the position.

16.63 The reasonableness or otherwise of a use of force appears to be treated as a mixed question of law and fact which ought properly be left to the jury.[58] However, practice has varied and continues to do so.[59]

16.64 Where the claim includes a claim in negligence, the judge could, in exercise of the court's case management powers, determine the matter, or put a series of factual matters to the jury, and determine the negligence claim upon the answers.[60]

16.65 Either party may submit to the judge that there is insufficient evidence on a particular issue for it to be left to the jury, as the jury could not properly

54 [1964] 2 All ER 610, CA.

55 *Dallison v Caffery* [1964] 2 All ER 610, CA.

56 *Ward v Chief Constable of The West Midlands* [1997] *Times* 15 December, CA.

57 [1997] EWCA Civ 1951.

58 *Pollard v Chief Constable of West Yorkshire* [1999] PIQR P219, CA; *Connor v Chief Constable of Merseyside* [2006] EWCA Civ 1549, [2007] HRLR 6; *McPherson v Chief Constable of Nottinghamshire Police* [2016] EWCA Civ 6 at para 14.

59 For example, the judge determined the reasonableness of force himself in *Magee v Chief Constable of Derbyshire Police* [2020] EWHC 3569 (QB) at para 125.

60 *Hutt v Commissioner of Police of the Metropolis* [2003] EWCA Civ 1911, (2003) *Times* 5 December.

conclude the point in the other party's favour. For example, this submission may be made by the defendant in relation to a false imprisonment and/or a malicious prosecution claim if there was, objectively viewed, sufficient evidence against the claimant to warrant arrest or prosecution, but the claimant challenges the honesty and propriety of the relevant officer's state of mind. An example of a judge declining at the end of the trial to put any questions to the jury at all is *Gerber v Commissioner of Police of the Metropolis*[61] in which the trial judge had taken the view that, to the extent that there were disputes of fact at all, the arrest of the claimant and force used to effect arrest would be considered lawful irrespective of how the jury resolved those disputed facts.

16.66 In *Dallison v Caffery*[62] Diplock LJ indicated that where there was reasonable and probable cause for an arrest or prosecution the judge should not leave the issue of the honesty of the officer's belief to the jury save in the unlikely event that there was cogent positive evidence that the officer himself did not believe the available material. However, it is important to understand what is meant by positive evidence in this context. Given that the evidence in question relates to the officer's state of mind, the claimant will rarely be in a position to lead specific evidence as to the officer's thought process at the time; rather the honesty or otherwise of the officer's belief is a matter of inference to be drawn from all the surrounding evidence. For example, the Court of Appeal in *Paul v Chief Constable of Humberside*[63] allowed an appeal from the trial judge's decision to withdraw the case from the jury and a re-trial was ordered, because the evidence indicated there was material from which the jury could have inferred that the decisions to arrest and prosecute were not based on an honest belief in the case put forward and/or were motivated by an improper consideration (in that case of diverting attention away from any police culpability in relation to the death in custody of one of the claimant's associates).

16.67 A party may also submit that an issue of fact need not go to the jury because even if the other party's case on the facts is believed, their claim/defence is bound to fail. For example, the claimant may submit that even on the officer's account of the events that precipitated the arrest, the officer's account did not give sufficient grounds to make a lawful arrest. Equally, a defendant may submit that on the claimant's admitted actions the officer exercised a legitimate power of arrest, irrespective of whether the claimant also behaved in a way that was the subject of disputed evidence.

16.68 The normal procedure is for counsel to prepare draft questions and to try to agree on the wording. The judge is then asked to approve the draft and to rule on any disputed issues. The form of the questions asked should be such that they can always be answered simply 'yes' or 'no'. The questions, or at least the questionnaire, should incorporate reference to where the burden and standard of proof lies. To avoid the risk of confusion it is desirable to refer to the parties by name.[64] Questions should be kept clear and concise,

61 [2018] EWHC 3549 (QB).

62 [1964] 2 All ER 610, CA.

63 [2004] EWCA Civ 308.

64 *Igwemma v Chief Constable of Greater Manchester* [2001] EWCA Civ 953, [2001] 4 All ER 751 provides a cautionary tale in this respect.

multiple sub-clauses should be avoided and no more questions should be asked than are strictly necessary for resolving the issues in dispute.

16.69 In assault cases there should normally be a separate question for each assault. Where the conduct said to amount to the assault is in dispute the question should be along the following lines: '*Has Mr Jackson [the claimant] satisfied you it is more likely than not that Officer Bloggs punched him in the face as he got out of the police van?*' If the force that was used is not in dispute, but there is an issue over whether that was reasonable in the circumstances, it is submitted that the jury should be asked in terms to decide this issue, as discussed at para 16.63 above.

16.70 In the more straightforward false imprisonment cases, where the arresting officer witnessed the events that are said to justify the arrest and the claimant contends that the officer's account of those events is false the jury needs to decide who is giving the truthful account and the question is focused accordingly, for example: '*Has the Chief Constable proved, on the balance of probabilities, that Mr Jackson [the claimant] kicked Officer Bloggs on the shin before he made the arrest?*'

16.71 If the arresting officer was not an eye-witness to the alleged offence and the arrest is justified by reference to information supplied by third parties, the jury may need to be asked questions about the material that the officer was aware of when the arrest was made and/or whether the officer honestly suspected that the claimant had committed the offence in question. Claims in false imprisonment may also be based on an officer's failure to give prescribed information on making the arrest. In those circumstances, if the defendant contends that the information was given on arrest, the jury will be asked a question along the lines of: '*Has the Chief Constable proved, on the balance of probabilities, that Officer Bloggs told Mr Jackson [the claimant] that he was under arrest / the grounds of his arrest at the time when the arrest was made?*'

16.72 Sometimes in false imprisonment cases the jury will also be asked to resolve factual issues relating to the length of the claimant's detention. In the more straightforward malicious prosecution cases, where officers claim to have witnessed the events that are said to justify the prosecution and the claimant contends that their account was false, the position is similar to false imprisonment. The jury needs to decide what actually happened and whether the relevant officers deliberately falsified their account. If the officers did so, the central disputed ingredients of the malicious prosecution claim will be established, namely lack of reasonable and probable cause for the prosecution and malice. Thus the question is normally formulated along the following lines: '*Has Mr Jackson [the claimant] proved, on the balance of probabilities, that PC Bloggs fabricated his account of Mr Jackson lunging towards him and kicking him?*'

16.73 In very exceptional cases, where the evidence only permits of one answer, a judge may determine the issue in favour of one party or the other rather than put the matter to the jury. However, the appellate courts have cautioned against doing so. In *McPhilemy v Times Newspapers Ltd* Simon Brown LJ warned that:[65]

65 [2001] EWCA Civ 871, [2001] EMLR 34 at para 33.

> . . . it will often be unwise for trial judges to withdraw issues from the jury and by the same token unwise for counsel to invite them to do so. Only when it is plain that one verdict alone would be rational and any other perverse should the issue be withdrawn. The risk of a successful appeal and the disproportionate expense of a re-trial is otherwise too great.

Closing speeches

16.74 Once the questions for the jury have been resolved and copies of the questions distributed to the jurors, both counsel will make their closing speeches. The defendant's speech is first. Both counsel will try to draw together their best points on the evidence and to meet the points raised by the other party, often focusing on the questions which the jury will have to answer as discussed above at paras 16.69–16.71.

The summing-up

16.75 The judge will outline to the jurors their respective roles, namely that the judge decides the law and the jury determine the crucial issues of disputed fact. The burden and standard of proof will be explained and any relevant legal directions will be given, for example as to the use the jury can make of evidence relating to past bad character (discussed at paras 16.29–16.37). The jurors will be taken through the questions they have to answer and the purpose of the questions will be explained. It is usual for the judge to summarise to the jury the ingredients of the causes of action and to refer to the police's relevant powers, so that the jury can understand the framework in which the questions are asked. However, the extent to which it is necessary or appropriate to do so will be governed by the particular circumstances. In *Ward v Chief Constable of the West Midlands*[66] the Court of Appeal allowed an appeal in relation to a summing up that failed to explain to the jury the legal ingredients of the offence for which the claimant was arrested or the torts relied upon, in a context where the jury had asked for further assistance and the elements of the offence were directly relevant to one of the questions they had to answer. However, in *Sutton v Commissioner of Police of the Metropolis*[67] the Court of Appeal emphasised that jurors should be told as much – and no more – of the law as they need to know in order to be able intelligently to play their part in the trial process; for example if the judge relies on words to which the law has given a particular meaning the judge must also explain that meaning to the jury. The judge should also remind the jury of the salient factual evidence.

The jury's decision on liability

16.76 A jury should endeavour to reach a unanimous verdict. In a civil trial there is no fixed time for which the jurors must deliberate before they are given a majority direction. They must be given such time as the court thinks

66 [1997] 12 WLUK 202, [1997] *Times* 15 December, CA.
67 [1998] 7 WLUK 864, CA.

reasonable having regard to the nature and complexity of the case.[68] In practice, judges rarely indicate to juries that a majority verdict can be accepted until they have been deliberating for at least two hours, and in a complex case the period would be longer. In a High Court case, the judge can accept a majority decision of 10:2 or 11:1.[69] In a county court case, seven of the jury must agree on the verdict.[70] A decision by a lower majority can only be accepted if both parties agree to this course.[71]

16.77 The judge must be careful not to direct the jury in a way that appears to put pressure on them to arrive at a verdict. If the jurors seem to be deadlocked and the judge feels that it may be useful to give them some guidance, the form of words identified by the Court of Appeal (Criminal Division) in *R v Watson*[72] can be used.[73] If the jury remains deadlocked and the parties cannot agree to accept a lower majority, the judge has to discharge the jury and order a re-trial.

16.78 If the jury is able to return answers to the questions it has been asked, the judge will then rule on the claimant's causes of action. As indicated above, in some instances the answers given by the jury will decide whether the claim succeeds, whereas in some circumstances the judge will have to make legal rulings to determine the outcome of the action once the judge has the jury's decision on the material facts. It may be that further submissions from counsel are required.

16.79 In *Igwemma v Chief Constable of Greater Manchester*[74] after the jury's decision had been announced in court, the foreman of the jury indicated that a mistake had been made and the jury was allowed to retire again briefly and then to give a different answer to one of the questions. The mistake had arisen as a result of the jury's confusion over which party was the claimant and which the defendant. The Court of Appeal decided that the trial judge was correct to let the jury alter its verdict, even though it had already been discharged by then. It was emphasised that it was important for the jury's findings to be effectively transmitted to the court, so that if there was some misunderstanding, it should be put right, if this could be done without causing injustice to either party. Whether or not injustice would result in such circumstances would depend upon factors such as the time that had elapsed since the original answers were returned; whether the jury itself raised the possibility of misunderstanding and whether the jury could have been persuaded to change its view by anything said or done since the original verdicts had been given, in particular if anything had since emerged that the jury would not have heard during the course of the evidence given at the trial.

68 Juries Act 1974 s17(4).

69 Juries Act 1974 s17(1).

70 Juries Act 1974 s17(2).

71 In *Morrison v Chief Constable of West Midlands Police* [2003] EWCA Civ 271, (2003) *Independent* 28 February, Lord Phillips MR queried whether a party's refusal to accept a majority below 7:1 was consistent with the overriding objective laid down by the CPR, given the attendant costs and use of court resources involved in the inevitable re-trial.

72 (1988) 87 Cr App R 1, CA.

73 *Morrison v Chief Constable of the West Midlands* [2003] EWCA Civ 271.

74 [2001] EWCA Civ 953, [2001] 4 All ER 751.

The jury's decision on quantum

16.80 If the claimant succeeds in whole or in part upon liability, following the answering of the questions by the jury and the application of the law thereafter by the judge, the claimant will be entitled to damages. In some cases the parties manage to agree a figure as to the appropriate amount at this stage. In the absence of such agreement, the jury will be asked to determine quantum. The directions that the jury should be given by the judge in relation to damages were set out by the Court of Appeal in *Thompson and Hsu v Commissioner of Police of the Metropolis*.[75] These are discussed in detail in chapter 17. The procedure usually adopted is that counsel address the judge in the absence of the jury as to the appropriate brackets of figures that the jury should be given as guidance in relation to the material heads of compensation. Counsel will normally ask the judge to rule upon whether it is an appropriate case for the jury to consider awarding aggravated and/or exemplary damages, if the defendant objects to these heads of damages being put to the jury. Submissions will be made upon any other issues of law on which the judge may need to direct the jury, for example whether it is a case where it is open to the jury to conclude that the claimant's conduct could reduce any award of aggravated or exemplary damages that would otherwise be made (see chapter 17).

16.81 Counsel will then address the jury on quantum, explaining their respective positions. The defendant's speech is made first, and then the claimant's. The judge will then sum up to the jurors, explaining to them the heads of damages that they need to consider, the basis upon which they can make an award or decline to make an award under any particular head and indicating to them the guideline figures they should bear in mind. As discussed in more detail in chapter 17, the jury will normally make a separate award of basic damages for each cause of action, such as false imprisonment, assault and malicious prosecution. An award for psychiatric injury is also normally given as a separate figure, although it may stem from two or more causes of action. Separate awards are also made of aggravated and exemplary damages (where appropriate). If a finding of fact is central to the quantum of the claim, but did not need to be resolved at the liability stage, the jury may be asked a specific question on that point, to help guide its assessment of damages. For example, questions might relate to features of the claimant's treatment in custody that are said to aggravate the damage caused, such as alleged denial of medical assistance or delay in permitting access to legal advice.

Costs

16.82 At the conclusion of the trial, the court will make an order as to costs. The ordinary position is that the unsuccessful party bears the costs of the successful party. Where there has been partial success, the court will need to consider how that should be reflected in the costs, and may make an award of a percentage of costs. Consideration will also need to be given to the effect of any settlement offers and particularly whether either party has

75 [1997] 2 All ER 762, CA.

'beaten' an offer made pursuant to CPR Part 36. Reference should be made to CPR Part 36, and the guidance provided by the White Book. In all cases, it is the judge who determines how the issue of costs will be decided, and the jury will have no role in this process. Detailed provisions on costs are contained in CPR Part 44.

Appeals

16.83 In this section the appeals procedure will be considered, namely; appeals in jury trials; and appeals in judge-only trials.

Appeals procedure

16.84 The conduct of appeals is the subject of a detailed framework set out in CPR Part 52 and the accompanying practice directions. Those details rules reflect, in part, various initiatives seeking to improve the efficiency of appeals in the Court of Appeal or High Court (as many appeals from county court cases will be heard there) (see below para 16.89) relating to, for example, the preparation of skeleton arguments and appeal bundles. This chapter does no more than point towards the key features of appeals, in particular as they relate to police claims. Careful regard should be had to CPR Part 52, as well as the helpful commentary in the White Book.

16.85 Permission to appeal is required from the court making the decision under challenge or from the appeal court.[76] If the application for permission is made to the lower court, it can be made orally at the end of the relevant hearing. The courts have encouraged the making of applications at the hearing itself, where possible, rather than adjournments for further submissions.[77] Importantly, where an application to adjourn the decision hearing is made, it should be accompanied by an application to extend time to file the appellant's notice. The ordinary position would be an extension of time to file the appellant's notice to 21 days from the decision on leave to appeal. This is to avoid the risk that the time to file the appellant's notice, which continues to run from the decision date, will run out. The lower court has no jurisdiction to consider a retrospective application for permission to appeal.[78]

16.86 If the application is made to the appeal court, it is made in a written appeal notice,[79] though the application can be renewed at an oral hearing if it is refused on a consideration of the papers.[80] The time for filing the appellant's notice is 21 days after the decision of the lower court 'or any adjournment of that hearing', unless the lower court directs otherwise.[81] That an appellant has not sought permission before the lower court, does

76 CPR 52.3.

77 *McDonald v Rose* [2019] EWCA Civ 4, [2019] 1 WLR 2828 at para 21.

78 *Lisle-Mainwaring v Associated Newspapers Ltd* [2018] EWCA Civ 1470, [2018] 1 WLR 4766 at para 15.

79 CPR 52.12.

80 CPR 52.4(2).

81 CPR 52.12(2).

not prevent permission being sought from the appellate court, although the courts have encouraged parties to seek an appeal from the judge in the lower court who is fully seized of the matter.[82]

16.87 The lower court can extend time for the application for permission to the lower court. It cannot vary the time limit for filing the appeal notice to the appeal court. Any such application must be to the appeal court itself.[83]

16.88 Permission will be granted if the proposed appeal has a real prospect of success or there is some other compelling reason why the appeal should be heard (such as where a point of substantial public interest is raised).[84] That is the single test which applies to all first appeals irrespective of the court.[85] However, applications for permission to appeal on questions of fact or on the evaluation of expert evidence must meet the high threshold described in *Grizzly Business Ltd v Stena Drilling Ltd*.[86]

16.89 The 'routes' for an appeal are now helpfully set out in CPR PD 52A (Appeals: General provisions). A decision of a district judge will be appealed to a circuit judge, and a decision of a circuit judge will generally be appealed to the High Court.[87] Appeals in High Court proceedings are to the Court of Appeal.[88] An appeal from the outcome of a trial will also be heard by the Court of Appeal.[89]

16.90 Where the circuit judge has made a decision on appeal, then the appeal will be to the Court of Appeal.[90] Second appeals to the Court of Appeal require permission from the Court of Appeal and are only permitted where an important point of principle or practice is raised.[91]

Appeals in jury trials

16.91 In general, the appeal court will allow an appeal where the decision of the court below was 'wrong' or was unjust due to a serious procedural or other irregularity.[92] In cases where a judge sits alone, a 'wrong' decision may involve an error of law, an error of fact or relate to the exercise of a discretion. However, in relation to a jury trial the scope for an appeal is more limited. The Court of Appeal will not overturn a jury's decision on the facts unless it is shown to be perverse, or flawed by legal error in the directions given to the jury by the judge. Thus the potential grounds of appeal from the outcome of a civil action jury trial are likely to be confined to one or more of the following:

82 *Municipio de Mariana v BHP Group Plc* [2020] EWHC 2471 (TCC) at paras 41–43 and 90.
83 CPR 52.15.
84 CPR 52.6(1).
85 *Wheeldon Brothers Waste Ltd v Millennium Insurance Co Ltd* [2018] EWCA Civ 2403 at paras 17–18.
86 [2017] EWCA Civ 94 at paras 39–40.
87 Access to Justice Act 1999 (Destination of Appeals) Order 2016 SI No 917 art 5.
88 Senior Courts Act 1981 s16(1), apart from Masters' decisions, which are appealed to High Court judges (see Access to Justice (Destination of Appeals) Order 2016 SI No 917 art 4.
89 County Courts Act 1984 s77(1).
90 Access to Justice Act 1999 (Destination of Appeals) Order 2016 SI No 917 art 6.
91 CPR 52.7.
92 CPR 52.21(3).

- error of law by the judge;
- wrongly withdrawing issues from the jury;
- perverse verdict by the jury;
- serious procedural irregularity in the course of the trial;
- bias on the part of the judge;
- new evidence.

Error of law by the judge

16.92 The decision may be quashed if the judge has misdirected the jury on the law, given the jury the wrong questions to decide, or failed to direct it on a material matter.[93] Similarly, an appeal will lie if the judge has erred in the questions of law that the judge had to decide. For example in *Balchin v Chief Constable of Hampshire*[94] the trial judge erred when ruling whether the officer had reasonable grounds to arrest the claimant, by making findings of fact that should have been left for the jury to determine.

Wrongly withdrawing issues from the jury

16.93 A clear example of wrongly withdrawing issues from the jury is *Paul v Chief Constable of Humberside*[95] where the judge erred in failing to leave questions relating to the honesty of the officers' beliefs and to the propriety of their motives to the jury in relation to a false imprisonment and malicious prosecution claims.

Perverse verdict by the jury

16.94 If perverse verdict by the jury arises at all, it is likely to arise in one of two ways. First, a decision may be quashed if a jury has arrived at a conclusion contradicted by the evidence. In *Masters v Chief Constable of Sussex*[96] the Court of Appeal allowed an appeal from a jury's conclusion that the claimant had been assaulted, where his own medical evidence contradicted his case and there was no supporting evidence for his account. They held that in the circumstances the assault claim should have been withdrawn from the jury.

16.95 Second, the jury's decision will also be quashed if it is perverse in the sense that inconsistent answers have been given to the questions asked. However, the test for establishing perversity is strict; it must be shown that there was a necessary inconsistency, sufficient to vitiate the trial on the ground that the jurors must have based their deliberations on a false approach or otherwise been sufficiently unreliable as to justify a re-trial.[97] It is not perverse for the jury to accept parts of each party's account and to reject others.[98] The House of Lords has emphasised that the Court of Appeal should not find a jury's verdict on liability perverse, unless there was no rational explanation for it.[99]

93 See *Ward v Chief Constable of The West Midlands* [1997] 12 WLUK 202.
94 [2001] EWCA Civ 538.
95 [2004] EWCA Civ 308.
96 [2002] EWCA Civ 1482.
97 *Abbassy v Commissioner of Police of the Metropolis* [1990] 1 All ER 193, CA.
98 *Purchase v Chief Constable of Thames Valley* [2001] EWCA Civ 682.
99 *Grobbelaar v News Group Newspapers Ltd* [2002] UKHL 40, [2002] 4 All ER 732.

Serious procedural irregularity in the course of the trial

16.96 Examples of cases where serious procedural irregularity in the course of the trial could arise might include placing undue pressure on a deadlocked jury to arrive at a verdict.

Bias on the part of the judge

16.97 It is not uncommon for claimants to feel that the trial judge has been unduly unsympathetic to their position, whether in terms of interjections during the trial or comments made during the summing-up. However, it is very difficult to mount a successful appeal on this basis, where the party would have to prove either actual bias on the part of the trial judge or that the judge's conduct was such that the claimant was deprived of a fair trial in breach of the guarantee contained in European Convention on Human Rights (ECHR) Article 6(1).[100] Comments that caused resentment at the time may appear less significant when reduced to a line or two in a lengthy written transcript.

New evidence

16.98 Appeals rarely succeed on the ground of new evidence, as the appellant usually needs to show that the evidence could not have been found with reasonable diligence at the time of the original trial, and that had it been adduced it would have had an important influence on the result.[101]

16.99 In the situations discussed, a successful ground of appeal is likely to lead to an order for a re-trial, unless the outcome of the case can be resolved without findings of fact being made (for example, if the Court of Appeal considers that an issue should have been withdrawn from the jury due to lack of evidence). Where the appeal relates to the jury's decision on damages, the Court of Appeal may be able to substitute its own conclusion, as it has the power to make an award of damages or to vary an award of damages made by the jury, rather than ordering a re-trial.[102] The Court of Appeal has the power to overturn a jury's award where it considers that the sum was excessive or inadequate, in the sense that a reasonable jury could not have made the award having regard to the guidelines given in *Thompson and Hsu v Commissioner of Police of the Metropolis*[103] and the court can then arrive at its own figure.

Appeals in judge-only trials

16.100 The scope for appeal in judge-only cases is equivalent to the position in civil cases generally. Judges' conclusions on the law or on the facts can be appealed. However, the Court of Appeal has frequently expressed caution

100 For one such case, not in the police context, see *Serafin v Malkiewicz* [2020] UKSC 23, [2020] 1 WLR 2455.

101 In *Commissioner of Police of the Metropolis v Lincoln* [2001] EWCA Civ 2110 the Court of Appeal held that in the light of new evidence relating to the credibility of the claimant's witness, the interests of justice did require a re-trial.

102 CPR 52.10(3).

103 [1998] QB 498, CA.

about overturning decisions of fact made by the judge who had the opportunity of hearing and evaluating the witnesses, unless the issue under challenge relates to inferences to be drawn from the primary facts found, rather than the primary facts themselves. Where the complaint relates to the judge's exercise of a discretion, the Court of Appeal will only interfere if the judge erred in law, or misdirected themself in some way or reached a conclusion outside of the generous ambit within which reasonable disagreement is possible.

16.101 An order may also be appealed where the judge has not given sufficient reasons. A judge is not required to address every argument raised nor all the evidence. Where the case turns on the credibility of the main witness(es), the judge must at least address the principal grounds upon which the evidence of the witness has been challenged.[104] Some helpful guidance is provided in *Simetra Global Asserts Ltd and another v Ikon Finance Ltd and others*.[105]

16.102 As with appeals in respect of a trial by jury, in a judge-only trial an appeal may be pursued on the basis of actual or perceived bias of the judge, but the bar for doing so is a high one. An example is *Goodenough v Chief Constable of Thames Valley*,[106] in which the appeal was pursued on the assertion that the rejection of the clam was 'premised on an unbalanced and seriously inadequate analysis of the issues and evidence that compromised the fairness of his decision'.[107] The perceived unfairness was said to be evident on the face of the judgment rather than deriving from any conduct at trial. It was said that the judgment was sarcastic about the victim and overly sympathetic to the officer.[108] The appeal was rejected.

104 *Harb v HRH Prince Abdul Aziz* [2016] EWCA Civ 556, per Lord Dyson at para 39.
105 [2019] EWCA Civ 1413, [2019] 4 WLR 112.
106 [2021] EWCA Civ 1422.
107 [2021] EWCA Civ 1422 at para 4(iv).
108 [2021] EWCA Civ 1422 at para 35.

CHAPTER 17

Damages

Introduction

17.1 Some victims of police misconduct bring a civil action against the police as a matter of principle and say that the amount of damages is very much a secondary consideration to vindicating their rights by obtaining a judgment in their favour or obtaining an apology. It is true that in some cases the police will offer an apology as part of a settlement of a case (see chapter 15), but there is no provision in the civil justice system for requiring this or for ordering disciplinary proceedings (although misconduct matters may be reconsidered if the police lose a case at trial).

17.2 It is also the position that an award of damages is not the only purpose of the law of tort, and that a public acknowledgement that the claimant has suffered a wrong may play as important a role as a monetary award.[1] However, in most cases, in practice, an award of damages is the main remedy available in a civil action, and is likely to be the main way in which the police seek to settle a case.

17.3 In this chapter:

- The major case on damages in police cases, *Thompson and Hsu v Commissioner of the Police of the Metropolis*,[2] is introduced in which guidance was provided by the Court of Appeal on levels and types of damages. The case is used as a benchmark in almost every civil action against the police, especially involving false imprisonment and malicious prosecution, and cases involving aggravated and exemplary damages, even though the case was decided in 1997. It is important to note that the indicative figures in the guidance need to be updated in line with inflation for present-day cases, and reminders of this will be set out at various points in this chapter.
- The chapter then describes in detail the various types of damages available, referring to the guidance in *Thompson and Hsu*.
- The chapter then describes the nature of damages for some of the particular causes of action described earlier in this book, as well as the damages under the Human Rights Act (HRA) 1998.

The issue of damages is also referred to at several other places in this book, in relation both to various causes of action and procedural matters. The most important of these are as follows and relate to damages:

- for psychiatric harm – paras 7.80–7.81;
- under the Protection from Harassment Act 1997 – para 7.104;
- under the Law Reform (Miscellaneous Provisions) Act 1934 – para 7.197;
- under the Fatal Accidents Act 1976 – paras 7.203–7.205;
- under the Data Protection Act 2018 – para 11.205;
- for misuse of private information – para 11.207;
- for defamation – para 11.216;
- under the Equality Act (EqA) 2010 – paras 12.127–12.137.

1 See *Ashley v Chief Constable of Sussex* [2008] UKHL 25, [2008] 1 AC 962. See also *MR v Commissioner of Police of the Metropolis* [2019] EWHC 1970 (QB), [2019] Costs LR 1441, where an offer by a claimant to accept no damages if an admission of liability was made by the police was accepted to be a valid Civil Procedure Rules 1998 (CPR) Part 36 offer (see further paras 15.139–15.146).

2 [1997] EWCA Civ 3083, [1998] QB 498.

Background to court of appeal guidelines for police damages

17.4 As will have been seen in chapter 15, cases involving false imprisonment and malicious prosecution provide in most circumstances for a right to jury trial in the civil courts. It is the role of the jury, where there is one, not only to assist the judge determine liability in a case (see chapter 16) but also, in the absence of agreement between the parties, to determine the level of damages to be awarded to a successful claimant. In cases heard by a judge alone (where the right to a jury has not been exercised or does not apply), it is the judge who determines the level of damages (absent agreement between the parties). The Court of Appeal guidelines described below are regularly applied by judges as well as used to assist juries.

17.5 The traditional approach of the courts was to provide juries with virtually no guidance as to how much might be an appropriate sum to award in a case where it was the jury's role to do so. For example, in a 1990 case (that is no longer good law) involving damages for false imprisonment Purchas LJ in the Court of Appeal said:[3]

> Parliament has seen fit to leave the assessment of damages to the judgment of the jury rather than the judge . . . these are areas where the question of damages is so utterly subjective to the individual facts involved that I think it would be wrong to attempt to influence by judicial interference consideration of damages by the jury.

17.6 Such an approach, though, meant there was little consistency in the awards made by juries and it was a number of improbably large awards which led to the appeals in *Thompson and Hsu* and in other cases. Prior to this there had already been some developments in statute and case-law relating to the award of damages by juries. In 1990 the Court of Appeal was given 'power to order a new trial on the ground that damages awarded by a jury are excessive or inadequate' and to 'substitute for the sum awarded by the jury such sum as appears to the court to be proper'.[4] Then in a series of appeals concerning libel damages awarded by juries, the Court of Appeal became more willing to provide guidance and to interfere with large awards.[5]

17.7 The *Thompson and Hsu* appeal considered two cases:

1) The first was that of Ms Thompson. She had been lawfully arrested for a driving offence but excessive force was used against her in the police station. She was maliciously prosecuted (and acquitted) for assault against her police officer assailants and taken to court in handcuffs. The jury awarded her £51,500 of which £50,000 constituted exemplary damages.
2) The second case was that of a Mr Hsu. He was arrested at his home when he tried to stop the police entering as they did not have a warrant. He was assaulted during the arrest and detained for 75 minutes at the police station. He was racially abused. The police fabricated a version of

3 *Abbassy v Commissioner of Police of the Metropolis* [1990] 1 All ER 193 at 204, CA.

4 Courts and Legal Services Act 1990 s8; and see CPR 52.20.

5 *John v MGN Ltd.* [1997] QB 586, [1996] 2 All ER 35, CA; and *Rantzen v. Mirror Group Newspapers (1986) Ltd* [1994] QB 670, [1993] 4 All ER 975, CA.

events whereby the arrest was justified as Mr Hsu had assaulted an officer. His premises were left unsecured and items were missing, and Mr Hsu suffered post-traumatic stress symptoms for some years. He was awarded £220,000 by a jury of which £200,000 was exemplary damages.

17.8 The police appealed these awards. Lord Woolf MR, in opening his judgment in the Court of Appeal, said:

> In a number of recent cases members of the public have been awarded very large sums of exemplary damages by juries against the Commissioner of Police for the Metropolis for unlawful conduct towards them by the police. As a result these two appeals have been brought by the Commissioner. The intention is to clarify the directions which a judge should include in a summing up to assist the jury as to the amount of damages, particularly exemplary damages, which it is appropriate for them to award a plaintiff who is successful in this type of action. As similar appeals are pending any guidance given by us on this subject should influence the outcome of those appeals in addition to providing guidance for the future.

17.9 The guidance is given in 14 numbered paragraphs. It is referred to at some length in the text below when the various types of damages are considered. The guidance relating specifically to false imprisonment and malicious prosecution is referred to in separate sections on damages for those torts (see paras 17.74–17.90 and 17.91–17.106). Although the Court of Appeal made it clear that the guidelines set no binding precedent, in practice they have been used in almost all related civil actions since the judgment and so provide the 'reasonable degree of predictability' sought by the Court of Appeal.

17.10 In the context of this book, it should also be noted that the Court of Appeal in *Thompson and Hsu* indicated that whilst it was 'highly desirable' that complainants co-operated with disciplinary investigations they were not legally obliged to do so. The fact that they did not do so could not be held against them in law so as to reduce the amount payable when assessing the compensation to which they are entitled.

Types of damages available

Basic damages

17.11 The usual categorisation of damages to compensate a claimant is into general and special damages. General damages constitute the compensation given as a remedy for the tortious actions of the defendant, and special damages to compensate for specific pecuniary loss such as loss of earnings or damage to property.

17.12 However, because 'aggravated damages' (see below) are also part of these compensatory damages, the *Thompson and Hsu* guidance introduced a further categorisation of compensatory damages so as to separate 'basic' damages from 'aggravated' damages.[6] Thus, in the terms used by the Court

6 See guidance number (2) in *Thompson*:'(2) As the law stands at present compensatory damages are of two types. (a) Ordinary damages which we would suggest should be described as basic, and (b) aggravated damages.'

of Appeal, 'basic' damages constitute all those damages (other than aggravated damages) awarded to compensate for damage suffered by a claimant. These might include damages for:

- personal injuries (pain, suffering and loss of amenity following an assault and any injuries caused by it);
- the harm done to the claimant's reputation, for example, by a malicious prosecution;
- the loss of liberty because of an unlawful detention and other consequential damage.

17.13 Damages for post-traumatic stress disorder (PTSD) and other psychiatric injuries caused by the tortious action of the police can be claimed under this heading. Future loss of earnings (often, for example, caused by physical or psychiatric injuries), can also be claimed.[7]

17.14 The Court of Appeal in *Thompson* stated that the jury should be given assistance in calculating basic damages:[8]

> The jury should be told that the basic damages will depend on the circumstances and the degree of harm suffered by the plaintiff. But they should be provided with an appropriate bracket to use as a starting point.

17.15 The 'brackets' mentioned will be based on the levels of damages described in the *Thompson and Hsu* case in false imprisonment and malicious prosecution cases, and on recognised levels of damages for personal injuries (including physical and psychiatric injuries).[9] These are discussed further below in the section describing damages awarded in cases for assault and battery.

17.16 The Court of Appeal said that special damages should be explained to a jury separately. Special damages are designed to make good the past financial loss which can be calculated at the date of trial, such as medical bills, repair bills and past loss of earnings. In a malicious prosecution case, they can also include travel expenses if, for example, a person has had to attend court on a number of occasions before being acquitted.

17.17 Where a claimant is being compensated for loss of reputation – for instance, after malicious prosecution or false imprisonment – then damages under this head can be lowered if the claimant had little reputation to lose, for example because they had previous convictions. However, basic damages should not be reduced even if the claimant's behaviour caused or contributed to the tortious behaviour of the police (for example, by violent behaviour which led to the involvement of the police in an incident), although this might be a factor to take into account when considering aggravated or exemplary damages (see below, para 17.18).

7 For someone who was in work at the time of the torts committed by the police and is consequentially now unable to work, this part of the claim may constitute the largest part of the claim. Practitioners should consult a work such as *Kemp & Kemp: Quantum of damages*, Sweet & Maxwell, for the approach to be taken to calculating such loss, which is beyond the scope of this book. Deductions in the calculation may be made through the DSS Compensation Recovery Unit where the claimant has received social security payments as a result of his/her inability to work following an injury caused by the police.

8 *Thompson*, guidance number (3).

9 See as a starting point *Judicial College guidelines for the assessment of general damages in personal injury cases*, OUP, 16th edn, 2022; and further below.

Aggravated damages

17.18 Aggravated damages may be payable in addition to general or special damages. They are conventionally seen as an extra element of compensation in recognition that the exceptional motives, conduct or manner of the defendant have aggravated the claimant's damage by intangible injury to personality (insult, humiliation, degradation, indignation, outrage, distress, hurt feelings, etc). The Court of Appeal in *Thompson and Hsu* described their application as follows:

> Such damages can be awarded where there are aggravating features about the case which would result in the plaintiff not receiving sufficient compensation for the injury suffered if the award were restricted to a basic award. Aggravating features can include humiliating circumstances at the time of arrest, or any conduct of those responsible for the arrest or the prosecution which shows that they had behaved in a high-handed, insulting, malicious or oppressive manner either in relation to the arrest or imprisonment or in conducting the prosecution. Aggravating features can also include the way the litigation and trial are conducted.

17.19 The Court of Appeal has held that a persistent denial of liability in the civil action in the face of a judge's indications could justify an aggravated damages award.[10]

17.20 Other examples of behaviour of the defendant after the incident giving rise to the litigation which might give rise to an award of aggravated damages include the clear lack of an apology for the behaviour of the police and the failure to record a complaint or to investigate it properly. Discriminatory abuse has been cited by the courts as a particular reason for awarding aggravated damages.[11]

17.21 The fact that the defendant's exceptional behaviour is a precondition to the award of aggravated damages casts doubt on the purely compensatory nature of aggravated damages and suggests that they also contain a punitive element as well. Indeed, the Court of Appeal in *Thompson and Hsu* recognised that:[12]

> . . . if aggravated damages are awarded such damages, though compensatory are not intended as a punishment, will in fact contain a penal element as far as the defendant is concerned.

17.22 As the Court of Appeal noted, this may have an impact on the availability of exemplary damages (see below). However, later cases have emphasised the fact that aggravated damages are part of compensatory damages. In the Court of Appeal in *Rowlands v Chief Constable of Merseyside*,[13] Moore-Bick LJ said:[14]

> [T]he important factor to bear in mind is that they are primarily intended to be compensatory, not punitive. It follows that any injury for which compensation has been given as part of the award of basic damages should not be the subject of further compensation in the form of an award of aggravated

10 *Marks v Chief Constable of Greater Manchester* [1991] 11 WLUK 354, (1992) 156 LG Rev 990, *Times*, 28 January 1992.

11 See, for example, *Mohidin and others v Commissioner of Police of the Metropolis* [2015] EWHC 2740 (QB) at para 366.

12 At, guidance number (11).

13 [2006] EWCA Civ 1773, [2007] 1 WLR 1065.

14 At 26.

damages. However, the distinction between basic and aggravated damages will continue to have a part to play as long as the right to recover for intangible consequences such as humiliation, injury to pride and dignity as well as for the hurt caused by the spiteful, malicious, insulting or arrogant conduct of the defendant attaches to some causes of action and not others.

17.23 The Court of Appeal in *Rowlands* decided that aggravated damages for these issues were available even where personal injury damages had been awarded for psychiatric damage caused by the police actions, and there was not necessarily an overlap between the two awards. The Court of Appeal said that the trial judge in that case was wrong to withdraw the question of aggravated damages from the jury where an award for psychiatric damage of £2000 had been made. The Court awarded, in 2007, £6,000 in aggravated damages in a case where a total of £6,350 had been awarded for assault, false imprisonment and malicious prosecution (with the jury finding that an officer had told deliberate falsehoods during the trial). In the 2006 case of *Manley v Commissioner of Police of the Metropolis*[15] (another case where there was assault, false imprisonment and fabricated evidence at court and a basic award of £10,500) the Court of Appeal decided that no jury could have awarded less that £10,000 aggravated damages. In *R (Deptka) v Secretary of State for the Home Department,*[16] a 2019 immigration detention case, aggravated damages of £8,500 per claimant were awarded for the aggravating features of the four-week separation of the claimants, the delay in admitting liability, the delay in making an apology, and the initial refusal of interim payments.

17.24 In *Rowlands* the Court of Appeal also recognised that damages for distress, humiliation and injury to feelings are sometimes, in fact, awarded as part of basic damages and cited *Richardson v Howie*[17] as an example of this. In this vein, more recently, the High Court declined to make an award of aggravated damages in a case involving false imprisonment and assault, the judge stating that instead: 'The compensation awarded in each of the claims above has been adjusted upward in the Claimants' favour where appropriate to take account of the circumstances of the incident'.[18] It is submitted that it might be easier in some cases to persuade a court to adjust upwards the amount of basic damages rather than make a separate award of aggravated damages, and the outcome in terms of the level of the award should be the same.[19]

17.25 The Court of Appeal in *Thompson and Hsu* stated that if aggravated damages are thought appropriate then a separate award should be considered for each tort, although in practice that does not always happen, and the court will sometimes make the award without making it clear as to which tort it is attached. If the circumstances were to be serious enough to merit an award of aggravated damages, the Court of Appeal felt that an award should not be less that £1,000 (which now needs to be updated for inflation from the 1997 figure).

15 [2006] EWCA Civ 879.

16 [2019] EWHC 503 (Admin). See also *Holownia v Secretary of State for the Home Department* [2019] EWHC 794 (Admin) where £6,000 was awarded for initial shock,

17 [2004] EWCA Civ 1127.

18 *Stewart v Commissioner of Police of the Metropolis* [2017] EWHC 921 (QB) at para 22.

19 See, for example, *BXB v Watch Tower & Bible Tract Society* [2020] EWHC 156 (QB), [2020] 4 WLR 42 at para 207.

17.26 In *Thompson and Hsu* the court felt it would be difficult to indicate a precise arithmetical relationship between basic damages and aggravated damages, but:[20]

> . . . we would not expect the aggravated damages to be as much as twice the basic damages except perhaps where, on the particular facts, the basic damages are modest.

17.27 Thus, for example, a minor assault and/or a short period of detention accompanied by racial abuse might only lead to a small award of basic damages but might justify a proportionately larger award of aggravated damages. The jury should be reminded (and a judge bear in mind) that the combination of basic damages and aggravated damages should not exceed fair compensation for the injury suffered by the claimant.

17.28 If the claim for aggravated (and exemplary) damages does include a claim for racial abuse or humiliation (or other forms of discrimination) then recourse can be had to case-law on quantum for race discrimination in employment law cases. In particular in the 2002 case *Vento v Chief Constable of Yorkshire Police (No 2)*[21] the Court of Appeal set out guidance on the bands of compensation (to be updated for inflation) for injury to feelings ranging from £25,000 for the worst cases involving a lengthy campaign to 'awards of between £500 and £5,000 are appropriate for less serious cases, such as where the act of discrimination is an isolated or one off occurrence'.[22] A number of cases have uprated these figures in line with inflation, for example in the 2017 case of *Alseran v Ministry of Defence*[23] where the court said:[24]

> Allowing for the increase in the RPI over the 15 years since December 2002 when the *Vento* case was decided . . . comparable current round figures are: i) £23,000 to £38,000 for the top band; ii) £7,500 to £23,000 for the middle band; and iii) £750 to £7,500for the lower band.

17.29 Thus, in the 2015 case of *Mohidin v Commissioner of Police of the Metropolis*[25] one of the claimants, a 16-year-old, was struck and wrestled violently to the ground by police officers during a wrongful arrest and was then made to kneel in handcuffs. He was also subjected to racist abuse and an unlawful strip search. The court put this this case at the top of the lowest *Vento* band and awarded £7,200 for injury to feelings, and also awarded damages for

20 At guidance number (10).

21 [2002] EWCA Civ 1871, [2003] Po LR 171, [2003] ICR 318, [2003] IRLR 102.

22 *Vento* para 65. See *Mohidin* at paras 378–283 for the application in 'one-off' abuse type cases. See further paras 12.125–12.131 for more guidance on damages for discrimination.

23 [2017] EWHC 3289 (QB), [2019] QB 1251. For up-to-date figures, see also: Presidential Guidance, *Employment Tribunal awards for injury to feelings and psychiatric injury following De Souza v Vinci Construction (UK) Ltd [2017] EWCA Civ 879. Fifth addendum to presidential guidance originally issued on 5 September 2017*, April 2022: 'a lower band of £900 to £9,900 (less serious cases); a middle band of £9,900 to 29,600 (cases that do not merit an award in the upper band); and an upper band of £29,600 to £49,300 (the most serious cases), with the most exceptional cases capable of exceeding £49,300' (www.judiciary.uk/wp-content/uploads/2013/08/Vento-bands-presidential-guidance-April-2022-addendum-1.pdf). See also *Durrant v Chief Constable of Avon and Somerset Constabulary* [2017] EWCA Civ 1808, [2018] ICR D1 and see further at paras 12.128–12.131.

24 At para 892.

25 [2015] EWHC 2740 (QB).

pain and suffering and false imprisonment. Another claimant in that case received an aggravated damages award of £2,500 where he had been racially abused, even though his award for false imprisonment was only £200.

17.30 Despite the guidance from the Court of Appeal, and the examples set out above, given the non-pecuniary and intangible losses that aggravated damages are designed to compensate, coupled with the relevance of the defendant's conduct and the possible inclusion of a punitive element, it is difficult to predict the level of an award. In serious cases, aggravated damages (often together with exemplary damages) can be substantial and sometimes outstrip the purely compensatory element in an award. In practice, though, courts are often reluctant to award aggravated damages absent specific identified wrongdoing by the police, and practitioners are reminded that they are not awarded as a matter of course where officers have mistakenly, but honestly, believed that they have, for example, the power to arrest someone.

17.31 Lastly, it should be noted that a claimant's own conduct, behaviour and provocation can be taken into account in calculating aggravated damages. As the Court of Appeal in *Thompson and Hsu* put it:[26]

> In an appropriate case the jury should also be told that even though the plaintiff succeeds on liability any improper conduct of which they find him guilty can reduce or even eliminate any award of aggravated or exemplary damages if the jury consider that this conduct caused or contributed to the behaviour complained of.

17.32 One example of this might be a claimant who racially abused an officer who later assaulted him during an arrest: the assault would still give rise to an award of basic damages but a court or jury may feel that the claimant's initial conduct meant that aggravated damages should be reduced or eliminated. Of course, there should be some causal connection between the claimant's behaviour and the tortious actions of the police for this to apply. Thus in *Mohidin* the trial judge commented that aggravated damages for racial abuse should not be reduced simply because the claimant had had previous dealings with the police as 'It bears with it the implication that the racist humiliation of a youth is somehow less serious if he has come to the attention of the police before'.[27]

17.33 Aggravated damages can be awarded for all the torts referred to in this book, although the need for conduct by the defendant that has led to additional suffering for the claimant means that it will be more difficult to envisage circumstances in which they would be appropriately awarded in negligence actions, other than in relation to manner in which the police have conducted the litigation in defending the claim, except perhaps where there has been a high degree of recklessness towards carrying out police duties.

Exemplary damages

Overview

17.34 The availability of exemplary damages is narrower than that of aggravated damages in that they are only generally available where the actions of the police fall into certain categories (see below at para 17.30).

26 At guidance number (14).

27 *Mohidin* at para 368.

17.35 Exemplary damages (unlike aggravated damages) are not designed to compensate the claimant for their loss. Rather, in the limited circumstances in which they are available, the purpose is to punish the defendant in the action over and above the requirement to compensate, and to mark the disapproval by the court of the defendant's acts. They can, therefore, be awarded in circumstances where an award of aggravated damages has not been made.[28]

17.36 Since the landmark case of *Rookes v Barnard (No. 1)*,[29] exemplary damages have only been available in three categories of cases, all of which relate to the defendant's conduct. Only one of these categories is usually relevant in police actions and is described in that case by Lord Reid as 'oppressive, arbitrary or unconstitutional action by servants of the government'.[30] The terms 'oppressive, arbitrary or unconstitutional action' should be read disjunctively. Thus, if it is found that a wrongful arrest is an unconstitutional act by the police, it is not necessary also to show that the arrest was oppressive or arbitrary before exemplary damages are available (if the circumstances of the case merited an award).[31]

17.37 However, although it might be expected that police officers will conduct themselves with higher standards than the rest of the public, generally there is no obligation on the court to award exemplary (or aggravated) damages in all cases of tortious acts by the police just because they were committed by a police officer. The court (the judge or the jury if there is one) retains a discretion whether or not to award exemplary damages. In practice, it is only in the most egregious of cases that they are awarded, as explained further below. Having said that, the most common example of exemplary damages being awarded in the 'oppressive, arbitrary or unconstitutional' category is in tort actions against the police.[32] As the Court of Appeal said in the case of *Rowlands v Chief Constable of Merseyside Police*:[33]

> If the citizen is liable to encounter arbitrary, oppressive or unconstitutional action on the part of servants of the government of a kind which involves interference with his personal liberty, it is more likely in the nature of things that he will do so at the hands of the police than of other public servants.

17.38 Although in cases involving police officers there will not be difficulty showing that action has been carried out by 'servants of the government', the position might not be so clear in cases involving private security firms or even medical staff from private firms providing services in police stations. Thus, in *AB v South West Water Services Ltd*[34] it was held that employees of a privatised water company could not be described as govern-

28 *Isaac v Chief Constable of the West Midlands* [2001] EWCA Civ 1405, where a jury awarded £5,000 exemplary damages in a malicious prosecution case.

29 [1964] AC 1129, [1964] 1 All ER 367, HL.

30 The other two categories encompass situations where the award of exemplary damages is authorised by statute, and where the wrongful conduct has been calculated to make a profit which may well exceed the compensation payable to the claimant.

31 *Holden v Chief Constable of Lancashire* [1987] QB 380, CA.

32 *Clerk & Lindsell on Torts*, Sweet & Maxwell, 23rd edn, para 27-138.

33 [2006] EWCA Civ 1773, [2007] 1 WLR 1065 at para 39.

34 [1993] QB 507, CA.

ment servants when the conduct they were engaged in was 'not an exercise of executive power derived from government, central or local'.

17.39 It is submitted that it is wrong in principle for the award of exemplary damages to depend on whether the abuse of power in question has been committed by an individual who happens to be a government servant rather than by an employee of a privatised company, and that functions, such as the care and transportation of prisoners, the handling of 999 calls and forensic examinations by scene of crime officers all involve the exercise of executive power. Indeed, in *Kuddus v Chief Constable of Leicestershire*,[35] Lord Nicholls doubted whether Lord Reid's distinction between abuse of power by government servants and others could be sustained:[36]

> Whatever may have been the position 40 years ago, I am respectfully inclined to doubt the soundness of this distinction today. National and international companies can exercise enormous power. So do some individuals. I am not sure it would be right to draw a hard-and-fast line which would always exclude such companies and persons from the reach of exemplary damages.

17.40 *Kuddus* considered directly the question as to whether exemplary damages could be awarded in a claim for misfeasance in public office. Until this case, it had been the accepted position that exemplary damages were only available in causes of action where there had been an award of such damages prior to 1964 (the date of the *Rookes v Barnard* case). In *Kuddus* it was accepted that this was an arbitrary approach which should no longer be followed, and that exemplary damages could be available in other common law torts. However, Lord Nicholls emphasised that:[37]

> . . . the essence of the conduct constituting the court's discretionary jurisdiction to award exemplary damages is conduct which was an outrageous disregard of the plaintiff's rights.

17.41 The majority of the court in *Kuddus* were inclined to agree with an important Law Commission report from 1997[38] that there remained a place for exemplary damages in English law. Lord Nicholls supported this view in *Kuddus*, commenting that:[39]

> The availability of exemplary damages has played a significant role in buttressing civil liberties, in claims for false imprisonment and wrongful arrest. From time to time cases do arise where awards of compensatory damages are perceived as inadequate to achieve a just result between the parties. The nature of the defendant's conduct calls for a further response from the courts. On occasion conscious wrongdoing by a defendant is so outrageous, his disregard of the plaintiff's rights so contumelious, that something more is needed to show that the law will not tolerate such behaviour. Without an award of exemplary damages, justice will not have been done. Exemplary damages, as a remedy of last resort, fill what otherwise would be a regrettable lacuna.

35 [2001] UKHL 29, [2002] 2 AC 122.

36 *Kuddus* at para 66.

37 *Kuddus* at para 68 per Lord Nichools.

38 *Aggravated, exemplary and restitutionary damages* (Law Com No 247), 16 December 1997, available at: www.lawcom.gov.uk/project/aggravated-exemplary-and-restitutionary-damages/.

39 *Kuddus* at para 63.

17.42 The Court of Appeal in *Muuse v Secretary of State for the Home Department*[40] stressed, in a false imprisonment case, that despite these comments there was no need to find that a defendant had acted with malice before exemplary damages would be available and so, for example, sheer incompetence would be sufficient. The court said that 'the award of punitive damages under the common law has a real role in restraining the arbitrary use of executive power and buttressing civil liberties'.[41]

17.43 Despite this reference to civil liberties, the House of Lords in *Kuddus* noted that there remained a question as to whether exemplary damages could be awarded in claims under the HRA 1998 or discrimination legislation such as the EqA 2010 (see para 12.135) but left the question open for argument in an appropriate case on the point.[42] In practice, exemplary damages have not been awarded in HRA 1998 cases, and this is sometimes explained because the power to award damages is linked to the European Court of Human Rights' power to award damages for 'just satisfaction', and that court has not described damages it awards as punitive or exemplary (see further below from para 17.121). There is still also uncertainty as to whether and when exemplary damages can be claimed in negligence cases, although if malice does not need to be established (see above para 17.142) there would seem to be nothing to prevent an award if negligent behaviour was sufficiently reckless, perhaps in cases involving police drivers or the deployment of police dogs.

17.44 The present situation, then, is that a trial judge (or jury) in a civil action against the police should apply the guidance in the *Thompson and Hsu* case set out in this section when considering an award of exemplary damages. The *Thompson* guidance describes the exceptional nature of exemplary damages and the circumstances in which they could be awarded. Where the evidence is capable of supporting a claim for exemplary damages, whether these are awarded is a matter which should be left to the jury (where there is one).[43] The Court of Appeal held that the jury should be told (or the judge consider) that:[44]

> . . . though it is not normally possible to award damages with the object of punishing the defendant, exceptionally this is possible where there has been conduct, including oppressive or arbitrary behaviour, by police officers which deserves the exceptional remedy of exemplary damages.

17.45 The court in *Thompson and Hsu* went on to list four further factors that should be explained to the jury when consideration is being given to whether to award exemplary damages, all designed to emphasise their exceptional nature:[45]

1) First, the jury should bear in mind that if they have awarded aggravated damages, these will already have compensated the claimant for the

40 [2010] EWCA Civ 453.

41 At para 77.

42 See Lord Hutton at para 94.

43 See *Rowlands* at para 34. The Court of Appeal went on to make an award of exemplary damages of £7,500 in a case involving assault, false imprisonment and malicious prosecution.

44 *Thompson*, guidance number (12), cited in *Kuddus* at para 64.

45 *Thompson*, guidance number (12), cited in *Kuddus* at para 64.

effects of any 'oppressive and insulting behaviour' of the police and that these damages will provide 'inevitably, a measure of punishment from the defendant's point of view'.

2) Second, a jury must be careful to award exemplary damages only in circumstances where basic and aggravated damages provide an 'inadequate punishment' for the police.
3) Third, the jury should be aware that the award of exemplary damages is 'in effect a windfall' for the claimant and that any award will come out of funds used for general policing on behalf of the public (although the court pointed out that this last point would not be relevant if the damages would be payable by insurers for the police).
4) Last, the court was anxious to emphasise that the sum awarded by way of exemplary damages 'should be sufficient to mark the jury's disapproval of the oppressive or arbitrary behaviour but should be no more than is required for this purpose'. Practitioners should also bear in mind issues which might arise in police cases where the chief officer is sued vicariously in relation to the actions of individual officers (see para 17.52).

17.46 As in the case for aggravated damages, the court in *Thompson and Hsu* noted that any improper conduct by the claimant which caused or contributed to the wrongdoing of the police could reduce or eliminate an award of exemplary damages.

17.47 The court in *Thompson and Hsu* also gave some very broad guidance on the amounts (at 1997 levels) that should be awarded:[46]

> Where exemplary damages are appropriate they are unlikely to be less than £5,000. Otherwise the case is probably not one which justifies an award of exemplary damages at all. In this class of action the conduct must be particularly deserving of condemnation for an award of as much as £25,000 to be justified and the figure of £50,000 should be regarded as the absolute maximum, involving directly officers of at least the rank of superintendent.

17.48 In a subsequent case, *Goswell v Commissioner of the Police of the Metropolis*,[47] Simon Brown LJ summed up the guidance in a sentence thus:

> . . . it seems to me that really what the court (generally the jury but now us) is required to do in these cases is to mark its disapproval of the oppressive or arbitrary conduct in question, tempering its outrage, of course, with the thought that the exemplary damage award will constitute a windfall for the plaintiff and a depletion of police funds to the possible disadvantage of the general public.

More than one victim of police misconduct

17.49 One question not addressed in *Thompson and Hsu* is what happens where there is more than one victim of the police misconduct. It has been decided (in a non-police case) that one award of exemplary damages should be made which should be shared between the victims, rather than separate awards of exemplary damages for each individual.[48]

46 *Thompson*, guidance number (13), cited in *Kuddus* at para 80.

47 [1998] 4 WLUK 569, CA per Simon Brown LJ.

48 *Riches v News Group Newspapers Ltd* [1986] QB 256, CA.

17.50 That approach was adopted in the 2019 case of *Rees v Commissioner of Police of the Metropolis*,[49] where the court awarded a total sum of £150,000 in exemplary damages to be shared between three claimants in a case involving very serious police misconduct. The award was challenged in the Court of Appeal as it was an award of exemplary damages beyond the 'absolute maximum' of £50,000 (£91,500 when adjusted for inflation) referred to in *Thompson and Hsu*. The court rejected the challenge.[50] It pointed out that the court in *Thompson and Hsu* had made it clear that its guidance was 'not intended to be applied in a mechanistic manner'.[51] The Court of Appeal found that the guidance was directed at the paradigm of a single claimant and that the number of persons wrongly detained or prosecuted 'must at least be capable of bearing on the quantum of any award of exemplary damages'.[52]

17.51 Conversely, in *R (Lumba) v Secretary of State for the Home Department*,[53] which was a judicial review case about the application of an unlawful immigration detention policy by the Home Office, potentially affecting large numbers of detainees, the Supreme Court cited the fact that not all potential claimants were before the court as one of the reasons for not making an award of exemplary damages. In practice, in private law police actions, this should not be an issue as all the claimants are likely to be before the court and parties to the action.

Vicarious liability in exemplary damages

17.52 A chief officer of police will normally be vicariously liable for the misconduct of the force's officers, see paras 14.120–14.128, and it is usual, in practice, for the chief officer to pay any exemplary damages awarded (although there have been cases where a chief officer has joined individual officers to a claim with a view to seeking an indemnity if damages are awarded).[54]

17.53 When calculating the appropriate exemplary sum of damages, it has been the practice of the court to take into account the defendant's capacity to pay. In the police context, if a case was brought against individual officers, it would be their means that would be at issue. How should this rule be applied in vicarious liability cases? As the Law Commission said:[55]

> One possibility was that any sum which an employer is liable to pay as exemplary damages could be subject to deduction on account of the employee's lack of means. Another, contrasting, possibility was that the means of the wrongdoing employee are irrelevant to the size of the sum which the employer is vicariously liable to pay.

17.54 In *Thompson and Hsu* the Court of Appeal addressed the issue as follows:[56]

49 [2019] EWHC 2339 (QB), [2019] 7 WLUK 554.
50 *Rees v Commissioner of Police of the Metropolis* [2021] EWCA Civ 49, [2021] 1 WLUK 159.
51 *Thompson*, guidance number (7).
52 *Rees*, para 54.
53 [2011] UKSC 12, [2012] 1 AC 245.
54 See *Mohidin*, above.
55 *Aggravated, exemplary and restitutionary damages* (Law Com No 247), 16 December 1997, para 1.154.
56 Page 517.

> In the case of exemplary damages we have taken into account the fact that the action is normally brought against the chief officer of police and the damages are paid out of police funds for what is usually a vicarious liability for the acts of his officers in relation to which he is a joint tortfeasor (see now s88 Police Act 1996). In these circumstances it appears to us wholly inappropriate to take into account the means of the individual officers . . .

17.55 In a later case, however, a direct challenge was made to the proposition that exemplary damages could be awarded against the chief officer only vicariously liable for the torts committed by individual officers. The Court of Appeal in *Rowlands v Chief Constable of Merseyside* rejected the challenge and said as follows:[57]

> . . . it is desirable as a matter of policy that the courts should be able to make punitive awards against those who are vicariously liable for the conduct of their subordinates without being constrained by the financial means of those who committed the wrongful acts in question. Only by this means can awards of an adequate amount be made against those who bear public responsibility for the conduct of the officers concerned.

17.56 However, the vicarious nature of the chief officer's role means that credit can be given to a chief officer who has punished officers through disciplinary proceedings for wrongdoing when the question of exemplary damages comes to be considered.[58] The instituting of disciplinary proceedings might also be relevant even where an officer has been cleared of wrongdoing (especially if the proceedings were conducted in front of an independent panel chair).

17.57 Where only the prospect of disciplinary proceedings is raised at the stage when exemplary damages are being considered the Court of Appeal in *Thompson and Hsu* said this should only be taken into account where:

> . . . there is clear evidence that such proceedings are intended to be taken in the event of liability being established and that there is at least a strong possibility of the proceedings succeeding.

17.58 It is submitted that where an officer has already been convicted of a criminal offence relating to the same subject matter as the civil action, exemplary damages could still be recovered from the chief officer, although the role played by the police force in bringing the officer to justice might be relevant to the issue.

17.59 Finally, it might also be relevant to the question of exemplary damages whether the chief officer has paid a penalty in another forum. Thus, for example, in a case for misfeasance arising from a breach of data protection law, if the chief officer has already paid a penalty fine imposed by the Information Commissioner for the breach, it may be argued that an award of exemplary damages would be unnecessary.

Nominal damages

17.60 Historically, certain legal rights have been considered so important that even a technical breach of them entitles a claimant to bring proceedings, without

57 [2006] EWCA Civ 1773, [2007] 1 WLR 1065 at para 47.

58 *Goswell v Commissioner of the Police of the Metropolis*, unreported, 7 April 1998, per Simon Brown J.

having to prove that they have suffered any 'real' loss. Claims for the torts of false imprisonment, assault and battery, trespass to land and to goods are actionable in this way.[59] Nominal damages (ie damages awarded in the absence of any real loss) are not intended to compensate, but rather demonstrate that an individual's rights were infringed. Even though nominal damages may be small, exemplary damages, exceptionally, may also be awarded and if so, may significantly increase the overall award of damages to a claimant. Although this is a legal possibility, it is hard to think of a police case, at least, where it would be appropriate to award exemplary damages but not compensatory damages.[60] The debate as to whether only nominal damages should be awarded in false imprisonment cases where a person has been deprived of their liberty, in circumstances where lawful detention would have been possible, is considered in more detail below at paras 17.84–17.86.

Interest on damages

17.61 Senior Courts Act (SCA) 1981 s35A and County Courts Act (CCA) 1984 s69 provide the court with the general power to award interest within its discretion on damages awards in the High Court and county court respectively. By SCA 1981 s35A(2)and CCA 1984 s69(3) the discretion must be exercised in favour of a claimant who recovers damages exceeding £200 for personal injuries or death 'unless the court is satisfied that there are special reasons to the contrary'.

17.62 Interest on general damages for pain and suffering and loss of amenities is usually awarded from the date of service of the claim form until the date of trial, and the rate of interest is usually at two per cent per annum.[61] Interest to be awarded on past special damages is normally based on the average rate of interest allowed on money in court placed on Special Account over the period for which the interest is awarded.[62]

17.63 However, personal injury cases are in a special category and interest is not usually awarded on damages for other non-economic losses in police cases, such as loss of liberty or loss of reputation. This was confirmed in the case of *Holtham v Commissioner of Police of the Metropolis*[63] where the Court of Appeal relied on this principle as set out in *Saunders v Edwards*.[64] The court also stated, however, that:

> This will cause no injustice since juries, when awarding damages, will no doubt take account of how long it has taken plaintiffs to establish that the arrest and imprisonment was unlawful and of any increase in their suffering due to this delay.

17.64 This approach was confirmed more recently in the case of *Rees v Commissioner of Police of the Metropolis*[65] where the Court of Appeal said that

59 *Williams v The Peel River Land Company* [1878] 55 LT 689, HL.

60 See *Cumber v Chief Constable of Hampshire* (1995) *Times* 28 January [1995] 1 WLUK 440, (1995) 92(8) LSG 39, CA where it was held that it had to be rare if not unique for an award of exemplary damages not to be coupled with one of compensatory damages.

61 *Birkett v Hayes* [1982] 1 WLR 816, CA.

62 *Jefford v Gee* [1970] 2 QB 130, CA.

63 [1987] WL 491956 (1987), CA.

64 [1987] 1 WLR 1116, CA.

65 [2021] EWCA Civ 49.

a judge should calibrate an award not only to take account of inflation (if the *Thompson and Hsu* guidelines were being used), but to take account of the fact that it was only at the date of judgment that a claimant's rights were being vindicated. If that approach is adopted, there would be no call for an award of interest. The court said it would be good practice for a judge to expressly state that that was the approach being adopted.[66] From a practitioner's point of view, it would also be sensible to ensure that an uplift in damages is expressly claimed in negotiations, or at the end of a case, to represent the delay in a claimant achieving vindication.

Damages for particular torts

17.65 This section deals with the heads under which damages can be awarded for the following torts:

- assault and battery;
- false imprisonment;
- malicious prosecution;
- misfeasance in public office;
- seizure of goods;
- damage to goods;
- trespass to land.

See para 17.3 for other references to damages in this book.

Damages for assault and battery

17.66 Assault and battery are torts actionable in their own right. This means that it is not necessary to prove that there has been damage before a claim can be brought, and the successful claimant will always be entitled to at least nominal damages, even if they cannot point to any real loss.[67] As was said in *Alseran v Ministry of Defence*, this 'kind of injury which is inherent in the wrong itself is often referred to as "moral injury"'.[68]

17.67 Although a claim for personal injuries will often form the bulk of a damages claim in a case for assault and battery, all consequences flowing from the unlawful act can lead to compensation including for the distress, misery, humiliation, anger and indignation that such a tort may cause.[69] Accordingly, a significant claim for damages can arise even if the assault has not occasioned serious injury, particularly if it occurred in circumstances that caused substantial fear or humiliation to the victim. As discussed above (para 17.24) it appears that these factors can be reflected in the award for basic damages or the award for aggravated damages.[70]

66 [2021] EWCA Civ 49 at paras 45-48.

67 See *Ashley v Chief Constable of Sussex* [2008] UKHL 25, [2008] 1 AC 962 at para 60.

68 [2017] EWHC 3289 (QB), [2019] QB 1251 at para 876.

69 *Wilson v Pringle* [1987] QB 237, CA.

70 Compare the approach in *Gerald v Commissioner of Police of the Metropolis* (1998) *Times* 26 June, CA with the case of *Richardson v Howie* [2004] EWCA Civ 1127.

17.68 However, where the assault has resulted in personal injury (be it physical or psychiatric injury), the claimant may recover damages for those injuries. The general principles that apply to any case of personal injury apply to cases of assault and battery, and the details are beyond the scope of this book. Where personal injury has been caused by other tortious actions, the same principles will apply. Both physical and psychiatric damage can be caused by police negligence (in a case involving police driving for example), and it is not uncommon for false imprisonment and malicious prosecution to lead to psychiatric injury.

17.69 In short, though, a claim can be made for:

- pain and suffering, both in the past and in the future;
- 'loss of amenity', eg full or partial loss of a limb or organ;
- loss of enjoyment of life, eg an amateur footballer who has to give up the game because of the injuries;
- financial loss due to medical expenses, loss of earnings and loss of earning capacity.

17.70 Consistency and predictability of damages awards are assisted by various scales and guidelines. Most often used are the *Guidelines for the assessment of general damages in personal injury cases* published by the Judicial College, which is now in its 16th edn, and which indicates appropriate levels of award across the whole range of physical and psychiatric injuries to the person. Police action practitioners should ensure they have access to a copy of such guidance. Where more serious injuries have been caused, the assessment of damages will often rely on expert medical reports which can make specific reference to the scales of assessment set out in guidance.

17.71 However, in many assault and battery cases, personal injury damages will be claimed for cuts, bruising and minor injuries which occur during the arrest process, sometimes including handcuffing. Often these are injuries which will resolve in a short period of time, and reference to guidelines is unlikely to be of assistance. As an example in the 2017 case of *Stewart v Commissioner of Police of the Metropolis*,[71] one claimant suffered 'reddening and some pain for a short period' which merited an award of £350, and another claimant was 'handcuffed in a public place, immediately outside his home address' which merited an award of £500.

17.72 In more serious cases, it is possible for damages to be assessed both at the conclusion of the case and again at some future date if the claimant's condition may seriously deteriorate or that they will develop a serious medical condition (for example, epilepsy from head injuries). A claimant can, accordingly, apply to receive provisional damages when the court first gives judgment and a further award at some later date.[72] In these more serious cases, practitioners should consider obtaining advice from a personal injury specialist for the purposes of properly drawing up schedules of loss and damage.

17.73 Basic damages (see above paras 17.11–17.17) for personal injury cannot be reduced by reason of the claimant's conduct. It was held in *Lane v*

71 [2017] EWHC 921 (QB) at para 14.
72 See CPR Part 41.

Holloway[73] that on principle, when considering what damages a claimant is entitled to as compensation for physical injury, the fact that the claimant may have behaved badly is irrelevant.

Damages for false imprisonment

17.74 Damages for false imprisonment are intended to compensate for loss of liberty, discomfort and inconvenience, injury to dignity and loss of reputation. This section deals with damages for the usually relatively short periods of time that a person is detained from the time of arrest until release, or production before a magistrates' court. For awards made in relation to longer periods of detention (usually in prison) following remand in custody or conviction, see the discussion below in relation to malicious prosecution cases (which have led to a person wrongly serving a sentence of imprisonment and/or spending time on remand awaiting trial).

17.75 In *Murray v Minister of Defence* Lord Griffiths said:[74]

> The law attaches supreme importance to the liberty of the individual and if he suffers a wrongful interference with that liberty it should remain actionable even without proof of special damage.

17.76 Clearly, the crucial factors when assessing damages for false imprisonment will be the length of time for which the claimant was imprisoned and the damage to the person's reputation.[75] In *Thompson and Hsu*[76] the Court of Appeal assessed the financial value as follows:

> In a straightforward case of wrongful arrest and false imprisonment, the starting point is likely to be about £500 for the first hour during which the plaintiff has been deprived of his or her liberty. After the first hour an additional sum is to be awarded, but that sum should be on a reducing scale so as to keep the damages proportionate with those payable in personal injury cases and because the plaintiff is entitled to have a higher rate of compensation for the initial shock of being arrested. As a guideline we consider, for example, that a plaintiff who has been wrongly kept in custody for twenty four hours should for this alone normally be regarded as entitled to an award of about £3,000. For subsequent days the daily rate will be on a progressively reducing scale.

17.77 As mentioned already, the figures need to be increased to take account of inflation. The Court of Appeal in *Thompson and Hsu* emphasised that these were guideline figures only for the jury, so that the amounts can be increased or reduced to take into account any particular features of the claimant, the nature of the detention or the effect it has on the claimant. Thus, for example, a wrongful detention which begins with an arrest at gun-point in public, might lead to a higher basis for an award than for a person politely but wrongly arrested while voluntarily attending a police station. A person who is no stranger to police cells might be entitled to a lower award than a person detained in a police station for the first time. The shock of detention might, likewise, be greater for a child or a vulnerable adult than for other people.

73 [1968] QB 379, CA.

74 [1988] 1 WLR 692 at 704, HL.

75 *Walter v Alltools* (1944) 61 TLR 39, HC.

76 [1997] EWCA Civ 3083, [1998] QB 498, at guidance number (5).

These are factors which may also be taken into account when considering an award of aggravated damages (see paras 17.18–17.33).

17.78 Some cases involving longer periods of false imprisonment (for example, because of unlawful immigration policies), have specifically considered how much to award for the 'initial shock' of detention. Thus, in the 2019 case of *R (Deptka) v Secretary of State for the Home Department*[77] awards of £5,000 were made for the initial shock of detention to claimants who had never been previously detained.

17.79 In *Mohidin*, decided in October 2015, one of the claimants (who was 16) was detained for almost 20 hours after a street arrest, and strip-searched in breach of Police and Criminal Evidence Act 1984 (PACE) Code C (see para 6.104), and was awarded £4,500 for false imprisonment. A co-claimant detained for only five minutes at the scene of the arrest was awarded £200.[78]

17.80 Other factors might increase the level of damages. Any claim for damage to reputation continues until the police admit the imprisonment was false.[79]

17.81 If the initial arrest and detention was lawful but subsequently becomes unlawful while a person is detained at the police station (see chapter 6), then the 'initial shock' of arrest described by the Court of Appeal will not be relevant. There may be cases where the false imprisonment is more 'technical' in nature, for example, as already mentioned where a person who has attended voluntarily at a police station (and so might have spent time at the station answering questions in any event) but is then unnecessarily arrested, then a claimant might expect only to recover limited damages. In *Commissioner of Police of the Metropolis v MR*, a claimant attended voluntarily at a police and was then unlawfully arrested (as his arrest was not necessary (see para 6.80)) and was detained for almost seven hours: he was awarded £2,750 in 2018.[80]

17.82 As mentioned above, it may be possible to claim personal injury damages for psychiatric injury caused as a result of the arrest and detention if medical evidence for this can be produced. It is not unusual for someone wrongly arrested and detained to develop symptoms of PTSD or depression, for example. It will be possible to claim damages for any cash loss, such as loss of earnings as a result of the false imprisonment.[81] The principles in relation to these heads of damages are explained above in the section relating to damages for assault and battery (see paras 17.66–17.73).

17.83 The courts have discussed the issue as to whether a claimant will be entitled to damages where it can be shown that even though the detention was unlawful, if the law had been correctly applied then in fact the detention would have been lawful.

17.84 One view was set out in the case of *Roberts v Chief Constable of Cheshire*,[82] where the Court of Appeal considered the situation of a claimant who had

77 [2019] EWHC 503 (Admin).

78 *Mohidin*, paras 362–363.

79 *Walter v Alltools Ltd* (1944) 171 LT 371 at 372, HC per Lawrence LJ, followed in *Hook v Cunard Steamship Co Ltd* [1953] 1 All ER 1021 at 1042H.

80 [2019] EWHC 888 (QB).

81 *Childs v Lewis* (1924) 40 TLR 870; *Harnett v Bond* [1925] AC 689, HL.

82 [1999] 2 All ER 326, CA.

been lawfully arrested and detained in a police station, but where there had been a delay in carrying out a statutory review of the detention under PACE s40. The Court of Appeal found that the claimant in that case should be entitled to substantive (rather than nominal) damages for the time he was detained without the review taking place, even where it was clear that, if the review had been carried out, the detention would have continued.

17.85 However, the Supreme Court in the case of *R (Lumba) v Secretary of State for the Home Department*[83] decided that was the wrong approach. In that case the claimants were detained by the Secretary of State pending the making of deportation orders against them, by virtue of an unpublished policy. At first instance the court had found that if the secretary of state had applied her published policy the appellants would have been lawfully detained, in any event. The majority of the Supreme Court confirmed that false imprisonment was a trespassory tort that was actionable per se whether or not the claimant had suffered harm. However, as the appellants had suffered no loss as a result of the unlawful exercise of the power to detain (it was inevitable that they would anyway have been detained had the published policy been applied), and there was no justification for either exemplary or vindicatory damages, the appellants were entitled to no more than nominal damages (see para 17.60).

17.86 The correct approach therefore is to consider what is called the 'counterfactual', that is, what would have happened if the tort had not been committed. In a case like *Roberts* for example what would have happened is that the PACE review would have been carried out and the continued detention would have been lawful, and so only nominal damages should have been awarded. As explained in the police case of *Parker v Chief Constable of Essex*:[84]

> The principles set out in *Lumba* lead to an award of nominal damages if no loss has been suffered because the results of the counterfactual are the same as the events that happened. If and to the extent that they diverge (eg because a lawful arrest would not have occurred at the time but would have occurred later) the Court will have to decide on normal tortious compensatory principles whether and to what extent a substantial award of damages is merited for the divergence in outcome.

17.87 Thus, in *Parker* two officers fully aware of the reasonable grounds to suspect the claimant of criminal offences were delayed in attending to arrest him, and a third officer, who was not in receipt of the same information (and therefore did not have the necessary reasonable grounds) arrested the claimant instead. It was accepted that the arrest was unlawful, but argued by the police that the claimant would have been lawfully arrested if it had been realised that the actual arrest was unlawful, and therefore he was only entitled to nominal damages, as he had suffered no loss. In the Court of Appeal, Sir Brian Levenson P confirmed that the appellant would only be entitled to nominal damages:[85]

83 [2011] UKSC 12, [2012] 1 AC 245. *Lumba* has been considered and applied by the Supreme Court in *R (Kambadzi) v Secretary of State for the Home Department* [2011] UKSC 23, [2011] 1 WLR 1299 and by the Court of Appeal in *Bostridge v Oxleas NHS Foundation Trust* [2015] EWCA Civ 79.

84 [2018] EWCA Civ 2788, [2019] 1 WLR 2238 at para 63 (quoting para 51 of the High Court judgment).

85 2018] EWCA Civ 2788, [2019] 1 WLR 2238 at para 108.

It is thus clear that substantial damages will not be awarded if, had the defendant acted lawfully, the claimant would have been detained in any case, on the basis that no harm had ultimately been caused. That is not to encourage sloppy practice but, rather, to reflect actual loss. It also permits the distinction to be drawn between those who would have suffered the detriment in any event (in this case, false imprisonment) and those who would not.

17.88 The potential difficulty with this approach is that it can lead to lengthy arguments about what would have happened if the police had realised that they were acting unlawfully, and whether an arrest and detention would have been lawful. It would also seem to mean that the police are insulated from paying more than nominal damages where reviews of detention are not carried out (as in *Roberts*), or where for example a police officer has arrested a person without providing the person with the grounds for the arrest (as required by PACE s28(3)) where, if the grounds had been given, then the arrest would have been lawful. However, it is doubtful whether this will make much difference in some cases in relation to the level of damages awarded. In *Goswell v Commissioner of Police of the Metropolis*,[86] decided in 1998 (before the *Lumba* decision), where the initial arrest and detention were unlawful because the claimant was not provided with the grounds for arrest (contrary to PACE s28(3)) but these were provided twenty minutes later at the police station by the custody officer, an award of only £100 was made. In this case, the arrest would otherwise have been lawful and the claimant 'cannot realistically have been in doubt as to why he was being arrested'.

17.89 In *Lumba*, there was also consideration by some members of the Supreme Court as to whether, in circumstances where only nominal damages for false imprisonment would be awarded (and aggravated and exemplary damages were not appropriate), another form of compensation, described as 'vindicatory damages' could be awarded as recognition of the wrong done to the claimant (albeit that no loss had been found to have occurred). The Supreme Court recognised that vindicatory damages had been awarded by the Privy Council in cases involving jurisdictions with written constitutions, as a way of compensating for the breach of constitutional rights.[87] However, the majority of the Supreme Court did not think the award of vindicatory damages was appropriate and, giving the lead judgment, Lord Dyson doubted whether it would ever be appropriate to award such damages in a private law tort claim.[88] Even if vindicatory damages can be claimed, they are likely to be awarded on a modest scale. In *Lumba*, for example, Lady Hale would have awarded a sum of £500 to the claimants.[89]

17.90 In addition to basic damages and special damages, aggravated and exemplary damages may be claimed where appropriate in cases of false imprisonment by the police (see above, paras 17.18–17.59). In practice,

86 [1998] 4 WLUK 569, CA.

87 See, for example, *Attorney General of Trinidad and Tobago v Ramanoop* [2005] UKPC 15, [2006] 1 AC 328.

88 *Lumba*, paras 100–101.

89 *Lumba*, para 217.

aggravated damages and (especially) exemplary damages are quite unusual in false imprisonment cases, unless it can be shown that officers were aware they had no grounds to arrest someone but proceeded in any event. Thus in cases where an officer establishes that they had an 'honest suspicion' that a person had committed an offence, aggravated and exemplary damages are unlikely even if it is shown that there were no 'reasonable grounds' for the suspicion.

Damages for malicious prosecution

17.91 As has been discussed in chapter 8, to bring an action for malicious prosecution it must be shown that at least one of three types of loss has been suffered:

1) loss of reputation;
2) the risk of loss of 'life, limb or liberty';
3) financial loss.[90]

17.92 It is not clear whether, having met one of these conditions, *damages* are then limited to these types of loss. The modern approach seems to be that they constitute a hurdle but, once over it, damages are not limited to the three heads and may include such things as the humiliation and indignity of having to face a charge and the distress or anxiety felt while awaiting trial (although it could also be said that these are issues which could come within the 'loss of reputation' head).

17.93 In *Thompson and Hsu*,[91] Lord Woolf MR said:

> In the case of malicious prosecution the figure should start at about £2,000 and for prosecution continuing for as long as two years, the case being taken to the Crown Court, an award of about £10,000 could be appropriate. If a malicious prosecution results in a conviction which is only set aside on appeal this will justify a larger award to reflect the longer period during which the plaintiff has been in peril and has been caused distress.

17.94 The 'starting point' of £2,000 (set in 1997) now needs to be increased to take into account inflation. The starting point also needs to be increased or reduced to take into account the personal features of the claimant. For example, the figure for a claimant with a long criminal record being prosecuted for an offence may not be the same as a claimant with no previous convictions prosecuted for the same offence, and this might be based on the fact that such a person has less of a reputation to lose. It is also true, though, that a person with previous convictions is more likely to be successfully prosecuted and might face a longer prison sentence. Thus in *Manley v Commissioner of Police of the Metropolis*[92] a man with previous convictions was prosecuted for threatening to kill a police officer and Waller LJ said that:[93]

> . . . albeit the reputation of a man convicted of a very serious offence of violence (as here) may not suffer greatly, he is entitled to be compensated for

90 See, for example, *Gregory v Portsmouth City Council* [2000] 1 AC 419, HL.
91 [1998] QB 498, [1997] 2 All ER 762 at guidance number (6).
92 [2006] EWCA Civ 879.
93 [2006] EWCA Civ 879 at para 27.

the fact that (a) there is greater risk of the malicious prosecution succeeding and (b) a risk that he will get a longer prison sentence as a result of it succeeding, all of which will cause stress and anxiety.

17.95 In *Rees v Commissioner of Police of the Metropolis*[94] where the claimants were wrongly charged with murder, the High Court said that 'even a convicted criminal is bound to suffer some added notoriety and stigma from such an accusation'.[95] The court also commented at that:[96]

> The impact of imprisonment (both initial and long-term) is also less for those who are already experienced in custody. Accordingly, I will reduce each of these elements of the award because the claimants were all previously convicted of offences attracting custodial terms, but in this case, on balance the reduction for the distress element of the basic award and the aggravated damages will be modest because of the gravity of the charge.
>
> I add that those with previous criminal histories are also more likely to be targeted for malpractice by police officers in the first place although this feature fits more properly into the consideration of exemplary damages.

17.96 The amount of the basic award can also be affected by factors such as the length of the proceedings; whether the prosecution involved a trial or was discontinued at an earlier stage; whether the claimant gave evidence at a trial; the number of court hearings the claimant had to attend; and the seriousness of the offence charged. In *Rees* the court declined to reduce the award 'substantially' on the basis that there had been no trial, noting that there had been a lengthy 'voir dire', and the prosecution had continued for months.[97] Awards of £27,000 for each claimant were made on the particular facts of the case involving a lengthy prosecution for murder, not including damages for loss of liberty, but incorporating a ten per cent reduction for previous criminality.

17.97 However, it seems that the claimant's behaviour prior to arrest should not be taken into account when considering the level of basic damages (as opposed to aggravated or exemplary damages (see above, paras 17.18–17.59) for malicious prosecution. This approach is illustrated by *Clark v Chief Constable of Cleveland*[98] where the Court of Appeal increased an award of basic damages from £500 to £2,000 on the ground that the figure should not be reduced to take into account the claimant's aggressive behaviour towards officers immediately prior to the events that they falsified for the prosecution, since the former could not begin to justify the officers' subsequent reprehensible conduct.

17.98 *Clark* (a 1999 case) also provides an insight into the quantum that the Court of Appeal determined as appropriate for the basic award for a fairly standard malicious prosecution. The court held that if the claimant had been a man of good character a figure of £4,000 – £5,000 would have been appropriate for criminal proceedings in the magistrates' court involving a public order charge,[99] where the claimant was required to attend court on six occasions including trial and the whole proceedings had lasted for just

94 [2019] EWHC 2339 (QB).
95 [2019] EWHC 2339 (QB) at para 18.
96 [2019] EWHC 2339 (QB) at paras 20–21.
97 [2019] EWHC 2339 (QB) at para 22.
98 (1999) *Times* 13 May.
99 Public Order Act 1986 s4.

under a year. This figure was then reduced to £2,000 to reflect the claimant's previous convictions.

17.99 False imprisonment cases involving the police tend to involve detention over a maximum of a few days before a person is released or brought before a court (after which time any continued detention will be authorised by the court and will not be the responsibility of the police). In relation to 'loss of liberty' caused by malicious prosecution, difficulties can occur where there has been detention over a long period of time (for instance, where a person has been held on remand, or after conviction) as a result of the malicious prosecution. In *Rees*, the judge commented that:[100]

> . . . where loss of liberty takes place alongside a malicious prosecution there should be separately identified damages. However, it is necessary to avoid double counting. It is also accepted practice to provide a global figure for periods in custody rather than a multiple of a daily rate or tariff. A tapering effect has also been acknowledged so that the longer liberty is lost for the less incremental harm is recognised: *R v Governor of HMP Brockhill ex parte Evans* [1999] QB 1043 at 1060.

17.100 There is a growing case-law in relation to the levels of quantum to be paid for longer periods when someone has been wrongly held in detention. The two areas which have featured most often are cases involving compensation for miscarriages of justice and, more frequently, cases involving damages for false imprisonment for unlawful immigration detention.

17.101 Immigration detention cases often arise where a person has been detained either in breach of a Home Office policy, or where the policy itself has been deemed to be unlawful. The applicability to police cases should be treated with some caution however. In *Rees* the Court of Appeal upheld the first instance judge taking a cautious approach to such cases, stating:[101]

> . . . in such cases the awards tend not to be broken down into constituent parts of distress etc. on the one hand and loss of liberty on the other hand. Further, the context can be very different. Such cases also may involve, amongst other things, the detainee being detained on an open-ended basis, in circumstances of having the particular stress of potentially facing forced return to a country where he fears persecution.

17.102 In *Rees* (a case where two of the claimants had been detained awaiting trial on murder charges for 682 days each), at first instance, the judge said that she did not find immigration detention awards 'ideal comparators' but 'some have provided a general, more or less contemporary check to the claims made and the defendant's counter submissions'.[102] A case which the judge specifically referred to was the 2016 case of *AXD v Home Office*[103] in which, she said:[104]

> . . . a man with previous convictions was unlawfully detained for nearly two years (after a period of lawful detention) and was subjected to physical and verbal abuse on the grounds of sexual orientation. He feared being returned

100 [2019] EWHC 2339 (QB) at para 24.
101 [2019] EWHC 2339 (QB) at para 29.
102 [2019] EWHC 2339 (QB) at para 28.
103 [2016] EWHC 1617 (QB).
104 [2019] EWHC 2339 (QB) at para 28.

to Somalia to persecution. An award of £80,000 recognised all of those features.

17.103 Further, in the case of *R (MK (Algeria)) v Secretary of State for the Home Department*[105] Laws LJ explained:

> There are three general principles which should be born in mind: 1) the assessment of damages should be sensitive to the facts and the particular case and the degree of harm suffered by the particular claimant ... 2) Damages should not be assessed mechanistically as by fixing a rigid figure to be awarded for each day of incarceration ... A global approach should be taken ... 3) While obviously the gravity of a false imprisonment is worsened by its length the amount broadly attributable to the increasing passage of time should be tapered or placed on a reducing scale.

17.104 In *MK* (a 2010 case), the claimant was removed from his home in the presence of his family and unlawfully detained for 24 days, during which time removal directions were set, in circumstances where it appeared that the Home Secretary knew that the detention was unlawful. The Court of Appeal increased the £8,500 awarded as basic damages to £12,500 (there was also an aggravated damages award of £5,000).

17.105 In relation to miscarriage of justice compensation claims, the judge in *Rees* summarised the position stating that the largest award was:[106]

> ... in *O'Brien and others v Independent Assessor* [2003] EWHC 855 (Admin), [2004] EWCA Civ 103 after the claimants had served almost 18 years in prison following wrongful convictions for murder. The awards of £140,000 (2019 equivalent £241,450) were reduced by a quarter or so to reflect their criminality.

The judge in *Rees* also thought it was helpful to have a cross-check with personal injury awards and in this case said:[107]

> ... that it is necessary to have regard, in respect of the basic and aggravated award, to the sort of sums awarded currently, for serious physical and psychiatric injury. I have taken into account the guidance issued by the Judicial College. The most helpful is the bracket for awards for moderately severe PTSD set at £20,000 to £50,000. No cross check is relevant to the exemplary damages award.

The judge did not explain why this was the appropriate comparator in this case, but given the awards for 682 days of £60,000 the judge presumably equated the damage done to the claimants as broadly equivalent to suffering from a high level of moderately severe PTSD.

17.106 The court also considered that 'the degree of loss of liberty must have some impact on the degree of damage in an individual case' which was relevant where the claimants had spent some time after conviction in a category A prison 'leading to a diminution in the residual liberty of the claimants'.[108] The court also took into account restrictive bail conditions during the time that the claimants had been on bail prior to conviction.

105 [2010] EWCA Civ 980 at para 8.
106 [2019] EWHC 2339 (QB) at para 29.
107 [2019] EWHC 2339 (QB) at para 30.
108 [2019] EWHC 2339 (QB) at para 25; and see *Karagozlu v Commissioner of Police of the Metropolis* [2006] EWCA Civ 1691, [2007] 1 WLR 1881.

Damages for misfeasance in a public office

17.107 As discussed in chapter 8 above, a successful claim for misfeasance in public office involves showing that a claimant has suffered 'damage' in the sense of financial loss, loss of liberty or a further restriction on liberty while detained,[109] physical or psychiatric injury or, possibly, loss of reputation. It is not enough to show that there has a breach of a so-called fundamental or constitutional right to establish the tort.[110]

17.108 Otherwise, if the claimant establishes that the misconduct led to one or more of the forms of harm referred to above, then the text above relating to other torts such as false imprisonment and malicious prosecution will give a guide to the level of damages which could be awarded. As was said by the Court of Appeal in *Karagozlu v Commissioner of Police of the Metropolis*[111] while discussing the *Thompson and Hsu* case:

> . . . we can see no reason in principle to hold that what is damage for the purposes of malicious prosecution is not damage for the purposes of misfeasance.

17.109 As is also considered in chapter 8, the level of damages has yet to be resolved by authority in circumstances where the misfeasance relates to the fabrication or other dishonest manipulation of evidence in support of a prosecution. If a claim in malicious prosecution cannot succeed because there is other evidence to support the criminal proceedings so that a lack of reasonable and probable cause cannot be proved, it is doubtful that the claimant would recover basic damages analogous to those awarded for malicious prosecution. However, any conduct involving misfeasance in a public office may well lead to a substantial award of aggravated and/or exemplary damages, because of the degree of wrongdoing necessarily involved in establishing liability, and any injury to feelings arising out of the humiliating and / or oppressive manner of the treatment, and the guidance in *Thompson and Hsu* and subsequent cases will be useful in considering the levels of such awards.

Damages for seizure of goods

17.110 Wrongful interference with goods is discussed in chapter 9. If only damages are sought (and not the return of the property from the police), at least the value of the goods at the time they were seized can be expected. However, it can sometimes be difficult to prove the value of items, unless they have an easily ascertainable worth, such as a motor car. If the claimant has not kept receipts relating to the items, efforts should be made to find out their likely purchase price; failing that the claimant will have to provide realistic estimates of value. Whether or not the return of the item seized is sought, damages can be awarded for loss of use during the time it was retained. Depending on the nature of the item, this may have occasioned the claimant financial loss and/or inconvenience. Provided the claimant has acted reasonably, costs of hiring a replacement can be recovered.

109 [2007] 1 WLR 1881 at para 34.

110 *Watkins v Secretary of State for the Home Department* [2006] UKHL 17, [2006] 2 AC 395.

111 [2006] EWCA Civ 1691, [2007] 1 WLR 1881.

17.111 If the action is in trespass to goods, the claimant may be entitled to at least nominal damages,[112] even if s/he cannot show any real loss[113] and, in appropriate cases, there may also be an award of aggravated and exemplary damages.[114] If the action is in conversion, the claim will fail if actual loss cannot be shown.

Compensation for damage to goods

17.112 If the police damage or destroy belongings – for example, while searching a home – there may be a claim for damages. Technically, the claim might be for 'trespass to goods' or 'negligence'.

17.113 If the police damage goods, their owner is entitled to the cost of repair.[115] If the goods are destroyed or damaged beyond repair, or if it would be uneconomic to repair them, then their owner is entitled to the value of their replacement. In addition to damages for repair or replacement, a claim can also be made for the loss of the use of an article – eg if a television is damaged, compensation for the loss of enjoyment while it was repaired or replaced can be claimed.

17.114 If the claim is for trespass to goods, liability may be established even if no loss or damage in the traditional sense is shown. In such circumstances, a claimant may still be able to recover for distress and/or obtain an award of aggravated and/or exemplary damages. However, if the claim was brought as a negligence action, the claim would fail if no damage was shown.

Damages for trespass to land

17.115 Trespass to land is also discussed in chapter 9. If a claimant's land is damaged by the police, the claimant is usually entitled to recover only the reduction in the value of the land as a result of the damage, and it will be rare that they will be able to successfully claim the cost of restoration or rebuilding.[116]

17.116 As with false imprisonment and assault, a person can sue for trespass to land without having to show any damage in the sense of financial or physical loss. The claimant can recover for distress, anxiety and inconvenience caused by the intrusion upon their home or other property. The manner and violence the police use to enter the property is relevant to the level of damages,[117] and may justify awards of aggravated or exemplary damages. In *R v Reading Justices ex p South West Meats Ltd*[118] exemplary damages of £22,000 were awarded in addition to compensatory damages of £3,000 for a trespass to land and goods following the unlawful exercise of a search warrant. This was a relatively unusual and serious case of misconduct, and should not be treated as a 'standard'. Special damages are payable to compensate for anything broken or damaged.

112 See full discussion in chapter 9.
113 *William Leitch & Co v Leydon* [1931] AC 90 at 106, HL.
114 *Sears v Lyons* (1818) 2 Stark 317; *Rookes v Barnard* [1964] AC 1129, HL.
115 *The Bernina* (1886) 55 LT 781.
116 *Ward v Cannock Chase DC* [1985] 3 All ER 537, ChD.
117 *Huxley v Berg* (1815) 1 Stark 98.
118 [1991] 11 WLUK 400, [1992] Crim LR 672, *Independent*,13 December 1991, QBD.

17.117 A case which provides a good example of the damages that may be expected for trespass where there have been procedural errors in executing the warrant is *Fisher v Chief Constable of Cumbria Police*[119] which involved the search of uninhabited commercial premises. This was a decision of the Court of Appeal delivered a few months after the *Thompson and Hsu* judgment, discussed above, and included Lord Woolf MR as part of the court. Roch LJ explained the background as follows:

> The act of trespass arose because the police did not leave a copy of the search warrant on the premises. That omission was due to mere forgetfulness. But for that inadvertent omission there would have been no trespass.

17.118 The judge in *Fisher* summarised the principles involved thus:

> If a [claimant] proves a trespass to his land, he is entitled to recover nominal damages, even if he has not suffered any actual loss. If the trespass has caused the [claimant] actual damage, he is entitled to receive such an amount as will compensate him for his loss. Where the defendant has made use of the [claimant's] land the [claimant] is entitled to receive by way of damages such a sum as should reasonably be paid for that use.

17.119 Applying these principles, Roch LJ in *Fisher* said:

> Here the trespass occurred because of mere forgetfulness by [an officer]. That was a mitigating feature . . . [T]he search was conducted with reasonable care so as to reveal drugs but not to cause unnecessary damage. That was another mitigating feature. The defendant had offered to pay for the cost of repairing the door into the premises. That was a further mitigating feature. The trespass lasted approximately two hours and had been concluded by the time the plaintiffs arrived at their shop that morning.
>
> The plaintiffs had to be compensated for this intrusion into their property, carrying with it, as it did the suggestion that they or one of them was somehow linked with illegal dealing in controlled drugs. There was in addition the physical disturbance of their property and the disruption and inconvenience of having to restore the contents of their property to their former order and the need to see that the use of dogs in the search had not compromised the hygiene of their premises.

17.120 Taking the guidelines in *Thompson and Hsu* into account in relation to other torts, the Court of Appeal in *Fisher* found that the proper bracket for general damages for the trespass to the claimants' premises in this case was one starting at £500 with a ceiling of £1,500. These figures would need to be updated to take into account inflation. This is a useful starting point for claimants in trespass to land cases. Clearly, if a case is more than a wrongful entry case and there is a prolonged and intrusive search of the claimant's home when the claim is present then the bracket would need to be much higher than this.

Damages under the Human Rights Act 1998

17.121 Claims under the HRA 1998 have been referred to in a number of cases in chapters 6–12 above. This section summarises the general principles applicable to the award and assessment of damages under the HRA 1998.

119 [1997] EWCA Civ 2232, [1997] 7 WLUK 603.

Some examples are also given of awards made in respect of those Articles most relevant to claims concerning the police.

Remedies 'necessary to afford just satisfaction'

17.122 By HRA 1998 s8(1), the court is empowered to 'grant such relief or remedy' as it considers 'just and appropriate'. That can include a declaration as to the fact of the claimant's rights having been violated. A declaration may be important as it provides 'a formal, reasoned, vindication of a person's legal rights and an acknowledgment in a public forum that they have been wronged' and is 'an integral part of the democratic process whereby a public body can be called to account'.[120]

17.123 The relief granted may also include damages, although there is no automatic entitlement. By HRA 1998 s8(3) no award of damages should be made unless, taking account of all the circumstances of the case, including any other relief granted, the court is 'satisfied that the award is necessary to afford just satisfaction to the person in whose favour it is made'.

17.124 It has been observed that the HRA 1998 is not primarily a tort statute and that the remedy of damages generally plays a less prominent role in actions based on breaches of the rights scheduled to the Act. The concern of a claim will often be to bring the infringement to an end and the question of compensation can be of secondary importance, if any.[121] As expressed in *Van Colle v Chief Constable of Hertfordshire*:[122]

> Where civil actions are designed essentially to compensate claimants for their losses, Convention claims are intended rather to uphold minimum human rights standards and to vindicate those rights.

17.125 However, damages can nonetheless be a vital part of affording an effective remedy and will be the primary objective of many claims. That can also be an important function of the HRA 1998, and the amount of compensation should adequately reflect the harm caused. Indeed, as Leggatt J observed in *Alseran v Ministry of Defence*, where harm has been suffered, to 'decline to award damages, or to make an award which affords only partial reparation, would be to deny the claimant an effective remedy'.[123]

17.126 Where the claimant has been sufficiently compensated in respect of the same harm in a parallel common law claim there will generally be no basis to make a further award under the HRA 1998.[124]

120 *D v Commissioner of Police of the Metropolis* [2014] EWHC 2493 (QB) at para 18, [2015] 1 WLR 1833 at 1842F.

121 See *R (Greenfield) v Secretary of State for the Home Department* [2005] UKHL 14, [2005] 1 WLR 673 at para 9; and, more recently, *DSD v Commissioner of Police of the Metropolis* [2018] UKSC 11 at paras 64–65.

122 [2008] UKHL 50, [2009] AC 225 at para 138.

123 [2017] EWHC 3289 (QB), [2019] QB 1251 at para 933.

124 *Dobson v Thames Water Utilities Ltd* [2009] EWCA Civ 28, [2009] 3 All ER 319.

Relevance of awards made by the European Court of Human Rights

17.127 HRA 1998 s8(4) requires the domestic courts in assessing the amount of damages to 'take into account the principles applied' by the European Court of Human Rights (ECtHR). Lord Bingham described in *Greenfield*'s case that domestic courts are not bound by the ECtHR but 'should not aim to be significantly more or less generous'.[125]

17.128 However, beyond some very general and consistently applied principles, the ECtHR rarely explains the basis upon which it has arrived at the sum awarded, generally referring instead to what it considers to be equitable in the particular case. In substance, that means that the ECtHR will assess damages at an amount judged by the court to be fair in the individual case, rather than precisely calculated.

17.129 Beyond the general principles considered below, the scope for discerning significant guidance from ECtHR as to the amount of damages appropriate in any particular case has its limitations. As Leggatt J observed in *Alseran*, the ECtHR 'hardly ever refers to amounts which it has awarded previously in other cases' and when assessing awards of non-pecuniary damages 'generally gives little or no explanation of how it has arrived at a particular figure'.[126] In the absence of such explanation, it is only possible to seek to extrapolate a principled approach from contrasting amounts in different cases and drawing inferences as to the factors the court is likely to have considered relevant. However, even that, in the view of Leggatt J, in the *Alseran* case 'assumes that there is a latent order or logic underlying awards' made by the ECtHR which is not explained, but there is 'good reason to think that it is not'.[127]

17.130 Similarly, in *Sturnham*'s case, Lord Carnwath JSC observed that the judges of the ECtHR no doubt seek to achieve a degree of internal consistency in the level of awards in different cases, but ultimately do not intend decisions to have precedential effect.[128] For Leggatt J, the awards made by the ECtHR can be little more than a 'cross-check' to ensure that damages awarded would not be perceived by the ECtHR as inadequate or as excessive.[129]

17.131 The task of seeking to infer from what is considered equitable in a case by the ECtHR to what may be necessary to afford just satisfaction in a domestic case is made more challenging by the fact that the ECtHR deals with cases from 47 countries and takes into account local economic circumstances. The relative value of an amount of euros may vary considerably across the different states, and that needs to be taken into account, as well as inflation.[130] Awards made by the ECtHR to applicants from countries where

125 *R (Greenfield) v Secretary of State for the Home Department* [2005] UKHL 14, [2005] 1 WLR 673 at para 19.

126 [2017] EWHC 3289 (QB), [2019] QB 1251 at 920.

127 [2017] EWHC 3289 (QB), [2019] QB 1251 at 921.

128 *R (Sturnham) v The Parole Board of England and Wales and another (No 2)* [2013] UKSC 47, [2013] 2 AC 254 at para 105.

129 [2017] EWHC 3289 (QB), [2019] QB 1251 at 923.

130 *D v Commissioner of Police of the Metropolis* [2015] EWHC 493 (QB), [2015] 1 WLR 1833 at paras 33–35; and *Alseran v Ministry of Defence* [2017] EWHC 3289 (QB), [2019] QB 1251 at para 919.

the cost of living is relatively low tend to be low by comparison with awards to applicants from countries where the cost of living is much higher.[131]

17.132 It has also been acknowledged that as the body of domestic case-law develops, with reference to ECtHR principles, the court can increasingly refer to and rely upon domestic rather than ECtHR precedent.[132]

The relevance of causation in assessing damages

17.133 As above, under the HRA 1998 the court must first decide whether it is necessary to award damages in order to afford the claimant just satisfaction. In assessing the amount of damages the general approach taken by the ECtHR is one of 'restitutio ad integrum'. That is, the aim is to restore the claimant to the position they would have been in if they had not suffered the violation of their right of which complaint is made.[133]

17.134 It follows that in order for the court to award damages, there must generally be a causal link between the violation of the right and the harm suffered by the claimant for which damages are sought. In *Kingsley v UK* the ECtHR explained:[134]

> . . . it is well established that the principle underlying the provision of just satisfaction . . . is that the applicant should as far as possible be put in the position he would have enjoyed had the proceedings complied with the Convention's requirements . . . The Court will award financial compensation under Article 41 only where it is satisfied that the loss or damage complained of was actually caused by the violation it has found . . . since the State cannot be required to pay damages in respect of losses for which it is not responsible.

17.135 Where there is no causal link with demonstrable harm, it may be that no damages are awarded. In Article 6 cases, which relate to the right to a fair trail, for example, it is not infrequently the case that it cannot be shown that the outcome of the trial would have been different, and no damages will be awarded.[135]

17.136 Precisely what causative link is required is less straightforward. The ECtHR applies a fairly flexible and contextual approach as equity demands in the particular case. As observed by Green J in *D v Commissioner of Police of the Metropolis*, the rules are 'not however applied in any absolute or inflexible manner and even where the alleged harm seems upon the face of the facts set out in the judgment remote or speculative the Court sometimes considers it nonetheless "equitable" to make an award'.[136]

17.137 Generally, however, a compelling case for significant damages requires some causative link. It will generally be sufficient to establish that the claimant has lost a 'real prospect' or 'substantial chance' of a difference outcome.[137] That may also be more relevant to the assessment of damages

131 *Sturnham*'s case [2013] UKSC 47, [2013] 2 AC 254 at para 38.

132 For example, see *Sturnham* [2013] UKSC 47, [2013] 2 AC 254 at para 29.

133 *Anufrijeva v Southwark LBC* [2003] EWCA Civ 1406, [2004] 2 WLR 603.

134 (2002) 35 EHRR 10 at para 40, ECtHR.

135 *Greenfield*'s case [2005] UKHL 14, [2005] 1 WLR 673 at para 8.

136 [2014] EWHC 2493 (QB) at para 21, [2015] 1 WLR 1833 at 1843E.

137 *Van Colle v Chief Constable of the Hertfordshire Police* [2008] UKHL 50, [2009] 1 AC 225 at para 138.

rather than liability. In *Sarjantson v Chief Constable of Humberside* the Court of Appeal considered in the context of an Article 2 claim that a failure to respond promptly to an emergency call should be judged against what was known at the time, and that in hindsight a prompt response would not have made a difference was irrelevant to liability but might mean there was no right to damages.[138]

17.138 In the context of pecuniary losses, the ECtHR adopts what appears to be a slightly more stringent approach, and looks to see whether a clear causal link has been established (considered further below at para 17.151).[139]

Non pecuniary damages

17.139 The ECtHR distinguishes between pecuniary and non-pecuniary damages, the former being harm which can be quantified in monetary terms.

17.140 Non-pecuniary damages are akin to general damages at common law, although the scope of injury which may fall within non-pecuniary damages for European Convention on Human Rights (ECHR) purposes is broad. Awards are not confined to psychiatric injury and damages may be awarded for injury to feeling variously described by the ECtHR as distress; anxiety; frustration; feelings of injustice or humiliation; prolonged uncertainty, disruption to life or powerlessness.[140] For example, in *Vistins v Latvia* the award made by the Grand Chamber was adjusted to reflect the 'powerlessness and frustration' felt by a land-owner dispossessed of his property.[141]

17.141 The ECtHR certainly does not require medical evidence in order to make such an award and is often prepared to simply infer injury to feelings (or similar) from the fact of the violation. However, medical evidence of physical or psychiatric injury may warrant a higher award.

The relevance of domestic scales for the assessment of damages

17.142 A question has arisen in a number of cases as to the extent to which domestic courts, in assessing the appropriate sum of non-pecuniary damages, should look to scales used in the assessment of damages in domestic tort law. In *Greenfield*'s case, the House of Lords rejected a submission that in awarding damages under the HRA 1998 the English courts should apply domestic scales of damages.[142] However, in *Alseran* Leggatt J considered that it does not follow that it is *never* relevant to consider levels of damages awarded in domestic law and, to the contrary, it was considered 'clear that in certain kinds of case it is not merely relevant but important to do so'.[143] He observed that certain HRA 1998 claims such as, for example, a claim for violation of Article 6 would not give rise to a

138 [2013] EWCA Civ 1252, [2014] QB 411.

139 See below under 'pecuniary losses'.

140 *Alseran and others v Ministry of Defence* [2017] EWHC 3289 (QB), [2019] QB 1251 at para 912.

141 (2012) 58 EHRR 107, ECtHR.

142 [2005] 1 WLR 673 at para 18.

143 [2017] EWHC 3289 (QB), [2019] QB 1251 at para 930.

claim in English law. However, claims for violations of Articles 3 and 5 often will. He considered that:[144]

> In such cases the same basic right – to bodily integrity or to liberty – is protected both by the law of tort and by the Human Rights Act. There is a powerful argument of principle that where, in such cases, a victim is being compensated under section 8 of the Human Rights Act for the defendant's unlawful act, he or she should receive similar compensation for the harm suffered to that which would be awarded on a parallel claim in tort. To award less compensation would be to treat the breach of a fundamental human right guaranteed by the Convention as less serious than breach of the equivalent right protected by the common law of tort. Unless some good reason is shown for taking a different approach, the amount of compensation awarded for the same injury caused by the same wrongful conduct should in principle be the same in each case. This principle seems to me to carry particular weight in the case of non-pecuniary damage for which any amount awarded in compensation can only be symbolic of the value which our society attributes to harm of the relevant kind.

17.143 Leggatt J went on to say that, in fact:[145]

> In a case where the unlawful act for which damages may be awarded under section 8 is also a tort, an English court would in my view be failing in its duty if it did not have regard to the level of damages which would be awarded as compensation in tort and ask whether it is necessary to award a similar sum to afford just satisfaction to the claimant or whether there is a good and sufficient reason which makes it just and appropriate to award a different sum.

17.144 Leggatt J's advocated approach of looking to domestic scales of damages, at least in respect of personal injury of a sort which may be compensated in tort, is yet to be endorsed by the higher courts, but seems to provide a clearer and more principled approach to the assessment of damages. It is also consistent with the symbiotic relationship between domestic and ECtHR approach to assessing damages, in which the ECtHR also looks for guidance in the approach in domestic cases. *Z v UK* is an example of a case in which sizeable awards were made by the ECtHR for psychiatric injury and consequential pecuniary losses such as loss of earnings and cost of medical treatment very largely based on claims calculated as they would be in a negligence claim.[146]

17.145 It follows, therefore, that in cases of personal injury reference can be made to domestic precedents in tort and scales such as the Judicial College Guidelines (referred to above at para 17.15).

The relevance of the conduct of the state

17.146 Aggravated and exemplary damages are not awarded under the HRA 1998, but the state's conduct may be taken into account in assessing the sum necessary to afford just satisfaction to the claimant. Accordingly, the amount of damages may be increased to reflect the seriousness and manner of the violation, in much the same way as aggravated and exem-

144 [2017] EWHC 3289 (QB), [2019] QB 1251 at para 931.
145 [2017] EWHC 3289 (QB), [2019] QB 1251 at para 932.
146 [2001] 2 FLR 612, ECtHR.

plary damages.[147] This is sometimes described as 'moral injury'. As stated by the Grand Chamber in *Varnava v Turkey*, in some situations [148]

> . . . the impact of the violation may be regarded as being of a nature and degree as to have impinged so significantly on the moral well-being of the applicant as to require something further.

Similarly, in *Al-Jedda v UK*, the Grand Chamber of the ECtHR described that its awards of non-pecuniary damage:[149]

> . . . serve to give recognition to the fact that moral damage occurred as a result of a breach of a fundamental human right and reflect in the broadest of terms the severity of the damage.

In *Assenov v Bulgaria* the ECtHR in determining the appropriate amount of non-pecuniary damages took into account the 'gravity and number of violations'.[150]

17.147 However, it remains the case that the purpose of the award of damages is to compensate the claimant for the harm suffered rather than to punish the state. As explained in *Varnava* the awards seek to reflect the severity of the damages, 'are not, nor should they be, intended to give financial comfort or sympathetic enrichment at the expense of the contracting party concerned'.[151]

17.148 That the responsible officers have faced misconduct proceedings is not a reason to reduce the amount of damages.[152]

The relevance of the conduct of the claimant

17.149 The behaviour of the claimant may also be taken into account in deciding what is equitable and necessary to afford just satisfaction, and may even lead the court to decline to make an award at all.

17.150 In *McCann v UK* the killing of IRA gunmen in Gibraltar by British soldiers involved a breach of Article 2, but the ECtHR declined to make any award of damage at all 'having regard to the fact that the three terrorist suspects who were killed had been intending to plant a bomb in Gibraltar'.[153] In *Neville v Commissioner of Police of the Metropolis* a claim related to a death during police restraint failed on its facts, but the judge indicated that, if successful, damages would have been reduced by half to reflect the claimant's own contribution by taking cocaine and entering into a self-induced state of psychosis.[154]

147 *Anufrijeva v Southwark LBC* [2003] EWCA Civ 1406, [2004] QB 1124 at para 68; and *Alseran and others v Ministry of Defence* [2017] EWHC 3289 (QB), [2019] QB 1251 at 915.

148 Reports of Judgments and Decisions 2009-V, p13 at para 224.

149 (2011) 53 EHRR 789 at 114, ECtHR.

150 (1998) 28 EHRR 652 at 175, ECtHR.

151 Reports of Judgments and Decisions 2009-V, p13 at para 224.

152 *Van Colle*'s case [2007] EWCA Civ 325, [2007] 1 WLR 1821 at para 124.

153 (1995) 21 EHRR 97 at para 219, ECtHR.

154 [2018] EWHC 20 (QB).

Pecuniary damages

17.151 Where it is shown that the violation has caused pecuniary damage (that is, financial loss) to the applicant, the court will normally award the full amount.

17.152 In contrast to pecuniary damages, the court tends to impose a more onerous approach to causation. In *Z v UK* the court considered Article 3 claims brought in respect of a sibling group who had suffered horrific familial abuse. They claimed, among other things, that the long-term psychiatric injury would impact upon their ability to enter gainful employment, and accordingly that they had suffered a loss of future earnings. The ECtHR explained:[155]

> As regards the applicants' claims for pecuniary loss, the Court's case-law establishes that there must be a clear causal connection between the damage claimed by the applicant and the violation of the Convention and that this may, in the appropriate case, include compensation in respect of loss of earnings . . .

17.153 In *Alseran and others v Ministry of Defence* Leggatt J surveyed the relevant case-law as to damages pursuant to the HRA 1998 and elicited a number of principles, one of which was that 'before the court will award financial compensation, a clear causal link must be established between the damage claimed and a violation found by the court'.[156]

17.154 However, provided that a clear causal connection is established between the violation and the loss, that there may be significant uncertainties in quantifying the *amount* of that loss does not preclude an award. The ECtHR has made clear that, provided a causal link can be established, an award may be made 'notwithstanding the large number of imponderables involved in the assessment of future losses', although in general the greater the lapse of time involved the more uncertain the link becomes between the breach and the damages.[157]

Examples of awards made under the Human Rights Act 1998

17.155 It is beyond the scope of this chapter to give a comprehensive account of awards that have been made in relation to the various rights protected by the HRA 1998. The circumstances in which HRA 1998 claims may arise against the police are broad. However, some key examples are given in relation to Articles 2, 3, 4 and 8. These Articles are discussed in depth in chapter 7 at paras 7.109–7.193. Article 8 is also covered in chapters 9 and 11. Damages in respect of unlawful detention will ordinarily either be pursued at common law and/or be assessed with reference to *Thompson and Hsu* (addressed above) rather than Article 5.

155 (2002) 34 EHRR 3 at para 119, ECtHR.
156 [2017] EWHC 3289 (QB), [2019] QB 1251 at para 910.
157 *Z v UK* (2002) 34 EHRR 3 at para 120, ECtHR.

Article 2

17.156 One factor relevant to the assessment of damages will likely be whether the underlying violation is of the negative obligation not to take life, or of positive obligations to protect life and/or to investigate the circumstances of the death (see paras 7.112–7.148). Cases of the state itself taking life are likely to be considered particularly seriousness given the fundamental nature of the right to life.

17.157 As described in chapter 7, Article 2 claims are generally brought by family members as 'indirect victims' of the violation. In *Rabone v Pennine Care NHS Trust* the Supreme Court noted that the range of awards by the ECtHR had been between £5,000 and £6,000.[158] The court set out key factors in considering awards for emotional distress, anguish and grief caused by violations of Article 2:[159]

> One would expect the court to have regard to the closeness of the family link between the victim and the deceased, the nature of the breach and the seriousness of the non-pecuniary damage that the victim has suffered. Factors which will tend to place the amount of the award towards the upper end of the range are the existence of a particularly close family tie between the victim and the deceased; the fact that the breach is especially egregious; and the fact that the circumstances of the death and the authority's response to it have been particularly distressing to the victims. Conversely, factors which will tend to place the award towards the lower end of the range are the weakness of the family ties, the fact that the breach is towards the lower end of the scale of gravity and the fact that the circumstances of the death have not caused the utmost distress.

17.158 Domestic awards for violations of Article 2 have been particularly modest. In *Rabone* itself the Supreme Court considered that the award of £5,000 was low, but was not under appeal. In *Savage v South Essex Partnership NHS Trust* the award (in 2010) in respect of a failure to protect a mental health patient from a known risk of suicide was £10,000. In *Van Colle v Chief Constable of Hertfordshire*[160] the award in respect of a failure by police to take preventative measures in respect of a known threat to the life of a prosecution witness attracted a combined award of £25,000. The component parts identified by the Court of Appeal were £10,000 to the estate and £7,500 to each parent, although the reasoning would indicate that the court was seeking to arrive at an overall amount consistent with awards made by the ECtHR (such as the award of £20,000 in *Edwards v UK*[161]). More recently, in *Neville v Commissioner of Police of the Metropolis* the court indicated, obiter, and in respect of a death under police restraint, that it would have awarded £20,000, albeit reduced by half to reflect the contribution made by the claimant to the circumstances of his death.[162]

17.159 Recent ECtHR cases in respect of failures to protect an individual from a real and immediate risk to life have tended to attract slightly higher

158 [2012] UKSC 2, [2012] 2 AC 72 at para 85, referring to and relying upon the survey of cases by Mackay J in *Savage (No 2)* [2010] EWHC 865 (QB).

159 [2012] UKSC 2, [2012] 2 AC 72 at para 85.

160 [2007] EWCA Civ 325, [2007] 1 WLR 1821.

161 (2002) 35 EHRR 487, ECtHR.

162 [2018] EWHC 20 (QB).

awards. Examples are *Laptev v Russia*[163] and *Trapeznikova v Russia*[164] in which sums of EUR23,000 and EUR26,000 respectively were made in respect of suicides of prisoners. Neither case had particularly exceptional aggravating factors.

17.160 Cases where there has been egregious conduct should attract a higher award. In *Semache v France,* the deceased had died after being restrained by the police and, on arrival at the police station, was left lying in his own vomit for 30 minutes before medical attention was sought. The ECtHR held that the police had a heightened obligation toward the deceased given his vulnerability as a result of his drunkenness and being subject to a dangerous restraint. The police's reaction had been negligent. €30,000 was awarded in respect of non-pecuniary damage.

17.161 These cases have all been concerned with the operational duty to take reasonable preventative measures to protect against a known risk to life. Where the claim relates solely to failures to adequately investigate a death, it may be that the award will be smaller. In *Goodenough v Chief Constable of Thames Valley* failures in the investigation of a death associated with the police warranted an award of £5,000.[165]

17.162 There is some basis to consider that a separate award pursuant to Article 2 can be made on behalf of the estate in a claim brought further to the Law Reform (Miscellaneous Provisions) Act 1934 (see paras 7.197–7.199). Pursuant to HRA 1998 s7, a claim may only be brought by a person who is a 'victim' of the violation for the purposes of ECHR Article 34. The ECtHR has indicated that a deceased person does not have standing to bring a complaint as a victim[166] and a question therefore arises as to whether the deceased's estate can properly be a victim. However, in *Keenan v UK* a claim brought by the mother of the deceased succeeded in respect of Article 3 and the court awarded £7,000 'to be held by the applicant [his mother] for his estate', and £3,000 to the applicant in her personal capacity.[167] The same approach was taken in *McGlinchey v UK*.[168] Those are both Article 3 cases, but in the Article 2 claim in *Van Colle v Chief Constable of Hertfordshire* awards were made to both the estate, and the parents of the deceased.[169] It is suggested that where damages might be payable in respect of suffering of the deceased in life (for example, between fatal injury and death), a claim on behalf of the estate may serve a particular purpose. Otherwise, it would appear that just satisfaction can generally be afforded by awards to the family as indirect victims.

Article 3

17.163 In the context of claims against the police, a violation of the negative obligation not to inflict inhumane or degrading treatment contrary to Article 3 will most commonly arise in relation to the use of excessive force. In

163 App No 36480/13, 9 February 2021, ECtHR.
164 App No 45115/09, 1 December 2016, ECtHR.
165 [2020] EWHC 1428 (QB).
166 *Dvoracek v Slovakia* (App No 3074/04), 28 July 2009, ECtHR.
167 (2001) 33 EHRR 38 at para 137.
168 (2003) 37 EHRR 41.
169 [2007] EWCA Civ 325, [2007] 1 WLR 1821.

Alseran v Ministry of Defence Leggatt J summarised five cases in which the ECtHR awarded damages in instances of physical violence by the police.[170] They range from an award of €5,000 in respect of non-pecuniary damage for harassment and a slap to the face in police custody,[171] to €45,000 in a case where the violence was so severe as to amount to torture.[172]

17.164 Another common area for claims will be in the context of violations by the police of the positive obligation to prevent and to investigate treatment between individuals which engages Article 3. In *D v Commissioner of Police of the Metropolis* Green J surveyed the relevant case law on non-pecuniary losses in the context of violations of Article 3 and identified that the ECtHR awards generally fell into the following brackets:[173]

a) €1,000–8,000 where the court wishes to make a nominal or low award;
b) €8,000–20,000 for a routine violation of Article 3 with no serious long-term mental health issues and no unusual aggravating factors;
c) €20,000–100,000 for cases where there are aggravating factors such as: i) medical evidence of material psychological harm; ii) mental harm amounting to a recognised medical condition; iii) where the victim has also been the victim of physical harm or a crime caused in part by the state; iv) long-term systemic or endemic failings by the state; v) morally reprehensible conduct by the state. This list is by no means exhaustive.

17.165 Where a violation (for example, in investigating a crime) would not have prevented the crime itself, the court will look to assess the extent to which harm suffered by the victim has directly been caused or aggravated by the failures in investigation. Thus, in a case relating to failures to investigate a rape, the court will seek to assess the distinct impact of the failures of the investigation and not the impact of the rape.[174]

17.166 In *D* itself the two claimants were victims of the Jon Worboys (the so-called 'black cab rapist'). The court identified wide ranging failures by the police in the investigation. Both claimants identified psychiatric injury which had been caused or aggravated by the failures in the police investigation. In 2015, the claimant *DSD* was awarded £20,000 in non-pecuniary damages and £2,500 in respect of the cost of future medical treatment. The claimant NBV was awarded £17,000 in non-pecuniary damages and £2,000 as a contribution to future treatment costs. In respect of NBV, the court had concluded that, absent police failures, the assault upon her would have been avoided. In those circumstances a larger award would have been warranted, but the amount was reduced to account for the fact that compensation had already been received by NBV in respect of the assault by way of a claim against the perpetrator himself, and also an award from the Criminal Injuries Compensation Authority.[175] See further at para 4.151 on the relationship between awards made by the CICA and civil claims.

170 [2017] EWHC 3289 (QB), [2019] QB 1251 at 924–925.
171 *Bouyid v Belgium* (2016) 62 EHRR 32, ECtHR.
172 *Cestaro v Italy* (App No 6884/11), 7 April 2015, ECtHR.
173 [2015] 1 WLR 1833 at para 68(7).
174 *D v Commissioner of Police of the Metropolis* [2014] EWHC 2493 (QB), [2015] 1 WLR 1833 at para 121.
175 [2014] EWHC 2493 (QB), [2015] 1 WLR 1833 at para 142.

17.167 Where a claim is limited to being an investigative failure, and where there is no evidence of psychiatric injury directly related to the investigative failure, the award may be more modest. An example is *O v Commissioner of Police of the Metropolis* in which £5,000 was awarded (in 2011) in respect of failures, contrary to both Articles 3 and 4, to investigate the claimants being forced to work as domestic slaves.[176] The claimants suffered 'distress and frustration' over a period of 12 to 15 months, and ultimately only one claimant was willing to support an investigation.

Article 4

17.168 Awards in respect of state failures to investigate indications of trafficking and slavery have been modest. In *SM v Croatia* the applicant had been trafficked by being forced into prostitution. The ECtHR held that, following the matter being brought to the attention of the state, the prosecuting authorities reacted promptly but they failed to follow-up on obvious areas of inquiry. The investigation had been deficient as the police had not contacted potential witnesses or reviewed her social media. The ECtHR awarded EUR5,000 for non-pecuniary damage.[177] As above, £5,000 was awarded in respect of a violation of Article 4 in *O v Commissioner of Police of the Metropolis* (above). Similar awards have been made in *CN v UK*[178] (€8,000) and *Zoletic v Azerbaijan*[179] (€5,000).

Article 8

17.169 Claims relating to the violation of bodily integrity which might otherwise breach Article 8 will generally proceed as an assault claim and damages will generally be assessed by applying domestic scales of damages (as above). However, that is not always so. In *Y.F v Turkey* €4,000 was awarded in respect of a forced gynaecological examination in the course of a police investigation.[180] In *Wainwright v United Kingdom* awards of €3,000 were made in respect of strip searches in a prison that had not been conducted in accordance with the relevant policies and procedures.[181]

17.170 Claims may also arise in the context of dissemination of private information. In *Khmel v Russia* the videoing of a person in police custody and subsequent dissemination of the footage to the public warranted an award of €5,000.[182] In *Nikolaishvili v Georgia* the release of a photograph of a detained person and associating the applicant as wanted in connection with a murder when in fact he was not accused violated Article 8 and resulted in an award of €8,000.[183] There had also been a violation of Article 5. The unlawful recording or surveillance of conversations in the course of

176 [2011] HRLR 29, ECtHR.
177 (2021) 72 EHRR 1, ECtHR.
178 (2013) 56 EHRR 24, ECtHR.
179 App No 20116/12, 7 October 2021, ECtHR.
180 App No 24209/94, 22 July 2003, ECtHR.
181 (2007) 44 EHRR 40, ECtHR.
182 App No 20383/04, 12 December 2013, ECtHR.
183 App No 37084/04, 13 January 2009, ECtHR.

covert police operations has resulted in awards of €1,000[184] and €7,500.[185] Claims for breach of Article 8 in respect of misuse of private information are considered further in chapter 11.

17.171 As discussed in chapter 7, claims under Article 8 in respect of positive obligations to protect an individual from a threat of harm by a third party are usually determined with reference to Articles 2 or 3, although in *Burlya v others v Ukraine* awards of £11,000 and £9,000 were made in favour of applicants whose homes had been the subject of an attack by a mob from which the police failed to protect them.[186]

17.172 Article 8 may be engaged by entry into a person's home, and in *Keegan v UK* awards of €3,000 and €2,000 were made in respect of an unlawful search and entry into the applicants' home.[187]

184 *Bykov v Russia* (App No 4378/02), 10 March 2009.
185 *Dragojevic v Croatia* (App No 68955/11), 15 January 2015.
186 App No 3289/10 (ECtHR, 6 February 2019).
187 (2007) 44 EHRR 33.

Index